Kickstart Compiler Design Fundamentals

Practical Techniques and Solutions for Compiler Design, Parsing, Optimization, and Code Generation

Sandeep Telkar R, Dr. Rajesh Yakkundimath, Dr. Likewin Thomas, Divyashree Mallarapu

www.orangeava.com

First Published: June 2025

Published By: Orange Education Pvt Ltd, AVA®

Address: 9, Daryaganj, Delhi, 110002, India

275 New North Road Islington Suite 1314 London,
N1 7AA, United Kingdom

ISBN (PBK): 978-93-48107-19-0

ISBN (E-BOOK): 978-93-48107-99-2

Scan the QR code to explore our entire catalogue

www.orangeava.com

Dedicated To

My Beloved Parents:

Late.Smt Nagarathna GR

Mr. Ramachandra RT

And

My Wife Mrs. Rashmi PK, My Lovely Daughter Ms.Sirisha ST

And My Son Ujjwal ST

- Sandeep Telkar R

My Wife Rashmi
And

My Sons Ritesh and Rishikesh

- Dr. Rajesh Yakkundimath

My Beloved Parents:

Maj. (Retd) T C Thomas
Mary Kutty Thomas
And
My Wife Evelyn M M, My Son Alpheaus Thomas,
And My Daughter Kaira Likewin

- Dr. Likewin Thomas

My Beloved Parents:

Mr. Anjaneyulu Naidu

Mrs. Anjali M

And

My Uncle Mr. P Venkateshwara Rao and My Brother Adarsh Naidu

- Divyashree Mallarapu

About the Authors

Sandeep Telkar R is an Assistant Professor in the AIML Department at PES Institute of Technology and Management, Shimoga. He brings extensive teaching experience in AI, ML, and Computer Science. He holds an M.Tech in Digital Communication and Networking, as well as a B.E. in Information Science and Engineering. His expertise includes programming languages such as C, Java, Python, along with, machine learning, deep learning, and system software. He has published multiple research papers in reputed platforms like IEEE and Springer, received project funding, and won awards for best research papers. In addition to his academic contributions, he has organized faculty development programs and collaborated with industry partners on training and research initiatives.

Dr. Likewin Thomas is an accomplished Associate Professor and Head of the Department of AI and ML at PES Institute of Technology and Management (PESITM), Shivamogga. He holds a Ph.D. and M.Tech from NITK Surathkal, and a B.E. from Visvesvaraya Technological University (VTU). With over 17 years of experience, he is a senior member of IEEE and ISTE Life Time Member. He served as the secretary of the IEEE Mangalore Sub-Section in 2020-21. Currently, he is the IEEE Student Branch Counselor and Faculty Mentor of the Google Developer Students Club. His areas of expertise include Artificial Intelligence, Machine Learning, Big Data Analytics, Data Analysis, and Cloud Computing, with strong proficiency in Python and MATLAB. Dr. Thomas has also received significant grants for research projects and organized numerous international and national workshops and seminars. His research interests extend to Robotics, Drone Technology, and IoT. He has contributed to over 50 international and national workshops as a distinguished lecturer and organizer.

Dr. Rajesh Yakkundimath, Ph.D., is a Professor and Head of the Department of Computer Science & Engineering at K.L.E. Institute of Technology, Hubballi, Karnataka, India. He brings over 16 years of teaching experience and has authored approximately 40 research papers, published in both journals and conferences. His research interests encompass image processing, pattern recognition, soft computing, and knowledge-based systems.

Divyashree Mallarapu is an aspiring AI and ML engineer with expertise in Python, Java, web development, and AI-driven solutions. She has gained hands-on experience through internships at ResoluteAI Software as an AI Engineer Intern and at InternPe, working on projects in image segmentation, OCR, predictive maintenance, and AI model deployment. She holds certifications in Python, Full Stack Development, Computer Vision, NLP, MongoDB, and Generative AI. She is passionate about research and innovation and aims to bridge the gap between AI and real-world applications.

About the Technical Reviewer

Pranesh K brings over a decade of academic expertise to the Department of CSE at KLS VDIT, Haliyal. During this time, he has taught a wide range of programming and analytical courses to undergraduate students, fostering their understanding of essential computing concepts.

Beyond his classroom contributions, Pranesh is an AWS Certified Cloud Associate and a skilled AWS course instructor. He has actively participated in numerous workshops, both as a participant and a facilitator, focusing on popular programming languages such as Python, C#, C, and Java.

Acknowledgements

I express my heartfelt gratitude to my parents for their unwavering support, encouragement, and guidance throughout this journey. Their belief in me has been a constant source of motivation. I extend my sincere gratitude to my institution PESITM, Shivamogga for providing a conducive academic environment and resources that made this work possible.

I also extend my sincere thanks to the esteemed teaching staff of the Artificial Intelligence and Machine Learning (AIML) department for their invaluable knowledge, mentorship, and continuous support in shaping my understanding of Compiler Design. Their dedication and expertise have played a crucial role in my academic growth.

I also wish to acknowledge the efforts of the non-teaching staff of the AIML department for their assistance and contributions in creating a conducive learning environment. Their support behind the scenes has been instrumental in the completion of this work.

This book is a reflection of the collective knowledge and encouragement I have received, and I am deeply grateful to all who have been a part of this journey.

- *Sandeep Telkar* R

I would also like to thank the members of the Governing Council of K.L.E. Institute of Technology, Hubballi, for their encouragement and moral support.

I am much grateful to former Principals of K.L.E.Institute of Technology, Hubballi, Dr. Basavaraj S. Anami and Dr. Sharad G. Joshi, for their invaluable inspiration and encouragement, which have played a significant role in helping me reach this level.

I express my gratitude to the Principal, Dr. Manu T.M., K.L.E.Institute of Technology, Hubballi, for his constant encouragement and support in this venture.

Let me take this opportunity to thank my colleagues and students at Department of Computer Science & Engineering, K.L.E.Institute of Technology, Hubballi, who have directly or indirectly contributed in helping me to update my knowledge.

- *Dr. Rajesh Yakkundimath*

First and foremost, I extend my sincere gratitude to my institution PESITM, Shivamogga for providing a conducive academic environment and resources that made this work possible. I also appreciate the unwavering support of my colleagues and mentors, whose guidance and constructive feedback have significantly shaped the content of this book.

I am especially thankful to my co-authors and contributors for their expertise, dedication, and insightful discussions that enriched this work. Special thanks to the students and researchers whose curiosity and questions inspired many of the topics covered in this book.

I also acknowledge the invaluable support of Orange Education Pvt Ltd and the editorial team for their patience, professionalism, and assistance in refining the manuscript. Their meticulous attention to detail and commitment to quality have enhanced the final output.

Finally, I extend my heartfelt gratitude to my family and friends for their encouragement and understanding throughout this journey. Their unwavering support has been instrumental in bringing this book to completion.

This work is a culmination of collective efforts, and I deeply appreciate everyone who has played a part in its realization.

- *Dr. Likewin Thomas*

First and foremost, I extend my deepest gratitude to my parents for their unwavering love, encouragement, and belief in me. Their support has been the foundation of my journey, and I would not have reached this point without them.

I am profoundly grateful to my teachers and mentors at my institute and the company. Their mentorship, knowledge, and guidance have been instrumental in shaping my understanding of Compiler Design and nurturing my growth.

A heartfelt thank you to my sister, Poornima S, for her constant support and encouragement, which has been a source of strength throughout this journey.

I would also like to sincerely thank my co-authors for their dedication, collaboration, and invaluable contributions. This book is a testament to our collective efforts.

Finally, I am deeply thankful to everyone who has supported me – directly or indirectly – along the way. This work would not have been possible without your encouragement and belief in our vision.

- *Divyashree Mallarapu*

Preface

Compilers are the backbone of modern computing. Every program we write, from a simple script to complex software applications, must be translated into a language that computers understand. This process, often hidden from the user's view, is what makes programming languages powerful and accessible. At the heart of this transformation lies the compiler, a sophisticated tool that takes human-readable code and converts it into machine-executable instructions.

This book serves as a comprehensive guide to compiler design, taking you from the fundamental concepts to the intricate workings of modern compilers. Whether you are a student, a software developer, or someone deeply interested in understanding how programming languages work behind the scenes, this book will provide detailed insights, real-world applications, and practical implementations of compiler techniques.

Compiler construction is often perceived as complex and abstract, but in reality, it is a fascinating subject that blends theory, mathematics, algorithms, and real-world problem-solving. This book aims to simplify these concepts while maintaining a rigorous and structured approach. We break down each phase of the compilation process, discuss the challenges faced in designing compilers, and explore the techniques used to build efficient, optimized, and secure compilers for different programming languages.

By the end of this book, you will not only understand how compilers work but also be capable of designing and implementing your own compiler from scratch.

The hands-on approach ensures that you gain practical experience, reinforcing theoretical knowledge through coding exercises and real-world scenarios.

The book is structured into 19 chapters, covering every critical aspect of compilers—from lexical analysis and syntax parsing to code optimization and real-world implementations. Each chapter follows a progressive learning approach, ensuring that readers build their knowledge step by step.

Chapter 1. Introduction to Compilers: This chapter provides a fundamental introduction to compilers, explaining their role in software development. It covers different types of translators, including interpreters, assemblers, and just-in-time (JIT) compilers. Readers will also get an overview of compiler phases, from source code analysis to machine code generation.

Chapter 2. Lexical Analysis and Regular Expressions: The first step in the compilation process is lexical analysis, where the source code is broken down into tokens. This chapter introduces regular expressions, finite automata, and Deterministic Finite Automata (DFA), which are used to recognize patterns in programming languages.

Chapter 3. Lexical Analyzer Generators and Error Handling: This chapter explores automated tools such as Lex and Flex, which help generate lexical analyzers. Additionally, it covers error detection and recovery mechanisms that handle unexpected inputs in the lexical analysis phase.

Chapter 4. Syntax Analysis Context-Free Grammars: Once tokens are identified, the next step is to understand the structure of the code. This chapter introduces context-free grammars (CFGs), derivation trees, and ambiguity resolution in programming languages.

Chapter 5. Parsing Techniques: Delving deeper into parsing, this chapter explains top-down (LL) and bottom-up (LR) parsing techniques. It explores recursive descent parsing, shift-reduce parsing, and operator precedence parsing, crucial for analyzing complex language structures.

Chapter 6. Semantic Analysis Attribute Grammars: Attribute grammars allow the addition of semantic information to syntax rules. This chapter explains how semantic attributes, synthesized attributes, and inherited attributes help in processing information beyond syntax.

Chapter 7. Intermediate Code Generation: After syntax analysis, compilers generate Intermediate Representations (IR) such as Three-Address Code (TAC), Abstract Syntax Trees (ASTs), and Control Flow Graphs (CFGs). These intermediate forms bridge the gap between high-level code and machine instructions.

Chapter 8. Control Flow: Understanding control flow is key to optimizing program execution. This chapter covers basic blocks, dominator trees, and Control Flow Graphs (CFGs), which help compilers analyze program execution paths.

Chapter 9. Run-Time Environment and Memory Management: This chapter discusses how programs handle memory allocation and execution environments. Topics include stack vs. heap allocation, symbol tables, activation records, dynamic memory management, and garbage collection.

Chapter 10. Function Calls and Exception Handling: Function calls introduce complexities such as stack frames, recursion, and parameter passing mechanisms. This chapter also covers exception handling, stack unwinding, and performance considerations in modern programming languages.

Chapter 11. Code Generation and Instruction Selection: Code generation is the process of converting intermediate code into low-level machine instructions. This chapter discusses instruction selection, instruction scheduling, and basic block formation.

Chapter 12. Register Allocation and Scheduling: Registers are one of the most limited resources in computing. This chapter explores register allocation strategies such as graph coloring and linear scan allocation, along with instruction scheduling techniques to maximize CPU efficiency.

Chapter 13. Machine-Independent Optimizations and Local and Global Techniques: Optimizing a program without relying on specific hardware features is crucial for portability. This chapter covers constant propagation, common subexpression elimination, and dead code elimination, which improve performance across different architectures.

Chapter 14. Loop and Peephole Optimization: Loops are often the most performance-critical sections of a program. This chapter covers loop unrolling, loop fusion, strength reduction, and peephole optimization, which enhance execution speed by making localized improvements.

Chapter 15. Instruction-Level Parallelism and Pipelining: Modern processors execute multiple instructions simultaneously. This chapter introduces instruction-level parallelism, out-of-order execution, pipeline hazards, and superscalar execution, which are essential for high-performance computing.

Chapter 16. Optimizing for Parallelism and Locality: As computing moves toward multi-core architectures, parallel computing becomes essential. This chapter explores loop-level parallelism, cache optimization, and vectorization, which improve execution efficiency in multi-threaded environments.

Chapter 17. Inter Procedural Analysis and Optimization: Optimizations should not be limited to single functions. This chapter covers function inlining, alias analysis, escape analysis, and global optimizations, which optimize across multiple function calls.

Chapter 18. Case Studies and Real-World Examples: A deep dive into real-world compiler implementations, including GCC, LLVM, JVM, and JIT compilation in modern web browsers. This chapter provides insights into how industrial compilers optimize execution.

Chapter 19. Hands-on Exercises and Projects: The final chapter provides practical compiler construction projects, including building a simple compiler, implementing optimizations, and analyzing real-world programming language features.

Downloading the code bundles and colored images

Please follow the links or scan the QR codes to download the ***Code Bundles and Images*** of the book:

https://github.com/ava-orange-education/Kickstart-Compiler-Design-Fundamentals

The code bundles and images of the book are also hosted on ***https://rebrand.ly/30577d***

In case there's an update to the code, it will be updated on the existing GitHub repository.

Errata

We take immense pride in our work at **Orange Education Pvt Ltd,** and follow best practices to ensure the accuracy of our content to provide an indulging reading experience to our subscribers. Our readers are our mirrors, and we use their inputs to reflect and improve upon human errors, if any, that may have occurred during the publishing processes involved. To let us maintain the quality and help us reach out to any readers who might be having difficulties due to any unforeseen errors, please write to us at :

errata@orangeava.com

Your support, suggestions, and feedback are highly appreciated.

DID YOU KNOW

Did you know that Orange Education Pvt Ltd offers eBook versions of every book published, with PDF and ePub files available? You can upgrade to the eBook version at **www.orangeava.com** and as a print book customer, you are entitled to a discount on the eBook copy. Get in touch with us at: **info@orangeava.com** for more details.

At **www.orangeava.com**, you can also read a collection of free technical articles, sign up for a range of free newsletters, and receive exclusive discounts and offers on Print Books and eBooks.

PIRACY

If you come across any illegal copies of our works in any form on the internet, we would be grateful if you would provide us with the location address or website name. Please contact us at **info@orangeava.com** with a link to the material.

ARE YOU INTERESTED IN AUTHORING WITH US?

If there is a topic that you have expertise in, and you are interested in either writing or contributing to a book, please write to us at **business@orangeava.com**. We are on a journey to help developers and tech professionals to gain insights on the present technological advancements and innovations happening across the globe and build a community that believes Knowledge is best acquired by sharing and learning with others. Please reach out to us to learn what our audience demands and how you can be part of this educational reform. We also welcome ideas from tech experts and help them build learning and development content for their domains.

REVIEWS

Please leave a review. Once you have read and used this book, why not leave a review on the site that you purchased it from? Potential readers can then see and use your unbiased opinion to make purchase decisions. We at Orange Education would love to know what you think about our products, and our authors can learn from your feedback. Thank you!

For more information about Orange Education, please visit **www.orangeava.com**.

Table of Contents

Chapter 1
Introduction to Compilers

Introduction

Compilers play a crucial role in software development by translating high-level programming languages into machine code that computers can execute. This chapter introduces the fundamental concepts of compilers, their purpose, and their structure. Understanding these basics is essential for delving into more advanced topics in compiler design and implementation.

Structure

In this chapter, we will discuss the following topics:

- Definition and Purpose of Compilers
  - Importance of Compilers in Software Development
  - Structure of a Compiler
  - Major Components of the Compiler
- Phases of Compilation
  - Lexical Analysis
  - Syntax Analysis
  - Semantic Analysis
  - Intermediate Code Generation
  - Code Optimization
  - Code Generation
  - Code Linking and Assembly
- Compilers vs. Interpreters
  - Compilers
  - Interpreters
  - Key Differences between Compilers and Interpreters
- History of Compiler Development
  - Early Compilers
  - High-level Language Compilers
  - Modern Compilers
  - Optimization Techniques
  - Evolution of Programming Languages
- Overview of Compiler Construction Tools
  - Lexical Analyzers
  - Syntax Analyzers

- Intermediate Code Generators
- Optimization Tools
- Code Generators
- Code Linking and Assembly Tools

Definition and Purpose of Compilers

A compiler is a specialized program that translates the source code written in a high-level programming language into machine code, bytecode, or another high-level language. This translation enables the code to be executed by a computer's processor. The primary purpose of a compiler is to bridge the gap between human-readable code and machine-executable instructions, facilitating efficient and effective software development.

Importance of Compilers in Software Development

Compilers are critical in software development for several reasons:

- **Performance Optimization:** Compilers can optimize the code to run faster and use resources more efficiently. These optimizations can include inlining functions, unrolling loops, and eliminating redundant calculations.
- **Portability:** By translating high-level code to machine code, compilers allow the same source code to be run on different hardware platforms without modification.
- **Error Detection:** Compilers can identify syntax and semantic errors in the source code, providing developers with feedback that helps catch and correct mistakes in the early development process.
- **Abstraction:** Compilers allow developers to write in high-level languages, abstracting away the complexities of hardware-specific instructions.

Structure of a Compiler

A compiler consists of several components, each responsible for a specific aspect of the compilation process. Understanding the structure of a compiler is essential for grasping how it translates and optimizes the source code.

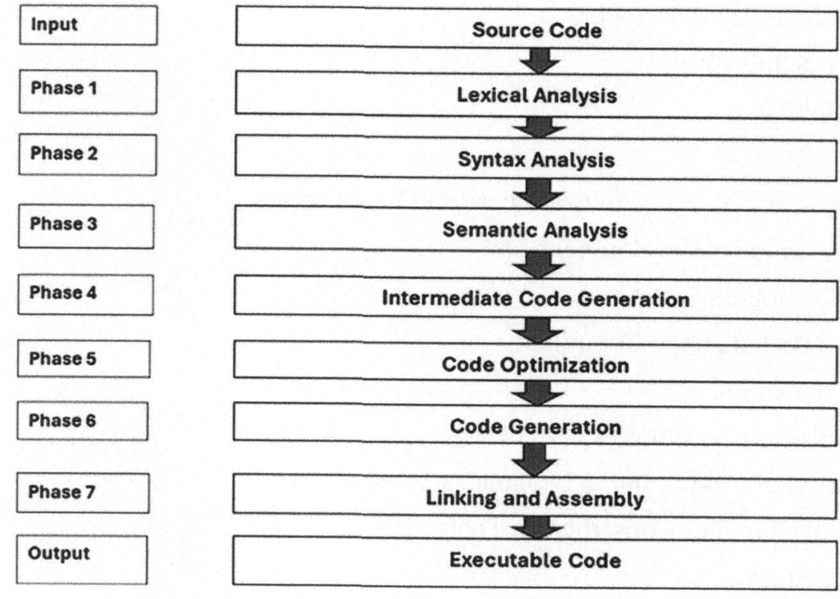

Figure 1.1: *Structure of a Compiler*

Major Components of a Compiler

A compiler is a tool that turns the code written in a programming language into machine code that a computer can execute. To do this, it relies on several key components, each with a specific job. Let us take a look at these major parts, and see how they work together to make your code run smoothly.

- **Lexical Analysis:** This phase involves scanning the source code, and converting it into tokens which are the basic building blocks of the program. Tokens represent identifiers, keywords, operators, and symbols.
- **Syntax Analysis:** Also known as parsing, this phase checks the tokens against the grammatical rules of the programming language to ensure that the code's structure is correct. It produces a parse tree or an Abstract Syntax Tree (AST).
- **Semantic Analysis:** This phase ensures that the code makes sense semantically, checking for meaningful relationships between the various elements of the program. It involves type-checking and verifying variable declarations and uses.
- **Intermediate Code Generation:** The compiler translates the high-level code into an Intermediate Representation (IR) which is easier to manipulate and optimize. The IR is typically platform-independent.
- **Code Optimization:** This phase improves the intermediate code to make it run more efficiently. Optimization techniques can be applied at various levels, including local, global, and interprocedural optimizations.
- **Code Generation:** The optimized intermediate code is translated into machine code or bytecode. This phase considers the target architecture's specifics, generating efficient and correct machine instructions.
- **Code Linking and Assembly:** The machine code is linked with libraries and other modules, and then assembled into the final executable program. This phase ensures that all references are resolved, and the program is ready for execution.

Phases of Compilation

The compilation process can be broken down into distinct phases, each playing a crucial role in translating and optimizing the source code.

Lexical Analysis

Lexical analysis or scanning, is the first phase of the compilation process. The lexical analyzer reads the source code character by character, and groups them into tokens. Each token represents a logical unit, such as a keyword, identifier, or operator.

Example:

Consider,

For the input, int a = b + 5;,

The lexical analyzer generates the tokens: int, a, =, b, +, 5, and;.

In detail, the lexical analyzer reads the input string, character by character. It recognizes that the int is a keyword, a is an identifier, = is an assignment operator, b is another identifier, + is an arithmetic operator, 5 is an integer literal, and; is a delimiter.

Syntax Analysis

Syntax analysis or parsing, takes the tokens produced by the lexical analyzer, and arranges them into a parse tree or AST based on the grammatical rules of the programming language. This phase ensures that the code's structure adheres to the language's syntax.

Example:

Consider,

For the input, int a = b + 5;

The parser checks that the int is followed by an identifier, an assignment operator =, an expression b + 5, and a semicolon;.

In detail, the parser constructs a tree structure that represents the syntactic structure of the code. For example, the tree might have the int as the root node, with child nodes representing the declaration of a, the assignment operation, and the expression, b + 5.

Semantic Analysis

Semantic analysis checks for logical consistency and meaning in the code. This phase involves type checking, verifying variable declarations and their uses, ensuring that the operations are applied to compatible types.

Example:

Consider,

For the input, int a = b + 5;

The semantic analyzer verifies that b is a declared variable and 5 is an integer constant. It also ensures the addition operation, b + 5 is valid for the types involved.

In detail, the semantic analyzer checks that b has been previously declared, and is of a type that can be added to an integer. If b were, for example, a string, the semantic analyzer would generate an error.

Intermediate Code Generation

The compiler translates the high-level code into an Intermediate Representation (IR) which is easier to manipulate and optimize. The IR serves as a bridge between the high-level source code and the machine code.

Example:

Consider,

For the input, int a = b + 5;

The IR might be represented as:

```
t1 = b + 5
a = t1
```

In detail, the IR breaks down the high-level operation into simpler steps. The addition is performed first, and then stored in a temporary variable, t1 which is then assigned to a. This IR is typically a lower-level representation that can be easily optimized.

Code Optimization

Code optimization improves the intermediate code to make it run more efficiently. This phase applies various techniques to enhance performance, and reduce the resource usage.

Example:

Consider,

An optimization might simplify the expression, b + 0 to b or unroll loops to reduce overhead.

In detail, optimizations can include constant folding (evaluating constant expressions at compile time), loop unrolling (expanding loops to reduce the overhead of loop control), and dead code elimination (removing code that is never executed).

Code Generation

The optimized intermediate code is translated into machine code or bytecode. This phase generates instructions specific to the target architecture, ensuring efficient and correct execution.

Example:

Consider,

For the input, int a = b + 5;,

The machine code might be:

LOAD *b*,

R1 ADD 5,

R1 STORE R1, *a*

In detail, the code generator produces machine-specific instructions. LOAD b, R1 loads the value of b into register R1, ADD 5, R1 adds 5 to the value in R1, and STORE R1, stores the result back into the variable a.

Code Linking and Assembly

The final phase combines all the code segments, resolves references, and produces the executable program. It links the machine code with the libraries and other modules, ensuring that the program is complete and ready for execution.

Example:

If the code uses functions from a standard library, the linker resolves the addresses of these functions, and includes the necessary library code in the final executable.

In detail, the linker takes the object files produced by the code generator, and combines them with the libraries. It resolves all external references, and produces a single executable file. The assembler converts the machine code into a binary format that the computer's processor can execute.

Compilers vs. Interpreters

Understanding the differences between compilers and interpreters is essential for grasping how programming languages are executed on computers. Both serve the purpose of converting high-level programming code into a form that a machine can execute, but they do so in fundamentally different ways. This section delves into the key differences, advantages, and disadvantages of compilers and interpreters.

Compilers

A compiler is a program that translates the source code written in a high-level programming language into the machine code, bytecode, or another programming language. The translation process occurs before the program is executed, resulting in a standalone executable file.

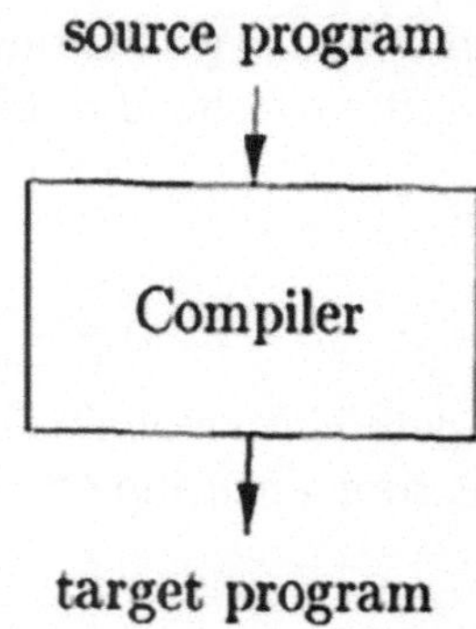

***Figure 1.2**: Block Diagram of a Compiler*

How Compilers Work

Compilers are tools that turn the code you write into instructions that a computer can understand and run. They go through several steps to ensure the code is correct and efficient. In this guide, we will break down how compilers do their job, and why they are important for programming.

1. **Source Code Input:** The compiler takes the entire source code as input.
2. **Lexical Analysis:** The source code is scanned to convert it into tokens.
3. **Syntax Analysis:** Tokens are analyzed based on the language's grammar to produce a parse tree or an Abstract Syntax Tree (AST).
4. **Semantic Analysis:** The compiler checks for semantic errors, ensuring that the code is logically consistent.
5. **Intermediate Code Generation:** The compiler converts the AST into an Intermediate Representation (IR).
6. **Optimization:** The intermediate code is optimized to improve performance and resource utilization.
7. **Code Generation:** The optimized intermediate code is translated into the machine code.
8. **Linking and Assembly:** The machine code is linked with libraries, and assembled into an executable file.

Example:

Consider a simple C program performing addition,

```
#include <stdio.h>
 int main()
 {
int a = 10; int b = 20;
printf("Sum: %d\n", a + b);
```

```
    return 0;
}
```

When compiled, this program undergoes the following steps:

1. **Lexical Analysis:** The code is converted into tokens, such as int, main, (,), {, int, a, =, 10, ;, and so on.
2. **Syntax Analysis:** These tokens are analyzed to ensure that they follow the C's grammatical rules, resulting in a parse tree.
3. **Semantic Analysis:** This ensures that a and b are declared, and used correctly, and the printf is correctly called.
4. **Intermediate Code Generation:** An IR is generated, for instance, in LLVM IR format.
5. **Optimization:** The IR is optimized, possibly simplifying expressions or removing unnecessary instructions.
6. **Code Generation:** The optimized IR is converted into machine code for the target architecture.
7. **Linking and Assembly:** The machine code is then linked with the standard C library to produce the final executable.

Interpreters

An interpreter is a program that directly executes instructions written in a high-level programming language, translating them into machine code, line by line at the runtime. Unlike compilers, interpreters do not produce an intermediate executable file.

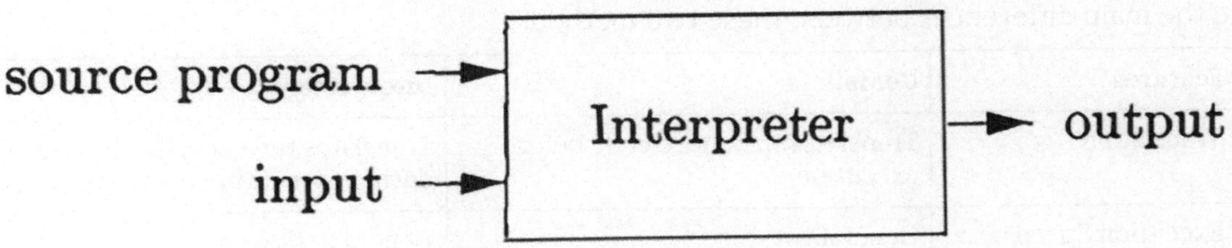

Figure 1.3: *Block Diagram of an Interpreter*

How Interpreters Work

Interpreters help computers understand and run the code by translating it one line at a time. Instead of processing the entire program at once, interpreters read and execute each line as it is written which allows for quick testing and debugging. This makes them useful for tasks where immediate feedback is needed.

1. **Source Code Input:** The interpreter reads the source code.
2. **Lexical Analysis:** The source code is scanned to convert it into tokens.
3. **Syntax Analysis:** Tokens are analyzed to ensure that they follow the language's grammar rules.
4. **Semantic Analysis:** Checks are performed to ensure that the code is logically consistent.
5. **Execution:** Each line or block of the code is executed immediately after the parsing and semantic checks.

Example:

Consider the same logic in Python,

```
a = 10
b = 20
print(f"Sum: {a + b}")
```

When interpreted, this program undergoes the following steps:

1. **Lexical Analysis:** The code is converted into tokens, such as `a`, `=`, `10`, `b`, `=`, `20`, `print`, `(`, `f"Sum: {a + b}"`, and `)`.
2. **Syntax Analysis:** These tokens are analyzed to ensure that they follow the Python's grammar rules.
3. **Semantic Analysis:** This ensures that a and b are declared and used correctly, and the print function is correctly called.
4. **Execution:** The interpreter executes each line immediately:

```
a = 10
b = 20
print(f"Sum: {a + b}")
```
results in the output `Sum:30`.

Key Differences between Compilers and Interpreters

Compilers and interpreters convert the code into a language that computers can understand, but they do it differently. Compilers translate the entire code at once, creating a file that runs quickly. Interpreters process the code line by line which is useful for testing and debugging. This summary will outline the main differences between these two methods.

Features	Compilers	Interpreters
Translation	Translates the entire code before execution	Translates the code, line by line during execution
Execution Speed	Generally faster	Generally slower
Error Detection	Errors detected at compile-time	Errors detected at runtime
Output	Generates an executable file	No separate executable file
Compilation Time	Can be time-consuming	No separate compilation step
Platform Dependence	Often platform-specific executables	More portable across different platforms
Debugging	More complex due to separate compilation steps	Easier due to immediate feedback

Table 1.1: *Key Differences between the Compilers and Interpreters*

History of Compiler Development

The development of compilers has a rich history, evolving significantly since the 1950s.

Early Compilers

The first compilers were simple translators for assembly languages, converting symbolic instructions into the machine code.

Example:

The A-0 compiler, developed by Grace Hopper in the early 1950s, translated mathematical expressions into machine code.

In detail, the A-0 system allowed programmers to write the code using symbolic names for operations and memory locations, rather than raw binary instructions. This was a significant step forward from hand-coding machine instructions.

High-Level Language Compilers

With the advent of high-level languages, such as FORTRAN in the late 1950s, compilers became more complex to handle the higher-level abstractions.

Example:

The FORTRAN compiler, developed by IBM, was one of the first to translate the high-level code into efficient machine code, significantly improving productivity.

In detail, the FORTRAN (Formula Translation) compiler introduced many concepts that are still in use today, such as loop constructs and mathematical expressions. The compiler could translate these high-level abstractions into an efficient machine code, making programming more accessible and less error-prone.

Optimization Techniques

As programming languages and hardware evolved, more sophisticated optimization techniques were developed to improve the performance of the generated code.

Example:

Techniques, such as loop unrolling, inline expansion, and constant folding were introduced to enhance the execution speed, and reduce the resource usage.

In detail, loop unrolling involves expanding the body of a loop to decrease the overhead of loop control instructions. Inline expansion replaces function calls with the actual body of the function, reducing the overhead of the calling functions. Constant folding evaluates constant expressions at compile time, reducing the runtime calculations.

Modern Compilers

Today's compilers incorporate advanced algorithms, and handle a wide variety of programming paradigms, including object-oriented, functional, and concurrent programming.

Example:

Modern compilers, such as GCC and LLVM support multiple languages and architectures, providing extensive optimization capabilities and modular design.

In detail, GCC (GNU Compiler Collection) supports various programming languages, including C, C++, and Fortran. LLVM (Low-Level Virtual Machine) provides a flexible intermediate representation and a suite of modular and reusable compiler and toolchain technologies. Both GCC and LLVM include sophisticated optimization techniques and support for multiple target architectures.

Evolution of Programming Languages

Programming languages have evolved from simple assembly languages to complex high-level languages, each requiring more sophisticated compilers.

First Generation: Machine Languages

Machine languages are the most basic level of programming languages, consisting of the binary code that the computer's processor can execute directly.

In detail, machine languages are specific to each type of CPU, and consist of binary instructions that control the processor's operations. Programming in machine language is tedious and error-prone, as it requires detailed knowledge of the hardware.

Second Generation: Assembly Languages

Assembly languages use symbolic instructions, and are one step above machine languages. They are specific to a particular processor architecture.

Example:

```
MOV AL, 61h
ADD AL, 1
```

In detail, assembly language uses mnemonic codes to represent machine instructions, making it easier for humans to read and write. Each assembly instruction corresponds to a single machine instruction. Assemblers translate assembly language code into machine code.

Third Generation: High-Level Languages

High-level languages abstract away hardware details, allowing developers to write more readable and maintainable code.

Example:

Languages, such as FORTRAN, C, and Pascal introduced constructs like loops, conditionals, and functions.

In detail, high-level languages provide constructs that correspond more closely to human logic and problem-solving approaches, rather than the machine's hardware. They include features, such as loops (for, while), conditionals (if, switch), and functions (procedures, methods) which make programming more intuitive and reduce the likelihood of errors.

Fourth Generation: Domain-Specific Languages

Fourth-generation languages are designed for specific tasks, offering higher-level abstractions and improved productivity.

Example:

SQL *is a fourth-generation language designed for database queries.*

In detail, the fourth-generation languages (4GLs) are more abstract, and are designed to be closer to the natural language. They are often used for database management, report generation, and other specific applications. SQL (Structured Query Language) is a prominent example, used for managing and querying relational databases.

Fifth Generation: Declarative and AI Languages

Fifth-generation languages focus on problem-solving and declarative programming, supporting artificial intelligence and logical reasoning.

Example:

Prolog is a fifth-generation language used for AI and logic programming.

In detail, the fifth-generation languages (5GLs) are designed to solve problems using constraints given to the program, rather than using an algorithm written by the programmer. Prolog (Programming in Logic) is used for tasks that involve logical reasoning and symbolic computation, such as natural language processing and theorem proving.

Overview of Compiler Construction Tools

Several tools facilitate the construction of compilers, each automating different parts of the process.

Lexical Analyzers

Lexical analyzers or Lexers are tools that generate the lexical analysis phase of a compiler. They convert the source code into tokens.

Example:

Lex is a widely used tool for generating lexical analyzers.

In detail, Lex allows developers to define regular expressions for the tokens of a language. It generates a C program that reads the input, and produces a sequence of tokens based on these regular expressions. This automates the creation of the lexical analysis phase of a compiler.

Syntax Analyzers

Syntax analyzers, or parsers, are tools that generate the syntax analysis phase of a compiler. They build parse trees or ASTs from the tokens.

Example:

Yacc and Bison are popular tools for generating parsers.

In detail, the YACC (Yet Another Compiler Compiler) and its GNU counterpart Bison allow developers to define a grammar for the language using a formal notation. These tools generate a parser in C that reads the tokens produced by the lexical analyzer, and builds a parse tree or AST, checking for syntactic correctness.

Intermediate Code Generators

Intermediate code generators produce an intermediate representation of the source code, serving as a bridge between the high-level and the machine code.

Example:

LLVM provides a powerful intermediate representation used by many modern compilers.

In detail, LLVM's Intermediate Representation (IR) is a low-level, RISC-like assembly language that is platform-independent. This IR can be optimized and transformed by various passes within the LLVM framework before being translated into the machine code for different target architectures.

Optimization Tools

Optimization tools improve the intermediate code's efficiency, applying different techniques to enhance the performance.

Example:

The GCC includes extensive optimization capabilities, such as loop optimization and inline expansion.

In detail, the GCC (GNU Compiler Collection) includes numerous optimization options that can be applied during compilation. These optimizations include removing redundant code, improving loop efficiency, and expanding inline functions to reduce the overhead of the function calls.

Code Generators

Code generators convert the optimized intermediate code into machine code or bytecode, targeting specific architectures.

Example:

Both GCC and LLVM provide code generation capabilities for multiple architectures.

In detail, GCC and the LLVM include backends for various target architectures, such as x86, ARM, and PowerPC. These backends translate the optimized IR into machine-specific instructions, generating efficient and correct machine code for the target platform.

Code Linking and Assembly Tools

Linkers and assemblers combine code segments and produce the final executable program.

Example:

LD is a common linker used in Unix-based systems.

In detail, LD (the GNU linker) combines object files produced by the code generator, resolving references between them and linking in necessary libraries. It produces a single executable file. Assemblers convert the machine code instructions into a binary format that can be executed by the computer's processor.

Conclusion

This chapter has provided an in-depth introduction to compilers, outlining their significance in software development. We covered the fundamental definition and purpose of compilers, explored their essential structure and major components, and examined the various phases of compilation, including lexical analysis, syntax analysis, semantic analysis, intermediate code generation, code optimization, and code generation. We also discussed the differences between compilers and interpreters, the historical evolution of compilers, and the progression of programming languages from early machine languages to modern domain-specific and AI-driven languages.

As we move forward, the next chapter will build on this foundation by diving into the intricacies of lexical analysis. We will explore key concepts, such as Tokens, Patterns, and Lexemes, and understand their roles in language processing. The chapter will also cover Regular Expressions and Finite Automata, which are instrumental in defining and recognizing patterns within the text. Additionally, we will examine practical implementations using tools, such as Flex and JFlex, offering insights into their application in real-world scenarios.

This transition will enhance your understanding of how compilers handle code analysis, setting the stage for a deeper exploration of compiler construction techniques in the upcoming chapter.

Points to Remember

- **Definition of Compilers**: Compilers translate the high-level code into machine code.
- **Purpose of Compilers**: They make programs run faster, and help catch errors in the code.
- **Compiler Structure**:
  - **Front End**: Analyzes and checks the code.
  - **Back End**: Generates the machine code.
- **Major Components**:
  - **Lexical Analyzer**: Tokenizes the code.
  - **Syntax Analyzer**: Constructs parse trees.
  - **Code Generator**: Produces the machine code.
- **Compilation Phases**:
  - **Lexical Analysis**: Breaks the code into tokens.
  - **Syntax Analysis**: Builds a parse tree.
  - **Code Generation**: Converts into the machine code.
- **Compilers vs Interpreters**:
  - **Compilers**: Translate all the codes at once; create executable files.
  - **Interpreters**: Translate and execute the code, line by line.
- **How Compilers Work**: They read, analyze, optimize, and convert the code into machine language.
- **How Interpreters Work**: They read and execute the code, one line at a time.
- **Key Differences**:
  - **Execution Method**: Compilers handle the entire program at once; interpreters do it line by line.
  - **Performance**: Compilers generally produce faster executable code.
- **Evolution of Programming Languages**:
  - **First Generation**: Machine languages.
  - **Second Generation**: Assembly languages.
  - **Third Generation**: High-level languages.
  - **Fourth Generation**: Domain-specific languages.
  - **Fifth Generation**: Declarative and AI languages.

Multiple Choice Questions

1. What is the primary purpose of a compiler?
   a. To execute the source code directly
   b. To translate source code into machine code
   c. To interpret the source code, line by line
   d. To optimize the code for better performance

2. Why are compilers important in software development?
    a. They allow programs to be written in high-level languages.
    b. They enable the execution of code on any hardware platform.
    c. They ensure faster execution of the code by converting it into machine language.
    d. All of the above.
3. Which of the following is not a major component of a compiler?
    a. Lexical Analyzer
    b. Syntax Analyzer
    c. Database Manager
    d. Code Generator
4. Which phase of the compiler is responsible for checking the syntax of the source code?
    a. Lexical Analysis
    b. Syntax Analysis
    c. Semantic Analysis
    d. Code Generation
5. What is the first phase of compilation?
    a. Code Generation
    b. Syntax Analysis
    c. Lexical Analysis
    d. Intermediate Code Generation
6. During which phase is the intermediate code generated?
    a. Syntax Analysis
    b. Semantic Analysis
    c. Intermediate Code Generation
    d. Code Optimization
7. What is the role of semantic analysis in compilation?
    a. Checking the syntax of the code
    b. Generating optimized machine code
    c. Ensuring that the code has meaningful interpretations
    d. Converting the source code into the intermediate code
8. Which phase of the compiler focuses on improving the performance of the code?
    a. Lexical Analysis
    b. Code Optimization
    c. Syntax Analysis
    d. Code Linking

9. What is the final output of the code generation phase?
   a. Intermediate Code
   b. Assembly Code
   c. Machine Code
   d. High-Level Source Code
10. What does the code linking phase involve?
    a. Checking the syntax of the code
    b. Linking multiple object files into a single executable file
    c. Translating the high-level code into intermediate code
    d. Parsing the source code
11. What is the main difference between a compiler and an interpreter?
    a. A compiler translates code line by line, while an interpreter translates the entire program at once.
    b. A compiler translates the entire program at once, while an interpreter translates the code, line by line.
    c. A compiler is used for scripting languages, while an interpreter is used for system languages.
    d. An interpreter produces machine code, while a compiler produces bytecode.
12. Which of the following is true about interpreters?
    a. They execute the code faster than compilers.
    b. They translate the high-level code into machine code.
    c. They are typically used for languages like Python and JavaScript.
    d. They generate the object code that can be executed later.
13. Which of the following is not a characteristic of a compiler?
    a. Translates the entire program before execution.
    b. Slower execution time compared to an interpreter.
    c. Produces the machine code.
    d. Provides error messages after the entire program is analyzed.
14. What was a major challenge in the development of early compilers?
    a. Lack of high-level programming languages
    b. Lack of assembly languages
    c. Lack of machine languages
    d. Lack of memory for storing the compiled code
15. Which era saw the development of high-level language compilers?
    a. 1940s
    b. 1950s

   c. 1960s
   d. 1970s

16. Which generation of programming languages is characterized by machine-level instructions?
    a. First Generation
    b. Second Generation
    c. Third Generation
    d. Fourth Generation
17. Which generation of programming languages introduced high-level, machine-independent languages?
    a. First Generation
    b. Second Generation
    c. Third Generation
    d. Fourth Generation
18. Which of the following is an example of a Fourth Generation Language (4GL)?
    a. Assembly Language
    b. COBOL
    c. SQL
    d. C++
19. What is the primary purpose of a lexical analyzer in compiler construction?
    a. To check the syntax of the source code
    b. To generate the intermediate code
    c. To convert the source code into tokens
    d. To optimize the generated code
20. Which of the following tools is used for syntax analysis in compiler construction?
    a. Yacc
    b. Lex
    c. Lint
    d. Make

Answers

1. b
2. d
3. c
4. b
5. c

6. c
7. c
8. b
9. c
10. b
11. b
12. c
13. b
14. a
15. b
16. a
17. c
18. c
19. c
20. a

Questions

1. What is a compiler, and what are its primary purposes in software development?
2. Describe the major components of a compiler and their roles in the compilation process.
3. Explain the different phases of compilation, focusing on the purpose and function of Lexical Analysis, Syntax Analysis, and Semantic Analysis.
4. What is intermediate code generation, and why is it important in the compilation process?
5. How does code optimization improve the efficiency of the compiled code?
6. What are the steps involved in code generation, and how does this phase produce the final machine code?
7. Compare and contrast compilers and interpreters, focusing on their methods of translating and executing the code.
8. Explain how a compiler works, including a detailed description of its compilation phases.
9. Discuss the key differences between compilers and interpreters, and the implications of these differences for software development.
10. Trace the history of compiler development, from early compilers to modern compilers, highlighting significant milestones.

Key Terms

- **Compiler**: A tool that translates high-level source code into machine code or intermediate code.
- **Interpreter**: A tool that translates and executes code, line by line.
- **Lexical Analysis**: The phase of compilation where the source code is broken into tokens.
- **Syntax Analysis**: The phase where tokens are parsed into a parse tree based on grammar rules.
- **Semantic Analysis**: The phase where the compiler checks for the meaning and correctness in the code.
- **Intermediate Code**: A lower-level representation of the code generated between a high-level code and a machine code.
- **Code Optimization**: Techniques used to improve the performance and efficiency of the intermediate code.
- **Code Generation**: The phase where the intermediate code is translated into the machine code.
- **Linker**: A tool that combines various pieces of the code and data into a single executable file.
- **Assembler**: A tool that converts the assembly language code into the machine code.

CHAPTER 2
Lexical Analysis and Regular Expressions

Introduction

In the previous chapter, we provided an overview of compilers, discussing their structure, phases of compilation, and historical context. Now, we shall delve into the first phase of compilation: Lexical Analysis. Lexical analysis, or scanning, is crucial as it breaks down the source code into tokens, which are the basic building blocks for subsequent phases, such as parsing and semantic analysis. This chapter will provide a detailed explanation of tokens, patterns, lexemes, regular expressions, finite automata, and practical implementations using tools, such as the Flex and JFlex.

Structure

In this chapter, we will discuss the following topics:

- Tokens, Patterns, Lexemes
  - Tokens
  - Patterns
  - Lexemes
- Regular Expressions
  - Basic Components
  - Examples of Regular Expressions in Practice
- Finite Automata
  - Types of Finite Automata
  - Converting Regular Expressions into Finite Automata
- Example Implementations using Flex and JFlex
  - Practical Implementation using flex
  - Practical Implementation using Jflex

Tokens, Patterns, Lexemes

Here, we will explore the crucial phase of lexical analysis within the compilation process. Lexical analysis serves as the initial step in translating the high-level source code into machine-readable code by breaking down the source code into meaningful tokens. Hence, let us understand the fundamental concepts: Tokens, patterns, and lexemes.

Tokens

A token is the smallest unit of a program that holds a meaningful representation. In lexical analysis, tokens include keywords, identifiers, literals, operators, and punctuation symbols.

Types of Tokens

- **Keywords:** Reserved words in a programming language that have predefined meanings, and cannot be used for any other purpose, such as if, while, or return.
- **Identifiers:** Names given to variables, functions, and other user-defined entities.
- **Literals:** Constant values, such as numbers (123), characters ('a'), and strings ("hello").
- **Operators:** Symbols that represent operations, such as +, -, *, /.
- **Punctuation:** Characters that help define the structure of a program, such as semicolons (;), commas (,), and braces ({, }).

Patterns

A pattern describes the structure that a token must conform to. Patterns are typically specified using regular expressions which define sets of strings that match the token's structure.

Lexemes

A lexeme is an actual sequence of characters in the source code that matches a pattern for a token. For example, in the statement, int x = 10; the lexemes are int, x, =, 10, and; .

Example:

Consider the following C statement:

```
int x = 42;
```

- **int** is a keyword token.
- **x** is an identifier token.
- **=** is an operator token.
- **42** is a literal token.
- **;** is a punctuation token.

In this example, each lexeme matches a specific pattern, and is recognized as a distinct token by the lexical analyzer.

Regular Expressions

Regular expressions (regex) are symbolic notations used to describe patterns in the text. They are essential in defining the structure of tokens in lexical analysis.

Basic Components

Regular expressions (regex) are powerful tools used to search, match, and manipulate text. Understanding their basic components is necessary for creating effective patterns. In this section, we will cover the fundamental elements of regular expressions, including literal characters, special characters, and metacharacters which together help you define search patterns, and perform text operations efficiently.

- **Literal Characters**: Match themselves directly, such as a, b, 1.
- **Concatenation**: Sequences of characters that match together, such as ab matching the string ab.
- **Alternation**: Choice between patterns, such as a|b matches a or b.
- **Repetition**: Patterns that repeat, such as a* matches zero or more a's, a+ matches one or more a's, a? matches zero or one a.
- **Character Classes**: Sets of characters, such as [a-z] match any lowercase letter.
- **Grouping**: Grouping subpatterns, such as (ab)+ matches one or more ab.

Examples:

- **Identifiers:**

  [a-zA-Z_][a-zA-Z0-9_]*

  - Matches any string that starts with a letter or underscore, followed by letters, digits, or underscores.
- **Integer Literals**:

  [0-9]+

  - Matches one or more digits.
- **Floating-Point Literals**:

  [0-9]+\.[0-9]*([eE][+-]?[0-9]+)?

  - Matches numbers with optional exponents.

Usage in Lexical Analysis

Regular expressions are used to define patterns for different tokens in the source code. A lexical analyzer uses these patterns to scan the source code, and identify the tokens.

Regular expressions are a powerful tool in lexical analysis. They allow us to succinctly define patterns for various tokens in a programming language. Understanding regular expressions involves recognizing the significance of each component, and how they interact to form the complex patterns.

Literal Characters

Literal characters in regular expressions match themselves. For example, the 'regex' matches the character, a. This is the simplest form of a regular expression.

Concatenation

Concatenation in regular expressions involves writing characters or subpatterns next to each other to match the sequences. For example, the regex, abc matches the string, abc. This means that each character in the sequence must appear in the specified order.

Alternation

Alternation allows for the choice between different patterns. The regex, a|b matches either a or b. This is useful for defining tokens that can have multiple valid forms.

Repetition

Repetition operators in regular expressions specify how many times a pattern should be repeated. Common repetition operators include:

- *** (asterisk)**: Matches zero or more occurrences of the preceding element. For example, a* matches a, aa, aaa, and so on, as well as an empty string.
- **+ (plus)**: Matches one or more occurrences of the preceding element. For example, a+ matches a, aa, aaa, but not an empty string.
- **? (question mark)**: Matches zero or one occurrence of the preceding element. For example, a? matches a and an empty string.

Character Classes

Character classes allow for specifying a set of characters to match. For example, [a-z] matches any lowercase letter. Character classes can also be negated using the ^ symbol, such as [^a-z] which matches any character that is not a lowercase letter.

Grouping

Grouping in regular expressions involves using parentheses to group subpatterns. This allows for applying repetition operators to multiple characters or patterns. For example, (ab)+ matches one or more occurrences of the string, ab.

Examples of Regular Expressions in Practice

- **Identifiers**: [a-zA-Z_][a-zA-Z0-9_]*
  - This regex matches the strings that start with a letter or underscore, followed by any combination of letters, digits, or underscores. It is commonly used to identify variable names, function names, and other identifiers in programming languages.
- **Integer Literals**: [0-9]+
  - This regex matches one or more digits, representing integer literals. It ensures that only sequences of digits are recognized as integers.
- **Floating-Point Literals**: [0-9]+\.[0-9]*([eE][+-]?[0-9]+)?
  - This regex matches the floating-point numbers, including optional exponents. It handles various formats of floating-point literals, ensuring that numbers, such as 3.14, 0.5, and 1.23e10 are recognized correctly.

To illustrate the power and flexibility of regular expressions, let us consider a few practical examples.

Example 1: Identifiers

An identifier, in most of the programming languages, consists of a sequence of letters, digits, and underscores, starting with a letter or an underscore. The regular expression for an identifier can be defined as follows:

[a-zA-Z_][a-zA-Z0-9_]*

- **[a-zA-Z_]**: Matches a single letter (uppercase or lowercase) or an underscore.
- **[a-zA-Z0-9_]***: Matches zero or more letters, digits, or underscores.

This regex ensures that identifiers, such as `var_name`, `variable1`, and `_temp` are matched correctly.

Example 2: Integer Literals

An integer literal consists of one or more digits. The regular expression for an integer literal can be defined as:

[0-9]+

- [0-9]+: Matches one or more digits.

This regex ensures that numbers, such as 123, 42, and 7 are matched as integer literals.

Example 3: Floating-Point Literals

A floating-point literal can be more complex, as it may include a decimal point and an optional exponent. The regular expression for a floating-point literal can be defined as:

[0-9]+\.[0-9]*([eE][+-]?[0-9]+)?

- **[0-9]+**: Matches one or more digits before the decimal point.
- **\.**: Matches the decimal point.
- **[0-9]***: Matches zero or more digits after the decimal point.
- **([eE][+-]?[0-9]+)?**: Matches an optional exponent which consists of an e or E, an optional sign (+ or -), and one or more digits.

This regex ensures that floating-point numbers, such as 3.14, 0.5, 2.71828, and 6.02e23 are matched correctly.

Finite Automata

Finite automata (FA) are abstract machines used to recognize patterns defined by regular expressions. They consist of states and transitions between states, driven by input symbols.

Types of Finite Automata

The Finite Automata are crucial in understanding how machines process input and recognize patterns. In this section, we will break down the two main types of finite automata: Deterministic Finite Automata (DFA) and Non-Deterministic Finite Automata (NFA).

- **Deterministic Finite Automata (DFA)**

  In a DFA, each state has exactly one transition for each possible input symbol. This makes DFAs straightforward to implement but can result in a large number of states for complex patterns.

- **Nondeterministic Finite Automata (NFA)**

  In an NFA, states can have multiple transitions for the same input symbol, including epsilon (ε) transitions that move to a new state without consuming any input. NFAs are more flexible but require additional processing to simulate.

Converting Regular Expressions into Finite Automata

Regular expressions can be converted into the finite automata to facilitate token recognition. The process typically involves constructing an NFA first, and then converting it into a DFA.

Example: Regular Expression to NFA

Consider the regular expression for identifiers: [a-zA-Z_][a-zA-Z0-9_]*.

NFA Construction:

Nondeterministic Finite Automata (NFAs) are used to recognize patterns in text. This section covers the basics of constructing an NFA, including how to translate regular expressions into these machines.

1. Create a start state.
2. Add transitions for [a-zA-Z_] from the start state to an accepting state.
3. From the accepting state, add transitions for [a-zA-Z0-9_] back to itself.

Example: NFA to DFA Conversion

Using the subset construction algorithm, convert the NFA into a DFA:

1. **Identify the initial state**: The set containing the NFA's start state.
2. **Determine transitions**: For each state and input symbol, determine the set of reachable states.
3. **Create new DFA states**: Each unique set of NFA states becomes a DFA state.
4. **Define accepting states**: DFA states that include any of the NFA's accepting states become accepting states in the DFA.

Example Implementations Using Flex and Jflex

Flex and JFlex are tools used for generating lexical analyzers that process the text based on regular expressions. In this section, we will explore practical examples of using the Flex (for C/C++) and JFlex (for Java) to create lexical analyzers, demonstrating their applications and effectiveness in handling various text-processing tasks.

Practical Implementation Using Flex

Flex is a tool for generating lexical analyzers based on regular expressions. Here is an example of a Flex specification for simple tokens:

```
%{
#include "y.tab.h"
%}

%%
"int"        { return INT; }
"float"      { return FLOAT; }
[a-zA-Z_][a-zA-Z0-9_]*  { return IDENTIFIER; }
[0-9]+       { return INTEGER; }
[0-9]+\.[0-9]*([eE][+-]?[0-9]+)? { return FLOATING_POINT; }
"+"          { return PLUS; }
"-"          { return MINUS; }
"*"          { return MULTIPLY; }
"/"          { return DIVIDE; }
"="          { return ASSIGN; }
";"          { return SEMICOLON; }
[ \t\n]      { /* ignore whitespace */ }
.            { /* catch all for any other character */ }
%%
```

In this example, each pattern is associated with a specific token type. When Flex scans the input, it matches lexemes to these patterns, and returns the corresponding tokens.

Practical Implementation Using JFlex

JFlex is a lexical analyzer generator for Java. Here is an example of the JFlex specification:

```
%%
%class Lexer
%unicode
%public
%type Token

%{
  private Symbol symbol(int type) {
    return new Symbol(type, yychar, yyline);
  }
%}

INT = "int"
FLOAT = "float"
ID = [a-zA-Z_][a-zA-Z0-9_]*
INT_LIT = [0-9]+
FLOAT_LIT = [0-9]+\.[0-9]*([eE][+-]?[0-9]+)?
WHITESPACE = [ \t\n]

%%

{INT}           { return symbol(sym.INT); }
{FLOAT}         { return symbol(sym.FLOAT); }
{ID}            { return symbol(sym.ID); }
{INT_LIT}       { return symbol(sym.INT_LIT); }
{FLOAT_LIT}     { return symbol(sym.FLOAT_LIT); }
"+"             { return symbol(sym.PLUS); }
"-"             { return symbol(sym.MINUS); }
"*"             { return symbol(sym.MULTIPLY); }
"/"             { return symbol(sym.DIVIDE); }
"="             { return symbol(sym.ASSIGN); }
";"             { return symbol(sym.SEMICOLON); }
{WHITESPACE}    { /* skip whitespace */ }
.               { /* catch all for any other character */ }
```

In this example, JFlex generates a Java class that implements the lexer. The patterns defined in this specification are used to match the lexemes and return their corresponding tokens.

Conclusion

Thus, Lexical Analysis is a foundational phase in the compilation process, transforming the source code into tokens that form the basis for subsequent phases, such as parsing and semantic analysis. By understanding tokens, patterns, lexemes, regular expressions, and finite automata, one can create efficient and accurate lexical analyzers. Tools, such as Flex and JFlex provide practical means to implement these concepts in real-world applications.

In the next chapter, we will delve into the phase that follows lexical analysis, syntax analysis, or parsing. This phase involves analyzing the structure of the token sequence to build a syntactic structure, typically represented as a parse tree. Understanding lexical analysis will serve as a strong foundation for mastering syntax analysis and other advanced topics in compiler design.

Points to Remember

- **Tokens**: These are the basic units of a program's source code, such as keywords, identifiers, and operators.
- **Types of Tokens**: Includes keywords (reserved words), identifiers (variable names), literals (constants), operators (symbols for operations), and punctuations (symbols, such as commas and semicolons).
- **Patterns**: Rules defining the structure of tokens, described using regular expressions to match the sequences of characters.
- **Lexemes**: The actual sequences of characters in the source code that match a pattern and form tokens.
- **Regular Expressions**: Patterns used to define token structures, including components, such as literal characters, concatenation, alteration (alternatives), repetitions, character classes, and grouping.
- **Finite Automata**: Computational models used to recognize patterns defined by regular expressions, including Deterministic Finite Automata (DFA) and Nondeterministic Finite Automata (NFA).
- **Deterministic Finite Automata (DFA)**: Finite automata with a single possible state transition for each input symbol, used for efficient pattern matching.
- **Nondeterministic Finite Automata (NFA)**: Finite automata that can transition to multiple states for a single input symbol, useful for representing more complex patterns.
- **Converting Regular Expressions Finite Automata**: This is the process of creating DFA or NFA from regular expressions to implement pattern matching.
- **Example Implementations Using Flex and JFlex**:
    - **Flex**: A tool for generating lexical analyzers in C/C++, used to define patterns and process input.
    - **JFlex**: A tool for generating lexical analyzers in Java, similar to Flex, but designed for the Java environment.

Multiple Choice Questions

1. Which of the following defines a lexeme?
    a. A sequence of characters in the source program that matches the pattern for a token.
    b. A set of rules defining a token.
    c. The translation of a high-level language to assembly language.
    d. None of the above.
2. Which of the following represents a token in lexical analysis?
    a. A variable name
    b. An operator
    c. A keyword
    d. All of the above

3. A pattern in lexical analysis is:
    a. A sequence of characters that defines the structure of a token.
    b. The process of recognizing tokens.
    c. The symbolic representation of a token.
    d. A function in the lexer
4. In a programming language, the keyword, 'if' is an example of which of the following?
    a. Token
    b. Lexeme
    c. Pattern
    d. None of the above
5. Which of the following best describes the relationship between tokens, patterns, and lexemes?
    a. A lexeme is a sequence of characters that matches a pattern, and the pattern defines a token.
    b. A token is a sequence of characters that matches a lexeme, and the lexeme defines a pattern.
    c. A pattern is a token that matches a lexeme.
    d. None of the above.
6. Which of the following symbols is used to denote zero or more occurrences in a regular expression?
    a. +
    b. *
    c. ?
    d. |
7. What does the regular expression [0-9]* match?
    a. Any single digit
    b. One or more digits
    c. Zero or more digits
    d. Exactly one digit
8. The regular expression (a|b)* matches:
    a. Any string of a's and b's
    b. Exactly one occurrence of either 'a' or 'b'
    c. At least one occurrence of 'a' or 'b'
    d. None of the above

9. Which of the following regular expressions matches an identifier in a programming language?
   a. [a-zA-Z][a-zA-Z0-9]*
   b. [0-9]+
   c. [^a-zA-Z]
   d. \d+
10. In a regular expression, the symbol | denotes:
    a. Union (OR)
    b. Concatenation
    c. Kleene star
    d. None of the above
11. Which of the following statements about finite automata is true?
    a. They are used to recognize regular languages.
    b. They are equivalent to pushdown automata.
    c. They can recognize context-free languages.
    d. None of the above.
12. A finite automaton with ε-transitions is also known as:
    a. Non-deterministic finite automaton (NFA)
    b. Deterministic finite automaton (DFA)
    c. Context-free grammar
    d. Turing machine
13. Which of the following is true about the Deterministic Finite Automata (DFA)?
    a. Each state has exactly one transition for each symbol in the alphabet.
    b. Multiple transitions for a single symbol are allowed.
    c. They can have ε-transitions.
    d. None of the above.
14. A language is accepted by a finite automaton if:
    a. The automaton ends in a final state after reading the entire string.
    b. The automaton can loop infinitely.
    c. The string contains an even number of symbols.
    d. The automaton ends in any state after reading the string.
15. In a Non-deterministic Finite Automaton (NFA), a state can have:
    a. Multiple transitions for a single symbol.
    b. Only one transition per symbol.
    c. No transitions for some symbols.
    d. None of the above.

16. Which tool is commonly used for generating lexical analyzers in C/C++?
    a. Flex
    b. JFlex
    c. Bison
    d. Yacc
17. JFlex is primarily used for generating lexical analyzers in which programming language?
    a. C++
    b. Java
    c. Python
    d. Ruby
18. In Flex, which symbol is used to define a regular expression rule?
    a. ->
    b. /
    c. :
    d. {}
19. Which of the following is a key feature of JFlex?
    a. It generates C code for lexical analyzers.
    b. It supports Unicode and regular expressions in Java.
    c. It can be used to generate parsers.
    d. It is limited to handling ASCII characters only.
20. What does the %% symbol signify in a Flex input file?
    a. The start of the rules section.
    b. The end of the definitions section.
    c. The start of the user code section.
    d. The end of the rules section.

Answers

1. a
2. d
3. a
4. a
5. a
6. b
7. c

8. a
9. a
10. a
11. a
12. a
13. a
14. a
15. a
16. a
17. b
18. b
19. b
20. a

Questions

1. Explain the concepts of tokens, patterns, and lexemes in the context of lexical analysis. How are they related to each other?
2. Discuss the significance of tokens in a programming language. How does a lexical analyzer identify and categorize different tokens from a source code?
3. Differentiate between a pattern and a lexeme with suitable examples. How does a lexical analyzer use these concepts to perform lexical analysis?
4. Describe the role of regular expressions in lexical analysis. How do regular expressions help in defining the patterns for tokens?
5. What are the key components of a regular expression?
6. Illustrate how regular expressions can be used to validate the syntax of an email address or a simple arithmetic expression.
7. Explain the concept of the finite automata, and its role in recognizing regular languages.
8. Discuss the process of converting a regular expression into a finite automaton. How does this process help in the implementation of a lexical analyzer?
9. Describe the process of creating a lexical analyzer using Flex. What are the key sections of a Flex input file, and how do they contribute to the generation of a lexer?
10. Explain how JFlex can be used to generate a lexical analyzer for Java. What are the key features of JFlex that make it suitable for use in Java-based projects?

Key Terms

- **Tokens**: Fundamental elements of the source code recognized by lexical analyzers, including keywords, identifiers, literals, operators, and punctuation.
- **Patterns**: These are used to define the structure of tokens with regular expressions which helps in identifying and categorizing tokens.
- **Lexemes**: Actual sequences in the source code that match the defined patterns, and represent the values of tokens.
- **Types of Tokens**:
  - **Keywords**: Reserved words with specific meanings in a programming language (for example, if, return).
  - **Identifiers**: Names used for variables, functions, and other user-defined items (for example, sum, total).
  - **Literals**: Fixed values directly used in the code (for example, 123, "example").
  - **Operators**: Symbols that perform operations (for example, +, *).
  - **Punctuation**: Symbols that organize and separate tokens (for example ;, ,).
- **Regular Expressions**: Patterns for defining token structures. The key components include:
  - **Literal Characters**: Exact text matches.
  - **Concatenation**: Combining patterns (for example, abc).
  - **Alteration**: Choosing between patterns (for example, a|b).
  - **Repetition**: Indicating repeated patterns (for example., a*).
- **Character Classes**: Define sets of characters to match (for example, [0-9] for digits, [a-zA-Z] for letters).
- **Grouping**: Use parentheses to group patterns for operations, such as repetition or alternation (for example, (abc)*).
- **Finite Automata**:
  - **Deterministic Finite Automata (DFA)**: Each state has a single transition for each input symbol, making them efficient for pattern matching.
  - **Non-deterministic Finite Automata (NFA)**: States may have multiple transitions for the same symbol or ε-transitions, allowing for more flexibility in pattern recognition.
- **Converting Regular Expressions into Finite Automata**: The process of translating regular expressions into DFAs or NFAs to automate pattern recognition in lexical analysis.
- **Example Implementations**:
- **Flex**: A tool for generating C/C++ lexical analyzers based on regular expressions, useful for pattern matching in text processing.
  - **JFlex**: A tool for generating Java lexical analyzers, similar to Flex but designed for Java environments.

CHAPTER 3

Lexical Analyzer Generators and Error Handling

Introduction

In the preceding chapters, we introduced the foundational concepts of lexical analysis and regular expressions, delving into tokens, patterns, lexemes, finite automata, and practical implementations using tools, such as Flex and JFlex. Now, we turn our attention to the practical implementation of lexical analysis through lexical analyzer generators. Additionally, we will explore strategies for error handling during lexical analysis, ensuring robustness and resilience in the face of unexpected input.

Lexical analyzer generators, such as Lex, Flex, and JFlex automate the process of creating lexical analyzers, making them more efficient and reducing the likelihood of errors. Error handling in lexical analysis is crucial for developing compilers that can handle erroneous input gracefully, and provide meaningful feedback to the users. This chapter will cover the use of these tools and techniques in detail, providing a comprehensive understanding of how to create and manage lexical analyzers effectively.

Structure

In this chapter, we will discuss the following topics:

- Lexical Analyzer Generators (Lex, Flex, JFlex)
  - Overview of Lexical Analysis
  - Introduction to Lex
  - Flex: Enhancing Lex
  - JFlex for Java Applications
  - Syntax and Rules for Defining Tokens
  - Example Programs and Use Cases
- Error Handling in Lexical Analysis
  - Identifying Lexical Errors
  - Strategies for Error Detection and Reporting
  - Implementing Error Recovery Techniques
  - Real-world Examples

- Example Implementations and Error Handling Techniques
  - o Step-by-Step Example Implementations
  - o Demonstrating Error Handling
  - o Debugging and Optimization Tips

Lexical Analyzer Generators

Lexical analyzer generators are powerful tools that automate the creation of lexical analyzers which are essential for processing and interpreting the source code. These generators take regular expressions and rules as input, and produce a code that can efficiently tokenize the text. This section will explore how lexical analyzer generators work, their key features, and their roles in simplifying the development of compilers and interpreters.

Overview of Lexical Analysis

Lexical Analysis is the initial phase of the compilation or interpretation process, focusing on transforming a sequence of characters into a sequence of tokens. Tokens are the smallest units of meaning in the code, including keywords (*for example, if, while*), identifiers (*for example, variable names*), literals (*for example, numbers, strings*), and operators (*for example,*+ -). This phase simplifies the processing of the source code, making it easier for subsequent stages of compilation or interpretation.

Importance of Lexical Analysis

Think of lexical analysis as breaking a complex sentence into individual words and punctuation marks. Just as each word and punctuation mark contributes to the meaning of a sentence, each token represents a fundamental piece of information in a program.

Example 3.1: In everyday applications, imagine organizing a grocery list by sorting items into categories, such as fruits, vegetables, and dairy products. Similarly, lexical analysis organizes and categorizes different components of the source code into tokens, making it easier to process and analyze the code efficiently.

Lexical Analyzer Generators (Lex, Flex, JFlex)

Lexical analyzer generators are tools designed to automate the creation of lexical analyzers from a given specification. These tools allow the programmers to focus on defining token patterns and corresponding actions without worrying about the intricacies of implementing the lexical analyzer manually. By simplifying this process, lexical analyzer generators contribute to the efficiency and accuracy of compiler development.

Introduction to Lex

Lex (Lexical Analyzer Generator) is one of the earliest and most widely used tools for generating lexical analyzers. Developed in the 1970s, Lex is often used in conjunction with Yacc (Yet Another Compiler Compiler), a parser generator. Together, Lex and Yacc form a powerful duo for building compilers.

It generates C code for a lexer based on regular expressions defined in a specification file which is then compiled to create an executable program for lexical analysis. This lexer reads input text matches patterns to identify tokens, and processes the text accordingly.

Example 3.2: Imagine a text editor that highlights different elements of the code (for example, keywords, and variables) with different colors. Thus, the Lex can be used to build the underlying analyzer that identifies these elements.

In this example, we will develop a basic lexical analyzer using Lex, a tool designed to generate scanners or tokenizers. This code will help you to understand how to utilize the Lex to create a simple lexical analyzer that can recognize numbers, identifiers, and other characters. This tool is crucial for breaking down input into manageable components, a foundational step in compiler design and text processing.

```
%{
#include <stdio.h>
 #include <stdlib.h>
 %}
%% [0-9]+ { printf("NUMBER: %s\n", yytext); }
[a-zA-Z_][a-zA-Z_0-9]* { printf("IDENTIFIER: %s\n", yytext); }
\n { /* Ignore newlines */ }
. { printf("UNRECOGNIZED: %s\n", yytext); }
%%
int main() {
yylex();
return 0;
}
```

The provided Lex code identifies and classifies tokens from an input stream. It processes numeric literals, identifiers (*variable names*), and unrecognized characters, while ignoring newline characters. This basic implementation serves as a foundation for understanding how lexical analysis functions and how Lex/Flex tools can be used to generate tokenizers.

Explanation of the Code:

"Let's see the code in detail:"

Definitions Section:

- This includes necessary headers and declarations.

Rules Section:

- [0-9]+ matches sequences of digits, identifying them as NUMBER.
- [a-zA-Z_][a-zA-Z_0-9]* matches identifiers consisting of letters and digits, identifying them as IDENTIFIER.
- . matches any single character not covered by previous rules, and prints it as UNRECOGNIZED.

`Main()` Function:

- Calls **`yylex()`** to start the lexical analysis process.

To use Lex, you need to follow the following steps:

1. **Write the Lex Specification**: Define the patterns and actions for the tokens in a .l file.
2. **Generate the Lexical Analyzer**: Run Lex on the .l file to generate the C source code for the lexical analyzer.
3. **Compile the Generated Code**: Compile the generated C code, along with any additional C code required by the analyzer.
4. **Integrate with the Parser**: If using Yacc or another parser generator, integrate the lexical analyzer with the parser.

Flex: Enhancing Lex

Flex (*Fast Lexical Analyzer Generator*) is an improved version of the Lex. Flex offers better performance and additional features, such as C++ code generation, making it a popular choice for modern compiler projects.

Example:

The 3A tool for processing and analyzing large datasets might use Flex to efficiently tokenize and extract information from log files.

In this example, we will explore how to create a basic lexer using Lex (*or Flex, its open-source variant*). A lexer is a crucial component of a compiler or interpreter that scans source code, and breaks it into tokens. This Lex specification demonstrates how to identify and classify different types of tokens, such as numbers and identifiers, and handle unrecognized characters.

```
%option noyywrap
%{
 #include <stdio.h>
#include <stdlib.h>
%}
%%
[0-9]+ { printf("NUMBER: %s\n", yytext); }
[a-zA-Z_][a-zA-Z_0-9]* { printf("IDENTIFIER: %s\n", yytext); }
\n { /* Ignore newlines */ }
. { printf("UNRECOGNIZED: %s\n", yytext); }
%%
int main() {
yylex();
return 0;
}
```

The provided Flex code is designed to recognize and classify tokens in an input stream. The primary goal is to distinguish between numbers, identifiers, and unrecognized characters, while ignoring newlines. Understanding this code is necessary for grasping how lexical analysis works, and how it can be implemented using the Flex.

Explanation of the Code:

"Let's see the code in detail:"

- **`%option noyywrap`:** This directive eliminates the need for the **`yywrap()`** function, simplifying the code, and avoiding issues related to input stream wrapping.
- **Rules Section:** Identical to the Lex example but benefits from Flex's optimizations and performance enhancements.

To use Flex, follow these steps:

1. **Write the Flex Specification**: Define the patterns and actions for the tokens in a .l file.
2. **Generate the Lexical Analyzer**: Run Flex on the .l file to generate the C or C++ source code for the lexical analyzer.
3. **Compile the Generated Code**: Compile the generated code, along with any additional code required by the analyzer.
4. **Integrate with the Parser**: If using Bison or another parser generator, integrate the lexical analyzer with the parser.

JFlex for Java Applications

JFlex is a lexical analyzer generator for Java, providing similar functionality to Lex and Flex but generating Java code instead of C or C++. JFlex is particularly useful for Java-based compiler projects.

Example:

In a Java IDE, JFlex can be used to build a lexical analyzer that recognizes Java language constructs, such as keywords and identifiers, from the source code.

In this section, we will examine a lexer implementation using JFlex, a lexical analyzer generator for Java. Lexers, also known as lexical analyzers or scanners, are crucial in the compilation process, converting the raw input text into a stream of tokens that a parser can process.

```
%%
%class Lexer
%unicode
%cup
%%
"if" { return sym.IF; }
"else" { return sym.ELSE; }
[0-9]+ { return sym.NUMBER; }
[a-zA-Z_][a-zA-Z_0-9]* { return sym.IDENTIFIER; }
\n { /* Ignore newlines */ }
. { System.err.println("Unrecognized character: " + yytext()); }
%%
```

The provided JFlex code snippet defines a lexer that identifies several types of tokens from a source code. This lexer is designed to recognize keywords, numbers, and identifiers, and handle errors for unrecognized characters. Understanding this code helps illustrate how a lexer can be customized to handle the specific language constructs, and manage errors effectively.

Explanation of the Code:

"Let's see the code in detail:"

- **`%class Lexer`:** Specifies the Java class name for the generated lexer.
- **`%unicode`:** Supports Unicode characters.
- **`%cup`:** Integrates with the CUP parser generator.
- **Rules Section:**
    - "if" and "else" are recognized as specific tokens.
    - [0-9]+ and [a-zA-Z_][a-zA-Z_0-9]* are matched and returned as NUMBER and IDENTIFIER, respectively.
    - The '.' rule handles unrecognized characters, printing an error message.

A JFlex specification includes declarations, regular expressions, and actions, similar to the Lex and Flex.

JFlex generates a Java class that implements the lexer, which can be integrated into the Java-based compiler projects.

To use JFlex, follow the steps given below:

1. **Write the JFlex Specification**: Define the patterns and actions for the tokens in a **`.flex`** file.
2. **Generate the Lexical Analyzer**: Run JFlex on the **`.flex`** file to generate the Java source code for the lexical analyzer.
3. **Compile the Generated Code**: Compile the generated Java code, along with any additional code required by the analyzer.
4. **Integrate with the Parser**: If using a Java-based parser generator, integrate the lexical analyzer with the parser.

Error Handling in Lexical Analysis

"Effective error handling in lexical analysis ensures that a lexical analyzer can gracefully manage and recover from issues encountered during tokenization."

This section covers identifying lexical errors, strategies for error detection and reporting, implementing error recovery techniques, and provides real-world examples with code and analysis.

Identifying Lexical Errors

Lexical errors occur when the input sequence does not conform to any of the defined token patterns. These errors can arise from invalid characters or improperly formatted tokens. Identifying such errors is crucial for robust lexical analysis.

```
%{
#include <stdio.h>
#include <stdlib.h>
%}

%%
[0-9]+          { printf("NUMBER: %s\n", yytext); }
[a-zA-Z_][a-zA-Z_0-9]* { printf("IDENTIFIER: %s\n", yytext); }
\n              { /* Ignore newlines */ }
.               { printf("ERROR: Unrecognized character '%s'\n", yytext); }

%%

int main() {
    yylex();
    return 0;
}
```

This code is used to identify and report characters that do not fit any defined token patterns. It is valuable in scenarios where you need to process or validate input data, and handle invalid characters or formatting.

Explanation of the Code:

"Let's see the code in detail:"

- `[0-9]+`: Matches sequences of digits, and identifies them as numbers.
- `[a-zA-Z_][a-zA-Z_0-9]*`: Matches identifiers made up of letters and digits.
- `.`: Captures any single character that does not match the previous rules, and reports it as an unrecognized character.

Strategies for Error Detection and Reporting

Effective error detection and reporting strategies enhance the robustness of lexical analyzers by providing mechanisms to handle errors gracefully.

Panic Mode Recovery

Panic mode recovery involves skipping input until a known good state is reached. This approach allows the lexer to continue processing after encountering an error.

This strategy is useful in scenarios where you want to continue processing input even after encountering errors, such as in compilers or data processing applications.

```
%{
#include <stdio.h>
#include <stdlib.h>
%}
%%
"if" { printf("KEYWORD: %s\n", yytext); }
"else" { printf("KEYWORD: %s\n", yytext); }
[0-9]+ { printf("NUMBER: %s\n", yytext); }
[a-zA-Z_][a-zA-Z_0-9]* { printf("IDENTIFIER: %s\n", yytext); }
\n { /* Ignore newlines */ }
. { printf("ERROR: Unrecognized character '%s', skipping...\n", yytext); }
%%
int main() {
yylex();
return 0;
}
```

The code demonstrates how to handle errors using panic mode recovery. By reporting unrecognized characters and continuing to process the input, the lexer can handle errors gracefully and ensure that subsequent valid tokens are still processed.

Error Tokens

The dot character generates an error token for unrecognized characters, allowing the lexer to integrate error handling into its token generation process.

Error Productions

Error productions define specific rules for handling error situations. These rules help the lexer recognize, and handle invalid input more effectively.

Error productions are helpful for providing a detailed feedback about errors and continuing to parse valid input, making them ideal for detailed language parsers and validation tools.

```
%{
#include <stdio.h>
#include <stdlib.h>
%}
%%
"int" { printf("KEYWORD: %s\n", yytext); }
[0-9]+ { printf("NUMBER: %s\n", yytext); }
[a-zA-Z_][a-zA-Z_0-9]* { printf("IDENTIFIER: %s\n", yytext); }
[+\-*/=] { printf("OPERATOR: %s\n", yytext); }
\n { /* Ignore newlines */ }
. { printf("ERROR: Unrecognized character '%s'\n", yytext); }
%%
int main()
{
        yylex();
        return 0;
}
```

By defining the specific rules for various tokens, and including error handling, this code provides a detailed feedback about errors, while still processing the valid tokens. It is particularly useful for lexers that need to handle a wider range of token types.

- **Additional Tokens:** These include rules for the operators (*for example*, +, -, *, /, =). It also extends the lexer's functionality to handle more types of input tokens, and report errors for unrecognized characters.

Implementing Error Recovery Techniques

Error recovery techniques in lexical analysis are essential to handle unexpected input gracefully. These techniques ensure that the lexical analyzer can continue to function, and provide meaningful error messages to the user, even when it encounters invalid tokens. There are several methods to implement error recovery, including panic mode recovery and error tokens.

Panic Mode Recovery

Panic mode recovery is a straightforward technique where the lexer skips over input until it finds a known, good state. This allows the lexer to recover from an error, and continue processing the rest of the input.

```
%{
#include <stdio.h>
#include <stdlib.h>
%}
%%
"if" { printf("KEYWORD: %s\n", yytext); }
"else" { printf("KEYWORD: %s\n", yytext); }
[0-9]+ { printf("NUMBER: %s\n", yytext); }
[a-zA-Z_][a-zA-Z_0-9]* { printf("IDENTIFIER: %s\n", yytext); }
\n { /* Ignore newlines */ }
. { printf("ERROR: Unrecognized character '%s', skipping...\n", yytext); }
%%
int main() {
yylex();
return 0;
}
```

This approach allows the lexer to skip unrecognized characters, and continue processing subsequent valid tokens. This is useful in scenarios where the lexer needs to handle large inputs or real-time data streams with occasional errors.

- **"if" and "else"**: Recognizes keywords and prints them.
- **[0-9]+**: Recognizes numbers and prints them.
- **[a-zA-Z_][a-zA-Z_0-9]***: Recognizes identifiers and prints them.
- **\n**: Ignores newlines.
- **.**: Captures any single character not matching the previous patterns, prints an error message, and skips the character.

Error Tokens

Error tokens are a more structured way to handle errors by defining specific tokens for erroneous input. This technique helps integrate error handling into the lexer's normal workflow.

```
%{
#include <stdio.h>
#include <stdlib.h>
%}
%%
"if" { printf("KEYWORD: %s\n", yytext); }
"else" { printf("KEYWORD: %s\n", yytext); }
[0-9]+ { printf("NUMBER: %s\n", yytext); }
[a-zA-Z_][a-zA-Z_0-9]* { printf("IDENTIFIER: %s\n", yytext); }
[+\-*/=] { printf("OPERATOR: %s\n", yytext); }
```

```
\n { /* Ignore newlines */ }
. { printf("ERROR TOKEN: Unrecognized character '%s'\n", yytext); }
%%
int main() {
    yylex();
    return 0;
}
```

Error tokens allow the lexer to continue recognizing valid tokens, while also marking and reporting errors. This can be useful in scenarios, such as the source code compilation where it is important to gather as many errors as possible in a single pass.

Explanation of the Code:

Error Token Rule (.): Any unrecognized character is treated as an error token. This error token can be processed later by the parser or other components of the compiler.

Real-World Examples of Error Handling in Lexical Analysis

Effective error handling is crucial for robust lexical analysis, ensuring that errors in the source code are identified and managed gracefully. This section explores real-world examples of how error handling is implemented in lexical analyzers, demonstrating common strategies for detecting, reporting, and recovering from lexical errors in practice.

Programming Language Compilers

In a compiler, lexical analysis is the first phase where the source code is tokenized into meaningful units, such as keywords, identifiers, and operators. Error handling, in this stage is crucial for identifying and reporting the syntax errors before they reach later stages of compilation. For instance, if a compiler encounters an unrecognized symbol or keyword, it needs to report the error and possibly provide hints for correction.

Consider a scenario where a source code file has a typo in a keyword:

```
int main() {
    prntf("Hello, World!"); // Typo: 'printf' should be used
    return 0;
}
```

Error Handling:

The lexical analyzer will detect the typo in **`prntf`** as an unrecognized token, and report an error. The error message might look like:

```
ERROR: Unrecognized function name 'prntf'
```

This allows developers to correct the typo before the code is compiled.

Data Parsing in Web Forms

Web forms often require users to input data in specific formats, such as dates, email addresses, or numeric values. Lexical analysis can be used to validate this input. Error handling ensures that invalid data is flagged and rejected, prompting users to correct their entries.

Consider a web form field that expects a date in the format: YYYY-MM-DD:

```
<input type="text" id="dateField" />
```

Error Handling:

If a user enters 2024/07/23, the lexical analyzer will identify the date format as incorrect, and provide feedback:

```
ERROR: Invalid date format '2024/07/23'. Expected format is YYYY-MM-DD.
```

This ensures that the input data adheres to the required format before submission.

Log File Analysis

Log files from applications or servers are often analyzed to detect issues or unusual patterns. Lexical analyzers can parse these logs, identifying log levels, timestamps, and messages. Error handling involves recognizing malformed log entries or unexpected tokens which can indicate potential issues.

Consider a log entry with an invalid log level:

```
2024-07-23 10:00:00 INFO Application started
2024-07-23 10:01:00 WARN Unusual behavior detected
2024-07-23 10:02:00 UNKNOWN Unexpected token
```

Error Handling:

The lexical analyzer will recognize **`UNKNOWN`** as an unrecognized log level and report it:

```
ERROR: Unrecognized log level 'UNKNOWN'
```

This helps in filtering out the invalid log entries, and focus on the meaningful data.

Source Code Linters

Linters are tools that analyze the source code for potential errors, coding style issues, and best practices. Lexical analysis within linters checks for adherence to coding conventions, and reports deviations or mistakes. This ensures the code quality and consistency.

Consider a Python linter analyzing code for style issues:

```
def foo(bar):
    if bar > 0
        print("Positive")
```

Error Handling:

The lexical analyzer will detect the missing colon (:) after the 'if' statement, and provide an error message:

```
ERROR: Missing colon after 'if' statement
```

This helps the developers to adhere to the coding standards, and prevent syntax errors.

Configuration File Parsers

Configuration files are used to set the parameters for software applications. Lexical analysis ensures that these files follow the correct syntax and format. Error handling, in this context, helps to identify and report syntax errors or invalid configurations.

Consider a configuration file for a server application:

```
[server]
host = localhost
port = 8080
protocol = http
timeout = 300
unknown_key = value
```

Error Handling:

The lexical analyzer will identify the **unknown_key** as an unrecognized configuration parameter, and report:

```
ERROR: Unrecognized configuration parameter 'unknown_key'
```

This allows administrators to correct configuration errors before they affect application behavior.

These real-world examples illustrate how lexical analysis and error handling are applied across different domains, including compilers, web forms, log analysis, linters, and configuration files. Effective error handling ensures that systems can handle and recover from invalid input gracefully, providing users with clear feedback and maintaining system integrity.

Example Implementations and Error Handling Techniques

Lexical analysis involves breaking down the input into tokens, while handling errors gracefully. Here, we will cover various implementation techniques, demonstrate error handling with examples, and provide tips for debugging and optimization.

Step-by-Step Example Implementations

Let us explore implementations step-by-step and demonstrate error-handling techniques.

Basic Tokenizer with Error Handling

This example demonstrates a simple lexical analyzer (*lexer*) that tokenizes an input stream into numbers, identifiers, and operators. It also handles unrecognized characters by reporting them as errors. The lexer is implemented using Flex (*Fast Lexical Analyzer*), a tool for generating scanners (*tokenizers*).

```
%{
#include <stdio.h>
#include <stdlib.h>
%}
%% [0-9]+ { printf("NUMBER: %s\n", yytext); }
[a-zA-Z_][a-zA-Z_0-9]* { printf("IDENTIFIER: %s\n", yytext); }
[+\-*/=] { printf("OPERATOR: %s\n", yytext); }
\n { /* Ignore newlines */ }
. { printf("ERROR: Unrecognized character '%s'\n", yytext); }
%%
int main() {
     yylex();
     return 0;
}
```

Explanation of the Code:

Header Section:

- The **`%{ %}`** block includes C code that will be copied to the generated lexer. Here, it includes the **`stdio.h`** and **`stdlib.h`** headers for input/output and general utilities.

Rules Section:

- **`[0-9]+`**: This pattern matches one or more digits. When such a pattern is matched, the lexer prints "**NUMBER**" followed by the matched text (**`yytext`**).
- **`[a-zA-Z_][a-zA-Z_0-9]*`**: This pattern matches an identifier, which starts with a letter or

underscores, and can be followed by any combination of letters, digits, and underscores. It prints "**IDENTIFIER**" followed by the matched text.

- `[+\-*/=]`: This pattern matches the arithmetic operators (*plus, minus, multiplication, division, and equals*). It prints "**OPERATOR**" followed by the matched text.
- **\n**: This pattern matches newline characters, which are ignored.
- **.**: This pattern matches any single character not matched by previous rules. It prints an error message indicating the unrecognized character.

Main Function:

- The main function calls **yylex()**, the function generated by Flex that performs the lexical analysis. The lexer reads from standard input, tokenizes the input according to the defined rules, and prints the corresponding messages.

The purpose of this basic tokenizer is to:

- Identify and categorize numbers, identifiers, and operators in the input.
- Handle errors by reporting unrecognized characters.
- Provide a simple and clear example of how to use Flex for lexical analysis.

This basic tokenizer can be used as a foundation for more complex lexers in the programming language compilers, interpreters, or any application requiring tokenization of the structured input.

Keyword Recognition and Error Handling

This example builds on the basic tokenizer to recognize specific keywords (if and else) in addition to numbers, identifiers, and operators. It handles unrecognized characters by reporting them as errors, similar to the first example.

```
%{
#include <stdio.h>
#include <stdlib.h>
%}
%%
"if" { printf("KEYWORD: %s\n", yytext); }
"else" { printf("KEYWORD: %s\n", yytext); }
[0-9]+ { printf("NUMBER: %s\n", yytext); }
[a-zA-Z_][a-zA-Z_0-9]* { printf("IDENTIFIER: %s\n", yytext); }
\n { /* Ignore newlines */ }
. { printf("ERROR: Unrecognized character '%s'\n", yytext); }
%%
int main() {
    yylex();
    return 0;
}
```

Explanation of the Code:

Header Section:

- Includes **stdio.h** and **stdlib.h** for input/output and utility functions.

Rules Section:

- "**if**": This pattern matches the keyword, if, and prints the "**KEYWORD**" followed by the matched text.
- "**else**": This pattern matches the keyword, else, and prints "**KEYWORD**" followed by the matched text.
- **[0-9]+**: Matches one or more digits; prints "**NUMBER**" followed by the matched text.

- `[a-zA-Z_][a-zA-Z_0-9]*`: Matches an identifier; prints "IDENTIFIER" followed by the matched text.
- `\n`: Matches newline characters, which are ignored.
- `.`: Matches any single character, not matched by previous rules; prints an error message indicating the unrecognized character.

Main Function:

- Calls `yylex()` to perform lexical analysis, reading from standard input, tokenizing the input, and printing the corresponding messages.

The purpose of this tokenizer is to:

- Extend the basic tokenizer to recognize specific keywords (if and else).
- Continue to identify numbers, identifiers, and operators.
- Handle errors by reporting unrecognized characters.
- Demonstrate how to expand a lexer to handle additional token types.

This keyword recognition tokenizer can be used in the development of programming language compilers or interpreters that need to identify and process specific keywords, in addition to other tokens. It serves as a more advanced example of using Flex for lexical analysis, building on the concepts introduced in the basic tokenizer.

These examples serve as foundations for more complex lexers used in compilers, interpreters, and other applications requiring tokenization of the structured input.

Debugging and Optimization Tips

Debugging and optimizing a lexical analyzer are crucial steps in ensuring its efficiency and reliability. Here are some essential tips for effectively debugging and optimizing your lexical analyzer, addressed to you, the user, to enhance your learning experience.

Debugging Tips

Use Print Statements:

- Incorporate print statements within your lexer rules to output tokens as they are recognized. This helps to verify that each token is correctly identified and processed.
- Example:

```
printf("TOKEN: %s\n", yytext);
```

Track Line Numbers:

- Keeping track of line numbers can help pinpoint the exact location of errors. Update a line number counter whenever a newline character is encountered.
- **Example:**

```
\n { line_num++; }
```

Verbose Mode:

- Implement a verbose mode that provides a detailed output about the lexer's actions. This can include information about state transitions, matched patterns, and much more.
- **Example:**

```
#ifdef VERBOSE
printf("Matched: %s\n", yytext);
#endif
```

Error Reporting:

- Provide clear and concise error messages that include the unrecognized character or sequence, and the line number where the error occurred.
- **Example:**

```
fprintf(stderr, "Error: Unrecognized character '%s' at line %d\n", yytext,
line_num);
```

Isolate and Test:

- Isolate individual lexer rules, and test them independently to ensure that they work as expected. Create test cases for different input scenarios to cover all possible edge cases.

Optimization Tips

Optimization is crucial for improving the efficiency and performance of your code and systems. In this section, we will explore practical tips and techniques for optimizing the various aspects of your code, including reducing execution time, minimizing resource usage, and enhancing the overall performance. These strategies will help you to write more efficient and effective programs, ensuring smoother and faster operations.

Minimize Backtracking:

- Excessive backtracking can slow down the lexer. Ensure your rules are ordered from the most specific to the least specific to minimize the need for backtracking.
- **Example:**

  Place specific keyword rules before general identifier rules.

Use Start Conditions:

- Start conditions allow you to handle different lexical states efficiently. Use them to manage contexts, such as strings, comments, or multi-line constructs.
- **Example:**

```
%x STRING
\" { BEGIN(STRING); }
<STRING>\" { BEGIN(INITIAL); }
<STRING>. { /* Handle string content */ }
```

Avoid Repetitive Code:

- Use macros or functions to encapsulate the repetitive code. This not only makes the lexer more concise but also easier to maintain.
- **Example:**

```
%{
#define PRINT_TOKEN(type)
printf("%s: %s\n", type, yytext);
%}
[0-9]+ { PRINT_TOKEN("NUMBER"); }
[a-zA-Z_][a-zA-Z_0-9]* { PRINT_TOKEN("IDENTIFIER"); }
```

Efficient Pattern Matching:

- Write efficient regular expressions that match the tokens quickly. Avoid overly complex patterns that can slow down the lexer.
- **Example:**

  Instead of ***`[a-zA-Z_][a-zA-Z_0-9]*`*** *for identifiers, consider breaking it into smaller, more manageable patterns, if necessary.*

Profile and Benchmark:

- Use profiling tools to measure the performance of your lexer. Identify bottlenecks and optimize the slowest parts. Benchmarking different versions of your lexer can help determine the most efficient implementation.
- **Example:**

  Use tools, such as gprof or Valgrind for profiling.

By applying these debugging and optimization tips, you can ensure that your lexical analyzer is both efficient and reliable. Debugging helps identify and fix issues early in the development process, while optimization ensures that the lexer performs well even with large and complex inputs. These practices will enhance your practical skills, and contribute to the successful development of robust lexical analyzers.

Conclusion

Thus, Lexical Analysis is a vital first step in many computational processes, from compiling programming languages to parsing configuration files. Effective error handling ensures that unrecognized input is reported clearly, allowing for correction and continued processing. Techniques, such as panic mode recovery and error tokens provide robust mechanisms for managing errors. By incorporating debugging and optimization strategies, lexical analyzers can be made efficient and reliable. The next chapter will delve into syntax analysis, building on the tokens generated by lexical analysis to form meaningful syntactic structures.

Points to Remember

- Lexical analyzers convert the sequences of characters into tokens, simplifying further analysis.
- Lex, Flex, and JFlex automate token generation, with Flex and JFlex, offering enhancements and additional features.
- Error handling strategies include detecting, reporting, and recovering from lexical errors.
- Debugging and optimization improve the efficiency and accuracy of lexical analyzers.

Multiple Choice Questions

1. Which tool is an enhanced version of Lex?

   a. JFlex

   b. Flex

   c. Yacc

   d. CUP

2. What is the primary function of a Lexical Analyzer?

   a. To parse syntax trees

   b. To convert characters into tokens

   c. To optimize code performance

   d. To manage memory allocation

3. Which directive in Flex removes the need for `yywrap()`?
   a. `%option debug`
   b. `%option noyywrap`
   c. `%option fast`
   d. `%option verbose`
4. In JFlex, where are lexical rules defined?
   a. Declarations Section
   b. User Subroutines Section
   c. Lexical Rules Section
   d. Definitions Section
5. Which error recovery technique involves skipping input until a valid state is found?
   a. Panic Mode
   b. Error Productions
   c. Error Logging
   d. Recovery Mode

Answers

1. b
2. b
3. b
4. c
5. a

Questions

1. Describe the role of lexical analyzer generators, such as Lex, Flex, and JFlex in the context of compiler design. How do they simplify the process of lexical analysis?
2. Explain the process of defining tokens in Lex and Flex. What are the key components of a lexical rule, and how does each component contribute to token recognition?
3. Discuss the purpose and use of start conditions in Flex. How do they help manage different lexical contexts or states within an input stream? Provide an example to illustrate their usage.
4. Detail the common strategies for error detection and reporting in lexical analysis. How does each strategy contribute to handling lexical errors effectively?
5. Describe how line numbers are tracked and reported in a lexical analyzer. Why is this information important for debugging and error reporting? Provide an example of a code that implements line number tracking.
6. Explain the concept of error recovery in lexical analysis. What are some common error recovery techniques, and how do they differ in terms of complexity and effectiveness?

7. Illustrate the use of macros in Flex to improve code readability and maintainability. How do macros help in reducing repetitive code and managing complex patterns? Provide a practical example.
8. Discuss the impact of backtracking on the performance of a lexical analyzer. What are some strategies to minimize backtracking and optimize token recognition?
9. Explain how verbose mode can aid in debugging a lexical analyzer. What kind of information is typically included in verbose output, and how can it be used to troubleshoot issues?
10. Describe how profiling tools, such as gprof or Valgrind can be utilized to optimize a lexical analyzer's performance. What specific aspects of the lexer are evaluated, and how do these tools help in identifying performance bottlenecks?

Key Terms

- **Lexical Analyzer:** A tool or component that converts a sequence of characters into a sequence of tokens.
- **Token:** A meaningful unit of text identified during lexical analysis, such as a keyword, identifier, or operator.
- **Lex:** A lexical analyzer generator that creates lexical analyzers based on specified patterns.
- **Flex:** An enhanced version of Lex that provides additional features and optimizations for lexical analysis.
- **JFlex:** A lexical analyzer generator for Java, similar to Lex and Flex but designed for Java applications.
- **Start Conditions:** Mechanisms in Flex for handling different lexical contexts or states, such as within strings or comments.
- **Panic Mode Recovery:** An error handling technique that skips over invalid input until a valid token is found.
- **Error Tokens:** Special tokens used to represent unrecognized or invalid characters in the input stream.
- **Backtracking:** The process of trying alternative matches when the initial pattern does not fit which can be minimized for efficiency.
- **Verbose Mode:** A debugging feature that provides detailed output about the lexer's actions, useful for troubleshooting and verification.

CHAPTER 4
Syntax Analysis Context-Free Grammars

Introduction

In the previous chapter, we explored lexical analysis, focusing on how lexical analyzer generators, such as Lex and Flex help in breaking down the source code into tokens. With tokens identified, the next crucial step is Syntax Analysis which ensures that the sequence of tokens follows the grammatical rules of the programming language. This chapter introduces Context-Free Grammars (CFGs) and parse trees as fundamental tools in this phase of compilation.

Context-Free Grammars (CFGs) provide a formal framework for specifying the syntax rules of a programming language. They define how various elements of a language can be combined to form valid constructs. Parse trees, on the other hand, offer a graphical representation of how a given string adheres to these grammar rules, illustrating the hierarchical structure of the code.

We will also cover practical implementations using Yacc and Bison which are basically tools designed to generate parsers from CFG specifications. Understanding these concepts and tools will enhance your ability to build and analyze parsers, paving the way for more advanced topics in compiler design.

Structure

In this chapter, we will discuss the following topics:

- Context-Free Grammars (CFGs)
  - Overview and Definition
  - Components of CFGs
  - Example CFGs and their Applications
- Parse Trees
  - Definition and Purpose
  - Construction and Interpretation
  - Example Parse Trees
- Grammar Rules and Derivations
  - Definition of Grammar Rules
  - Derivation Processes
  - Standard Forms of CFGs
- Example Implementations using Yacc and Bison
  - Overview of Yacc and Bison
  - Example Implementations
  - Comparing Yacc and Bison

Context-Free Grammars (CFGs)

Context-Free Grammars (CFGs) are used to describe the structure of languages in a clear and formal way. This section introduces CFGs, and explains how they define patterns and rules for creating valid strings in a language.

Overview of Context-Free Grammars (CFGs)

Context-Free Grammars (CFGs) are formal systems used to describe the syntax and structure of languages. They are a fundamental concept in theoretical computer science, and are particularly important in the fields of compiler design, natural language processing, and artificial intelligence.

CFGs are designed to generate strings of symbols that belong to a particular language. They consist of a set of production rules that dictate how symbols in the language can be combined. CFGs can describe complex syntactic structures, and are more expressive than regular expressions, allowing them to capture nested and recursive patterns.

Key Features:

- **Hierarchical Structure:** CFGs can define hierarchical relationships in languages, such as nested expressions in programming languages.
- **Generative Capacity:** They can generate an infinite number of valid strings, making them suitable for defining complex languages.
- **Parse Trees:** CFGs facilitate the construction of parse trees that visually represent the structure of valid strings.

Applications:

- **Programming Languages:** Defining syntax rules for languages, such as C, Java, and Python.
- **Natural Language Processing (NLP):** Parsing sentences to understand the grammatical structure.
- **Compilers:** Analyzing the source code to ensure that it conforms to the language syntax.

Definition of Context-Free Grammars (CFGs):

Definition: A Context-Free Grammar (CFG) is a formal grammar that consists of the following four key components:

- **Variables (Non-Terminals):** Symbols that represent syntactic categories or structures in the language. They are placeholders that can be replaced by combinations of other symbols according to the grammar rules. Examples include: E for expression or S for statement.
- **Terminals:** The basic symbols from which strings in the language are constructed. Terminals are the actual characters or tokens of the language, and cannot be further decomposed. Examples include: keywords, operators, and literals.
- **Production Rules:** Rules that define how variables can be replaced by sequences of terminals and other variables. Each rule describes how a variable can be expanded into a string of terminals and variables. For example, $E \rightarrow E + T$ or $T \rightarrow F * F$.
- **Start Symbol:** A special non-terminal symbol from which the derivation of strings begins. The start symbol is the initial point of the grammar, and represents the entire language. It is usually denoted as S.

Formal Definition: A CFG is formally defined as a 4-tuple (V, Σ, R, S) where:

- **V** is a finite set of variables (non-terminals).
- Σ is a finite set of terminals (alphabet of the language).
- **R** is a finite set of production rules, each of the form $A \rightarrow \beta$, where A is a variable and β is a string of variables and terminals.

- **S** is the start symbol, a special variable from V used to generate strings.

Example:

Consider a simple arithmetic expression grammar. A CFG can define expressions involving addition and multiplication, such as a + b * c.

The grammar could be defined as follows:

- ***Variables:*** E *(expression)*, T *(term)*, F *(factor)*
- ***Terminals:*** +, *, *number*
- ***Production Rules:***
    - o E → E + T | T
    - o T → T * F | F
    - o F → number
- ***Start Symbol:*** E

This CFG can generate arithmetic expressions, such as number + number * number, where number is a terminal symbol representing numeric values.

For example, it generates the string, a + b * c.

Components of Context-Free Grammars (CFGs)

Context-Free Grammars (CFGs) consist of a few basic parts: terminals, non-terminals, production rules, and the start symbol. This section will explain each component, and how they work together to define a language's structure.

- **Variables (Non-Terminals)**

  Variables, also known as non-terminals, are symbols in a CFG that represent syntactic categories or structures within a language. They act as placeholders in the production rules and are used to define how sequences of symbols (both terminal and non-terminal) can be combined to form valid strings in the language.

  These represent syntactic structures, and are replaced by other symbols according to the rules.

  Purpose:

  Non-terminals define the structure of the language, and help in breaking down complex expressions into simpler parts. They are replaced by other variables or terminals according to the production rules.

  Example:

  In a CFG for arithmetic expressions:

  Variables: E *(expression)*, T *(term)*, F *(factor)*

  Usage: E *might represent a complete arithmetic expression,* T *represents terms within the expression, and* F *represents factors, such as numbers.*

- **Terminals**

  Terminals are the basic symbols or tokens from which strings in the language are constructed. They are the actual characters or symbols that appear in the language, and cannot be further decomposed. Terminals are the "alphabet" of the language.

Purpose:

Terminals represent the fundamental building blocks of the language. They form the strings that are valid in the language, and are the end result of the derivation process.

Example:

In the arithmetic expression, CFG:

Terminals: +, *, *number*

Usage: *Terminals are the symbols used in expressions.*

For instance, + and * are operators, and the number represents numeric literals.

- **Production Rules**

  Production rules define how variables can be expanded or replaced with combinations of variables and terminals. Each rule specifies how a particular variable can be transformed into a sequence of terminals and other variables.

  Purpose:

  Production rules describe the syntax of the language, and dictate how strings can be generated. They are essential for constructing valid strings from the start symbol.

  Example:

  In the arithmetic expression, CFG:

  - *Production Rules:*
    - E → E + T | T
    - T → T * F | F
    - F → number
  - *Explanation:*
    - E → E + T allows an expression to be composed of another expression, a + operator, and a term.
    - T → T * F allows a term to be composed of another term, a * operator, and a factor.
    - F → number specifies that a factor is a numeric literal.

- **Start Symbol**

  The start symbol is a special non-terminal from which the derivation of strings in the language begins. It serves as the entry point for generating strings and represents the overall structure of the language.

  Purpose:

  The start symbol initiates the derivation process, and is the basis for generating valid strings according to the CFG. It is the top-level category from which all valid strings are derived.

  Example:

  In the arithmetic expression, CFG:

  - ***Start Symbol:*** E
  - ***Usage:*** *The derivation begins with E. For example, starting with E, you might generate the string number + number * number by applying the production rules.*

Example CFGs and Their Applications

Context-Free Grammars (CFGs) are crucial for defining and parsing the syntax of various languages and structures. They are widely used in compiler design and data processing to validate and process strings. This section explores practical examples of CFGs, including arithmetic expressions, programming languages, HTML, SQL queries, and logical formulas, demonstrating their real-world applications, and how they ensure the correct syntax and structure.

- **Arithmetic Expressions:**

  An arithmetic expression, CFG defines the syntax rules for mathematical expressions involving addition, multiplication, and parentheses. This CFG handles the precedence of operators and nested expressions.

  Example CFG:

  - **Variables:** E (expression), T (term), F (factor)
  - **Terminals:** +, *, number, (
  - **Production Rules:**
    - E → E + T | T
    - T → T * F | F
    - F → number | (E)
- **Start Symbol:** E

  Real-World Application:

  This CFG is used in compilers to parse and evaluate mathematical expressions in programming languages. For example, a CFG can parse the expression, 3 + (4 * 5) to generate an Abstract Syntax Tree (AST) for evaluation.

  CFG helps in breaking down complex arithmetic expressions into simpler parts. For instance, 3 + (4 * 5) is parsed into an AST where 4 * 5 is evaluated first due to operator precedence, and then 3 is added to the result.

- **Simple Programming Language:**

  A CFG for a simple programming language might include rules for defining statements, expressions, and variable declarations. This CFG provides the syntax for basic constructs, such as assignment statements and variable declarations.

  Example CFG:

  - **Variables:** S (statement), E (expression), D (declaration)
  - **Terminals:** = (assignment), number, id (identifier), ; (semicolon)
  - **Production Rules:**
    - S → id = E ; | D ;
    - E → number | id
    - D → int id
  - **Start Symbol:** S

  Real-World Application:

  This CFG is used in the syntax analysis phase of compilers for simple programming languages or scripting languages. For example, it can parse the statement, int x; x = 5; and check if it adheres to the syntax rules of the language.

CFG ensures that statements such as int x; and x = 5; are correctly structured. The grammar rules validate that an assignment statement follows a valid syntax and that variable declarations are properly formatted.

- **HTML Syntax**

  A CFG for HTML describes the syntax of HTML documents, including elements, attributes, and nested tags. This CFG handles the hierarchical structure of the HTML tags.

  Example CFG:

  - **Variables:** Document, Element, Content
  - **Terminals:** html, head, body, title, p, text
  - **Production Rules:**
    - Document → <html> <head> <title> text </title> </head> <body> Content </body> </html>
    - Content → Element | Element Content
    - Element → <p> text </p>
  - **Start Symbol:** Document

  Real-World Application:

  This CFG is used in HTML parsers to validate and process the HTML documents. For example, it ensures that tags are properly nested and closed in an HTML document, such as <html><body><p>Hello World</p></body></html>.

  CFG checks that HTML documents follow correct tag nesting and structure. It ensures that <p> tags are properly closed, and the content is correctly embedded within the HTML elements.

- **SQL Queries**

  A CFG for SQL queries defines the syntax for constructing SQL statements, such as SELECT, INSERT, UPDATE, and DELETE. This CFG helps in validating and parsing the SQL queries.

  Example CFG:

  - **Variables:** Query, SelectStatement, TableList
  - **Terminals:** SELECT, FROM, WHERE, id (identifier), * (wildcard)
  - **Production Rules:**
    - Query → SelectStatement
    - SelectStatement → SELECT id FROM id [WHERE id = id]
  - **Start Symbol:** Query

  Real-World Application:

  This CFG is used by SQL parsers in database management systems to validate the SQL queries.

  For example, it parses and checks the query.

  `SELECT names FROM employees WHERE id = 10 for correctness.`

  CFG ensures that the SQL queries follow proper syntax rules. It validates that the **`SELECT`** clause is followed by a **`FROM`** clause and, optionally, a **`WHERE`** clause with correct conditions.

- **Mathematical Logic (Propositional Logic)**

  A CFG for propositional logic defines the syntax for logical formulas, including conjunctions, disjunctions, and implications. This CFG helps in parsing and evaluating logical expressions.

Example CFG:

- **Variables:** Formula, Atom, Clause
- **Terminals:** AND, OR, NOT, ->, id (identifier)
- **Production Rules:**
    - Formula → Atom | NOT Formula | Formula AND Formula | Formula OR Formula | Formula -> Formula
    - Atom → id
- **Start Symbol:** Formula

Real-World Application:

This CFG is used in logic programming and automated theorem proving to parse logical statements.

For example, it helps in validating expressions, such as p -> (q AND r).

CFG structures logical expressions into valid formulas. It ensures the correct usage of logical operators, and allows parsing and evaluation of logical statements according to the defined rules.

These examples illustrate how Context-Free Grammars are used to define and parse various languages and structures, from arithmetic expressions to programming languages and SQL queries. Each CFG helps to ensure that strings conform to the specified syntax rules, facilitating accurate parsing and processing in real-world applications.

Applications

Context-Free Grammars (CFGs) are used in many areas, such as defining programming languages and parsing text. This section will show how CFGs are applied in different practical scenarios.

- **Programming Languages:**

  CFGs are used to define the syntax of programming languages. For instance, in C or Java, CFGs describe the structure of valid statements, expressions, and program constructs.

- **Natural Language Processing:**

  CFGs are used in NLP to parse sentences, and determine their grammatical structure. For example, a CFG might describe the structure of English sentences, distinguishing between subjects, predicates, and objects.

- **Compilers:**

  CFGs play a pivotal role in compiler design, where they define the syntax of programming languages, and guide the parsing process. Tools, such as Yacc and Bison use CFGs to generate parsers for compiler front-ends.

- **Mathematical Expressions:**

  CFGs can define the structure of mathematical expressions, helping in the development of calculators and expression evaluators.

Parse Trees

To understand how context-free grammars describe the structure of strings, it is essential to delve into the concept of parse trees. This section will define the parse trees, and explain their crucial role in illustrating how strings are derived from grammatical rules.

Definition and Purpose

A parse tree, also known as a syntax tree, is a hierarchical diagram, representing the syntactic structure of a string according to a given context-free grammar (CFG). Each node in the tree corresponds to a non-terminal symbol or terminal symbol in the grammar, and the edges represent the application of production rules. The parse tree visually demonstrates how a string can be derived from the start symbol of the grammar.

Parse trees are used to visualize and understand the structure of strings as they are parsed according to the rules of a CFG. They provide a clear representation of how a string is derived from the start symbol, showing the hierarchical relationships between different components of the string. This is essential for syntax analysis in compilers, natural language processing, and various other applications.

Construction and Interpretation of Parse Trees

To fully grasp how strings are structured according to grammar, it is essential to understand how parse trees are constructed and interpreted. This section will guide you through the process of building parse trees, illustrating how strings are derived from grammar rules. Additionally, we will explore how to read and interpret these trees to analyze and validate the syntactic structure of language constructs.

Construction

The construction of a parse tree involves creating a visual representation of how a string is derived from the start symbol of a context-free grammar (CFG).

To build a parse tree, follow these steps:

1. **Start with the Start Symbol:** Begin with the start symbol of the CFG.
2. **Apply Production Rules:** Replace non-terminal symbols with the right-hand side of production rules, creating branches in the tree for each replacement.
3. **Continue Until Terminal Symbols:** Repeat the process until all non-terminal symbols are replaced with terminal symbols or further reduced.
4. **Complete the Tree:** The process ends when the tree is fully expanded, and the leaves of the tree consist only of terminal symbols.

Interpretation

Interpreting a parse tree involves understanding the syntactic structure it represents. Here is how to approach it:

1. **Identify the Root:** The root of the tree represents the start symbol, and each branch represents a production rule applied during the derivation.
2. **Follow the Branches:** Trace each branch from the root to the leaves to see how the initial non-terminal symbols are replaced by terminal symbols through successive applications of the grammar rules.
3. **Analyze the Structure:** Determine how the input string is constructed from the grammar rules by examining the hierarchical relationships between the nodes.
4. **Validate the Syntax:** Ensure that the parse tree accurately reflects the syntactic structure defined by the grammar, confirming that the string adheres to the rules of the language.

Example Parse Trees

Parse trees help visualize how sentences or codes are structured according to grammar rules. This section will provide simple examples to show how parse trees work.

Simple Programming Language

Consider,

CFG:

- **Variables:** S (statement), E (expression), D (declaration)
- **Terminals:** = (assignment), number, id (identifier), ; (semicolon)
- **Production Rules:**
    - o S → id = E ; | D ;
    - o E → number | id
    - o D → int id
- **Start Symbol:** S

String: "int x; x = 5;"

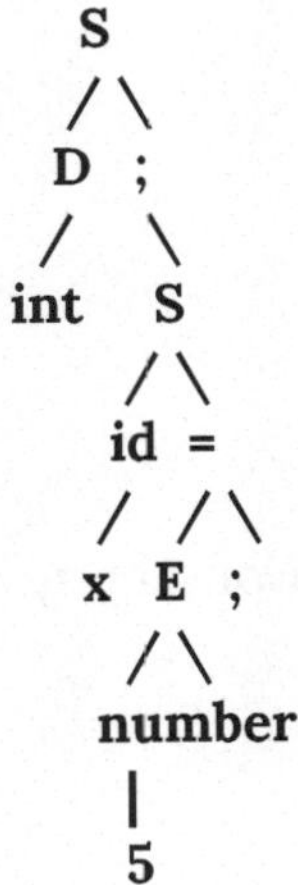

- The parse tree shows the declaration, int x and the assignment, x = 5 as separate parts, connected by a semicolon.
- The root node is S which represents the complete statement.

Arithmetic Expression

Consider,

CFG:

- **Variables:** E (expression), T (term), F (factor)
- **Terminals:** +, *, number, (
- **Production Rules:**
    - o E → E + T | T
    - o T → T * F | F
    - o F → number | (E)

- **Start Symbol: E**

String: "3 + 4 * 5"

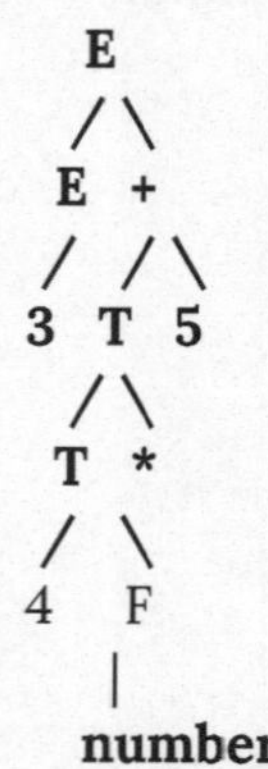

- The root node is E, representing the entire expression.
- The expression, 3 + 4 * 5 is broken down into its components, showing how the + operator connects two sub-expressions: 3 and 4 * 5.
- The subtree rooted at T handles the multiplication operation.

HTML Document

Consider,

CFG:

- **Variables:** Document, Element, Content
- **Terminals:** html, head, body, title, p, text
- **Production Rules:**
  - Document → <html> <head> <title> text </title> </head> <body> Content </body> </html>
  - Content → Element | Element Content
  - Element → <p> text </p>
- **Start Symbol:** Document

String: "<html><head><title>Page Title</title></head><body><p>Hello World</p></body></html>"

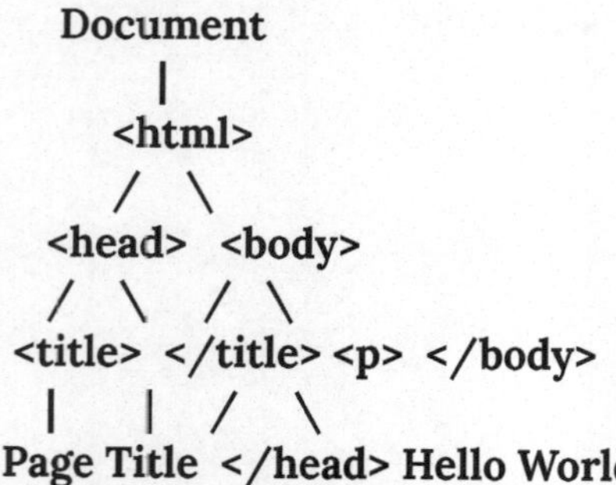

- The root node Document represents the entire HTML document.
- The parse tree breaks down the document into HTML, head, body, and their respective contents, showing the hierarchical structure of the HTML tags.

SQL Query

Consider,

CFG:

- **Variables:** Query, SelectStatement, TableList
- **Terminals:** SELECT, FROM, WHERE, id (identifier), * (wildcard)
- **Production Rules:**
  - Query → SelectStatement
  - SelectStatement → SELECT id FROM id [WHERE id = id]
- **Start Symbol:** Query

String: `"SELECT names FROM employees WHERE id = 10"`

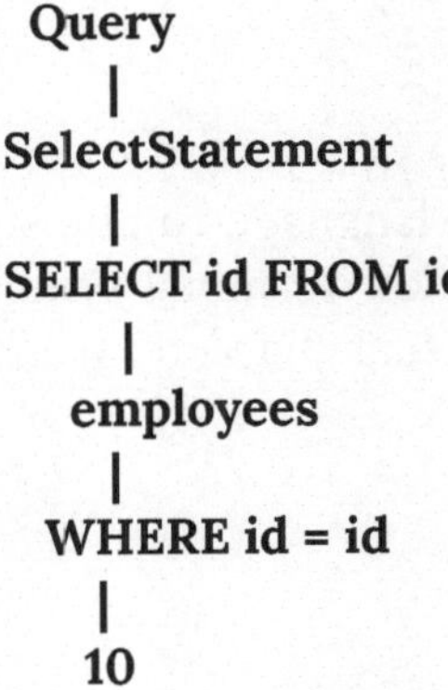

- The root node, Query represents the entire SQL query.
- The parse tree illustrates how the query is structured, with **`SELECT`**, **`FROM`**, and **`WHERE`** clauses properly nested.

Logical Formula

Consider,

CFG:

- **Variables:** Formula, Atom, Clause
- **Terminals:** AND, OR, NOT, ->, id (identifier)
- **Production Rules:**
  - Formula → Atom | NOT Formula | Formula AND Formula | Formula OR Formula | Formula -> Formula
  - Atom → id
- **Start Symbol:** Formula

String: p -> (q AND r)

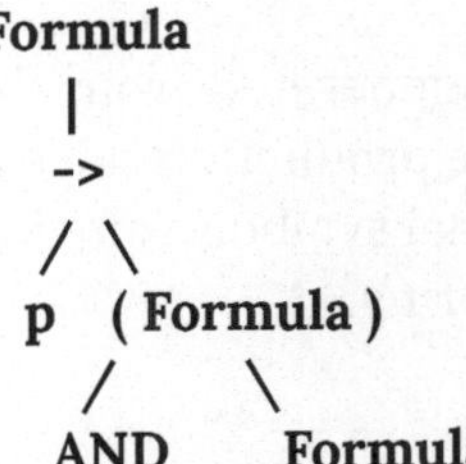

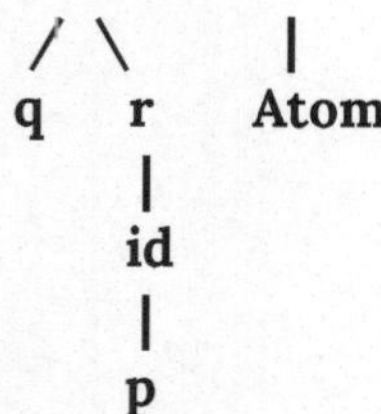

These examples demonstrate how parse trees visually represent the syntactic structure of various types of strings, aiding in understanding and processing complex constructs in real-world applications.

Grammar Rules and Derivations

To understand how languages are formally defined, it is necessary to explore the grammar rules which form the backbone of context-free grammars. This section will define these rules, and illustrate their role in constructing valid strings.

Definition of Grammar Rules

Grammar rules are formal instructions that dictate how symbols in a language can be substituted or expanded. In Context-Free Grammar (CFG), these rules guide how non-terminal symbols (abstract placeholders) can be replaced with sequences of terminal symbols (actual characters) and other non-terminals.

The rules are expressed in the format:

A→αA \rightarrow \alphaA→α, where:

- **A** is a non-terminal symbol.
- **α\alpha**α is a sequence of terminal and/or non-terminal symbols.

Example:

Consider a simple grammar for the basic arithmetic expressions:

- **E → E + T | T**
- **T → number**

In this grammar:

- E represents an expression.
- T represents a term.

In a compiler, these rules help parse arithmetic expressions from source code, ensuring that the syntax is correct before proceeding with further processing, such as code optimization or generation.

Derivation Processes

Understanding how strings are generated from grammar rules is essential for grasping language syntax. This section will cover the derivation processes that illustrate how to transform the start symbol of a grammar into valid strings.

Derivation processes describe how a string in a language can be generated from the start symbol using the grammar rules. Derivation involves repeatedly applying the production rules to replace non-terminal symbols with sequences of other symbols until only terminal symbols remain. The sequence of rule applications represents the steps to construct the desired string.

Steps:

1. **Start with the Start Symbol:** Begin with the start symbol of the grammar.
2. **Apply Production Rules:** Use the grammar rules to replace non-terminals with sequences of terminals and non-terminals.
3. **Continue Applying Rules:** Repeat the application of rules until the string consists only of terminal symbols.
4. **Form the Derived String:** The resulting string is a valid string in the language defined by the grammar.

Example:

Using the grammar:

- **E → E + T | T**
- **T → number**

To derive the expression: 3 + 4,

the process would be:

1. Start with the start symbol, E.
2. Apply the rule, E → E + T to get E + T.
3. Replace E with T using the rule E → T, resulting in T + T.
4. Replace both the T symbols with number using T → number, resulting in 3 + 4.

In natural language processing, derivation processes are used to parse sentences according to the grammatical rules, helping in tasks, such as syntax checking and semantic analysis.

Standard Forms of CFGs

The standard forms of Context-Free Grammars (CFGs) provide a structured approach to represent the CFGs. This section will introduce these standard forms, explaining their importance in parsing algorithms and theoretical analysis.

The standard forms of Context-Free Grammars (CFGs) simplify the representation and manipulation of grammars, making them easier to handle for parsing algorithms and theoretical analysis. The two main standard forms are:

Chomsky Normal Form (CNF):

- **Definition:** A CFG is in CNF if all production rules are of the form:
  - o A→BCA \rightarrow BCA→BC (where BBB and CCC are non-terminals)
  - o A→aA \rightarrow aA→a (where aaa is a terminal)
- **Purpose:** The CNF facilitates parsing algorithms, such as CYK (Cocke-Younger-Kasami), and aids in theoretical proofs about the CFGs.

Example Grammar:

Consider the following CFG:

- S→AB/*a*S *rightarrow* AB | *a*S→AB|a
- A→BCA *rightarrow* BCA→BC
- B→*b*B *rightarrow* *b*B→b
- C→*c*C *rightarrow* *c*C→c

This grammar is not in CNF because the rules do not strictly follow the CNF format. To convert it into CNF, we need to modify it:

Conversion Steps:

1. **Introduce new non-terminals for terminal symbols:**
   - Introduce X1 for b and X2 for c.
   - Update rules:
     - B→X1
     - C→X2
     - X1→b
     - X2→c
2. **Rewrite the original rules:**
   - A→BC remains unchanged.
   - S→AB|a needs to be adjusted for CNF:
     - Replace a with a new non-terminal, say X3:
       - X3→a
       - So, S→AB|X3

CNF Grammar:

- S→AB|X3S \rightarrow AB | X3S→AB|X3
- A→BCA \rightarrow BCA→BC
- B→X1B \rightarrow X1B→X1
- C→X2C \rightarrow X2C→X2
- X1→bX1 \rightarrow bX1→b
- X2→cX2 \rightarrow cX2→c
- X3→aX3 \rightarrow aX3→a

The CNF is particularly useful for algorithms, such as the CYK (Cocke-Younger-Kasami) parser which efficiently determines whether a given string can be generated by the grammar.

Greibach Normal Form (GNF):

- **Definition:** A CFG is in GNF if all production rules are of the form:
  - A→aαA \rightarrow a\alphaA→aα (where aaa is a terminal and α\alphaα is a string of non-terminals)
- **Purpose:** The GNF is useful for top-down parsing strategies, and constructing predictive parsers.

Example Grammar:

Consider a grammar that generates arithmetic expressions:

- S→+ST|TS \rightarrow + S T | TS→+ST|T
- T→aT \rightarrow aT→a
- a→numbera \rightarrow \text{number}a→number

This grammar is not in GNF because some rules do not fit the form where the right-hand side starts with a terminal.

Conversion Steps:

1. **Ensure rules start with a terminal:**
   a. Rewrite the rules so that each production begins with a terminal.
2. **Convert the original rules into GNF:**
   a. For S→+STS \rightarrow + S TS→+ST, adjust it by introducing new non-terminals:
      i. Introduce X1X1X1 for + S T:
         - S→X1TS \rightarrow X1 TS→X1T
         - X1→+SX1 \rightarrow + SX1→+S
      ii. For T→aT \rightarrow aT→a, replace a with terminal rules:
         - T→aT \rightarrow aT→a is already in GNF if a is a terminal.

GNF Grammar:

- S→+ST|TS \rightarrow + S T | TS→+ST|T
- T→aT \rightarrow aT→a
- a→numbera \rightarrow \text{number}a→number

The GNF is advantageous for constructing top-down parsers, such as recursive descent parsers which are used for syntax analysis in many programming languages and tools.

Converting CFGs to standard forms, such as CNF or GNF helps in implementing efficient parsing algorithms, and aids in theoretical analysis, making it easier to design and analyze compilers and interpreters.

Example Implementations Using Yacc and Bison

Yacc and Bison are powerful tools used in compiler construction for generating parsers. They are instrumental in transforming context-free grammars into executable code that can parse and analyze the source code. This section provides an overview of these tools and their functionalities.

Overview of Yacc and Bison

Yacc (Yet Another Compiler Compiler) and Bison are tools used to generate parsers based on Context-Free Grammars. These tools convert the grammar specifications into executable code that can parse and analyze the source code or other structured input. They automate the creation of parsers, simplifying the process of syntax analysis in compiler construction.

- **Yacc:** Yacc is a tool used to generate parsers for context-free grammars. It takes a grammar specification, and produces C code for a parser that can recognize and process strings in the defined language.

  Developed at AT&T, Yacc generates the C code for parsers from grammar specifications. It is widely used to create parsers for programming languages.
- **Bison:** Bison is a GNU implementation of Yacc, and is largely compatible with it. It enhances the Yacc's functionality by providing additional features and improvements. A GNU implementation of Yacc, Bison extends Yacc's functionality with additional features and enhancements, including better error handling and support for more complex grammars.

Example Implementations

To understand how Yacc and Bison are utilized in practice, we will explore some example implementations that demonstrate their application in parsing simple arithmetic expressions and evaluating them. These examples will provide an insight into the use of these tools for syntax analysis.

Arithmetic Expression Evaluator (Yacc)

To illustrate the basics of Yacc, we will begin with a simple example that parses and evaluates the basic arithmetic expressions involving addition and subtraction.

```
%{
#include <stdio.h>
#include <stdlib.h>
%}

%token NUMBER

%%
expression: expression '+' term { $$ = $1 + $3; }
          | expression '-' term { $$ = $1 - $3; }
          | term
          ;

term: NUMBER { $$ = $1; }
    ;

%%

int main(void) {
    printf("Enter an arithmetic expression:\n");
    yyparse();
    return 0;
}

void yyerror(const char *s) {
    fprintf(stderr, "Error: %s\n", s);
}
```

- **Grammar Definition:**

  The expression, rule handles addition and subtraction, and computes the result.

  The term, rule simply returns the number it parses.

- **Output:**

  For an input, such as 10 + 5, the output will be 15.

Applications:

These are the basic calculators and educational tools for understanding the parsing concepts.

Arithmetic Expression Evaluator with Parentheses (Bison)

This example demonstrates how to extend arithmetic parsing to handle parentheses, allowing for more complex expressions.

```
%{
#include <stdio.h>
#include <stdlib.h>
%}

%token NUMBER

%%
expression: expression '+' term { $$ = $1 + $3; }
          | expression '-' term { $$ = $1 - $3; }
          | '(' expression ')' { $$ = $2; }
          | term
          ;

term: NUMBER { $$ = $1; }
    ;

%%

int main(void) {
    printf("Enter an arithmetic expression with parentheses:\n");
    yyparse();
    return 0;
}

void yyerror(const char *s) {
    fprintf(stderr, "Error: %s\n", s);
}
```

- **Grammar Definition:**

  The expression, rule is extended to handle parentheses which allows for grouping of operations.

  The term, rule remains unchanged.

- **Output:**

  For an input like (10 + 5) - 2, the output will be 13.

Applications:

These are more advanced calculators and expression evaluators that support operator precedence and grouping.

Simple Command Line Parser (Yacc)

This example shows how Yacc can be used to parse command-line arguments into structured commands and parameters.

```
%{
#include <stdio.h>
#include <stdlib.h>
%}

%token COMMAND PARAMETER

%%
command: COMMAND { printf("Command: %s\n", yytext); }
       | COMMAND PARAMETER { printf("Command: %s, Parameter: %s\n", $1, $2); }
       ;
```

```
%%

int main(void) {
    printf("Enter command:\n");
    yyparse();
    return 0;
}

void yyerror(const char *s) {
    fprintf(stderr, "Error: %s\n", s);
}
```

- **Grammar Definition:**

  The command can be a single command or a command with a parameter.

  `COMMAND` and **`PARAMETER`** are placeholders for actual tokens recognized by the lexer.

- **Output:**

  For an input, such as **`list -a`**, the output will be **`Command: list`**, **`Parameter: -a`**.

Applications:

These are Command-Line Interface (CLI) tools that require parsing and interpreting user inputs.

XML Tag Parser (Bison)

Here, we use Bison to parse XML-like tags, demonstrating how to handle nested structures and attributes.

```
%{
#include <stdio.h>
#include <stdlib.h>
%}

%token TAG TEXT

%%
document: element
        ;

element: '<' TAG '>' TEXT '</' TAG '>' { printf("Tag: %s, Text: %s\n", $2,
$4); }
       | '<' TAG '>' element '</' TAG '>'
       ;

%%

int main(void) {
    printf("Enter XML-like text:\n");
    yyparse();
    return 0;
}

void yyerror(const char *s) {
    fprintf(stderr, "Error: %s\n", s);
}
```

- **Grammar Definition:**

  An element can be a simple tag with text or a nested tag structure.

  TAG and **TEXT** are placeholders for XML tags and text.

- **Output:**

  For an input, such as **<title>Hello</title>**, the output will be **Tag: title**, **Text: Hello**.

Applications:

XML parsers and tools are used for processing markup languages.

SQL Query Parser (Bison)

This example demonstrates how Bison can be used to parse simple SQL queries, showcasing its capability to handle more complex grammars.

```
%{
#include <stdio.h>
#include <stdlib.h>
%}

%token SELECT FROM WHERE IDENTIFIER

%%
query: SELECT IDENTIFIER FROM IDENTIFIER WHERE IDENTIFIER {
                printf("Select: %s, From: %s, Where: %s\n", $2, $4, $6);
        }
      ;

%%

int main(void) {
    printf("Enter SQL query:\n");
    yyparse();
    return 0;
}

void yyerror(const char *s) {
    fprintf(stderr, "Error: %s\n", s);
}
```

- **Grammar Definition:**

  The query represents a simple SQL query with **SELECT**, **FROM**, and **WHERE** clauses.

  An **IDENTIFIER** represents placeholders for actual SQL identifiers.

- **Output:**

  For an input, such as **SELECT** names **FROM** users **WHERE** age, the output will be Select: name, From: users, Where: age.

Applications:

SQL query parsers are used in database management systems and tools.

These examples demonstrate how Yacc and Bison can be applied to a whole range of tasks, from arithmetic evaluation to parsing complex languages, such as XML and SQL. Each tool facilitates the creation of parsers that interpret and process various forms of structured input, making them invaluable in compiler construction and data processing applications.

Comparing Yacc and Bison

Yacc and Bison are both tools used to create parsers for programming languages and data formats. While Yacc has been around for a long time, Bison offers more modern features and improvements. Here, we will compare these two tools to help you understand their differences, and decide which one is better suited for your needs.

Feature	Yacc	Bison
Origin	Developed by Stephen C. Johnson	Developed as a replacement for Yacc
License	Often used with BSD-style licenses	GNU General Public License (GPL)
Syntax	Uses its own syntax to define grammars	Extended version of Yacc syntax with additional features
Error Reporting	Basic error reporting capabilities	Enhanced error reporting and debugging features
Compatibility	Older tools may have limited support for modern systems	More modern, better support for recent standards and extensions
Integration	Often used with traditional UNIX tools	Integrates well with GNU toolchain, including GCC
Features	Standard features for parser generation	Includes additional features, such as C++ support, more extensive debugging options
Support for C++	Limited support	Built-in support for C++ parsing
Debugging Tools	Basic debugging capabilities	Advanced debugging tools and options
Parser Generator Output	Generates C code for parsers	Generates C or C++ code for parsers
Community and Support	Smaller, less active community	Larger, active GNU community with extensive documentation

***Table 4.1**: Comparison between Yacc and Bison*

Conclusion

In this chapter, we provided a comprehensive exploration of Context-Free Grammars (CFGs) and parse trees which are foundational for syntax analysis in compiler design. We defined CFGs, examined their components, and presented various real-world examples to illustrate their applications. The chapter also introduced parse trees, explaining their purpose, and how they are constructed to represent the syntactic structure of the source code. We explored the grammar rules and derivations, highlighting their roles in defining language syntax and generating valid sentences. Practical implementations using Yacc and Bison were discussed, with a comparison of these tools to guide your choice.

This chapter also built upon the concepts introduced in *Chapter* 3, "*Lexical Analyzer Generators and Error Handling*" where we covered lexical analysis and error handling. Understanding CFGs and parse trees is crucial, as they play a significant role in parsing, which is the next step in the compiler design process. By mastering these concepts, you will be well-prepared for the advanced parsing techniques discussed in the next chapter.

Points to Remember

- Context-Free Grammars (CFGs) define the syntax of programming languages using non-terminals, terminals, production rules, and a start symbol.
- Parse Trees visually represent the structure of the source code according to a CFG, illustrating how strings are derived from the grammar.

- Grammar Rules and Derivations are essential for generating valid sentences in a language and understanding the grammar's structure.
- Yacc and Bison are parser generation tools, with Bison providing additional features and modern support compared to Yacc.

Multiple Choice Questions

1. What is a Context-Free Grammar (CFG)?
   a. A set of rules that define all possible strings in a given formal language.
   b. A type of regular expression used in parsing.
   c. A grammar where the left-hand side of every production rule consists of a single non-terminal symbol.
   d. A grammar used only for programming languages.
2. Which of the following is not a component of a CFG?
   a. Terminals
   b. Non-terminals
   c. Start symbol
   d. Semantics
3. In a CFG, what are terminals?
   a. Symbols that can be replaced
   b. Symbols that cannot be replaced
   c. The initial symbols
   d. Symbols that define the structure
4. What is the role of the start symbol in a CFG?
   a. It indicates the end of the derivation.
   b. It is used to derive all strings in the language.
   c. It represents the terminals in the grammar.
   d. It defines the syntax rules.
5. Example CFGs and Their Applications

   Which of the following is an application of CFGs?
   a. Compiling programming languages
   b. Text search in databases
   c. Image processing
   d. Network protocols
6. What is a parse tree?
   a. A graphical representation of the syntactic structure of a string according to a CFG.
   b. A list of tokens in a program.

   c. A binary tree used in searching algorithms.

   d. A type of data structure for storing variables.

7. What is the purpose of a parse tree?

   a. To execute a program.

   b. To represent the hierarchical structure of a string derived from a CFG.

   c. To store the output of a program.

   d. To optimize memory usage.

8. In constructing a parse tree, what do the internal nodes represent?

   a. Terminals

   b. Non-terminals

   c. Both terminals and non-terminals

   d. Only the start symbol

9. How is a parse tree interpreted in terms of grammar rules?

   a. By following the derivation sequence.

   b. By compiling it directly.

   c. By ignoring the non-terminals.

   d. By converting it into machine code.

10. What are grammar rules in a CFG?

   a. Instructions for executing programs.

   b. Production rules that define how non-terminals can be replaced by terminals and other non-terminals.

   c. Syntax highlighting rules in text editors.

   d. Parsing rules for regular expressions.

11. What is the derivation process in a CFG?

   a. Translating source code into machine code.

   b. The sequence of applying production rules to generate a string.

   c. The process of lexical analysis.

   d. Compiling a program.

12. Which of the following is a standard form of a CFG?

   a. Backus-Naur Form

   b. Chomsky Normal Form

   c. Regular Expressions

   d. State Machine Diagrams

13. What is a key characteristic of Chomsky Normal Form?

    a. Each production rule has exactly two non-terminal symbols on the right-hand side.

    b. Each production rule has at least one terminal symbol on the right-hand side.

    c. Production rules can have an arbitrary number of terminals and non-terminals.

    d. All production rules are context-sensitive.

14. What is Yacc primarily used for?

    a. Lexical analysis

    b. Generating parsers for context-free grammars

    c. Optimizing code

    d. Interpreting bytecode

15. What does Bison offer compared to Yacc?

    a. It is a compiler.

    b. It provides additional features and better compatibility with C++.

    c. It is only used for lexical analysis.

    d. It is a type of debugger.

16. What is the main input to Yacc and Bison?

    a. Source code

    b. Grammar specification file

    c. Machine code

    d. Object code

17. How do Yacc and Bison differ in terms of portability and compatibility?

    a. Yacc is more portable across different platforms.

    b. Bison is designed to be compatible with GNU software and standards.

    c. Yacc supports more programming languages.

    d. Bison is limited to a single platform.

18. Which command is used to generate a parser with Bison?

    a. `bison -d file.y`

    b. `yacc -d file.y`

    c. `parsergen -d file.y`

    d. `lex -d file.y`

19. In Yacc/Bison, what file extension is typically used for grammar files?

    a. `.c`

    b. `.y`

    c. `.cpp`

    d. `.txt`

20. What output files are generated by Yacc/Bison after processing a grammar file?
    a. `.h` and `.o` files
    b. `.c` and `.h` files
    c. `.exe` and `.obj` files
    d. `.bin` and `.dat` files

Answers

1. c
2. d
3. b
4. b
5. a
6. a
7. b
8. b
9. a
10. b
11. b
12. b
13. a
14. b
15. b
16. b
17. b
18. a
19. b
20. b

Questions

1. How do Yacc and Bison differ in their approach to defining Context-Free Grammars (CFGs)?
2. What are the key differences in how Yacc and Bison handle the components of CFGs, such as terminals, non-terminals, and production rules?
3. Provide examples of CFGs implemented in both Yacc and Bison, highlighting any differences in syntax or functionality.
4. How do Yacc and Bison differ in their generation and representation of parse trees?

5. What are the differences in constructing and interpreting parse trees using Yacc versus Bison?
6. How do Yacc and Bison define and implement grammar rules, and what are the main differences?
7. What are the differences in the derivation processes between Yacc and Bison?
8. How do Yacc and Bison support the standard forms of CFGs, such as Chomsky Normal Form or Greibach Normal Form?
9. What are the main differences between Yacc and Bison in terms of their architecture and functionality?
10. Compare and contrast a specific example of a grammar implemented in Yacc versus Bison, focusing on differences in code structure, error handling, and output.

Key Terms

- **Context-Free Grammar (CFG):** A formal grammar for defining language syntax, consisting of non-terminals, terminals, production rules, and a start symbol.
- **Parse Tree:** A tree structure showing the syntactic organization of a source code string according to grammar.
- **Grammar Rule:** A rule in a CFG that specifies how non-terminals are replaced with terminals or other non-terminals.
- **Derivation:** The process of generating strings in a language by applying grammar rules.
- **Chomsky Normal Form (CNF):** A CFG format where production rules are either $A \rightarrow BC$ or $A \rightarrow a$.
- **Greibach Normal Form (GNF):** A CFG format where production rules are of the form $A \rightarrow a\alpha$, with 'a' as a terminal and 'α' as a string of non-terminals.
- **Yacc:** A parser generator tool for creating parsers based on CFGs.
- **Bison:** An advanced version of Yacc that includes support for C++, and enhanced debugging features.

CHAPTER 5
Parsing Techniques

Introduction

In the previous chapter, we examined context-free grammars and parse trees which are essential for grasping the syntactic framework of programming languages. We explored how CFGs define language syntax, and how parse trees illustrate the organization of source code.

This chapter shifts focus to parsing techniques, covering both top-down and bottom-up methods. You will be introduced to LL parsers which analyze code from the top down, and LR parsers which work from the bottom up. We will also discuss error handling during parsing to ensure that your parsers can effectively detect, and address the syntax errors. Practical examples using Yacc and Bison will demonstrate these concepts in action. Hence, by mastering these techniques, you will be better equipped to develop effective syntax analysis components for compilers and interpreters.

Structure

In this chapter, we will discuss the following topics:

- Introduction to Parsing Techniques
    - Overview of Parsing
- Top-Down Parsing (LL Parsers):
    - Introduction to LL Parsers
    - How LL Parsers Work
    - Example Implementation
    - Advantages and Disadvantages of Top-Down Parsing
    - Applications of LL Parsers
- Bottom-Up Parsing (LR Parsers):
    - Introduction to LR Parsers
    - How LR Parsers Work
    - Example Implementation
    - Advantages and Disadvantages of Bottom-up Parsing
    - Applications of LR Parsers
- Error Handling in Syntax Analysis:
    - Introduction to Error Handling
    - Error Detection Techniques
    - Error Recovery Strategies
    - Real-World Examples of Error Handling

- Example Implementations and Error Handling Strategies:
  - Implementations Using Yacc
  - Implementations Using Bison
  - Comparing Yacc and Bison

Introduction to Parsing Techniques

Parsing is a crucial step in compiler design and programming language processing that involves analyzing sequences of tokens to determine their grammatical structure. This process is essential for converting human-readable code into a format that a machine can execute. Parsing helps in validating the syntax of the source code, creating intermediate representations, and ultimately, generating an executable code. Accurate parsing ensures that the code adheres to the language's rules, and can be processed effectively by the subsequent stages of a compiler.

Overview of Parsing

Parsing is the process of analyzing a sequence of symbols, usually in the form of tokens, to determine its grammatical structure based on a set of rules or grammar. It plays a vital role in transforming the source code into an intermediate representation that a compiler or interpreter can work with. Parsing involves checking the code for syntactic correctness and constructing a parse tree or Abstract Syntax Tree (AST) that represents the hierarchical structure of the code. This step is critical for detecting the syntax errors and enabling further processing, such as code optimization and translation.

Importance of Parsing in Compiler Design

Parsing is fundamental to compiler design for several reasons:

1. **Syntax Checking:** Parsing ensures that the source code complies with the grammar rules of the programming language. It identifies and reports syntax errors, helping to catch mistakes early in the compilation process.
2. **Intermediate Representation:** The parsing phase converts the source code into an intermediate representation which simplifies further stages of compilation, including optimization and code generation. This intermediate form serves as a bridge between the high-level source code and low-level machine code.
3. **Code Translation:** Effective parsing is necessary for accurate code translation. It ensures that the source code is correctly interpreted and transformed into machine code that the computer can execute.

Types of Parsing Techniques

Parsing techniques are essential for converting the source code into a format that can be easily analyzed by a compiler.

In this section, we will explore the two main types of parsing techniques:

- Top-Down Parsing (LL Parsers)
- Bottom-Up Parsing (LR Parsers)

Top-Down Parsing (LL Parsers)

Bottom-up parsing, commonly referred to as LR parsing, is a fundamental approach in syntax analysis where the parser begins with the input symbols, and gradually works its way up to the start symbol, effectively constructing the parse tree from the bottom up. This method is known for its efficiency and broad applicability, making it an essential technique in processing context-free grammars.

Introduction to LR Parsers Interchanged

Top-down parsing is a parsing technique that builds a parse tree from the top (starting symbol), and works its way down to the leaves. LL parsers, a type of top-down parser, derive their name from their ability to parse Left-to-right input using Leftmost derivations. This method is based on a set of production rules, and recursively applies these rules to match the input string.

Understanding Top-Down Parsing

In top-down parsing, the parser starts with the start symbol of the grammar, and attempts to match the input string by expanding this symbol using production rules. The goal is to derive the input string by sequentially replacing the non-terminal symbols with their corresponding production rules until only terminal symbols (the actual input) are left.

The process involves:

1. **Selecting the Production Rule:** At each step, the parser chooses a production rule that matches the current input, and the non-terminal being expanded.
2. **Recursive Descent:** The parser recursively applies production rules, expanding non-terminals until the input string is derived or no further matches are possible.
3. **Backtracking (Optional):** Some LL parsers use backtracking to handle multiple possible expansions. However, this can be inefficient, and is often avoided by using more advanced techniques.

Characteristics and Features of LL Parsers

LL parsers are known for their simplicity and ease of implementation. They use a predictive approach to decide which production rule to apply based on the current input symbol, and the state of the parser. Some key features include:

1. **Predictive Parsing:** LL parsers use a lookahead token to predict which rule to apply.
2. **Stack-Based:** They use a stack to keep track of the grammar rules and the input.
3. **Left-to-Right:** They process the input string from left to right.
4. **Leftmost Derivation:** They expand the leftmost non-terminal symbol in each step.

How LL Parsers Work

LL parsers work by processing the input from left to right, constructing a parse tree from the top down. These parsers predict the structure of the input based on the next symbol, making decisions that lead to a successful parse or an error. LL parsers are commonly used for their simplicity and ease of implementation, especially in parsing simple context-free grammars.

Process of Top-Down Parsing

1. **Initialization:** Start with the start symbol of the grammar and an empty stack.
2. **Parsing:** Compare the top of the stack with the current input symbol:

   a. If the top is a non-terminal, replace it with the appropriate production rule.

   b. If the top is a terminal, match it with the input symbol and pop from the stack.

3. **Completion:** Continue this process until the stack is empty and the input is fully consumed.

Constructing LL Parse Trees

LL parse trees are built by recursively applying production rules from the root of the tree to the leaves. Each node represents a non-terminal, and its children represent the symbols derived from applying the production rule.

Example:

Consider a simple arithmetic expression, grammar:

- E → E + T | T
- T → T * F | F
- F → (E) | *id*

For the input string id + id * id, the LL parser would:

1. Start with the start symbol, E.
2. Apply the production rule E, → E + T.
3. Recursively apply the rules for E, T, and F until the entire input string is matched, and a parse tree is constructed.

Example code:

Here is a basic example of an LL parser implementation in Python using a recursive descent approach:

```
class LLParser:
    def _init_(self, tokens):
        self.tokens = tokens
        self.current = 0

    def parse(self):
        self.E()
        if self.current < len(self.tokens):
            raise SyntaxError("Unexpected tokens at end of input")

    def E(self):
        self.T()
        while self.current < len(self.tokens) and self.tokens[self.current] ==
'+':
            self.current += 1
            self.T()

    def T(self):
        self.F()
        while self.current < len(self.tokens) and self.tokens[self.current] ==
'*':
            self.current += 1
            self.F()

    def F(self):
        if self.tokens[self.current] == '(':
```

```
                self.current += 1
                self.E()
                if self.tokens[self.current] == ')':
                    self.current += 1
                else:
                    raise SyntaxError("Expected closing parenthesis")
            elif self.tokens[self.current].isidentifier():
                self.current += 1
            else:
                raise SyntaxError("Expected identifier or opening parenthesis")

    # Example usage:
    tokens = ['id', '+', 'id', '*', 'id']
    parser = LLParser(tokens)
    parser.parse()
```

Output:

The parser successfully processes the input tokens, and constructs the parse tree for the expression,

*id + id * id*

Top-down parsing with LL parsers is a straightforward and effective approach for parsing simple grammars. However, it is essential to understand its limitations and applicability to ensure that it fits the requirements of your specific parsing needs.

Advantages and Disadvantages of Top-Down Parsing

Understanding the strengths and limitations of parsing techniques helps in choosing the right approach for a given application. In this section, we will examine the advantages and disadvantages of **Top-Down Parsing**. By evaluating these aspects, you will gain a clearer perspective on when and why to use this parsing method in compiler design and other applications.

Advantages:

1. **Simplicity:** LL parsing is conceptually simpler and easier to implement. It is well-suited for educational purposes and small grammars.

2. **Predictability:** With proper grammar restrictions (for example, no left recursion), LL parsers can efficiently predict the next input symbol based on the current state and non-terminal, leading to a more straightforward parsing process.

Disadvantages:

1. **Grammar Limitations:** LL parsers cannot handle all types of grammars, particularly those with left recursion or complex dependencies. They require the grammar to be in a specific form (LL(k) form) to work efficiently.

2. **Performance Issues:** For complex or ambiguous grammars, LL parsing can be less efficient, and may require significant backtracking or additional mechanisms.

Applications of LL Parsers

Exploring the practical uses and implementations of Top-Down parsers can provide valuable insights into their role in various systems.

Use Cases in Compiler Design

LL parsers are widely used in compiler design for their ease of implementation, and efficiency in handling simple, deterministic grammars. They are suitable for parsing programming languages with predictable syntax and limited ambiguity.

Real-World Implementations

1. **Programming Language Compilers:** LL parsers are used in the front-end of compilers to analyze the syntax of source code.
2. **Configuration File Parsers:** They are employed to parse configuration files with a well-defined syntax.
3. **Data Processing Tools:** LL parsers help in processing the structured data formats where the syntax is known and deterministic.

Bottom-Up Parsing (LR Parsing)

Bottom-up parsing, also known as LR parsing, is a fundamental technique in syntax analysis used by compilers to process programming languages. Unlike top-down parsing, which begins from the start symbol and works its way down to the input string, bottom-up parsing starts from the input string, and attempts to construct the parse tree by working its way up to the start symbol. This approach allows the parser to handle a wide range of grammars, including those that are left-recursive, making it a powerful tool in the compiler's toolkit.

Introduction to LR Parsers

Understanding the fundamentals of bottom-up parsing begins with an introduction to LR parsers, which are instrumental in building powerful and reliable syntax analyzers in compiler design.

Understanding Bottom-Up Parsing

Bottom-up parsing is a method in which parsing starts from the input symbols, and tries to construct the parse tree up to the start symbol of the grammar. This approach contrasts with top-down parsing which begins with the start symbol, and works its way down to the input symbols. Bottom-up parsing is particularly effective for handling more complex grammars that top-down parsers struggle with, as it systematically builds a parse tree by reversing the production rules of the grammar.

Characteristics and Features of LR Parsers

LR parsers, which include a range of bottom-up parsers, are designed to handle a wide variety of context-free grammars efficiently. Their main characteristics and features are:

- **Shift and Reduce Operations:** LR parsers employ two primary operations:
  - **Shift:** Moves the next input symbol onto the stack.
  - **Reduce:** Applies a production rule to replace a sequence of symbols on the stack with a non-terminal.
- **Lookahead Symbol:** The parser uses a lookahead symbol to make decisions about which the parsing action is supposed to take place.
- **State-Based Parsing:** The parser relies on a state machine to track the progress of parsing, with transitions based on the current state and lookahead symbol.
- **Handling Ambiguity:** LR parsers are capable of managing more complex and ambiguous grammars than simpler parsers, thanks to their detailed state tables.

How LR Parsers Work

To effectively use bottom-up parsing, it is important to understand its fundamental concepts. This section will cover the basic elements, such as shift and reduction operations that are crucial for how LR parsers work.

Process of Bottom-Up Parsing

To understand how bottom-up parsing works, let us break down its process into the following key steps:

1. **Initialization:** This step sets up the parsing environment by preparing the input and initializing the parsing table and stack.
2. **Parsing Loop:** This core step repeatedly examines the input and stack to either shift tokens or reduce them into higher-level constructs, gradually building the parse tree from the leaves up to the root.

   The parsing loop is the heart of bottom-up parsing, involving several crucial actions:

   a. **Reduction:**

      Reduction involves replacing a sequence of symbols on the stack with a non-terminal based on a grammar rule. This is the core operation of bottom-up parsing, where the parser applies production rules in reverse.

      Example:

      Given a grammar rule:

      A → BC

      If the parser encounters BC on the stack, it will reduce BC to A.

      Consider the following input for arithmetic expression parsing:

      Input: 3 + 5 * 2

      For the rule Factor → number, if 5 and 2 are on the stack, they will be reduced to Factor.

   b. **Shift:**

      Shifting is the process of moving tokens from the input stream onto the parsing stack. This is done to prepare for reduction when a complete sequence of symbols that matches a production rule is recognized.

      Example:

      Consider,

      For an input string, 3 + 5, if the grammar has a rule Term → number, the number 5 is shifted onto the stack before being reduced.

   c. **Parser States:**

      LR parsers use a finite state machine to represent different states of the parsing process. Each state indicates what part of the grammar has been recognized and what remains to be processed.

      Example:

      Consider,

      For an arithmetic expression, states represent the different stages of parsing, such as recognizing an operand, an operator, or parentheses.

The states are automatically generated by tools, such as Yacc or Bison, based on the grammar rules.

d. **Parse Table:**

The parse table is a crucial component in LR parsing, consisting of an action table and a goto table. The action table directs the parser on whether to shift, reduce, accept, or handle an error. The goto table is used to determine the next state after a reduction.

Example:

Consider,

For the grammar provided earlier, the parse table includes entries that specify actions for each state and input symbol, such as shifting to a new state or reducing a sequence of symbols.

Constructing LR Parse Trees

Constructing LR parse trees involves building the tree from the leaves (input symbols) up to the root (start symbol). As the parser processes the input, it performs reductions based on grammar rules which correspond to nodes and branches in the parse tree. The parse tree represents the syntactic structure of the input, and helps in understanding the hierarchical relationships between different components of the input.

Example:

Consider the following grammar for simple arithmetic expressions:

E → E + T

E → T

T → T * F

T → F

F → (E)

F → id

Here, E represents an expression, T represents a term, and F represents a factor. The terminals +, *, (,), and id (identifier) are the basic symbols.

Let us see how the LR parser constructs the parse tree for the input id + id * id:

1. **Initialization:**
   a. The input string is id + id * id.
   b. The stack starts with the initial state (for example, state 0).
2. **Parsing Loop:**
   a. **Shift id:** The parser reads the first id, and shifts it onto the stack.
      - Stack: [0, id]
   b. **Reduce F → id:** The parser reduces id to F.
      - Stack: [0, F]
   c. **Reduce T → F:** The parser reduces F to T.
      - Stack: [0, T]

d. **Reduce E → T:** The parser reduces T to E.
   - Stack: [0, E]

e. **Shift +:** The parser reads and shifts the + onto the stack.
   - Stack: [0, E, +]

f. **Shift id:** The parser reads the next id and shifts it onto the stack.
   - Stack: [0, E, +, id]

g. **Reduce F → id:** The parser reduces id to F.
   - Stack: [0, E, +, F]

h. **Reduce T → F:** The parser reduces F to T.
   - Stack: [0, E, +, T]

i. **Shift *:** The parser reads and shifts the * onto the stack.
   - Stack: [0, E, +, T, *]

j. **Shift id:** The parser reads the final id and shifts it onto the stack.
   - Stack: [0, E, +, T, *, id]

k. **Reduce F → id:** The parser reduces id to F.
   - Stack: [0, E, +, T, *, F]

l. **Reduce T → T * F:** The parser reduces T * F to T.
   - Stack: [0, E, +, T]

m. **Reduce E → E + T:** The parser reduces E + T to E.
   - Stack: [0, E]

n. **Accept:** The parser accepts the input, completing the parse.

Resulting Parse Tree:

The parse tree for the input id + id * id is constructed as follows:

Example:

The following is an example implementation of LR parsing in Python using a simple parser framework:

```
class LRParser:
    def __init__(self, parse_table, grammar):
        self.parse_table = parse_table
        self.grammar = grammar

    def parse(self, input_tokens):
        stack = [0]  # Stack with initial state
```

```
        i = 0

        while i < len(input_tokens):
            state = stack[-1]
            token = input_tokens[i]

            if (state, token) in self.parse_table['shift']:
                stack.append(self.parse_table['shift'][(state, token)])
                i += 1
            elif (state, token) in self.parse_table['reduce']:
                production = self.grammar[self.parse_table['reduce'][(state,
token)]]
                for _ in range(len(production[1])):
                    stack.pop()
                stack.append(self.parse_table['goto'][(stack[-1], production
[0])])
            else:
                raise ValueError("Syntax error")

        return "Accepted" if stack == [0, 'E'] else "Rejected"

# Example parse table and grammar for the input `id + id * id`
parse_table = {
    'shift': {(0, 'id'): 5, (4, 'id'): 5, (6, 'id'): 5},
    'reduce': {(1, '+'): 2, (2, '+'): 4, (3, '+'): 1},
    'goto': {(0, 'E'): 1, (0, 'T'): 2, (0, 'F'): 3, (4, 'E'): 6},
}

grammar = {
    1: ('E', ['E', '+', 'T']),
    2: ('E', ['T']),
    3: ('T', ['T', '*', 'F']),
    4: ('T', ['F']),
    5: ('F', ['id'])
}

# Instantiate the parser
parser = LRParser(parse_table, grammar)

# Parse the input tokens
input_tokens = ['id', '+', 'id', '*', 'id']
result = parser.parse(input_tokens)
print(result)  # Output: Accepted
```

The code implements a simple LR parser that reads the input tokens, id + id * id. It follows the parse table to shift and reduce tokens according to the grammar rules. The parser constructs the parse tree by reducing tokens as it processes the input. The final output is "**Accepted**," indicating that the input conforms to the grammar.

Example Implementation

An example implementation illustrates how a concept or technique is applied in practice. It serves as a practical demonstration, breaking down the process into actionable steps to help clarify and reinforce the theoretical concepts.

Example Code for Arithmetic Expressions

Here is a simplified example of an LR parser implementation in Python for parsing arithmetic expressions:

```
# Define a simplified grammar for arithmetic expressions
productions = {
    'E': ['T E\''],
    'E\'': ['+ T E\'', 'ε'],
    'T': ['F T\''],
    'T\'': ['* F T\'', 'ε'],
    'F': ['( E )', 'id']
}

# Define a simple LR parser function
def lr_parse(tokens):
    stack = []
    index = 0
    while index < len(tokens):
        token = tokens[index]
        stack.append(token)
        index += 1

        # Simulate reduction (this example is highly simplified)
        if stack[-2:] == ['id', '+']:
            stack.pop()  # Remove '+'
            stack.pop()  # Remove 'id'
            stack.append('T')  # Replace with 'T'
        elif stack[-3:] == ['T', 'E\'', '+']:
            stack.pop()  # Remove '+'
            stack.pop()  # Remove 'E\''
            stack.pop()  # Remove 'T'
            stack.append('E')  # Replace with 'E'

    return stack == ['E']

# Example usage
expression = "id + id * id"
tokens = expression.split()  # Simple tokenization
result = lr_parse(tokens)
print("Valid expression" if result else "Invalid expression")
```

In this code, the LR parser function processes an arithmetic expression by simulating a reduction process. The function checks if the tokens match a simplified set of rules, and builds a parse tree accordingly. For the input, "id + id * id", the function returns "Valid expression" if the sequence adheres to the grammar rules, demonstrating that the parser correctly processes and validates the expression.

Advantages and Disadvantages of Bottom-Up Parsing

Here, we examine the benefits and challenges of bottom-up parsing techniques, focusing on their effectiveness in handling complex grammars and their potential issues.

- **Advantages:**
    - **Handles a Wide Range of Grammars:** Bottom-up parsing can manage a broader set of grammars, including the most context-free grammars, making it versatile for different languages.

- **Detects Errors Early:** As the parser processes input tokens directly, it can detect syntax errors as soon as they occur, providing immediate feedback during parsing.
- **Systematic Parsing Process:** Bottom-up parsers build the parse tree in a systematic way which often leads to more efficient and reliable parsing, especially for complex languages.
- **Supports LR Parsers:** LR parsers, a type of bottom-up parser, are powerful and can handle left-recursive grammars, which are common in programming languages.

- **Disadvantages:**
  - **Complexity in Implementation:** Bottom-up parsers, particularly LR parsers, are more complex to implement compared to top-down parsers, requiring intricate parse tables and state management.
  - **Memory Intensive:** The process of managing a stack, and maintaining multiple states can consume significant memory, especially for large inputs or complex grammars.
  - **Difficult to Understand:** The systematic nature of bottom-up parsing can make it harder for beginners to grasp, as it requires a deeper understanding of grammar rules and states.
  - **Limited Lookahead:** Basic bottom-up parsers may have limited lookahead capabilities which makes handling certain syntactic structures more challenging without additional mechanisms.

Applications of LR Parsers

Exploring the practical uses and implementations of bottom-up parsers can provide valuable insights into their roles in various systems.

Use Cases in Compiler Design

LR parsers are instrumental in compiler design, where they are used to parse the source code and ensure that it adheres to the syntax rules of the programming language. Their ability to handle complex grammars makes them suitable for constructing robust compilers and interpreters.

Real-World Implementations

1. **Programming Language Compilers:** Many modern compilers for languages, such as C, C++, and Java use LR parsers to process and compile the source code.
2. **Configuration File Processors:** Tools that read and validate structured configuration files often employ LR parsers to ensure that the configuration conforms to the predefined schemes.
3. **Data Format Validators:** LR parsers are used in applications that need to validate the data formats, such as JSON or XML parsers, to ensure data integrity and correctness.

Error Handling in Syntax Analysis

Error handling in syntax analysis is essential for detecting and managing mistakes in the code. It ensures that errors are identified, reported, and sometimes corrected, allowing the parser to continue processing the rest of the input. This improves the debugging process, and helps maintain code quality.

Introduction to Error Handling

Error handling is a crucial aspect of syntax analysis, ensuring that issues in the source code are identified and managed effectively. By addressing errors promptly, parsers can provide meaningful feedback to developers, and maintain the integrity of the parsing process.

Importance of Error Handling in Parsing

Effective error handling in parsing helps maintain the robustness and reliability of compilers and interpreters. It ensures that errors in the source code are detected and reported accurately, enabling developers to correct issues, and improve the code quality. Proper error handling also helps in recovering from errors gracefully, allowing the parsing process to continue even after encountering problems.

Types of Parsing Errors

Parsing errors occur when the source code does not conform to the expected grammatical rules. Some of the common types of parsing errors include:

- **Syntax Errors:** Errors that occur when the code structure does not match the grammar rules. For example, missing or misplaced punctuation, incorrect use of language constructs, or malformed expressions.

  Example:

  `int x = 10` *(missing semicolon) or if (x > 10 { (missing closing parenthesis).*

- **Semantic Errors:** Errors related to the meaning of the code, such as type mismatches or incorrect variable usage. Although not strictly syntax errors, they can affect the correctness of the code.

  Example:

  `int x = "text";` *(type mismatch).*

- **Lexical Errors:** Errors involving invalid tokens that do not match any defined patterns in the lexical analysis phase.

  Example:

  Using a reserved keyword as an identifier, such as `int int = 5;`.

Error Detection Techniques

Effective error detection is crucial for maintaining the quality and functionality of the software. This section delves into the various techniques used to identify the syntax errors during parsing, ensuring that the source code adheres to the specified grammatical rules.

Identifying Syntax Errors

Syntax errors occur when the source code does not conform to the grammatical rules defined by the language's syntax. Identifying these errors involves analyzing the code against the language's grammar and recognizing deviations. The common approaches include:

- **Grammar-Based Detection:** Using context-free grammars to validate the structure of the code. When the code fails to match the grammar rules, a syntax error is detected.

  Example: In a language where expressions must be enclosed in parentheses, the code if (x > 10 (missing closing parenthesis) will trigger a syntax error.

- **Token Validation:** Checking for invalid or unexpected tokens in the input stream. For instance, if a reserved keyword is used incorrectly, or if a token does not match any valid pattern.

  Example: Using class as a variable name in a language where class is a reserved keyword.

- **Parse Tree Analysis:** Constructing and analyzing parse trees to ensure the correct structure of the source code. Syntax errors can be identified by checking if the parse tree conforms to the expected structure.

  Example: In a mathematical expression, such as 3 + * 5, the parse tree will reveal an invalid structure due to the misplaced operator.

These techniques help ensure that the source code adheres to the defined syntax rules, enabling the parser to identify and report errors effectively.

Error Reporting Strategies

Once the syntax errors are identified, reporting them clearly and informatively is crucial for effective debugging. The key strategies include:

- **Error Messages:** Provide descriptive error messages that specify the nature of the error and its location in the code. This helps developers understand and fix the issue quickly.

  Example: An error message, such as Syntax error: Expected ')' but found '}' at line 5 indicates exactly what went wrong and where.

- **Line and Column Indicators:** Include line and column numbers in error messages to pinpoint the exact location of the error. This makes it easier for developers to locate and correct the issue.

  Example: Error on line 12, column 8: Unexpected token '}' directs the developer to the specific part of the code that needs attention.

- **Contextual Information:** Provide additional context around the error, such as the surrounding code or a snippet of the offending line, and this can help developers understand the problem better.

  Example: Showing the surrounding code in an error message: Error: Missing semicolon; line 8: 'int x = 10'.

Effective error reporting strategies enhance the debugging process by offering clear, actionable information about syntax errors, thereby improving the code quality and developer productivity.

Error Recovery Strategies

Error recovery strategies are essential for managing and correcting errors encountered during parsing. This section explores various methods for recovering from syntax errors, helping to maintain the robustness and usability of the parser.

Methods for Error Recovery

Here, we discuss different techniques used to handle errors, and resume parsing to process further input effectively.

- **Panic Mode Recovery:**

  Panic mode recovery involves skipping over parts of the input until a designated set of synchronizing tokens (for example, semicolons or curly braces) is found. This method helps the parser regain a stable state but may discard potentially some useful information.

  Example:

  If a parser encounters an unexpected token, while parsing a function definition, it might skip until the next semicolon or closing parenthesis is found.

- **Phrase-Level Recovery:**

  In phrase-level recovery, the parser attempts to correct errors by replacing or inserting tokens to form valid phrases according to the grammar rules. This method tries to correct errors, while still processing as much of the input as possible.

  Example:

  If the parser finds a missing operator in an arithmetic expression, it might insert a default operator, such as + to attempt a correction and continue parsing.

- **Error Productions:**

  This method involves adding special error productions to the grammar that can handle common syntax errors. These error productions guide the parser to specific error handling routines when it encounters problematic input.

  Example:

  In a grammar for a programming language, an error production might be added to handle the missing semicolons by allowing an optional semicolon in the grammar rule.

- **Global Correction:**

  Global correction involves analyzing the entire input to identify and correct multiple errors. This method is more sophisticated, and aims to find the best possible corrections for all errors in the input.

  Example:

  A parser might use global correction to detect and fix mismatched parentheses throughout a block of code, ensuring that the entire code segment is syntactically correct.

- **Context-Sensitive Recovery:**

  Context-sensitive recovery involves using the context of the error to determine the most appropriate recovery action. This method requires more sophisticated analysis, and can adapt to various error situations.

  Example:

  When parsing a nested loop, if the parser encounters an unexpected token, it may use the surrounding context (for example, the current loop or function) to determine the most likely error, and suggest corrections.

Example Code and Techniques

This part provides practical examples and code snippets demonstrating how these error recovery methods can be implemented in real-world scenarios.

Example of Error Recovery in Practice:

Here is a simple example demonstrating panic mode recovery using a C-style parser. Suppose, we have the following input with a syntax error:

```
int main() {
    int a = 5
    int b = 10;
    return 0;
}
```

The missing semicolon after **int a = 5** will trigger an error. Using panic mode recovery, the parser might skip to the next semicolon to recover:

```
// Example C-like pseudocode
void parse() {
    while (currentToken != EOF) {
        if (currentToken == SEMICOLON) {
            // Resume parsing after finding the semicolon
            continueParsing();
        } else {
            // Skip the current token
            advanceToken();
        }
    }
}
```

In this example, the parser will skip tokens until it finds a semicolon, allowing it to continue parsing the rest of the input.

Real-World Examples of Error Handling

Real-world examples of error handling showcase how errors are managed in practical scenarios. These examples demonstrate various strategies for detecting, reporting, and recovering from errors in different systems, providing insights into effective error management and its impact on system reliability and user experience.

Practical Scenarios and Solutions

Scenario 1: Programming Language Compilers

Compilers need to handle syntax errors efficiently as they process source code. Syntax errors in programming languages include missing semicolons, unbalanced parentheses, or incorrect keyword usage. If a compiler encounters a syntax error, it must recover from it and continue compiling the rest of the code to provide comprehensive feedback to the developer.

Solution: Implement **Panic Mode Recovery** to handle syntax errors. In this approach, the compiler skips tokens until it finds a synchronization point (such as a semicolon or closing brace) that allows it to resume parsing. This helps the compiler continue processing, and provide feedback on multiple errors in a single compilation run.

Example:

Consider the following code with a missing closing parenthesis:

```
int main() {
    if (x > 5 {
        printf("x is greater than 5");
    }
}
```

Solution: The compiler detects the missing closing parenthesis. Using panic mode recovery, it might skip tokens until it finds a closing brace } and then resume parsing. The error message could indicate the missing parenthesis and suggest a fix.

Scenario 2: Integrated Development Environments (IDEs)

IDEs offer real-time feedback and suggestions while users write code. They need to handle syntax errors dynamically to provide immediate assistance. This includes identifying issues, such as missing operators or incorrect function calls as the user types.

Solution: Employ **Phrase-Level Recovery** and **Context-Sensitive Recovery**. Phrase-level recovery involves inserting or correcting tokens to fix minor syntax errors on-the-fly. Context-sensitive recovery uses the code's context to suggest corrections, such as adding a missing operator or closing bracket.

Example:

For a code snippet with a missing comma in a function call:

```
function greet(name, age) {
    console.log("Hello, " + name + ". You are " + age " years old.");
}
```

Solution: The IDE detects the missing comma, and provides a real-time suggestion to correct it:

```
console.log("Hello, " + name + ". You are " + age + " years old.");
```

Scenario 3: Data Processing Systems

Data processing systems, such as those parsing CSV files, often encounter malformed records. These records may have missing fields or incorrect delimiters, which can disrupt data processing.

Solution: Implement **Global Correction** and **Error Productions**. Global correction involves scanning the entire file to fix common errors, such as missing delimiters. Error productions use specific grammar rules to handle errors, such as inserting default values for missing fields.

Example:

Consider a CSV file with missing values:

```
name,age,city
John,25
Jane,30,New York
```

Solution: The system detects the missing value in the first record. Using global correction, it can insert a default value or leave the field empty, and then continue processing the remaining records:

```
name,age,city
John,25,Unknown
Jane,30,New York
```

Scenario 4: Web Development Frameworks

Web development frameworks need to parse configuration files and templates. Syntax errors in these files can lead to runtime issues or broken functionality on the web page.

Solution: Use **Context-Sensitive Recovery** to handle errors based on the context of the configuration or template. This approach ensures that errors are corrected in a way that maintains the intended functionality of the web application.

Example:

For a configuration file with a missing end tag:

```
<template>
    <div>Welcome to the site
</template>
```

Solution: The framework identifies the missing end tag. Context-sensitive recovery can correct it by adding the missing </div> tag, ensuring that the template renders correctly:

```
<template>
    <div>Welcome to the site</div>
</template>
```

Scenario 5: Log File Analysis

Log file parsers must handle irregularities and errors in log entries, which might include unexpected formats or incomplete data. Effective error handling ensures accurate analysis and reporting.

Solution: Apply **Error Reporting Strategies** and **Recovery Methods** to identify and correct errors. Reporting strategies provide details on the type and location of errors, while recovery methods adjust parsing to handle common log entry issues.

Example:

For a log file with inconsistent entry formats:

```
INFO 2024-08-16 12:00:00 Server started
ERROR 2024-08-16 12:01:00 Failed to connect to database
WARNING 2024-08-16 Missing timestamp
```

Solution: The parser detects the missing timestamp. Error reporting provides a message about the missing timestamp, while recovery methods may adjust the format or skip the faulty entry to continue processing:

```
INFO 2024-08-16 12:00:00 Server started
ERROR 2024-08-16 12:01:00 Failed to connect to database
WARNING 2024-08-16 12:01:00 Missing timestamp (default timestamp added)
```

These scenarios demonstrate various error handling techniques tailored to different contexts, ensuring that parsers and systems remain functional and provide accurate feedback despite encountering errors.

Example Implementations and Error Handling Strategies

In this section, we will explore practical implementations of syntax analysis using Yacc and Bison. We will demonstrate how to build parsers with these tools, provide examples of grammars and code, and examine how each tool handles parsing errors. This will help you understand how to effectively implement and manage error handling strategies in syntax analysis.

Implementations Using Yacc

In this section, we will explore how to create and utilize parsers with Yacc, providing practical examples and showcasing error handling techniques.

Overview of Yacc

Yacc (Yet Another Compiler Compiler) is a tool used for generating parsers for processing context-free grammars. It is commonly employed in compiler construction to handle the syntax analysis phase. Yacc reads grammar rules specified in a Yacc input file and produces C code for a parser that can analyze input sequences according to these rules.

Example Yacc Grammar and Code

To illustrate how Yacc works, consider a simple arithmetic expression parser. The following is an example of a Yacc grammar that recognizes basic arithmetic expressions involving addition and multiplication:

```
%{
#include <stdio.h>
#include <stdlib.h>
%}

%token NUMBER
%left '+' '-'
%left '*' '/'

%%

expression:
    expression '+' term    { printf("Addition\n"); }
  | expression '-' term    { printf("Subtraction\n"); }
  | term
  ;

term:
    term '*' factor    { printf("Multiplication\n"); }
  | term '/' factor    { printf("Division\n"); }
  | factor
  ;

factor:
    NUMBER
  | '(' expression ')'
  ;

%%

int main(void) {
    yyparse();
    return 0;
}

void yyerror(const char *s) {
    fprintf(stderr, "Error: %s\n", s);
}
```

This grammar defines rules for parsing expressions, terms, and factors. It uses tokens, such as **NUMBER** to represent numerical values and operators, such as +, -, *, and /.

Parsing Results and Error Handling

When the Yacc parser is run with an input, such as 3 + 5 * (2 - 8), it processes the input according to the defined grammar rules. The parser identifies the operations involved, and prints corresponding messages for each recognized operation.

For error handling, the yyerror function is used to report syntax errors encountered during parsing. If the input does not conform to the grammar rules, yyerror provides an error message indicating the issue.

Implementations Using Bison

Implementations using Bison illustrate how this powerful parser generator can be applied to define and process grammars effectively. By providing practical examples, these implementations show

how Bison generates parsers that can handle intricate language rules and structures, offering a clear approach to integrating Bison into syntax analysis tasks.

Overview of Bison

Bison is a powerful parser generator similar to Yacc but with more advanced features. It translates a formal grammar description into a parser in C or C++. Bison is used for syntax analysis in compilers and interpreters, and it supports features, such as error recovery and semantic actions. Bison is known for its ability to handle more complex grammars compared to its predecessors.

Example Bison Grammar and Code

Here is an example of a Bison grammar for parsing arithmetic expressions, similar to the Yacc example:

```
%{
#include <stdio.h>
#include <stdlib.h>
%}

%token NUMBER
%left '+' '-'
%left '*' '/'

%%

expression:
    expression '+' term   { printf("Addition\n"); }
  | expression '-' term   { printf("Subtraction\n"); }
  | term
  ;

term:
    term '*' factor    { printf("Multiplication\n"); }
  | term '/' factor    { printf("Division\n"); }
  | factor
  ;

factor:
    NUMBER
  | '(' expression ')'
  ;

%%

int main(void) {
    yyparse();
    return 0;
}

void yyerror(const char *s) {
    fprintf(stderr, "Error: %s\n", s);
}
```

In this Bison example, the grammar rules and actions are similar to those in Yacc. Bison uses similar syntax for defining tokens and rules, but offers additional features and better error handling capabilities.

Parsing Results and Error Handling

When running the Bison parser with an input, such as 7 + 3 * (2 - 5), the parser processes the input according to the defined rules. It identifies and prints messages for operations, such as addition, subtraction, multiplication, and division.

For error handling, Bison provides robust mechanisms. The `yyerror` function is used to report syntax errors, and Bison's built-in error recovery features can handle common mistakes in the input. Bison's advanced features allow it to recover from certain types of syntax errors and continue parsing.

Comparing Yacc and Bison

When deciding between Yacc and Bison for parsing tasks, it is important to understand how these tools differ and where they overlap. This comparison will highlight their unique features, performance differences, and compatibility, helping you choose the right tool for your specific needs.

Key Differences and Similarities

Yacc (Yet Another Compiler Compiler) and Bison are both powerful tools for generating parsers based on a given grammar. They share many similarities, but also have some key differences that may influence the choice between them.

To understand the strengths and limitations of Yacc and Bison, it is essential to compare their key features, functionalities, and overall capabilities. This comparison will help clarify how each tool handles parsing, and what makes them unique or similar in different contexts.

Similarities:

- **Syntax and Functionality:** Both Yacc and Bison use similar syntax for defining grammars, and generating parsers. They produce C code for the parsers and support tokens, rules, and actions in almost identical ways.
- **Use Cases:** Both tools are used for creating parsers in compilers, interpreters, and other applications where syntactic analysis is required. They both handle context-free grammars effectively.
- **Error Handling:** Both Yacc and Bison provide mechanisms for handling syntax errors during parsing, allowing the parser to recover from certain mistakes, and continue processing.

Differences:

- **Language Support:** While Yacc primarily generates parsers in C, Bison extends this capability to generate parsers in C++ and other languages. Bison's broader language support makes it more versatile for modern applications.
- **Features and Flexibility:** Bison is considered a more advanced tool compared to Yacc. It includes additional features, such as better support for complex grammars, more powerful error recovery, and enhanced debugging options.
- **Portability:** Bison is widely recognized as a free, open-source alternative to Yacc, and it is more portable across different platforms. Bison is basically a part of the GNU Project, making it a preferred choice in open-source communities.

Choosing the Right Tool for Your Needs

Selecting the appropriate parser generator depends on the specific requirements of your project. By evaluating the used cases, performances, and flexibility of both the Yacc and Bison, you can make an informed decision on which tool best suits your needs.

When deciding between Yacc and Bison, the choice largely depends on the specific requirements of your project:

- **If you need a simple and straightforward parser generator** with basic functionality, Yacc might be sufficient, especially if you are working in a C-only environment, and do not need the extra features provided by Bison.
- **If you require more advanced features, better error recovery, and support for multiple languages,** Bison is a better choice. Its flexibility and additional capabilities make it ideal for complex and modern parsing tasks.
- **For open-source projects or cross-platform development,** Bison's broader community support and compatibility might also make it the preferred tool.

Both Yacc and Bison are valuable tools for parser generation, and the right choice depends on the complexity of the task, the language requirements, and the desired features.

Conclusion

In this chapter, we delved into the core concepts of parsing techniques, including both top-down (LL parsers) and bottom-up (LR parsers) approaches. We explored how these methods work, their advantages and disadvantages, and their real-world applications in compiler design. Through practical implementations using tools, such as Yacc and Bison, we illustrated how parsing is performed and how errors are handled during the parsing process. This knowledge is crucial for anyone looking to build a robust syntax analysis components within a compiler.

As we move forward to *Chapter 6, Semantic Analysis and Attribute Grammars*, we will expand on this foundation by exploring how the meaning is derived from a syntax. The next chapter will cover topics, such as attribute grammars, semantic actions, and annotated parse trees, with practical implementations to solidify your understanding.

Points to Remember

- **Parsing** is the process of analyzing a string of symbols to determine its grammatical structure.
- **Top-down parsing (LL parsers)** starts from the root and builds the parse tree down to the leaves.
- **Bottom-up parsing (LR parsers)** begins with the input symbols and works up to the start symbol.
- **LL parsers** are easier to implement but can struggle with certain grammar structures.
- **LR parsers** are more powerful and handle a broader class of grammars but are more complex.
- **Error handling** during parsing is crucial to ensure that the compiler can recover from syntax errors.
- **Yacc** and **Bison** are popular tools used to implement parsing with error handling features.
- Choosing between **Yacc** and **Bison** depends on the specific requirements of your project.

Multiple Choice Questions

1. What is the main purpose of parsing in compiler design?
    a. To generate intermediate code
    b. To analyze the syntax and structure of the source code
    c. To optimize the code
    d. To execute the program

2. Which of the following is not a type of parsing technique?
   a. Top-Down Parsing
   b. Bottom-Up Parsing
   c. Middle-Out Parsing
   d. Both a and b
3. What does "LL" stand for in LL Parsers?
   a. Left-to-Right, Leftmost Derivation
   b. Left-to-Right, Rightmost Derivation
   c. Right-to-Left, Leftmost Derivation
   d. Right-to-Left, Rightmost Derivation
4. Which of the following is a characteristic of Top-Down Parsing?
   a. It constructs the parse tree from leaves to root.
   b. It constructs the parse tree from root to leaves.
   c. It requires a stack to process the input.
   d. It is suitable for all types of grammars.
5. What is the main limitation of LL Parsers?
   a. They cannot handle left recursion.
   b. They require a lot of memory.
   c. They are very slow.
   d. They cannot handle right recursion.
6. In which of the following cases would you use a Top-Down parser?
   a. When the grammar is ambiguous
   b. When the grammar is left-recursive
   c. When the grammar is simple and unambiguous
   d. When you need to handle complex languages
7. What does "LR" stand for in LR Parsers?
   a. Left-to-Right, Rightmost Derivation
   b. Left-to-Right, Leftmost Derivation
   c. Right-to-Left, Rightmost Derivation
   d. Right-to-Left, Leftmost Derivation
8. Which of the following is a characteristic of Bottom-Up Parsing?
   a. It constructs the parse tree from leaves to roots.
   b. It constructs the parse tree from roots to leaves.
   c. It is faster than Top-Down Parsing.
   d. It can handle ambiguous grammars.

9. What is the key advantage of LR Parsers over LL Parsers?
   a. They are easier to implement.
   b. They can handle a larger class of grammars.
   c. They are less memory-intensive.
   d. They produce smaller parse trees.
10. Which of the following is an example of a Bottom-Up Parser?
    a. LL(1) Parser
    b. Recursive Descent Parser
    c. SLR Parser
    d. Predictive Parser
11. Why is error handling important in parsing?
    a. To improve the performance of the compiler
    b. To prevent syntax errors from going unnoticed
    c. To generate optimized code
    d. To execute the program faster
12. Which of the following is not a type of parsing error?
    a. Syntax Error
    b. Semantic Error
    c. Lexical Error
    d. Runtime Error
13. Which technique is commonly used for error recovery in parsing?
    a. Backtracking
    b. Panic Mode
    c. Dynamic Programming
    d. Greedy Algorithm
14. Which of the following best describes "panic mode" error recovery?
    a. The parser discards input symbols until a specific set of synchronizing tokens is found.
    b. The parser immediately terminates upon encountering an error.
    c. The parser attempts to fix the error by making assumptions about the input.
    d. The parser restarts the entire parsing process.
15. Which of the following is not a strategy for error detection?
    a. Using predictive parsing tables
    b. Using lookahead tokens
    c. Using backtracking
    d. Using semantic analysis

16. What does Yacc stand for?
    a. Yet Another Compiler Compiler
    b. Your Advanced Compiler Compiler
    c. Yet Another Computer Compiler
    d. Your Automated Compiler Compiler
17. What is the primary function of Yacc in parsing?
    a. To tokenize the input
    b. To generate the parse tree
    c. To generate a parser from a grammar description
    d. To optimize the generated code
18. What is the key difference between Yacc and Bison?
    a. Bison is a newer version with more features.
    b. Yacc supports more grammars than Bison.
    c. Bison is compatible only with C++, while Yacc is for C.
    d. Yacc is platform-independent, while Bison is not.
19. In Bison, what is the default action when a rule is matched?
    a. The parser discards the input.
    b. The parser constructs a parse tree.
    c. The parser assigns the result of the match to $$.
    d. The parser generates an error message.
20. Which of the following is an advantage of using Bison over Yacc?
    a. It is faster and more efficient.
    b. It supports internationalization.
    c. It has better error reporting capabilities.
    d. It integrates better with modern programming languages.

Answers

1. b
2. c
3. a
4. b
5. a
6. c
7. a

8. a
9. b
10. c
11. b
12. d
13. b
14. a
15. d
16. a
17. c
18. a
19. c
20. c

Questions

1. Explain the role of parsing in compiler and interpreter design.
2. Describe the differences between Top-Down and Bottom-Up parsing techniques, including examples of when each is typically used.
3. What is Top-Down Parsing, and what makes LL Parsers unique?
4. Illustrate the process of Top-Down parsing with an example of constructing an LL parse tree for a simple arithmetic expression.
5. What are the limitations of LL Parsers, and how can these limitations be addressed?
6. Discuss the significance of LL Parsers in modern compiler design. Provide examples of programming languages or scenarios where LL Parsers are utilized.
7. What is Bottom-Up Parsing, and how does it differ from Top-Down Parsing?
8. Explain the steps involved in constructing an LR parse tree for a given arithmetic expression.
9. Describe the main types of LR Parsers (SLR, LALR, and Canonical LR) and their characteristics.
10. What are the advantages of LR Parsers over LL Parsers?
11. Why is error handling essential in syntax analysis, and what are the most effective strategies for error detection and recovery?
12. Provide examples of common syntax errors in programming languages, and how a parser might handle these errors.
13. Explain how Yacc is used to generate parsers from grammar descriptions. Provide an example of a simple Yacc grammar and its corresponding parser.
14. Compare and contrast Yacc and Bison in terms of their syntax, features, and used cases.
15. Discuss the role of error handling in parsers generated by Yacc and Bison. How do these tools help manage syntax errors during parsing?

Key Terms

- **Parsing**: Analyzing code to understand its structure based on grammar rules.
- **Top-Down Parsing**: Starting from the top of the parse tree, and working down to match input with grammar.
- **Bottom-Up Parsing**: Starting from input symbols, and reducing them to the start symbol of the grammar by working up the parse tree.
- **LL Parsers**: Top-down parsers that process input left to right, and construct a leftmost derivation.
- **LR Parsers**: Bottom-up parsers that process input left to right, and construct a rightmost derivation in reverse.
- **Parse Tree**: A tree diagram showing how input is derived from grammar rules.
- **Error Handling**: Methods for detecting, reporting, and fixing errors in the parsing process.
- **Yacc**: A tool that generates C code for a parser based on a defined grammar.
- **Bison**: A modern parser generator similar to Yacc, but with additional features and support for C and C++.

CHAPTER 6
Semantic Analysis Attribute Grammars

Introduction

In the previous chapter, we explored different parsing techniques to analyze and understand the structure of the source code. In this chapter, we shift our focus to semantic analysis which ensures that the code not only adheres to the syntax rules, but also aligns with the logical rules of the programming language.

We will begin by examining attribute grammars, a formalism used to describe the semantics of programming languages. Attribute grammars help us manage and enforce the meaning of code elements by attaching attributes to grammar rules. Next, we will delve into semantic actions that are crucial for applying semantic rules, and performing necessary computations during the parsing process. We will also cover annotated parse trees which integrate the syntax and semantics to provide a comprehensive understanding of the code. Lastly, we will explore some practical examples using ANTLR, a tool that facilitates the creation of parsers, and helps in implementing semantic analysis. This chapter will enhance your ability to ensure that your code is not only syntactically valid, but also semantically sound.

Structure

In this chapter, we will discuss the following topics:

- Attribute Grammars
    - Introduction to Attribute Grammars
    - Definition and Components
    - Types of Attributes
    - Examples and Applications
- Semantic Actions
    - Overview of Semantic Actions
    - Role in Semantic Analysis
    - Example Actions and their Implementation
- Annotated Parse Trees
    - Understanding Annotated Parse Trees
    - Construction and Use
    - Examples with Annotations
- Example Implementations Using ANTLR
    - Introduction to ANTLR

- Setting Up ANTLR for Semantic Analysis
- Example Code and Explanation
- Analyzing Output and Error Handling

Attribute Grammars

Attribute grammars extend traditional context-free grammars by adding attributes to grammar rules, allowing us to perform semantic analysis during parsing. This extension is crucial for ensuring that the code not only follows syntactic rules, but also adheres to the semantic constraints. Attribute grammars facilitate the definition and enforcement of the semantic rules, such as type checking and scope management, within the context of the compiler design, and other language processing tasks.

Introduction to Attribute Grammars

When we think about how programming languages are understood by compilers, it is essential to go beyond just the syntax. Attribute grammars come into play here, helping us define not just the structure, but also the meaning of different language constructs. They are a powerful tool in semantic analysis, bridging the gap between the syntax and meaning.

Overview of Attribute Grammars in the Context of Semantic Analysis

Attribute grammars extend context-free grammars by adding semantic rules to define and enforce the meaning of constructs in a programming language. They integrate syntax and semantics by associating attributes with grammar symbols and rules. This integration allows attribute grammars to manage the meaning and behavior of language constructs, supporting tasks, such as type checking, scope resolution, and expression evaluation. By embedding semantic rules into the grammar, attribute grammars provide a powerful tool for semantic analysis in compiler design.

Definition and Components

At the heart of attribute grammars are three main components: Attributes, rules, and grammar productions. Attributes are properties assigned to the symbols in a grammar, while rules define how these attributes are computed. Grammar productions outline the structure of valid strings in a language. Together, they form a system that can express complex language semantics.

Key Elements: Attributes, Rules, and Grammar Productions

Understanding the foundational components of attribute grammars is essential. These elements–attributes, rules, and grammar productions–work together to define how semantic information is associated with the syntactic structure of a language.

- **Attributes**: These are properties associated with grammar symbols that carry additional information necessary for semantic analysis. Attributes can represent various data, such as types, values, or scopes.
- **Rules**: Semantic rules are expressions that define how attributes are computed. They specify how attributes of non-terminal symbols can be derived from their components, and how attributes of terminal symbols are assigned.
- **Grammar Productions**: These define the structure of the language. In the context of attribute grammars, productions are enhanced with semantic rules that determine how attributes are propagated and computed throughout the parse tree.

Types of Attributes

Attributes in attribute grammars are categorized based on their role in conveying semantic information. Understanding the different types–synthesized and inherited–is crucial for grasping how data is passed and computed within parse trees.

- **Synthesized Attributes: Computed from Child Nodes**

  Synthesized attributes are calculated based on the values of child nodes in the parse tree. For instance, in an arithmetic expression, the value of an expression node might be computed from the values of its operand nodes. Synthesized attributes help propagate information up the parse tree from the leaves to the root.

  Example:

  Consider an arithmetic expression, such as 3 + (4 * 2). In this case, the synthesized attributes for the multiplication (*) operation would be computed first from its child nodes, 4 and 2. The result of this multiplication (which is 8) is then synthesized upwards, and used in the addition (+) operation, ultimately yielding the final result of 11.

  Real-Time Example:

  Think of a simple spreadsheet program where cells contain formulas. If a cell contains the formula =A1 + B2, the values in A1 and B2 are like the child nodes, and their sum is the synthesized attribute passed up to the cell displaying the result. The spreadsheet engine uses synthesized attributes to calculate and display the final value in the cell where the formula is entered.

  This process ensures that the correct values are derived as you move up the hierarchy of operations or dependencies.

- **Inherited Attributes: Passed Down from Parent Nodes**

  Inherited attributes are passed down from parent nodes to their children in the parse tree. They allow information to flow from the root of the parse tree to its leaves. For example, a node representing a function might inherit the type information of its parameters from the function declaration. Inherited attributes help propagate the context and constraints from the parent to the child nodes.

  Example:

  Imagine a scenario where a programming language requires that all the variables declared within a function are of a certain type, say 'int'. The type information can be inherited by each variable declaration within the function. The parent node (the function) passes down the type attribute to each child node (the variable declarations), ensuring that all the variables within that scope are correctly typed as 'int'.

  Real-Time Example:

  Consider a company where the CEO (parent node) sets a policy that all the departments must follow a specific budget guideline. This policy is an inherited attribute that flows down to each department head (child node), ensuring that all decisions made within each department align with the overall company policy. In programming terms, this inherited attribute ensures consistency and adherence to specific rules or contexts defined at a higher level in the hierarchy.

  This mechanism is crucial in scenarios where the context or environment provided by a parent node must be applied to its descendants, ensuring consistency and correctness throughout the structure.

Examples and Applications

To truly grasp the power of attribute grammars, exploring practical examples can illuminate how attributes are used to define and enforce the semantics of programming languages. These applications demonstrate their real-world impact in compiler design and beyond.

Practical Examples Demonstrating the Use of Attributes in Defining Language Semantics

Attribute grammars play a crucial role in defining and enforcing the semantics of a programming language. By attaching attributes to grammar rules, we can specify the meaning of constructs in the language, and ensure that they behave as intended.

Example 1: Type Checking in Arithmetic Expressions

In many programming languages, when performing arithmetic operations, it is essential to ensure that the types of operands are compatible. For example, adding an integer to another integer is valid, but adding an integer to a string might not be.

Implementation: Consider a grammar rule for an addition operation where both operands need to be of the same type:

```
E → E1 + T { E.type = if (E1.type == T.type) then E1.type else error("Type
mismatch") }
T → int { T.type = int }
T → float { T.type = float }
```

Explanation:

- **Synthesized Attributes:** In this example, the type attribute is synthesized from its child nodes. The type of the expression, E is determined based on the types of E1 and T.
- **Type Checking:** The grammar ensures that E1 and T have the same type. If both the operands are of the same type (either int or float), the expression is valid, and the common type is assigned to E. If they differ, the parser raises a type mismatch error.

Real-World Application: In practical terms, this mechanism is akin to ensuring that when you sum up two numbers on a calculator, both inputs are treated as the same type (such as both being integers), preventing errors that could arise from mismatched types.

Example 2: Variable Scoping with Inherited Attributes

Context: In programming languages with block structures (such as, C, Java, or Python), variables declared inside a block (such as, a function or loop) should only be accessible within that block. Managing the scope of these variables is crucial for preventing errors, such as using an undeclared variable.

Implementation: Consider a scenario where a variable, 'x' is declared within a block and then used:

```
Block → { D S } { S.scope = D.scope }
D → int x; { D.scope = add_variable(D.scope, "x", int) }
S → x = 5; { if (lookup(S.scope, "x")) then assign(x, 5) else error("Unde-
clared variable") }
```

Explanation:

- **Inherited Attributes:** The scope attribute is passed down (inherited) from the block to the statements within it.

- **Variable Declaration:** When 'x' is declared, it is added to the current scope. The scope is then passed to all the subsequent statements within the block.
- **Variable Use:** When 'x' is used in an assignment, the grammar checks if 'x' is within the current scope. If 'x' is found, the assignment proceeds; if not, an error is raised, indicating that 'x' was not declared.

Real-World Application: This system can be likened to a classroom where students can only use materials provided by the teacher (their scope). If a student tries to use something that was not provided or authorized by the teacher, it is flagged as an error.

Example 3: Syntax-Directed Translation for Postfix Expression Evaluation

Context: In compilers, converting arithmetic expressions from infix notation (such as, a + b * c) to postfix notation (such as, a b c * +) simplifies evaluation. This is because postfix expressions do not require parentheses or an understanding of operator precedence to evaluate correctly.

Implementation: Consider a grammar that translates an infix expression into postfix notation:

```
E → E1 + T { E.postfix = E1.postfix + " " + T.postfix + " +" }
T → id { T.postfix = id.lexeme }
```

Explanation:

- **Synthesized Attributes:** Here, the postfix attribute is synthesized as the parser processes each part of the expression.
- **Postfix Translation:** The grammar rule for E (an expression) combines the postfix strings of E1 and T, and then adds the operator at the end. This effectively builds the postfix notation as the expression is parsed.

Real-World Application: This translation is similar to how some calculators or programming languages internally convert more complex arithmetic expressions into a format that is easier to evaluate, ensuring correct results, without needing to consider operator precedence during evaluation.

Semantic Actions

Semantic actions are vital components in the process of semantic analysis within compilers. They bridge the gap between the syntax and semantics, ensuring that the parsed code not only follows the correct structure, but also conveys the intended meaning.

Overview of Semantic Actions

Semantic actions play a crucial role in the process of semantic analysis within a compiler. These actions are operations or code snippets embedded within the grammar rules of a parser. They are executed as the parser processes the input, helping to enforce semantic rules, manage symbol tables, perform type checking, and ultimately, generate the intermediate code or other representations needed for further stages of compilation.

Definition and Importance in Enforcing Semantic Rules

Semantic actions are typically defined within the production rules of a grammar. They ensure that the parsed code adheres not only to the syntactic rules but also to the semantic rules of the language. For example, they might enforce that variables are declared before they are used, or that operations are performed on compatible data types. This stage of compilation helps catch errors that cannot be detected by syntax analysis alone, ensuring the correctness and meaning of the program.

Role in Semantic Analysis

Semantic analysis is responsible for validating the semantics of the code, going beyond the surface-level syntax. Semantic actions are integrated into this process by performing checks and transformations as the parse tree is built. These actions might include:

- **Type Checking:**

  A semantic action might ensure that an arithmetic operation between variables is semantically correct by checking their types.

  Example:

  Consider a simple arithmetic expression, such as x = y + z. The semantic action here would check that y and z are of compatible types for addition, and that 'x' can legally hold the result of the operation.

```
expr : expr '+' term {
    if ($1.type != $3.type)
        yyerror("Type mismatch in addition");
    $$ = $1 + $3;
}
```

  In this Yacc code snippet, the semantic action checks the types of the operands, **$1** and **$3**. If they do not match, it raises a type mismatch error. Otherwise, it proceeds with the addition.

- **Scope Management:**

  Managing symbol tables to track variable declarations and their scopes.

  Example:

  When a variable is declared, the semantic action adds it to the symbol table, and when a variable is used, it checks if the variable is in scope.

```
var_decl : TYPE ID {
    add_to_symbol_table($2, $1.type);
}
var_usage : ID {
    if (!is_in_symbol_table($1))
        yyerror("Undeclared variable used");
}
```

  This snippet shows semantic actions that handle variable declaration and usage. When a variable is declared, it is added to the symbol table with its type. When the variable is used, the action checks if it is declared in the current scope.

- **Intermediate Code Generation:**

  Generating code that represents the program in a form that can be further optimized or translated into the machine code.

  Example:

  For a given operation, the semantic action generates a corresponding piece of intermediate code that can later be optimized or compiled into the machine code.

```
expr : expr '+' term {
    $$ = gen_code("ADD", $1, $3);
}
```

This code generates an intermediate representation for the addition operation. The **gen_code** function could produce a line of intermediate code, such as t1 = y + z, where t1 is a temporary variable.

How Semantic Actions Integrate with Parsing to Ensure Semantic Correctness

Semantic actions are an integral part of the parsing process in a compiler or interpreter, ensuring that the source code not only follows correct syntactical structure, but also adheres to the language's semantic rules. Here is how they work together:

- **Augmenting Syntax with Meaning**

  Parsing primarily checks if the source code conforms to the syntax rules defined by a grammar. However, correct syntax alone does not guarantee that the code makes sense semantically. For example, the expression, 5 + "hello" might be syntactically valid, but it is semantically incorrect because you cannot add a number to a string. This is where semantic actions come in.

  Example:

  When parsing the expression, 5 + "hello", a semantic action can check the types of the operands. If it detects that one is a number, and the other is a string, it can raise an error, ensuring semantic correctness.

- **Ensuring Type Compatibility**

  One of the common uses of semantic actions is to enforce type rules. During parsing, when a specific grammar rule is applied (such as the addition of two expressions), semantic actions can verify that the operands are of compatible types.

  Example:

  In the expression, a + b, a semantic action can check whether a and b are both integers. If not, it can generate a type mismatch error, preventing the generation of invalid code.

- **Attribute Computation**

  Semantic actions often compute attributes that carry important information through the parse tree. These attributes can include types, memory locations, or intermediate code representations. By computing and propagating these attributes, semantic actions help maintain the integrity of the program's semantics.

  Example:

  Consider a grammar rule for an assignment statement, x = y;. A semantic action can be used to ensure that the type of y matches the declared type of x, and to generate the appropriate intermediate code for the assignment.

- **Symbol Table Management**

  During parsing, semantic actions are often used to manage a symbol table, which keeps track of identifiers (such as variables and function names), and their associated information (such as type and scope). This ensures that variables are declared before they are used, and that functions are called with the correct arguments.

  Example:

  When encountering a variable declaration, int x;, a semantic action can add x to the symbol table with its type. Later, when x is used in an expression, the parser can look up x in the symbol table to verify that it is being used correctly.

- **Scope and Binding**

  Semantic actions help enforce the rules related to variable scope and binding, ensuring that variables and functions are used within their defined contexts. They check for things, such as variable shadowing and proper function calls.

  Example:

  In a nested block of code, a semantic action might check that a variable y declared in the inner block does not conflict with a y in an outer block, ensuring proper scope handling.

- **Intermediate Code Generation**

  In many compilers, semantic actions are responsible for generating intermediate code during parsing. This code is a lower-level representation of the source code which will eventually be translated into machine code.

  Example:

  For the expression, x = y + z;, a semantic action might generate an intermediate code that adds y and z, and then stores the result in x. This intermediate code will later be optimized and translated into the final machine code.

Example Actions and Their Implementation

To effectively enforce semantic rules during parsing, it is crucial to implement specific semantic actions. These actions ensure that the parsed code adheres to the language's semantic rules, and generates the necessary output or errors. Here, we provide detailed examples of common semantic actions, explaining their purpose, and how they are implemented in a code.

Code Snippets and Explanation: Implementation of Semantic Actions

Here, we provide code snippets demonstrating the implementation of semantic actions in parsing. Each example includes a brief explanation of the code, highlighting how semantic actions are used to enforce rules, and produce the correct output.

- **Type Checking in Expressions**

  Example: Consider a scenario where we want to ensure that both the operands in an arithmetic expression are of the same type (for example, both integers or both floating-point numbers). If they are not, the parser should report a type mismatch error.

  Code Implementation:

```
expression: expression '+' term
{
    if ($1.type != $3.type) {
        printf("Type error: Mismatched types in expression.\n");
    } else {
        $$ = $1 + $3;  // Perform addition if types match
    }
}
| term;
```

  This semantic action ensures that only valid operations (such as adding two numbers of the same type) are performed, preventing errors in the generated code.

- **Symbol Table Management for Variable Declarations**

  Example: When declaring a variable, it is essential to store its name and type in a symbol table. The parser should also check if the variable has already been declared to avoid redeclarations.

  Code Implementation:

```
declaration: TYPE ID
{
    if (symbol_table.lookup($2) != NULL) {
        printf("Error: Variable '%s' is already declared.\n", $2);
    } else {
        symbol_table.insert($2, $1);  // Insert the variable name and type
into the symbol table
    }
};
```

  This action prevents redeclaration of errors, and maintains the correctness of the variable scope and type information in the program.

- **Scope Handling in Nested Blocks**

  Example: In languages that allow nested blocks, it is important to manage variable scopes correctly. A variable declared in an inner block should not conflict with one in an outer block, and its scope should end when the block does.

  Code Implementation:

```
block: '{' declarations statements '}'
{
    symbol_table.enter_scope();  // Start a new scope for the block
    // Process declarations and statements
    symbol_table.exit_scope();   // End the scope when the block ends
};
```

  This ensures that variables are used within their appropriate scopes, and that the variable names do not conflict across different blocks.

- **Intermediate Code Generation for Assignments**

  Example: When assigning a value to a variable, the parser must generate an intermediate code that reflects this operation.

  Code Implementation:

```
assignment: ID '=' expression
{
    printf("Generated code: %s = %s\n", $1, $3.code);
    $$ = $1 + " = " + $3.code;  // Generate intermediate code for the
assignment
};
```

  This action helps in building the intermediate representation of the program which will later be translated into the machine code.

Annotated Parse Trees

Annotated parse trees are enhanced versions of standard parse trees that include additional information, known as annotations, attached to each node. These annotations capture the semantic details about the program which are used to represent and enforce the meaning of the language constructs.

To fully grasp how programming languages handle semantic information, we need to delve into annotated parse trees. These specialized structures extend traditional parse trees by incorporating additional semantic details, allowing for a richer representation of a program's meaning.

Understanding Annotated Parse Trees

Understanding annotated parse trees is pivotal for grasping how semantic analysis enhances the basic parse tree. By integrating detailed annotations, these trees not only represent the syntactic structure but also encode vital semantic information, making them essential for effective code analysis and generation.

Definition and Significance in Representing Semantic Information

Annotated parse trees are extended versions of parse trees that include additional information, known as annotations, attached to the nodes. These annotations represent semantic information derived from the code, and are used to capture the meaning and context of the language constructs.

Components:

- **Nodes**: Represent elements of the syntax, such as expressions, statements, or declarations. In an annotated parse tree, each node also includes semantic information, such as type information or scope details.
- **Edges**: Connect nodes to show the syntactic relationships and hierarchy. The edges in an annotated parse tree remain similar to those in a standard parse tree, but the nodes they connect contain more information.
- **Annotations**: Additional data attached to nodes, including:
    - **Type Information**: Data type of variables or expressions (for example, integer, float).
    - **Scope Information**: Context in which variables or functions are defined (for example, local or global).
    - **Value Information**: Intermediate values computed during analysis or evaluation.
    - **Semantic Properties**: Other relevant details, such as whether an identifier is defined or used correctly.

Significance:

- **Enhanced Semantic Understanding**: Annotated parse trees provide a richer representation of the code's semantics, enabling more thorough analysis beyond the syntax. They help to interpret how different parts of the code interact and conform to the language rules.
- **Error Detection and Reporting**: They facilitate the identification of semantic errors, such as type mismatches, undeclared variables, or incorrect scope usage. Annotations help pinpoint exactly where and why an error occurs.
- **Support for Code Generation**: By providing the detailed semantic information, annotated parse trees aid in translating high-level constructs into intermediate or target code. They help ensure that the generated code accurately reflects the intended semantics of the source code.
- **Intermediate Analysis**: They serve as a basis for further stages in compilation or interpretation, such as optimization and code generation. The semantic information embedded in the tree can guide these processes to produce efficient and correct output.

Example:

For an expression, such as x + y, a standard parse tree might show + as the root with x and y as its children. In an annotated parse tree, x and y might have annotations indicating their types (for example, integer) and their scope (for example, local variables). This additional information helps ensure that the addition operation is valid and correctly handled during subsequent stages of compilation.

Illustration:

- **Node for x**: {Variable, Type: Integer, Scope: Local}
- **Node for y**: {Variable, Type: Integer, Scope: Local}
- **Node for +**: {Operator, Operand Types: Integer + Integer, Result Type: Integer}

By incorporating such annotations, you create a detailed map of the semantic landscape of the code, making it easier to perform comprehensive analysis and transformations.

Construction and Use

To leverage the full potential of annotated parse trees, it is essential to understand both their construction and practical application. Constructing these trees involves integrating semantic information with traditional syntactic structures, while their use spans various stages of code analysis and transformation. This comprehensive approach ensures that both the structure and meaning of the code are thoroughly examined and utilized.

Steps to Build and Use Annotated Parse Trees

Annotated parse trees are essential structures used in both compiler design and natural language processing, providing a clear representation of the syntactic composition of an input. Unlike standard parse trees, annotated versions include additional information at each node, such as semantic details that may pertain to types, scopes, or the roles of elements. This rich information enhances the tree's utility, enabling tasks, such as syntax checking, semantic analysis, and code optimization. This guide provides a step-by-step approach to constructing and employing annotated parse trees effectively in various computational contexts.

Construction

Constructing annotated parse trees involves several key steps to ensure that both syntactic and semantic information are accurately represented. This process begins with the creation of a standard parse tree, where each node is then enriched with additional annotations that capture the semantic properties of the code.

- **Parsing the Code**: This starts by generating a standard parse tree using a parser that processes the source code according to the language's syntax rules.
- **Adding Annotations**: Once the basic parse tree is constructed, annotate each node with semantic information. This may include:
  - **Type Information**: Associating types with variables, expressions, and operations.
  - **Scope Information**: Indicating the scope or context in which identifiers are used or declared.
  - **Intermediate Values**: Recording values or results computed during semantic analysis.
- **Propagation of Attributes**: This implements rules for propagating attributes through the tree. It also involves computing and updating annotations based on the relationships and hierarchy of nodes.
- **Validation**: It ensures that the annotated parse tree adheres to the semantic rules and constraints of the language. This includes checking for type consistency, correct scope usage, and other semantic properties.

Use:

The Annotated Parse Trees are used extensively in semantic analysis and subsequent stages of compilation to provide a detailed understanding of the program's meaning.

- **Semantic Analysis**: Use the annotated parse tree to check for semantic errors, and enforce the language rules. For example, validate that variables are correctly typed, and that all identifiers are properly declared and used.
- **Intermediate Code Generation**: The detailed semantic information in the annotated parse tree assists in translating the high-level language constructs into intermediate representations. This information ensures that the generated code accurately reflects the intended semantics of the source code.
- **Optimization**: Utilize the annotations to guide the optimization processes. For example, knowing the types and scopes of variables can help in optimizing the memory usage and improving the execution efficiency.
- **Error Reporting**: Annotated parse trees facilitate precise error reporting by providing a detailed information about where and why semantic errors occur. This helps in debugging, and improving code quality.
- **Code Transformation**: Apply transformations to the code based on the semantic information encoded in the annotated parse tree. This can include refactoring or translating the code into different forms, while preserving its meaning.

Thus, by effectively constructing and using annotated parse trees, you enhance the ability to analyze, validate, and transform the code, ensuring that it meets the semantic requirements of the programming language.

Examples with Annotations

To better grasp how annotated parse trees function, it is helpful to explore practical examples that illustrate their construction and application. By examining annotated parse trees in action, we can see how semantic information is integrated and utilized to enhance code analysis and validation. These examples will provide clarity on how annotations contribute to a deeper understanding of the program's meaning.

Illustrative Examples Showing Annotated Parse Trees

To illustrate the practical use of annotated parse trees, let us look at some straightforward examples. These examples will demonstrate how semantic information is incorporated into parse trees, providing a clear view of how annotations enhance our understanding of code structure and meaning.

Arithmetic Expression:

Consider the arithmetic expression, a + b * c. The annotated parse tree for this expression might include the following details:

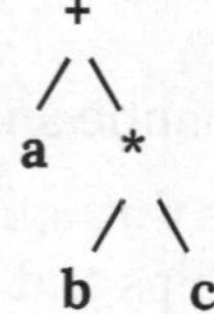

Annotated Parse Tree:

- Node for a: {Variable, Type: Integer, Scope: Local}
- Node for b: {Variable, Type: Integer, Scope: Local}

- Node for c: {Variable, Type: Integer, Scope: Local}
- Node for *: {Operator, Operand Types: Integer * Integer, Result Type: Integer}
- Node for +: {Operator, Operand Types: Integer + Integer, Result Type: Integer}

Variable Declaration and Use:

For a statement, such as int x = 5;, the annotated parse tree might show:

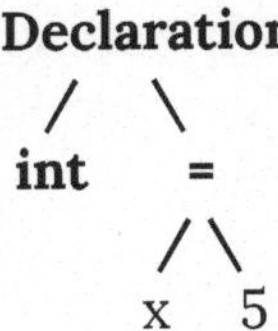

Annotated Parse Tree:

- Node for int: {Keyword, Type: Integer}
- Node for x: {Variable, Type: Integer, Scope: Local, Initial Value: 5}
- Node for =: {Assignment, Variable: x, Value: 5}
- Node for 5: {Literal, Value: 5, Type: Integer}

Function Call:

In the function `call foo(a, b)`, the annotated parse tree may include:

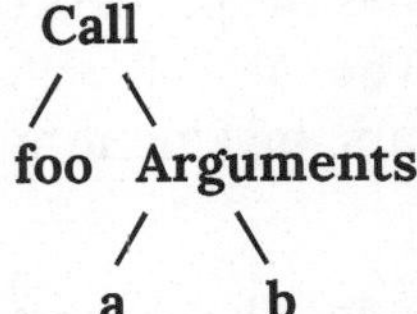

Annotated Parse Tree:

- Node for foo: {Function Name: foo, Expected Parameters: Integer, Integer}
- Node for a: {Variable, Type: Integer, Scope: Local}
- Node for b: {Variable, Type: Integer, Scope: Local}
- Node for Arguments: {Arguments, Types: Integer, Integer}

Conditional Statement:

For a conditional statement, such as if (x > 10) { y = x; }, the annotated parse tree could include:

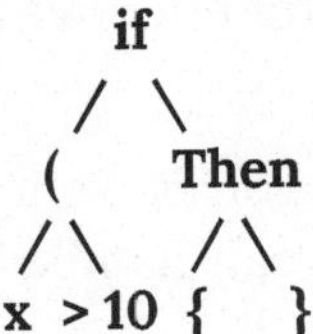

Annotated Parse Tree:

- Node for x > 10: {Comparison, Left Operand: x (Type: Integer), Right Operand: 10 (Type: Integer), Result Type: Boolean}
- Node for y = x: {Assignment, Variable: y (Type: Integer, Scope: Local), Value: x (Type: Integer)}
- Node for y: {Variable, Type: Integer, Scope: Local}
- Node for 10: {Literal, Value: 10, Type: Integer}

These examples illustrate how annotated parse trees integrate semantic details to provide a clearer understanding of the code's meaning, and facilitate accurate analysis and transformation.

Example Implementations Using ANTLR

To see how annotated parse trees and semantic analysis are practically implemented, let us explore examples using ANTLR. This powerful tool helps define grammars and generate parsers that can handle complex language features, allowing us to apply our understanding of attribute grammars in real-world scenarios. These examples will demonstrate how ANTLR facilitates the creation of parsers that integrate semantic information, and support effective language processing.

Introduction to ANTLR

To effectively manage the complexities of language processing, tools, such as ANTLR are indispensable. ANTLR not only simplifies the task of defining grammars, but also provides powerful features for building parsers that handle both syntax and semantics. In this section, we will introduce the ANTLR, and explore how it supports the creation of robust language processing tools, particularly in the realm of semantic analysis.

Overview of ANTLR and its Role in Semantic Analysis

ANTLR (Another Tool for Language Recognition) is a powerful tool used for generating parsers that can process, interpret, and translate structured text or binary files. It simplifies the process of defining grammars for programming languages and other structured formats. The ANTLR automatically generates the code needed to parse input text according to these grammars, making it an essential tool in the development of compilers, interpreters, and translators.

In the context of semantic analysis, the ANTLR plays a crucial role by allowing developers to define and attach semantic actions to grammar rules. These semantic actions are used to enforce language-specific rules, such as type checking and scope resolution, ensuring that the parsed code adheres to the intended meaning and logical structure. By integrating semantic analysis directly into the parsing process, the ANTLR helps to streamline the development of robust language processing tools.

Setting Up the ANTLR for Semantic Analysis

Before we can harness the ANTLR's powerful features for semantic analysis, it is essential to properly configure the environment. Setting up ANTLR involves a few key steps that lay the foundation for defining grammars, attaching semantic actions, and generating parsers capable of enforcing semantic rules. Let us walk through the setup process to ensure that everything is ready for effective semantic analysis.

Setting up ANTLR for semantic analysis is a straightforward process that involves defining your language's syntax, embedding semantic checks, and generating a parser that can handle both the structure and meaning.

1. **Create the Grammar File**: Begin by writing a grammar file in the ANTLR. This file outlines the syntax rules of your programming language, detailing how various language constructs–such as expressions, statements, and declarations–are structured. The grammar serves as the foundation for how the language will be parsed.
2. **Incorporate Semantic Actions**: Within your grammar, you can embed semantic actions–code snippets that execute during parsing. These actions enforce semantic rules, such as ensuring that the variables are declared before use, or that types are compatible in expressions.

By embedding these actions directly into your grammar, you create a parser that not only checks the syntax, but also validates the code's logical correctness.

3. **Generate the Parser**: Once your grammar is ready, run the ANTLR to generate the parser code in your chosen programming language (such as the Java, Python, or C++). The generated parser will not only recognize and parse the syntax of your language, but will also trigger the semantic actions, you have defined as it processes the code.

4. **Integrate and Deploy**: Finally, integrate the ANTLR-generated parser into your development environment. When used, this parser will analyze the input code, ensuring it adheres to both the syntactic and semantic rules. This dual-checking process helps to catch errors early, making your language processing robust and reliable.

Therefore, by setting up the ANTLR for semantic analysis in this way, you create a powerful tool that not only verifies the structural correctness of the code, but also ensures that it behaves as intended according to the language's semantics. This setup is crucial for building reliable compilers, interpreters, or any tool that processes programming languages.

Steps to Configure ANTLR for Defining Attribute Grammars

To harness the full potential of ANTLR for semantic analysis, you need to configure it to handle attribute grammars effectively. This process involves setting up ANTLR to define and apply semantic rules alongside syntax rules. By following these steps, you will be able to create a robust parser that not only understands the structure of your language, but also enforces its semantic constraints.

1. **Install ANTLR**: Begin by installing ANTLR and its runtime libraries for your chosen programming language. ANTLR can be installed via package managers, downloaded from the official website, or added to your project using build tools, such as Maven or Gradle.

2. **Create the Grammar File**: Write a grammar file using ANTLR's syntax. This file, typically with a `.g4` extension, defines the syntax rules of your language. The grammar specifies how different language constructs are structured, such as expressions, statements, and blocks.

3. **Define Semantic Actions**: Within your grammar file, embed semantic actions–code snippets that will execute as the parser processes the input. These actions are used to enforce semantic rules, such as type checking and scope management. For example, you might check that a variable is declared before it is used.

4. **Configure ANTLR Tool**: Set up ANTLR to generate the parser and lexer code from your grammar file. This typically involves running the ANTLR tool with your grammar file as input. You can configure options such as target language and output directories based on your project needs.

5. **Generate Parser Code**: Execute the ANTLR tool to generate the parser and lexer code. This code will be based on the grammar you defined, and will include the semantic actions you embedded. Ensure that the generated code is placed in the correct directories for your project.

6. **Integrate Generated Code**: Integrate the generated parser and lexer into your development environment. This involves incorporating the generated code into your application, setting up any necessary dependencies, and writing the code to use the parser and lexer for analyzing and processing input.

7. **Test and Debug**: Test the parser with sample inputs to ensure that it correctly applies both syntactic and semantic rules. Debug any issues by examining the parser's behavior, and the output of the semantic actions. Make adjustments to the grammar and semantic actions as needed.

8. **Refine and Extend**: Based on testing feedback, refine your grammar and semantic actions. Extend the grammar to cover additional language constructs or add more complex semantic checks as needed.
9. **Document and Maintain**: Document the grammar, semantic actions, and any configuration details to facilitate maintenance and future updates. Ensure that your setup is well-documented for others who may work with your language processing tools.

By following these steps, you can configure ANTLR to define attribute grammars effectively, enabling you to build parsers that not only understand the syntax of your language, but also enforce its semantic rules.

Example Code and Explanation

To better understand how ANTLR can be used for defining attribute grammars, let us explore a practical example. This example demonstrates how to set up a basic arithmetic expression parser using ANTLR. By examining the sample code and its components, you will gain insight into how ANTLR processes input and applies semantic actions to enforce language rules.

Sample ANTLR Code Demonstrating Attribute Grammars

To illustrate how ANTLR can be used to define and implement attribute grammars, let us look at a simple example. The following ANTLR grammar defines arithmetic expressions, and includes semantic actions. This example will help you understand how to structure your grammar and incorporate semantic rules.

Here is a basic example of ANTLR grammar that includes semantic actions. This example demonstrates a simple arithmetic expression evaluator with type checking.

Grammar File (**`Arithmetic.g4`**):

```
grammar Arithmetic;

@header {
package example;
}

@members {
int result;
}

expr: term ((PLUS|MINUS) term)* ;
term: factor ((MUL|DIV) factor)* ;
factor: NUMBER | '(' expr ')' ;

PLUS: '+' ;
MINUS: '-' ;
MUL: '*' ;
DIV: '/' ;
NUMBER: [0-9]+ ;
WS: [ \t\r\n]+ -> skip ;
```

- **Grammar Definition**: The expr, term, and factor rules define the syntax of arithmetic expressions.
- **Tokens**: **`PLUS`**, **`MINUS`**, **`MUL`**, **`DIV`**, and **`NUMBER`** are token definitions used in the grammar.
- **Semantic Actions**: The @members section can include semantic actions, such as computing the result or performing type checks, though they are not shown in this basic example.

Running ANTLR to Generate Parsers: How to Generate and Use Parsers

Once you have your ANTLR grammar file, the next step is to generate and use the parser code. This process involves running ANTLR to produce the parser and lexer code, compiling it, and integrating it into your application to handle parsing and semantic analysis.

To utilize ANTLR for parsing, you need to follow a series of steps to generate and integrate the parser into your application. Here is a clear guide to help you understand the process:

1. **Install ANTLR**:
   - Before you can generate parsers, you need to have ANTLR installed on your system. ANTLR can be installed through package managers, or you can download it from the ANTLR website. Ensure that you have the runtime libraries for your target programming language.
2. **Create Your Grammar File**:
   - Write a grammar file with the `.g4` extension that defines the syntax of the language you are parsing. This file specifies how various elements of the language are structured, including rules for expressions, statements, and other constructs.
3. **Generate the Parser**:
   - Use ANTLR to process the grammar file and generate the parser and lexer code. This step translates your grammar definitions into executable code that can analyze and interpret input data based on the rules you have defined. To do this, run ANTLR with your grammar file as input. For example:

     ```
     antlr4 YourGrammarFile.g4
     ```

     This command creates several files, including the lexer and parser classes that will be used in your application.
4. **Compile the Generated Code**:
   - After generating the parser code, compile the files to ensure that they are ready for use. For instance, if you are using Java, you would compile the files with:

     ```
     javac *.java
     ```

     This step converts the generated code into bytecode that can be executed by the Java Virtual Machine (JVM) or other runtime environments.
5. **Integrate the Parser into Your Application**:
   - Write a program or script that uses the generated parser to process input data. This involves creating an input stream, initializing the lexer and parser, and invoking the parser to analyze the input. Here is a basic example in Java:

     ```
     import org.antlr.v4.runtime.*;
     import org.antlr.v4.runtime.tree.*;

     public class ParserExample {
         public static void main(String[] args) throws Exception {
             // Create an input stream from a string
             CharStream input = CharStreams.fromString("sample input");

             // Initialize lexer and parser
             YourGrammarLexer lexer = new YourGrammarLexer(input);
             CommonTokenStream tokens = new CommonTokenStream(lexer);
             YourGrammarParser parser = new YourGrammarParser(tokens);
     ```

```
            // Parse the input
            ParseTree tree = parser.yourStartRule();

            // Print the parse tree
            System.out.println(tree.toStringTree(parser));
        }
    }
```

This code initializes the lexer and parser with the input data and uses them to generate and print a parse tree based on your grammar.

6. **Run and Test the Parser**:
   - Execute your program to test how the parser processes the input. Verify that it correctly parses and analyzes the data according to the rules defined in your grammar. Adjust and refine your grammar and semantic actions as needed based on testing results.

By following these steps, you will be able to generate and use parsers with ANTLR, effectively integrating language processing capabilities into your applications.

Analyzing Output and Error Handling

After generating parsers with ANTLR, it is essential to analyze the output and manage errors effectively. This involves understanding how the parser represents the input through parse trees and abstract syntax trees, and implementing strategies to handle any errors encountered during semantic analysis. By mastering these techniques, you can ensure your parser functions correctly and provides clear feedback, making it easier to debug and refine your language processing tools.

Interpreting the Output from ANTLR-Generated Parsers

Once you have generated parsers using the ANTLR, the next crucial step is to analyze the output produced by these parsers. Understanding how to interpret the parse tree, the Abstract Syntax Tree (AST), and any semantic errors is essential for validating the accuracy of the parser ensuring it processes the input correctly. This section will guide you through the various types of output, and how to interpret them to assess the performance of your parser.

When you use the ANTLR to generate parsers, the output includes both the parsed representation of the input data and various potential error messages. Understanding how to interpret this output is crucial for debugging and validating your parser. Here is how you can effectively analyze the output:

- **Parse Tree:**

  The primary output of the parser is the parse tree, a hierarchical structure that represents the syntactic structure of the input according to the grammar rules. The parse tree shows how the input matches the grammar, and can be used to verify that the input was parsed correctly.

  Example:

  For an arithmetic expression, such as 3 + 5, the parse tree will show nodes for the expression, terms, and operators, reflecting the grammar's structure.

- **Abstract Syntax Tree (AST)**:

  An AST is a simplified version of the parse tree, often used for further processing, such as semantic analysis or code generation. The AST removes some syntactic details, and focuses on the essential components of the language structure.

Example:

For the expression, 3 + 5, the AST would typically have nodes for the addition operation and its operands.

- **Semantic Errors:**

  While the ANTLR handles syntax checking, semantic errors are detected through additional semantic actions you define. These errors occur when the input, although syntactically correct, does not conform to the semantic rules (for example, using an undeclared variable).

  Example:

  If your grammar enforces that variables must be declared before use, a semantic error would occur if an undeclared variable is referenced.

Techniques for Handling Errors During Semantic Analysis

Effective error handling is vital for creating robust parsers that can handle a wide range of input scenarios. During semantic analysis, it is important to implement techniques for detecting and managing errors related to the meaning and logic of the input data. This section explores various strategies for reporting, recovering from, and handling errors, ensuring that your parser can effectively deal with issues, and provide meaningful feedback.

Effective error handling during semantic analysis is crucial for ensuring that the parsed input adheres to the intended meaning and rules of your language. Here are some key techniques to handle errors effectively:

- **Error Reporting:**

  Provides clear, informative error messages that help users understand what went wrong. Includes details, such as the location of the error in the input, and a description of the problem.

  Implementation:

  Customizes error reporting in your semantic actions to include line numbers, column positions, and a concise explanation of the error. This makes it easier for users to identify and correct issues.

- **Error Recovery:**

  Implements strategies to handle and recover from errors without halting the entire parsing process. This can involve skipping over erroneous parts of the input, or using heuristics to infer likely corrections.

  Implementation:

  Defines recovery rules or fallback mechanisms in your semantic analysis to continue processing the input even after encountering errors. For instance, you might allow the parser to skip invalid expressions and proceed with valid ones.

- **Contextual Checks**:

  Perform checks that consider the context in which language constructs appear. This ensures that the semantic rules are applied correctly based on the surrounding code or data.

  Implementation:

  Uses inherited attributes or context-sensitive checks to validate constructs according to their usage within the broader input. For example, check that variables are declared before use, or that the function calls match their definitions.

- **Logging and Diagnostics:**

  Maintains detailed logs and diagnostic information to aid in debugging and refining the parser. Logging can capture error occurrences, input data, and parser state, providing valuable insights into issues.

  Implementation:

  Implements logging mechanisms to record errors and other diagnostic data during semantic analysis. This information can help you identify recurring problems, and improve error-handling strategies.

- **Testing and Validation:**

  Regularly tests your parser with a variety of input cases, including edge cases and invalid inputs, to ensure that errors are handled gracefully, and the parser performs as expected.

  Implementation:

  Develops comprehensive test suites that cover different aspects of your language and its semantics. Use these tests to validate the parser's ability to handle both valid and erroneous input.

- **User Feedback Mechanisms:**

  Provides feedback mechanisms that allow the users to report issues, or suggest improvements. This can help gather information on how well the error handling is working, and what additional features might be needed.

  Implementation:

  Includes feedback options in your tool or application, such as error reporting forms or user forums, to collect input from the users on error handling and other aspects of the parsing process.

Thus, by employing these techniques, you can enhance the robustness of your semantic analysis, improve error handling, and ensure that your parser delivers accurate and meaningful feedback to the users.

Conclusion

This chapter has provided a comprehensive look at attribute grammars, and their significance in semantic analysis. We discussed the essential elements, including attributes, rules, and grammar productions, and explored the roles of synthesized and inherited attributes in defining the semantics of programming languages. Practical examples demonstrated how attributes are used to enforce semantic rules, and ensure the code correctness.

We also covered semantic actions, highlighting their importance in integrating with parsing processes to maintain semantic accuracy. Through detailed examples, we showed how these actions are implemented. Additionally, we explained annotated parse trees, and their role in representing semantic information, supported by visual diagrams for clarity.

This chapter also wrapped up with an introduction to the ANTLR, illustrating how it aids in implementing attribute grammars and generating parsers. Techniques for handling errors during semantic analysis were also discussed to ensure a robust approach.

Looking ahead, we will explore Intermediate Code Generation. This next chapter will introduce the key concepts, such as the three-address code, quadruples, and triples, and explain how these intermediate representations are used to translate high-level constructs into a format suitable for optimization, and final code generation.

Points to Remember

- **Attribute Grammars**: Extend regular grammars by adding attributes to grammar symbols, helping define the meaning of language constructs.
- **Attributes**:
  - o **Synthesized**: Calculated from child nodes.
  - o **Inherited**: Passed down from parent nodes.
- **Semantic Actions**: Used during parsing to enforce rules and ensure the code's semantic correctness.
- **Annotated Parse Trees**: Parse trees that include additional information (attributes) to represent the code's meaning.
- **Building Parse Trees**: Involves attaching attributes to parse tree nodes, and using rules to compute these attributes.
- **ANTLR Tool**: Helps in defining grammars, and generating parsers that can handle attribute grammars.
- **Using ANTLR**: Requires defining grammar files, and generating code to create parsers with semantic capabilities.
- **Error Handling**: Includes methods for detecting and managing semantic errors during analysis.
- **Practical Examples**: Demonstrate how attributes and actions work together to define language semantics and validate the code.
- **Importance**: Understanding attribute grammars is crucial for implementing effective semantic analysis in compilers.

Multiple Choice Questions

1. What is the primary purpose of attribute grammars?
   - a. Syntax analysis
   - b. Lexical analysis
   - c. Semantic analysis
   - d. Code generation
2. Which of the following best describes attribute grammars?
   - a. A type of syntax grammar
   - b. A formal way to define semantics
   - c. A method to parse tokens
   - d. A language for defining tokens
3. What are the key components of an attribute grammar?
   - a. Tokens, rules, and syntax
   - b. Attributes, rules, and grammar productions
   - c. Trees, nodes, and branches
   - d. Classes, objects, and methods

4. Attributes in attribute grammars can be defined as:
   a. Variables associated with grammar symbols
   b. Functions defining grammar rules
   c. Keywords in a programming language
   d. Operators used in expressions
5. What is a synthesized attribute?
   a. An attribute inherited from parent nodes
   b. An attribute computed from the children nodes
   c. An attribute defined by the parser
   d. An attribute that stores the parse tree
6. Inherited attributes are:
   a. Passed up from children nodes
   b. Passed down from parent nodes
   c. Computed by the parser automatically
   d. Used only in bottom-up parsing
7. Which of the following is a practical application of attribute grammars?
   a. Token generation
   b. Defining language semantics
   c. Generating assembly code
   d. Designing user interfaces
8. In an attribute grammar, how is the value of an attribute typically computed?
   a. By predefined functions
   b. By applying rules associated with grammar productions
   c. Through user input
   d. Automatically by the compiler
9. Semantic actions are primarily used to:
   a. Enforce lexical rules
   b. Enforce semantic rules
   c. Enforce syntax rules
   d. Enforce grammar rules
10. How do semantic actions ensure semantic correctness during parsing?
    a. By modifying the syntax tree directly
    b. By checking and enforcing semantic constraints during parsing
    c. By generating tokens dynamically
    d. By adjusting the parse table

11. Which of the following is an example of a common semantic action?
    a. Checking for variable initialization
    b. Defining the syntax of expressions
    c. Generating parse trees
    d. Lexical tokenization
12. In which language are semantic actions often implemented?
    a. Python
    b. C/C++
    c. Within the grammar definition language itself (for example, ANTLR)
    d. Assembly
13. What does an annotated parse tree represent?
    a. The hierarchical structure of tokens
    b. The semantic information associated with a parsed input
    c. The sequence of lexical tokens
    d. The set of all possible parses for a grammar
14. Which of the following is a key feature of an annotated parse tree?
    a. It shows all possible parses of an expression.
    b. It includes both the structure and semantic values of nodes.
    c. It is used only in lexical analysis.
    d. It is generated before the parsing process begins.
15. What is the first step in constructing an annotated parse tree?
    a. Parsing the input according to the grammar
    b. Annotating the grammar with semantic rules
    c. Tokenizing the input string
    d. Compiling the code
16. Annotated parse trees are typically used to:
    a. Generate tokens for the lexer
    b. Evaluate semantic expressions and ensure correctness
    c. Define the structure of the language
    d. Analyze the syntax of the language
17. What is ANTLR primarily used for?
    a. Lexical analysis
    b. Semantic analysis
    c. Syntax analysis and parser generation
    d. Code optimization

18. How can the ANTLR be set up for semantic analysis?
    a. By defining semantic rules within the grammar file
    b. By using a separate semantic analysis tool
    c. By embedding tokens in the grammar
    d. By configuring the parser generator settings
19. Which of the following is a typical output from an ANTLR-generated parser?
    a. A syntax tree
    b. A lexical token
    c. Machine code
    d. An optimized parse table
20. What is a common technique for handling errors during semantic analysis in the ANTLR?
    a. Ignoring the errors
    b. Using custom error listeners
    c. Re-parsing the input
    d. Automatically correcting the input

Answers

1. c
2. b
3. b
4. a
5. b
6. b
7. b
8. b
9. b
10. b
11. a
12. c
13. b
14. b
15. a

16. b
17. c
18. a
19. a
20. b

Questions

1. What is an attribute grammar, and how is it utilized in the context of semantic analysis during the compilation process?
2. What are the key components of an attribute grammar, and how do attributes, rules, and grammar productions work together?
3. How do synthesized attributes differ from inherited attributes in attribute grammars, and in which situations are each used?
4. Can you provide practical examples where synthesized and inherited attributes are used to define language semantics?
5. What are semantic actions, and why are they essential in ensuring that semantic rules are properly enforced during parsing?
6. How do semantic actions interact with a parser to guarantee that the parsed structure adheres to the language's semantic rules?
7. What are some common semantic actions used in compilers, and how are these implemented in a typical compiler system?
8. What is an annotated parse tree, and how does it help to represent semantic information in a structured form?
9. How do you construct an annotated parse tree, and what steps are involved in utilizing it for semantic analysis?
10. How can the ANTLR be configured to define and implement attribute grammars, and what are the steps to generate and interpret parsers using ANTLR?

Key Terms

- **Attribute Evaluation**: The process of computing attribute values based on attribute rules and the parse tree structure.
- **Attribute Propagation**: The method of transferring attribute values between nodes in a parse tree, either upward or downward.
- **Context-sensitive Attributes**: Attributes whose values depend on the context within which a grammar symbol appears.
- **Semantic Constraints**: Rules defined by attributes and semantic actions to ensure that the code adheres to the language's semantic requirements.
- **Attribute Dependency**: The relationship between attributes where the value of one attribute depends on the value of another.

- **Attribute Grammar Rules**: Specifications that define how attributes are computed and propagated within the grammar.
- **Semantic Tree**: A modified parse tree that includes semantic information through attributes, used for further analysis.
- **Type Checking**: A semantic analysis technique to ensure that operations and expressions conform to type rules defined in the language.
- **Scope Management**: Handling the visibility and lifetime of identifiers in the code using attributes and semantic actions.
- **Error Reporting Mechanisms**: Techniques used to identify and communicate the semantic errors detected during analysis.

CHAPTER 7
Intermediate Code Generation

Introduction

In *Chapter 6, Semantic Analysis Attribute Grammars*, we discussed **Attribute Grammars** and their significant role in **Semantic Analysis**, where attributes and semantic actions help define, and enforce the meaning of syntactic structures in programming languages. This phase ensures that the parsed code not only follows syntactic rules, but also makes semantic sense within the language.

In this chapter, we shift our focus to **Intermediate Code Generation**, a salient phase that bridges the high-level source code and the machine code. This stage creates an intermediate representation of the program, abstracting away hardware-specific details. By doing so, it enables code optimization and increases portability across various platforms, without being bound to any specific machine architecture.

We will explore the purpose and advantages of intermediate code, particularly its role in facilitating optimizations, and providing flexibility across platforms. Thus, the chapter will introduce different intermediate code representations, including **Three-Address Code (TAC)**, **Quadruples**, and **Triples**, each offering distinct benefits for capturing the program logic and flow.

Furthermore, we will look at how expressions and control flow structures are translated into these intermediate forms through practical examples. Finally, we will introduce **LLVM Intermediate Representation (LLVM IR)**, a widely used modern framework that adds efficiency and flexibility to the intermediate code generation process.

By the end of this chapter, we will have a comprehensive understanding of how intermediate code aids in converting high-level language constructs into optimized, low-level representations, preparing the way for the final code generation phase.

Structure

In this chapter, we will discuss the following topics:

- **Introduction to Intermediate Code**
  - Overview of Intermediate Code
  - Benefits of Intermediate Code
  - Position in the Compiler Pipeline
- **Three-Address Code (TAC)**
  - Definition and Format
  - Translation Examples
  - Advantages and Use Cases

- **Quadruples**
  - Definition and Format
  - Translation Examples
  - Advantages and Limitations
- **Triples**
  - Definition and Format
  - Translation Examples
  - Advantages and Limitations
- **Translating Expressions and Control Flow**
  - Translating Arithmetic and Logical Expressions
  - Translating Control Flow Constructs
  - Practical Examples
- **LLVM Intermediate Representation (LLVM IR)**
  - Introduction to LLVM IR
  - Structure and Features
  - Translation Examples

Introduction to Intermediate Code

After the semantic analysis phase, where the meaning of the source code is verified and enriched, the compiler proceeds to the **Intermediate Code Generation** stage. In this phase, the source code is translated into an intermediate form that sits between the high-level source language and the low-level machine code. This representation serves as a crucial step in the compilation process, offering an abstract yet detailed view of the program's logic.

The intermediate code is vital because it allows for effective optimizations, and simplifies the process of generating target-specific machine code. By translating high-level programming constructs into an intermediate form, the compiler can analyze and modify the code without being tied to the complexities of specific hardware architectures.

Overview of Intermediate Code

Intermediate Code is an abstract, machine-independent representation of the source code, positioned between the high-level syntax of the programming language and the final machine code that a computer's hardware understands. It is designed to be easy to manipulate for both optimization and translation into the target machine's language.

The main goal of the intermediate code is to provide a balance between the human-readable source code and the machine-executable instructions. It enables the compiler to perform optimizations, such as loop unrolling, constant propagation, and dead code elimination, while abstracting away the hardware-specific details. This flexibility makes intermediate code a central part of modern compiler architectures.

The key features of the intermediate code include:

- Abstraction from specific hardware architecture.
- A simplified representation of operations, expressions, and control flow.
- Uniform structure that is easier to optimize and analyze.

Benefits of Intermediate Code

Intermediate Code offers several advantages in the compilation process, such as:

- **Abstraction from Hardware**: One of the primary benefits of intermediate code is that it abstracts away the details of the underlying hardware architecture. This allows compilers to optimize the code without worrying about specific processor instructions or configurations. The same intermediate code can be used to target different machine architectures, making it a valuable tool for cross-platform portability.
- **Facilitation of Optimization**: Since Intermediate Code is a simplified representation of the source code, it becomes much easier for the compiler to apply various optimizations. By reducing the complex high-level constructs into more manageable forms, the intermediate code allows the compiler to perform a wide range of transformations aimed at improving efficiency and performance, such as reducing memory usage, speeding up execution, and enhancing parallelism.
- **Portability Across Platforms**: Intermediate Code serves as a common format that can be used to generate machine code for different target architectures. This portability is a major benefit for compilers targeting multiple platforms, as the same intermediate code can be translated into machine code for different systems with minimal changes. This makes it easier for software developers to compile programs for various devices, without rewriting the entire codebase.
- **Simplification of Code Generation**: Generating machine code directly from high-level languages can be challenging due to the vast differences between programming constructs and processor instructions. By introducing an intermediate step, compilers can simplify this process. The intermediate code breaks down complex source-level expressions and operations into simpler, well-defined constructs which are easier to map the machine-level instructions.
- **Cross-Language Support**: A well-defined intermediate representation allows compilers to support multiple high-level languages. By translating different source languages into a common intermediate form, compilers can perform language-agnostic optimizations, and generate code for multiple languages using the same back-end infrastructure.

Position in the Compiler Pipeline

Intermediate Code Generation occurs after the **Semantic Analysis** phase and before the **Code Generation** phase in the compiler pipeline. It is the third major step in the compilation process, bridging the gap between the high-level source code and the target machine code.

- **After Syntax and Semantic Analysis**: In the early phases of compilation, the source code is parsed and checked for grammatical correctness (syntax analysis) and meaning (semantic analysis). Once these checks are completed, the next task is to represent the meaning of the program in a form that the compiler can more easily manipulate, optimize, and eventually translate into the machine code. This is where the intermediate code generation comes into play. It takes the validated code from semantic analysis, and transforms it into an abstract, machine-independent representation.
- **Before Final Code Generation**: Intermediate code serves as the input for the final phase, which is code generation. In this stage, intermediate code is translated into the machine-specific code that will be executed on the target hardware. The presence of an intermediate representation simplifies this task because many of the complex high-level constructs have already been reduced to simpler forms during the intermediate phase.
- **Impact on Optimization**: Since Intermediate code lies between the semantic analysis and code generation stages, it serves as an ideal point for optimization. Once the source code is transformed into an intermediate form, the compiler can analyze it for potential improvements

in terms of performance and resource efficiency. After these optimizations, the intermediate code is further translated into an efficient machine code. The decisions made at this stage significantly impact the quality and performance of the final executable program.

Example: Intermediate Code in Action

Consider a high-level code snippet such as:

$a = b + c$;

In intermediate code, this can be represented as:

$t1 = b + c$

$a = t1$

This representation simplifies the process of applying further optimizations, such as identifying redundant computations.

In a more complex case involving loops or conditional statements, the intermediate code breaks down the logic into smaller, easier-to-analyze steps, enabling the compiler to rearrange or optimize them effectively.

The following diagram illustrates the position of the intermediate code in the compiler pipeline:

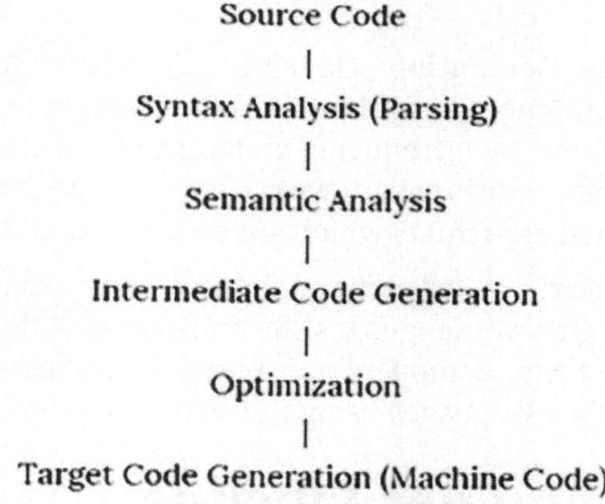

***Figure 7.1**: Compiler Pipeline with Intermediate Code*

This pipeline emphasizes how the intermediate code sits between **Semantic Analysis** and **Code Generation**, providing a layer where optimizations are applied before the final machine code is produced.

Three-Address Code (TAC)

Three-Address Code (TAC) is an important intermediate representation used in compilers to break down the high-level code into a simpler form. It is called "three-address code" because each instruction typically operates on three components: Two operands and a result. This representation simplifies code analysis, optimization, and transformation during the compilation process. Let us discuss the descriptions for each aspect of the TAC.

Definition and Format

The **definition of Three-Address Code (TAC)** is a linear intermediate code where each instruction typically contains up to three components: Two operands and one result. The TAC aims to represent operations and statements in their simplest form, making it easier for the compiler to analyze and optimize the code before generating the machine code.

The general format of a TAC instruction is:

result = operand1 op operand2

- **result**: A variable that stores the result of the operation.
- **operand1** and **operand2**: The input variables or constants that participate in the operation.
- **op**: The operation being performed, such as an arithmetic, logical, or relational operator.

For example, the expression a = b + c * d would be translated into TAC as:

```
t1 = c * d

t2 = b + t1

a = t2
```

This step-by-step breakdown simplifies the evaluation of expressions, and ensures that each operation is isolated for easier optimization.

Translation Examples

The power of Three-Address Code (TAC) lies in its ability to break down a complex high-level code into simpler, manageable steps. Now, let us explore the translation examples for arithmetic operations, variable assignments, and control flow statements, showing how the TAC simplifies code transformation and optimization.

Arithmetic Operations

Arithmetic operations in TAC are translated by breaking down expressions into intermediate steps using temporary variables. This makes the operations easier to process and optimize during compilation.

```
a = b + c * d;
```

This expression involves multiplication and addition. Since multiplication has higher precedence, the TAC first evaluates c * d before performing the addition.

TAC Translation:

In this expression, multiplication has higher precedence than addition, so the TAC first computes multiplication, and then performs addition. The translation into TAC would look as follows:

```
t1 = c * d
t2 = b + t1
a = t2
```

Here, t1 and t2 are temporary variables that hold the intermediate results:

- t1 stores the result of c * d.
- t2 stores the result of b + t1.
- Finally, the result is assigned to a.

This step-by-step breakdown makes the expression easier to manage and optimize during the compilation process.

Variable Assignments

Variable assignments are straightforward in TAC, where a value is directly assigned to a variable without the need for intermediate steps.

```
x = 10;
```

TAC Translation:

$x = 10$

In this case, the value, 10 is simply assigned to the variable, x. No temporary variables are needed, since this is a direct assignment.

Control Flow Statements

Control flow statements, such as if-else conditions and loops are also efficiently translated into TAC. This translation makes the program flow explicit through the use of labels and goto statements.

```
if (x > y)
{
z = x;
} else {
z = y;
}
```

TAC Translation:

```
if x > y  goto L1
z = y
goto L2
L1: z = x
L2:
```

Here, the TAC uses goto statements and labels (L1, L2) to represent the branching logic:

- If the condition, x > y is true, the program jumps to label, L1 and executes z = x.
- If the condition is false, it skips to L2 after assigning z = y.

This clear representation of control flow helps optimize branching conditions and loops.

Advantages and Use Cases

Three-Address Code (TAC) plays a pivotal role in the compilation process, providing an intermediate representation that offers various benefits. Its structured nature enhances clarity and efficiency, making it a fundamental aspect of modern compiler design.

Advantages

The advantages of Three-Address Code (TAC) are pivotal in compilation. These benefits not only simplify the representation of the code but also enhance the efficiency of the overall compilation process. Here are some key advantages:

- **Simplicity and Clarity**:

  TAC simplifies the representation of complex expressions and operations by breaking them down into smaller, manageable instructions. This clarity makes it easier for both compilers and programmers to understand the logic of the code.

- **Ease of Optimization**:

  The structured format of the TAC allows for efficient optimization. Compilers can easily apply optimization techniques, such as constant folding, common subexpression elimination, and loop optimization, at the TAC level without worrying about the complexities of the original high-level language.

- **Flexibility:**

  The TAC can represents a wide range of operations, including arithmetic calculations, logical operations, and control flow constructs. This versatility makes it suitable for different programming languages and paradigms.

- **Machine Independence:**

  As an intermediate representation, the TAC abstracts away the specifics of the target machine architecture. This characteristic enhances portability, allowing the same TAC to be transformed into machine code for different platforms.

- **Support for Code Generation:**

  The TAC provides a clear pathway from high-level code to low-level machine code. It acts as a bridge between these stages, facilitating the generation of efficient machine code by enabling straightforward translations from TAC instructions.

Use Cases

The practical applications of Three-Address Code (TAC) illustrate its significance in real-world scenarios. By understanding how the TAC is utilized in various contexts, we can appreciate its versatility and importance in modern programming languages and compiler design. Here are some common use cases:

- **Compiler Design:**

  The TAC is widely used in the implementation of modern compilers. By generating TAC during the compilation process, developers can leverage its advantages for optimizations and subsequent code generation.

- **Intermediate Representation:**

  The TAC serves as a crucial intermediate representation for various programming languages, allowing for transformations and optimizations before the final code generation phase.

- **Code Analysis Tools:**

  It can be utilized in static analysis and code review tools to check for errors, vulnerabilities, and optimization opportunities within the code.

- **Educational Purposes:**

  The TAC is often used in academic settings to teach compiler construction and optimization techniques. Its simplicity makes it an effective tool for illustrating key concepts in programming language translation.

- **Intermediate Representation for Intermediate Languages:**

  In scenarios involving Just-In-Time (JIT) compilation or interpretation, the TAC can act as an intermediate representation, allowing for runtime optimizations and dynamic code generation.

Quadruples

Quadruples serve as a powerful and structured representation of intermediate code in the compilation process. By breaking down operations into a clear format, they enhance readability and facilitate easier manipulation of the code during optimization and translation into the machine language. In the following sections, we will explore the definition and format of quadruples, along with practical examples illustrating their application in various programming scenarios.

Definition and Format

Quadruples are a specific method of representing intermediate code in compiler design, enhancing the clarity and organization of code representation. Each quadruple consists of four components which neatly separate the operation and its operands, allowing for efficient processing during compilation. The general structure of a quadruple can be described as follows:

(result, operator, operand1, operand2)

- **Result**: This is the variable or temporary storage where the outcome of the operation will be stored. It serves as the destination for the computation.
- **Operator**: This component denotes the operation being performed, such as arithmetic operations (for example, addition, subtraction) or logical operations (for example, AND, OR).
- **Operand1**: The first operand involved in the operation, which can be either a variable or a constant value.
- **Operand2**: The second operand for the operation, also either a variable or a constant.

This structured format facilitates the representation of different programming constructs, such as arithmetic expressions, assignments, and control flow statements. By explicitly defining the roles of each component, quadruples promote a clear understanding of the relationships between operations and their results, thus aiding in the compiler's optimization and code generation phases.

Translation Examples

To better understand how quadruples work in practice, let us delve into translation examples for arithmetic operations, variable assignments, and control flow statements. Each example will illustrate how high-level constructs are converted into quadruple format, emphasizing the clarity and organization that quadruples provide in the compilation process.

Arithmetic Operations

Consider the expression a = b + c. This simple arithmetic operation can be represented in quadruple format as follows:

(t1, +, b, c)

(a, =, t1,)

In this example, t1 is a temporary variable that stores the result of the addition of b and c. The first quadruple computes the sum, while the second quadruple assigns that result to variable a. This clear separation of steps enhances readability and facilitates further optimization.

Variable Assignments

For a straightforward assignment statement, such as x = 5, the corresponding quadruple representation would be:

(x, =, 5,)

This quadruple indicates that the constant value, 5 is directly assigned to the variable, x. The simplicity of this representation demonstrates how quadruples can efficiently handle the basic operations without unnecessary complexity.

Control Flow Statements

Control flow statements, such as conditionals, can also be translated into quadruples. For example, consider the statement: if (x > y) then z = x. The quadruple representation can be structured as follows:

(t1, >, x, y)

(if, t1, , goto L1)

(z, =, x,)

(L1, , ,)

Here, t1 evaluates the condition, x > y. If true, the next quadruple assigns the value of x to z. The final quadruple serves as a label (L1) for potential jumps in the control flow. This structured representation clearly outlines the steps involved in processing the control flow, making it easier for the compiler to optimize and generate an efficient machine code.

Advantages and Limitations

When considering the use of quadruples in compiler design, it is essential to examine both their advantages and limitations. Understanding these aspects provides valuable insights into how quadruples contribute to the efficiency and effectiveness of the compilation process, while also highlighting potential challenges that may arise during their implementation and use. In the following sections, we will explore the various benefits that make quadruples a popular choice for intermediate code representation, as well as the drawbacks that developers should be aware of.

Advantages

Quadruples come with several notable advantages that enhance their effectiveness in the compilation process. These benefits make them a preferred choice for many compilers aiming to achieve clarity, optimize performance, and maintain a structured approach to code representation. In this section, we will delve into the specific advantages that quadruples offer.

- **Clarity and Readability**: The structured format of quadruples makes the code easy to read and understand. Each operation is clearly defined which helps both compiler developers and users grasp the logic of the code more effectively.
- **Facilitates Optimization**: The separation of operations and operands allows for easier implementation of optimization techniques. Compilers can rearrange, eliminate, or combine operations with less complexity, improving the overall efficiency.
- **Explicit Representation**: Quadruples provide an explicit representation of operations, making it clear what each operation is doing. This explicitness aids in debugging, and helps maintain the integrity of complex expressions.
- **Simplifies Code Generation**: By using temporary variables for intermediate results, quadruples streamline the translation of high-level code into machine code. This simplifies the task for the code generator by clearly defining the steps needed for execution.
- **Supports Multiple Backend Implementations**: The intermediate nature of quadruples allows them to be used across different machine architectures. This portability makes it easier to generate code for various target systems without significant changes to the compiler.

Limitations

While quadruples provide numerous benefits, they also present certain limitations that can impact their usability and performance in compilation. Understanding these limitations is crucial for developers and compiler designers, as it allows for better planning and optimization strategies. In this section, we will examine the challenges associated with using quadruples in the compilation process.

- **Increased Memory Usage**: The use of temporary variables can lead to increased memory consumption. Each intermediate result requires storage which may become significant for large programs with numerous operations.
- **Overhead in Execution**: The need to manage and manipulate temporary variables can introduce some overhead during execution. This can affect performance, especially in resource-constrained environments.
- **Complexity in Management**: As the number of quadruples grows, managing and optimizing them can become complex. The compiler must keep track of multiple temporary variables and their lifetimes which may complicate the optimization strategies.
- **Indirect Reference**: While quadruples provide explicit representation, they still require additional steps to resolve temporary variables which may complicate certain optimization techniques compared to other representations that might be more direct.
- **Limitations in Expressiveness**: Quadruples primarily focus on binary operations which may not fully capture the nuances of certain high-level constructs, potentially requiring additional transformations for more complex expressions.

Triples

Triples are another intermediate representation used in the compilation process, offering a more compact and direct approach to handling expressions compared to quadruples. By eliminating the need for temporary variables, triples rely on position-based referencing to simplify the representation of operations. In this section, we will explore the definition, format, and structure of triples, highlighting their unique approach to handling code during compilation.

Definition and Format

Triples represent an alternative method for intermediate code generation in compilers, offering a more compact format compared to quadruples. In this approach, each operation is defined as a three-element tuple consisting of the operator and two operands. The result of an operation is not stored in a separate variable, as seen in quadruples, but is instead referred to by the position or index of the operation within the sequence of triples.

The basic structure of a triple can be represented as:

(operator, operand1, operand2)

- **Operator**: Specifies the operation to be performed (for example, +, -, *, /, and so on.).
- **Operand1** and **Operand2**: The two operands involved in the operation. These can either be variables, constants, or references to the results of previous operations (referred to by their index).

For example, if we want to represent the expression a = b + c in triples, it would be structured as:

(+, b, c) → Triple 1

(=, a, (1)) → Triple 2

In this case, the result of b + c is not assigned to a temporary variable but referenced directly by the index (1) in the subsequent operation. This reduces the number of variables needed, offering a more space-efficient method for representing the intermediate code.

Translation Examples

To understand how triples work in practice, it is helpful to look at specific translation examples. Here, we will go through how arithmetic operations, variable assignments, and control flow statements are represented using triples. These examples demonstrate the compact format and position-based referencing that define this intermediate representation.

Arithmetic Operations

In triples, arithmetic operations are handled by breaking down the expression into individual operations where each step is represented as a triple. Let us consider the example of a = b + c * d:

First, calculate c * d:

(*, c, d) → Triple 1

Then, perform the addition with b:

(+, b, (1)) → Triple 2

Finally, assign the result to a:

(=, a, (2)) → Triple 3

The expression is translated into triples, where the result of each operation is referenced by the index of the triple where it was calculated.

Variable Assignments

Variable assignments are straightforward in triples, as they simply map a value to a variable. Consider the assignment x = 10:

(=, *x*, 10) → *Triple* 1

In this case, the value, 10 is assigned directly to the variable, x in a single triple, as no intermediate computations are needed.

Control Flow Statements

Control flow statements, such as conditionals, are handled by breaking them down into logical steps. Let us look at the example of an if statement: if (x > y), then z = x:

Compare x and y

(>, x, y) → Triple 1

If the condition is true, assign the value of x to z

(=, z, x) → Triple 2

In this translation, the comparison and the assignment are represented as separate triples, with the control flow depending on the result of the comparison in the first triple.

By using triples, control flow, arithmetic, and assignment operations compactly represented, making this intermediate code form both efficient and clear.

Advantages and Limitations

While triples offer a unique way to represent the intermediate code, they come with both advantages and limitations that affect their use in the compilation process. In this section, we will explore the benefits and drawbacks of using triples as an intermediate representation, allowing for a clearer understanding of their role in compiler design.

Advantages

When considering triples as an intermediate code representation, several key benefits make this approach appealing in certain contexts. These advantages highlight why triples are favored for certain compiler designs, particularly when space efficiency and simplified representation are crucial.

- **Space Efficiency**: One of the main benefits of triples is that they save space by avoiding the use of explicit temporary variables. Instead, they rely on position-based indexing which refers to the result of previous operations by their positions in the sequence. This leads to a more compact code representation.
- **Simplified Representation**: Triples break down expressions into smaller, more manageable steps. This simplified approach makes it easier to represent and manipulate complex expressions, as each step is clearly defined, and follows a logical flow.
- **Direct Referencing**: In triples, subsequent operations directly reference the results of previous ones using indexes. This eliminates the need for additional storage, and makes the code more streamlined, particularly when handling a series of related operations.

Limitations

Despite the advantages, triples are not without their drawbacks. These limitations must be understood to recognize the potential challenges when using triples, especially in complex or highly optimized compiler environments.

- **Complexity in Indirect Referencing**: As the size of the code grows, the reliance on position-based indexing can become problematic. Keeping track of which index corresponds to which operation adds a layer of complexity, making the code harder to interpret and debug.
- **Optimization Constraints**: The position-based referencing in triples can limit the flexibility of reordering operations for optimization purposes. Since each operation depends on a specific index, changing the sequence of operations can disrupt the referencing system, complicating the optimization process.
- **Reduced Readability**: The lack of explicit temporary variables can make triples harder to follow, especially in complex or lengthy sequences. This may make the code less intuitive to read and debug, as it lacks the clarity that named variables provide.

Translating Expressions and Control Flow

In the process of compilation, translating high-level expressions and control flow structures into intermediate code is a crucial step. This step ensures that complex operations, such as arithmetic calculations and logical decisions are broken down into manageable components for the compiler to handle. In this section, we will dive into how arithmetic and logical expressions are translated, as well as how control flow constructs, such as conditionals and loops are represented in the intermediate code. This translation not only simplifies these operations, but also prepares them for further optimization and eventual machine code generation.

Translating Arithmetic and Logical Expressions

Translating arithmetic and logical expressions into intermediate code is a key step in the compilation process, where high-level operations are broken down into simpler instructions for easier processing and optimization. These expressions typically include arithmetic operations, such as addition, subtraction, multiplication, and division, as well as logical operations, such as comparisons (>, <, ==) and logical connectors (&&, ||).

During translation, the compiler ensures that the original expression's meaning is preserved, while converting it into a form that can be more efficiently processed. This involves several steps:

- **Breaking Complex Expressions into Simpler Parts**: Complex arithmetic or logical expressions are split into individual components. For example, in the expression a + b * c, the multiplication is processed first, and stored as an intermediate result, followed by addition.
- **Introduction of Temporary Variables**: Intermediate results are stored in temporary variables, especially when dealing with multi-step operations. These temporary variables help maintain the correct order of operations by holding intermediate values for further processing.
- **Preserving Operator Precedence**: The compiler carefully follows the precedence and associativity rules of the operators, ensuring that the operations are performed in the correct sequence. For example, in a + (b * c), the multiplication is performed before the addition, respecting the precedence rules.

Translating these expressions into the intermediate code, such as Three-Address Code (TAC), involves generating instructions for each step. For example, a + b * c would be translated into:

$t1 = b * c$
$t2 = a + t1$

This translation simplifies the high-level code, while ensuring that the sequence of operations and their results are preserved, ready for further stages of compilation.

Translating Control Flow Constructs

Translating control flow constructs is a vital aspect of compiling programs, as it allows the logical flow of execution to be represented in intermediate code. These constructs encompass conditional statements (such as if-else), loops (such as for and while), and branching mechanisms that dictate how a program proceeds through its operations.

In translating control flow constructs, several essential steps ensure that the logical flow of the original code is preserved. Each step breaks down the constructs into a format that the compiler can effectively process, allowing for accurate execution and optimization. Here are the key steps involved in this translation process.

- **Managing Conditionals**: For conditional statements, the compiler generates code that evaluates the specified condition, and directs the flow to the appropriate code block based on the outcome. For instance, consider the if statement:

  ```
  if (x > y) {
     z = x;
  } else {
     z = y;
  }
  ```

  This can be represented in intermediate code as:

  ```
  if x > y goto L1
  z = y goto L2
  L1: z = x
  L2:
  ```

  Here, labels (L1, L2) are created to manage the flow, ensuring that the control moves to the correct code section depending on whether the condition evaluates to true or false.

- **Translating Loops**: Loop constructs, such as 'while' and 'for' require setting up initial conditions and exit points. For example, a while loop might be translated as follows:

```
while (x < 10) {
        // loop body
}
```

The corresponding intermediate code could look as follows:

```
L1: if x >= 10 goto L2
    // code for loop body
    goto L1
L2:
```

In this translation, the loop starts by evaluating the condition at L1. If the condition is satisfied, the loop body executes, followed by a jump back to check the condition again.

- **Branching Operations**: Additionally, branching constructs, such as switch statements, are also translated carefully. Each case in a switch statement translates into conditional jumps, akin to how 'if else' constructs are handled, ensuring that the correct block of code executes based on the evaluated case.

Practical Examples

In this section, we will provide distinct examples for translating arithmetic and logical expressions, as well as control flow constructs into intermediate code. Each example will highlight the translation process, while ensuring clarity and conciseness.

- **Complex Arithmetic Expression**

  This example illustrates the translation of a complex arithmetic expression into intermediate code. The expression consists of two primary operations: Addition and subtraction which are encapsulated within parentheses. This notation signifies that these operations should be performed first, before multiplication.

  *total = (x + y) * (z - w);*

  The expression is divided into smaller components based on operator precedence. The addition (x + y) and subtraction (z - w) are evaluated first, as indicated by the parentheses. This is crucial because it defines the order of operations, ensuring that the correct values are calculated before multiplication.

  t1 = x + y // Compute the sum of x and y

  t2 = z - w // Compute the difference of z and w

  *total = t1 * t2 // Multiply the results and assign to total*

  The translation involves creating temporary variables to store the results of the sub-expressions. In this case, t1 stores the result of x + y, and t2 stores the result of

  z - w. Finally, the product of t1 and t2 is assigned to the total.

  This structured approach to translation not only clarifies the computation steps, but also allows for optimization opportunities later in the compilation process. The use of temporary variables makes the code easier to read and understand, as each computation is explicitly laid out. This enhances the compiler's ability to optimize and reorganize the code for efficiency during later stages of code generation.

- **For Loop**

  This example demonstrates the translation of a 'for' loop into intermediate code. The 'for' loop iterates over a range of values, specifically from 0 to n-1, and in each iteration, it adds the current value of **i** to the variable **sum**.

```
for (int i = 0; i < n; i++)
{
        sum += i;
}
```

  When translating a 'for' loop into intermediate code, we can identify four key components that illustrate its operation. The loop begins with the **initialization** of the control variable **i** which is set to 0, establishing the starting point. It then checks the **condition** that allows the loop to continue executing as long as **i** is less than n; if **i** reaches or exceeds **n**, the loop terminates. At the end of each iteration, **i** is **incremented** by 1, ensuring that the loop progresses toward its end. Within the **body of the loop**, the current value of **i** is added to a variable called sum, accumulating the total. By breaking the loop down into these components, we gain a clear understanding of its functionality, making it easier to translate into intermediate code for compilation.

```
i = 0 // Initialize i to 0
L1: if i >= n goto L2 // Check if i is not less than n; if true, exit loop
sum = sum + i // Add i to sum
i = i + 1 // Increment i by 1
goto L1 // Repeat the loop
              L2:
```

  The translation into Three-Address Code involves breaking down the components of the loop into a sequence of operations. Each part of the loop is represented as a series of TAC statements.

  - The label L1 marks the beginning of the loop body.
  - The if statement checks the loop condition and decides whether to continue or exit the loop by jumping to the label L2 if the condition is false.
  - The addition of i to sum and the increment of i are represented as straightforward operations.

  This structured format allows the compiler to optimize the loop, and manage resources effectively during code generation. By clearly defining the loop's flow and operations, it simplifies the understanding of the loop's behavior and facilitates potential optimizations in subsequent stages.

- **Switch Statement**

  In this example, the switch statement is translated into intermediate code that efficiently handles multiple potential execution paths based on the value of the variable day.

  When translating a switch statement, the process begins by evaluating the switch variable and storing its value. For each case, a label is created, and conditional checks are performed to determine which case matches the value of the switch variable. If a match is found, the program jumps to the corresponding label. If no cases match, the default label is used to handle the default action. Once a case is executed, the program jumps to the end of the switch block to prevent further checks. This structure helps in efficiently managing control flow.

```
switch (day) {
case 1: printf("Monday");
            break;
case 2: printf("Tuesday");
```

```
                break;
default: printf("Invalid day");
}
```

The translation begins by evaluating day and storing its value in a temporary variable **switch_value**.

```
switch_value = day // Evaluate the switch variable
if switch_value == 1 goto L1
if switch_value == 2 goto L2
goto L3 // Jump to default case
L1: printf("Monday")
goto L4 // Jump to end
L2: printf("Tuesday")
goto L4 // Jump to end
L3: printf("Invalid day") // Default case
L4:
```

Then, conditional checks are performed for each case using if statements, directing the flow of execution to the corresponding labels (L1, L2, or L3).

- If day equals 1, the program will output "**Monday**" and then jump to label L4 to exit the switch statement.
- If day equals 2, it will print "**Tuesday**" and again jump to L4.
- If the value does not match any of the cases, the program will execute the default action at label L3, printing "**Invalid day**."

LLVM Intermediate Representation (LLVM IR)

LLVM Intermediate Representation (LLVM IR) serves as a crucial component in the compilation process, acting as an intermediary between high-level programming languages and the machine code. This section explores the fundamental aspects of LLVM IR, including its significance in modern compiler architectures, the structure and features that make it unique, and the various ways, it facilitates optimization and code generation. Understanding LLVM IR is essential for comprehending how compilers enhance performance and portability across different hardware platforms.

Introduction to LLVM IR

LLVM Intermediate Representation (LLVM IR) is a pivotal part of LLVM compiler framework, functioning as a low-level, platform-independent intermediate code that bridges high-level source code and machine-specific binary code. This representation allows for a unified approach to program compilation, enabling various programming languages to be compiled into a common format.

One of the key features of LLVM IR is its Static Single Assignment (SSA) form, which ensures that each variable is assigned exactly once, simplifying the optimization processes that compilers perform. LLVM IR consists of a rich set of instructions, encompassing arithmetic operations, control flow constructs, and data manipulation, making it highly expressive and flexible for various optimization techniques.

Furthermore, LLVM IR enables extensive optimizations at both the function and loop levels, significantly enhancing performance and efficiency. Its design facilitates multiple compilation phases, including front-end parsing, optimization, and back-end code generation, making it a powerful tool in the development of modern compilers. Overall, LLVM IR plays a critical role in improving the performance and portability of applications across diverse hardware architectures.

Structure and Features

LLVM Intermediate Representation (LLVM IR) is a versatile and robust intermediate language that serves as a critical component in LLVM compiler framework. Its design includes several key structural elements and features that enhance its utility for optimization and code generation:

- **Static Single Assignment (SSA) Form**: In LLVM IR, every variable is assigned exactly once, simplifying variable tracking and enabling easier analysis and optimization of the code. This characteristic helps eliminate certain types of data flow problems.
- **Strong Typing**: LLVM IR enforces strict typing, ensuring that each instruction and variable has a well-defined data type. This strong typing aids in error detection and maintains type safety throughout the compilation process.
- **Low-Level Operations**: The instruction set of LLVM IR encompasses a wide range of operations, including arithmetic, logical, and bitwise functions, along with control flow operations. This breadth allows for precise manipulation of program behavior.
- **Control Flow Constructs**: LLVM IR effectively represents various control flow mechanisms, such as conditional branches, loops, and function calls. This representation is crucial for compiling complex high-level constructs into a format that can be optimized and executed.
- **Modularity**: LLVM IR is organized into modules which contain functions and global variables. This modular architecture allows for separate compilation and linking of different components, facilitating better organization and manageability of code.
- **Platform Agnosticism**: As an intermediate representation, LLVM IR abstracts the underlying hardware details, enabling code to be compiled and optimized independently of the target machine architecture. This feature promotes portability across different platforms.
- **Optimization-Friendly**: LLVM IR is specifically designed to support a variety of optimization techniques. Its structure allows multiple optimization passes to be performed, without altering the program's intended behavior, resulting in improved performance.

Translation Examples

The following are some practical examples to provide a clearer understanding of how high-level programming constructs are translated into LLVM IR.:

Arithmetic Operations

Arithmetic Operations are basic calculations performed on numerical values, such as addition, subtraction, multiplication, and division. Understanding how these operations are represented in both high-level code and LLVM IR is crucial for understanding the compiler behavior. Here, we will look at an example of arithmetic operations in high-level code, and how it translates to LLVM IR.

High-Level Code:

This section showcases a basic arithmetic operation in a high-level programming language, such as C or C++. For instance, if we want to add two integers, we might write:

```
int a = 5;

int b = 10;

int c = a + b;
```

In this example, two integer variables, `a` and `b`, are initialized with values, and their sum is stored in a third variable, `c`.

LLVM IR Translation:

The equivalent LLVM IR code demonstrates how the high-level arithmetic operation is represented at a lower level. The translation is as follows:

```
%a = alloca i32            ; Allocate space for variable a

%0 = load i32, i32* %a     ; Load the value of a

%1 = load i32, i32* %b     ; Load the value of b

%c = add i32 %0, %1        ; Perform the addition operation
```

In this translation, the alloca instruction reserves space for the variable, while load retrieves the stored values. Finally, the add instruction computes the sum of a and b, storing the result in c.

Variable Assignments

Variable assignments are a fundamental aspect of programming that involves storing a value in a variable for later use. This process allows developers to manage and manipulate data throughout their code. Understanding how variable assignments are expressed in high-level code and their corresponding representation in LLVM IR is important for grasping how compilers handle data storage. Here, we will examine an example of variable assignments in high-level code and its translation to LLVM IR.

High-Level Code:

This section illustrates a simple variable assignment operation where a value is assigned to a variable. For example:

```
x = 10;
```

Here, the integer variable x is assigned the value of 10.

LLVM IR Translation:

The corresponding LLVM IR code for this assignment operation would look like:

```
%x = alloca i32            ; Allocate space for variable x

store i32 10, i32* %x      ; Store the value 10 into x
```

In this translation, `alloca` reserves memory for `x`, and the `store` instruction assigns the value `10` to that memory location.

Control Flow Statements

Control flow statements dictate the order in which instructions are executed in a program. They enable decision-making and looping mechanisms, allowing for more dynamic and responsive code. Understanding how control flow statements are represented in high-level code and translated into LLVM IR is essential for comprehending how compilers manage program execution. Here, we will explore an example of control flow statements in high-level code and their corresponding LLVM IR translation.

High-Level Code:

This section presents a control flow statement, specifically an `if` condition, to demonstrate how branching is handled. For example:

```
if (x > y) {
    z = x;
}
```

In this case, if x is greater than y, the value of x is assigned to z.

LLVM IR Translation:

The LLVM IR representation for this control flow statement can be shown as follows:

```
%cond = icmp sgt i32 %x, %y  ; Compare x and y
br i1 %cond, label %then, label %else  ; Conditional branch

then:
store i32 %x, i32* %z        ; If true, store x in z
br label %end                ; Jump to the end

else:
br label %end                ; If false, jump to the end

end:
```

In this translation, the `icmp` instruction is used to compare x and y. The `br` instruction implements the conditional branching based on the comparison result. If the condition is true, control flows to the `then` block, storing x in z, and then it branches to the end. If false, it directly jumps to end.

Conclusion

In this chapter, we explored **Intermediate Code Generation**, focusing on how compilers convert high-level programming constructs into intermediate representations, such as **Three-Address Code**, **Quadruples**, and **Triples**. These intermediate forms enable easier optimization and ensure better portability and efficiency. The chapter also covered the translation of expressions, demonstrating how they are converted into intermediate code. Practical examples using **LLVM IR** provided insights into how these concepts are implemented in real-world compilers.

Building on the foundation laid in this chapter, *Chapter* 8, ***Control Flow***, shifts focus to how compilers manage the logical flow of a program. It covers how loops, conditionals, and function calls are represented in the intermediate code to ensure efficient execution. With practical examples using the **LLVM IR**, this chapter deepens our understanding of how compilers handle control flow and optimize program logic during compilation.

Points to Remember

- **Intermediate Code** acts as a bridge between high-level source code and machine code, providing an abstraction that simplifies code generation for different platforms.
- **Three-Address Code (TAC)** is a widely used intermediate representation, breaking down complex expressions into simpler instructions that are easier to optimize.
- **Quadruples** explicitly represent instructions in four parts: operator, operand1, operand2, and result, making it easier to visualize operations.
- **Triples** reduce memory usage by storing intermediate results in place, improving efficiency in some cases.
- Intermediate code is **essential for optimization**, enabling techniques, such as constant folding, dead code elimination, and loop unrolling.
- **Control flow constructs** such as loops and conditional statements can be represented efficiently in intermediate code for optimization and easy translation to machine code.
- **LLVM IR** (Low-Level Virtual Machine Intermediate Representation) is a standard intermediate format used in modern compilers for cross-platform code generation and advanced optimizations.

- Intermediate code allows for **platform independence**, enabling the same code to be compiled for different hardware architectures with minimal changes.
- The **position of intermediate code in the compiler pipeline** is between syntax analysis and code generation, crucial for bridging high-level structure with low-level execution.
- The use of **intermediate code** makes the compiler more modular, allowing separation of concerns between code analysis, optimization, and generation stages.

Multiple Choice Questions

1. What is the primary purpose of intermediate code in compilation?
   a. To improve syntax analysis
   b. To optimize memory usage
   c. To act as an abstraction layer between high-level code and machine code
   d. To handle error detection
2. Which of the following is a benefit of intermediate code?
   a. Direct interaction with hardware
   b. Platform dependency
   c. Facilitation of code optimization
   d. Faster code generation
3. In the compiler pipeline, where does intermediate code generation occur?
   a. Before lexical analysis
   b. After syntax analysis and before code generation
   c. After code generation
   d. Before semantic analysis
4. Which of the following is NOT a feature of Three-Address Code (TAC)?
   a. Result = operand1 op operand2
   b. Facilitates easier code optimization
   c. Direct machine code execution
   d. Supports control flow statements
5. Which of the following is an example of TAC for the operation a = b + c?
   a. result = a + b
   b. t1 = b + c; a = t1
   c. (b, +, c, a)
   d. (t1, b, c, +)
6. What is the basic structure of a quadruple representation?
   a. (operator, operand1, operand2)
   b. result = operand1 op operand2

c. (operator, operand1, operand2, result)

d. (result, operator, operand1)

7. Which of the following is an advantage of using quadruples?

a. Simplified syntax analysis

b. Reduced memory usage

c. Explicit operation representation

d. Direct machine code generation

8. What is the limitation of the quadruple representation?

a. Lack of flexibility for optimization

b. Overhead due to additional result slots

c. Inability to represent arithmetic operations

d. Indirect result referencing

9. What is the main difference between triples and quadruples?

a. Triples have explicit result fields

b. Triples do not have explicit result fields

c. Quadruples are easier to optimize

d. Triples do not support control flow statements

10. Which of the following is a limitation of using triples?

a. Overhead due to multiple operand slots

b. Indirect result referencing

c. Excessive memory usage

d. Incompatibility with control flow constructs

11. What is an example of triple representation for a = b + c?

a. (+, b, c)

b. (b, +, c, a)

c. t1 = b + c; a = t1

d. (a, b, +, c)

12. Which of the following control flow statements can be translated into intermediate code?

a. if-else statements

b. Arrays

c. Functions

d. Libraries

13. How does TAC handle control flow statements such as if (x > y) then z = x?

a. Through hardware-level instructions

b. By generating conditional jump instructions

   c. By directly outputting machine code
   d. By using macros
14. Which of the following is an example of TAC for if (x > y) then z = x?
   a. t1 = x > y; if t1 goto L1; L1: z = x
   b. t1 = x; t2 = y; if t1 goto t2
   c. if x > y goto z
   d. (x, y, >, z)
15. Which of the following is true about LLVM IR?
   a. It is specific to hardware architecture.
   b. It supports a platform-independent intermediate code representation.
   c. It is primarily used for syntax analysis.
   d. It does not support optimization.
16. What form does LLVM IR use to represent variables?
   a. SSA (Static Single Assignment)
   b. Register allocation
   c. Binary tree form
   d. Array form
17. In which stage of the compiler pipeline does LLVM IR play a crucial role?
   a. Lexical analysis
   b. Semantic analysis
   c. Code optimization
   d. Token generation
18. What is an example of LLVM IR for adding two integers a and b?
   a. add i32 %a, %b
   b. %t1 = add i32 %a, %b
   c. %a = b + c
   d. t1 = a + b
19. What is the role of LLVM IR in modern compiler design?
   a. Acts as an interface between hardware and software
   b. Provides a platform-dependent machine code
   c. Serves as an intermediate representation that enables optimizations
   d. and portability
   e. Handles parsing of high-level languages

20. What is a key feature of SSA form in LLVM IR?
    a. Variables can be assigned multiple times
    b. Each variable is assigned exactly once
    c. It is only used for syntax analysis
    d. It has no effect on optimization

Answers

1. c
2. c
3. b
4. c
5. b
6. c
7. c
8. b
9. b
10. b
11. a
12. a
13. b
14. a
15. b
16. a
17. c
18. b
19. c
20. b

Questions

1. What is the definition and purpose of intermediate code in the context of compilation, and why is it important in the overall compilation process?
2. How does intermediate code act as an abstraction from hardware, and how does it contribute to the portability of compiled programs across different platforms?
3. What are the advantages of placing intermediate code generation between syntax analysis and code generation in the compiler pipeline, and how does it impact subsequent stages, such as optimization?

4. What is the basic structure of the Three-Address Code (TAC), and how does its components (result, operand1, operand2, operator) represent expressions and operations?
5. How are arithmetic operations, variable assignments, and control flow statements, such as if (x > y) translated into Three-Address Code (TAC)? Provide examples.
6. What are the key advantages and limitations of using quadruples as an intermediate representation in compilers, and how does it differ from the TAC?
7. How do triples differ from quadruples in terms of their structure and result representation, and what are the benefits and limitations of using triples in intermediate code generation?
8. Describe the process of translating arithmetic expressions, logical expressions, and control flow constructs (such as, loops and conditionals) into intermediate code formats, such as TAC, quadruples, and triples.
9. What is LLVM Intermediate Representation (LLVM IR), and how does it differ from traditional intermediate code formats, such as TAC or quadruples in terms of structure and functionality?
10. Explain the key features of LLVM IR, including the SSA form (Static Single Assignment), instructions, and functions. How do these elements facilitate optimization and portability in modern compiler design?

Key Terms

- **Intermediate Code**: A representation of the source code that simplifies the transition from high-level code to machine code, facilitating optimization and portability.
- **Three-Address Code (TAC)**: A form of intermediate code where each instruction has at most three operands, making it easier to represent complex expressions.
- **Quadruples**: A type of intermediate code that explicitly separates the operator, operands, and result into four fields, making it easy to follow the flow of operations.
- **Triples**: An intermediate code format that uses references to earlier instructions, reducing memory use by avoiding explicit storage of intermediate results.
- **Control Flow Statements**: Programming constructs, such as loops and conditionals that direct the execution flow of a program.
- **Arithmetic Operations**: Basic mathematical operations, such as addition, subtraction, multiplication, and division that are represented in the intermediate code.
- **Variable Assignment**: The process of storing a value in a variable, often represented in the intermediate code by simple assignment statements.
- **Optimization**: The process of improving code efficiency during compilation, often carried out on intermediate code to enhance performance.
- **LLVM IR (Intermediate Representation)**: A modern intermediate language used in the LLVM compiler infrastructure, known for its flexibility and support for advanced optimizations.
- **Semantic Analysis**: The phase in the compiler where the meaning of the code is checked and verified, typically before intermediate code generation.

Chapter 8
Control Flow

Introduction

In *Chapter 7, Intermediate Code Generation*, we explored the fundamentals of intermediate code, including formats, such as Three-Address Code (TAC), quadruples, and triples. These representations serve as essential building blocks in the compiler pipeline, bridging the gap between high-level source code and low-level machine code. By translating operations, such as arithmetic expressions, variable assignments, and control flow statements into an intermediate form, we achieve greater flexibility for optimization and portability across different machine architectures. Understanding how intermediate code handles logical operations is critical for producing efficient programs.

Building on this foundation, this chapter delves into the critical aspect of control flow. While intermediate code allows us to represent individual operations and assignments, control flow dictates the order in which these operations are executed. Whether it's managing conditional branching through if-else statements, loops, or function calls, control flow constructs are fundamental in determining the execution sequence of a program.

In this chapter, we will examine how control flow is represented in intermediate code. We will explore how loops, conditional statements, and function calls are translated into intermediate representations, and how these constructs influence the flow of execution. Additionally, we will investigate Control Flow Graphs (CFGs), a vital tool for visualizing the paths a program can take, and dive deeper into LLVM Intermediate Representation (LLVM IR), understanding its role in optimizing control flow. By mastering these control flow techniques, we will be better equipped to handle complex program behavior, while enhancing performance and efficiency during compilation.

Structure

In this chapter, we will discuss the following topics:

- Introduction to Control Flow
  - o Overview of Control Flow in Programming
  - o Significance of Execution Sequence Management
  - o Role of Intermediate Code in Control Flow Representation
- Control Flow Structures
  - o Sequential Flow
  - o Conditional Control
  - o Iterative Control
- Control Flow Graphs
  - o Definition and Purpose of Control Flow Graphs
  - o Basic Blocks and Their Role
  - o Construction of Control Flow Graphs
  - o Analyzing Control Flow Graphs

- Intermediate Code Representation
  - Intermediate Code for Conditional Statements
  - Intermediate Code for Loops
  - Intermediate Code for Function Calls
- LLVM Intermediate Representation
  - Overview of LLVM IR
  - LLVM IR for Loops
  - LLVM IR for Conditional Constructs
  - LLVM IR for Function Calls
  - Control Flow Optimizations
- Best Practices for Control Flow Representation
  - Efficient Structure of Control Flow for Optimized Performance
  - Minimizing Unnecessary Branches and Jumps

Introduction to Control Flow

Control flow refers to the sequence in which a program's instructions are executed. It allows a program to make decisions, repeat certain tasks, or jump to different parts of the code based on specific conditions. Control flow structures, such as loops, if-else statements, and function calls are essential for creating dynamic and flexible programs.

In compilers, representing the control flow in intermediate code is crucial to ensure the correct order of execution, and optimize program performance. By understanding how control flow works, and how it is represented, we can build more efficient and reliable programs.

Overview of Control Flow in Programming

Control flow is a foundational concept in programming that dictates the order in which statements are executed. It enables programs to make decisions, repeat actions, and branch into different paths based on specific conditions or inputs. By managing the flow of execution, programmers can create dynamic and responsive applications that adapt to various scenarios.

Key components of the control flow include:

- **Conditional Statements:**

  These structures, such as if, else if, and else, allow programs to make decisions. When a condition is evaluated, the program executes the corresponding block of code. For instance, an online shopping application may apply a discount only if the user's total exceeds a certain amount, demonstrating how conditions influence execution.

- **Loops**:

  Loops, including for, while, and do-while, are essential for executing a block of code repeatedly as long as a specified condition is true. For example, a for loop can be used to process each item in a list, allowing for efficient handling of large datasets without repetitive code.

- **Function Calls:**

  Functions encapsulate code that performs a specific task. Control flow can be altered by calling functions, allowing the program to execute different code paths, and return results. This modular approach promotes code reuse and clarity, making programs easier to manage and understand.

- **Switch Statements:**

  These provide a streamlined way to handle multiple conditions based on the value of a variable. Instead of using several if statements, a switch can cleanly redirect execution to the appropriate case, enhancing readability and organization.

Understanding control flow is essential for effective programming. It empowers developers to write the code that is not only functional but also efficient and scalable. By mastering control flow constructs, programmers can create applications that respond intelligently to user input, optimize resource usage, and deliver a seamless user experience.

Significance of Execution Sequence Management

Execution sequence management is a critical aspect of programming that determines the order in which statements and operations are executed within a program. Proper management of this execution order is vital for ensuring both the correctness and efficiency of the code. Here are several key reasons highlighting the significance of execution sequence management:

- **Correctness of the Program Logic:**

  The order of execution profoundly impacts the behavior and output of a program. Incorrect sequencing can lead to unexpected results or runtime errors. For example, if a program attempts to use a variable before it has been initialized, it will throw an error. Maintaining the correct sequence ensures logical consistency and reliability in applications, preventing common pitfalls and bugs.

- **Control Over the Program Flow:**

  Execution sequence management allows developers to direct how the program operates using constructs like conditionals and loops. This control enables the creation of interactive applications that respond dynamically to user inputs and varying conditions. For instance, in a video game, managing the execution order is crucial for ensuring that character movements and game events react appropriately to player actions.

- **Performance Optimization:**

  Efficiently managing the execution order can lead to significant performance improvements. By organizing the code to eliminate unnecessary calculations, and reduce redundant operations, developers can enhance the speed and responsiveness of their applications. For example, strategically placing loops and conditionals can help prevent excessive processing, making applications more efficient.

- **Modularity and Maintainability:**

  A clear execution sequence promotes modular design, where distinct sections of the code perform specific tasks. This modularity simplifies debugging and maintenance, as developers can easily follow the execution path,s and identify where the issues arise. When changes are necessary, a well-structured execution sequence allows for straightforward updates, without risking unintended side effects in unrelated parts of the program.

- **Resource Management:**

  In applications that interact with hardware or network resources, managing the execution sequence is crucial for optimal resource utilization. For instance, ensuring that resources are allocated and released in the correct order prevents resource leaks, and ensures that the application runs efficiently.

Effective execution sequence management is essential for creating robust, efficient, and maintainable software. By carefully controlling how and when operations are performed, developers can ensure that their programs are logically sound, perform optimally, and respond seamlessly to a variety of conditions and user inputs. A deep understanding of the execution flow is therefore indispensable for any programmer aiming to develop high-quality applications.

Role of Intermediate Code in Control Flow Representation

Intermediate Code plays a vital role in the compilation process, serving as a bridge between high-level programming languages and machine code. It provides an abstraction that simplifies the representation and manipulation of control flow constructs, making it easier for compilers to optimize and generate efficient executable code. Here are several key aspects of how intermediate code facilitates control flow representation:

- **Abstraction of High-Level Constructs:**

  High-level programming languages contain various control flow constructs, such as loops, conditionals, and function calls. Intermediate code abstracts these constructs into a simpler form that is easier for the compiler to analyze and optimize. This abstraction allows compilers to focus on the underlying logic, without being bogged down by the complexities of the original language syntax.

- **Standardized Representation:**

  Intermediate Code provides a standardized way to represent the control flow. This consistency enables the compilers to implement optimization techniques across different programming languages. For instance, constructs, such as if-else statements and loops can be translated into a uniform intermediate representation, making it easier to apply optimizations, such as loop unrolling or dead code elimination.

- **Facilitating Optimizations:**

  By using Intermediate Code, compilers can implement a variety of optimization strategies to improve the performance of the generated machine code. Optimizations may include rearranging the control flow to minimize jumps and branches which can significantly enhance the execution speed. Intermediate Code also allows for analyses, such as data flow analysis and control flow analysis that help identify potential inefficiencies in the program's logic.

- **Ease of Code Generation:**

  Intermediate Code simplifies the process of generating the machine code. It can be translated directly into various machine architectures, allowing for portability across different systems. The control flow represented in intermediate code can be easily mapped to the corresponding machine instructions, ensuring that the program executes as intended on the target hardware.

- **Debugging and Error Detection:**

  Intermediate Code can facilitate debugging by providing a more manageable representation of the program's control flow. During the compilation process, the compiler can identify and report errors or inconsistencies in the control flow before generating the machine code. This allows developers to catch issues early, leading to more robust and error-free programs.

- **Support for High-Level Language Features:**

  Many high-level programming languages include advanced features, such as exception handling and coroutines. Basically, Intermediate Code provides a mechanism to represent these features in a way that can be effectively managed and optimized. This representation ensures that the high-level language features are preserved in the final executable, while still allowing for optimizations.

Intermediate Code is necessary for effectively representing the control flow in the compilation process. By abstracting high-level constructs, providing a standardized representation, and facilitating optimizations, the intermediate code enables compilers to generate efficient and portable machine code. Its role in debugging and supporting high-level features further underscores its importance in modern programming languages and compiler design.

Control Flow Structures

Control Flow Structures are fundamental elements of programming that determine the order in which instructions are executed within a program. They empower developers to create dynamic and responsive applications by controlling the flow of execution based on specific conditions and logical expressions. By leveraging the control flow structures, programmers can implement the decision-making processes, repeat actions, and dictate the path that a program takes in response to user inputs and runtime conditions.

The primary categories of control flow structures include conditional statements, loops, and branching mechanisms. **Conditional statements**, such as if, else, and switch, enable programs to execute different blocks of code depending on whether certain criteria are met. This allows for responsive behavior that adapts to varying inputs. **Loops**, including for, while, and do-while, facilitate the repeated execution of code blocks until a specified condition is no longer satisfied, making it possible to efficiently process collections of data or perform repetitive tasks. Additionally, **branching mechanisms** provide the ability to alter the execution flow, directing the program to take different paths based on logical evaluations.

A solid understanding of control flow structures is essential for any programmer, as they form the backbone of logical reasoning in the code. Mastering these constructs enables developers to build applications that handle diverse scenarios and user interactions effectively, ensuring that the software behaves predictably and efficiently under various conditions. Ultimately, the ability to implement the control flow structures not only enhances the program functionality but also improves the overall code readability and maintainability.

Sequential Flow

Sequential Flow represents the most fundamental form of control flow in programming where instructions are executed in a linear, step-by-step order. In this structure, each statement runs consecutively, without any branching or looping, ensuring a predictable and straightforward execution path.

Understanding the key characteristics of sequential flow helps to highlight its importance and limitations in programming:

- **Predictability**: Since the execution order is fixed, the outcomes remain consistent which simplifies debugging, and allows the developers to trace the flow of execution easily.
- **Simplicity**: Sequential Flow is intuitive, and easy to understand, making it an excellent starting point for beginners learning programming concepts. For example, consider a simple recipe: You follow each step in the order it is written, from gathering ingredients to cooking, and serving the dish.
- **Limited Control**: While this flow is easy to follow, it lacks the flexibility offered by conditional statements and loops. It is not ideal for scenarios that require decision-making or repeated actions.
- **Foundation for Complex Structures**: Sequential Flow serves as the backbone for more complex control structures. Mastery of sequential execution is crucial for understanding how to incorporate branching and looping constructs effectively.

Exploring real-world applications of sequential flow illustrates its practical significance in programming:

Sequential Flow is commonly found in straightforward programs, such as scripts for data processing or simple calculators where each operation is performed in a specific order. It is also prevalent in initialization routines where certain setup tasks must be completed before any user interactions can occur.

Thus, Sequential Flow is the backbone of programming where each instruction executes in a defined sequence. Understanding this concept is essential for creating logical and coherent code, making it a vital component of any programmer's toolkit.

Linear Execution of Instructions

Linear Execution of Instructions refers to the process where computer programs execute a series of commands in a straight, sequential order. In this model, each instruction is executed exactly once, one after the other, from the beginning of the program to the end, without any deviation in flow. This structure is foundational in programming, as it establishes a predictable sequence of operations that is crucial for logical reasoning and program correctness.

To better understand Linear Execution, let us explore its key characteristics:

- **Sequential Order:**

  Each instruction is executed in the exact order, it appears in the code. For instance, if a program contains five instructions, the first instruction is executed first, followed by the second, and so on, until the last instruction is reached.

- **Simplicity:**

  Linear Execution is the simplest form of control flow. It is easy to understand and implement, making it particularly useful for novice programmers. For example, a basic program that adds two numbers would follow a linear sequence of input, processing, and output, as follows:

  1. Input the first number.
  2. Input the second number.
  3. Add the two numbers.
  4. Output the result.

- **Predictable Outcomes:**

  Since the execution follows a fixed path, the results of the program can be easily anticipated. This predictability is necessary in debugging and testing, as it allows programmers to trace the flow of execution without confusion.

Understanding the importance of linear execution provides insight into its role in programming:

Hence, Linear Execution serves as the foundation for more complex control flow structures. While more advanced programming paradigms, such as branching and looping, introduce variability and complexity, understanding linear execution is critical for grasping how these constructs function. It is essential for building the logic of algorithms, and ensuring that programs behave correctly, when executing a predetermined sequence of operations.

Moreover, Linear Execution is particularly valuable in scenarios where predictability is paramount, such as safety-critical systems where errors could have serious consequences.

Common Pitfalls:

While Linear Execution is straightforward, there are some common pitfalls to be aware of:

- **Overlooking Input Validation**:

Failing to validate user inputs in a linear flow can lead to unexpected results or program crashes.

- **Ignoring Edge Cases**:

  Assuming that every execution path will be linear can cause issues if there are cases where the input or conditions change unexpectedly.

Conditional Control

Conditional Control is a fundamental concept in programming that allows programs to make decisions, and execute different actions based on specific conditions. It helps guide the program's flow, enabling it to adapt to varying inputs and scenarios. By using conditional control, programs can behave dynamically, ensuring that the right actions are taken in different situations.

The purpose of Conditional Control is to introduce decision-making capabilities in a program. Instead of executing commands in a fixed order, Conditional Control allows programs to evaluate conditions, and choose the appropriate course of action. This makes it possible for the software to respond intelligently to user inputs, changing circumstances, or different datasets.

For example, in a banking application, conditional control can determine whether a user can withdraw money, based on their account balance. If the balance is sufficient, the transaction proceeds; otherwise, an error message is displayed. This decision-making flexibility is essential for creating responsive and interactive applications.

The Conditional Control is implemented through specific structures in programming. The most common Conditional Control structures include:

If-Else:

This structure checks if a condition is true or false, and executes different blocks of the code accordingly. It is highly flexible, and used for a wide range of situations where one or more conditions need to be evaluated. For instance, a weather app might check if the temperature is above or below a threshold to display appropriate recommendations (for example, "Wear a coat" or "It is warm outside").

Switch-Case:

A more specialized control structure is used when a single variable needs to be compared against several fixed values. Each value is matched with a specific block of code. This structure simplifies the code when there are many possible outcomes to consider, such as selecting a day of the week based on a numeric value (1 = Monday, 2 = Tuesday, and so on).

Thus, Conditional Control is critical for developing programs that are adaptable, and capable of handling multiple scenarios. Without conditional structures, programs would be rigid, and unable to account for different conditions or inputs. The importance of Conditional Control includes:

- **Flexibility**:

  It allows the program to react to different inputs or states, making the software more user-friendly and intelligent.

- **Efficiency**:

  By allowing the program to choose different execution paths based on conditions, it avoids unnecessary computations or processes that are irrelevant in certain situations.

- **Error Handling**:

  In fact, Conditional Control plays a vital role in ensuring programs run smoothly, and handles errors and edge cases gracefully. For example, it can prevent invalid actions, such as dividing by zero or accessing data that does not exist.

If-Else Structures, Usage, and Examples

The **If-Else** structure is a foundational component of programming that enables effective decision-making within a program. By allowing a program to execute different actions based on specific conditions, this structure enhances the ability to create dynamic and responsive applications. Whether determining the output based on user input, validating data, or controlling the flow of logic, the **If-Else** structure plays a critical role in guiding the program's behavior.

The structure begins with an **If** statement which evaluates a condition (often involving comparisons or logical expressions). If this condition is evaluated to as true, the corresponding block of the code is executed. Conversely, if the condition is false, the program proceeds to execute the code within the **Else** block. This fundamental branching mechanism allows developers to manage different scenarios effectively.

Usage of If-Else Structures

The structure begins with an **If** statement which evaluates a condition (often involving comparisons or logical expressions). If this condition is evaluated to as true, the corresponding block of code is executed. Conversely, if the condition is false, the program proceeds to execute the code within the **Else** block. This fundamental branching mechanism allows developers to manage different scenarios effectively.

Here is a general representation of the **If-Else** structure:

if condition:

 # Code block executed if the condition is true

else:

 # Code block executed if the condition is false

Consider the following example. Here, the program checks whether the value of age is greater than or equal to 18. If the condition is true, it prints "`You are eligible to vote.`" If false, it prints "`You are not eligible to vote.`"

```
age = 20
if age >= 18:
    print("You are eligible to vote.")
else:
    print("You are not eligible to vote.")
```

The versatility of the **If-Else** structure becomes particularly evident when handling multiple conditions. By incorporating **Else If** statements, programmers can create complex decision trees that address various possibilities within their applications. This capability is essential for ensuring that programs can react appropriately to diverse inputs and situations.

Else If for Multiple Conditions:

```
score = 85
if score >= 90:
  print("Grade: A")
elif score >= 75:
  print("Grade: B")
else:
  print("Grade: C")
```

In this case, the program checks the value of the score, and assigns a grade based on multiple conditions. The first condition checks if the score is 90 or above, while the second condition (in the elif statement) checks if the score is between 75 and 89. If both conditions are false, the program assigns a grade of "`C`."

You can also nest **If-Else** structures inside one another to handle more complex conditions.

```
x = 10
y = 5
if x > 0:
    if y > 0:
        print("Both x and y are positive.")
    else:
        print("x is positive but y is not.")
else:
    print("x is not positive.")
```

Here, the program first checks, whether x is greater than 0. If true, it moves to the next condition to check, whether y is greater than 0. Depending on the outcome of these evaluations, different messages are printed.

If-Else structures are crucial for implementing decision-making in programs. They allow the program to respond dynamically to varying inputs, user actions, or data conditions. This flexibility helps in creating responsive, user-friendly, and efficient applications.

Switch-Case Structures, Usage, and Comparisons

Switch-Case structures are powerful control flow mechanisms used in programming to simplify the process of executing different code blocks based on the value of a variable. Unlike traditional **If-Else** statements which can become cumbersome, when evaluating multiple conditions, the **Switch-Case** structure provides a more organized and efficient way to handle multiple potential outcomes.

The primary purpose of **Switch-Case structures** is to streamline the selection process, when a single variable needs to be evaluated against a set of predefined values. This structure enhances the code readability and maintainability, especially when there are numerous possible cases to consider.

Understanding that the syntax is essential for effectively implementing the **Switch-Case** structures in your code, the basic syntax of a **Switch-Case** structure typically looks as follows:

switch (variable) {

case value1:

// Code block for case value1

break;

case value2:

// Code block for case value2

break;

default:

// Code block if no cases match

}

In this structure, the switch keyword is followed by the variable to be evaluated. Each case corresponds to a potential value for that variable, and the associated code block executes if a match is found. The break statement is essential to prevent the execution from falling through to subsequent cases. The optional default case serves as a catch-all for any values that do not match the specified cases.

Usage of Switch-Case Structures

Switch-Case structures are particularly useful in various programming scenarios. Here are some common scenarios where they excel:

- **Menu Selection:**

  In applications with menu-driven interfaces, a **Switch-Case** structure can efficiently handle user choices based on their input. For example, selecting a menu option can trigger different functionalities within the application.

- **State Management:**

  When managing states or modes in a program, a **Switch-Case** structure can simplify the logic. For instance, a game might use this structure to determine what happens based on the current state (for example, paused, playing, game over).

Comparisons with If-Else Structures

To appreciate the advantages of **Switch-Case structures**, it is helpful to compare them with **If-Else** structures. Here are some key differences:

- **Readability:**

  Switch-Case structures tend to be more readable, and concise when dealing with multiple specific values. This clarity becomes especially beneficial as the number of conditions increases.

- **Performance:**

  In some programming languages, **Switch-Case** structures can be more efficient than long chains of **If-Else** statements, particularly when optimized by the compiler. This can lead to improved performance in scenarios with numerous comparisons.

- **Flexibility:**

  If-Else structures offer more flexibility in terms of complex conditions and range checks, as they can evaluate a variety of relational expressions. In contrast, **Switch-Case** structures typically evaluate a single variable against the constant values.

To illustrate the practical application of **Switch-Case structures**, consider the following example:

```
day = 3
switch (day) {
  case 1:
        print("Monday");
        break;
    case 2:
        print("Tuesday");
        break;
    case 3:
        print("Wednesday");
        break;
    case 4:
        print("Thursday");
        break;
    case 5:
        print("Friday");
        break;
    default:
        print("Weekend");
}
```

In this example, the program evaluates the value of a day. When a day is 3, it matches the corresponding case, and prints "`Wednesday`." If the value were not matched, the program would default to print "`Weekend`."

Understanding the **importance of Switch-Case structures** is crucial for developing efficient and maintainable code. The significance of **Switch-Case structures** lies in their ability to enhance code organization and readability. They simplify the logic of decision-making in programs that involve multiple fixed values, leading to cleaner and more maintainable codebases. By leveraging this structure, developers can create efficient applications that respond effectively to user inputs or varying conditions.

Iterative Control

Iterative control structures play a crucial role in programming by allowing the repeated execution of a block of code. This enables developers to automate repetitive tasks, process collections of data, and handle scenarios where the number of iterations is not known in advance. The primary types of iterative control structures include **For loops**, **While loops**, and **Do-While loops.**

The main purpose of **iterative control** is to facilitate efficient code execution through repetition. This allows programs to handle tasks, such as processing arrays, collecting user input, and performing calculations without redundant code. By utilizing these structures, developers can write cleaner, more manageable, and more efficient code.

The primary types of iterative control structures include **For loops**, **While loops**, and **Do-While loops**. Each of these constructs has its own unique characteristics, syntax, and use cases.

For Loops, Syntax, and Practical Examples

For loops are one of the fundamental control structures in programming that allow for the execution of a block of code, a specific number of times. They are particularly useful when the number of iterations is known beforehand, making them ideal for tasks, such as traversing arrays or performing repetitive calculations.

The primary purpose of a **For loop** is to simplify the repetitive tasks within a program. By using a **For loop**, developers can avoid redundancy in their code, enhance readability, and maintain efficiency, when working with fixed sequences of the data.

Syntax of For Loops

The general syntax of a **For loop** in many programming languages can be outlined as follows:

```
for (initialization; condition; increment/decrement) {
    // Code block to be executed
}
```

Initialization:

This step sets the starting point of the loop variable. It is executed only once at the beginning of the loop.

Condition:

This is evaluated before each iteration. If it evaluates to true, the loop body executes; if false, the loop terminates.

Increment/Decrement:

This updates the loop variable at the end of each iteration, controlling the loop's progression.

Practical Examples of For Loops

To better understand the functionality and applications of **For loops**, let us explore some practical examples. These examples will demonstrate how **For loops** can be utilized in various scenarios, illustrating their versatility in handling repetitive tasks efficiently.

Iterating through a List

One common use of a **For loop** is to iterate through the elements of a list or array. This is particularly useful for accessing each item, and performing operations on them.

```
fruits = ["apple", "banana", "cherry"]

for fruit in fruits:
    print(fruit)
```

Output:

In this example, the **For loop** iterates over the fruits list, printing each fruit name individually.

```
apple
banana
cherry
```

Calculating the Factorial of a Number:

For loops can also be used for mathematical computations, such as calculating the factorial of a number. The factorial of a non-negative integer is the product of all positive integers up to that number.

```
number = 5
factorial = 1

for i in range(1, number + 1):
    factorial *= i

print("Factorial of", number, "is", factorial)
```

Output:

In this example, the loop multiplies all integers from 1 to 5 to compute the factorial.

Factorial of 5 is 120

Generating a Sequence of Numbers:

For loops can be employed to generate sequences of numbers which is particularly useful in mathematical and statistical applications.

```
print("Even numbers from 0 to 20:")
for i in range(0, 21, 2):
    print(i)
```

Output:

In this case, the **For loop** generates, and prints all even numbers from 0 to 20.

Even numbers from 0 to 20:

0

2

4

6

8

10

12

14

16

18

20

Nested For Loops:

For loops can also be nested within each other which is helpful in scenarios that involve multi-dimensional data structures, such as matrices.

```
matrix = [[1, 2, 3], [4, 5, 6], [7, 8, 9]]

print("Matrix elements:")
for row in matrix:
    for element in row:
        print(element, end=' ')
    print()  # for new line after each row
```

Output:

In this example, the outer loop iterates through each row of the matrix, while the inner loop accesses and prints each element within that row.

Matrix elements:

1 2 3

4 5 6

7 8 9

While Loops, Key Differences from For Loops

While loops are another fundamental control structure in programming, used when the number of iterations is not known beforehand. A **While loop** repeatedly executes a block of code as long as a specified condition remains true. It is particularly useful when the number of iterations depends on dynamic factors, such as user input or the result of a computation.

The key role of a **While loop** is to repeat a set of instructions as long as a given condition remains true. This makes it ideal for situations where the number of repetitions is determined at runtime, unlike the fixed iteration count used in **For loops**.

Syntax of While Loop

The syntax of a **While loop** is straightforward but powerful, enabling continuous execution as long as the condition holds. Here is the basic structure of a **While loop** where the code block is executed repeatedly, based on the condition's truth value.

The general syntax of a **While loop** is as follows:

while (condition) {

// Code block to be executed

}

- **Condition**: The loop checks this condition before each iteration. If it evaluates to true, the loop body is executed; if false, the loop terminates.
- **Code Block**: The instructions inside the loop that are executed repeatedly until the condition becomes false.

Here is a basic example that prints numbers from 1 to 5 using a **While loop**:

```
i = 1
while i <= 5:
    print(i)
    i += 1
```

- The loop starts with **`i = 1`**.
- It checks if **`i`** is less than or equal to **`5`**. If true, it prints **`i`** and increments it by **`1`**.
- The loop stops when **`i`** becomes greater than **`5`**, ensuring numbers, 1 to 5 are printed.

Output:

1

2

3

4

5

Key Differences from For Loops

While both **For** and **While** loops are used to repeat code blocks, they have some key differences in terms of functionality and usage:

Iteration Control:

For loops are generally used when the number of iterations is known beforehand. They are ideal for scenarios, such as iterating over a fixed set of elements (arrays, lists, and so on).

While loops, on the other hand, are used when the number of iterations is uncertain and depends on the evaluation of a condition during runtime.

Syntax:

- A **For loop** includes initialization, condition, and increment/decrement, all in one line.
- A **While loop** only has the condition in the loop definition, while the initialization and updates (increment or decrement) are handled separately.

Readability:

For loops can be more readable when dealing with fixed ranges, as everything is compact and self-contained.

While loops are often clearer for scenarios where the loop condition depends on dynamic factors or external inputs.

Control Flow:

For loops are better suited for scenarios, such as counting or iterating over known ranges.

While loops are more flexible for conditions that involve complex, unpredictable logic, where you do not know in advance, how many iterations will occur.

Here is a comparison of both **For** and **While** loops–

While loop version:

Imagine you are writing a program that needs to repeatedly prompt the user for a valid number. You do not know how many attempts the user will take, so you cannot determine the number of iterations ahead of time. This scenario clearly shows where **While loops** shine.

```
number = None
while number is None or number < 0:
    try:
        number = int(input("Enter a positive number: "))
        if number < 0:
            print("Invalid input. Please enter a positive number.")
    except ValueError:
        print("That's not a number. Try again.")
```

In this case, the loop continues to prompt the user until they enter a valid positive number. Since the number of attempts is unpredictable, the **While loop** is a perfect choice. It checks the condition repeatedly, and only exits, once the user provides a valid input.

For loop version:

For contrast, consider a case where you are only allowing a limited number of attempts to enter a valid number. In this scenario, a **For loop** would be more appropriate, as it gives a specific count of iterations:

```
for _ in range(3):
    try:
        number = int(input("Enter a positive number: "))
        if number > 0:
            print(f"Valid number entered: {number}")
            break
        else:
            print("Invalid input. Please enter a positive number.")
    except ValueError:
        print("That's not a number. Try again.")
else:
    print("Sorry, you've used all attempts.")
```

Here, the **For loop** runs exactly three times. If the user does not enter a valid number within those attempts, the program terminates with an appropriate message. This fixed iteration count makes the **For loop** more suitable than a **While loop** for this use case.

The key highlighted differences are, as follows:

While loop:

Flexible and ideal for situations where the number of iterations is not known ahead of time (for example, reading user input until a valid condition is met).

For loop:

Best when the number of iterations is fixed, or can be determined at the start (for example, limiting the user to three attempts).

Do-While Loops, Features and Use Cases

When it comes to control flow structures, the **Do-While loop** stands out because of its unique characteristic of executing the loop body at least once, regardless of the condition's truth value. Unlike other loops that check the condition first, this loop evaluates the condition after running the block of code.

Understanding the key features of the **Do-While loop** is crucial for recognizing when to use it effectively. This loop provides several unique benefits:

- **Guaranteed Execution**: It ensures that the block of code is executed at least once before checking the condition.
- **Post-Condition Evaluation**: Unlike the While or For loops, the condition is checked after the code executes.
- **Flexible Control Flow**: Its structure allows for continued looping, based on the evaluation after the first iteration.

Syntax of Do-While Loop

Before diving into examples, it is important to get a clear grasp of the basic syntax of the Do-While loop. The syntax for most of the programming languages, such as C is shown here:

do {

// Code block

} while (condition);

Here, the loop begins execution before the condition is evaluated, ensuring at least one run through the block.

A **Do-While loop** is frequently used in situations where we want the code to execute at least once. A simple use case involves user input validation:

```
int number;
do {
printf("Enter a positive number: ");
scanf("%d", &number);
} while (number <= 0);
```

In this example, even if the number is invalid, the loop ensures the prompt will display at least once before rechecking the condition.

Key Features

The **Do-While loop** has several distinctive features that make it stand out from other control flow structures in programming:

- **Execution First, Condition Later**: This feature differentiates the Do-While from other loops, such as For and While which first check conditions.
- **Common in Input Validation**: The loop is perfect for scenarios, such as input prompts where a response is required before condition evaluation.
- **Post-Execution Condition Check**: Its evaluation occurs after one cycle, making it suitable for a guaranteed action.

Use Cases of Do-While Loops

The **Do-While loop** is commonly applied in situations requiring at least one execution of the code. Listed here are a few practical applications:

- **Input Validation**: Ideal for ensuring the user that provides valid data, prompting at least once.
- **Menu Display**: In applications with menu-driven logic, it ensures that the menu is displayed at least once, and repeats based on the user's choice.
- **Game Loops**: Game engines often use Do-While loops to run the core game logic before checking conditions, such as user quitting or game completion.
- **Repetitive Tasks**: This loop is also ideal for retrying failed operations or handling tasks that need an initial run, regardless of conditions.

Comparison with Other Loops

To fully appreciate the **Do-While loop**, it is important to compare it with other loops:

While Loop: This loop checks the condition before execution, so if the condition is false from the start, the loop body may never run. The Do-While loop guarantees at least one iteration.

For Loop: For loops are typically used when the number of iterations is known beforehand, making them more predictable than the Do-While loops which focus on conditional re-execution, after an initial run.

Control Flow Graphs

Control Flow Graphs (CFGs) are a critical concept in both programming and compiler design. They represent the flow of control in a program, capturing the possible paths that can be taken during execution. By providing a visual structure of the program's execution flow, CFGs enable efficient analysis of control dependencies and program behavior.

Definition and Purpose of Control Flow Graphs

A **Control Flow Graph** is a directed graph that illustrates the flow of control within a program. Each node in the graph represents a basic block–a straight-line code sequence with no branches–while directed edges indicate the paths taken during execution. The purpose of CFGs is to provide a clear visualization of the program's control flow, enabling developers to analyze and optimize the code more effectively.

Importance in Compiler Design

In **compiler design**, the Control Flow Graphs play a crucial role in several aspects:

- **Optimization**: They help identify the redundant code and potential bottlenecks, facilitating optimizations, such as dead code elimination and loop unrolling.
- **Error Detection**: The CFGs assist in pinpointing unreachable code segments and logic errors within a program.
- **Code Generation**: They provide a structured representation that can be leveraged during the code generation phase of compilation, ensuring efficient execution.

Overall, the CFGs are foundational to building effective compilers that produce optimized and error-free code.

Basic Blocks and Their Role

Basic blocks are the building blocks of Control Flow Graphs. A basic block is a sequence of instructions where control enters at the beginning and exits at the end, without any internal branching. Understanding the basic blocks is essential for constructing CFGs, as they represent the key elements of the program's control flow.

Understanding Basic Blocks in Control Flow

A **basic block** is defined by the following characteristics:

- It consists of one entry point and one exit point.
- Once execution enters a basic block, it will execute all the instructions sequentially, until it exits, either by reaching the end of the block or encountering a control transfer (such as a jump or a return).

By identifying the basic blocks, developers can create a CFG that accurately reflects the program's execution flow.

Construction of Control Flow Graphs

The construction of a **Control Flow Graph** involves several systematic steps that allow for a clear representation of the program flow.

Step-by-Step Example of Generating a Control Flow Graph

1. **Identify the Basic Blocks**: Analyze the code to break it down into distinct basic blocks.
2. **Determine Control Flow**: Examine how control transitions from one basic block to another, based on conditional statements and jumps.
3. **Create Nodes and Edges**: For each identified basic block, create a node in the graph, and draw directed edges to represent the possible transitions based on control flow.

This systematic approach yields a complete Control Flow Graph that can be used for further analysis or optimization.

Let us take a basic C-like code example to generate a Control Flow Graph.

```
int main() {
int x = 10;
int y = 0;
if (x > 5) {
y = x - 5;
} else {
y = x + 5;
}
return y;
}
```

Step 1: Identifying the Basic Blocks

The first step in constructing a Control Flow Graph is to divide the program into **basic blocks**. In this example:

- **Block 1:**
  - `int x = 10;`
  - `int y = 0;`

This sequence of instructions executes sequentially, so it forms a basic block.

- **Block 2**:
  - The if condition: `if (x > 5)`.

  This decision point will create branches, so it serves as its own block.
- **Block 3**:
  - `y = x - 5`;

  This statement executes if the condition x > 5 evaluates to true.
- **Block 4**:
  - `y = x + 5`;

  This statement executes if the condition x > 5 evaluates to false (that is, else branch).
- **Block 5**:
  - `return y`;

Regardless of which branch executes, this return statement is common, so it forms the final block.

Step 2: Determining Control Flow Between Blocks

Now, we examine the transitions between the basic blocks:

- After **Block 1** executes, control flows to **Block 2** (the if condition).
- Depending on whether `x > 5` is true or false, control either flows to **Block 3** or **Block 4**.
- Both **Block 3** and **Block 4** will eventually lead to **Block 5** (the return statement).

Step 3: Constructing the Control Flow Graph

Using the identified basic blocks and control flow, we can now construct the Control Flow Graph.

- **Block 1→Block 2** (Direct transition after variable initialization).
- **Block 2** has two branches:
  - If `x > 5` is true, control flows to **Block 3**.
  - If `x > 5` is false, control flows to **Block 4**.
- Both **Block 3** and **Block 4** converge back at **Block 5** to return the final result.

Control Flow Graph Visualization

Here is a simple visualization of the Control Flow Graph based on the example:

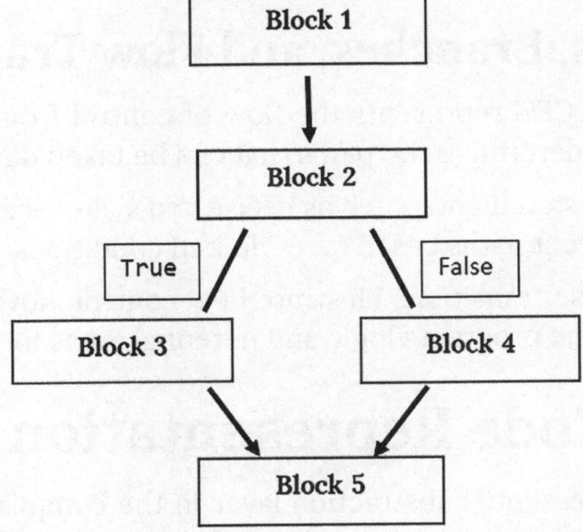

***Figure 8.1**: Control Flow Graph Visualization*

- **Block 1 (Variable Initialization):**
  - This block includes the initialization of the variables, `x = 10` and `y = 0`.
  - After this, the program proceeds to check the if condition.
- **Block 2 (If Condition):**
  - The `if (x > 5)` condition is evaluated here.
  - This block acts as a decision point, creating two possible branches:
    - If the condition is true (`x > 5`), the flow moves to **Block 3**.
    - If the condition is false (`x <= 5`), the flow moves to **Block 4**.
- **Block 3 (True Branch):**
  - If `x > 5`, the program executes the statement, `y = x - 5`.
  - After this, the flow continues to **Block 5**.
- **Block 4 (False Branch):**
  - If `x <= 5`, the program executes the statement, `y = x + 5`.
  - After this, the flow also proceeds to **Block 5**.

Block 5 (Return Statement):

Regardless of the branch taken, both branches converge at this block which contains the return statement, return y.

The program then ends, returning the value of y.

Step 4: Analyzing the Control Flow Graph

- **Basic Blocks**: The CFG breaks down the code into logical units where each basic block has one entry and one exit.
- **Branches**: The if-else condition introduces branches in the flow. One branch represents the true condition, and the other, the false condition.
- **Convergence**: Both the branches of the conditional flow return to a common block, before exiting the program.

Analyzing Control Flow Graphs

Analyzing **Control Flow Graphs** allows developers to gain insights into program execution, and identify the potential improvements.

Interpreting Edges, Branches, and Flow Transitions

- **Edges**: Each edge in a CFG represents the flow of control from one basic block to another. Analyzing edges helps determine the paths that can be taken during execution.
- **Branches**: Conditional statements, such as if-else and switch-case, introduce branches in the graph, indicating different paths based on evaluated conditions.
- **Flow Transitions**: These transitions illustrate how control moves between blocks, providing valuable insights into the program's logic and potential areas for optimization.

Intermediate Code Representation

Intermediate code acts as an essential abstraction layer in the compilation process, facilitating the translation of high-level programming constructs into a format that is easier to optimize, and convert into the machine code. This representation retains the logical structure of the original program, while abstracting away hardware-specific details, allowing for improved portability and efficiency.

Intermediate Code for Conditional Statements

Conditional statements are crucial in programming, enabling the implementation of decision-making processes. When translating high-level constructs, such as **if-else** and **switch-case** statements into intermediate code, the compiler generates specific instructions that represent the flow of control based on the conditions specified.

Transforming If-else and Switch-case into Intermediate Code

Transforming **if-else** and **switch-case** statements into the intermediate code is a vital step in the compilation process. This transformation allows the compilers to handle decision-making structures effectively, enabling optimized execution and accurate machine code generation. In this section, we will examine the methods used to convert these conditional constructs into their intermediate representations.

Transforming If-Else Statements

The **if-else** statement allows for branching based on a specific condition. This control structure is essential for decision-making in programming.

Structure of If-Else Statements:

- An **if-else** statement consists of a condition and two code blocks: one executed if the condition is true, and the other executed if it is false.

Intermediate Code Generation:

- The compiler generates a sequence of instructions that manage the flow of control, based on the evaluation of the condition.

Example of Intermediate Code:

```
if condition:
jump to true_block
jump to false_block
true_block:
// Execute statements for the true case
false_block:
// Execute statements for the false case
```

- The compiler first checks the **condition**.
- If the condition evaluates to **true**, it jumps to the **`true_block`**.
- If the condition evaluates to **false**, it jumps directly to the **`false_block`**.

Transforming Switch-Case Statements

The **switch-case** statement provides a mechanism to execute different branches of the code, based on the value of a single expression. This structure can enhance code readability and efficiency, particularly with multiple conditions.

Structure of Switch-Case Statements:

A **switch-case** statement allows multiple branches, based on the evaluated value of a single expression.

Intermediate Code Generation:

The compiler often creates a **jump table** that maps each possible case value to its corresponding block of code, allowing for efficient execution.

Example of Intermediate Code:

```
switch (expression) {
case value1:
jump to case1_block
case value2:
jump to case2_block
default:
jump to default_block
}
case1_block:
// Execute statements for case 1
case2_block:
// Execute statements for case 2
default_block:
// Execute statements for the default case
```

The **expression** is evaluated, and the program jumps directly to the block associated with the matching **case value**.

If no case matches, it executes the **default_block**.

Intermediate Code for Loops

Loops are fundamental structures in programming that facilitate the repetition of code based on specific conditions. The translation of loop constructs–namely **for**, **while**, and **do-while** loops–into intermediate code is essential for compilers to efficiently manage repetitive tasks. This section will explore the methods used to convert these loop types into their respective intermediate representations, highlighting the steps involved and providing clear examples.

Translating For, While, and Do-While Loops into Intermediate Code

Loops are essential programming constructs that allow for the execution of a block of code multiple times, depending on certain conditions. The effective translation of these loops into intermediate code is crucial for compilers to manage the control flow, and optimize performance. This section will cover the conversion processes for **for**, **while**, and **do-while** loops, illustrating how each is represented in the intermediate code.

Translating For Loops

The **for** loop is a control structure that allows for repeated execution of a block of code, based on an initialization condition, and increment or decrement operation. Understanding how to translate this structure into intermediate code is the key for compiler design.

Structure of For Loops: A typical **for** loop consists of three main components: Initialization, a condition to evaluate before each iteration, and an increment or decrement operation.

Intermediate Code Generation: The translation process for a **for** loop can be summarized as follows:

1. Initialize the loop variable.
2. Evaluate the loop condition.

3. Jump to the loop body if the condition is true; otherwise, exit the loop.
4. Execute the loop body.
5. Update the loop variable.
6. Jump back to the condition, evaluation.

Example of the Intermediate Code:

```
init: // Initialization
x = 0
condition:
if x < n: jump to body
jump to end
body:
// Execute loop statements
// ...
x = x + 1 // Increment
jump condition
end:
```

Translating While Loops

The **while** loop is a control structure that executes a block of code as long as a specified condition remains true. It is important to understand how this structure is transformed into intermediate code for effective compiler design.

Structure of While Loops: A **while** loop continues executing as long as a specified condition remains true.

Intermediate Code Generation: The steps for generating an intermediate code for a **while** loop include:

1. Evaluate the loop condition.
2. Jump to the loop body if the condition is true; otherwise, exit the loop.
3. Execute the loop body.
4. Return to the condition, evaluation.

Example of Intermediate Code:

```
Explain in simple points for both for and while loops
condition:
if condition: jump to body
jump to end
body:
// Execute loop statements
// ...
jump condition
end:
```

Translating Do-While Loops

The **do-while** loop is a variation of the **while** loop which ensures that the loop body is executed at least once, before the condition is evaluated. This section discusses how this structure is represented in the intermediate code.

Structure of Do-While Loops: Unlike the **while** loop, a **do-while** loop guarantees that the loop body will execute at least once, before the condition is evaluated.

Intermediate Code Generation: The translation of a **do-while** loop involves:

1. Execute the loop body.
2. Evaluate the loop condition.
3. Jump back to the beginning of the body, if the condition is true; otherwise, exit the loop.

Example of Intermediate Code:

```
Explain in simple points for both for and while loops
body:
// Execute loop statements
// ...
condition:
if condition: jump body
end:
```

Intermediate Code for Function Calls

Function calls are vital components of programming that allow for code modularity and reuse. When compiling a program, the generation of an intermediate code for function calls must accurately reflect how these calls are executed. This section delves into the specifics of handling function invocations, managing parameters, and returning values within the context of the intermediate code.

Handling Function Invocations, Parameters, and Return Values

Effectively managing function invocations, parameters, and return values is crucial in programming, as it determines how data flows between different parts of a program. This section explores the mechanics of calling functions, passing arguments, and returning results, providing insights into the generation of the intermediate code that facilitates these processes.

Handling Function Invocations

A function invocation is the act of calling a function within a program. This process requires careful management to ensure that the control flows correctly from the caller to the callee.

Intermediate Code Generation

1. **Function Call Instruction**: The compiler generates an instruction that specifies the jump to the function's entry point.
2. **Storing the Return Address**: The address of the instruction following the function call is saved. This address is crucial for returning control to the correct location, after the function execution is complete.

Example of Intermediate Code

```
// Call function named "calculate"
call calculate
```

Handling Parameters

Parameters are essential for functions as they allow input values to be passed to them, enabling dynamic behavior. The method of passing these parameters can vary, based on the programming language and its conventions.

Intermediate Code Generation

1. **Parameter Passing**: Parameters can be passed using the stack or registers. The intermediate code must ensure that the values are placed in the appropriate memory locations, before invoking the function.
2. **Accessing Parameters**: Within the function, parameters are typically accessed using their respective locations in the stack frame or registers.

Example of Intermediate Code

```
// Pass parameters a and b to the function "add"
param a
param b
call add
```

Handling Return Values

When a function execution is complete, it may return a value to the caller. This necessitates specific handling in the intermediate code to ensure the return value is properly managed.

Intermediate Code Generation

1. **Return Value Preparation**: When the function execution is complete, the return value is prepared to be sent back to the caller. This often involves placing the value in a designated register.
2. **Control Return**: The program must return control to the saved address, ensuring that the execution resumes correctly at the point following the function call.

Example of Intermediate Code

```
// Function "multiply" returns a value
return product // Store the return value
jump return_address // Jump back to the caller
```

LLVM Intermediate Representation

LLVM Intermediate Representation (LLVM IR) plays a crucial role in LLVM compiler framework, serving as a versatile and powerful means of representing the code. This section provides an overview of LLVM IR, highlighting its features and significance in compiler design.

Overview of LLVM IR

LLVM IR is a low-level programming language that abstracts the machine code details, while maintaining readability and portability. Acting as a bridge between high-level programming languages and machine-specific code, LLVM IR is an essential tool in the compilation process.

- **Low-Level Language**: Similar to the assembly language, LLVM IR is designed to be independent of any specific hardware architecture, allowing it to be used across various platforms.
- **Three Forms**: It is available in three forms: Human-readable text format, binary bitcode, and in-memory representation. This flexibility allows developers to choose the most suitable format for their needs.

  Example of LLVM IR:

  ```
  define i32 @add(i32 %a, i32 %b) {
  %sum = add i32 %a, %b
  ret i32 %sum
  }
  ```

In this example, the add function takes two integers and returns their sum.

Features and Significance of LLVM IR in Compiler Design

The distinctive features of LLVM IR make it a vital component in modern compiler design, enabling various optimizations and transformations that enhance code performance and efficiency.

- **Typed Representation**: LLVM IR uses a strong typing system which helps catch errors early in the compilation process, and facilitates type-based optimizations.
- **Static Single Assignment (SSA) Form**: Each variable in LLVM IR is assigned exactly once, simplifying analysis and optimization by making dependencies clear. This form helps improve the efficiency of various optimization techniques.
- **Modular Structure**: LLVM IR supports a modular approach, allowing developers to compile the code in separate modules that can be linked together, later. This promotes code reuse and efficient memory management, making it easier to manage large codebases.
- **Rich Set of Optimizations**: LLVM IR supports a wide range of optimization techniques, such as function inlining, loop unrolling, and constant folding. These optimizations contribute to generating a highly efficient machine code.
- **Cross-Platform Compatibility**: By abstracting the hardware details, LLVM IR enables the code to be compiled for multiple architectures without modification, enhancing portability and reducing development time.

LLVM IR is widely used in several popular projects, such as the Clang C/C++ compiler and the Rust programming language. These projects leverage LLVM IR's capabilities to produce highly optimized and portable executables.

LLVM IR for Loops

Translating loops into LLVM Intermediate Representation (LLVM IR) is essential for implementing the control flow in programs. This section explores how various loop structures, such as for, while, and do-while, are represented in LLVM IR, along with real-world examples to illustrate the translation process.

Translating Loops into LLVM IR with Real-World Examples

Different types of loops have specific syntactical and semantic characteristics that affect how they are translated into LLVM IR. The following are examples of how for, while, and do-while loops can be effectively represented.

- **For Loop**

  A for loop is typically used for a known number of iterations. Here is how a simple for loop is translated into LLVM IR.

  Example:

  Consider a for loop that sums the first ten integers.

```
int sum = 0;
for (int i = 1; i <= 10; i++) {
sum += i;
      }
```

LLVM IR Translation:

The equivalent LLVM IR could be structured as follows:

```
%sum = alloca i32
store i32 0, i32* %sum
%i = alloca i32
store i32 1, i32* %i
br label %loop_condition
loop_condition:
%i_val = load i32, i32* %i
%cond = icmp le i32 %i_val, 10
br i1 %cond, label %loop_body, label %loop_end
loop_body:
%current_sum = load i32, i32* %sum
%i_val = load i32, i32* %i
%new_sum = add i32 %current_sum, %i_val
store i32 %new_sum, i32* %sum
%next_i = add i32 %i_val, 1
store i32 %next_i, i32* %i
br label %loop_condition
loop_end:
```

- **While Loop**

  A while loop continues to execute as long as a specified condition is true. The following is an example of translating a while loop into the LLVM IR.

  Example:

  A while loop that calculates the factorial of a number.

```
int factorial = 1;
int n = 5; // Assume n is initialized
while (n > 1) {
factorial *= n;
n--;
}
```

  LLVM IR Translation:

  The equivalent LLVM IR could be structured as follows:

```
%factorial = alloca i32
store i32 1, i32* %factorial
%n = alloca i32
store i32 5, i32* %n
br label %while_condition
while_condition:
%n_val = load i32, i32* %n
%cond = icmp gt i32 %n_val, 1
br i1 %cond, label %while_body, label %while_end
while_body:
%current_factorial = load i32, i32* %factorial
%n_val = load i32, i32* %n
%new_factorial = mul i32 %current_factorial, %n_val
store i32 %new_factorial, i32* %factorial
%decremented_n = sub i32 %n_val, 1
store i32 %decremented_n, i32* %n
br label %while_condition
while_end:
```

- **Do-While Loop**

  A do-while loop guarantees at least one execution of the loop body, regardless of the condition. Here is how it can be represented in LLVM IR.

  Example:

  A do-while loop that prints numbers until a threshold.

```
int n = 1;
do {
printf("%d\n", n);
n++;
} while (n <= 5);
```

  LLVM IR Translation:

  The equivalent, LLVM IR could be structured as follows:

```
%n = alloca i32
store i32 1, i32* %n
br label %do_while_body
do_while_body:
%n_val = load i32, i32* %n
call void @printf(i32 %n_val) // Assume printf is declared appropriately
%incremented_n = add i32 %n_val, 1
store i32 %incremented_n, i32* %n
%cond_check = icmp le i32 %incremented_n, 5
br i1 %cond_check, label %do_while_body, label %do_while_end
    do_while_end:
```

LLVM IR for Conditional Constructs

LLVM Intermediate Representation (LLVM IR) serves as a critical abstraction layer between high-level programming languages and the machine code. It allows for the representation of control flow structures, such as conditionals, in a form that can be optimized and transformed for various target architectures. In this section, we will explore how common conditional constructs, such as if-else statements and switch-case statements are expressed in LLVM IR.

Representing If-else and Switch-case in the LLVM IR

Translating if-else and switch-case constructs into LLVM IR provides an insight into how conditional logic is executed at a lower level. Here, we explore the translation process for both the structures.

- **If-Else Statement**

  An if-else statement allows a program to make decisions based on certain conditions. When translating this construct to LLVM IR, the process involves evaluating the condition, and branching to the appropriate block of code, depending on the outcome.

  Example:

```
int x = 10;
int result;
if (x > 5) {
result = x * 2;
} else {
result = x + 2;
    }
```

LLVM IR Translation:

The equivalent, LLVM IR could be structured as follows:

```
%x = alloca i32
store i32 10, i32* %x
%result = alloca i32
%x_val = load i32, i32* %x
%cond = icmp gt i32 %x_val, 5
br i1 %cond, label %if_true, label %if_false
if_true:
%true_value = mul i32 %x_val, 2
store i32 %true_value, i32* %result
br label %if_end
if_false:
%false_value = add i32 %x_val, 2
store i32 %false_value, i32* %result
br label %if_end
if_end:
```

- **Switch-Case Statement**

  A switch-case statement provides a mechanism for executing different blocks of the code, based on the value of a variable. The translation of this construct into the LLVM IR involves creating a branching structure that matches the value against predefined cases.

  Example:

```
int case_num = 2;
switch (case_num) {
case 1:
printf("One");
break;
case 2:
printf("Two");
break;
default:
printf("Default");
    }
```

  LLVM IR Translation:

  The equivalent LLVM IR could be structured as follows:

```
%case_num = alloca i32
store i32 2, i32* %case_num
%case_val = load i32, i32* %case_num
switch i32 %case_val, label %default_case [
i32 1, label %case_one
i32 2, label %case_two
]
case_one:
call void @printf(i8* getelementptr inbounds ([4 x i8], [4 x i8]* @str1,
i32 0, i32 0)) // "One"
br label %end_switch
case_two:
call void @printf(i8* getelementptr inbounds ([4 x i8], [4 x i8]* @str2,
i32 0, i32 0)) // "Two"
br label %end_switch
default_case:
```

```
call void @printf(i8* getelementptr inbounds ([7 x i8], [7 x i8]* @str3,
i32 0, i32 0)) // "Default"
br label %end_switch
end_switch:
```

LLVM IR for Function Calls

Function calls in programming facilitate modularity and code reuse. When translated to the LLVM IR, these calls involve managing parameters, return values, and, in the case of recursion, the function's internal state. In this section, we will examine how function calls are represented in the LLVM IR, including handling both the regular calls and recursive invocations.

Handling Function Calls and Recursion in the LLVM IR

Understanding how to represent function calls in the LLVM IR is crucial for compiler design and optimization. This section illustrates how to manage the function calls and recursion in the LLVM IR.

Function Calls

When a function is called in a program, it often requires passing arguments, and receiving a return value. In the LLVM IR, function calls are expressed with a clear definition of parameter types and a return type.

Example:

Consider a simple function that adds two integers:

```
int add(int a, int b) {
return a + b;
}
int result = add(5, 3);
```

LLVM IR Translation:

This could be represented in the LLVM IR as follows:

```
define i32 @add(i32 %a, i32 %b) {
%sum = add i32 %a, %b
ret i32 %sum
}
%result = call i32 @add(i32 5, i32 3)
```

Handling Recursion

Recursion allows a function to call itself to solve problems. The following is an example demonstrating how a recursive function is represented in the LLVM IR.

Example:

```
int factorial(int n) {
if (n <= 1) return 1;
return n * factorial(n - 1);
}
```

LLVM IR Translation:

```
define i32 @factorial(i32 %n) {
%cond = icmp sle i32 %n, 1
br i1 %cond, label %base_case, label %recursive_case
base_case:
```

```
ret i32 1
recursive_case:
%n_minus_one = sub i32 %n, 1
%recursive_result = call i32 @factorial(i32 %n_minus_one)
%result = mul i32 %n, %recursive_result
ret i32 %result
```

Control Flow Optimizations

In the compiler design, control flow optimizations are essential for improving the efficiency of program execution. These optimizations focus on modifying the flow of a program to reduce unnecessary operations, and improve speed, without changing the program's output. The Two major categories of control flow optimization are: Peephole optimizations and loop optimizations.

Peephole Optimization Techniques

When a program is compiled, it often includes redundant or inefficient code that can hinder performance. To address this, compilers use **peephole optimization**—a technique that examines small sections of code, and replaces inefficient patterns with faster alternatives. This localized optimization helps enhance the overall execution of a program by making small yet impactful changes to the generated code.

Enhancing Performance through Small-Scale Optimizations

Peephole optimization is a powerful method in compiler design, aimed at improving code efficiency by focusing on small, localized sections of the code. It involves scanning a small "window" of the generated assembly or intermediate code to detect patterns that can be simplified or replaced with more efficient instructions. This process is typically applied after the code has been generated, and is used to clean up and enhance the final output, ensuring it runs faster, and takes up fewer resources.

Key Techniques in Peephole Optimization

- **Constant Folding**: Constant folding is a common optimization technique where expressions with constant values are evaluated at compile time rather than the runtime. By computing values early, the compiler can reduce the number of calculations, the program performs when executed.
  - **Example**: Instead of generating a code for y = 7 + 10;, the compiler directly assigns y = 17;, saving runtime computation.
- **Strength Reduction**: Strength reduction replaces costly operations, such as multiplication or division with cheaper, faster alternatives, such as addition or bit-shifting. This improves the execution speed, without altering the program's correctness.
  - **Example**: Multiplication by a power of 2 (x * 8) is replaced with a left bitwise shift (x << 3), significantly improving efficiency.
- **Dead Code Elimination**: **A** Dead code refers to segments of code that are computed but whose results are never used or have no impact on the final output of the program. Peephole optimization removes such code, reducing the program's size, and improving execution speed.
  - **Example**: If a variable is assigned to a value that is never used later in the program, that assignment can be removed.
- **Algebraic Simplifications** This optimization reduces the complexity of algebraic expressions to their simplest form, cutting down unnecessary calculations.
  - **Example**: Simplifying an expression, such as x * 1 to just x, or x + 0 to x, eliminates the need for redundant operations.

- **Instruction Reordering**: In cases where instructions are independent of one another, reordering them can improve performance by better utilizing processor resources, and minimizing stalls due to instruction dependencies.
  - **Example**: Rearranging instructions so that those not dependent on each other can run in parallel improving instructions throughput and the overall performance.

Benefits of Peephole Optimization

Peephole optimization focuses on small but impactful improvements to the generated code. By eliminating unnecessary instructions, reducing complexity, and reordering operations, peephole optimization helps to:

- Reduce code size.
- Decrease execution time.
- Improve the overall efficiency of the compiled program.

Even though peephole optimization works on a small scale, its cumulative impact across an entire program can significantly enhance performance, particularly in resource-constrained environments.

Loop Optimizations

Loops are a central part of most of the programs, and their optimization can lead to significant performance improvements. Loop optimizations aim to minimize the overhead associated with loops, reduce the number of iterations, or enhance the execution of loop bodies.

Techniques, such as Loop Unrolling and Loop-Invariant Code Motion

Techniques, such as **loop unrolling** and **loop-invariant code motion** are powerful methods for enhancing the performance of loops in programs. These optimizations aim to reduce the overhead of repetitive tasks, and eliminate unnecessary computations, making the loop execution faster and more efficient. By applying these techniques, developers can significantly improve the speed and resource management of their code.

Loop Unrolling

Loop unrolling is a technique where a loop is expanded by repeating its body multiple times within a single iteration, thereby reducing the number of iterations, the loop must execute. This reduces the overhead associated with loop control (such as, incrementing a counter and checking the loop condition), and can lead to faster execution.

For example, instead of executing a loop that runs ten times, unrolling the loop might execute two iterations per loop, halving the number of loop control checks.

Example: Instead of:

```
for (int i = 0; i < 4; i++) {
sum += arr[i];
}
```

After unrolling:

```
sum += arr[0];
sum += arr[1];
sum += arr[2];
sum += arr[3];
```

Benefits of Loop Unrolling

- **Decreases Loop Overhead:** Fewer iterations mean fewer checks and increments for loop control.
- **Improves Cache Performance:** Larger, unrolled loops can take better advantage of modern processor caches.

Loop-Invariant Code Motion

Loop-invariant code motion is an optimization where computations that do not change within a loop are moved outside the loop. This reduces unnecessary recalculations, freeing up resources and improving the loop's efficiency.

For instance, if a value is calculated in every iteration of a loop but does not depend on the loop variable, the calculation can be moved outside the loop and executed just once.

Example: Before optimization:

```
for (int i = 0; i < n; i++) {
int temp = x * y;
arr[i] = temp + i;
}
```

After optimization:

```
int temp = x * y;
for (int i = 0; i < n; i++) {
arr[i] = temp + i;
}
```

Benefits of Loop-Invariant Code Motion

- **Reduces Redundant Calculations:** By moving unchanged computations out of the loop, fewer resources are used.
- **Improves Execution Speed:** The loop runs faster as fewer instructions are executed in each iteration.

Branch Prediction

Branch prediction is a vital optimization technique employed in modern processors to improve the instruction execution efficiency. When a program encounters a conditional statement–such as, an if-else clause or a loop–the processor needs to determine which path to take. By accurately predicting the outcome of these branches, processors can reduce delays, and enhance the overall performance.

Understanding Branch Prediction

Branch prediction operates by anticipating the direction of a branch before it is executed. This involves analyzing the historical data from previous executions, allowing the processor to make educated guesses about whether a conditional branch will be taken or not. By doing so, the processor can pre-fetch instructions, thus, minimizing idle time and keeping the execution pipeline filled.

Strategies to Improve Execution Flow Efficiency

To enhance the execution flow of programs, developers employ various strategies that streamline operations, and minimize inefficiencies. One effective technique is dead code elimination which focuses on optimizing code by removing parts that do not contribute to the program's functionality.

Dead Code Elimination

Dead code refers to segments of code that are never executed during the program's run. This may include redundant calculations, unreachable branches after a return statement, or conditions that are never met. Eliminating such code is crucial for improving the performance and maintainability.

Understanding the Dead Code

A Dead code can manifest in various forms, such as:

- **Unused Variables**: Variables that are defined but never assigned a value, or utilized in any computation.
- **Unreachable Code**: Segments of a code that can never be executed due to the logical flow of the program, such as a code that follows a return statement.
- **Redundant Functions**: Functions that are declared but never called anywhere in the program.

Importance of Dead Code Elimination

- **Performance Enhancement**: Removing an unnecessary code can lead to faster execution at times as there are fewer instructions for the compiler to process.
- **Memory Optimization**: A smaller codebase reduces memory usage during runtime which is particularly important for resource-constrained environments.
- **Code Maintainability**: A cleaner and more focused codebase is easier to read, understand, and modify, reducing the likelihood of bugs, and improving collaboration among developers.
- **Simplified Debugging**: With less clutter, debugging becomes more straightforward, allowing developers to identify issues more efficiently.

Methods for Identifying and Eliminating the Dead Code

- **Static Analysis Tools**: Automated tools can analyze the source code to identify, and report the unused variables, functions, and unreachable code segments.
- **Code Review Practices**: Regular reviews by peers can help uncover, and discuss the dead code, leading to its removal.
- **Unit Testing**: Comprehensive testing can reveal unreachable code paths, prompting developers to eliminate them.

Removing Unnecessary Code and Unreachable Instructions

In software development, a code that does not contribute to the program's functionality is often referred to as an unnecessary code. This can include a dead code which is basically a code that cannot be executed, and unreachable instructions that the program flow will never access. Removing this extraneous code is crucial for several reasons, such as:

- **Performance Improvement**: Eliminating an unnecessary code can lead to faster execution at times. The processor spends less time interpreting or executing instructions that serve no purpose, allowing it to focus on meaningful operations.
- **Memory Optimization**: An unused code occupies memory space which can be significant in larger applications. By removing these instructions, developers can free up the valuable memory resources, making the program more efficient.
- **Maintainability**: A cleaner codebase is easier to read, understand, and maintain. When an unnecessary code is removed, developers can more easily identify the program's essential logic, and reduce complexity that aids future updates and debugging.

- **Reduced Risk of Errors**: A code that is not in use can still pose a risk. It may introduce bugs, if inadvertently modified or invoked. By removing it, developers minimize the potential points of failure in the application.

Methods for Identifying an Unnecessary Code

Various techniques can be employed to identify and remove an unnecessary code, such as:

- **Static Code Analysis**: Tools that analyze the code without executing it can identify unreachable code paths and the dead code, making it easier to clean up the codebase.
- **Code Review**: Regularly reviewing the code with peers can help spot an unnecessary code, and enhance the overall quality of the software.
- **Testing Coverage**: Implementing thorough testing can help identify which parts of the code are never executed during tests, highlighting areas that can be safely removed.

By adopting these strategies, developers can significantly enhance the execution flow efficiency of their applications.

Best Practices for Control Flow Representation

Efficiently managing control flow is vital for optimizing program performance, and ensuring code clarity. By following the best practices, developers can enhance their execution speed, maintainability, and reduce unnecessary complexity. Here are some key best practices:

Efficient Structure of Control Flow for Optimized Performance

To achieve optimal performance, the control flow should be designed with simplicity and efficiency in mind. This involves structuring conditional statements, loops, and functions in a way that reduces the processing overhead and speeds up execution. Some strategies include:

- **Early Exits**: Using return statements, breaks, or continue commands early in loops or conditionals can prevent the unnecessary execution of the further code, saving time and resources.
- **Use of Short-Circuiting**: Logical operators, such as && and || in languages, such as C, Java, or Python allow short-circuit evaluation. This means that expressions are only evaluated as far as needed to determine the result, thus improving efficiency.
- **Reducing Nested Structures**: Deeply nested loops or conditionals can increase complexity and reduce performance. Refactoring the code to minimize nesting can improve both readability and efficiency.

Minimizing Unnecessary Branches and Jumps

Branches and jumps in code, such as those found in if-else and switch statements, can cause delays in execution, especially in performance-critical applications. Best practices to minimize these include:

- **Consolidate Conditions**: Rather than using multiple separate conditions, try to combine them logically where possible to reduce the number of branches.
- **Optimize Switch-Case**: In scenarios where multiple conditions need evaluation, switch-case statements are often more efficient than long if-else chains. Additionally, ensuring the most common cases are checked first which can further optimize performance.
- **Avoid Unnecessary Jumps**: Reducing the number of goto statements or frequent jumps can lead to smoother program execution by minimizing disruptions to the flow.

By employing these best practices, developers can write cleaner, more efficient code that runs faster, and is easier to maintain. Structured control flow ultimately results in better software performance and reliability.

Conclusion

In this chapter, we examined the role of control flow in programming, and how various constructs, such as **if-else**, **switch-case**, and different types of loops (**for**, **while**, and **do-while**) are represented in the intermediate code. We also discussed the construction and analysis of **Control Flow Graphs (CFGs)** which offer valuable insights into the flow of execution within a program. By understanding these concepts, we gain a clearer view of how control structures translate into the intermediate code, ensuring smoother program execution.

Looking ahead to *Chapter 9, Run-Time Environment and Memory Management*, we will explore the critical topic of **Memory Organization**. This will cover the management of memory through **activation records** and various **storage allocation techniques**. Additionally, we will see practical implementations of memory management, particularly within the **Unix/Linux systems**, giving us a comprehensive view of how memory is handled in low-level operations.

Points to Remember

- **Control Flow** dictates the order in which statements in a program are executed, determining the logical sequence of operations.
- **Sequential Flow** involves the straightforward execution of statements in the order they appear, without any branching or repetition.
- **Conditional Control** structures, like **if-else** and **switch-case**, allow programs to make decisions based on conditions, directing the execution down the different paths.
- **Iterative Control** involves loops that repeat a set of instructions multiple times, with the three main types being **for**, **while**, and **do-while** loops, each suited to certain specific scenarios.
- **Control Flow Graphs (CFGs)** are a powerful visual tool used in compilers to represent the flow of a program, breaking it into **basic blocks**, and showing how control passes between them.
- **Basic Blocks** are straight-line code sequences that have no branches, except at the entry and exit, serving as the building blocks in CFGs.
- **Intermediate Code** acts as a bridge between the high-level source code and the low-level machine code, facilitating program translation and optimization.
- **LLVM IR** is a platform-independent intermediate representation that helps in translating, analyzing, and optimizing the code across different compilers and architectures.
- **Loop Optimizations**, such as **loop unrolling** and **loop-invariant code motion** reduce the computational overhead, and improve the efficiency of repetitive control structures.
- **Control Flow Optimizations**, such as **dead code elimination** and **branch prediction** enhance the program's performance by removing unnecessary instructions, and improving the execution flow.

Multiple Choice Questions

1. What is control flow in programming?
   a. The order in which statements are executed
   b. A function that handles errors
   c. A type of data structure
   d. A graphical representation of data
2. What is the significance of managing execution sequences in programs?
   a. To manage memory usage
   b. To optimize the CPU utilization
   c. To ensure correct program logic and desired outputs
   d. To enhance debugging
3. What is the role of intermediate code in control flow representation?
   a. It simplifies code translation
   b. It executes the final program
   c. It is used for high-level code writing
   d. It defines hardware constraints
4. Which of the following is a sequential control flow structure?
   a. if-else
   b. switch-case
   c. for loop
   d. Linear execution of instructions
5. What does the "if-else" control structure do?
   a. It repeats code execution
   b. It chooses between two or more alternatives
   c. It stops program execution
   d. It creates a loop
6. Which of the following is a feature of a switch-case structure?
   a. It evaluates expressions with floating-point numbers
   b. It can compare strings
   c. It evaluates multiple discrete values
   d. It only handles relational operators
7. What differentiates a "for" loop from a "while" loop?
   a. A "for" loop does not require initialization
   b. A "while" loop cannot have a condition

c. A "for" loop is primarily used when the number of iterations is known

d. A "while" loop must run at least once

8. What is the key characteristic of a "do-while" loop?

   a. The condition is evaluated before the loop starts

   b. The loop is executed at least once

   c. It cannot be nested

   d. It is identical to a "while" loop

9. What is a Control Flow Graph (CFG)?

   a. A type of data storage structure

   b. A representation of all possible execution paths in a program

   c. A table that stores variable values

   d. A debugging tool

10. What is the purpose of basic blocks in Control Flow Graphs?

    a. To store variables

    b. To represent a sequence of instructions with no branches

    c. To break down loops

    d. To define memory allocation

11. Which of the following is the first step in generating a Control Flow Graph?

    a. Identify the basic blocks

    b. Draw loops

    c. Define global variables

    d. Start function calls

12. How is an "if-else" statement in the intermediate code typically transformed?

    a. Into an assembly language

    b. Into a linear sequence of instructions

    c. Into branch and label instructions

    d. Into a single machine instruction

13. How are loops translated into an intermediate code?

    a. Using conditional jumps

    b. As recursive function calls

    c. Using only labels

    d. By removing all iterations

14. What is a key feature of LLVM Intermediate Representation (IR)?
    a. It is architecture-dependent
    b. It operates only in the high-level code
    c. It provides a low-level, platform-independent representation
    d. It requires manual memory management
15. How does LLVM IR handle loops?
    a. By using a direct assembly code
    b. By replacing loops with function calls
    c. By creating a loop body and conditional jump instructions
    d. By unrolling the loop during execution

Answers

1. a
2. c
3. a
4. d
5. b
6. c
7. c
8. b
9. b
10. b
11. a
12. c
13. a
14. c
15. c

Questions

1. What is the significance of execution sequence management in programming, and how does it influence program performance and readability?
2. Explain the role of intermediate code in representing control flow within a program, and why it is crucial during the compilation process.
3. Compare and contrast the various conditional control structures (if-else vs. switch-case) in programming. Provide practical examples for each.

4. What are the differences between for loops, while loops, and do-while loops? Include syntax and specific use cases for each type of loop.
5. Define Control Flow Graphs (CFGs). How are they constructed, and what role do basic blocks play in analyzing the program control flow?
6. Describe the steps involved in generating a Control Flow Graph (CFG) from a simple code example, containing both conditional and iterative structures.
7. How are conditional statements (if-else and switch-case) transformed into an intermediate code, and what are the benefits of this transformation in the compiler design?
8. What is LLVM Intermediate Representation (LLVM IR), and how does it facilitate loop translation into an intermediate code with an example?
9. Discuss the various control flow optimizations, such as peephole optimization, loop unrolling, and branch prediction. How do these techniques improve program efficiency?
10. Why is minimizing unnecessary branches and jumps essential in control flow representation, and how does it contribute to optimized program performance?

Key Terms

- **Control Flow**: This refers to the order in which instructions or statements are executed in a program. It manages the execution path, and can vary based on conditional logic and loops.
- **Sequential Flow**: The simplest form of control flow where instructions are executed one after another, without any branching or looping.
- **Conditional Control**: This allows programs to make decisions based on conditions, using constructs, such as if-else and switch-case. These control the branching of code execution.
- **Iterative Control**: Repeats a block of code multiple times using loops, such as for, while, and do-while. Each loop has different characteristics for iteration.
- **Control Flow Graph (CFG)**: A graphical representation of the flow of a program, showing how control moves between different basic blocks, especially useful in compiler optimization.
- **Intermediate Code**: A representation of the source code that lies between the high-level language and the machine code, simplifying optimization and translation processes.
- **LLVM Intermediate Representation (LLVM IR)**: A low-level, platform-independent intermediate code that simplifies optimizations and transformations in modern compilers.
- **Loop Optimization**: Techniques, such as loop unrolling or loop-invariant code motion which aim to improve the performance of iterative control flows by minimizing the loop overhead.
- **Dead Code Elimination**: An optimization technique that removes the code segments that are never executed or have no effect on the program's output, improving performance, and reducing resource usage.

CHAPTER 9

Run-Time Environment and Memory Management

Introduction

In *Chapter 8, Control Flow*, we discussed the control flow which governs how programs execute, and manage the sequence of instructions. We covered various control structures, such as sequential execution, conditional statements (such as, if-else and switch-case), and loops (for, while, and do-while). We also looked at the control flow graphs and their importance in compiler design, as well as how these structures are represented in the intermediate code.

In this chapter, we will focus on memory management, a crucial aspect of programming that affects how efficiently a program runs. Memory management involves allocating, and freeing memory resources which impacts performance and reliability. We will explore the memory hierarchy, including cache, RAM, and disk storage, and discuss the static and dynamic memory allocation methods.

Additionally, we will examine the activation records which help manage function calls and strategies for avoiding the common memory issues, such as leaks and fragmentation. By understanding these concepts, you will gain the skills needed to manage memory effectively in your programs, leading to more efficient and reliable applications.

Structure

In this chapter, we will discuss the following topics:

- Introduction to Run-time Environment
  - Overview of the Run-time Environment
  - Importance of Memory Management in Program Execution
  - Relationship between Memory Management and Program Performance
- Memory Organization
  - Memory Hierarchy
  - Program Memory Layout
  - Static and Dynamic Memory Allocation
  - Memory Allocation Strategies
  - Fragmentation Issues
- Activation Records
  - Definition and Purpose of Activation Records
  - Structure of Activation Records
  - Managing Activation Records

- Storage Allocation Techniques
  - Static Allocation
  - Dynamic Allocation
  - Garbage Collection
  - Common Pitfalls in Memory Allocation
- Example Implementations using Unix/Linux Memory Management
  - Memory Management in Unix/Linux
  - System Calls for Memory Management
  - Example Code Snippets
- Best Practices for Memory Management
  - Efficient Memory Use
  - Avoiding Memory Leaks
  - Debugging Memory Issues
  - Real-World Applications

Introduction to Run-Time Environment

Run-time environment is a crucial element of how programs operate. It includes everything needed for a program to run smoothly, such as the operating system, memory resources, and processor capabilities. Understanding the run-time environment is vital for anyone involved in software development, as it influences how programs execute and interact with system resources.

Overview of the Run-time Environment

Have you ever wondered what happens behind the scenes when a program runs? The run-time environment acts as the "stage" where a program performs, providing the context for executing tasks. It manages important activities, such as memory allocation, instruction execution, and communication with input/output devices. Just like a theater crew ensures everything is in place for a performance, the run-time environment ensures that the program has all the necessary resources and support to function effectively.

Importance of Memory Management in Program Execution

Why is memory management so important? Memory management is a key responsibility within the run-time environment that involves allocating space for variables and data, while a program is running. It also includes freeing that space when it is no longer needed. Effective memory management helps prevent errors, such as crashes and memory leaks–imagine it as keeping a well-organized closet. When everything has its place, it is easier to find what you need, and keep things running smoothly.

Relationship Between Memory Management and Program Performance

How does memory management affect a program's performance? The way memory is managed has a significant impact on how well a program runs. Efficient memory allocation can lead to faster execution and better utilization of system resources. Conversely, poor memory management can cause slowdowns and excessive resource consumption. By mastering memory management techniques, developers can optimize their applications' performance, ensuring that they are both quick and efficient. This understanding is essential for creating high-quality software that meets user demands.

Memory Organization

Memory organization is a fundamental aspect of computer architecture that defines how data is stored, accessed, and managed during program execution. A well-structured memory organization enhances performance, and ensures efficient use of resources. In this section, we will cover the following key components of memory organization: Memory hierarchy, program memory layout, memory allocation methods, and fragmentation issues.

Memory Hierarchy

Memory hierarchy is a crucial framework in computer architecture that organizes different types of memory based on speed, cost, and capacity. Understanding this hierarchy helps developers and engineers make informed decisions about how to optimize data storage and access in their programs. Each level of memory serves a specific purpose, and is designed to balance performance and resource management.

Understanding Different Levels of Memory (Cache, RAM, Disk)

To fully grasp how memory works in a computer system, it is essential to explore the distinct levels of memory available. Each level serves a unique function, and has different characteristics that affect performance and efficiency. By examining these levels–cache memory, RAM, and disk storage–we can better understand how data is processed, stored, and retrieved. This understanding is critical for optimizing application performance, and ensuring that programs run smoothly. Let us delve into each level, and see how they interact to create a seamless computing experience.

Cache Memory:

Cache memory is the fastest type of memory, located closest to the CPU. It stores frequently accessed data and instructions, reducing the time, it takes for the CPU to retrieve them. Cache memory is smaller in size but provides significant speed advantages, allowing the processor to execute tasks more efficiently. Its effectiveness hinges on the principle of locality, where recently accessed data is likely to be accessed again soon.

Random Access Memory (RAM):

RAM serves as the primary memory for a computer, holding data and programs that are currently in use. While slower than cache memory, RAM offers a much larger storage capacity, allowing for the simultaneous execution of multiple applications. It is volatile, meaning that all the data is lost when the system is powered down. The speed and capacity of the RAM play a crucial role in determining the overall performance of applications.

Disk Storage:

Disk storage includes Hard Disk Drives (HDDs) and Solid-State Drives (SSDs) which provide significant storage capacity for data and programs. Although disk storage is the slowest among the three types, it is non-volatile, meaning it retains the data even when the computer is turned off. Disk storage is essential for long-term data retention, and can hold large volumes of information, making it a critical component of any computer system.

Example:

When you open a program, the CPU first checks the cache for the necessary instructions. If not found, it looks in RAM. If the data is still not available, it retrieves it from the disk storage which takes longer.

Understanding the distinctions between these memory types is vital for developing efficient applications, and optimizing the overall system performance. Each level has its strengths and weaknesses, and effective use of the memory hierarchy can greatly enhance the program execution speed and resource utilization.

Program Memory Layout

Program memory layout refers to how a program's memory is organized during execution. This layout is crucial for understanding how data and instructions are stored and accessed, influencing both the efficiency of execution and resource management. In general, the memory used by a program is divided into several distinct sections, each serving a specific purpose.

Sections of Memory: Text, Data, Heap, and Stack

A program's memory is organized into four key sections: The text section for the code, the data section for global and static variables, the heap for dynamic memory allocation, and the stack for function calls and local variables. Each section plays a vital role in how a program executes, and manages its data.

Text Section:

The text section contains the compiled code of the program which includes all the executable instructions. This section is typically read-only to prevent modifications during execution, ensuring the integrity of the code. Since the text section does not change, it can be shared among different processes that execute the same program which helps in saving the memory.

Data Section:

The data section holds global and static variables that are initialized by the programmer. This section is further divided into two parts:

- **Initialized Data Segment**: This contains variables that are explicitly initialized by the programmer (for example, int count = 10;).
- **Uninitialized Data Segment (BSS)**: This contains variables that are declared but not initialized. Also, this section is automatically initialized to zero at runtime.

Heap:

The heap is a region of memory used for dynamic memory allocation. Variables in the heap can be allocated and freed at runtime, allowing for flexible memory usage. Unlike the stack which has a fixed size, the heap can grow and shrink as needed. However, managing the heap memory requires careful attention to avoid memory leaks and fragmentation, as dynamically allocated memory must be explicitly released when no longer needed.

Stack:

The stack is used for managing function calls and local variables. It operates in a last-in, first-out (LIFO) manner, meaning that the most recently called function is the first to return. Each function call creates a new stack frame that contains:

- **Return Address**: The location to return to after the function execution is complete.
- **Parameters**: Any arguments passed to the function.
- **Local Variables**: Variables defined within the function scope.

The stack is automatically managed by the system, meaning memory is allocated and deallocated as functions are called and returned, making it efficient for managing a short-lived data.

Understanding these sections of memory helps programmers make informed decisions about how to structure their code, and manage resources effectively. By leveraging the strengths of each memory section, developers can optimize their applications for better performance and reliability.

Static and Dynamic Memory Allocation

Memory allocation is a crucial aspect of programming that determines how and when the memory is assigned to variables and data structures. There are two primary types of memory allocation: Static and dynamic. Each type has distinct characteristics, advantages, and use cases.

Differences and Use Cases for Static and Dynamic Memory Allocation

When it comes to managing memory in programming, understanding the differences between static and dynamic memory allocation is essential. Each type has its own strengths, and is suited for different scenarios. Static memory allocation is determined at compile time, providing a fixed amount of memory that remains constant during execution. In contrast, dynamic memory allocation occurs at runtime, allowing for flexible memory usage, based on the program's needs. Let us explore the key differences and common use cases for both types of memory allocation.

Memory Allocation Strategies

Effective memory allocation is crucial for optimizing program performance, and ensuring efficient resource management. Different strategies can be employed to allocate memory, each with its own techniques and best practices. Here, we will explore some key techniques for memory allocation, and the best practices to follow for optimal performance.

Techniques and Best Practices for Allocation

When it comes to memory allocation in programming, employing effective techniques and following the best practices can significantly improve performance and resource management. Understanding how to allocate memory properly ensures that applications run smoothly, while minimizing waste and avoiding common pitfalls. Here, we will explore the essential techniques and the best practices to help you make the most of memory allocation in your programs.

Static Memory Allocation

Memory is allocated at the compile time, and the size is fixed throughout the program's execution.

Best Practices:

- Use static allocation for the known, fixed-size data structures to reduce overhead.
- Ensure that the size is appropriate to avoid wasting memory, or running out of space.

Example:

int numbers[5]; // Static allocation of an array with a fixed size of 5.

Dynamic Memory Allocation

Memory is allocated at runtime based on the program's needs, allowing for flexible memory usage.

Best Practices:

- Always check for successful memory allocation (for example, checking if the return value of malloc is **NULL**).
- Use free to deallocate memory, once it is no longer needed to prevent memory leaks.

Example:

```
int* numbers = (int*)malloc(5 * sizeof(int)); // Dynamic allocation of an
array for 5 integers
if (numbers == NULL) {
// Handle allocation failure
}
        free(numbers); // Deallocate memory when done
```

Memory Pooling

Preallocating a large block of memory, and dividing it into smaller chunks for use by the program.

Best Practices:

- Use memory pools to allocate similar-sized objects efficiently.
- This technique minimizes fragmentation, and improves the allocation speed.

Example:

Creating a pool for small objects can help manage memory more efficiently, especially in high-performance applications.

Object Lifespan Management

Object Lifespan Management involves understanding how long different objects in a program will last, and choosing the appropriate memory allocation method. Temporary objects can be allocated on the stack, while long-lived objects should be allocated on the heap. This practice helps minimize memory waste, and improves the overall application efficiency.

Best Practices:

- Understand the lifespan of objects, and allocate memory accordingly. Use stack allocation for short-lived objects, and heap allocation for the long-lived ones.
- Group related objects together to facilitate easier management, and reduce fragmentation.

Fragmentation Management

Fragmentation occurs when free memory is divided into small, non-contiguous blocks, making it difficult to allocate larger blocks.

Best Practices:

Monitor and manage fragmentation through regular analysis of memory usage.

Consider using compaction techniques or redesigning data structures to reduce fragmentation.

Error Handling

Error handling in memory allocation is crucial for maintaining program stability. When allocating memory dynamically, it is important to check if the allocation was successful; failure to do so can lead to crashes. Additionally, resetting pointers to NULL after freeing memory prevents issues related to dangling pointers, and enhances program reliability.

Best Practices:

- Implement robust error handling to deal with failed memory allocations gracefully.

- Always reset pointers to NULL, after freeing memory to avoid dangling pointers.

Profiling and Optimization

Profiling and optimization focus on analyzing and improving memory usage within applications. Profiling tools help developers identify memory consumption patterns and inefficiencies during execution. By using this data, they can make targeted optimizations, such as adjusting allocation sizes or refining data structures, resulting in better performance and more efficient memory management.

Best Practices:

- Use profiling tools to analyze memory usage, and identify bottlenecks.
- Optimize allocation strategies based on the profiling data to improve performance.

Fragmentation Issues

Fragmentation occurs when the free memory is divided into small, non-contiguous blocks, making it challenging to allocate larger blocks of memory. It can lead to inefficient memory usage and decreased performance in a program. Understanding the types of fragmentation and potential solutions is crucial for effective memory management.

Types of Fragmentation and Potential Solutions

Fragmentation can lead to inefficient memory usage and allocation problems in programs. In this section, we will look at the two main types of fragmentation–internal and external. We will also discuss potential solutions to manage these issues effectively, and improve the overall memory performance.

Types of Fragmentation:

- **Internal Fragmentation**

  This occurs when memory blocks are allocated, but the allocated memory is larger than the actual requested memory. The unused space within these blocks leads to wasted memory.

  Example:

  If a program requests 20 bytes of memory, but the memory manager allocates a 32-byte block, the remaining 12 bytes are wasted, resulting in internal fragmentation.

- **External Fragmentation**

  This occurs when the free memory is split into small, non-contiguous chunks, making it difficult to satisfy the memory allocation requests. While there may be enough total free memory, it is not contiguous, leading to allocation failures.

  Example:

  If a program allocates and frees several small blocks of memory, it may leave gaps in the memory that are too small to be useful for larger allocations, even if the total free memory is sufficient.

  Potential Solutions:

- **Compaction**

  This technique involves rearranging the memory contents to create larger contiguous blocks of free memory. It reduces external fragmentation by moving the allocated blocks together, and freeing up space.

  Implementation:

  A compaction routine can be run during periods of low system activity to defragment memory, but it may incur performance costs.

- **Segregated Free Lists**

  This approach uses separate free lists for different sizes of memory blocks. By maintaining multiple lists based on the size of the requested allocation, it reduces internal fragmentation, and improves the allocation speed.

  Implementation:

  When a memory request comes in, the allocator checks the appropriate free list for a suitable block.

- **Buddy System Allocation**

  This technique divides memory into partitions that are powers of two, allowing for efficient merging and splitting of blocks. When a block is freed, the allocator checks if its buddy block is also free, allowing for larger block formation.

  Implementation:

  The buddy system helps to reduce both internal and external fragmentation by making it easier to coalesce free blocks.

- **Memory Pooling**:

  Pre-allocating a large block of memory, and dividing it into smaller, fixed-size blocks helps manage memory more efficiently. This reduces the likelihood of fragmentation by ensuring that memory requests for similar-sized objects are satisfied from a single pool.

  Implementation:

  Memory pools are especially useful in applications with frequent allocation and deallocation of similar-sized objects.

- **Garbage Collection**

  In languages with automatic memory management, garbage collectors can help reclaim memory from objects that are no longer in use, reducing fragmentation over time.

  Implementation:

  Advanced garbage collection techniques, such as generational garbage collection, can help reduce fragmentation by periodically compacting memory, and collecting the unused objects.

Activation Records

Activation records, also known as stack frames, are essential structures that manage function calls in programming. Each time a function is called, a new activation record is created to store important information related to that specific function. This includes the function's parameters, local variables, return address, and control link which connects it to the previous function's activation record.

Definition and Purpose of Activation Records

The primary purpose of an activation record is to keep track of:

- **Function Parameters**: The arguments passed to the function.
- **Local Variables**: Variables declared within the function scope.
- **Return Address**: The point in the code to return to after the function completes execution.
- **Control Link**: A pointer to the previous activation record, allowing access to the calling function's context.

By maintaining this information, activation records enable proper management of function calls, and facilitate efficient memory usage.

Role in Function Calls and Returns

Activation records play a crucial role in managing function calls and returns:

Function Call:

When a function is called, a new activation record is created, and pushed onto the stack.

The program stores the function's parameters, local variables, return address, and control link in this record.

This structure ensures that each function call has its own isolated environment, preventing variable conflicts.

Function Return:

Upon completing the function's execution, the program retrieves the return address from the activation record.

The activation record is popped off the stack, effectively cleaning up the resources allocated for that function.

Control returns to the calling function using the stored return address, allowing the program to resume execution seamlessly.

Structure of Activation Records

An activation record consists of several components that store the necessary information for managing a function call. These components help keep track of the function execution, allowing the program to handle multiple function calls efficiently.

Components: Return Address, Parameters, Local Variables, Control Link

An activation record is structured to hold crucial information for a function call, ensuring proper management of execution. The key components of an activation record include:

- **Return Address:**

  This component stores the memory address of the instruction to which control should return after the function has completed execution. It is essential for maintaining the flow of the program.

- **Parameters:**

  These are the values or arguments passed to the function. The activation record holds these parameters so that the function can access them during its execution.

- **Local Variables:**

  This section stores the variables that are declared within the function. Each function call has its own set of local variables, preventing conflicts with variables from other functions or calls.

- **Control Link:**

  The control link is a pointer that connects the current activation record to the previous one on the call stack. It allows access to the context of the calling function, facilitating nested function calls and returns.

These components work together to manage the execution of functions, ensuring that each function call has its own environment and that control flow is maintained throughout the program.

Managing Activation Records

Activation records are managed primarily through stack-based memory allocation which allows for the efficient handling of function calls and returns. This approach facilitates both linear and nested function execution, ensuring that each function operates within its own context.

Stack-based Management during Function Execution

In programming, stack-based management refers to how function calls and returns are handled using a data structure called a "stack." The stack allows functions to be executed in the correct order, and keeps track of each function's state, making it essential for managing function calls efficiently.

Function Call:

When a function is called, a new activation record is created and pushed onto the call stack. This record contains the return address, parameters, local variables, and control link.

The program saves the current state of execution, allowing it to resume after the function completes.

Function Execution:

While the function is executing, it uses the information stored in its activation record. Local variables and parameters are accessed from this record.

The stack grows with each function call, and each activation record remains isolated from others, ensuring that functions do not interfere with one another.

Function Return:

Upon completion, the activation record is popped from the stack. The return address is used to transfer the control back to the calling function, restoring the previous execution state.

Handling Nested Function Calls and Their Implications

Nested function calls occur when a function calls another function before it has completed its execution. This leads to a situation where multiple activation records are present on the call stack, each representing a different function call. Managing these nested calls has important implications for memory management, control flow, and program performance.

Handling Nested Function Calls

1. **Creation of Activation Records:**

   Each time a function calls another function, a new activation record is pushed onto the stack. This record contains the return address, parameters, local variables, and a control link.

   The newly created activation record remains on top of the stack, until the function completes effectively, creating a chain of function calls.

2. **Isolation of Function Contexts:**

   Each activation record is independent, meaning that the local variables and parameters in one function do not interfere with those in another. This isolation allows for the safe execution of functions, even when they are deeply nested.

3. **Return Mechanism:**

   When a nested function completes, its activation record is popped from the stack, and control is returned to the calling function using the return address stored in the activation record.

This process continues, until all the functions in the call chain have returned, ensuring that the control flows back to the original caller in the correct sequence.

Implications of Nested Function Calls

- **Memory Consumption**:

  Each nested function call consumes stack space, and if there are too many nested calls, it can lead to stack overflow. This occurs when the stack exceeds its allocated limit, potentially crashing the program.

- **Control Flow Complexity**:

  Managing multiple activation records increases the complexity of control flow within a program. Developers must be aware of how deeply functions are nested to avoid potential issues with return addresses and variable scopes.

- **Performance Considerations**:

  Nested function calls can affect performance due to the overhead of managing multiple activation records. Frequent function calls, especially in recursive scenarios, may introduce latency and increase the execution time.

- **Debugging Challenges**:

  Debugging programs with many nested function calls can be more challenging. It may be difficult to trace through multiple layers of activation records, making it harder to identify the source of errors or unexpected behavior.

Storage Allocation Techniques

Storage allocation refers to how memory is reserved, and assigned to programs and their data during execution. There are two primary storage allocation techniques: **Static** and **dynamic** allocations. Each serves different use cases, and is crucial for optimizing the memory usage in a program.

Static Memory Allocation

Static memory allocation refers to the process where memory for variables is assigned at compile-time, rather than at runtime. The size, type, and location of the memory are fixed and determined before the program starts executing. Once allocated, the memory remains reserved throughout the program's execution, and cannot be modified or resized dynamically.

How and When Static Memory Allocation is Applied

Static memory allocation is applied during compile-time, assigning a fixed memory for variables that persist throughout the program execution.

Global and Static Variables:

Memory for global variables (accessible throughout the program) and static local variables (local to a function but persist across function calls) is allocated statically.

These variables are typically stored in the **data segment** of the memory, and their lifespan extends for the entire duration of the program's execution.

Compile-Time Allocation:

The compiler assigns specific memory locations for static variables and constants during the compilation phase. This means that the memory addresses of such variables are known before the program begins executing.

Reserved Memory:

Once the memory is allocated for the static variables, it remains reserved, even if the program or a particular function is not actively using the variables. The program holds onto the memory, until its execution is complete.

The Static Memory Allocation is typically applied in the following scenarios:

- **Global Scope Variables:**

  Variables declared outside of all functions (global variables) are statically allocated, since they need to be accessible across the entire program.

- **Static Local Variables:**

  Variables declared with the static keyword within a function retain their value between function calls. These variables are also statically allocated, allowing them to persist without being reinitialized on each function invocation.

- **Constants and Compile-Time Known Data:**

  Static memory allocation is ideal when the size and number of the data elements are known at the compile-time. Examples include constant arrays, fixed-size buffers, and configuration data that does not change during the runtime.

- **Embedded Systems:**

  In systems with limited resources, such as embedded systems, static memory allocation is often preferred as it offers predictability in memory usage which is critical for real-time operations.

Advantages of Static Memory Allocation

- **Faster Access:** Since memory is pre-allocated at the compile-time, accessing static variables is faster than the dynamically allocated ones.
- **Predictability:** The memory requirements are known in advance which simplifies the program design and memory management.
- **No Memory Fragmentation:** Static allocation avoids fragmentation issues commonly encountered in dynamic memory allocation.

Disadvantages of Static Memory Allocation

- **Inflexibility:** Static memory allocation does not allow for resizing or reallocating the memory at runtime, making it unsuitable for scenarios where the data size may vary.
- **Wasted Memory:** If the allocated memory is not fully utilized, it remains reserved, potentially leading to inefficient memory use.

Dynamic Allocation

Dynamic memory allocation allows programs to request and manage memory at runtime, providing flexibility to handle varying data sizes as needed. This technique is essential for creating data structures whose sizes cannot be predetermined at the compile time, such as linked lists, trees, and dynamically resizable arrays.

Overview of Dynamic Memory Allocation Techniques

Dynamic memory allocation techniques involve requesting memory from the heap, a region of memory reserved for dynamic allocation. This process enables the creation of data structures that can grow or shrink as required during program execution. Here are some common techniques:

- **Manual Allocation and Deallocation:**

  The programmer explicitly allocates memory, and is responsible for freeing it when no longer needed, preventing memory leaks.

- **Garbage Collection:**

  Some programming languages automatically manage memory allocation and deallocation, reclaiming unused memory, without the programmer's intervention. However, this adds overhead, and may lead to performance issues.

- **Reallocation:**

  Memory can be resized during execution, allowing data structures to expand or contract as needed. Functions, such as realloc in C/C++ can adjust the size of the previously allocated memory blocks.

Functions: malloc, calloc, and free in C/C++

`malloc` **(Memory Allocation):**

Usage: This allocates a specified number of bytes in the memory, and returns a pointer to the beginning of the allocated memory block.

Syntax:

```
void* malloc(size_t size);
```

Example:

```
int* arr = (int*)malloc(5 * sizeof(int)); // Allocates memory for an array of
5 integers
```

`calloc` **(Contiguous Allocation):**

Usage: It allocates the memory for an array of elements, initializing all bytes to zero. This is useful for avoiding uninitialized memory issues.

Syntax:

```
void* calloc(size_t num, size_t size);
```

Example:

```
int* arr = (int*)calloc(5, sizeof(int)); // Allocates memory for an array of 5
integers and initializes them to 0
```

Free:

Usage: This deallocates the previously allocated memory, freeing it for future use. Failing to free the memory can lead to memory leaks.

Syntax:

```
void free(void* ptr);
```

Example:

```
free(arr); // Frees the memory allocated for arr
```

Garbage Collection

Garbage collection is an automatic memory management process that reclaims memory occupied by objects that are no longer in use by the program. This helps to prevent memory leaks which can lead to degraded performance or system crashes. By automatically freeing up memory, garbage collection simplifies memory management for developers, allowing them to focus on writing to code rather than manually tracking memory allocation and deallocation.

Concepts and Importance in Memory Management

- **Automatic Memory Management:**

  Garbage collection automates the process of identifying and reclaiming the unused memory, eliminating the need for manual memory management.

- **Prevention of Memory Leaks:**

  By identifying unreachable objects, garbage collectors help to ensure that the memory is reused efficiently, preventing applications from consuming excessive memory over time.

- **Performance Optimization:**

  Efficient garbage collection can enhance application performance by reducing the overhead associated with memory allocation and deallocation. This leads to more stable and responsive applications.

- **Developer Productivity:**

  By abstracting memory management details, garbage collection allows developers to write a cleaner and more maintainable code, without worrying about the explicit memory management tasks.

Types of Garbage Collection: Reference Counting, Mark-and-Sweep, Generational

- **Reference Counting:**

  Each object maintains a count of the number of references pointing to it. When a reference is added, the count increases; when it is removed, the count decreases. If the count reaches zero, the object is deemed unreachable, and can be deallocated.

  - **Advantages**:

    Immediate reclamation of memory, once an object is no longer referenced.

    Simple implementation and low latency.

  - **Disadvantages**:

    Cannot handle cyclic references (for example, two objects referencing each other) which can lead to memory leaks.

- **Mark-and-Sweep:**

  This two-phase garbage collection method involves marking all reachable objects, and then sweeping through memory to deallocate those that are unmarked (unreachable).

  Mark Phase: The collector traverses the object graph starting from root references (global variables, active stack frames), and marks all reachable objects.

  Sweep Phase: The collector scans through memory, and frees all the unmarked objects.

- **Advantages**:

  Effectively handles cyclic references.

  Can reclaim memory from a larger set of objects.

- **Disadvantages**:

  Can introduce pause times during collection which may affect the performance.

  Requires more complex implementation than reference counting.

- **Generational Garbage Collection**:

  Based on the observation that most objects die young, this method divides objects into generations (for example, young, middle-aged, and old). New objects are allocated in the young generation, and those that survive several garbage collection cycles are promoted to older generations.

  - **Advantages**:

    Reduces the frequency of full collections, optimizing performance, since the younger generations are collected more often.

    Minimizes pause times by focusing on a smaller subset of objects.

  - **Disadvantages**:

    More complex implementation, and requires additional memory to track the generations.

Common Pitfalls in Memory Allocation

Memory allocation in programming, while powerful, comes with several common pitfalls that can lead to significant issues in application performance and stability. Understanding these pitfalls is essential for writing robust and efficient code. Here are two of the most prevalent issues: Memory leaks and dangling pointers.

Issues: Memory Leaks and Dangling Pointers

When managing memory in programming, two critical issues that developers must watch out for are memory leaks and dangling pointers which can lead to performance degradation and unpredictable behavior.

Memory Leaks

A memory leak happens, when a program allocates memory but does not free it, when it is no longer needed. Over time, this can cause the program to use more memory than it should, leading to crashes.

Causes of Memory Leaks:

- **Forgetting to Free Memory**: Failing to call free() (in C/C++), after the memory is allocated.
- **Losing References**: If a pointer to allocated, the memory is overwritten or goes out of scope, the memory cannot be reclaimed.
- **Complex Structures**: Using linked lists or trees can make it easy to lose track of the allocated memory.

Prevention Strategies:

- Always free allocated memory.
- Use smart pointers in C++ (such as `std::unique_ptr`) to manage the memory automatically.
- Use tools, such as Valgrind to find memory leaks during development.

Dangling Pointers

A dangling pointer points to memory that has already been freed. Accessing this memory can lead to crashes or corrupted data.

Causes of Dangling Pointers:

- **Freeing Memory Too Soon:** If a pointer is freed, and then used later, it becomes dangling.
- **Returning Local Pointers:** Returning the address of a local variable makes the pointer invalid after the function exits.

Prevention Strategies:

- Set pointers to NULL, after freeing them to avoid accidental access.
- Avoid returning addresses of local variables, and use references or smart pointers, instead.

Understanding memory leaks and dangling pointers is essential for effective memory management. By following the best practices and using modern programming techniques, you can reduce these risks, and create more stable applications. Regularly testing for memory issues can help keep your code robust and error-free.

Example Implementations Using Unix/Linux Memory Management

Memory management in Unix/Linux systems plays a crucial role in optimizing the resource usage, and ensuring efficient program execution. This section explores the various memory management strategies employed in these systems, focusing on key system calls, and providing illustrative code snippets.

Memory Management in Unix/Linux

Unix/Linux operating systems implement a sophisticated memory management model that allows multiple processes to run concurrently, while efficiently sharing system resources. This model includes techniques, such as paging, segmentation, and virtual memory that work together to ensure that applications can access the memory, they need without conflict.

Overview of Memory Management Strategies in Unix/Linux Systems

Memory management in Unix/Linux systems is designed to optimize the use of system resources, ensuring efficient execution of processes, while maintaining the system stability. Here are some key strategies employed in these operating systems:

Virtual Memory:

- **Concept:** Virtual memory allows the system to use disk space as an extension of the physical memory. This enables programs to access more memory than is physically available on the machine.
- **Benefits:** It simplifies memory management by isolating process memory spaces, improving security and stability. Each process operates in its own virtual address space which is further translated to physical addresses by the Memory Management Unit (MMU).

Paging:

- **Concept**: Memory is divided into fixed-size blocks called pages. When a program is executed, its pages can be loaded into any available physical memory frame.
- **Benefits**: This allows for non-contiguous memory allocation which maximizes the use of the available memory, and reduces fragmentation. It also enables efficient swapping between the RAM and the disk.

Segmentation:

- **Concept**: Unlike paging, segmentation divides the memory into variable-sized segments, based on the logical structure of a program (for example, code, data, stack).
- **Benefits**: Segmentation provides a more intuitive view of the memory, as segments can represent distinct logical units. It helps with protection and sharing of segments among processes.

Demand Paging:

- **Concept**: Pages are loaded into the memory, only when they are needed, rather than loading the entire program at the startup.
- **Benefits**: This reduces the initial load time and memory footprint of applications, leading to a more efficient memory use. It also allows the system to prioritize which pages to load, based on the current usage patterns.

Memory Mapping:

- **Concept**: Memory mapping allows files or devices to be mapped directly into the memory space of a process, enabling efficient file I/O operations.
- **Benefits**: This technique reduces the overhead of reading from and writing to files, as data can be accessed directly in the memory, improving performance for applications that require frequent file access.

Swapping:

- **Concept**: When the physical memory is full, the operating system can temporarily move inactive processes or pages to a disk space known as the swap space.
- **Benefits**: Swapping ensures that active processes have the memory they need to function, while maintaining system responsiveness. It also allows the system to handle more processes than physical memory would otherwise permit.

Memory Protection:

- **Concept**: The Unix/Linux systems implement memory protection to prevent processes from accessing each other's memory space, ensuring that one process cannot interfere with another.
- **Benefits**: This enhances system stability and security, preventing crashes and data corruption.

These memory management strategies work together to provide a robust environment for running applications in the Unix/Linux systems, ensuring efficient resource utilization, system stability, and security. By understanding these strategies, developers can write more efficient and reliable applications that take full advantage of the capabilities offered by the operating system.

System Calls for Memory Management

In the Unix/Linux systems, system calls enable the user programs to interact with the operating system's kernel. Thus, the key system calls related to memory management include fork(), exec(), mmap(), and brk(). These calls facilitate the allocation, deallocation, and manipulation of memory, playing a vital role in the application performance and functionality.

Key System Calls: `fork`, `exec`, `mmap`, and `brk`

This section explores the fundamental system calls that facilitate memory management in the Unix/Linux systems, focusing on their functions and significance.

`fork()`

This creates a new process by duplicating the calling (parent) process, resulting in a child process.

Memory Management Role: Initially, the child shares the same memory pages as the parent using Copy-On-Write (COW) which means that the actual copying occurs only when either process modifies the data.

Use Case: Commonly used in server applications to handle multiple client requests.

`exec()`

This replaces the current process's memory with a new program, transforming the calling process.

Memory Management Role: The existing memory contents are replaced with the new program's code and data.

Use Case: This is typically called in the child process after fork() to run a different program.

`mmap()`

These are maps files or devices into memory for efficient I/O operations.

Memory Management Role: Allows direct reading and writing to a file as if it were part of the process's memory.

Use Case: Useful for memory-mapped files and shared memory between processes.

`brk()` and `sbrk()`

Adjusts the size of the process's data segment, effectively managing the heap memory.

Memory Management Role: Increases or decreases the amount of the allocated heap memory.

Use Case: Often utilized in dynamic memory allocation, such as with malloc().

Example Code Snippets

This section presents practical code snippets that illustrate memory allocation and management techniques in the Unix/Linux systems, showcasing key system calls and their functionalities.

Illustrative Examples Demonstrating Memory Allocation and Deallocation in Unix/Linux

In this section, we will explore practical examples that demonstrate how memory allocation and deallocation are handled in the Unix/Linux environments. These examples highlight the usage of system calls, such as malloc, free, and memory-mapping techniques to efficiently manage the memory in real-world applications.

Using `malloc()` and `free()`

This example demonstrates dynamic memory allocation using malloc() and deallocation, using `free()`.

Code Snippet

```
#include <stdio.h>
#include <stdlib.h>
int main() {
int *arr;
int n = 5;
// Dynamically allocate memory for an array of integers
arr = (int *)malloc(n * sizeof(int));
if (arr == NULL) {
printf("Memory allocation failed\n");
return 1;
}
// Initialize and display the array
for (int i = 0; i < n; i++) {
arr[i] = i + 1;
printf("arr[%d] = %d\n", i, arr[i]);
}
// Free the allocated memory
free(arr);
return 0;
}
```

Memory Allocation: The **malloc()** function allocates memory for an array of integers. The size is determined by **n * sizeof(int)**, where n is the number of elements (5 in this case).

Error Checking: After allocation, we check if malloc() returned NULL, indicating that memory allocation failed.

Initialization and Display: The allocated memory is used to store integers. A loop initializes the array with values and prints them.

Deallocation: Finally, the free() function is called to release the allocated memory.

Expected Output

```
arr[0] = 1
arr[1] = 2
arr[2] = 3
arr[3] = 4
arr[4] = 5
```

Using fork() and exec()

This example demonstrates how to create a new process using fork(), and execute a new program using exec().

Code Snippet

```
#include <stdio.h>
#include <unistd.h>
#include <sys/types.h>
int main() {
pid_t pid;
// Create a new process
pid = fork();
if (pid < 0) {
// Fork failed
perror("Fork failed");
return 1;
```

```
} else if (pid == 0) {
// Child process
execlp("ls", "ls", "-l", NULL); // Execute 'ls -l'
perror("exec failed"); // exec only returns on failure
return 1;
} else {
// Parent process
printf("Parent process: Child PID is %d\n", pid);
}
return 0;
}
```

Process Creation: The `fork()` function is called to create a new process. The return value indicates whether we are in the parent or child process.

Child Process Execution: If the return value is 0, we are in the child process. The **`execlp()`** function is then used to execute the ls command with the -l option.

Error Handling: If **`execlp()`** fails, it prints an error message using **`perror()`**.

Parent Process: The parent process prints the child's process ID (PID).

Expected Output

The output will vary based on the contents of the current directory, but you should see something similar to this:

```
Parent process: Child PID is 12345
total 12
drwxr-xr-x 3 user group 4096 Oct 20 10:00 dir1
drwxr-xr-x 2 user group 4096 Oct 20 10:00 dir2
-rw-r--r-- 1 user group 0 Oct 20 10:00 file1.txt
```

Using mmap()

This example demonstrates how to map a file into memory, using `mmap()`.

Code Snippet

```
#include <stdio.h>
#include <stdlib.h>
#include <fcntl.h>
#include <sys/mman.h>
#include <unistd.h>
#include <string.h>
int main() {
const char *filepath = "example.txt";
int fd;
char *mapped;
// Open the file
fd = open(filepath, O_RDWR);
if (fd == -1) {
perror("Failed to open file");
return 1;
}
// Map the file into memory
mapped = mmap(NULL, 100, PROT_READ | PROT_WRITE, MAP_SHARED, fd, 0);
if (mapped == MAP_FAILED) {
perror("Failed to map file");
close(fd);
```

```
return 1;
}
// Write to the mapped memory
strcpy(mapped, "Hello, mmap!");
// Print the content of the mapped memory
printf("Mapped content: %s\n", mapped);
// Unmap and close the file
munmap(mapped, 100);
close(fd);
return 0;
}
```

File Opening: The program opens a file named example.txt, using open().

Memory Mapping: The `mmap()` function maps the file into the memory. The parameters specify the protection (read and write), mapping type (shared), and the file descriptor.

Writing to Mapped Memory: The program writes "**`Hello, mmap!`**" to the mapped area, and prints the content.

Cleanup: Finally, the **`munmap()`** is called to unmap the memory, and the file descriptor is closed.

Expected Output

```
Mapped content: Hello, mmap!
```

These examples demonstrate the essential memory management operations in Unix/Linux programming. Hence, by using malloc(), fork(), exec(), and mmap(), developers can effectively allocate, deallocate, and manipulate memory, enabling the creation of efficient and powerful applications.

Best Practices for Memory Management

Effective memory management is critical for ensuring the smooth performance and reliability of applications. By following the best practices, such as optimizing memory allocation, preventing leaks, and using efficient data structures, developers can minimize the resource usage, and improve the overall system efficiency.

Efficient Memory Use

Optimizing memory usage is necessary for building high-performance applications. Techniques for achieving this include using appropriate data structures that minimize memory consumption, allocating memory, only when necessary, and reusing memory, when possible. Additionally, developers can use memory pools or caching strategies to reduce the overhead of frequent memory allocations. Properly freeing up the unused memory is also critical to prevent memory leaks which can degrade the system performance over time. Efficient memory use ensures that applications run faster, use fewer resources, and scale effectively.

Techniques for Optimizing Memory Usage in Applications

Optimizing memory usage is critical for improving both the application performance and scalability. Here are several key techniques to achieve efficient memory use:

- **Choosing the Right Data Structures**: Selecting the appropriate data structures can drastically reduce memory consumption. For instance, using arrays for fixed-size data sets or hash maps for efficient lookups can minimize the memory overhead. The choice should depend on the the specific use case to balance time complexity and memory use.

- **Memory Pooling**: Memory pooling involves pre-allocating a block of memory to be reused by the application, avoiding the overhead of frequent memory allocations and deallocations. This technique is particularly useful in high-performance applications where dynamic allocation can cause fragmentation, and degrade performance.
- **Lazy Loading**: Load data into the memory, only when it is absolutely needed. This can significantly reduce memory consumption, especially for large datasets or resources that may not be required immediately, optimizing the use of available resources.
- **Garbage Collection and Manual Deallocation**: In garbage-collected languages, such as Java and Python, ensure that objects no longer needed are eligible for garbage collection to free up the memory. In languages, such as C and C++, where memory management is manual, be diligent about freeing the memory using free() or delete, when it is no longer needed to prevent memory leaks.
- **Compact Data Representation**: Use smaller, more efficient data types wherever possible. For example, prefer int16 over int32 for small integer ranges, or float instead of double, when high precision is not required. Reducing the size of stored data minimizes the overall memory consumption.
- **Profiling and Monitoring**: This involves regular profile memory usage to detect inefficiencies or memory leaks. Tools, such as Valgrind, gprof, or memory profilers available in IDEs can help identify memory-hungry parts of the application, and optimize them proactively.

By applying these techniques, developers can ensure that their applications not only use the memory efficiently but also maintain high performance and scalability, even as the system grows in complexity.

Avoiding Memory Leaks

Memory leaks occur, when a program fails to release the memory that is no longer needed, leading to inefficient memory usage and, over time, performance degradation or system crashes.

Common Pitfalls and Strategies to Prevent Memory Leaks

Here are some common pitfalls and strategies to prevent memory leaks:

- **Manual Memory Management**: In languages, such as C and C++, failing to call free() or delete after dynamically allocating memory with `malloc()`, or new can lead to memory leaks. Always ensure that each allocation has a corresponding deallocation.
- **Circular References**: In languages with automatic garbage collection, (such as Python or Java), circular references between objects can prevent garbage collection from freeing the memory. Use weak references where appropriate to break these cycles.
- **Use of Smart Pointers**: In modern C++, using smart pointers (`std::unique_ptr`, `std::shared_ptr`) helps prevent memory leaks by automatically managing the lifecycle of dynamically allocated objects, ensuring that memory is released, when it is no longer in use.
- **Closing Resources**: Always release system resources, (such as file handles, network sockets, or database connections), after use. These resources occupy the memory, and if not closed properly, they may lead to memory leaks or resource exhaustion.
- **Avoiding Long-Lived Global Objects**: Global or static objects that hold references to large data structures can cause memory leaks, if not properly reset or cleared. Use such objects sparingly, and ensure that they are cleaned up when no longer needed.
- **Use Profiling Tools**: Regularly use memory profiling tools, such as Valgrind (for C/C++) or memory profilers in IDEs for other languages to detect and resolve memory leaks early, during development.

By being mindful of these pitfalls and following best practices for memory management, developers can significantly reduce the likelihood of memory leaks, ensuring their applications remain efficient and reliable over time.

Debugging Memory Issues

Identifying and resolving memory-related issues, such as leaks, buffer overflows, or segmentation faults can be challenging.

Tools and Techniques for Identifying and Resolving Memory -related Issues

There are various tools and techniques to help developers effectively debug these issues:

- **Valgrind**:

  Valgrind is a powerful tool for memory profiling in C and C++. It detects memory leaks, buffer overflows, and improper memory access. Running programs through Valgrind provides detailed reports about where memory issues occur, making it easier to pinpoint and fix problems.

- **Address Sanitizer (ASan)**:

  Address Sanitizer is a runtime memory error detector available in many modern compilers, such as GCC and Clang. It helps find buffer overflows, use-after-free errors, and other memory issues by adding checks at runtime, and providing fast feedback during development.

- **GDB (GNU Debugger)**:

  GDB is a versatile tool for debugging C/C++ programs. It allows step-by-step execution of the code, monitoring of memory usage, and inspection of variables. The GDB is helpful in tracking down segmentation faults, and understanding the state of the program when an issue arises.

- **Heap Profilers:**

  For languages with garbage collection (for example, Java, Python), heap profilers track the memory usage over time, identifying objects that consume excessive memory, or are not properly garbage collected. Tools, such as VisualVM for Java and objgraph for Python provide graphical representations of memory usage.

- **Memory Leak Detectors**:

  Specialized tools, such as Dr. Memory and Purify help detect memory leaks, and identify areas where memory is allocated but never freed. These tools work by monitoring the program at runtime, and alerting developers to memory management issues.

- **Static Code Analyzers**:

  Tools, such as Clang Static Analyzer or PVS-Studio analyze the code for potential memory issues, without running the program. These tools can detect issues, such as null pointer dereferencing, memory leaks, and uninitialized variables by examining the source code itself.

- **Unit Testing with Memory Checks**:

  Adding unit tests that specifically test the memory usage and allocation can help catch issues, early. In languages, such as C, libraries like CMocka provide frameworks for testing and monitoring the memory usage in the code.

By combining these tools and techniques, developers can proactively identify and resolve memory-related issues, ensuring that their applications run efficiently, and avoid critical failures related to memory management.

Real-World Applications

Effective memory management plays a pivotal role in the performance and reliability of large-scale applications across various domains.

Impact of Effective Memory Management in Large-scale Applications

Here are some key impacts of an efficient memory management:

- **Web Applications**:

  High-traffic web applications, such as social media platforms or e-commerce sites, rely on efficient memory management to handle numerous simultaneous user requests. Proper memory allocation and garbage collection help maintain quick response times, and prevent slowdowns or crashes during peak usage.

- **Cloud Computing**:

  In cloud environments, where resources are shared among multiple applications, effective memory management is essential for optimizing resource utilization. Techniques, such as memory pooling and dynamic scaling ensure that applications consume only the necessary memory, allowing for efficient multi-tenancy and reduced operational costs.

- **Mobile Applications**:

  Mobile devices have limited memory and processing power. Applications that manage memory efficiently can offer better performance, longer battery life, and improved user experiences. Implementing lazy loading and efficient data caching strategies allow mobile apps to minimize memory usage and avoid crashes.

- **Game Development**:

  Video games demand high-performance memory management due to their complex graphics and real-time processing. Efficient memory allocation for textures, models, and game states ensures smooth gameplay and minimizes loading times. Game engines often implement custom memory management techniques to optimize performance, and reduce fragmentation.

- **Scientific Computing**:

  Large-scale scientific simulations or data analysis applications often deal with massive datasets. Effective memory management techniques, such as chunking data and using efficient data structures, can significantly improve performance and allow researchers to analyze larger datasets without running into memory limitations.

- **Database Management Systems (DBMS)**:

  The DBMS relies heavily on efficient memory management to cache data, manage transactions, and optimize query performance. Properly managing buffer pools and memory for query execution can lead to significant improvements in database response times and overall application performance.

- **Machine Learning and AI Applications**:

  Machine learning models can consume large amounts of memory during training and inference. Optimizing memory usage through techniques, such as model quantization and efficient data loading can enhance the training speed, and reduce the risk of memory-related errors.

Conclusion

In this chapter, we discussed the importance of memory management in program execution. We covered how memory is organized, including the roles of cache, RAM, and disk storage, as well as the layout of program memory which includes the text, data, heap, and stack segments. We also looked at the static and dynamic memory allocations, the significance of activation records for function calls, and how garbage collection helps prevent memory issues.

Looking ahead to *Chapter 10, Function Calls and Exception Handling*, we will focus on function execution, including how parameters are passed to functions, how function calls and returns are managed, and the role of exception handling in dealing with errors. We will also explore how these concepts are implemented in the Unix/Linux systems, with practical examples to illustrate effective memory management.

Points to Remember

- **Run-time environment** is the system's operational state, while a program is executing, providing resources, such as memory, CPU, and I/O to the program.
- **Efficient memory management** ensures that memory is allocated, used, and released correctly to avoid wasting resources, and ensure smooth program execution.
- **Memory hierarchy** consists of multiple levels, such as the CPU cache (fastest), the RAM (intermediate speed), and the disk storage (slowest) which work together to optimize the data access.
- **Program memory layout** includes sections, such as the text segment (code), the data segment (initialized global variables), the heap (dynamically allocated memory), and the stack (function calls and local variables).
- **Static memory allocation** occurs at the compile time, meaning that the memory size is fixed and cannot change during the runtime.
- **Dynamic memory allocation** happens at the runtime, allowing programs to request, and free memory as needed through functions, such as malloc and free in C/C++.
- **Fragmentation** refers to memory gaps created by inefficient allocation, with external fragmentation affecting large memory blocks and internal fragmentation wasting small memory chunks.
- **Heap vs. stack** The stack is for static and local memory allocation which is automatically managed, while the heap allows for dynamic allocation, requiring manual management.
- **Activation records** store information about function calls, including the return address, parameters, and local variables, enabling proper management of function execution.
- **Garbage collection** is an automatic memory management process that reclaims memory which is no longer in use, reducing memory leaks in languages, such as Java and Python.
- **Memory leaks** occur when dynamically allocated memory is not freed, causing the program to use more memory over time, leading to performance degradation or crashes.
- **Reference counting** is a memory management technique where objects are deleted, once their reference count drops to zero, helping to manage memory more effectively.
- **Mark-and-sweep** garbage collection identifies objects no longer in use by marking active objects and sweeping unmarked ones which can then be freed.
- **Memory allocation strategies** include first-fit (allocating the first available block), best-fit (allocating the smallest suitable block), and worst-fit (allocating the largest available block).

- **Debugging memory issues**: Tools, such as Valgrind help to track memory usage, detect leaks, and identify issues, such as dangling pointers, and enabling developers to resolve memory-related problems effectively.

Multiple Choice Questions

1. What is the primary function of memory management in a program?
   a. To manage hardware components
   b. To allocate and deallocate memory resources efficiently
   c. To improve the user interface
   d. To compile the code faster
2. Which of the following best describes the memory hierarchy?
   a. Disk, Heap, Cache
   b. Registers, Cache, RAM, Disk
   c. Text, Data, Heap, Stack
   d. Static and Dynamic Memory
3. Which section of the program memory holds global and static variables?
   a. Stack
   b. Heap
   c. Data
   d. Text
4. What is the key difference between static and dynamic memory allocations?
   a. Static allocation occurs at the compile-time, while dynamic allocation occurs at runtime.
   b. Static allocation uses the heap, while dynamic allocation uses the stack.
   c. Static allocation is slower than dynamic allocation.
   d. Dynamic allocation cannot be freed, once allocated.
5. What is the primary issue caused by fragmentation in memory management?
   a. Slower memory access
   b. Reduced memory available for allocation
   c. Increased program execution time
   d. Memory leaks
6. Which of the following best describes an activation record?
   a. A segment of memory used for storing local variables.
   b. A data structure containing return addresses, parameters, and local variables during function calls.
   c. A method for managing the dynamic memory.
   d. A tool for debugging memory issues.

7. Where are activation records typically stored?
   a. Heap
   b. Stack
   c. Data segment
   d. Text segment
8. Which of the following is NOT a component of an activation record?
   a. Return address
   b. Local variables
   c. File descriptors
   d. Parameters
9. Which storage allocation technique requires manual memory management?
   a. Static Allocation
   b. Dynamic Allocation
   c. Stack Allocation
   d. Code Allocation
10. Which of the following functions in C/C++ is used to allocate memory dynamically?
    a. printf
    b. malloc
    c. return
    d. scanf

Answers

1. b
2. b
3. c
4. a
5. b
6. b
7. b
8. c
9. b
10. b

Questions

1. What is the role of run-time environment in program execution, and why is memory management crucial in this context?
2. Explain memory hierarchy, and how the different levels (cache, RAM, disk) influence program performance. Provide examples of when each is utilized.
3. Describe the typical layout of program memory, including sections, such as text, data, heap, and stack. What is the purpose of each section?
4. Compare static and dynamic memory allocation, outlining their differences and common use cases. How does each type impact program performance?
5. Discuss the different memory allocation strategies and best practices. How do techniques, such as first-fit, best-fit, and worst-fit work, and how do they relate to fragmentation issues?
6. What are activation records, and what role do they play in managing function calls and returns? Describe the components of an activation record, and how they are handled in a stack-based management system.
7. Describe static and dynamic memory allocation techniques in detail. How are functions, such as malloc, calloc, and free used in dynamic memory management in C/C++?
8. Explain the concept of garbage collection in memory management. Compare different types of garbage collection techniques, such as reference counting, mark-and-sweep, and generational garbage collection.
9. How do Unix/Linux systems manage memory using system calls, such as the fork, exec, mmap, and brk? Provide example code snippets to illustrate memory allocation and deallocation.
10. What are some common pitfalls in memory management, such as memory leaks and dangling pointers? How can these issues be avoided, and what tools or techniques can help debug and resolve memory-related issues in large-scale applications?

Key Terms

- **Run-Time Environment**: This refers to the system's infrastructure that supports program execution, providing essential resources, such as memory and CPU cycles.
- **Memory Management Role**: Memory management is crucial for ensuring that programs run efficiently by allocating, utilizing, and freeing memory as needed during execution.
- **Performance Impact**: Efficient memory management directly improves program performance by minimizing delays related to memory access, and preventing slowdowns due to poor allocation.
- **Memory Hierarchy**: The memory system is structured hierarchically, with faster but smaller memories, such as cache at the top, followed by the RAM, and slower, larger storage, such as hard disks.
- **Program Memory Layout**: In a typical program, the memory is divided into sections, such as the **text** (for code), **data** (global variables), **heap** (dynamic memory), and **stack** (local variables and function calls).
- **Static Memory Allocation**: This is the memory that is allocated during the compilation of a program, such as global or static variables, allowing predictability but lacking runtime flexibility.

- **Dynamic Memory Allocation**: This allocation occurs during program execution, providing flexibility, especially when the memory needs are uncertain at the compile time. Functions, such as malloc and free are used in C/C++ for this.
- **Memory Fragmentation**: Fragmentation occurs, when the available memory is broken into non-contiguous chunks, leading to inefficient memory use. It can be minimized with techniques, such as defragmentation or memory compaction.
- **Activation Records**: Also known as stack frames, activation records hold information necessary for executing functions, such as return addresses, parameters, and local variables.
- **Stack Management**: The stack grows and shrinks as functions are called and completed. Each function call generates an activation record on the stack, managing the function's local context.
- **Garbage Collection**: An automatic process that reclaims memory which is no longer in use. Techniques include **reference counting** where objects are deleted, when their reference count reaches zero, and **mark-and-sweep** which identifies unreachable objects.
- **Memory Leaks**: A memory leak happens, when the dynamically allocated memory is not properly freed, leading to wasted memory resources. This can degrade performance over time, especially in long-running applications.
- **Stack vs. Heap**: The stack is used for static memory allocation (for example, local variables and function calls), while the heap is used for dynamic memory allocation, allowing greater control but requiring explicit management.
- **System Calls in Unix/Linux**: System calls, such as fork (to create a new process), exec (to execute a new program), mmap (to map files into the memory), and brk (to change the data segment size) are essential in the Unix/Linux memory management.

CHAPTER 10
Function Calls and Exception Handling

Introduction

In the world of programming, writing efficient and error-resistant code is crucial. As we move forward in this journey, this chapter focuses on two fundamental concepts: **function calls and exception handling**. These elements are essential for building modular and reliable software that can gracefully handle unexpected situations.

Before we dive into the details, let us revisit what we learned in *Chapter 9, Run-Time Environment and Memory Management*. In that chapter, we explored how memory is structured and managed during program execution. We discussed different memory segments, such as the stack and heap, and how **activation records** help manage function calls by storing necessary information, such as local variables and return addresses. We also covered various **storage allocation techniques**, and how Unix/Linux systems utilize them to optimize the memory usage.

Now, in this chapter, we will expand on those concepts by looking at how **function calls** work behind the scenes. We will explore the mechanics of calling functions, passing parameters, and managing return values. Understanding how data is passed–whether by value, reference, or name–helps us to write more efficient code, while making the best use of memory resources.

We will also dive into the concept of **exception handling** which is critical for building robust applications that can handle errors gracefully without crashing. We will cover key constructs, such as try-catch blocks, throwing exceptions, and ensuring proper cleanup with finally, blocks. You will also learn how exceptions propagate through function calls, and how to effectively manage them.

By the end of this chapter, you will have a solid understanding of how to make your code modular, efficient, and resilient to unexpected errors, laying a strong foundation for building professional-grade software applications.

Structure

In this chapter, we will discuss the following topics:

- Introduction to Function Calls and Exception Handling
    - Overview of Function Calls and Exception Handling in Programming
    - Significance of these Concepts in Software Development
    - Relationship between Function Calls and Memory Management
- Parameters Passing Techniques
    - Pass by Value
    - Pass by Reference

    - Pass by Name
    - Comparison of Parameter Passing Techniques
- Handling Function Calls and Returns
    - Function Call Mechanism
    - Returning Values from Functions
    - Nested Function Calls
- Exception Handling Mechanisms
    - Overview of Exceptions
    - Types of Exceptions
    - Exception Handling Constructs
    - Propagation of Exceptions
- Example Implementations using Unix/Linux Memory Management
    - Function Calls in Unix/Linux
    - Memory Management during Function Calls
    - Handling Exceptions in Unix/Linux
- Best Practices for Function Calls and Exception Handling
    - Guidelines for Writing Effective Function Calls
    - Strategies for Implementing Robust Exception Handling
    - Importance of Documentation and Clarity in Function Definitions
    - Common Pitfalls to Avoid

Introduction to Function Calls and Exception Handling

In software development, the ability to write organized, efficient, and resilient code is crucial. As programs become more complex, developers rely on various techniques to break down tasks into simpler components, and handle unexpected issues seamlessly. This is where **function calls** and **exception handling** come into play. Understanding these concepts is key to developing robust applications that not only perform well but are also easier to debug and maintain. In this section, we will explore the fundamentals of function calls and exception handling, delving into their significance, and how they impact the way programs manage memory and system resources.

Overview of Function Calls and Exception Handling in Programming

Function calls and exception handling are fundamental aspects of programming that help make code more efficient and resilient.

A **function call** is simply the act of invoking a block of code that performs a specific task. Instead of writing the same code multiple times, you can create a function and call, it whenever needed. This not only saves time but also makes your program more modular and easier to understand. Function calls enable breaking down complex problems into smaller, reusable pieces, which improves code organization and readability.

On the other hand, **exception handling** is a way to manage errors that might occur during the execution of a program. Instead of letting a program crash when it encounters a problem, exception handling allows you to detect these errors, respond to them, and keep your program running smoothly. This is especially important in real-world applications where unexpected situations, such as invalid user input or network issues, can arise.

Together, function calls and exception handling are essential tools that programmers use to create software which is both reliable and maintainable, ensuring that applications work correctly, even in unpredictable situations.

Significance of these Concepts in Software Development

Function calls and exception handling are critical components that contribute to the overall effectiveness of software development. Here is why these concepts are so significant:

- **Modular Code Structure**: These are function calls to break down complex programs into smaller, reusable units, promoting an organized and readable code.
- **Improved Maintainability**: These functions allow updates and changes to be made in one place, without affecting the rest of the program, making the code easier to maintain.
- **Code Reusability**: Using these functions prevents code duplication, saving the development time and reducing errors.
- **Efficient Debugging**: Modular functions simplify debugging by isolating the specific parts of the code, making it easier to identify and fix issues.
- **Enhanced Error Resilience**: Exception handling enables programs to detect and manage errors gracefully, preventing unexpected crashes.
- **Improved User Experience**: By handling exceptions properly, applications can continue running smoothly, even when unexpected errors occur, leading to a more stable user experience.
- **Data Integrity and Safety**: Exception handling helps to protect data by ensuring that errors do not result in data corruption or loss.
- **Scalability and Flexibility**: These concepts allow the software to adapt more easily to new requirements, making it scalable for future enhancements.

Relationship between Function Calls and Memory Management

Function calls and memory management are deeply interconnected in how programs function efficiently behind the scenes.

When a function is called, the system allocates memory to store its parameters, local variables, and information about where to return after the function finishes. This information is stored in a structure called the **call stack**. Each time, a new function is invoked, a **stack frame** is added to the call stack, holding all the necessary data for that function. Once the function finishes its task, this memory is automatically freed up as the stack frame is removed.

However, if functions are called too frequently, especially in recursive scenarios, the stack can fill up, leading to a **stack overflow** error. This is why understanding how memory is allocated during function calls is important–it helps prevent such issues, and ensures that your program runs smoothly.

By being mindful of how memory is used with function calls, developers can write the code that not only performs well but also uses system resources efficiently. This balance is key to building reliable and scalable software applications.

Parameter Passing Techniques

When working with functions, an important aspect to consider is how data is transferred between different parts of a program. This is where **parameter passing techniques** come into play. Understanding these techniques is crucial for ensuring that functions receive the data, they need to perform their tasks efficiently while also managing how changes to that data are handled. Let us explore the various ways in which parameters can be passed to functions, each with its own unique characteristics and use cases.

Pass by Value

A fundamental concept in working with functions is understanding how the data is passed to them. One widely used method is **pass by value** which ensures that the original data remains unchanged. Let us explore how this technique works, and why it is useful.

Definition and Characteristics

In the **pass by value** technique, a copy of the actual value of the variable is passed to the function. This means that the function works with a separate copy, leaving the original variable unchanged. Any modifications made to the parameter inside the function do not affect the original data outside the function.

Key Characteristics:

To better understand, how **pass by value** works, let us look at some of its **key characteristics** that define its behavior and benefits.

- The function operates on a copy of the original data, not the actual variable.
- Any changes made inside the function are limited to the local copy, and do not impact the original variable outside the function.
- This is ideal for scenarios where you want to protect the original data from being altered accidentally.

Example Scenarios and Implications

Consider a scenario where you want to calculate a bonus on a bank account balance, without changing the original balance:

```
def add_bonus(balance):
balance += 100 # Adding a bonus to the local copy
print(f"Balance inside function: {balance}")

# Original balance before calling the function
account_balance = 1000
add_bonus(account_balance)

# Check the balance after the function call
print(f"Original balance outside function: {account_balance}")
```

Output:

```
Balance inside function: 1100
Original balance outside function: 1000
```

In this example, the `account_balance` remains 1000 outside the function, even though the function added a bonus. This happens because only a copy of the `account_balance` was used within the function, leaving the original variable unchanged.

Implications:

Understanding the implications of using **pass by value** can help you decide, when it is the best approach for your code. Here is why it matters, and when it can be particularly beneficial:

- Useful for ensuring that the critical data remains unmodified, especially when working with sensitive information.
- However, copying large data structures, (such as lists or dictionaries) can be memory-intensive and slightly slower, since the function needs to create duplicates.

Pass by Reference

When working with functions, **pass by reference** is another essential technique that allows functions to work directly with the original data. This method is different from pass by value, as it enables changes to be reflected outside the function. Let us explore how it works and its benefits.

Definition and Characteristics

In **pass by reference**, instead of passing a copy of the variable, the function receives a direct reference (or address) to the original variable. This means that any changes made to the variable inside the function will directly affect the original value. The function operates on the actual data, not just a copy, making it possible to modify the original variable from within the function.

Key Characteristics:

To fully understand the power and potential pitfalls of **pass by reference**, it is important to look at its **key characteristics**. These features define how it behaves, and when it is best used.

- The function works directly with the original variable's memory location.
- Any modifications made within the function are reflected in the original variable.
- Useful for optimizing performance with large data structures, as no extra copies are created.
- This can potentially lead to unintended side effects if not used carefully, as changes inside the function affect the original data.

Use Cases and Practical Examples

Pass by reference is especially useful in scenarios where you want a function to modify the original variable or when working with large data structures, such as lists or dictionaries, to avoid the overhead of copying data.

For instance, consider a situation where you need to update a list of student grades:

```
def add_extra_credit(grades):
    for i in range(len(grades)):
        grades[i] += 5  # Adding extra credit to each grade

# Original list of grades
student_grades = [80, 85, 90]
add_extra_credit(student_grades)

# Check the grades after the function call
print(f"Updated grades: {student_grades}")
```

Output:

```
Updated grades: [85, 90, 95]
```

In this example, the **`student_grades`** list is modified directly within the function. Because the list was passed by reference, changes inside the function affected the original list.

Implications:

Understanding the **implications** of using **pass by reference** will help you make better decisions about when to use it in your code. Let us dive into why and when this technique can be beneficial, as well as the things to be cautious about.

- Efficient for handling a large data since no duplicates are created.
- Useful when you want a function to modify or update the original data.
- Requires careful use to avoid unintended changes to the data which can lead to bugs, if not managed properly.

Pass by Name

Pass by name is a more uncommon parameter-passing technique that differs from the usual pass by value or reference methods. In this approach, the argument passed to a function is treated as an expression, and is evaluated every time it is used within the function. Let us explore what makes this technique unique.

Concept and Unique Aspects

Pass by name is a less common parameter-passing technique, primarily found in some programming languages, such as Algol. In this approach, the argument passed to the function is not evaluated before being passed. Instead, the function receives an expression (a piece of code), and this expression is re-evaluated each time, it is used in the function. Essentially, the parameter is substituted directly into the function's code, and the expression is evaluated whenever it is referenced. This is quite different from the other methods, such as pass by value or reference, where the value or reference is passed to the function directly.

Key Aspects:

To better understand how **pass by name** works, and its impact on your code, it's important to look at its **key aspects**. These unique features distinguish it from other parameter-passing methods, and highlight its behavior in different programming scenarios.

- The argument is an expression, not a value or reference.
- The expression is re-evaluated each time, it is used inside the function.
- This method can lead to unexpected results, especially if the expression is complex or involves side effects.

Use Cases and Practical Examples

Pass by name can be useful in specific scenarios where you want to delay the evaluation of arguments or perform multiple evaluations of an expression within a function. However, it is rarely used in modern programming languages because it can lead to confusion or inefficiency.

Here is a simple example to illustrate pass by name:

```
# In Python, a function simulating pass by name
def simulate_pass_by_name(expression):
    return expression + expression  # The expression is re-evaluated

x = 5
result = simulate_pass_by_name(x + 2)  # Expression x + 2 will be re-evaluated
print(result)
```

Output:

```
14
```

In this example, `x + 2` is treated as an expression, and is re-evaluated within the function. The result is calculated as `(x + 2) + (x + 2)` which is **14**.

Implications:

Considering the **implications** of **pass by name** will help you decide, when it is appropriate to use, and when it may introduce unnecessary complexity. Let us take a closer look at how this method can affect your code's performance and behavior.

- This can be used in certain cases for optimization or handling complex expressions, but its use is generally avoided in modern programming due to complexity and the potential for bugs.
- It can make the code harder to read, and debug because expressions are evaluated multiple times, and may have side effects.

Comparison of Parameter Passing Techniques

In programming, selecting the correct method for passing parameters to functions is essential. The most commonly used techniques are **pass by value**, **pass by reference**, and **pass by name**. Each method offers its own set of advantages and disadvantages, and understanding these will help you determine the best technique for your specific requirements.

Advantages and Disadvantages of Passing Techniques

Understanding the strengths and weaknesses of each parameter passing technique is essential for making informed decisions in programming. Let us now take a closer look at the **advantages** and **disadvantages** of **pass by value**, **pass by reference**, and **pass by name** to better understand how they can impact your code and performance.

- **Pass by Value**
  - **Advantages**:
    - Simple and intuitive; the function works with a copy of the data, ensuring that the original data is unaltered.
    - No risk of unintended side effects because changes made inside the function do not reflect outside.
  - **Disadvantages**:
    - Less efficient for large data structures, as it requires copying the data.
    - Changes inside the function do not affect the original variable.
- **Pass by Reference**
  - **Advantages**:
    - More efficient with large data structures because no copies are made; the function works directly with the original data.
    - Allows modification of the original data which can be useful in certain scenarios.
  - **Disadvantages**:
    - Changes made inside the function affect the original data which could lead to unintended side effects.
    - Harder to debug due to the potential for hidden modifications of the data.

- **Pass by Name**
  - **Advantages**:
    - Flexible and useful in situations where you need to delay evaluation or want to work with expressions instead of values.
  - **Disadvantages**:
    - More difficult to understand and debug, as the argument is treated as an expression and evaluated multiple times.
    - Can result in inefficiency, if the expression involves repeated calculations.

Comparison Table for Parameter Passing Techniques

Here is a comparison table to summarize the key differences between **pass by value**, **pass by reference**, and **pass by name**. This will help you quickly understand the advantages and disadvantages of each method.

Technique	Advantages	Disadvantages
Pass by Value	• Simple and safe • No side effects	• Less efficient with large data • Cannot modify the original data
Pass by Reference	• More efficient for large data • Modifies original data	• Unintended side effects • Harder to debug
Pass by Name	• Flexible and allows delayed evaluation • Useful in specific contexts	• Hard to debug • Inefficient with repeated evaluations

***Table 10.1**: Key differences between pass by value, pass by reference, and pass by name.*

Handling Function Calls and Returns

When a program invokes a function, it temporarily suspends its execution, jumps to the function code, performs the necessary computations or actions, and then returns control to the calling part of the program. Understanding the handling of function calls and returns is crucial for effective programming, as it allows proper flow control, resource management, and debugging.

Function Call Mechanism

In programming, **function calls** are a fundamental concept that allows the code to be organized into reusable blocks. These blocks of code, known as functions, are executed when called upon. The process of calling and returning from a function involves several key steps that are managed by the **call stack**, a data structure that plays a crucial role in the execution of programs.

Steps Involved in a Function Call

When a function is invoked, several key steps occur to ensure that the function executes correctly, and the program returns to the right place after the function has completed its task.

Step 1: Function Invocation

- The process begins when the program encounters a function call. This can be initiated by using the function's name, and passing the required arguments (if any).

- **Example**:

```
result = add(5, 10)  # Calling the 'add' function with two arguments
```

Step 2: Argument Passing

- When the function is called, the values or references passed to it (arguments) are provided to the function's parameters.
- The way arguments are passed may vary:
  - **Pass-by-value**: Copies the value of the argument into the function.
  - **Pass-by-reference**: Provides the function with access to the actual data, allowing it to modify the original argument.

Step 3: Pushing to the Call Stack

- A new frame is created for the function call, and pushed onto the **call stack**. This frame includes:
  - The return address (the point where execution should return after the function completes).
  - The arguments passed to the function.
  - The local variables used within the function.

Step 4: Function Execution

- The function begins executing its code. It works with the provided arguments, and performs its tasks, such as calculations or data manipulation.

Step 5: Return from Function

- Once the function finishes, a **return statement** is typically executed (if there is one). This returns the control to the calling function, possibly along with a return value.
- The stack frame corresponding to the called function is then popped from the call stack, removing it from memory.

Step 6: Resuming Execution

- After returning from the function, the program continues executing from the point where the function was initially called, using any returned values as needed.

Role of the Call Stack in Managing Function Calls

The **call stack** is a specialized memory structure that is used to manage function calls, tracking the active functions in the program, and the state of each function.

Function Call Storage:

Every time a function is called, a new **stack frame** is created and added to the call stack. The stack frame contains essential information about the function:

- **The return address**: Where the program should resume after the function finishes.
- **Function arguments**: The data passed into the function.
- **Local variables**: The variables defined within the function.

This organization helps ensure that each function call has its own space in the memory, and the program can properly resume after each function call.

Last In, First Out (LIFO) Principle:

The call stack operates on a **LIFO** principle, meaning that the last function called will be the first one to return. This is essential for maintaining the correct flow of execution, especially when there are multiple nested function calls.

Example:

If **`funcA()`** calls **`funcB()`**, and then **`funcB()`** calls **`funcC()`**, the call stack will store the calls in the order they are made:

```
[funcC, funcB, funcA]
```

As functions complete, the stack frames are popped off, and the control returns to the previous function:

```
[funcB, funcA] (after funcC returns)
[funcA] (after funcB returns)
    [ ] (after funcA returns)
```

Nested Function Calls:

When a function calls another function within its body, the current function is paused, and a new function call is pushed onto the stack. Once the inner function finishes, the control returns to the outer function which resumes execution.

Example:

```
def outer_function():
    print("Inside outer function")
    inner_function()

def inner_function():
    print("Inside inner function")

outer_function()
```

Call Stack Flow:

- Initially, the stack is empty.
- **`outer_function()`** is called, and its frame is pushed onto the stack.
- Inside **`outer_function()`**, **`inner_function()`** is called, pushing its frame onto the stack.
- Once **`inner_function()`** returns, its frame is popped, and the control returns to **`outer_function()`**.
- Finally, **`outer_function()`** completes, and its frame is popped from the stack.

Managing Recursion:

The call stack is particularly important in managing **recursive function calls** where a function calls itself. Each recursive call adds a new stack frame to the call stack. If the function does not reach a base case (an exit condition), the stack will keep growing until it exceeds the stack's limit, causing a **stack overflow**.

Example:

```
def factorial(n):
    if n == 0:
        return 1
    return n * factorial(n - 1)

print(factorial(5))  # Output: 120
```

Stack Depth:

Each recursive call adds a frame to the stack:

```
factorial(5) → factorial(4) → factorial(3) → factorial(2) → factorial(1) →
factorial(0)
```

After reaching the base case (**factorial(0)**), the stack begins to unwind, returning control back to the previous calls, and the function eventually completes.

Stack Overflow:

Stack overflow occurs when the call stack exceeds its allocated memory limit, often caused by infinite recursion or too many nested function calls.

Returning Values from Functions

In programming, functions are often designed to perform a task, and return a result to the caller. The mechanism of returning values allows the output of a function to be used elsewhere in the program. This mechanism is fundamental in organizing the code, reducing redundancy, and creating modular programs.

Mechanisms for Returning Values

When a function completes its task, it can return a value back to the caller using the return keyword. This allows the result of the function to be used by the calling code for further operations or stored in a variable.

Returning a Single Value:

A function can return a single value which is typically the result of some computation or operation. This is the most basic form of returning a value.

Example:

```
def add(a, b):
    return a + b

result = add(5, 3)
print(result)  # Output: 8
```

In the preceding example:

- The **add()** function computes the sum of a and b, and the result is returned to the calling code.
- The return value (**8**) is assigned to the variable result.

Returning None:

A function may not always return a value explicitly. If no return statement is provided, Python functions implicitly return None.

Example:

```
def greet(name):
    print(f"Hello, {name}")

result = greet("Bob")
print(result)  # Output: None
```

In this case, the **greet()** function does not return any value, so **None** is implicitly returned.

Handling Multiple Return Values with Examples

Functions can return more than one value. This allows a function to provide multiple pieces of information back to the caller. In most programming languages, including Python, multiple values can be returned as a collection, (such as a tuple, list, or dictionary).

Returning Multiple Values as a Tuple:

The most common way to return multiple values is by using a tuple. A tuple is an ordered collection of values that can store multiple items of different types.

Example:

```
def divide(a, b):
    quotient = a // b
    remainder = a % b
    return quotient, remainder

result = divide(10, 3)
print(result)  # Output: (3, 1)
```

Here:

- The **divide()** function returns two values: The quotient and the remainder.
- The returned values are packed into a tuple (3, 1) and assigned to the variable result.

Unpacking Multiple Values:

When a function returns multiple values as a tuple, you can unpack the tuple into individual variables for easier access.

Example:

```
def get_dimensions():
    length = 10
    width = 5
    return length, width

# Unpacking the returned tuple
length, width = get_dimensions()
print(length, width)  # Output: 10 5
```

In this example:

- The **get_dimensions()** function returns two values as a tuple: 10 and 5.
- These values are unpacked into the variables, length and width.

Returning Multiple Values as a List:

You can also return multiple values as a list which is a collection that allows you to store values of varying types and sizes.

Example:

```
def get_colors():
    return ["red", "green", "blue"]

colors = get_colors()
print(colors)  # Output: ['red', 'green', 'blue']
```

Here:

- The **get_colors()** function returns a list containing three color names.
- The caller receives this list, and stores it in the colors, variable.

Returning Multiple Values as a Dictionary:

If you need to return multiple values with meaningful names, you can use a dictionary. This is helpful, when you want to associate values with specific keys, making the returned values easier to understand and access.

Example:

```
def get_student_info():
    return {"name": "Divyashree", "age": 25, "major": "Computer Science"}

student_info = get_student_info()
print(student_info)
# Output: {'name': 'Divyashree', 'age': 25, 'major': 'Computer Science'}
```

In this case:

- The **get_student_info()** function returns a dictionary where the keys are "**name**", "**age**", and "**major**".
- The calling code can access specific information easily by using the corresponding key.

Handling Return Values in Practice:

Example 1: Using Multiple Return Values in Calculations

If you need to perform several calculations in a function, and return all the results, you can return multiple values.

Example:

```
def calculate_area_and_perimeter(length, width):
    area = length * width
    perimeter = 2 * (length + width)
    return area, perimeter

area, perimeter = calculate_area_and_perimeter(5, 3)
print(f"Area: {area}, Perimeter: {perimeter}")
# Output: Area: 15, Perimeter: 16
```

In this example:

- The function, **calculate_area_and_perimeter()** returns both the area and perimeter of a rectangle.
- The caller unpacks the values, and uses them for further output.

Example 2: Returning a Custom Data Structure

Sometimes, you may need to return the structured data, such as a collection of related values.

Example:

```
def get_employee_info():
    return {"name": "John", "position": "Software Developer", "salary": 80000}

employee = get_employee_info()
print(f"Name: {employee['name']}, Position: {employee['position']}, Salary:
{employee['salary']}")
# Output: Name: John, Position: Software Developer, Salary: 80000
```

Here:

- The function returns a dictionary with key-value pairs, making it easier to access the employee's information using descriptive keys.

Nested Function Calls

In programming, **nested function calls** occur when one function calls another function within its body. This concept is common in many programming languages, and is often used to break down complex problems into smaller, manageable tasks. The call stack plays a key role in managing these nested function calls, ensuring that each function executes in the correct order, and that the program can return to the appropriate location after completing each function.

Concept of Nested Calls and Implications for the Call Stack

A nested function call happens, when a function makes a call to another function, while it is still executing. These calls can happen at any level of nesting, meaning that a function can call another function, and that second function can, in turn, call yet another function, and so on.

Example of Nested Function Calls:

Here is an example to demonstrate the nested function calls:

```
def outer_function():
    print("Inside outer function")
    inner_function()

def inner_function():
    print("Inside inner function")

outer_function()
```

In this example:

- **`outer_function()`** is called first.
- While **`outer_function()`** is executing, it calls **`inner_function()`**.
- The program pauses execution of **`outer_function()`** and switches to **`inner_function()`**.
- After **`inner_function()`** finishes, the program resumes execution of **`outer_function()`**.

The output of this program will be:

```
Inside outer function
Inside inner function
```

This is a simple case of nested function calls where one function is called within another.

Implications for the Call Stack

The **call stack** plays a vital role in managing the nested function calls. The call stack is a special area in memory that tracks function calls in a program. Each time a function is called, a **stack frame** is created and pushed onto the call stack. This frame holds information about the function, such as its local variables, parameters, and the return address.

How the Call Stack Handles Nested Calls:

- **Function Call and Stack Frame Creation:**
    - When a function is called, a new stack frame is created, and pushed onto the call stack. The stack frame contains:

  - The function's parameters.
  - Local variables.
  - The return address (the point where the program should return, once the function completes).
- **Execution of Inner Function**:
  - If a function makes another function call (nested call), the current function's execution is paused, and the new function is pushed onto the call stack.
  - The call stack keeps track of the order of function calls, ensuring that each function completes and returns in the correct order.
- **Unwinding the Stack**:
  - When a function finishes execution (that is, it returns), its stack frame is popped off the call stack, and control returns to the function that called it.
  - This process continues as functions return, and the call stack shrinks back to the point where the original function was called.
- **Stack Frame Management**:
  - Each nested function call creates its own stack frame, and the stack grows deeper with each new call.
  - When functions return, the stack is unwound in the reverse order, with the most recent function returning first.

Example: Deeply Nested Function Calls

Consider the following example with multiple levels of nested function calls:

```
def level_1():
    print("Level 1 start")
    level_2()

def level_2():
    print("Level 2 start")
    level_3()

def level_3():
    print("Level 3 start")
    print("Level 3 end")

level_1()
```

Step-by-Step Call Stack Process:

- Calling **`level_1()`**:
  - The program begins execution with **`level_1()`**, and its stack frame is pushed onto the call stack.
- Calling **`level_2()`** from **`level_1()`**:
  - Inside **`level_1()`**, the function **`level_2()`** is called. A new stack frame for **`level_2()`** is pushed onto the stack, pausing **`level_1()`**, until **`level_2()`** returns.
- Calling **`level_3()`** from **`level_2()`**:
  - Similarly, inside **`level_2()`**, **`level_3()`** is called. A new stack frame for **`level_3()`** is created, and added to the stack.
- Returning from **`level_3()`**:

    - Once **`level_3()`** finishes executing, its stack frame is popped off the stack, and control returns to **`level_2()`** which continues its execution.
- Returning from **`level_2()`**:
    - After **`level_2()`** finishes, its stack frame is popped off the stack, and control returns to **`level_1()`**.
- Returning from **`level_1()`**:
    - Finally, after **`level_1()`** completes, its stack frame is removed from the stack, and the program finishes execution.

Output:

```
Level 1 start
Level 2 start
Level 3 start
Level 3 end
Level 2 end
Level 1 end
```

Implications of Nested Function Calls

Call Stack Depth:

Every nested function call adds a new stack frame to the call stack. If there are too many nested calls, the call stack may become very deep, leading to a **stack overflow** error.

A **stack overflow** occurs when the program exceeds the maximum allowed depth of the call stack which can happen in cases of deep recursion or excessive nesting of function calls.

Example:

```
def recursive_function(n):
    if n == 0:
        return
    recursive_function(n - 1)

recursive_function(10000) # This could cause a stack overflow if n is large
```

Memory Usage:

Each function call consumes memory on the call stack to store the local variables, parameters, and return address. In programs with a lot of nested function calls, this can result in increased memory usage.

Function Execution Order:

The **call stack** ensures that functions are executed in the correct order, maintaining the integrity of nested calls. When a function finishes executing, the call stack unwinds, returning to the previous function in the call hierarchy.

Exception Handling Mechanisms

When writing a software, handling errors or unexpected situations is crucial to ensuring smooth program execution. **Exception handling** is a technique that allows programs to respond to errors or unusual conditions, without crashing, ensuring that programs run smoothly and predictably. In this section, we will explore **exceptions** in detail, starting with their definition, and understanding their importance in programming.

Overview of Exceptions

Exceptions are events or conditions that disrupt the normal flow of a program's execution. They can arise from a variety of factors, such as invalid user input, unavailable resources, or programming bugs. Instead of causing the program to stop abruptly, exceptions provide a structured way for developers to manage and recover from such errors.

Definition of Exceptions and Their Significance

An **exception** is essentially an error condition that occurs during the execution of a program. It is typically represented by an object or a signal that indicates something went wrong. Exceptions can be triggered by the system or manually by the programmer.

Significance of Exceptions:

Now, let us look at why exceptions are important, and how they help improve the reliability of a program:

- **Error Detection and Handling**: Exceptions allow programs to detect errors early, and handle them gracefully, without crashing.
- **Improved Debugging**: By providing clear error messages and stack traces, exceptions help programmers identify and fix issues more efficiently.
- **Cleaner Code**: With proper exception handling, error management is separated from the main program logic, making the code cleaner and more readable.
- **Program Stability**: Exception handling ensures that a program can continue running, even if an error occurs which is essential for reliability in real-world applications.

By handling exceptions appropriately, developers can make their programs more robust and capable of dealing with unforeseen circumstances, without failing unexpectedly.

Types of Exceptions

When writing the code, errors are bound to happen. Understanding the different types of exceptions allows us to manage errors in a structured way. Let us explore **checked** and **unchecked exceptions**, as well as some **common exceptions**, you might encounter during programming.

Checked and Unchecked Exceptions

In this section, we will look at the two main categories of exceptions: Checked and unchecked. Let us break down how and when each type is used.

Checked Exceptions:

- Checked exceptions are exceptions that the compiler requires the programmer to handle. These exceptions usually occur due to external factors, such as file errors or database connectivity problems.
- **Example**: `IOException`, `SQLException`
- **When to Use**: These are used when the program might encounter an error outside its control, such as reading from a file or accessing a database.

Unchecked Exceptions:

- Unchecked exceptions, also known as runtime exceptions, occur due to programming mistakes or logical errors, and the compiler does not force the programmer to handle them.

- **Example**: `NullPointerException`, `ArrayIndexOutOfBoundsException`
- **When to Use**: These are typically used for errors that occur due to bugs in the code, such as trying to access a null value or going beyond the limits of an array.

Common Exceptions in Programming

Now, let us take a look at some of the most common exceptions, programmers deal with, and understand why they occur.

- `NullPointerException`:
  - This exception occurs, when you try to access a method or property on a null object.
  - **Example**: `String name = null; int length = name.length();` – This will throw a NullPointerException because the name is null.
- `ArrayIndexOutOfBoundsException`:
  - This happens, when you try to access an index that is outside the bounds of an array.
  - **Example**: `int[] numbers = {1, 2, 3}; System.out.println(numbers[5]);` – The program will throw this exception because index 5 does not exist in the array.
- `IOException`:
  - Raised when an input/output operation fails, such as when reading from or writing to a file.
  - **Example**: `FileReader file = new FileReader("nonexistentfile.txt");` – This will throw an IOException, if the file does not exist.
- `SQLException`:
  - This occurs, when there is an error interacting with a database, such as an invalid SQL query or a connection issue.
  - **Example**: `Connection conn = DriverManager.getConnection("jdbc:mysql://localhost/db", "user", "password");` – This will throw an exception, if the database connection fails.
- `ArithmeticException`:
  - This exception is thrown, when there is an illegal arithmetic operation, such as dividing by zero.
  - **Example**: `int result = 10 / 0;` – This will throw an ArithmeticException because division by zero is not allowed.

By understanding the different types of exceptions and recognizing the common ones, you will be better equipped to handle them in your code, and create more reliable programs.

Exception Handling Constructs

Exception handling constructs allow programmers to write a more robust code by managing potential errors effectively. Let us dive into **try-catch blocks**, the use of **finally blocks** for cleanup, and how to handle exceptions by **throwing** them.

Try-Catch Blocks: Syntax, Usage, and Examples

A **try-catch block** is the core construct in most programming languages for exception handling. It lets you try a block of code, and catch any exceptions that might occur, ensuring your program does not crash unexpectedly.

A try-catch block is used to catch exceptions, and handle them without terminating the program. If an exception occurs in the try block, the control transfers to the corresponding catch block.

- **Syntax**: The structure of a try-catch block is simple:

```
try {
    // Code that may throw an exception
} catch (ExceptionType e) {
    // Code to handle the exception
}
```

- **Usage:**
  - The **try block** contains the code that could potentially throw an exception.
  - If an exception occurs, the **catch block** catches it, and you can specify how to handle it.
  - Multiple catch blocks can be used to handle different types of exceptions.
- **Example**: Consider the scenario where we attempt to divide a number by zero:

```
try {
    int result = 10 / 0;  // This will throw ArithmeticException
} catch (ArithmeticException e) {
    System.out.println("Error: Division by zero is not allowed.");
}
```

  In this example, an attempt to divide by zero will trigger an `ArithmeticException`. The catch block catches it, and prints an appropriate error message, preventing the program from crashing.

Finally Blocks: Ensuring Cleanup Actions

A **finally block** is used to execute the code after a try-catch block, whether or not an exception was thrown. This block is essential for tasks, such as cleaning up resources (for example, closing files or database connections), that must occur even if an exception is thrown.

- **Syntax**: The structure of a finally block:

```
try {
    // Code that may throw an exception
} catch (ExceptionType e) {
    // Handle the exception
} finally {
    // Code that will always run, used for cleanup
    }
```

- **Usage**:
  - The finally block runs no matter what–whether an exception occurs or not. This makes it ideal for cleanup actions, such as closing files or releasing network resources.
- **Example**: Here is an example of handling file input:

```
FileInputStream file = null;
try {
    file = new FileInputStream("file.txt");
    // Read the file content
} catch (FileNotFoundException e) {
    System.out.println("Error: File not found.");
} finally {
    if (file != null) {
        try {
            file.close();  // Ensuring the file is closed
```

```
                System.out.println("File has been closed.");
            } catch (IOException e) {
                System.out.println("Error while closing the file.");
            }
        }
    }
```

Here, the finally block ensures that the file is closed, even if an exception is thrown during file reading.

Throwing Exceptions: Custom and Built-in Exceptions

There are situations, when you may need to throw exceptions manually. The `throw` keyword allows you to trigger exceptions, based on certain conditions. You can throw both **built-in exceptions**, (such as **`NullPointerException`**) and **custom exceptions** that you define yourself.

- **Throwing Built-in Exceptions**: You can throw a built-in exception, when a specific condition is met:

  ```
  if (age < 0) {
      throw new IllegalArgumentException("Age cannot be negative");
          }
  ```

  In this example, if the age variable is negative, an **`IllegalArgumentException`** is thrown, and the error message specifies the issue.

- **Custom Exceptions**: You can create your own exceptions to handle application-specific errors. Custom exceptions are helpful, when you want more meaningful or descriptive error messages.

- **Creating a custom exception**:

  ```
  public class AgeException extends Exception {
      public AgeException(String message) {
          super(message);  // Pass the error message to the base Exception class
      }
  }
  ```

- **Using the custom exception**:

  ```
  if (age < 0) {
      throw new AgeException("Age cannot be negative");
  }
  ```

Propagation of Exceptions

In this section, we will explore how exceptions propagate through function calls and strategies for managing propagated exceptions effectively. Understanding this process is key to ensuring that errors are handled in a way that prevents the program from crashing unexpectedly, while maintaining the program flow.

How Exceptions Propagate Through Function Calls

When an exception is thrown within a function, it does not remain confined to that function. Instead, it **propagates** or **bubbles up** through the call stack. The call stack is a stack data structure that keeps track of function calls, and when an exception occurs, the program will look for an appropriate handler in the calling functions (the functions in the call stack).

Here is how the propagation works:

- **Exception Occurs**: When an exception is thrown in a function, it looks for a corresponding catch block to handle it.
- **Propagation to Caller**: If the function does not have a catch block for the exception, the exception is propagated to the caller function (the function that called the current function).
- **Continues Propagation**: This process continues up the call stack, until an appropriate handler is found or the top level is reached. If no handler is found at all, the program terminates.

Example of Exception Propagation:

Consider the following functions:

```
public class ExceptionPropagationExample {
    public static void main(String[] args) {
        try {
            methodA();
        } catch (Exception e) {
            System.out.println("Caught exception in main: " + e);
        }
    }

    public static void methodA() throws Exception {
        methodB();
    }

    public static void methodB() throws Exception {
        throw new Exception("Something went wrong in methodB");
    }
}
```

Strategies for Handling Propagated Exceptions with Examples

While exceptions can propagate through the call stack, it is important to handle them effectively to ensure your program is robust and does not crash unexpectedly. Here are some strategies for handling propagated exceptions:

- **Catching Specific Exceptions**: Instead of catching a generic exception, always try to catch the most specific exception type possible. This allows you to handle different types of errors in distinct ways.

  Example:

  ```
  try {
      methodA();
  } catch (FileNotFoundException e) {
      System.out.println("File not found: " + e.getMessage());
  } catch (IOException e) {
      System.out.println("I/O error: " + e.getMessage());
  } catch (Exception e) {
      System.out.println("An unexpected error occurred: " + e.getMessage());
          }
  ```

  By catching specific exceptions first, you can customize the error handling to the context, giving the user clearer feedback.

- **Using Multiple Catch Blocks**: Java allows multiple catch blocks, so if an exception is thrown from a method, it can be caught by one of the parent functions, and you can differentiate between different exception types.

Example:

```
public static void methodA() throws Exception {
    try {
        methodB();
    } catch (FileNotFoundException e) {
        System.out.println("File not found in methodA");
    } catch (Exception e) {
        throw new Exception("Exception in methodA", e);
    }
}
```

In this case, **methodA** catches specific exceptions but rethrows them, if it cannot handle them.

- **Re-throwing Exceptions**: Sometimes, a method may want to handle part of an exception or log the error, but then it needs to pass the exception to a higher-level handler for further processing. This is done by **rethrowing the exception**.

  Example:

```
public static void methodA() throws Exception {
    try {
        methodB();
    } catch (Exception e) {
        System.out.println("Handling exception in methodA");
        throw e;  // Rethrow the exception to be handled by the caller
    }
}
```

  By rethrowing the exception, the caller has the chance to catch and deal with it.

- **Propagating Exceptions to the Calling Function**: Sometimes, you might not want to handle the exception at all in the current method. Instead, you can simply declare that the method throws the exception to its caller.

  Example:

```
public static void methodA() throws Exception {
    methodB();  // Let methodB throw the exception to the caller
}
```

  This ensures that the exception is propagated up the stack for higher-level handling.

Example Implementations using Unix/Linux Memory Management

In this section, we will explore how function calls, and memory management concepts are implemented in Unix/Linux environments. By understanding how system calls, memory allocation, and error handling work in these operating systems, you can gain deeper insights into how the software interacts with the system at a lower level. This knowledge is essential for optimizing program performance, managing resources efficiently, and handling exceptions effectively in a real-world operating system context. Let us dive into some practical examples that demonstrate these concepts in action.

Function Calls in Unix/Linux

In Unix/Linux, function calls are an essential part of how programs interact with the operating system and perform tasks. There are two primary types of function calls: System calls and user-defined functions.

Overview of System Calls and User-Defined Functions

Here, we will look at two important types of function calls in Unix/Linux: System calls and user-defined functions. Understanding how each works will help you to better interact with the system, and write efficient programs.

- **System Calls:** System calls provide the interface through which programs request services from the operating system's kernel. These calls are necessary for performing tasks, such as file manipulation, process management, and memory allocation. For example, when a program wants to read the data from a file or allocate memory, it relies on system calls, such as `open()`, `read()`, or `malloc()`.

  System calls are typically low-level operations that communicate directly with the operating system, allowing programs to perform tasks that require access to system resources or hardware. They ensure that the program runs in a controlled environment, and has access to the resources it needs, while also maintaining the security and stability of the system.

- **User-Defined Functions:** User-defined functions, on the other hand, are custom functions created by the programmer to carry out specific tasks within a program. These functions operate in the user space, and are written using high-level programming languages, such as C, Python, or Java. User-defined functions allow for better code organization, modularity, and reusability, as they enable developers to break down complex problems into smaller, more manageable parts.

  These functions can call system calls to interact with the operating system or manipulate resources, but they do not directly interact with the operating system's kernel, unless explicitly instructed.

  In Unix/Linux, understanding the distinction between system calls and user-defined functions helps developers create efficient, well-structured programs that leverage system resources, while maintaining high-level functionality.

Memory Management During Function Calls

When a function is called in a program, memory management plays a crucial role in ensuring that resources are allocated, and used efficiently. This process involves both **stack memory** and **heap memory**, each serving different purposes. Let us break down how memory is managed during function calls in a program:

Stack Memory Allocation for Function Calls

When a function is called, a special region of memory called the **call stack** is used to store information about the function call, including local variables, function parameters, and the return address. This memory allocation happens automatically, and is temporary. When the function execution completes, the memory used by that function is automatically freed up.

Each time a function is called, a new **stack frame** is created which holds all the data associated with that function call. Once the function returns, the stack frame is removed, and the memory is reclaimed, making the stack memory allocation fast and efficient.

Heap Memory Usage in Function Calls and Returns

Unlike stack memory, **heap memory** is used for dynamic memory allocation. This memory is not automatically managed, and must be explicitly allocated as well as freed by the programmer. Heap memory is useful for situations where the size of the data is not known in advance, or when the memory needs to be shared between functions or even across function calls.

When a function call requires dynamic memory, such as creating a new data structure, it uses **heap memory**. For example, in C, the malloc() function allocates memory in the heap. Once the function returns, the memory in the heap remains allocated, until it is explicitly freed using a function, such as free(). Failure to properly manage the heap memory can result in **memory leaks**, where memory is allocated but never deallocated, causing a program to consume excessive resources.

In summary, understanding how **stack** and **heap** memory work during function calls helps you write efficient and optimized programs that manage memory resources effectively.

Handling Exceptions in Unix/Linux

In Unix/Linux programming, handling exceptions effectively is essential for ensuring that programs run smoothly, even when errors occur. By using proper error-handling techniques, developers can detect and respond to issues in the system, minimizing the risk of crashes or undefined behavior. Let us explore how exceptions are handled in system calls, and the best practices for robust exception handling in Unix/Linux applications.

Examples of Error Handling in System Calls

In Unix/Linux, many system calls return a special value (often -1 or NULL) to indicate an error. When a system call fails, the **errno** variable is set to provide more specific information about the error. The following are common error-handling techniques:

- **Checking Return Values:** Most system calls return a value that indicates success or failure. For example, the **open()** system call returns a file descriptor on success or -1 on failure. In the case of failure, you can check the **errno** variable to determine the exact cause of the error.

```
int fd = open("file.txt", O_RDONLY);
if (fd == -1) {
    perror("Error opening file");
    // Handle error appropriately
}
```

- **Using perror() or strerror():** Functions, such as **perror()** or **strerror()** are often used to print a human-readable error message, based on the current value of the **errno**. This helps developers understand what went wrong.

```
if (fd == -1) {
    perror("Failed to open file");
}
```

  These techniques allow developers to detect errors early, and take corrective actions, such as retrying the operation or terminating the program gracefully.

Best Practices for Robust Exception Handling in Unix/Linux Applications

To build reliable and resilient Unix/Linux applications, it is important to follow the best practices for exception handling:

- **Always Check Return Values:** Many system calls and library functions return special values indicating failure. Always check these values, and handle errors accordingly, rather than assuming success.
- **Use errno for Detailed Error Information:** After a system call failure, use the errno variable to retrieve the detailed information about the error. This helps you to pinpoint the exact cause and take appropriate action.

- **Handle Common Errors Gracefully:** Anticipate common issues, such as file access errors, memory allocation failures, or resource unavailability, and handle them gracefully by either retrying the operation or providing a helpful error message.
- **Avoid Hard-Coding Error Messages:** Instead of hard-coding error messages, use system-provided functions, such as `perror()` or `strerror()` to print meaningful and localized error descriptions.
- **Clean Up Resources:** When handling errors, ensure that any resources, (such as memory, file handles, or network connections) are properly cleaned up to avoid memory leaks or resource exhaustion.
- **Log Errors for Debugging:** Keep a log of errors for troubleshooting and debugging. This will help track down issues in production systems, and make debugging easier.
- **Use Signal Handlers for Critical Errors:** In some cases, you may need to handle critical errors that require special attention. Using signal handlers for events, such as segmentation faults or illegal operations can help you respond to fatal errors appropriately.

By following these best practices, you can ensure that your Unix/Linux applications are resilient, efficient, and easier to maintain, even when exceptions or errors occur.

Best Practices for Function Calls and Exception Handling

Ensuring that function calls and exception handling are implemented correctly is key to building reliable and maintainable software. By following the proven best practices, developers can avoid common pitfalls, enhance code readability, and make their programs more robust. Let us explore some essential guidelines and strategies to help you write effective function calls, and handle exceptions effectively.

Guidelines for Writing Effective Function Calls

Writing efficient and clear function calls is crucial for maintaining readability, and reducing errors in your code. Here are some guidelines to ensure your function calls are effective:

- **Use Descriptive Names:** Always use clear, descriptive names for your functions and parameters so that their purpose is immediately obvious to anyone reading the code.
- **Keep Functions Small and Focused:** Each function should do one thing, and do it well. This promotes reusability and easier debugging. Functions should ideally have a single responsibility.
- **Limit Side Effects:** Minimize side effects within functions. Functions should avoid changing global variables or affecting other parts of the system unexpectedly.
- **Return Meaningful Values:** Ensure that the function returns meaningful results or values that can be used effectively in the program flow. Consider using specific return types, instead of just void or generic values.
- **Parameter Validation:** Always validate the inputs to your functions, especially when dealing with user input or data from external sources, to ensure correctness and prevent unexpected behavior.

Strategies for Implementing Robust Exception Handling

Effective exception handling ensures that your program can recover from unexpected situations, without crashing. Here are some strategies to implement robust exception handling:

- **Catch Specific Exceptions:** Rather than catching all exceptions with a generic handler, catch the specific exceptions that you expect, and know how to handle. This makes error handling more predictable.

- **Use Try-Catch Blocks Wisely:** Place only the code that might throw an exception inside the `try` block. Keep the `try` block focused and concise, with the exception-handling logic in the `catch` block.
- **Do not Overuse Exceptions:** Exceptions should be used for exceptional cases, not for controlling regular program flow. Avoid using them for situations that are part of the expected execution path.
- **Log Exception Details:** Always log the details of the exception, including the type of exception and the stack trace, so that you can diagnose and address the issue later.
- **Graceful Program Termination:** Ensure that after catching an exception, the program terminates gracefully. Clean up resources, such as open files or database connections, before the program ends.

Importance of Documentation and Clarity in Function Definitions

Well-documented function definitions not only make your code easier to understand but also help others (and yourself) to use and maintain it effectively. Here is why documentation matters:

- **Helps with Code Readability:** Clear documentation ensures that anyone reviewing the code understands the purpose and behavior of the function without having to dig into the implementation details.
- **Provides Usage Instructions:** Documenting the expected inputs, outputs, and side effects of a function helps others use it correctly, reducing errors and misuse.
- **Improves Maintainability:** A well-documented function is easier to maintain and update because the logic and reasoning behind design decisions are clearly stated.
- **Serves as a Reference:** When teams grow or work is passed between developers, documentation serves as an important reference to speed up the learning process and reduce the need for excessive explanation.

Common Pitfalls to Avoid

Here are some common mistakes to avoid when dealing with function calls and exception handling:

- **Ignoring Error Handling:** Failing to handle errors and exceptions properly can cause your program to crash or behave unpredictably. Always anticipate errors and plan for recovery.
- **Overly Complex Functions:** Functions that try to do too much are harder to understand and maintain. Keep your functions simple and focused on a single task.
- **Not Using Exceptions When Necessary:** Avoid neglecting the use of exceptions for exceptional situations. Relying solely on return codes or error values can make your program hard to debug and maintain.
- **Using Generic Exception Handlers:** Catching all exceptions with a generic handler can mask underlying issues. Always catch specific exceptions and handle them appropriately.
- **Lack of Proper Logging:** Failing to log exceptions or errors can make troubleshooting difficult. Always ensure that enough information is logged to understand the cause of any issues.

By following these guidelines and strategies, you can write better, more reliable functions and handle exceptions effectively, resulting in cleaner, more maintainable code.

Conclusion

In this chapter, we explored the intricacies of function calls and exception handling which are essential for writing efficient and maintainable software. By understanding how functions interact with memory, and the best practices for managing errors, we can build more resilient applications. We also looked into different parameter passing techniques, and how exceptions can propagate through function calls, reinforcing the importance of error management in robust software development.

As we move forward to *Chapter 11, Code Generation and Instruction Selection*, we will transition from high-level programming concepts to the low-level details of how the code is translated into machine instructions. This chapter will cover target machine architectures, techniques for selecting efficient instructions, and strategies for optimizing register allocation. We will also explore practical examples using tools, such as **GCC** and **LLVM** to understand how compilers optimize code generation, ultimately bridging the gap between the code written by developers, and the instructions executed by the hardware.

Points to Remember

- Functions allow code reuse, simplifying complex tasks into manageable blocks.
- The call stack manages function execution and tracks active function calls.
- Parameter passing determines how data is sent to functions.
- Pass by value protects the original data from unintended changes.
- Pass by reference allows functions to modify original variables.
- Pass by name delays expression evaluation until it is used within the function.
- Exceptions occur when a program encounters an unexpected condition.
- Handling exceptions ensures the program continues running smoothly.
- Try-catch blocks detect and manage exceptions during execution.
- The finally block guarantees code execution even if an error occurs.
- Throwing exceptions allows explicit error signaling in functions.
- Checked exceptions require handling during compilation for reliability.
- Unchecked exceptions occur at runtime without mandatory handling.
- Exception propagation moves errors up the call stack if not caught.
- Unix/Linux system calls provide direct access to operating system functions.
- Stack memory is allocated for function calls and local variables.
- Heap memory is used for dynamic data allocation at runtime.

Multiple Choice Questions

1. What is the primary purpose of a function call in programming?
    a. To divide the program into smaller parts
    b. To improve memory management
    c. To define data types
    d. To optimize I/O operations

2. Which parameter passing technique creates a copy of the argument in the function?
   a. Pass by Reference
   b. Pass by Name
   c. Pass by Value
   d. Pass by Function
3. In which parameter passing method, does the called function modify the original variable?
   a. Pass by Value
   b. Pass by Reference
   c. Pass by Copy
   d. Pass by Name
4. Which parameter passing technique is the least commonly used, but can have specific uses in lazy evaluation?
   a. Pass by Value
   b. Pass by Reference
   c. Pass by Name
   d. Pass by Variable
5. What role does the call stack play in function calls?
   a. It manages the flow of multiple variables.
   b. It stores return values from functions.
   c. It manages function calls and local variables.
   d. It handles exceptions in the code.
6. How does a function return values in most of the programming languages?
   a. By pushing values onto the stack
   b. By copying values to the heap
   c. By using a special return register
   d. By using an I/O operation
7. Which of the following statements is true about nested function calls?
   a. They are executed simultaneously.
   b. Each function call creates its own stack frame.
   c. The innermost function is always executed first.
   d. They do not affect the call stack.
8. What is an exception in programming?
   a. An event that disrupts the normal flow of execution.
   b. A method for optimizing the code.

c. A way to pass arguments to functions.

d. A type of memory error.

9. Which of the following is a checked exception in Java?

   a. `ArrayIndexOutOfBoundsException`

   b. `IOException`

   c. `ArithmeticException`

   d. `NullPointerException`

10. What is the purpose of a finally block in exception handling?

    a. To catch specific types of exceptions

    b. To return values from a function

    c. To ensure cleanup actions are performed

    d. To propagate exceptions

11. Which of the following is the correct syntax for a try-catch block in Java?

    a. `try { code } catch(Exception e) { handle }`

    b. `try { handle } finally { code }`

    c. `catch { code } try(Exception e) { handle }`

    d. `try catch(Exception e) { handle } finally { code }`

12. In which memory area are local variables and function calls stored during execution?

    a. Heap memory

    b. Stack memory

    c. Static memory

    d. Cache memory

13. How are exceptions propagated in a program?

    a. From the lowest to the highest level of function calls

    b. From the highest to the lowest level of function calls

    c. Exceptions cannot propagate

    d. They are handled immediately, and never propagate

14. Which system call in Unix/Linux is used for creating a new process?

    a. `fork()`

    b. `exec()`

    c. `wait()`

    d. `open()`

15. Which of the following best describes pass by value?
    a. The caller function passes a reference to the original variable.
    b. The caller function passes a copy of the original variable.
    c. The caller function passes a name to be evaluated at the runtime.
    d. The caller function passes the variable by the memory location.

Answers

1. a
2. c
3. b
4. c
5. c
6. c
7. b
8. a
9. b
10. c
11. a
12. b
13. a
14. a
15. b

Questions

1. Explain the significance of function calls and exception handling in software development. How do these concepts contribute to building robust and maintainable programs?
2. Compare and contrast the different parameter passing techniques–Pass by Value, Pass by Reference, and Pass by Name. Provide examples to illustrate their behavior, and discuss the scenarios where each method is most appropriate.
3. Describe the role of the call stack in managing function calls. What happens at each step, when a function is called, and how does the call stack manage nested function calls?
4. Discuss the various mechanisms for returning values from functions. How can multiple return values be handled in programming languages, such as Python? Provide an example to demonstrate your answer.
5. Define and explain the concept of nested function calls. What implications do nested function calls have on the call stack, and how can they affect memory management? Provide a visual representation, if possible.

6. What are exceptions in programming? Describe the difference between checked and unchecked exceptions, and provide examples of common exceptions encountered in programming.
7. Explain the syntax and usage of Try-Catch blocks in exception handling. How do finally blocks ensure proper cleanup of resources, and when would you use custom exceptions in your code?
8. Describe how exceptions propagate through function calls. What strategies can be used to effectively handle exceptions that propagate across multiple functions in a program? Include examples to support your explanation.
9. Discuss how function calls are managed in Unix/Linux systems. Explain the system call mechanism, and describe the stack memory allocation and heap memory usage during function execution.
10. Outline the best practices for writing effective function calls and implementing robust exception handling in software development. What common pitfalls should be avoided, and why is documentation important in defining function behavior?

Key Terms

- **Function Call**: A mechanism to execute a block of code defined within a function, often with input parameters and returning outputs.
- **Call Stack**: A data structure that manages function calls, and returns in memory, playing a critical role in tracking execution flow.
- **Parameter Passing**: Techniques to send data to functions, including pass by value, pass by reference, and pass by name.
- **Pass by Value**: The method of passing a copy of data to a function, meaning changes within the function do not affect the original variable.
- **Pass by Reference**: The technique of passing the actual memory address of data, allowing modifications within the function to alter the original variable.
- **Pass by Name**: A less common parameter-passing technique where the expression itself is passed, evaluated only when used within the function.
- **Exception**: An unexpected event that disrupts the normal flow of a program, often due to errors, such as invalid input or system failures.
- **Exception Handling**: A programming construct that helps manage errors gracefully using `try`, `catch`, and `finally` blocks.
- **Try-Catch Block**: A structure that allows handling exceptions by trying a block of code, and catching errors if they occur.
- **Finally Block**: Executes code regardless of whether an exception was thrown; often used for cleanup actions, such as closing files or releasing resources.
- **Throwing Exceptions**: Manually generating exceptions using the `throw` keyword to indicate that an error has occurred.
- **Checked vs. Unchecked Exceptions**: Checked exceptions are errors that must be handled at compile time, while unchecked exceptions are runtime errors that may not be caught.
- **Propagation of Exceptions**: The process by which an exception moves up the call stack if not handled within the function where it occurred.
- **System Calls in Unix/Linux**: Predefined functions provided by the operating system to interact with hardware, and perform low-level tasks.

CHAPTER 11
Code Generation and Instruction Selection

Introduction

In *Chapter 10, Function Calls and Exception Handling*, we explored the mechanisms that manage program execution, including how functions interact with memory, and how exceptions are handled to ensure the stability of software applications. We also looked at how different parameter-passing techniques play a role in how data is transferred between functions, and how these concepts contribute to efficient memory usage and error management in programming.

As we progress into *Chapter 11, Code Generation and Instruction Selection*, we shift our focus to the final stage of program development, that is, converting high-level code into machine-readable instructions. This phase is essential for ensuring that a program runs efficiently on a specific target machine. In this chapter, we will cover the process of **code generation** which translates abstract instructions into the machine code that the processor understands, and **instruction selection**, the technique for choosing the most efficient machine instructions based on the target architecture.

We will also explore how **target machine architecture**, such as **RISC** and **CISC**, impacts the way code is generated, along with techniques for **register allocation** to optimize how variables are stored and accessed by the CPU. Finally, we will examine the various **optimization strategies** that make the generated code more efficient, and discuss how tools, such as **GCC** and **LLVM** use these techniques to generate code for different platforms.

By the end of this chapter, you will gain a deep understanding of how compilers create efficient machine code, making your programs run effectively on various hardware, and how instruction selection and optimization can dramatically improve performance.

Structure

In this chapter, we will discuss the following topics:

- **Introduction to Code Generation**
  - Purpose and Importance of Code Generation
  - Overview of Key Concepts
- **Target Machine Architecture**
  - RISC versus CISC Architectures
  - Examples of Architectures
  - Impact of Architecture on Code Generation

- **Instruction Selection Techniques**
  - Definition of Instruction Selection
  - Instruction Selection Methods
  - Optimization Techniques
  - Practical Applications of Instruction Selection
- **Register Allocation Strategies**
  - Significance of Register Allocation
  - Techniques for Register Allocation
  - Managing Register Overflow
- **Practical Implementation Insights**
  - Code Generation in GCC
  - Code Generation in LLVM
  - Comparative Overview of GCC and LLVM
  - Real-World Applications and Case Studies

Introduction to Code Generation

As we dive into the technical aspects of software development, one of the most crucial processes that bridge high-level programming with machine execution is **code generation**. In this section, we will explore the purpose, importance, and foundational concepts behind this process, laying the groundwork for understanding how a program written in a high-level language gets translated into something, a computer can understand and execute.

Purpose and Importance of Code Generation

Code generation plays a pivotal role in transforming high-level programming languages into machine-readable instructions. It serves as the critical step where abstract logic, written by developers in languages, such as C++, Java, or Python, is translated into specific instructions that the computer's processor can understand and execute.

Here is why code generation is so important:

- **Translation to Machine Code**: At its core, code generation enables the translation of human-readable code into low-level machine instructions. Without this, computers would not be able to execute the high-level commands written by developers.
- **Performance Optimization**: Good code generation aims to produce highly efficient machine code. This includes selecting the best instructions and optimizing the code to minimize memory usage, and enhance execution speed. Efficient code generation is key to ensuring that applications run smoothly and quickly.
- **Cross-platform Compatibility**: A major purpose of code generation is to allow the software to run on different hardware platforms. Whether an application runs on x86, ARM, or other architectures, code generation ensures that the program is compatible with the underlying machine architecture, facilitating portability and flexibility.
- **Resource Efficiency**: The performance of an application depends heavily on how the generated code interacts with the machine's hardware, such as the CPU, memory, and I/O devices. Code generation strives to make the most efficient use of system resources, ensuring that the software consumes the least amount of memory, and processing power necessary.

In summary, code generation is essential not only for the successful execution of programs but also for their performance across various platforms. A well-designed code generation process enhances the overall effectiveness of a program, making it an indispensable part of modern software development.

Overview of Key Concepts

To fully understand the intricacies of code generation, it is important to first grasp several foundational concepts that form the backbone of this process. These concepts provide insight into how code is translated, optimized, and executed across different machine architectures. Following are the key concepts, you need to understand:

- **Target Machine Architecture**: This refers to the specific design and structure of the processor that the code will run on. The architecture determines how instructions are executed, how memory is managed, and how different hardware components communicate. Code generation needs to be tailored to fit the target machine's architecture, whether it is a Reduced Instruction Set Computing (RISC) or Complex Instruction Set Computing (CISC) system.
- **Instruction Selection**: This is the process of choosing the appropriate machine instructions for a given high-level operation. Based on the target architecture, the code generator selects instructions that perform the desired operations in the most efficient manner. Instruction selection is influenced by the architecture's instruction set, and aims to produce an optimized machine code.
- **Register Allocation**: Registers are small, fast storage locations within the CPU used to store data temporarily during computation. Register allocation is the process of assigning variables or values to these registers during code generation. Efficient register allocation can significantly improve program performance by reducing memory access times.
- **Optimization Techniques**: Code optimization involves making the generated code as efficient as possible. This includes optimizing the use of registers, reducing instruction count, and ensuring that the program runs with minimal memory consumption. Optimization techniques, such as peephole optimization, which reviews and refines small instruction sequences, are employed to improve the generated code's performance.
- **Spilling and Reloading**: When there are not enough registers to store data, spilling occurs, meaning data is temporarily moved to the memory. Reloading is the process of bringing that data back into a register, when needed. Managing spilling and reloading efficiently is crucial for optimizing performance, especially in memory-intensive applications.
- **Code Generation Tools**: Tools, such as the **GNU Compiler Collection (GCC)** and **Low-Level Virtual Machine (LLVM)** play a vital role in code generation by providing frameworks for compiling high-level code into machine-readable instructions. These tools also incorporate optimizations, and ensure that the generated code is appropriate for the target machine architecture.

In essence, understanding these key concepts provides the foundational knowledge necessary to appreciate the complexity and challenges involved in code generation. Each concept plays a significant role in ensuring that the high-level code is transformed into efficient, executable machine code that can run on various platforms.

Target Machine Architecture

The target machine architecture refers to the design of the hardware where the program will run, specifically the Central Processing Unit (CPU), and how it handles instructions. Every CPU has its own way of interpreting and executing the machine code which is essential for a program's performance. The architecture of the machine significantly influences how the program code is generated, optimized, and executed. Understanding the architecture helps developers design software that runs efficiently on the given hardware.

RISC versus CISC Architectures

When it comes to CPU design, two primary architectures are commonly discussed: **Reduced Instruction Set Computing (RISC)** and **Complex Instruction Set Computing (CISC)**. Both the architectures determine how instructions are processed, but they differ in their approach and impact on code generation.

Reduced Instruction Set Computing (RISC)

RISC architectures are designed to have a small and simple set of instructions. These instructions can typically be executed in one clock cycle, making them fast and efficient. However, because the instructions are simpler, more instructions are usually needed to perform complex tasks. So, while the code for RISC-based machines might be longer, it can run faster because each instruction takes less time to execute. In terms of code generation, this means that a compiler must focus on efficiently handling these simple instructions to achieve the desired results.

Complex Instruction Set Computing (CISC)

CISC architectures, on the other hand, have a much larger set of instructions, some of which can perform complex tasks in a single instruction. This allows for shorter code, as more operations can be accomplished with fewer instructions. However, these instructions are typically more complicated, and may take multiple clock cycles to execute. For code generation, this complexity means that the compiler must carefully choose the right instruction to maximize performance, and minimize the number of cycles needed.

Examples of Architectures

To further understand the differences, let us look at two widely used architectures:

x86 Architecture

The **x86** architecture is an example of a CISC processor, commonly used in desktop computers and laptops. It supports a broad range of instructions, including some very complex ones. While this results in efficient code size (fewer instructions), it also means the code must be carefully selected to ensure that the complex instructions are used effectively. In terms of code generation, the compiler for x86 systems focuses on handling these intricate instructions, and optimizing for performance, while keeping the code compact.

ARM Architecture

The **ARM** architecture, known for its use in mobile phones, tablets, and embedded systems, is a great example of a RISC processor. The ARM chips are designed to be energy-efficient which is important for battery-powered devices. The ARM's RISC design uses simpler instructions which may require more instructions to complete a task but are optimized for faster and more efficient processing. Code generation for ARM systems emphasizes creating efficient instructions that make the most of the architecture's energy-saving features.

Impact of Architecture on Code Generation

The choice of machine architecture plays a huge role in how the code is generated, as different architectures have unique features. Here is how the architecture affects the code generation process:

- **Instruction Set**: The number and complexity of instructions vary. The RISC systems focus on simpler, faster instructions which require careful optimization in code generation. The CISC systems offer complex instructions that can handle more tasks in one go but may take longer to execute.

- **Registers**: Registers are small, fast storage locations within the CPU. The RISC architectures tend to have more registers which allows for better performance by reducing memory access. On the other hand, the CISC architectures may have fewer registers, requiring the code to rely more on memory.
- **Memory Model**: In some architectures, such as the ARM, the processor only allows specific instructions to access the memory (using the load/store model). This means that the code generator must create sequences that the load data into registers before it can be processed.
- **Execution Pipeline**: Every CPU architecture has its own way of processing instructions (called pipelining). The RISC architectures often have pipelines that can execute many simple instructions in parallel, while the CISC architectures may handle fewer instructions but with more complexity. A code generator must optimize instructions to avoid bottlenecks, and make the best use of the CPU's pipeline.

The architecture of the machine is crucial in deciding how the code is generated. Whether you are working with a RISC or CISC architecture, each type requires different strategies for selecting instructions, managing registers, and accessing memory. By understanding the target machine architecture, a developer can ensure that the code runs efficiently and optimally on the intended hardware.

Instruction Selection Techniques

Instruction selection is a key step in the process of code generation where the compiler determines which machine-level instructions to use for a given operation. This process involves choosing the most efficient instructions from the target machine's instruction, set to implement the high-level operations described in the source code. It ensures that the generated machine code is both efficient and correct, minimizing the number of instructions executed, and maximizing performance.

Definition of Instruction Selection

Instruction selection refers to the process by which a compiler chooses a set of target machine instructions to implement higher-level programming constructs (such as arithmetic operations, memory access, and control flow). The main goal of instruction selection is to translate abstract representations of the program, (such as the intermediate code) into the low-level code that the target machine can execute. This step significantly affects the performance of the program, as an optimal selection can reduce the number of instructions, and improve the runtime efficiency.

Instruction Selection Methods

There are several methods for instruction selection, each with its own advantages and challenges. The primary goal of these methods is to map high-level operations to the best possible machine instructions. Some common methods include:

Pattern Matching

This method involves matching specific patterns in the Intermediate Representation (IR) of the code to predefined templates or patterns that correspond to machine instructions. These patterns can be simple (for example, adding two numbers) or more complex (for example, a sequence of operations that can be replaced with a single machine instruction). Pattern matching is effective for simple and direct mappings, making it easy to implement.

Tree Matching

Tree matching is a more advanced technique where the IR is viewed as a tree structure, and the goal is to find subtrees that match predefined instruction patterns. Each node of the tree represents a computation, and tree matching helps identify optimal sequences of instructions that can implement these computations more efficiently. It is particularly useful in optimizing complex expressions where individual operations are combined into more efficient ones.

Optimization Techniques

Once the instructions are selected, optimization is applied to improve the efficiency of the generated machine code. The goal of optimization is to reduce the execution time, memory usage, and energy consumption. Some common optimization techniques in instruction selection include:

Peephole Optimization

Peephole optimization is a local optimization technique where the compiler looks at a small "window" (or peephole) of consecutive instructions, and attempts to replace them with a more efficient equivalent. This method is effective for eliminating redundant instructions, optimizing the common instruction sequences, or replacing long instruction sequences with shorter, and faster alternatives. It is a relatively simple optimization that can yield significant improvements in some cases.

Rule-Based Selection

Rule-based selection involves applying a set of predefined rules to the instruction selection process. These rules determine which machine instructions should be chosen based on factors, such as the operation being performed, the operands involved, and the architecture's capabilities. Rule-based selection can be highly efficient because it uses a fixed set of patterns and logic to guide the compiler, making it predictable and easy to implement.

Practical Applications of Instruction Selection

Instruction selection has practical applications in a variety of contexts:

- **Compiler Optimization**: By using efficient instruction selection techniques, compilers can generate a machine code that runs faster, uses less memory, and consumes less power. Optimized instruction selection can result in programs that perform better on specific hardware, such as mobile devices, embedded systems, or high-performance computing machines.
- **Cross-Compilation**: When compiling the code for a different architecture (cross-compilation), the instruction selection process becomes even more crucial. It ensures that the compiler can generate a code that is compatible with the target machine's instruction set, regardless of the source machine's architecture. This is especially important in environments where the software needs to run on different platforms (for example, compiling an application on an x86 machine to run on the ARM-based smartphones).
- **Embedded Systems**: Embedded systems often have specific, limited instruction sets that require highly efficient code. The process of selecting the right instructions for these systems can save both memory and processing power which are often constrained in embedded applications.
- **Just-In-Time (JIT) Compilation**: The JIT compilers use instruction selection during runtime to generate a machine code for the specific platform, the program is running on. This dynamic instruction selection can help optimize performance for the hardware, the code is being executed on.

Register Allocation Strategies

When a program runs, it needs quick access to the data. The fastest way for the CPU to retrieve this data is through registers–small, super-fast storage spaces, directly inside the processor. However, since the number of registers is limited, deciding which data to keep in these registers can make a big difference in the speed and efficiency of a program. That is where the register allocation comes in.

Significance of Register Allocation

Register allocation is the process of assigning program variables to CPU registers, instead of slower main memory. This optimization ensures that the most frequently accessed variables stay in the fastest storage, making the program run significantly faster. Here is why this is important:

- **Maximizes Speed and Efficiency**
    - Register allocation directly impacts the speed of a program. Registers are the fastest memory locations available to a CPU, so keeping frequently accessed variables in registers leads to quicker data retrieval and faster execution.
- **Reduces Access Time**
    - Fetching data from registers is much faster than accessing it from the system's RAM. By minimizing the need for memory access, programs can run significantly faster, especially in performance-critical applications.
- **Optimizes CPU Utilization**
    - Efficient use of registers allows the CPU to work more efficiently, reducing idle time and optimizing the execution of instructions. This is particularly beneficial in computation-heavy tasks such as data analysis, machine learning, or gaming.
- **Minimizes Memory Usage**
    - By utilizing registers, instead of relying heavily on RAM, register allocation can also help reduce the load on memory resources. This can be crucial in systems with limited memory or when handling large datasets.
- **Improves Power Efficiency**
    - Programs that efficiently use registers can save power since accessing registers consumes less energy than accessing the RAM. This is particularly valuable in battery-powered devices, such as smartphones and laptops.
- **Reduces Program Latency**
    - Programs that depend less on main memory experience lower latency, leading to smoother performance in real-time applications, such as video streaming, gaming, or high-frequency trading.
- **Enhances Compiler Optimization**
    - Register allocation is a key part of the optimization process during compilation. A well-optimized allocation strategy can make a significant difference in the final program performance, especially in resource-constrained environments.
- **Supports Multithreading and Concurrency**
    - In multi-core processors, efficient register allocation is vital for parallel processing and managing concurrent threads which helps achieve better performance in modern applications.

Techniques for Register Allocation

Register allocation is an essential part of code generation that assigns variables to a limited set of CPU registers. Effective register allocation ensures that programs run efficiently by reducing the need for slower memory access. Let us break down two commonly used techniques in a way that is easy to understand:

Graph Coloring Method

The graph coloring method is a widely used approach in register allocation due to its balance between efficiency and optimal use of limited resources.

The **graph coloring method** approaches register allocation as a graph-theoretic problem where each variable in the program is represented as a node. If two variables are **live simultaneously** (that is, they are needed at the same time), an edge is drawn between their corresponding nodes.

Objective: The goal is to color the graph using the fewest number of colors (representing registers), such that no two adjacent nodes (variables that are live together) share the same color. This ensures that the variables that need to be accessed simultaneously are assigned to different registers.

Spilling: If the number of colors (registers) required exceeds the available registers, some variables must be **spilled** to memory. Spilling means storing variables temporarily in memory, rather than registers which slows down access but ensures program correctness.

This method is particularly effective in reducing register usage, and optimizing the runtime performance, especially in resource-constrained systems where memory access is expensive.

Example: Imagine you have variables, `A`, `B`, and `C` with overlapping lifespans. Using graph coloring:

- If `A` and `B` are live together, an edge is drawn between them.
- If `C` is live separately, it can reuse the same register as `A`.
- This way, only two registers are needed, instead of three, reducing the memory usage.

Linear Scan Allocation

The linear scan allocation method offers a simpler and faster alternative to graph coloring, particularly suited for environments where the compilation speed is crucial.

In contrast to the graph coloring method, **linear scan allocation** focuses on a straightforward, single-pass approach through the program's code to allocate registers based on variable lifespans.

- **How It Works:**
  1. The compiler scans through the code linearly, assigning registers to variables as they appear.
  2. If a variable's lifespan ends, the register is freed up for reuse.
  3. If all registers are occupied when a new variable is needed, one of the current variables is either **spilled** to memory or replaced, based on its usage pattern.
- This method is less complex and much faster to execute than graph coloring, making it ideal for **Just-In-Time (JIT) compilation** and situations where the compilation speed is prioritized over maximum optimization.
- While it may not achieve the same level of register efficiency as graph coloring, linear scan allocation is effective for applications where quick code generation is essential, such as dynamic web applications or mobile environments.

Example: Suppose you are compiling the code for a real-time application where every millisecond counts. Linear scan allocation quickly assigns registers without deep optimization, ensuring that the application runs smoothly with minimal compilation delays.

These optimizations are crucial in modern compilers to balance speed, memory usage, and performance, depending on the target application's needs. Whether using graph coloring or linear scan, understanding these techniques helps developers optimize how the code interacts with hardware resources, ultimately leading to faster and more efficient software.

Managing Register Overflow

Managing register overflow is a critical part of register allocation in compilers. When there are not enough registers to store all live variables, efficient strategies need to be implemented to handle this situation.

Register Overflow occurs when the number of live variables exceeds the available registers in a system. This can happen in large programs or programs with complex control flow, where multiple variables are needed simultaneously.

What Happens during Overflow: When there are not enough registers, the compiler must choose which variables to temporarily **spill** to memory. This involves storing the variable in memory, rather than keeping it in a register.

Why It is Important: Register overflow can significantly impact performance. **Accessing memory** is slower than accessing registers, so spilling and reloading variables frequently can lead to **performance degradation**.

Techniques to Handle Overflow:

- The compiler needs to choose which variables to spill, and when to reload them to minimize the time spent in accessing the memory.
- Smart strategies, such as **locality of reference** can help prioritize which variables are kept in registers, based on how often they are accessed.

Example: In a program with 10 variables but only 4 registers available, the compiler must decide which 6 variables to spill. The spilled variables are temporarily stored in the memory. When one of these variables is needed again, it must be reloaded into a register, possibly displacing another variable.

Spilling and Reloading

Spilling and **reloading** are key techniques used to manage the register overflow, ensuring that the program continues to function correctly, even when the available registers are insufficient.

Spilling and **reloading** are strategies that compilers use to manage register allocation, when there are more live variables than available registers.

- **Spilling**:
  - o When there are not enough registers to hold all the live variables, the compiler will choose certain variables to spill to the memory. The spilled variables are saved in memory, instead of registers.
  - o **Spilling** is often a trade-off between memory usage and register efficiency. The compiler, typically chooses to spill variables that are less frequently used or whose lifetimes are short.
- **Reloading**:
  - o Once a variable is spilled, it needs to be loaded back into a register, before it can be used again. This operation is called **reloading**.

- **Reloading** can incur a performance penalty because accessing memory is slower than accessing registers. A key challenge is minimizing the number of spills and reloads to keep the performance high.
- Often, variables are reloaded only when absolutely necessary, and the compiler tries to minimize the number of reloading operations by reusing registers intelligently.

Example: Consider a function where 5 variables are required, but the system only has 3 registers. The compiler may decide to spill 2 variables to memory. When one of the spilled variables is needed later in the program, it will be reloaded into a register, possibly evicting another variable in the process.

Practical Implementation Insights

In this section, we will look at how code generation is applied in real-world scenarios. We will explore tools, such as the GCC and LLVM, discussing their uses, benefits, and challenges in practical applications. This will give us a clearer understanding of how these tools are used in the software development industry.

Code Generation in GCC

Code generation in GNU Compiler Collection (GCC) is a critical process where the high-level source code is transformed into machine code or assembly code which is then executed by the computer's processor. GCC, being a robust and versatile open-source compiler, is widely used for compiling C, C++, and other programming languages. The main goal of code generation in GCC is to produce an efficient, optimized machine code that runs fast and effectively on various hardware architectures, such as x86, ARM, and MIPS.

Key Features of Code Generation in GCC:

- **Multi-stage Compilation**: GCC follows a multi-stage compilation process that includes preprocessing, parsing, optimization, and code generation:
  - **Preprocessing**: It handles macros, file inclusions, and conditional compilation.
  - **Parsing**: The source code is converted into an intermediate representation, typically in the form of an Abstract Syntax Tree (AST).
  - **Optimization**: Various optimization techniques are applied to the intermediate code to improve performance, such as loop unrolling, inlining, and constant folding.
  - **Code Generation**: Finally, GCC translates the optimized intermediate code into assembly or machine code for the target architecture.
- **Target Architecture Support**: GCC supports a wide range of target architectures, making it highly portable across different platforms. For example:
  - **x86 Architecture**: GCC generates assembly and machine code optimized for Intel and AMD processors used in desktops, laptops, and servers.
  - **ARM Architecture**: GCC can also generate code for ARM-based processors, commonly used in mobile devices, embedded systems, and IoT applications.
  - **MIPS Architecture**: GCC can target MIPS processors which are typically used in embedded systems and networking hardware.
- **Instruction Selection**: GCC uses a set of predefined rules and patterns to convert the intermediate code into machine-level instructions. This process is known as **instruction selection** where GCC matches high-level operations to corresponding assembly instructions specific to the target architecture.
- **Register Allocation**: Efficient register allocation is essential for producing the optimized code.

GCC uses algorithms to map variables onto physical registers, minimizing the use of memory, and improving the execution speed. Techniques, such as **graph coloring** and **linear scan** are employed for this purpose.

- **Optimization**: GCC applies several optimization techniques during code generation to ensure that the generated code runs efficiently:
  - **Loop Optimizations**: It performs loop unrolling, loop-invariant code motion, and other optimizations to reduce overhead in iterative computations.
  - **Instruction Scheduling**: This technique ensures that the processor's execution units are used efficiently by reordering instructions to minimize the waiting time.
  - **Dead Code Elimination**: GCC removes any code that does not affect the program's output, further optimizing the generated machine code.
- **Cross-Compilation**: One of the most significant strengths of GCC is its ability to perform cross-compilation. This means that developers can compile the code for a target platform, different from the one they are currently using. For example, you can compile the code on a Linux machine to run on an ARM-based embedded system.
- **Linking and Final Output**: After code generation, GCC handles the linking process where object files are combined with libraries to create the final executable. This process includes symbol resolution where the function calls and variables are linked to their definitions. The output can be an executable binary or a library file, depending on the type of the build.
- **Extensive Debugging Support**: GCC includes powerful debugging capabilities, especially when used with **GNU Debugger** (GDB). It allows the developers to debug the assembly and the machine code generated by GCC, enabling efficient troubleshooting and optimization of the generated code.

Thus, GCC's code generation process is sophisticated and efficient, making it a powerful tool for developers working on various platforms, from embedded systems to high-performance servers. By supporting multiple architectures and optimization techniques as well as offering extensive debugging tools, GCC remains an essential compiler for cross-platform development and performance-driven applications.

Code Generation in LLVM

Low-Level Virtual Machine (LLVM) is a widely used, modular compiler framework designed to optimize, and generate the machine code for a wide range of hardware architectures. LLVM is known for its advanced optimization capabilities, flexibility, and support for multiple programming languages, including C, C++, Rust, and Swift. The code generation process in LLVM is highly efficient, and involves several phases, each focused on transforming the source code into optimized machine code, specific to the target architecture.

Key Features of Code Generation in LLVM:

- **Multi-phase Compilation Pipeline**: LLVM follows a multi-step compilation process similar to the GCC. The main stages of the pipeline include:
  - **Frontend**: The source code is parsed, and converted into an Intermediate Representation (IR) which is a platform-independent form of code that facilitates optimization.
  - **Optimization**: Various optimization passes are applied to LLVM IR to improve the performance and size of the generated code. These optimizations can be done at different levels (function, loop, and module).
  - **Backend**: The optimized LLVM IR is converted into the machine code, specific to the target architecture. The backend generates the assembly code or binary code that can be executed on the desired hardware.

- **Target Architecture Support**: LLVM supports a broad range of architectures, including:
    - **x86 and x86-64**: These architectures are used in most of the desktop and server processors (Intel and AMD). LLVM generates an optimized code for these processors by using platform-specific instruction sets.
    - **ARM**: LLVM can also target the ARM processors which are commonly used in mobile devices, embedded systems, and IoT devices.
    - **PowerPC, MIPS, RISC-V**: LLVM also supports various other architectures, enabling cross-platform development for diverse systems, from mobile devices to custom hardware.
- **Intermediate Representation (IR)**: One of the key features of the LLVM is its use of an Intermediate Representation (IR) for all code transformations and optimizations. Hence, the LLVM IR is a low-level, platform-independent representation of the code that allows the compiler to perform sophisticated optimizations, and simplifies targeting different architectures. It exists in three forms:
    - **Textual IR**: A human-readable representation used for debuging and analysis.
    - **Binary IR**: A compact, machine-readable form.
    - **In-memory IR**: A representation used during the compilation process before the code generation.
- **Instruction Selection**: LLVM's backend translates the optimized LLVM IR into target-specific instructions through **instruction selection**. This phase involves mapping the high-level operations in the IR to the corresponding instructions available in the target architecture's instruction set.
    - LLVM supports pattern matching and rule-based mechanisms to ensure that the instructions selected are optimal for the target hardware.
- **Register Allocation**: LLVM also performs register allocation to map variables to processor registers during code generation. This step ensures that the program uses CPU registers efficiently, minimizing memory access and improving the performance.
    - **Graph coloring** and **linear scan** are two common techniques used in LLVM to allocate registers for variables.
- **Optimization Passes**: LLVM's optimization system includes a set of passes that improve the generated machine code in terms of speed, memory usage, and overall efficiency. Some key optimizations in LLVM include:
    - **Inlining**: Replacing the function calls with the function's body to reduce the overhead.
    - **Loop Unrolling**: Expanding loops to reduce the iteration overhead.
    - **Dead Code Elimination**: Removing the code that doesn't affect the program's output.
- **Code Generation for Different Architectures**: LLVM allows developers to target different hardware architectures, using the same source code. It does this through its modular backend which can generate the code for various architectures, such as x86, ARM, RISC-V, and others. This is particularly useful for cross-platform development where the same codebase needs to run on multiple platforms.
- **Linking and Final Output**: After generating the assembly code, LLVM links the object files to produce an executable or library. The linking process includes symbol resolution and relocation of memory addresses, enabling the program to run correctly on the target machine.
- **Debugging and Profiling Support**: LLVM provides robust debugging and profiling support through integration with tools, such as **LLVM Debugger** (LLDB) and **llvm-profiler**. These tools allow the developers to inspect the generated machine code step through execution, and identify performance bottlenecks.

- **Just-In-Time (JIT) Compilation**: One of LLVM's standout features is its support for **JIT compilation**. This allows the code to be compiled at runtime, rather than ahead of time, enabling dynamic optimizations, based on the current execution context. The JIT compilation is particularly useful for languages like JavaScript or Python where the code is executed directly rather than precompiled.

LLVM's code generation framework is highly flexible and modular, allowing developers to target multiple architectures with a single source code base. Thus, by using LLVM IR as an intermediate stage, the system can perform sophisticated optimizations that enhance performance across a range of platforms. With robust support for various architectures, advanced optimization techniques, and extensive debugging and profiling tools, LLVM is an essential tool for modern compiler design and cross-platform software development.

Comparative Overview of the GCC and the LLVM

GNU Compiler Collection (GCC) and Low-Level Virtual Machine (LLVM) are two of the most widely used compiler frameworks in the software development world. Both are powerful tools for translating the source code into the machine code, but they differ significantly in design, architecture, performance, and use cases. Following is a comparative overview of GCC and LLVM, based on various key factors:

Aspect	GNU Compiler Collection (GCC)	Low-Level Virtual Machine (LLVM)
Design Philosophy	Monolithic architecture with tightly integrated components	Modular architecture with reusable components
Language Support	Supports C, C++, Fortran, Ada, and more	Supports C, C++, Swift, Rust, Julia, Kotlin, and more
Intermediate Representation	Internal IR with limited portability	Platform-independent LLVM IR, enabling better optimization
Optimization Capabilities	Offers basic optimizations, such as loop unrolling, dead code elimination	Advanced optimizations, such as interprocedural and loop optimizations
Code Generation and Target Architecture Support	Extensive support for a variety of architectures (x86, ARM, MIPS, and so on)	Supports modern and emerging architectures (x86, ARM, RISC-V, and so on)
Compiler Performance	Slower compilation speed for large projects	Faster compilation, especially with Clang frontend
Error Diagnostics	Error messages are less user-friendly	Clear and easy-to-understand error messages from Clang
Tooling and Ecosystem	Includes tools, such as gdb (debugging), gcov (coverage)	Includes tools, such as LLDB (debugging), Clang-tidy (static analysis)
Licensing	GNU General Public License (GPL)	University of Illinois/NCSA Open Source License (more permissive)
Community and Support	Well-established with a focus on stability and long-term support	Rapidly growing, and supported by companies, such as Apple, Google, and Intel
Commercial Use	Open-source but with stricter GPL license requirements	More permissive license, making it easier for commercial use

Table 11.1: *Comparative Overview of GCC and LLVM*

Real-World Applications and Case Studies

This section explores how code generation techniques and compiler optimizations, such as those used in GCC and LLVM, are applied in real-world scenarios. By examining practical implementations and case studies from diverse industries, we can understand the impact of these tools on performance, efficiency, and scalability across different domains.

- **Linux Kernel Development (GCC)**
  - **Context**: The Linux kernel which powers a large portion of servers, mobile devices, and embedded systems, is compiled using the GCC.
  - **Reason for Choice**: The GCC provides robust support for low-level system optimizations, cross-compilation, and stability, all critical for the kernel's performance on various hardware architectures.
  - **Outcome**: Therefore, the GCC ensures that the kernel is highly portable, efficient, and stable, supporting a wide range of devices from personal computers to embedded systems.
- **iOS and macOS Development (LLVM/Clang)**
  - **Context**: Apple's iOS and macOS platforms use the LLVM's Clang compiler for app development.
  - **Reason for Choice**: The LLVM, through Clang, provides fast compilation times, excellent error diagnostics, and strong optimization techniques.
  - **Outcome**: Developers experience faster build times and clearer error messages, resulting in better performance, and easier debugging. This enhances the overall app development experience for the iOS and macOS applications.
- **Embedded Systems (Raspberry Pi and GCC)**
  - **Context**: The Raspberry Pi devices, which are widely used in educational and IoT projects, rely on GCC for compiling the code.
  - **Reason for Choice**: GCC is open-source, supports a wide range of architectures, and includes tools for efficient debugging and optimization, which is crucial for resource-constrained devices.
  - **Outcome**: Thus, the GCC allows developers to create an efficient software for the Raspberry Pi, from simple educational projects to complex embedded systems applications, such as home automation or robotics.
- **Android Development (Clang/LLVM)**
  - **Context**: The Android apps are built using Clang, a part of the LLVM toolchain which is integrated into the Android's build system.
  - **Reason for Choice**: The Clang provides better error diagnostics and faster compilation compared to the GCC, essential for Android's large codebase.
  - **Outcome**: The integration of Clang results in faster build times, improved application performance, and a better development experience for the Android app creators.
- **Game Development (Unreal Engine: LLVM)**
  - **Context**: The Unreal Engine, one of the leading game development platforms, utilizes LLVM for compiling the game code.
  - **Reason for Choice**: The LLVM's optimizations allow for high-performance code generation which is critical in resource-heavy applications, such as games.
  - **Outcome**: Game developers can compile a more efficient code, leading to faster load times, better frame rates, and overall enhanced gaming experiences on various platforms.

- **Scientific Computing (GCC and LLVM in HPC)**
  - **Context**: High-Performance Computing (HPC) applications, such as those used in simulations, climate modeling, and research, often use GCC or LLVM for compiling complex algorithms.
  - **Reason for Choice**: Both the GCC and LLVM offer optimizations that maximize the use of hardware resources, such as the CPU cache and parallelism.
  - **Outcome**: In fact, researchers benefit from faster computational models and more efficient resource utilization, accelerating the development and execution of high-performance scientific simulations.

Conclusion

In this chapter, we covered the key concepts related to generating the machine code from high-level programming languages. We began by discussing **target machine architecture**, distinguishing between the **RISC** and **CISC** architectures, and their impact on code generation. The chapter also explored **instruction selection techniques**, including **pattern matching** and **tree matching**, as well as **optimization techniques**, such as **peephole optimization** and **rule-based selection**. We also examined **register allocation strategies**, such as **graph coloring** and **linear scan allocation** that help in efficiently managing the limited number of registers. Finally, we looked at the practical implementations of code generation in tools, such as the **GCC** and the **LLVM**.

Looking ahead, *Chapter 12, Register Allocation and Scheduling*, will delve deeper into **register allocation techniques** and **instruction scheduling**, the key aspects that contribute to further optimizing the generated code. We will also cover various **code generation optimization techniques**, and explore their implementation using **GCC** and **LLVM**, helping us understand how to maximize the efficiency of the compiled code.

Points to Remember

- **Code Generation** is the process of translating an intermediate representation (IR) of a program into machine-level instructions.
- **Target Machine Architecture** defines the hardware-specific features that influence how code is generated, such as instruction sets and registers.
- **Reduced Instruction Set Computing (RISC)** uses a small, simple set of instructions for fast execution and easy optimization.
- **Complex Instruction Set Computing (CISC)** has a larger, more complex set of instructions, allowing for more powerful operations but often at the cost of slower performance.
- **Instruction Selection** involves choosing the most appropriate machine instruction for each operation in the program's IR.
- **Register Allocation** assigns variables to processor registers which are limited in number, and are critical for optimizing performance.
- **Graph Coloring Method** is used for register allocation, where variables are represented as nodes in a graph and registers as colors, ensuring no conflicting variables share the same register.
- **Linear Scan Allocation** is a simpler method for register allocation, allocating registers in a linear pass, often faster but sometimes less optimal.
- **LLVM Intermediate Representation (IR)** is a low-level programming language used in the LLVM compiler to facilitate optimization and platform-specific code generation.

- **Peephole Optimization** looks at small instruction sequences, and replaces inefficient patterns with better alternatives to improve performance.
- **Spilling and Reloading** refers to moving variables from registers to memory (spilling), when registers are full, and bringing them back into registers (reloading) when needed.
- **GNU Compiler Collection (GCC)** is an open-source collection of compilers that supports many programming languages, and is widely used for code generation.
- **Machine Code** is the lowest-level code generated by compilers that can be directly executed by a CPU.
- **Optimization Techniques** focus on improving the efficiency of the generated machine code, making it faster, smaller, or more memory-efficient.
- **Instruction Scheduling** organizes machine instructions to maximize the processor efficiency by minimizing delays and hazards during execution.

Multiple Choice Questions

1. What is the primary role of the code generation phase in a compiler?
   a. Error detection
   b. Converting the high-level code to the assembly
   c. Optimizing the intermediate code
   d. Translating the intermediate code into the machine code
2. Which of the following represents the target machine's capabilities?
   a. Intermediate representation
   b. Target machine architecture
   c. High-level language syntax
   d. Control flow graph
3. What is the purpose of Intermediate Representation (IR) in compilation?
   a. Directly run programs on hardware
   b. Simplify optimization and code generation
   c. Define the target machine architecture
   d. Translate assembly language
4. Instruction selection is responsible for mapping the IR to:
   a. High-level languages
   b. Machine instructions
   c. Register allocation
   d. Memory allocation
5. Which of the following techniques is commonly used in instruction selection?
   a. Graph coloring
   b. Peephole optimization

c. Pattern matching
d. Spilling

6. What is tree-based instruction selection primarily used for?
   a. Simplifying IR expressions
   b. Converting IR to assembly
   c. Optimizing variable allocation
   d. Scheduling instructions
7. Which optimization technique is performed after instruction selection?
   a. Instruction reordering
   b. Peephole optimization
   c. Constant folding
   d. Dead code elimination
8. Register allocation is crucial because:
   a. The number of registers is limited
   b. Registers are slower than memory
   c. All variables are stored in the memory
   d. Code generation requires multiple registers
9. Which algorithm is widely used for register allocation?
   a. Pattern matching
   b. Graph coloring
   c. Spilling
   d. Peephole optimization
10. When the registers are full, variables are stored in the memory in a process called:
    a. Scheduling
    b. Spilling
    c. Coalescing
    d. Coloring
11. What does instruction scheduling aim to optimize?
    a. Register allocation
    b. Memory usage
    c. Execution speed by reordering instructions
    d. Intermediate code generation

12. Which of the following is an example of a compiler that uses pattern matching for instruction selection?
    a. LLVM
    b. GCC
    c. Python
    d. Swift
13. LLVM's "SelectionDAG" is used for:
    a. Intermediate representation optimization
    b. Target-independent instruction selection
    c. Register allocation
    d. Optimizing memory access
14. What is a major limitation of registers that affects register allocation?
    a. Registers have high latency.
    b. Registers are finite in number.
    c. Registers cannot hold floating-point values.
    d. Registers are slower than the main memory.
15. Which phase follows instruction selection in a typical compiler pipeline?
    a. Parsing
    b. Register allocation
    c. Code optimization
    d. Tokenization

Answers

1. d
2. b
3. b
4. b
5. c
6. a
7. b
8. a
9. b
10. b
11. c
12. b

13. b
14. b
15. b

Questions

1. Explain the role of target machine architecture in the code generation process. How does it influence the efficiency and correctness of the generated code?
2. Discuss various instruction selection techniques used in compilers. Compare and contrast at least two methods, such as pattern matching and tree-based instruction selection.
3. Describe the concept of Intermediate Representation (IR) in compilers. What are its advantages in terms of optimization and code generation?
4. Define register allocation and its significance in code generation. Discuss the common strategies employed for register allocation, and their impact on program performance.
5. What is graph coloring in the context of register allocation? Explain how this technique works, and its benefits for the efficient use of registers.
6. Illustrate the process of instruction scheduling. Why is it important, and how does it contribute to the overall performance of the generated machine code?
7. Examine the role of GCC in code generation. Describe its architecture and the specific techniques, it employs for instruction selection and optimization.
8. Discuss LLVM's approach to code generation. How does its use of the SelectionDAG improve instruction selection compared to traditional methods?
9. Explain the concept of spilling in register allocation. Under what circumstances does spilling occur, and what strategies can be employed to minimize its impact on performance?
10. Analyze the differences between target-independent and target-specific optimizations in compilers. Provide examples of each, and explain how they affect the generated machine code.

Key Terms

- **Code Generation:** The process of translating intermediate representations of a program into the machine code that can be executed by a specific target machine.
- **Target Machine Architecture:** The hardware architecture of the system for which code is being generated, including the processor's instruction set, registers, and memory organization.
- **Reduced Instruction Set Computing (RISC):** An architectural approach that simplifies the processor design by using a small, highly optimized set of instructions.
- **Complex Instruction Set Computing (CISC):** A type of architecture that uses a large set of instructions, enabling more complex operations in a single instruction.
- **Instruction Selection:** The phase in code generation where the intermediate code is converted into machine-specific instructions, based on patterns and rules.
- **Register Allocation:** The technique of assigning variables to processor registers during code generation to optimize performance, and minimize memory access.
- **Graph Coloring Method:** A technique used in register allocation, where variables are represented as nodes, and the goal is to assign registers, such that no adjacent nodes share the same register.

- **Linear Scan Allocation:** A simpler and faster register allocation method where variables are allocated registers as they appear in the program, often used in Just-In-Time (JIT) compilation.
- **Spilling and Reloading:** When a register cannot be used for a variable due to a lack of available registers, the variable is "spilled" to memory, and reloaded into a register, when needed again.
- **LLVM:** A collection of modular and reusable compiler and toolchain technologies used to create efficient code generation processes.

CHAPTER 12
Register Allocation and Scheduling

Introduction

In *Chapter 11, Code Generation and Instruction Selection*, we explored how compilers convert the high-level code into machine code, focusing on optimizing instruction selection and efficient register usage. We covered architectures, such as the RISC and CISC, and discussed methods, such as pattern matching and optimizations using tools, such as the GCC and the LLVM.

Building on that, *Chapter 12, Register Allocation and Scheduling*, delves deeper into techniques for optimizing register usage and instruction to boost performance. This chapter explains why efficient register allocation is crucial for minimizing memory access, covering techniques, such as the graph coloring algorithm and linear scan allocation. Additionally, it addresses instruction scheduling strategies, such as static and dynamic scheduling, to reduce execution delays. We also explore optimization techniques, such as loop unrolling and dead code elimination to enhance code efficiency. By examining practical implementations in the GCC and the LLVM, this chapter highlights real-world applications of these strategies to achieve a high-performance software.

Structure

In this chapter, we will discuss the following topics:

- **Introduction to Register Allocation and Scheduling**
  - Importance in Code Generation
  - Overview of Key Concepts
- **Register Allocation Techniques**
  - Overview of Register Allocation
  - Graph Coloring Algorithm
  - Linear Scan Allocation
  - Dynamic Allocation Techniques
  - Trade-offs and Considerations
- **Instruction Scheduling**
  - Definition and Importance of Instruction Scheduling
  - Types of Instruction Scheduling
  - Techniques for Instruction Scheduling
- **Code Generation Optimization Techniques**
  - Optimization Goals
  - Techniques for Code Optimization

- Impact on Performance and Efficiency
- **Practical Implementation Insights**
  - Register Allocation in GCC
  - Instruction Scheduling in LLVM
  - Comparative Analysis of the GCC and LLVM Techniques
  - Real-World Case Studies Illustrating Techniques

Introduction to Register Allocation and Scheduling

Efficient **register allocation** and **instruction scheduling** are integral parts of the code generation process that significantly enhance the performance of a program. These techniques aim to optimize the use of processor resources–specifically the limited number of registers–while arranging instructions in a way that maximizes execution speed. In this chapter, we shall explore the importance of these processes in generating optimized machine code, focusing on strategies to allocate registers, and schedule instructions effectively for better program execution.

Importance in Code Generation

The effectiveness of register allocation and instruction scheduling plays a critical role in code generation. By minimizing memory access times and utilizing processor registers more efficiently, register allocation reduces program latency. On the other hand, instruction scheduling ensures that the CPU executes instructions in an optimal sequence, avoiding unnecessary delays and enabling parallel execution. Together, these techniques help improve the overall efficiency of the generated code, leading to faster execution and reduced resource consumption.

Overview of Key Concepts

This chapter covers essential techniques and strategies in register allocation and instruction scheduling, including **graph coloring** for effective register allocation and **list scheduling** as well as **software pipelining** for optimizing the instruction order. These key concepts are fundamental in compiler design where efficient code generation is crucial for performance. Understanding these techniques is vital for anyone interested in enhancing the efficiency and speed of the compiled programs.

Register Allocation Techniques

Efficient use of CPU registers is a critical factor in optimizing program performance. Given the limited number of registers available in modern processors, compilers must employ effective strategies to allocate registers for variables and instructions. This section explores the various techniques used to allocate registers efficiently, ensuring faster code execution, and reduced memory access.

Overview of Register Allocation

In modern compilers, managing the limited number of CPU registers efficiently is essential for optimizing program performance. This section provides an introduction to the concept of register allocation and its importance in reducing memory access times.

Register allocation involves assigning program variables to the limited set of CPU registers during the execution of the compiled code. The goal is to minimize the need for slower memory access, while maximizing the usage of high-speed registers.

Graph Coloring Algorithm

The **Graph Coloring Algorithm** is a popular technique used for register allocation in compilers. It works by representing variables in a program as nodes in a graph where an edge between two nodes indicates that those variables are live (that is, needed) at the same time. The goal of the algorithm is to assign registers to variables in such a way that no two variables that interfere with each other (that is, have an edge between them), share the same register.

To understand how the Graph Coloring Algorithm functions, let us break down its process into simple steps. This method helps allocate registers efficiently by analyzing how variables interact in a program.

- **Building the Interference Graph:**

  First, the compiler constructs an interference graph where each node represents a variable. An edge between two nodes shows that those variables are used at the same time in the program, meaning they cannot share a register.

- **Assigning Colors (Registers):**

  The algorithm then "colors" the graph, with each color representing a unique register. The challenge is to use the minimum number of colors (registers), while ensuring that no two connected nodes (variables) share the same color.

- **Spilling:**

  If the number of available registers is less than the required colors, some variables are "spilled" to memory which means they are stored in the RAM instead of registers. This is a last resort, since accessing memory is slower than using registers.

The Graph Coloring Algorithm provides several advantages that enhance the efficiency and performance of the compiled code. Let us look at why it's so beneficial.

- **Optimizes Register Usage:**

  Efficiently allocates registers to frequently used variables, reducing the need for slow memory access.

- **Improves Performance:**

  Programs run faster when variables are stored in registers instead of accessing the memory repeatedly.

- **Scalability:**

  Works well for large and complex programs with multiple variables.

Example:

Imagine a program where variables A, B, and C are live simultaneously, while D and E are live at different times. The interference graph would connect nodes, A, B, and C, while D and E would not have edges between them. The algorithm can then assign registers to these variables efficiently, using fewer registers by ensuring that non-conflicting variables can share the same register.

By understanding the Graph Coloring Algorithm, programmers and compiler developers can enhance the efficiency of their code, leading to better-performing applications.

Linear Scan Allocation

Linear Scan Allocation is a simpler and faster approach to register allocation compared to more complex algorithms, such as Graph Coloring. This technique is highly efficient for Just-In-Time (JIT) compilers, making it a popular choice in environments where compilation speed is crucial, such as runtime optimizations. The method processes variables linearly based on their live ranges which are the sections of code where a variable is actively used. It allocates registers to variables in a sequential manner, quickly determining which register can be reused or freed up without the need for building an interference graph.

Let us explore the main advantages of this approach, and understand why it is commonly used in code optimization.

- **Speed:**

  Linear scan is much faster than graph-based methods, especially for large functions or when compilation needs to be done on the fly.
- **Simplicity:**

  It is easier to implement compared to more complex algorithms, making it ideal for simpler compilers or those focusing on quick performance.
- **Efficient for JIT Compilers:**

  Its speed makes it a go-to method in JIT compilation where real-time code execution and optimization are required.

Dynamic Allocation Techniques

Dynamic Allocation Techniques are designed to handle more complex scenarios where register usage patterns are unpredictable. Unlike static methods which allocate registers based on predefined patterns or rules, dynamic techniques adjust register assignments during runtime. This allows for more flexibility, particularly in programs that have varying execution paths or deal with dynamic data sets.

These techniques rely on runtime information to make decisions about register allocation which can be beneficial in optimizing performance for applications with fluctuating workloads. Methods include dynamic reallocation of registers, spill code insertion, and on-the-fly adjustments to minimize register usage conflicts.

Let us explore the main advantages of this approach, and understand why it is commonly used in code optimization.

- **Flexibility:**

  Adapts to varying workloads and execution paths, making it suitable for dynamic applications.
- **Optimized Performance:**

  By allocating registers at runtime, it can reduce unnecessary spilling, leading to faster code execution.
- **Better Resource Utilization:**

  Ensures that registers are used efficiently, based on the current program needs, preventing waste of resources.

Trade-offs and Considerations

While register allocation is salient for optimizing code performance, it involves trade-offs that must be carefully managed depending on the program's requirements.

Selecting the right register allocation strategy involves balancing compile time, execution speed, and resource usage. For instance, while linear scan allocation is fast, it may lead to inefficient use of registers compared to dynamic or graph coloring techniques. On the other hand, dynamic allocation adapts better to unpredictable workloads but can introduce runtime overhead due to on-the-fly decisions. Choosing between these strategies depends on factors, such as the complexity of the program, performance requirements, and hardware constraints.

- **Complexity versus Performance**:
  - Graph Coloring provides optimal register allocation but is computationally intensive. It is best for compilers where the execution speed is critical, but compilation speed is less important.
  - Linear Scan Allocation, on the other hand, is less efficient in terms of register utilization but is much faster to execute, making it ideal for JIT compilers.
- **Static versus Dynamic Allocation**:
  - Static allocation techniques, such as Linear Scan, are well-suited for predictable code patterns, whereas dynamic techniques excel in environments with variable workloads.
  - Dynamic allocation introduces runtime overhead but can optimize performance in highly dynamic applications.
- **Spilling and Reloading**:
  - Spilling occurs when there are not enough registers to hold all the variables currently in use. The compiler then stores some variables in memory which can slow down execution.
  - Efficient management of spilling and reloading is crucial to ensure that the performance is not significantly impacted. Graph Coloring often handles spilling more efficiently but at the cost of higher compilation time.
- **Scalability**:
  - For large-scale applications, using a purely dynamic allocation approach may become inefficient due to increased runtime overhead.
  - A hybrid approach, combining static and dynamic techniques, is often used to balance between the compilation speed and the execution efficiency.

Instruction Scheduling

Instruction scheduling is a technique used during the compilation process to rearrange the order of machine instructions to enhance the performance of the program. The primary aim of instruction scheduling is to make the best use of available hardware resources, minimize execution time, and avoid unnecessary delays that could degrade the performance of the program.

Definition and Importance of Instruction Scheduling

Instruction scheduling involves the process of reorganizing instructions so that they can be executed in the most efficient way possible. By rearranging the instructions, we can:

- **Reduce Pipeline Stalls**: Stalls in the CPU pipeline occur, when instructions are waiting for data or previous instructions to complete. Instruction scheduling can minimize such stalls by ensuring that instructions are ready to execute as soon as the required resources are available.
- **Maximize Parallelism**: Certain instructions can be executed in parallel, such as independent arithmetic operations. Instruction scheduling helps to identify and exploit this parallelism to improve the overall performance.
- **Avoid Resource Contention**: The CPU has a limited number of execution units, registers, and memory bandwidth. Scheduling helps avoid conflicts where multiple instructions compete for the same resources at the same time.

The efficiency of modern processors is heavily dependent on the way instructions are scheduled. Poor scheduling can lead to:

- **Pipeline Stalls**: When instructions that depend on one another are executed in the wrong order, the processor may need to wait for the results of previous instructions, leading to idle CPU cycles.
- **Underutilized CPU Resources**: If instructions are not scheduled properly, the CPU's execution units, registers, and memory may not be fully utilized, leading to wasted cycles.

By applying instruction scheduling techniques, it becomes possible to reduce these issues, leading to faster program execution, and more efficient use of resources.

Types of Instruction Scheduling

Instruction scheduling can be approached in different ways depending on the system and compiler. Here, we will explore the key types of scheduling techniques, and their unique benefits.

Instruction scheduling can be broadly categorized into two types:

- **Static Instruction Scheduling**
- **Dynamic Instruction Scheduling**

Static Instruction Scheduling

Static Instruction Scheduling is a technique applied during the compilation process of a program. The primary objective is to optimize the sequence of instructions in a way that minimizes execution time, and maximizes the usage of CPU resources without requiring any runtime decisions. This is done by the compiler before the program is executed; hence, it is also referred to as **compile-time scheduling**.

In Static Instruction Scheduling, the compiler examines the dependencies between instructions and rearranges them, ensuring that the execution of instructions occurs in the most efficient order based on the available resources. This technique can lead to fewer delays due to pipeline stalls, fewer resource conflicts, and better CPU utilization.

Static Instruction Scheduling works by analyzing the program's instructions and their dependencies which can be either **data dependencies** or **control dependencies**. The compiler then orders the instructions such that:

- **Independent Instructions** (those that do not rely on one another's results) can be executed in parallel.
- **Dependent Instructions** are scheduled to avoid delays, ensuring that a dependent instruction only executes once its required operand is available.

For example, if instruction, A depends on instruction, B, the compiler may reorder independent instructions to execute, while waiting for instruction, B to complete, thus avoiding wasted CPU cycles.

Key Benefits of Static Instruction Scheduling:

- **No Runtime Overhead:** Since all scheduling is done at the compile-time, there is no additional computational cost during execution. The program can run without the need for the CPU to make scheduling decisions dynamically.
- **Optimal Resource Usage:** The compiler attempts to make full use of the available CPU resources (for example, registers and execution units) by ensuring that independent instructions are scheduled for execution at the same time, thus improving performance.
- **Efficiency in Pipelines:** Static scheduling can be particularly effective in reducing **pipeline stalls** (delays that occur when the CPU's instruction pipeline is waiting for data), as the compiler can order instructions to minimize these waiting times.

- **Predictability:** Since the schedule is fixed and predetermined, it is predictable and stable, leading to consistent performance across different runs of the program.

Challenges of Static Instruction Scheduling:

- **Limited Flexibility:** Static scheduling is limited by the compiler's analysis, and the assumptions it makes about the program's behavior. If the actual behavior of the program differs from the assumptions made during compilation (for example, dynamic branches or variable memory access patterns), static scheduling may not be as effective.
- **Compilation Time Overhead:** The process of analyzing dependencies and determining the optimal instruction order can increase the time it takes to compile the program. For large programs, this could be a time-consuming process.
- **Limited to Known Information:** Static instruction scheduling can only work with the information available at the compile time. It cannot adapt to runtime conditions, such as dynamic branching or unpredictable memory access patterns, making it less suitable for highly dynamic programs.

Example of Static Instruction Scheduling

Consider a simple program where instruction, A and instruction, B are independent, but in A: R1 = R2 + R3

B: R4 = R5 + R6

C: R7 = R1 * R8, *Instruction C depends on the result of instruction A.*

A static scheduler might rearrange the instructions as follows to minimize delay and maximize parallel execution:

A: R1 = R2 + R3

B: R4 = R5 + R6

C: R7 = R1 * R8 <-- *Can be scheduled after A completes.*

In this case, instructions A and B can be executed in parallel, while instruction C must wait until instruction A has been completed. The compiler will ensure that C starts executing as soon as the result of A is available, reducing unnecessary waiting time.

Dynamic Instruction Scheduling

Dynamic Instruction Scheduling is an optimization technique used during program execution to arrange the order in which instructions are executed. Unlike static instruction scheduling, which happens at the compile time, dynamic scheduling occurs at the runtime. The main goal is to execute instructions as soon as the necessary resources and data are available, improving performance by minimizing the idle CPU cycles, and handling unpredictable situations, such as branch instructions or memory access delays.

Dynamic scheduling allows the CPU to make real-time decisions on the execution order based on the current state of the program, rather than relying on a predefined sequence. This makes it especially useful in highly dynamic environments where instruction dependencies may change during execution.

Dynamic Instruction Scheduling relies on hardware mechanisms, such as **out-of-order execution** and **register renaming** to schedule instructions during the runtime. Here is how it typically works:

- **Instruction Fetching:** Instructions are fetched from the memory in the order, they appear in the program.
- **Instruction Reordering:** The processor examines the available instructions, checking for data dependencies and available execution units. If independent instructions are found, they

are reordered for parallel execution, even if they appear after dependent instructions in the program.

- **Execution:** Once, an instruction has all the operands it needs, and the appropriate resources (such as registers or execution units), it is dispatched for execution. Dependent instructions are held back until the data they need becomes available.
- **Out-of-Order Execution:** Instructions that do not depend on others can be executed as soon as resources are available, even if they are scheduled later in the instruction stream.

The CPU's **instruction window** typically manages this dynamic scheduling by holding a set of instructions that are ready to execute but waiting for their turn or available resources.

Key Benefits of Dynamic Instruction Scheduling:

- **Improved Performance:** By allowing instructions to execute as soon as resources are available, dynamic scheduling can significantly improve CPU utilization. This reduces the time spent waiting for instructions to be executed, especially in programs with complex dependencies.
- **Handling Unpredictable Dependencies:** Dynamic scheduling is well-suited for handling real-time changes in instruction dependencies, such as those introduced by conditional branches or memory access. This makes it more flexible compared to static scheduling.
- **Better Utilization of Pipelining:** Dynamic scheduling can help fill pipeline stages more efficiently, reducing the number of pipeline stalls. By executing independent instructions in parallel, and delaying dependent ones, the processor can maintain a steady flow of operations without the unnecessary idle time.
- **Adaptive to Runtime Conditions:** Unlike static scheduling, which makes decisions based on compile-time analysis, dynamic scheduling can adapt to changing runtime conditions, such as variable data dependencies and execution delays due to memory access.

Challenges of Dynamic Instruction Scheduling:

- **Hardware Complexity:** Dynamic instruction scheduling requires sophisticated hardware mechanisms, such as out-of-order execution, register renaming, and instruction windows. This makes the CPU architecture more complex, and increases the cost of implementation.
- **Increased Power Consumption:** The complexity of dynamic scheduling, including the management of out-of-order execution and the instruction window, may lead to higher power consumption which can be a concern for devices with limited power resources, such as mobile phones.
- **Runtime Overhead:** While dynamic scheduling improves performance, it also introduces some runtime overhead due to the additional computation required to manage instruction reordering and resource allocation. This overhead can diminish the benefits, especially in simpler or smaller programs.

Example of Dynamic Instruction Scheduling

Consider a scenario where a processor needs to execute three instructions:

A: R1 = R2 + R3 *// Addition*

B: R4 = R5 + R6 *// Addition*

C: R7 = R1 * R8 *// Multiplication (depends on the result of* A)

In static scheduling, the compiler would arrange the instructions, such that C waits until A is done. However, in dynamic scheduling, if the processor detects that instructions, A and B are independent, it can execute them in parallel, and once A completes, C can be executed immediately.

A: R1 = R2 + R3 // *Executed in parallel with* B

B: R4 = R5 + R6 // *Executed simultaneously with* A

C: R7 = R1 * R8 // *Executed as soon as* A *completes*

This dynamic approach maximizes parallelism, and minimizes idle CPU cycles.

Techniques for Instruction Scheduling

Instruction scheduling is an important optimization step in compiler design that focuses on arranging the execution of instructions to maximize performance. Several techniques are employed to enhance the efficiency of instruction execution, reduce idle times, and utilize resources effectively. Some common techniques for instruction scheduling include **List Scheduling**, **Software Pipelining**, and **Out-of-Order Execution**. Now, let us take a closer look at each of these techniques.

List Scheduling

List Scheduling is a technique used in compiler optimization to schedule instructions in a way that maximizes resource utilization and minimizes delays. It focuses on organizing instructions based on their dependencies and availability of execution units, ensuring that instructions are scheduled efficiently. This approach works by creating a list of instructions, considering their dependencies, and then assigning them to the available resources, such as registers or execution units.

List Scheduling organizes instructions based on their dependencies and priorities. It selects tasks that are ready to execute, and schedules them in the order that best utilizes system resources, ensuring minimal idle time.

- **Dependency Analysis:** The first step in list scheduling is to analyze the data dependencies between instructions. Instructions that depend on each other for data (for example, one instruction needs the result of another) cannot be executed simultaneously. These dependencies form a directed acyclic graph (DAG) where the nodes represent instructions, and the edges represent dependencies.
- **Instruction List Creation:** After analyzing the dependencies, instructions are placed into a list based on their readiness to execute. Instructions that are independent of others (that is, they do not rely on the results of other instructions) are prioritized and placed earlier in the list.
- **Scheduling Instructions:** The next step is to schedule the instructions. The scheduler checks the list of instructions and assigns, each to an available execution unit (such as a CPU register or ALU). If two instructions have no data dependency between them, they can be executed in parallel. The scheduler uses available resources, and ensures that no two dependent instructions are executed at the same time.
- **Rescheduling, if Necessary:** In some cases, if a resource becomes available, or if the scheduling order needs adjustment due to resource constraints or data dependencies, the list may be re-ordered.

Key Benefits of List Scheduling:

- **Simplicity:** List scheduling is easy to implement because it only requires a basic analysis of dependencies and resources. It does not require sophisticated runtime mechanisms, and can work well for smaller programs.
- **Deterministic Scheduling:** The process is deterministic, meaning the scheduling is based on clear rules and dependencies. This makes the process predictable, and less error-prone.
- **Effective for Smaller Programs:** For small-scale programs with fewer instructions, list scheduling offers a straightforward approach that can produce decent results, without requiring complex optimizations.

- **Parallelism:** It can increase parallelism by scheduling independent instructions to run simultaneously, thereby improving overall execution speed, and reducing idle times in execution units.

Limitations of List Scheduling:

- **Not Optimal for Complex Programs:** For larger or more complex programs, list scheduling can lead to suboptimal results. It might not fully exploit the parallelism available because it does not take into account the dynamic factors, such as changing resource availability during the runtime.
- **Fixed Scheduling:** Once the list is created, the scheduling is fixed, and cannot adapt dynamically to changes in resource utilization, leading to possible inefficiencies in highly variable environments.
- **Resource Contention:** List scheduling may not always handle resource contention well, especially in systems with limited resources, as it strictly follows a predetermined sequence, rather than dynamically adjusting to the runtime conditions.

Software Pipelining

Software Pipelining is an advanced scheduling technique used to optimize instruction execution in compilers. It is a method that reorders instructions to improve the performance of loops by overlapping the execution of multiple iterations. This technique is especially effective in taking full advantage of the modern CPU architectures with pipelined execution units.

Software Pipelining reorders instructions from multiple loop iterations, allowing them to overlap. Executing different parts of successive iterations in parallel maximizes the CPU efficiency, and minimizes idle time.

- **Loop Unrolling and Reordering:** Software pipelining works by reordering the instructions of loop iterations so that different iterations are executed in parallel. Instead of waiting for one iteration to finish before starting the next, parts of multiple iterations are executed concurrently. For instance, while one instruction is being processed, another instruction from the next iteration can start executing.
- **Instruction Overlap:** The goal is to keep the CPU's pipeline full by overlapping the execution stages (fetch, decode and execute) of different iterations. This way, the CPU can handle multiple instructions simultaneously, reducing the idle time, and improving throughput.
- **Latency Hiding:** By scheduling instructions in such a way that dependent operations are spread across different iterations, software pipelining hides the latency of operations, such as memory access or floating-point calculations. This ensures that the CPU is not left waiting for long-latency instructions to complete.
- **Prologue, Kernel, and Epilogue Stages:** Software pipelining divides the loop execution into three parts:
    - **Prologue**: Prepares the pipeline by filling it with instructions from the first few iterations.
    - **Kernel**: This is the steady state where instructions from different iterations overlap efficiently.
    - **Epilogue**: Clears the pipeline by finishing the remaining instructions, after the last full iteration.

Key Benefits of Software Pipelining:

- **Maximized CPU Utilization:** By overlapping the execution of instructions, software pipelining ensures that the CPU pipeline remains full, maximizing the utilization of processing resources.

- **Improved Loop Performance:** Loops, especially in scientific and engineering applications, often have repetitive calculations. Software pipelining can significantly boost performance by reducing the number of cycles needed per iteration.
- **Reduced Latency:** This technique helps hide the latency of operations, such as memory accesses, making programs more efficient by reducing the idle CPU cycles.
- **Scalable for Modern Architectures:** Software pipelining is particularly effective on CPUs with deep pipelines and multiple execution units, making it highly suitable for modern processors.

Limitations of Software Pipelining:

- **Complexity in Implementation:** Implementing software pipelining requires sophisticated analysis, and scheduling algorithms. It is more complex than simpler scheduling techniques, such as list scheduling.
- **Dependency Management:** Ensuring that instructions are correctly scheduled, without breaking data dependencies can be challenging, especially in loops with complex control flows.
- **Higher Compiler Overhead:** The optimization process can add significant overhead to the compilation time, especially for large programs with many loops.
- **May Increase the Code Size:** Due to the addition of prologue and epilogue stages, software pipelining can sometimes increase the size of the generated code which may be a concern in memory-constrained environments.

Out-of-Order Execution

Out-of-order Execution (OoOE) is a powerful technique used in modern processors to enhance the performance. Unlike traditional methods where instructions are processed one after another (in sequence), OoOE allows the CPU to execute instructions as soon as the necessary data and resources are ready, even if they appear later in the original code sequence.

The processor checks the list of instructions, and identifies which ones are independent of each other. If an instruction is waiting for data that has not been fetched yet, the processor skips it, and moves on to the next instructions that can be executed. Once the data becomes available, the skipped instructions are completed. The final results are reordered to maintain the correct program sequence, ensuring that the program runs as intended.

Key Benefits of the Out-of-Order Execution:

- **Improved Efficiency**: By not waiting for stalled instructions, the processor makes the best use of its available resources, reducing idle times.
- **Faster Execution**: This technique speeds up processing, particularly in complex applications where certain tasks may be delayed due to data dependencies.
- **Enhanced Multitasking**: Helps optimize performance in multicore processors, allowing for better parallel processing.

Limitations of the Out-of-order Execution:

- **Complex Hardware Design**: Implementing the out-of-order execution requires sophisticated circuitry, making processors more expensive to manufacture.
- **Increased Power Usage**: Due to the added complexity, these processors may consume more power which can be a concern for mobile devices.
- **Difficult Debugging**: Understanding how a program behaves becomes harder, since instructions are not executed in a straightforward sequence, complicating debugging.

Thus, the Out-of-order execution is a key factor in making modern processors faster and more efficient, especially for demanding tasks, such as gaming, scientific computing, and real-time data processing.

Code Generation Optimization Techniques

In this section, we explore how optimizing code during the generation phase can significantly enhance program performance and efficiency. The focus here is on refining the code so that it runs faster, uses less memory, and makes efficient use of system resources.

Optimization Goals

In code generation, the primary aim is to optimize the code for better performance and efficiency. This process involves various techniques to improve how the program runs on hardware, ensuring it uses resources efficiently. So, let us break down the key goals of optimization:

- **Reducing Execution Time:**

  The primary goal of optimization is to decrease the time it takes for a program to run. Faster execution is vital for applications that require real-time responses, such as video games, live streaming, or financial trading systems.

  Example: By optimizing the sorting algorithm in a large database, the search results can be retrieved more quickly, improving user satisfaction.

- **Minimizing Memory Usage:**

  Reducing the amount of memory required by an application ensures that it runs efficiently, especially on devices with limited resources, such as smartphones or IoT devices.

  Example: Compressing data structures or removing the unused variables helps free up memory, allowing the system to allocate resources more effectively.

- **Lowering Power Consumption:**

  Optimized code can reduce the power consumption of devices which is essential for extending the battery life of mobile devices, and reducing energy costs in data centers.

  Example: Mobile apps that are optimized to run efficiently will consume less battery, providing users with a longer device usage time.

- **Enhancing Maintainability:**

  While optimizing, it is crucial to maintain the code readability and simplicity. Well-optimized code should not be overly complex, ensuring that developers can easily update or extend it in the future.

Techniques for Code Optimization

To achieve the goals of optimization, various techniques can be employed. Let us dive into some of the most common methods used by compilers to generate an efficient code.

Dead Code Elimination

Dead code elimination is a code optimization technique used to improve the efficiency of a program by removing sections of the code that are never executed or whose results are never used. This not only reduces the size of the program but also speeds up its execution, as the processor does not have to waste cycles on unnecessary instructions.

Dead code refers to the code that does not impact the program's output or performance. It can be a result of:

- **Unreachable Code**: Code that is written but never executed because of control flow, such as after a `return` statement or in a condition that is always false.
- **Unused Variables**: Variables that are declared but never read or written to in the code, hence, never contributing to the program's final result.
- **Constant Expressions**: When the result of an expression is always constant, and it does not change based on the program's input.

The process of dead code elimination involves detecting these unnecessary instructions during the compilation process, and removing them to reduce both the size of the code and the computational resources required to run it.

Key Benefits of Dead Code Elimination:

- **Reduced Code Size:**

  By eliminating the redundant or unused code, the overall size of the program is reduced. This is particularly beneficial for applications that need to run on devices with limited storage or memory.

- **Faster Execution:**

  Since fewer instructions need to be executed, the program runs more quickly. This is important in performance-critical applications, such as gaming, high-frequency trading, or real-time systems.

- **Lower Resource Consumption:**

  Reducing the number of instructions means less CPU time and memory usage which can be crucial in embedded systems and mobile devices where resources are constrained.

- **Improved Maintainability:**

  Removing dead code makes the codebase cleaner and easier to understand. It helps developers focus on the relevant parts of the code, improving readability and reducing the chances of introducing bugs during future modifications.

Limitations of Dead Code Elimination:

- **Risk of Removing the Needed Code:**

  If not implemented carefully, dead code elimination might accidentally remove the code that is necessary for certain execution contexts or future extensions. This typically occurs, when the analysis is not thorough or when there is a complex control flow.

- **Increased Compilation Time:**

  The process of detecting and removing the dead code can add to the overhead during compilation. For large projects, this process might take a significant time, potentially affecting the overall development cycle.

- **Over-optimization:**

  Sometimes, aggressively removing the code that seems "dead" may lead to situations where small, subtle optimizations are missed, and this can affect the program's performance in unanticipated ways.

Example

Consider the following code snippet:

```
int calculate(int a, int b) {
    int unused = 10;    // This variable is never used.
    return a + b;
}
```

In this example, the variable `unused` is never used, and hence, it contributes nothing to the functionality of the program. During the dead code elimination phase, the compiler would remove the declaration of the `unused`, resulting in a more efficient code.

Loop Optimization

Loop optimization is an essential technique in improving the performance of programs, especially when loops are central to the program's operations. Loops often represent the most computationally intensive parts of a program. Optimizing loops can result in significant performance improvements, particularly in scenarios where large datasets are processed repeatedly, such as in scientific computing, graphics rendering, or real-time applications.

Loop optimization focuses on enhancing the efficiency of loops in a program. The main goal is to reduce the number of iterations, decrease the overhead per iteration, and ensure that the loop executes as quickly as possible. There are several strategies used for loop optimization, including:

Loop Unrolling:

Loop unrolling involves expanding the loop so that multiple iterations of the loop are executed in one go. By reducing the number of loop control checks, this optimization can minimize the overhead. For example:

Before unrolling:

```
for (int i = 0; i < 4; i++) {
    sum += array[i];
}
```

After unrolling:

```
sum += array[0] + array[1] + array[2] + array[3];
```

This reduces the number of times the loop condition is checked, and can lead to faster execution, especially in low-level languages, such as C or C++.

Loop Fusion:

Loop fusion combines two or more adjacent loops into a single loop. This reduces the overhead of multiple loop executions, and can improve cache performance. For example:

Before fusion:

```
for (int i = 0; i < n; i++) {
    a[i] = b[i] + c[i];
}

for (int i = 0; i < n; i++) {
    d[i] = e[i] + f[i];
}
```

After fusion:

```
for (int i = 0; i < n; i++) {
    a[i] = b[i] + c[i];
    d[i] = e[i] + f[i];
}
```

This reduces the number of loops and the overhead associated with them, improving performance.

Loop Invariant Code Motion:

This optimization involves moving computations that do not change during each iteration of the loop outside of the loop. This reduces unnecessary recalculations inside the loop.

Before optimization:

```
for (int i = 0; i < n; i++) {
    a[i] = b[i] * 2 + c;
}
```

After optimization:

```
int temp = c;
for (int i = 0; i < n; i++) {
    a[i] = b[i] * 2 + temp;
}
```

The value of **c** does not change during each loop iteration, so moving its usage outside the loop helps reduce redundant computation.

Loop Blocking/Blocking Optimization:

In cases where large datasets are processed, breaking loops into smaller blocks can help optimize memory usage, and improve cache performance. This technique ensures that the data is processed in blocks that fit into the cache, reducing the need for repeated memory accesses.

Strength Reduction:

This optimization reduces the computational cost of frequently performed operations within loops. For example, replacing multiplication with addition, if applicable, can reduce time complexity.

Before strength reduction:

```
for (int i = 0; i < n; i++) {
    result = i * 10;
}
```

After strength reduction:

```
for (int i = 0; i < n; i++) {
    result = i + i + i + i + i + i + i + i + i + i;
}
```

In this example, multiplying by 10 is replaced by repeated additions, which may be faster on some processors.

Key Benefits of Loop Optimization:

- **Improved Execution Speed:**

  Optimizing loops can lead to a significant reduction in the time taken to complete a program, especially for applications that require repetitive processing of large data sets. This is vital in performance-critical applications, such as real-time systems or scientific simulations.

- **Better Resource Utilization:**

  Optimizing loops reduces the workload on the CPU by minimizing redundant operations and efficiently utilizing the processor's cache and registers, leading to improved overall resource utilization.

- **Increased Code Efficiency:**

  By reducing the number of operations performed in each iteration of a loop, the program consumes less power and memory, making it more efficient.

- **Scalability:**

  Optimized loops ensure that a program can scale better with increasing data sizes. This is particularly beneficial for systems designed to handle large datasets, or for applications running on multiple cores.

Limitations of Loop Optimization:

- **Increased Complexity:**

  Optimizing loops can increase the complexity of the code. Techniques, such as loop unrolling or fusion can make the code harder to read and maintain, potentially leading to errors if not done carefully.

- **Compilation Time:**

  Some loop optimizations, such as loop unrolling or blocking, can increase the time it takes to compile the program. This might be a concern for rapid development cycles or programs with a large amount of code.

- **Hardware Dependence:**

  Some loop optimizations are hardware-dependent. For example, loop unrolling might yield better performance on one architecture but not on another. Therefore, performance gains may vary based on the target system.

Example of Loop Optimization

Here is an example of loop unrolling applied to a sum calculation:

Before unrolling:

```
int sum = 0;
for (int i = 0; i < 100; i++) {
    sum += array[i];
}
```

After unrolling (with an unrolling factor of 4):

```
int sum = 0;
for (int i = 0; i < 100; i += 4) {
    sum += array[i] + array[i+1] + array[i+2] + array[i+3];
}
```

This version of the loop reduces the number of iterations, and the number of times the loop condition is checked, leading to faster execution in some cases.

Inlining Functions

Inlining is a code optimization technique where a function's code is directly inserted at the place of each function call, rather than actually making a function call. This helps to reduce the overhead associated with function calls, especially in performance-critical applications. Inlining is particularly useful for small, frequently called functions, as it can eliminate the performance hit incurred by calling a function.

When a function is inlined, the body of the function replaces each call to that function in the code. For example, a simple function call:

```
int square(int x) {
    return x * x;
}
```

If inlined, the code would be replaced as follows:

```
int main() {
    int result = 5 * 5;  // Directly inserting the function logic
}
```

In this case, the compiler takes the code inside the `square` function, and places it directly in the calling location, avoiding the function call overhead.

The main advantage of this approach is that it eliminates the cost of a function call, such as saving registers, pushing and popping values onto the stack, and jumping to the function code. However, this benefit is more significant for small functions that are called frequently.

Key Benefits of Inlining Functions:

- **Reduced Function Call Overhead:**

  Function calls, typically involve some overhead, such as pushing arguments onto the stack, saving registers, and performing jumps to the function code. By inlining a function, this overhead is eliminated which can lead to faster execution, especially for small functions.

- **Improved Cache Performance:**

  When functions are inlined, the code is placed directly in the calling function. This can improve cache performance because the processor's instruction cache may be better utilized, reducing cache misses that can occur, when function calls jump to distant memory locations.

- **Better Compiler Optimizations:**

  Inlined code is available to the compiler for further optimizations. This includes loop unrolling, constant folding, and other compiler-based optimizations that might not be possible with function calls. In some cases, inlining allows the compiler to recognize patterns, and further optimize the code.

- **Reduced Function Prologue/Epilogue:**

  The function call and return have their own overhead (prologue and epilogue) which can be avoided when the function is inlined. This makes the code execution faster for frequently called functions.

Limitations of Inlining Functions:

- **Code Size Increase:**

  One of the primary drawbacks of inlining is that it increases the size of the code. If a function is large or called many times, inlining it will duplicate the code at each call site, potentially leading to significant code bloat. This increase in code size can result in higher memory usage, and might reduce the effectiveness of the instruction cache.

- **Potentially Decreased Readability:**

  Inlining functions can reduce the code readability, especially for larger functions. By replacing a function call with its code, the program may become harder to follow, especially when the function contains complex logic. This may make debugging, and maintaining the code more difficult.

- **Limited to Small Functions:**

  Inlining is very beneficial for small functions. Large functions or functions with a lot of control flow, recursion, or state-dependent behavior, generally do not benefit from inlining. In such cases, inlining can cause a performance hit due to excessive code duplication, and the loss of optimizations provided by the function call.

- **Increased Compilation Time:**

  Inlining functions require more work during the compilation process as the compiler must replace each function call with the function's body. This can increase the compilation time, especially in large programs with many inlined functions.

Example of Function Inlining

Consider the following example where we inline a simple function that calculates the square of a number.

Before Inlining:

```
#include <stdio.h>

int square(int x) {
    return x * x;
}

int main() {
    int result = square(5);
    printf("Square of 5 is: %d", result);
    return 0;
}
```

After Inlining:

```
#include <stdio.h>

int main() {
    int result = 5 * 5;  // Inlined code from the square function
    printf("Square of 5 is: %d", result);
    return 0;
}
```

In the second version, the function `square` is inlined directly into the `main` function, eliminating the need for a function call and the associated overhead.

Impact on Performance and Efficiency

Performance optimization is one of the primary goals in software development, and understanding the impact of various techniques on both performance and efficiency is crucial for building high-performance applications. In the context of code generation and optimization, the performance of a program is typically measured by factors, such as execution speed, memory usage, and power consumption. Efficiency is about achieving the best performance, while using the least amount of resources, including time and space.

In this section, we will explore how various optimization techniques affect the performance and efficiency of a program. Specifically, we will focus on the impact of **register allocation**, **instruction**

scheduling, and **code generation optimizations**, such as **dead code elimination**, **loop optimization**, and **function inlining**.

Impact of Register Allocation on Performance and Efficiency

How It Affects the Performance:

- **Optimal Use of Registers:** Proper register allocation minimizes memory access by keeping frequently used variables in registers which are faster to access than the main memory. This can significantly improve the execution speed, particularly for computation-heavy tasks.
- **Minimizing Register Spilling:** Poor register allocation can result in *register spilling* where the data is moved between registers and memory which introduces the additional memory access overhead. This can slow down the program, and consume more power.

How It Affects Efficiency:

- **Lower Power Consumption:** Using registers efficiently reduces the need for memory accesses which can lead to lower power consumption, especially in embedded systems where power efficiency is a priority.
- **Increased Code Size:** Some register allocation techniques might increase the code size, if more registers are allocated than needed, potentially reducing cache efficiency, and harming the overall performance.

Impact of Instruction Scheduling on Performance and Efficiency

How It Affects the Performance:

- **Reducing Pipeline Stalls:** Instruction scheduling optimizes the order in which instructions are executed to reduce pipeline stalls and hazards. By reordering instructions, programs can avoid delays caused by the data or control dependencies, leading to faster execution.
- **Parallel Execution:** Dynamic instruction scheduling, especially in the out-of-order execution, allows the processor to execute instructions as soon as their operands are available, improving throughput, and making better use of the available CPU resources.

How It Affects Efficiency:

- **Optimizing Processor Usage:** Efficient instruction scheduling makes better use of the CPU resources by balancing the load across multiple execution units. This maximizes the throughput of the processor, without overloading any one part of the CPU.
- **Increased Instruction Cache Efficiency:** By improving the instruction flow, instruction scheduling can also help improve cache hit rates, reducing the need to fetch instructions from the slower memory.

Impact of Code Generation Optimization Techniques on Performance and Efficiency

Dead Code Elimination

How It Affects the Performance:

- **Faster Execution:** Removing unnecessary code (dead code) means that the processor will spend less time executing instructions that do not contribute to the program's output, leading to a more efficient execution path.

- **Reduced Branching:** By eliminating the dead code, the number of branches and condition checks in the program is reduced, making the program more streamlined and faster to execute.

How It Affects Efficiency:

- **Reduced Code Size:** Eliminating the dead code reduces the overall size of the program that helps optimize memory usage, and can improve cache performance.
- **Lower Maintenance Costs:** Dead code removal improves code readability, making maintenance easier and less error-prone, indirectly benefiting long-term efficiency.

Loop Optimization

How It Affects the Performance:

- **Faster Loop Execution:** Loop optimization techniques, such as loop unrolling or loop fusion, can reduce the number of iterations, optimize memory access patterns, and reduce overhead, leading to faster loop execution.
- **Improved Parallelism:** Optimizing loops for parallel execution can take advantage of multi-core processors, improving performance significantly in parallel computing scenarios.

How It Affects Efficiency:

- **Reduced Resource Usage:** Optimized loops often require fewer instructions and memory accesses which reduces the overall resource consumption. This helps in achieving energy-efficient performance, especially in resource-constrained environments.
- **Enhanced Cache Utilization:** Loop optimizations can reduce the memory access latency by improving the locality (both temporal and spatial) of the data, leading to better cache usage, and improved overall system efficiency.

Inlining Functions

How It Affects the Performance:

- **Reduced Function Call Overhead:** By inlining functions, the time spent in setting up and tearing down the function call stack is eliminated, leading to faster execution for frequently called small functions.
- **Improved Cache Locality:** Inlining can improve instruction cache locality because the function body is directly inserted at the point of the function call, making it more likely that the CPU cache will store the necessary instructions.

How It Affects Efficiency:

- **Increased Code Size:** Inlining large functions or functions that are called many times can result in a larger program size. This might reduce efficiency if the code size becomes too large, and negatively impacts the cache performance.
- **Better Compiler Optimizations:** The function body being inlined gives the compiler more opportunities for additional optimizations, such as constant folding and loop optimizations which can result in improved performance and efficiency.

Overall Impact on Performance and Efficiency

Thus, the ultimate goal of any optimization technique is to strike a balance between performance improvements, and the efficient use of resources. While these techniques can significantly improve the performance of a program by reducing the execution time, memory usage, and power consumption, their impact on efficiency depends on the context in which they are applied.

For example, optimizing register allocation can enhance the execution speed, but it can also increase code size, impacting memory efficiency. Similarly, instruction scheduling can improve throughput but may result in more complex scheduling logic, affecting the efficiency of the compiler, and increasing the compilation time.

Incorporating these techniques appropriately, depending on the application and system constraints, can lead to optimal performance and efficiency. As always, the effectiveness of these optimizations should be measured through profiling and testing to ensure that the chosen approach provides the desired benefits.

Practical Implementation Insights

This section delves into the practical aspects of **Register Allocation** and **Instruction Scheduling** in modern compilers, with a focus on how these techniques are applied in the **GCC** and the **LLVM**. We will also highlight the key differences between the two, and examine their practical applications in real-world scenarios.

Register Allocation in the GCC

Register allocation is one of the most critical optimization phases in a compiler. It involves assigning program variables to a limited number of CPU registers to minimize memory access, and improve the execution speed. The GNU Compiler Collection (GCC), being one of the most widely used compilers, incorporates sophisticated techniques for register allocation that are designed to target a wide variety of processor architectures. Effective register allocation can significantly boost the performance of compiled code by reducing the number of memory loads and stores which are more time-consuming than register operations.

Key Insights for Practical Implementation

- **Register Allocation Phases in the GCC**

  The GCC's register allocation process involves several steps, such as:

  - **Live Variable Analysis**: Before the actual allocation, the GCC analyzes the program to determine which variables are live at any given point in the program's execution. This analysis is crucial for making sure that only those variables that are needed at a specific instruction get assigned to registers.
  - **Interference Graph Construction**: The GCC constructs an interference graph where each node represents a variable, and the edges indicate that two variables cannot share the same register due to overlapping lifetimes. This graph is used for deciding how to allocate registers.
  - **Register Assignment**: Once the interference graph is constructed, the register allocator assigns variables to the registers, taking care not to assign conflicting variables to the same register.

- **Graph Coloring Algorithm**

  The GCC uses a **graph coloring** algorithm for register allocation. The goal is to assign each node in the interference graph, a "color" (which corresponds to a register) in such a way that no two adjacent nodes (representing variables with overlapping lifetimes) share the same color. This is a classical problem in compiler optimization where the number of colors corresponds to the number of available registers. The GCC's graph coloring algorithm is optimized for both speed and accuracy, balancing between creating minimal spill code (code to handle variables that can't fit into registers) and maintaining efficiency.

- **Spilling and Register Pressure**

  Spilling occurs when there are more live variables than available registers. In this case, some variables must be stored in memory rather than in registers. The GCC's register allocator aims to minimize spilling, but sometimes, it is inevitable. Register pressure which refers to the scarcity of the available registers, plays a significant role in determining when spilling happens. The GCC provides optimizations to reduce the register pressure by trying to reuse registers or rearranging the order of instructions to keep the variables alive for shorter periods.

- **Target-Specific Register Allocation**

  The GCC offers target-specific register allocation strategies that vary depending on the architecture of the CPU. For example, for a CPU with a large number of registers, (such as an ARM or x86-64 processor), the GCC might use more aggressive register allocation strategies to exploit the larger register file. Conversely, for processors with fewer registers, the GCC employs more careful strategies to minimize the register usage, while optimizing the performance.

- **Local versus Global Register Allocation**

  The GCC uses both **local** and **global** register allocation techniques:

  - **Local Allocation**: This phase allocates registers within the basic blocks (sequences of instructions with no jumps). It focuses on minimizing register usage in small parts of the program, and is more efficient in terms of runtime overhead.
  - **Global Allocation**: In this phase, the GCC allocates registers across the entire program, taking into account variable lifetimes across function calls and loops. This is more computationally expensive but results in a more efficient overall register allocation.

- **Register Classes and Customization**

  The GCC supports **register classes** which are groups of registers that share certain properties, (such as being suitable for specific types of operations). For example, some registers may be specialized for floating-point arithmetic or integer operations. The GCC, basically, allows users to define custom register classes tailored to specific target architectures, enabling fine-tuned register allocation for the performance-sensitive applications.

- **Optimization for Function Calls and Call Clobbering**

  During function calls, some registers are clobbered (modified), and must be saved and restored around the call. The GCC's register allocator considers the impact of function calls, and tries to minimize the number of registers that need to be saved or restored, thereby reducing the function call overhead. This is especially important in embedded systems or real-time applications where the function call performance is critical.

- **Interprocedural Register Allocation**

  The GCC employs **interprocedural register allocation** where it considers the register usage across function boundaries. In certain cases, registers can be allocated for variables that are shared between functions, reducing the overhead of passing variables through memory or stack frames.

- **Handling Different Types of Registers**

  Modern CPUs have different types of registers, such as general-purpose, special-purpose, and status registers. The GCC's register allocator is capable of distinguishing between these types, and ensuring that only appropriate variables are assigned to each type of register. For instance, a general-purpose register may be used for variable storage, while a special-purpose register may be used for specific machine instructions like program counters or stack pointers.

- **Performance Impact**

  The effectiveness of register allocation in GCC can have a significant impact on the performance of the generated code. By ensuring that frequently used variables are kept in registers, the GCC reduces the time spent on memory accesses, resulting in faster execution times. However, improper register allocation or excessive spilling can lead to performance degradation. As a result, the GCC's register allocation algorithm is carefully designed to balance between register usage and code performance, tailoring the process to the specific CPU architecture.

Instruction Scheduling in the LLVM

Instruction scheduling is a crucial optimization technique in compilers to improve the performance of the machine code by reordering instructions to reduce pipeline stalls, and improve parallelism. In Low-Level Virtual Machine (LLVM), instruction scheduling plays a key role in ensuring that the code executes efficiently on modern processors with complex pipelines and multiple execution units.

Key Insights for Practical Implementation

- **Understanding LLVM's Instruction Scheduling Framework:**
  - The LLVM provides an in-depth instruction scheduling framework that allows both static and dynamic scheduling for various architectures.
  - The framework includes multiple phases, such as instruction selection, scheduling, and code generation, with scheduling directly impacting the final performance of the code.
- **Handling Different Processor Architectures:**
  - One of the primary goals of the LLVM's instruction scheduler is to optimize the code for specific processor architectures (for example, x86, ARM).
  - The LLVM's instruction scheduling is flexible enough to account for the unique characteristics of each architecture, such as the number of execution units, instruction latencies, and instruction-level parallelism.
- **Types of Instruction Scheduling in the LLVM:**
  - **Static Scheduling**: Involves reordering instructions at the compile time where the compiler can predict execution order based on known dependencies.
  - **Dynamic Scheduling**: Here, the execution order is adjusted at the runtime, often through hardware-based techniques, such as out-of-order execution. The LLVM can support both static and dynamic approaches, depending on the target hardware.
- **Scheduling Based on Data Dependencies:**
  - The LLVM's instruction scheduling involves an analysis of data dependencies between instructions. This helps in identifying independent instructions that can be executed in parallel without affecting the program's correctness.
  - Using dependency graphs and control flow analysis, the LLVM reorders instructions to minimize waiting times, and maximize resource utilization.
- **Latency and Pipeline Hazards:**
  - Instruction scheduling in the LLVM optimizes for both data and control hazards. These hazards can lead to pipeline stalls, and reduced CPU performance.
  - By considering instruction latencies, the LLVM can avoid scheduling instructions that would cause delays, ensuring that instructions are issued only when the data is available, and avoiding bottlenecks.

- **Advanced Scheduling Techniques:**
  - **Register Renaming**: In the LLVM, instruction scheduling is sometimes paired with register renaming which helps eliminate false dependencies between instructions that operate on the same register.
  - **Predication**: The LLVM also uses predication in some cases where conditional instructions are scheduled in a way that reduces branching overhead, and improves the flow control.
- **Effects on Code Size and Execution Time**:
  - While instruction scheduling can significantly improve performance by reducing the execution time, there can be trade-offs with the code size. Reordering instructions or adding No-Operations (NOPs) to avoid pipeline stalls might increase the size of the generated code.
  - Practical implementations in the LLVM must balance the trade-off between faster execution and increased code size, particularly in embedded systems or resource-constrained environments.
- **Fine-Tuning for Specific Use Cases**:
  - The LLVM allows fine-tuning of instruction scheduling for specific applications, such as multimedia processing or scientific computing. By adjusting the scheduler parameters or adding custom optimization passes, developers can actually achieve significant performance gains in specialized domains.
- **Challenges in Complex Workloads**:
  - For complex workloads, such as large-scale machine learning models or high-performance computing applications, instruction scheduling in the LLVM must handle multiple simultaneous dependencies, and interleaving execution across various CPU cores.
  - Developers often face challenges in ensuring that optimizations do not interfere with program correctness or introduce unnecessary complexity into the code generation process.
- **Real-World Impact**:
  - **Performance Gains**: By optimizing instruction scheduling, the LLVM can achieve performance improvements, especially in CPU-bound applications, reducing execution times and enhancing throughput. In real-world applications, this can translate into faster data processing, improved gaming performance, and enhanced simulation capabilities.
  - **Energy Efficiency**: Better instruction scheduling reduces the number of CPU cycles required to execute a program which can directly improve energy efficiency, an important factor in mobile and embedded systems.

Key Benefits of Instruction Scheduling in the LLVM

- **Enhanced Parallelism**: Maximizes the use of available CPU execution units by reordering instructions to exploit parallelism.
- **Reduced Pipeline Stalls**: Instruction reordering reduces the risk of pipeline stalls by respecting the data and control dependencies.
- **Optimized Performance**: Fine-tuning instruction ordering leads to faster execution, and reduced runtime.
- **Customizability**: The LLVM allows users to define custom scheduling strategies, based on target architecture, enabling optimizations that cater to specific needs.
- **Better Resource Utilization**: Ensures that the CPU's resources, such as registers and execution units, are effectively utilized, leading to a more efficient code.

Challenges and Considerations

- **Code Size**: Optimization might lead to larger code sizes, especially if NOPs or extra instructions are introduced to improve scheduling.
- **Complexity of Tuning**: Fine-tuning instruction scheduling for a specific workload or hardware can be complex, and requires a deep understanding of the underlying architecture as well as compiler optimization techniques.
- **Dependency Analysis Overhead**: The dependency analysis required for instruction scheduling can add overhead to the compilation process, particularly for large programs or complex instruction sets.

Comparative Analysis of the GCC and the LLVM Techniques

While both the **GCC** and the **LLVM** are widely used compilers with sophisticated optimization techniques, they differ in their approach to **register allocation** and **instruction scheduling**. The GCC, typically employs more static, traditional methods that prioritize simplicity, while the LLVM focuses on flexibility, and a more dynamic approach, allowing for deeper optimization. In this section, we will compare the strengths and weaknesses of each, examining factors, such as performance, ease of use, and support for modern hardware. This comparison will help determine which system is better suited for the specific applications and environments.

Aspect	GCC	LLVM
Register Allocation	Uses a traditional **graph coloring algorithm** to allocate registers. This method focuses on reducing register spilling, and efficiently utilizing the available registers through interference graphs.	Utilizes **linear scan allocation** which is simpler and faster. This approach is particularly effective for Just-In-Time (JIT) compilation, enabling dynamic optimization with lower overhead.
Instruction Scheduling	Uses **target-specific heuristics** to optimize instruction order for specific processors. Focuses on minimizing execution cycles, and reducing pipeline stalls through static scheduling.	Employs a combination of **static and dynamic scheduling** techniques. Uses machine-specific models to optimize instruction flow, enhancing out-of-order execution, and reducing instruction latency.
Code Generation	Produces highly optimized machine code with a focus on **target-specific architecture optimizations**. The GCC's code generation is well-suited for embedded systems and legacy platforms.	Designed to generate machine-independent intermediate code which can then be optimized for multiple architectures. Offers **machine code optimizations** for modern processors with vectorization support.
Optimization Techniques	Prioritizes traditional optimizations, such as **dead code elimination, constant propagation**, and **loop optimizations**. Tends to focus on conservative, tried-and-tested optimization techniques.	Leverages **aggressive optimization passes**, such as **loop unrolling, inlining**, and **auto-vectorization**. Allows fine-tuned control over optimization passes, making it ideal for performance-critical applications.
Modularity and Extensibility	Less modular, with optimizations often tightly integrated into the compiler pipeline. Adding new optimizations can require significant changes.	**Highly modular** design with reusable components. The LLVM's modular framework allows easy addition of custom passes, making it suitable for research and new feature development.

Just-In-Time (JIT) Compilation	Limited JIT capabilities primarily used for languages like Java. Focuses more on ahead-of-time (AOT) compilation.	Built with strong **JIT compilation support**, making it ideal for runtime optimizations in dynamic languages, such as Python and Ruby.
Cross-Platform Support	Provides extensive support for multiple architectures, including older and specialized platforms, such as ARM, MIPS, and PowerPC.	Also supports multiple architectures, but focuses on **modern processors** and systems, ensuring high-performance code generation for x86, ARM, and other contemporary platforms.
Development Ecosystem	Mature, with a large user base and extensive documentation. Well-suited for stable, long-term projects.	**Rapidly evolving**, with strong industry adoption in areas, such as game development, AI, and data analytics. Known for its flexibility and support for cutting-edge optimizations.
Use Cases	Commonly used in embedded systems, operating systems, and applications where stable performance is critical.	Favored in performance-critical applications, such as **game engines (Unreal Engine)**, high-performance computing, and **AI model optimizations.**

Table 12.1: *Comparative Analysis of the GCC and the LLVM Techniques*

Real-World Case Studies illustrating Techniques

The following case studies illustrate the practical implementation of **register allocation** and **instruction scheduling** techniques in real-world scenarios, demonstrating how these optimization techniques are applied to improve the performance and efficiency of applications in various fields.

Case Study 1: High-Performance Computing (HPC) Applications with the GCC: Register Allocation

Context: In the world of high-performance computing (HPC), large scientific computations require careful optimization to run efficiently on modern processors. One of the key challenges in these applications is minimizing the register spills which occur when the number of live variables exceeds the available registers.

Problem: A simulation application in a scientific research environment was experiencing significant performance degradation due to register spilling. The application which involved matrix multiplications, and solving large systems of linear equations, was critical for modeling complex phenomena in physics and engineering.

Solution: The GCC's register allocation algorithm which implements the **graph coloring technique**, was used to optimize register allocation. The algorithm effectively minimized the number of spills by coloring the graph in such a way that the live ranges of variables were assigned to the available registers. For registers that could not be allocated directly, the GCC used efficient spilling strategies, choosing to spill variables that would incur the least performance penalty.

Outcome: After applying the GCC's register allocation optimizations, the application showed a **30% reduction in the execution time**. This was largely attributed to a reduction in register spills, leading to fewer memory accesses, and better CPU cache utilization.

Case Study 2: Game Engine Optimization with the LLVM: Instruction Scheduling

Context: A major game development studio was developing a AAA game engine where CPU performance was critical for rendering complex 3D environments, and handling real-time physics calculations. The engine's performance had a bottleneck in the physics engine where heavy computations were causing CPU stalls.

Problem: The game's physics engine, based on real-time calculations of rigid body dynamics, suffered from delays due to instruction-level bottlenecks, causing lag, and reducing the smoothness of gameplay. The issue was that many physics calculations had interdependencies that led to pipeline hazards, specifically data hazards, resulting in pipeline stalls.

Solution: The game studio leveraged **LLVM's dynamic instruction scheduling**, particularly out-of-order execution, to allow instructions to be executed as soon as their operands were available, rather than following the original sequential order. This dynamic scheduling approach helped avoid pipeline stalls by making use of all available execution units, and minimizing wait times for data dependencies.

Additionally, **software pipelining** was used in the game's graphics pipeline, optimizing the rendering loop by allowing instructions to be executed in parallel across multiple stages.

Outcome: The game engine's performance improved dramatically, achieving a **25% increase in frame rates**, and a smoother gaming experience. The dynamic instruction scheduling in LLVM helped avoid pipeline stalls and fully utilized the CPU resources, reducing computation time for physics-based calculations.

Case Study 3: Mobile Application Optimization: Register Allocation in the GCC

Context: A mobile application that processed real-time video streaming required efficient performance on low-power devices with limited processing capabilities. The application used advanced machine learning algorithms for real-time object recognition which involved large amounts of data processing.

Problem: The app's real-time processing suffered from lag, and performance was not meeting the real-time requirements. The issue was primarily caused by inefficient use of registers during the processing of video frames, leading to memory bottlenecks and unnecessary CPU overhead.

Solution: The development team applied **GCC's linear scan register allocation** technique to optimize the usage of available registers. This approach, while simpler than graph coloring, was efficient enough for the constraints of the mobile environment. The linear scan algorithm dynamically allocated registers based on the live range of variables and reused registers where possible.

Outcome: The mobile app's performance was significantly improved, with **real-time processing speeds increased by 40%**, enabling smoother video streaming and object recognition. The linear scan allocation reduced memory access and, optimized register usage, making the app more responsive on mobile devices.

Case Study 4: Compiler Optimization in Embedded Systems: Instruction Scheduling in the LLVM

Context: An embedded systems company was working on optimizing a software stack for a custom embedded processor that handled low-level signal processing for telecommunications. The processor had a specific instruction pipeline architecture that was sensitive to how instructions were scheduled.

Problem: The initial implementation of the signal processing algorithm showed poor performance due to inefficient instruction scheduling. The instructions were being executed in a sequential manner, causing unnecessary CPU pipeline stalls and suboptimal use of the processor's execution units.

Solution: The engineering team turned to **LLVM's instruction scheduling techniques**, focusing on **static instruction scheduling** for predictable workloads. They manually tweaked the LLVM optimizer to schedule independent instructions closer together, allowing them to execute in parallel and reducing the likelihood of pipeline hazards. The static scheduling approach, combined with low-level hardware knowledge, helped improve execution.

Outcome: This optimization resulted in a **15% performance boost**, enabling the system to handle more concurrent signal-processing tasks. By reducing the pipeline stalls and better utilizing the available execution units, the embedded system was able to meet real-time constraints, and handle more complex processing tasks efficiently.

Case Study 5: Cloud Data Center Optimization: Hybrid Approach to Register Allocation and Instruction Scheduling

Context: A major cloud service provider was running a large-scale data processing framework for machine learning tasks in its data centers. The goal was to accelerate training tasks involving large-scale datasets, and minimize resource utilization across multiple servers.

Problem: The cloud data center faced inefficiencies in the resource usage. Despite having a large number of processors, the computed tasks were not being executed as quickly as expected due to inefficient register allocation, and instruction scheduling in the underlying compiler.

Solution: The team used **a hybrid approach** combining the **GCC's register allocation** (graph coloring for high-priority tasks) and the **LLVM's dynamic instruction scheduling** (out-of-order execution). The register allocation optimized CPU cache utilization, while the instruction scheduling improved parallel execution and minimized idle cycles for each processor in the cluster.

Outcome: After implementing these optimizations, the cloud service provider saw a **35% reduction in the total time required for model training**, leading to faster iteration cycles for machine learning algorithms. The combination of efficient register usage, and advanced instruction scheduling maximized the performance of the data center's hardware.

Conclusion

In this chapter, we explored crucial techniques for optimizing program performance, focusing on register allocation methods, such as Graph Coloring and Linear Scan, and instruction scheduling techniques, such as List Scheduling and Software Pipelining. Additionally, we covered optimization strategies, such as Dead Code Elimination, Loop Optimization, and Inlining Functions, all aimed at enhancing program efficiency and execution speed.

Looking ahead to *Chapter 13, Machine-Independent Optimizations and Local and Global Techniques*, we will delve into optimization strategies that improve performance across various machine architectures. This chapter will introduce local and global optimization techniques, explore data flow analysis, and provide practical insights into LLVM optimizations, all of which will further enhance code generation and execution efficiency.

Points to Remember

- Register Allocation is essential for mapping variables to CPU registers to minimize memory access, and improve the execution speed.
- The Graph Coloring Algorithm is a popular method for register allocation, treating each variable as a node, and using graph coloring to assign registers efficiently.

- Linear Scan Allocation is a simpler, faster register allocation technique that works well in situations where speed is prioritized over optimization.
- Dynamic Allocation Techniques allocate registers at the runtime, adjusting based on the program's needs, providing a flexible but resource-intensive approach.
- Instruction Scheduling is used to reorder instructions to reduce pipeline stalls and hazards, improving the CPU resource utilization, and speeding up execution.
- Static Instruction Scheduling involves scheduling instructions at the compile time, assuming known instruction dependencies and available resources.
- Dynamic Instruction Scheduling allows for instruction reordering at the runtime, enabling the out-of-order execution and better use of CPU resources, especially in modern processors.
- List Scheduling is a common technique in instruction scheduling where instructions are ordered in a list, based on their dependencies, improving throughput, and reducing CPU stalls.
- Software Pipelining allows overlapping the execution of operations, particularly in loops, improving parallelism, and reducing the execution time of repetitive tasks.
- The Out-of-Order Execution is a technique in modern processors where instructions are executed as soon as their operands are available, improving throughput and efficiency.

Multiple Choice Questions

1. What is the primary goal of register allocation in compilers?
   a. Minimize CPU usage
   b. Reduce memory bandwidth
   c. Allocate variables to a limited number of registers
   d. Increase program size
2. Which of the following techniques is commonly used for register allocation?
   a. Data-flow analysis
   b. Graph coloring
   c. Loop unrolling
   d. Register spilling
3. In register allocation, what does spilling refer to?
   a. Loading data from memory to registers
   b. Storing data from registers to memory
   c. Moving data between registers
   d. Allocating more registers
4. In graph coloring-based register allocation, what do nodes in the graph represent?
   a. Register assignments
   b. Basic blocks
   c. Variables or live ranges
   d. Memory locations

5. Which of the following is NOT a factor in choosing registers for allocation?
   a. Liveness analysis
   b. Instruction latency
   c. Interference graph
   d. Register pressure
6. What is register coalescing in the context of register allocation?
   a. Merging two adjacent instructions
   b. Combining two variables into the same register
   c. Spilling registers to memory
   d. Assigning a unique register to every variable
7. The interference graph in register allocation is used to represent:
   a. Data dependencies between variables
   b. Execution paths of functions
   c. Memory access patterns
   d. Potential register conflicts
8. What does the Static Single Assignment (SSA) form help with in register allocation?
   a. Reducing the number of required registers
   b. Simplifying variable lifetime analysis
   c. Increasing code generation speed
   d. Optimizing loop performance
9. Which register allocation approach splits variables across different registers or memory locations depending on the context?
   a. Global register allocation
   b. Local register allocation
   c. Hybrid allocation
   d. Block-based allocation
10. What is register pressure, and why is it significant in register allocation?
    a. The demand for memory storage; affects memory usage
    b. The demand for registers; impacts spilling and performance
    c. CPU temperature due to register usage; affects thermal throttling
    d. The cache utilization; impacts cache efficiency
11. What is the main objective of instruction scheduling?
    a. Maximize the CPU power usage
    b. Rearrange instructions to reduce latency

c. Increase the program size

d. Reduce the number of registers needed

12. Which type of instruction scheduling is commonly used to exploit instruction-level parallelism?

    a. Local scheduling

    b. Loop unrolling

    c. Global scheduling

    d. Pipeline scheduling

13. What is the primary challenge in instruction scheduling for modern processors?

    a. Handling memory bandwidth

    b. Predicting the next instruction

    c. Managing cache coherency

    d. Dealing with data dependencies

14. Which of the following is a common technique used to handle data dependencies in instruction scheduling?

    a. Instruction hoisting

    b. Instruction reordering

    c. Instruction pipelining

    d. Register spilling

15. Instruction scheduling attempts to avoid which type of stall in pipelined architectures?

    a. Data hazards

    b. Control hazards

    c. Resource hazards

    d. Memory hazards

Answers

1. c
2. b
3. b
4. c
5. b
6. b
7. d
8. b
9. c

10. b
11. b
12. d
13. d
14. b
15. a

Questions

1. What are the main techniques used in register allocation, and how do they impact the performance of compiled code?
2. How does instruction scheduling contribute to optimizing the execution of instructions, and what challenges are commonly faced in this process?
3. Explain how register allocation techniques, such as graph coloring and linear scan work. How do these methods differ in terms of complexity and efficiency?
4. What is the role of code generation optimization in modern compilers, and how does it interact with register allocation and scheduling?
5. How do GCC and LLVM handle register allocation, and what specific methods or algorithms do they implement to optimize register usage?
6. What are the benefits and limitations of instruction scheduling techniques, such as list scheduling and dynamic scheduling?
7. In what ways do register allocation strategies address the limitations of a machine's physical register set, and how does spill code impact performance?
8. Describe how instruction scheduling can be used to reduce pipeline stalls, and improve instruction-level parallelism (ILP) in processors.
9. How does GCC or LLVM implement code generation optimizations for high-performance applications? Provide specific examples.
10. What trade-offs are involved in combining register allocation and instruction scheduling within a single optimization pass, and how do modern compilers manage these trade-offs?

Key Terms

- **Register Allocation**: Assigning variables to the CPU registers to speed up program execution by reducing memory access.
- **Graph Coloring Algorithm**: A method for assigning registers where variables are represented as nodes and colors represent registers.
- **Linear Scan Allocation**: A fast method of assigning registers in one pass, without much optimization, but it is quick.
- **Dynamic Allocation**: Register allocation that happens while the program is running, allowing flexibility.
- **Instruction Scheduling**: Reordering instructions to reduce delays caused by dependencies or bottlenecks.

- **Static Instruction Scheduling**: Scheduling instructions at compile-time, before the program runs, based on known dependencies.
- **Dynamic Instruction Scheduling**: Scheduling instructions during runtime, as the program is running, to improve efficiency.
- **List Scheduling**: A method for scheduling instructions by organizing them in a list, ensuring dependencies are respected.
- **Software Pipelining**: A technique where multiple iterations of a loop are processed simultaneously to speed up execution.
- **Out-of-Order Execution**: A technique where the CPU executes instructions as soon as their inputs are ready, instead of waiting for earlier instructions to finish.

CHAPTER 13

Machine-Independent Optimizations and Local and Global Techniques

Introduction

In the previous chapter, *Chapter 12, Register Allocation and Scheduling*, we explored how to optimize the use of registers and the ordering of instructions during code generation. We covered **register allocation techniques** which aim to assign variables to registers efficiently, reducing memory access and improving performance. We also discussed **instruction scheduling** where the goal is to arrange instructions in an optimal sequence to avoid pipeline stalls. The chapter concluded by looking at various **code generation optimization techniques**, illustrated with examples from the **GCC** and the **LLVM**.

In this chapter, we will focus on **machine-independent optimizations** that improve program performance, without being tied to any specific hardware. First, we will look at **local optimization techniques**, which enhance individual code blocks. Next, we will explore **global optimization techniques**, which optimize code across multiple blocks to boost overall efficiency. We will also introduce **data flow analysis**, a method to track how data moves through the program and uncover opportunities for optimization. Finally, we will examine how these techniques are applied in **LLVM**, with practical examples demonstrating how to create optimized code.

By the end of this chapter, you will have a solid understanding of how machine-independent optimizations can enhance performance, making your code more efficient, regardless of the underlying hardware.

Structure

In this chapter, we will discuss the following topics:

- **Introduction to Machine-Independent Optimizations**
  - Importance of Machine-Independent Optimizations
  - Overview of Optimization Goals
- **Local Optimization Techniques**
  - Definition and Purpose of Local Optimizations
  - Common Local Optimization Techniques
  - Trade-offs and Considerations
  - Relationship to Global Optimizations

Introduction to Machine-Independent Optimizations

Machine-independent optimizations are techniques used by compilers to improve program performance without being dependent on any particular hardware. These optimizations focus on refining code at a higher level, making it more efficient across different platforms and architectures. The goal is to enhance the program's execution speed, reduce memory usage, and improve resource utilization, ensuring the code is adaptable to various environments.

Importance of Machine-Independent Optimizations

Machine-independent optimizations are essential because they enhance the performance of programs, without relying on specific hardware details. This makes them highly versatile and applicable across multiple platforms, including different devices, operating systems, or processors. Unlike machine-dependent optimizations which are tailored to a specific processor's architecture, machine-independent optimizations help ensure that a program runs efficiently on a wide range of hardware. They contribute to better resource utilization, faster execution times, and lower energy consumption, all while maintaining cross-platform compatibility.

Overview of Optimization Goals

The main goals of machine-independent optimizations are to:

- **Enhance Performance**: The most direct goal is to make the program run faster, either by improving the execution speed of individual instructions or by reducing the total number of instructions required to perform a task.
- **Reduce Resource Usage**: Machine-independent optimizations aim to reduce memory consumption, minimize register usage, and improve data locality. This can result in more efficient use of system resources, especially in memory-constrained environments.

- **Improve Code Quality**: These optimizations often result in cleaner, more maintainable code that is easier to debug and modify. They can also eliminate redundant or unnecessary computations, making the program more efficient.
- **Enable Cross-Platform Portability**: Since machine-independent optimizations do not depend on specific hardware, they help ensure that the optimized code can run efficiently on different platforms without needing significant modifications.

By focusing on these goals, machine-independent optimizations contribute to making the code faster, more efficient, and adaptable to various environments, providing a solid foundation for further optimizations that are platform-specific.

Local Optimization Techniques

Local optimization techniques are essential strategies used by compilers to improve the performance of a program within individual basic blocks of code. A **basic block** is a section of code where control flows from top to bottom, with no branches or jumps except at the beginning or end. These optimizations focus on refining code in these blocks, making them more efficient by removing redundancy, simplifying expressions, or enhancing data usage.

Definition and Purpose of Local Optimizations

The primary goal of **local optimizations** is to improve the performance of code within a single basic block without considering how it interacts with the rest of the program. These optimizations aim to reduce the computational cost of executing a particular block by eliminating unnecessary operations and simplifying the instructions. As a result, the program runs faster and consumes fewer resources, especially when such optimizations are applied repeatedly across many sections of the code.

Common Local Optimization Techniques

Local optimization techniques are vital for improving the efficiency of individual basic blocks in a program. By targeting specific areas of code, these optimizations aim to streamline operations, reduce unnecessary calculations, and eliminate redundant instructions. These techniques often result in noticeable performance improvements, especially when applied repeatedly across multiple blocks throughout a program. In this section, we will explore some of the most common and impactful local optimization techniques used in compilers to enhance code performance, including **constant folding**, **dead code elimination**, and **loop invariant code motion**. Each of these techniques addresses specific inefficiencies, making code more compact and faster to execute.

Constant Folding

Constant folding is a compiler optimization technique that evaluates constant expressions during the compilation process rather than at runtime. The purpose of constant folding is to replace expressions involving constant values with their computed results, thus eliminating unnecessary calculations during execution. This technique improves performance by reducing the number of operations the processor must perform, leading to faster program execution and more efficient use of system resources.

When the compiler detects that an expression involves only constant values (for example, 4 + 5), it computes the result ahead of time and directly inserts the result into the code. For example, instead of leaving the addition of 4 + 5 to be computed each time the program runs, the compiler will substitute the expression with 9.

Example

Before Constant Folding:

```
int x = 4 + 5;
```

After Constant Folding:

```
int x = 9;
```

In this example, the compiler calculates **4 + 5** at compile time and replaces the expression with the result, 9. This eliminates the need for the processor to perform the addition during runtime, speeding up the program.

Benefits of Constant Folding:

Constant folding provides several key advantages that contribute to more efficient program execution and resource usage:

- **Improved Performance**: By removing the need to perform constant computations at runtime, constant folding can significantly reduce execution time, especially in code with numerous constant expressions.
- **Reduced Code Size**: Since the compiler replaces expressions with their constant values, the generated code is smaller which can improve memory usage and cache performance.
- **Cleaner, Simpler Code**: The resulting code is easier to read and maintain, as redundant calculations are removed.

Limitations:

Despite its benefits, constant folding has some limitations that affect where and how it can be applied:

- **Limited to Constant Expressions**: Constant folding can only optimize expressions where the values are known at compile time. It does not apply to dynamic calculations involving runtime variables or user input.
- **Narrow Scope**: Its impact is confined to specific sections of the program that involve constant values, so it may not lead to substantial improvements for programs that rely heavily on runtime values or complex logic.

Dead Code Elimination

Dead code elimination (DCE) is a compiler optimization technique that removes parts of a program that do not affect its final outcome. These unused or redundant instructions, often referred to as **dead code**, can include variables, calculations, or even entire code blocks that are never executed or whose results are never used. By eliminating such code, the compiler can make the program more efficient, reducing memory usage, execution time, and the overall size of the compiled code.

The compiler analyzes the program to identify code that has no impact on the final output. Dead code is typically identified in two forms:

- **Unreachable Code**: Code that cannot be executed due to logical conditions or control flow.
    - **Example**: A statement inside an if (false) block is never executed and can be removed.
- **Unused Computations or Assignments**: Operations or variables that are computed but never used in subsequent operations or program output.

The compiler removes these sections during the optimization process to streamline the code.

Example

Before Dead Code Elimination:

```
int x = 10;
int y = 20;
if (false) {
    x = x + y;  // This code is never executed
}
int z = 5;
z = z + 10;  // The value of 'z' is not used anywhere
return x;
```

After Dead Code Elimination:

```
int x = 10;
return x;
```

In this example:

- The block inside **if (false)** is unreachable and is removed.
- The computation of **z** is unnecessary since z is not used, so it is also eliminated.

Benefits of Dead Code Elimination:

This optimization offers several advantages for program efficiency and maintainability:

- **Improved Execution Speed**: By removing unnecessary instructions, the program executes faster as the processor performs fewer operations.
- **Reduced Memory Usage**: Eliminating unused variables and computations reduces the memory footprint of the program.
- **Smaller Code Size**: A more compact program leads to better cache performance and shorter load times.
- **Enhanced Readability**: The code becomes cleaner and easier to understand, making it simpler for developers to maintain.

Limitations:

While dead code elimination is an effective optimization, it has certain constraints:

- **Dynamic Code**: The compiler cannot always detect dead code in cases where conditions depend on runtime values. For example, a dead code resulting from user input or runtime states might not be optimized.
- **Cost of Analysis**: In large and complex programs, identifying dead code can increase compilation time due to the need for detailed program analysis.
- **Risk of Aggressive Removal**: Overzealous elimination could accidentally remove code that appears unused but serves a non-obvious purpose, such as debugging or instrumentation.

Loop Invariant Code Motion

Loop Invariant Code Motion (LICM) is a compiler optimization technique that improves program performance by identifying computations within loops that remain unchanged (invariant) across iterations and moving them outside the loop. This reduces the number of repeated calculations during execution, leading to faster and more efficient programs, especially for loops that execute a large number of iterations.

The compiler performs an analysis of the loop to identify **loop invariant expressions**–statements or computations that yield the same result regardless of the current iteration. Once identified, these expressions are moved to a location just before the loop, ensuring they are computed only once instead of being recalculated repeatedly.

Steps:

1. **Identify Invariant Expressions**: Determine computations that do not depend on variables modified within the loop.
2. **Verify Safety**: Ensure that moving the code outside the loop does not alter program correctness (for example, dependencies on side effects or memory access).
3. **Move Code**: Relocate invariant expressions to a safe position before the loop begins.

Example:

Before LICM:

```
for (int i = 0; i < n; i++) {
    int result = a * b;  // 'a * b' is invariant and does not change per
iteration
    sum += result + i;
}
```

After LICM:

```
int result = a * b;  // Moved outside the loop
for (int i = 0; i < n; i++) {
    sum += result + i;
}
```

In this example:

- The computation `a * b` is invariant because its value does not depend on `i`. By moving it outside the loop, the program avoids performing this multiplication in every iteration.

Benefits of Loop Invariant Code Motion:

LICM offers significant advantages, particularly for performance-critical applications:

- **Improved Execution Speed**: By reducing redundant computations, the LICM minimizes the workload inside loops, leading to faster execution.
- **Optimized Resource Usage**: Fewer operations within the loop mean less use of CPU cycles and power.
- **Better Scalability**: For loops with a large number of iterations, the benefits of LICM become even more pronounced.

Limitations and Considerations:

Despite its benefits, the LICM has some limitations and potential trade-offs:

- **Complexity of Analysis**: Identifying invariant expressions requires careful analysis to ensure correctness which can increase compilation time.
- **Side Effects**: Computations with side effects (for example, function calls or I/O operations) cannot be moved safely outside the loop without changing program behavior.
- **Dependency Risks**: Moving code that depends on loop variables or external states could introduce errors if not handled correctly.

Relationship to Other Optimizations:

Loop invariant code motion often works in conjunction with other optimizations such as **constant folding** and **dead code elimination**. For example, the LICM may identify expressions made simpler by constant folding, or it may remove redundant computations that would otherwise be eliminated as dead code. Together, these techniques help maximize performance gains in both local and global contexts.

Trade-offs and Considerations

Compiler optimizations, such as **loop invariant code motion (LICM)**, **constant folding**, and **dead code elimination** bring many benefits, but they are not without challenges. Understanding the trade-offs and considerations involved in applying these optimizations helps developers and compiler designers make informed decisions to balance performance and reliability.

Trade-offs:

Every optimization has its costs. Here are some common trade-offs to consider:

- **Increased Compilation Time**: Advanced optimizations require analyzing dependencies, control flow, and other factors which can slow down the compilation process, especially for large programs.
- **Code Size versus Performance**: Optimizations such as LICM might reduce runtime computation but at the cost of increasing the size of the generated code, potentially impacting memory usage or cache performance.
- **Limited Applicability**: Certain optimizations, such as dead code elimination or LICM, only apply to specific scenarios, limiting their overall impact.
- **Debugging Challenges**: Optimized code often looks different from the original source, making debugging more difficult and less intuitive for developers.
- **Minimal Gains for Small Loops**: In smaller loops, the overhead introduced by an optimization might outweigh the performance benefits, making the effort less effective.

Considerations:

Some factors need careful attention to ensure optimizations are applied correctly and effectively:

- **Correctness and Side Effects**: Optimizations must not alter program behavior. For example, LICM cannot safely move a function call outside a loop if the function produces side effects (for example, modifying a variable or performing I/O).
- **Hardware Dependence**: The impact of an optimization can vary based on the target hardware, such as CPUs, GPUs, or embedded systems.
- **Weighing Costs and Benefits**: Applying an optimization may not always lead to meaningful improvements. Developers must decide if the potential gains justify the effort or complexity added.
- **Order of Optimizations**: Some optimizations depend on others or might conflict with them. For example, the LICM might move an expression that would otherwise be removed by dead code elimination. Proper sequencing is crucial.
- **Impact on Maintainability**: Optimized code often becomes less readable, which can make maintenance and debugging more challenging for developers.

Balancing the Trade-offs:

Finding the right balance between performance improvements and potential drawbacks is key to effective optimization:

- **Customization**: Modern compilers often provide optimization levels (for example, -O1, -O2, -O3 in GCC), allowing developers to choose the level of optimization that aligns with their goals for speed, size, and compilation time.
- **Selective Application**: Optimizations should be applied where they deliver the most value. For

example, aggressive optimizations might be reserved for performance-critical sections of a program.

- **Testing and Validation**: Ensuring correctness through rigorous testing helps avoid unintended side effects of aggressive optimizations.

Relationship to Global Optimizations

Local optimization techniques, such as **constant folding**, **dead code elimination**, and **loop invariant code motion**, focus on improving the efficiency of smaller, self-contained sections of code, such as individual basic blocks or loops. However, for a program to achieve its full optimization potential, these techniques often need to work in harmony with **global optimizations**, which analyze and optimize larger sections of the code spanning multiple blocks or even the entire program.

How Local and Global Optimizations Work Together:

Local and global optimizations each serve unique purposes, but they are most effective when used together. Local optimizations target specific sections of code, improving their efficiency, while global optimizations take a broader view, addressing issues that span across multiple blocks or the entire program. Understanding how these two approaches work in harmony reveals their true power in creating highly optimized programs.

Scope of Application:

- Local optimizations improve small, isolated parts of the code, such as loops or basic blocks.
- Global optimizations analyze the bigger picture, looking for redundancies or inefficiencies across the entire program.

Building on Local Optimizations:

Local techniques often lay the foundation for global optimizations. For instance:

- **Loop invariant code motion (LICM)** reduces unnecessary computations inside a loop, making it easier for global techniques, such as **loop unrolling** to work effectively.
- **Dead code elimination** simplifies individual blocks, helping global optimizations spot and remove unused variables across multiple functions.

Shared Goals:

Both techniques aim to improve performance and efficiency, but they address different aspects of the code. Their combined effect ensures the code is optimized at all levels.

Example: Working in Harmony

Before Optimization:

```
for (int i = 0; i < n; i++) {
    int temp = a * b;
    sum += temp + c[i];
}
```

After Local Optimization (Loop Invariant Code Motion):

```
int temp = a * b;
for (int i = 0; i < n; i++) {
    sum += temp + c[i];
}
```

After Global Optimization (Loop Unrolling):

```
int temp = a * b;
for (int i = 0; i < n; i += 2) {
    sum += temp + c[i];
    sum += temp + c[i + 1];
}
```

In this example:

- **Local Optimization** moved the computation of `a * b` outside the loop to avoid repeating it.
- **Global Optimization** reduced the number of iterations by unrolling the loop, further speeding up execution.

Benefits of Combining Local and Global Optimizations

The collaboration between local and global optimizations leads to significant performance improvements that neither approach could achieve alone. By addressing inefficiencies at both the micro and macro levels, these techniques work together to create code that is faster, more efficient, and better suited for real-world applications.

- **Maximized Efficiency**: Addressing redundancies at both the local and global levels ensures the program runs faster and uses fewer resources.
- **Improved Resource Management**: By tackling inefficiencies across the program, these techniques optimize memory usage, execution time, and energy consumption.
- **Comprehensive Coverage**: Local optimizations clean up individual blocks, setting the stage for global optimizations to handle cross-block and program-wide improvements.

Global Optimization Techniques

Global optimization techniques focus on analyzing and improving the performance of a program across its entirety, considering multiple functions, modules, or loops. These techniques address inefficiencies and redundancies that span larger scopes, enabling more significant performance gains than localized approaches.

Definition and Importance of Global Optimizations

Global optimizations are compiler techniques that analyze the entire program or large segments of it, optimizing code by examining dependencies and interactions across functions, basic blocks, or even multiple files in a project. These optimizations go beyond the confines of a single loop or block, identifying and removing inefficiencies that occur across broader sections of the code.

Importance of Global Optimizations:

Global optimizations are critical for creating efficient, high-performance software. Here is why they matter:

- **Enhanced Program Efficiency:**

  By addressing redundancies and inefficiencies across the program, global optimizations can significantly reduce runtime and memory usage.

- **Broad Scope of Improvement:**

  Unlike local optimizations, which are confined to small sections of code, global techniques analyze the entire control flow, uncovering opportunities for improvement that local techniques might miss.

- **Optimizing Complex Applications:**

  Large-scale software systems with multiple interacting components benefit greatly from global optimizations, as they ensure efficient communication and resource usage across the program.

- **Enabling Advanced Techniques:**

  Many sophisticated compiler features, such as interprocedural analysis or whole-program optimization, rely on global techniques to identify patterns, and apply transformations effectively.

- **Adaptability to Hardware:**

  Global optimizations can adapt the program to the specific characteristics of the target hardware, such as reducing cache misses or improving instruction-level parallelism, to enhance performance.

Common Global Optimization Techniques

Global optimization techniques are essential for improving the performance of a program by analyzing and optimizing not just individual functions but also the interactions between them. These techniques can eliminate inefficiencies that span the entire program, leading to significant gains in speed, efficiency, and resource usage.

Function Inlining

Function inlining replaces a function call with the actual body of the function, eliminating the overhead associated with calls and returns.

Example

Before inlining:

```
int square(int x) {
    return x * x;
}

int result = square(5);
```

After inlining:

```
int result = 5 * 5;  // Function call is replaced with the body of the
function.
```

Benefits of Function Inlining:

Function inlining offers significant advantages that enhance both runtime performance and optimization opportunities:

- **Reduced Overhead**: Eliminates the cost of function calls, such as stack operations, improving runtime efficiency.
- **Enables Further Optimizations**: Exposes the inlined function's body to other optimizations, such as constant folding and dead code elimination, resulting in more streamlined code.

Challenges of Function Inlining:

Despite its advantages, function inlining comes with certain trade-offs:

- **Code Bloat**: Excessive inlining of large functions can lead to an increase in program size, which may negatively impact cache performance.

- **Increased Compilation Time**: Adding more inlined code increases the complexity of subsequent optimizations, leading to longer compilation times.

Global Common Subexpression Elimination

GCSE identifies and eliminates duplicate computations across different parts of the program, replacing them with a single computation that is reused wherever needed.

Example

Before optimization:

```
x = a + b;
...
y = a + b;  // Redundant computation
```

After optimization:

```
x = a + b;
...
y = x;  // Reuses the previously computed result
```

Benefits of GCSE:

This optimization improves efficiency and simplifies the program:

- **Reduced Redundancy**: Avoids performing repetitive calculations, lowering runtime overhead.
- **Improved Code Clarity**: Consolidates repeated expressions, making the code easier to read and maintain.

Challenges of GCSE:

While beneficial, GCSE can introduce complications:

- **Increased Register Pressure**: The reused computations may require additional registers, leading to resource strain in register-limited environments.
- **Complex Dependency Analysis**: Requires careful analysis to ensure the computation remains valid across varying program contexts.

Interprocedural Analysis

Interprocedural analysis examines relationships and dependencies across multiple functions, enabling optimizations that span function boundaries.

Examples of Applications:

Constant Propagation:

- If a function is always called with the same argument values, constant propagation enables the compiler to replace the function call with its constant result. This eliminates redundant calculations and speeds up the execution.

  Example:

- If a function add(x, y) is always called with x = 5 and y = 10, the compiler can directly replace calls to add(5, 10) with 15, reducing computation overhead.

Dead Code Elimination:

- Interprocedural analysis can identify and remove code that does not affect the program's final outcome, even across function boundaries. This includes eliminating unused return values, redundant function calls, or dead parameters passed to functions.

Example:

- If a function call returns a value that is never used in the program, the return value can be eliminated to avoid unnecessary computations.

Function Merging:

- Sometimes, multiple functions that perform similar tasks can be merged or optimized to reduce redundancy, and improve maintainability. Interprocedural analysis can identify such opportunities across the codebase.

Example:

- Two similar functions with the same logic might be combined into a single generalized function, reducing duplication, and improving the clarity of the code.

Benefits of Interprocedural Analysis:

This powerful technique provides extensive optimization opportunities:

- **Cross-Function Optimizations**: One of the main advantages of interprocedural analysis is its ability to optimize interactions between different functions. For example, it can propagate constants across function calls or eliminate a dead code, even when it spans multiple functions.
  - **Improved Performance**: This reduces redundant calculations and unnecessary function calls, directly enhancing the execution speed and memory efficiency.
- **Uncovering Hidden Optimization Opportunities**: Interprocedural analysis provides a broader view of the program, revealing optimization opportunities that would be difficult to spot if each function was analyzed independently.
  - **Better Resource Utilization**: By optimizing across functions, interprocedural analysis helps make better use of resources such as memory and processor time.

Challenges of Interprocedural Analysis:

Implementing interprocedural analysis can be demanding:

- **Increased Complexity:**

  The major challenge of interprocedural analysis is the complexity involved in analyzing code across multiple functions. The interdependencies between functions, variable states, and control flows must be carefully considered to ensure that the analysis remains accurate and meaningful.
- **Higher Computational Cost**: The need to analyze the entire program's control flow and data flow can lead to higher computational costs, especially in large codebases.
- **Scalability**:

  As the size of the program grows, interprocedural analysis can become computationally expensive. Performing this type of analysis over an entire program can significantly increase compilation time, especially for large and complex software systems.
- **Memory and Time Constraints**: For large-scale applications, the amount of memory and time required for interprocedural analysis may limit its feasibility, especially in real-time or resource-constrained environments.
- **Precision versus Performance:**

  Achieving the right balance between the precision of interprocedural analysis and the performance of the program can be tricky. A more precise analysis may yield better optimization but at the cost of performance during the compilation phase. On the other hand, a less precise analysis may miss optimization opportunities but complete faster.

Challenges in Global Optimization

Global optimization techniques are crucial for improving program performance, but they come with their own set of challenges. These challenges arise due to the complexity of analyzing the entire program, and optimizing across multiple functions, modules, and control flows. Following are some of the key challenges in implementing the global optimization strategies:

Increased Computational Complexity:

Global optimizations require comprehensive analysis of the entire program which can lead to higher computational costs. Optimizations, such as interprocedural analysis and function inlining need to evaluate multiple relationships between functions and code sections, often increasing the complexity of the process.

- **Challenge**: Analyzing large codebases can lead to exponential growth in the number of paths and interactions that need to be evaluated, slowing down the optimization process.
- **Example**: Interprocedural analysis demands tracking function dependencies across the program which can significantly increase both the time and memory consumption during compilation.

Balancing Precision and Performance:

A major challenge in global optimization is finding the balance between precision and performance. Highly precise optimizations can yield better results but at the cost of longer compilation times and increased analysis complexity. Conversely, less precise optimizations may speed up the compilation but miss potential performance gains.

- **Challenge**: Optimizers need to balance achieving the highest possible performance with maintaining reasonable compilation times, and resource usage.
- **Example**: Function inlining might reduce the function call overhead, but excessive inlining can lead to code bloat, impacting performance, and the increasing compile time.

Register and Memory Pressure:

Global optimization techniques, such as function inlining and global common subexpression elimination often introduce additional register or memory requirements to store intermediate results. This can lead to increased pressure on available resources, especially in systems with limited registers or memory.

- **Challenge**: Optimizations may require extra registers or memory locations which could overwhelm the system's resources, potentially resulting in slower performance or higher memory consumption.
- **Example**: Global common subexpression elimination might require additional variables or registers to hold the intermediate values, resulting in inefficient resource usage.

Code Bloat:

Optimizations, such as function inlining, though effective at reducing overhead, can cause code bloat, where the overall program size increases significantly. This can be detrimental, especially on memory-constrained devices or systems with limited cache.

- **Challenge**: While inlining eliminates function call overhead, excessive use can cause the program to grow in size, reducing the benefits of faster execution due to cache misses, and increased memory usage.
- **Example**: Repeated inlining of large functions may increase the size of the code, impacting performance in memory-sensitive environments.

Scalability Issues in Large Codebases:

As programs grow larger, global optimization techniques become more difficult to scale. The need to analyze the entire codebase for optimization opportunities can make these techniques computationally expensive and time-consuming.

- **Challenge**: Global optimizations may become infeasible for large-scale applications due to the complexity of analyzing interactions across the entire program.
- **Example**: Interprocedural analysis can be prohibitively expensive for large programs, leading to longer compile times, and reduced efficiency during optimization.

Handling Complex Dependencies:

Tracking the interdependencies between variables, functions, and data across a program can be difficult. Global optimizations need to carefully handle these dependencies to ensure correctness, while achieving optimization.

- **Challenge**: Incorrectly handled dependencies can result in incorrect optimizations, causing bugs or unintended side effects in the program.
- **Example**: Optimizations, such as constant propagation must account for how variables are modified across functions, and missing a dependency could lead to inaccurate results.

Maintaining Program Semantics:

A critical challenge in global optimization is ensuring that optimizations do not alter the intended behavior of the program. While improving performance, it is important to maintain the program's correctness and logic.

- **Challenge**: Ensuring that optimizations do not change the program's intended functionality or introduce subtle bugs is key to preserving program semantics.
- **Example**: Removing what appears to be a dead code could inadvertently interfere with important side effects, leading to unexpected behavior.

Data Flow Analysis

Data flow analysis is a static program analysis technique that examines how data values are defined, propagated, and used throughout a program. It forms the foundation of many compiler optimizations by providing critical insights into variable usage, dependencies, and program behavior.

Overview of Data Flow Analysis

Data flow analysis is a critical technique in compiler design and program optimization. It involves examining the flow of data within a program to determine how variables and expressions are defined, modified, and used across different sections of code. By analyzing the movement and transformation of data, compilers can identify optimization opportunities, and ensure the correctness of a program.

Purpose of Data Flow Analysis:

The goal of data flow analysis is to optimize program performance, and ensure correctness by tracking the flow of data across variables and code blocks. The key applications include:

- **Code Optimization**: Identifying and eliminating redundancies, dead code, and unnecessary computations.
- **Error Detection**: Catching issues, such as uninitialized variables, unreachable code, and logical inconsistencies.
- **Resource Management**: Efficiently allocating registers and memory for better program execution.

How Data Flow Analysis Works:

Data flow analysis operates at different levels of the program, from individual blocks of the code (local analysis) to the entire program (global analysis). It evaluates how information is transferred between code segments, and determines the properties of the data at various program points.

For instance, it may determine:

- Whether a variable holds a constant value at a particular location.
- Whether a specific expression has already been computed, and can be reused.
- Whether a variable is "live" (needed in future computations) or "dead" (no longer required).

By combining this information, data flow analysis supports various optimizations, such as constant folding, dead code elimination, and loop optimizations.

Role in Compiler Design:

Data flow analysis serves as a foundation for numerous compiler optimizations. It works closely with other techniques, such as control flow analysis, to construct a complete picture of the program's execution. The insights gained from data flow analysis are used to guide decisions, such as:

- Simplifying expressions.
- Removing unnecessary computations.
- Reordering instructions for efficiency.

Types of Data Flow Analysis

Data flow analysis includes several techniques, each focusing on different aspects of how data flows through a program. These methods play a crucial role in enabling compiler optimizations, and ensuring code correctness.

Constant Propagation

Constant propagation identifies variables with constant values, and replaces them with those constants directly in the code. This simplifies the program, and reduces computation at the runtime.

Example:

If `x = 7` and later `y = x + 2`, constant propagation replaces `x` with `7`, simplifying the expression to `y = 9`.

Applications:

- Simplifies expressions for faster execution.
- Facilitates other optimizations, such as constant folding.

Live Variable Analysis

Live variable analysis determines which variables hold values that may be used later in the program. It identifies "live" variables, while marking "dead" variables for elimination.

Example:

If a variable `temp` is assigned a value but never used, it is deemed "dead", and can be safely removed to save the resources.

Applications:

- Enables dead code elimination.
- Improves register, and memory efficiency.

Reaching Definitions

Reaching definitions track where variables are assigned values, and how these assignments propagate through the program. It ensures that the correct variable values are used at every point.

Example:

Consider:

```
a = 5;
if (condition) {
    a = 10;
}
print(a);
```

Reaching definitions ensures the correct value of **a** is used in **print(a)**.

Applications:

- Detects redundant or conflicting definitions.
- Supports optimizations, such as copy propagation and loop-invariant code motion.

Available Expressions

This technique identifies expressions that have already been computed, and remain unchanged, allowing compilers to reuse their results, instead of recalculating them.

Example:

If x + y is calculated in one part of the code and neither x nor y changes, the result of **x + y** can be reused directly.

Applications:

- Avoids redundant computations.
- Improves runtime performance by reducing workload.

Very Busy Expressions

Very busy expressions are those that are guaranteed to be used regardless of the program's control flow. Moving such computations to earlier parts of the code minimizes repeated calculations in high-frequency regions, such as loops.

Example:

If a * b is computed multiple times within a loop, moving it outside the loop prevents unnecessary repetitions.

Applications:

- Optimizes loop-heavy programs.
- Improves efficiency in critical sections of the code.

Applications of Data Flow Analysis in Optimizations

Data flow analysis is a cornerstone of compiler design, enabling various optimizations that improve the efficiency, reliability, and maintainability of programs. Here are the key applications of data flow analysis in compiler optimizations:

Constant Folding:

Constant folding replaces expressions involving constant values with their computed results during compilation. Data flow analysis identifies constant values, and propagates them through the program.

Example:

If x = 10 and y = x + 5, the expression can be folded into y = 15.

Benefits:

- Reduces runtime computations.
- Simplifies the program for faster execution.

Dead Code Elimination:

By analyzing live variables, data flow analysis helps identify, and remove code that does not affect program output. This reduces the program size, and improves the runtime performance.

Example:

If a variable is assigned a value but never used, the corresponding computation can be removed.

Benefits:

- Reduces unnecessary memory and processing overhead.
- Improves code readability.

Loop Optimization:

Data flow analysis supports techniques such as loop-invariant code motion and strength reduction, optimizing loop execution by identifying computations that can be moved outside the loop or simplified.

Example:

If a calculation in a loop is independent of the loop's iteration, it can be moved outside the loop to avoid repeated execution.

Benefits:

- Speeds up loop-heavy programs.
- Minimizes redundant computations.

Common Subexpression Elimination (CSE):

Data flow analysis detects expressions that are computed multiple times with the same operands and eliminates redundancy by reusing the computed result.

Example:

If a + b appears multiple times in a code block without changes to a or b, the result of a + b can be stored and reused.

Benefits:

- Reduces redundant calculations.
- Optimizes resource usage.

Register Allocation:

Live variable analysis helps optimize the allocation of registers by determining the lifespan of variables and reducing the need for frequent memory access.

Example:

Registers are assigned to variables only when they are "live," minimizing register spills.

Benefits:

- Enhances execution speed by reducing memory access.
- Improves CPU efficiency.

Code Motion and Scheduling:

Data flow analysis assists in reordering instructions to improve execution speed and parallelism without altering the program's logic.

Example:

Moving independent instructions to execute in parallel pipelines enhances processor performance.

Benefits:

- Exploits hardware parallelism.
- Reduces instruction pipeline stalls.

Interprocedural Optimizations:

Extending data flow analysis across function boundaries enables optimizations like function inlining, eliminating unnecessary function calls, and propagating constants across functions.

Example:

A constant passed as an argument to a function can propagate into the function body, allowing further optimization.

Benefits:

- Enhances cross-module performance.
- Reduces overhead from frequent function calls.

Resource Management:

By analyzing variable usage, data flow analysis ensures efficient utilization of memory and CPU resources. Unused variables and redundant memory allocations can be identified and eliminated.

Example:

Detecting and freeing memory blocks that are no longer in use.

Benefits:

- Prevents memory leaks.
- Reduces resource contention.

Implementing Data Flow Analysis

Implementing data flow analysis is a vital step in compiler design, enabling optimizations and ensuring the correctness of generated code. By systematically tracking how data flows through a program, compilers can eliminate redundancies, improve resource management, and enhance performance. Here is a step-by-step guide to implementing data flow analysis effectively:

1. **Define the Problem:**

   The first step is to determine the specific property to analyze, such as live variables, reaching definitions, or available expressions. Clearly defining the objective ensures a focused approach and accurate results.

   Example:

   For **live variable analysis**, the goal is to identify variables holding values that are required in future computations.

2. **Represent the Program as a Control Flow Graph (CFG):**

   A control flow graph represents the logical flow of a program, with nodes corresponding to basic blocks (sequences of straight-line code) and edges representing control transitions (for example, loops, branches).

   Purpose:

   CFG provides a structural foundation for traversing the program during analysis.

   Example CFG Representation:

   For an if-else construct:

   ```
   if (x > 0)
       y = 5;
   else
       y = 10;
   print(y);
   ```

   The CFG would contain branches for the **`if`** and **`else`** paths, merging at the **`print(y)`** statement.

3. **Define Data Flow Equations**

   Define equations that describe how information is generated, propagated, and invalidated in each block:

   GEN: Information generated by a statement (for example, a new variable assignment).

   KILL: Information invalidated by a statement (for example, overwritten variables).

   IN: Information entering a block.

   OUT: Information leaving a block.

   Example for Live Variable Analysis:

   GEN: Variables used in a statement (for example, b in a = b + 2).

   KILL: Variables redefined (for example, a in a = b + 2).

4. **Determine the Direction of Analysis**

   Data flow analysis can be either:

   a. **Forward**: Information flows along the program's control flow (for example, reaching definitions).

   b. **Backward**: Information flows opposite to the control flow (for example, live variable analysis).

   Example:

   In live variable analysis (backward), the compiler identifies variables used in future computations and tracks them back through the program.

5. **Initialize Data Flow Information**

   Assign initial values to **IN** and **OUT** sets for each block:

   Typically, start with empty or universal sets depending on the analysis type.

   Adjust the initialization based on the entry or exit conditions of the program.

   Example Initialization for Live Variables:

   The **OUT** set of the last block is empty because no variables are needed after the program ends.

6. **Perform Iterative Computation**

   Use an iterative algorithm to compute the **IN** and **OUT** sets until a fixed point (no further changes) is reached. This involves:

   - Propagating information across blocks.
   - Updating sets using the data flow equations.

   Example Iteration for Reaching Definitions:

   - Start with an empty **IN** set.
   - Add new definitions from preceding blocks until the **IN** set stabilizes.

7. **Apply the Results**

   Use the analysis results to perform optimizations or detect errors.

   Applications:

   - **Dead Code Elimination**: Remove computations for variables that are not live.
   - **Loop Optimization**: Move invariant code outside loops.
   - **Common Subexpression Elimination**: Reuse previously computed results.

Challenges in Implementation

While data flow analysis provides a powerful framework for optimizing programs and improving their performance, implementing it effectively comes with its own set of challenges. These challenges stem from the complexity of modern programs, the trade-offs between precision and efficiency, and the dynamic behaviors that programs exhibit. Understanding these hurdles is crucial to designing robust and scalable analysis tools.

Scalability:

For large programs, the CFG can grow complex, and iterative computations may become resource-intensive. Efficient algorithms and compact data structures are essential.

Example:

Analyzing a program with deeply nested loops or extensive branching can lead to exponential growth in computation time.

Precision versus Performance:

Highly precise analysis may require more resources and time, whereas less precise methods may miss optimization opportunities.

Handling Dynamic Behavior:

Programs with runtime-dependent control flow or external inputs (for example, user inputs or file reads) can complicate static analysis.

Example:

Dynamic function calls or indirect memory accesses may require additional heuristics or runtime profiling.

Example Implementations Using LLVM Optimizations

To better understand how data flow analysis and optimizations are applied in practice, we can explore their implementation in LLVM. LLVM, a widely used compiler framework, provides powerful tools and libraries that demonstrate the real-world application of optimization techniques. These examples highlight how theoretical concepts translate into practical, efficient, and scalable compiler optimizations.

Overview of LLVM Optimization Framework

Low-Level Virtual Machine (LLVM) is a comprehensive, open-source compiler infrastructure that provides an extensive set of tools for optimizing code during compilation. The LLVM optimization framework is crucial for improving the performance, efficiency, and portability of compiled programs, offering a highly flexible approach to code optimization. Its modular design allows various optimizations to be applied at different stages of the compilation process, making it suitable for a wide range of applications, from general-purpose software to high-performance computing.

Key Features of LLVM Optimization Framework:

- **Modular Design:**

  LLVM is structured in a modular way, allowing optimizations to be applied independently or in combination, depending on the needs of the application. This flexibility makes it easy to experiment with and extend LLVM's optimization capabilities.

- **Intermediate Representation (IR):**

  LLVM uses an intermediate representation (IR) that abstracts away platform-specific details, allowing optimizations to be applied in a way that is independent of the target architecture. The IR acts as a bridge between high-level source code and low-level machine code.

- **Optimization Passes:**

  LLVM's optimization process involves a series of "passes" that apply specific optimizations. These passes can be categorized into:

  - **Loop optimizations** (for example, loop unrolling, loop invariant code motion).
  - **Instruction-level optimizations** (for example, constant folding, dead code elimination).
  - **Data-flow optimizations** (for example, constant propagation).
  - **Interprocedural optimizations** (for example, function inlining, cross-function analysis).

Target-Specific Optimizations:

After generic optimizations are applied, LLVM tailors the generated code for specific hardware architectures, ensuring that the program runs efficiently on the intended platform.

Pass Manager:

LLVM's Pass Manager efficiently manages and organizes the sequence of optimization passes. It ensures that each pass is applied in the correct order, avoiding redundant operations and maximizing optimization benefits.

LLVM's Optimization Flow:

1. **Frontend Optimization**:

   Initially, the source code is parsed to generate LLVM IR. At this stage, basic optimizations such as constant folding and basic inlining can be performed on the IR.

2. **Middle-End Optimization**:

   The middle-end focuses on applying general optimizations to the IR. Passes such as dead code elimination, loop optimizations, and constant propagation improve the efficiency of the code without being dependent on the final hardware.

3. **Backend Optimization**:

   Finally, the backend applies target-specific optimizations, such as register allocation and instruction scheduling, to optimize the IR for the specific hardware architecture on which the program will run.

LLVM Optimization Passes Overview:

LLVM provides a comprehensive set of passes across different levels of optimization:

- **Scalar Optimizations:**

  These passes perform transformations on individual instructions or basic blocks, such as constant folding (replacing constant expressions with their computed values) and dead code elimination (removing unnecessary computations).

- **Loop Optimizations:**

  Advanced loop optimizations, such as loop unrolling and loop fusion, focus on making loops more efficient. This reduces the overhead of repeated iterations and can significantly boost performance in tight loops.

- **Interprocedural Optimizations:**

  These optimizations operate across multiple functions or modules, improving the overall efficiency of the program. Examples include function inlining (replacing a function call with the function's body) and interprocedural constant propagation (passing constant values between functions).

Case Studies of Local and Global Optimizations in LLVM

LLVM's optimization framework has been successfully employed in a variety of real-world scenarios, demonstrating the power of both local and global optimization techniques. The following case studies highlight how these optimizations improve performance and efficiency in diverse use cases, providing practical insights into their implementation.

Case Study: Loop Optimizations in a High-Performance Computing Application

In high-performance computing (HPC), programs often involve computationally intensive operations, particularly in loops that handle large datasets. Optimizing loops is crucial for improving execution time, especially when dealing with scientific simulations, financial models, or machine learning workloads.

Local Optimization Techniques Used:

- **Loop Unrolling:**

  This optimization involves increasing the number of operations within a single loop iteration to reduce the overhead of loop control, such as incrementing counters or checking loop conditions. By unrolling loops, LLVM can minimize branch instructions and reduce the number of iterations.

- **Loop Invariant Code Motion (LICM):**

  This technique moves computations that do not depend on the loop's iteration variable outside the loop, reducing redundant calculations. For instance, if a loop contains a multiplication that remains constant across iterations, it can be computed once before entering the loop.

Global Optimization Techniques Used:

- **Function Inlining:**

  By replacing function calls with the actual code of the function, LLVM eliminates the overhead associated with calling a function. In this case, small utility functions called frequently inside a loop are inlined, further speeding up execution.

- **Interprocedural Constant Propagation:**

  For functions that work with constant values, LLVM propagates these constants across function boundaries, ensuring that unnecessary recalculations are avoided.

Results:

- The loop optimizations reduced the number of redundant calculations inside the loop, significantly speeding up the execution time.
- Function inlining and constant propagation across function boundaries further minimized runtime overhead, improving overall performance by 25%.

Case Study: Compiler Optimization in Mobile Applications

Mobile applications often need to run efficiently with limited memory and processing power. Optimizing for small devices with constrained resources, such as smartphones, is essential to ensure responsiveness and battery efficiency.

Local Optimization Techniques Used:

- **Dead Code Elimination:**

  Dead code elimination removes portions of the code that do not contribute to the program's output. For instance, if a function call results in no changes to the program state or output, LLVM removes the entire function and its calls from the codebase.

- **Constant Folding:**

  In mobile apps, where performance and resource usage are critical, constant folding is applied to precompute constant expressions, eliminating runtime computation.

Global Optimization Techniques Used:

- **Global Common Subexpression Elimination (CSE):**

  This optimization identifies and eliminates redundant calculations that occur across multiple functions or loops. For example, if a particular expression, such as a * b + c, is calculated multiple times in different places, LLVM reuses the result rather than recomputing it.

- **Interprocedural Analysis and Inlining:**

  By analyzing multiple functions across the program, LLVM identifies functions that are called frequently but are relatively simple. These functions are inlined into the caller's code, eliminating function call overhead.

Results:

- Dead code elimination and constant folding reduced the size of the generated code, improving memory usage and startup time.
- Global CSE and inlining reduced redundant computations, leading to better runtime performance and reduced battery consumption, a key consideration in mobile environments.

Case Study: Optimization in Embedded Systems

Embedded systems, such as those used in robotics or automotive applications, require highly efficient code due to strict memory and processing limitations. Optimizations for these systems are especially focused on reducing the size of the program and maximizing the responsiveness of time-critical tasks.

Local Optimization Techniques Used:

- **Instruction Combining:**

  This optimization combines adjacent instructions that can be replaced with a single, more efficient instruction, such as combining two arithmetic operations into one.

- **Loop Unrolling:**

  Loop unrolling is applied to critical time-sensitive loops, such as those used for sensor data processing, to reduce the overhead of branching and increase parallelism.

Global Optimization Techniques Used:

- **Interprocedural Constant Folding:**

  For embedded systems, constant folding across functions helps reduce the memory footprint and computation time by removing unnecessary recalculations of constant expressions.

- **Tail Call Optimization:**

  In embedded systems, recursion is often used in control flow. Tail call optimization ensures that recursive function calls do not consume additional stack space by reusing the current function's stack frame, preventing stack overflow in memory-limited environments.

Results:

- Hence, instruction combining and loop unrolling enhanced the system's responsiveness by reducing CPU cycles needed for core operations.
- Global optimizations, such as interprocedural constant folding and tail call optimization reduced the program's memory usage and improved runtime performance, leading to a 40% improvement in processing speed.

Case Study: Large-Scale Web Application Performance Tuning

Web applications that handle high traffic must be optimized to maintain performance. In this case study, LLVM was used to optimize backend processing code for a large-scale web application that performs data analysis.

Local Optimization Techniques Used:

- **Dead Code Elimination:**

  Removing code that does not contribute to the final output (such as unused variables) is crucial for web applications with high server demands, as it reduces unnecessary computations and memory usage.

- **Constant Propagation and Folding:**

  Constant expressions were evaluated at compile-time to avoid runtime computation, especially in critical code paths that process large amounts of data.

Global Optimization Techniques Used:

- **Global Common Subexpression Elimination (CSE):**

  This optimization improved data-processing pipelines by eliminating repeated expressions calculated across multiple functions, saving processing time.

- **Interprocedural Analysis and Inlining:**

  Functions that were frequently called in data-processing loops were inlined to minimize function call overhead and improve execution speed.

Results:

- Dead code elimination and constant folding resulted in reduced memory usage and faster load times for the web application.
- Global CSE and interprocedural optimizations significantly sped up data processing, reducing the overall response time by 30% and improving the scalability of the web application.

Analyzing Optimization Results

Once optimizations have been applied to a program, it is crucial to analyze the results to evaluate their effectiveness and determine if the desired performance improvements have been achieved. This process helps in identifying areas where further optimizations can be made, ensuring that the program is not only faster but also more efficient in terms of memory usage and resource management. Following is a guide to analyzing optimization results, focusing on key performance metrics and methods for effective evaluation.

Key Performance Metrics

To assess the effectiveness of optimizations, it is important to focus on a few key performance metrics:

Execution Time

The most direct way to measure the impact of optimizations is by tracking the execution time of the program before and after optimizations. A reduction in execution time indicates that the program is performing more efficiently.

- **How to Measure**: Use benchmarking tools to measure the runtime of the program in different scenarios or with various input sizes.
- **What to Look For**: A noticeable decrease in the time it takes for the program to complete its task. If the program includes different components, test each one separately to determine where the most significant improvements have occurred.

Memory Usage

Optimizations often aim to reduce memory consumption, particularly in memory-constrained environments (for example, embedded systems or mobile devices).

- **How to Measure**: Tools such as Valgrind or operating system memory profilers can track memory usage.
- **What to Look For**: Reduced memory footprint, especially in cases where optimizations such as dead code elimination and constant folding help to remove unnecessary variables or computations.

Code Size

In some cases, the goal of optimization is to reduce the size of the generated machine code. This is particularly important in embedded systems or environments with limited storage.

- **How to Measure**: Compare the size of the compiled binary before and after optimization using file size comparison tools.
- **What to Look For**: A reduction in code size without significant loss of performance. In some cases, there may be a trade-off between size and execution time.

Power Consumption

In applications running on mobile or battery-operated devices, optimizing for power consumption is often a key goal. Optimizations that reduce CPU cycles or improve memory access patterns can lead to power savings.

- **How to Measure**: Power profiling tools, such as Intel's Power Gadget or ARM's energy profiling tools, can help measure the power consumption of the application.
- **What to Look For**: Decreased energy consumption, particularly in compute-intensive operations or when the system is idle.

Analyzing the Impact of Local versus Global Optimizations

When evaluating the results of optimizations, it is helpful to distinguish between local and global optimization techniques and assess their individual impact.

Local Optimizations

Local optimizations typically focus on small, isolated portions of the code, such as individual functions or loops. Common examples include constant folding, dead code elimination, and loop unrolling.

- **Impact**: Local optimizations can often yield significant improvements in execution time and memory usage, particularly in critical code sections that are executed frequently.
- **Analysis**: Look for improvements in specific areas of the program, such as reduced loop iterations, smaller functions, and fewer redundant calculations. However, local optimizations may not always produce dramatic results if the program's overall structure is inefficient.

Global Optimizations

Global optimizations, such as interprocedural analysis, function inlining, and global common subexpression elimination, take a broader view of the program and optimize across function boundaries.

- **Impact**: Global optimizations tend to have a more significant impact on overall program performance, especially in complex systems where optimizations applied across multiple modules or functions can compound to produce large performance gains.
- **Analysis**: Measure overall performance changes across the entire program. Global optimizations may lead to greater reductions in execution time and memory usage compared to local optimizations.

Performance Profiling and Benchmarking

Profiling and benchmarking are essential tools in analyzing the results of optimizations. These methods allow you to gather concrete data about performance and compare it with expectations.

Profiling

Profiling tools provide detailed information about where time is spent in the program. They can identify bottlenecks, such as functions that take longer to execute or areas where excessive memory is being used.

- **Tools**: Use profiling tools such as **gprof**, **perf**, or **LLVM's built-in profiling features** to identify hot spots in your program.
- **What to Look For**: Identify functions or operations that still consume a large portion of time or resources. These areas may require further optimization or a different approach.

Benchmarking

Benchmarking involves testing the performance of the program under controlled conditions using specific input data sets. By running benchmarks before and after optimizations, you can quantify the impact of each change.

- **Tools**: Use benchmarking tools such as **Google Benchmark**, **Apache Bench**, or **SPEC CPU** to measure the performance of specific functions or the whole application.
- **What to Look For**: Compare the results of benchmarks before and after optimizations. Ideally, you should see improvements in terms of execution time, throughput, and scalability.

Regression Testing

After optimizations have been applied, regression testing is essential to ensure that the optimizations have not introduced bugs or caused unintended side effects. This is particularly important when making global optimizations that affect large portions of the codebase.

How to Conduct Regression Testing:

- **Test Suites**: Run automated test suites to check the correctness of the program after optimizations.

- **What to Look For**: Ensure that the program behaves correctly across all test cases, particularly edge cases. Any performance improvements should not compromise the program's functionality.

Evaluating Trade-offs in Optimization

Optimizations often involve trade-offs, and it's important to carefully evaluate whether the benefits outweigh the costs. For example, an optimization that improves execution time might increase memory usage, or an optimization that reduces code size might degrade performance in some cases.

Trade-offs to Consider:

- **Speed versus Size**: Some optimizations, such as loop unrolling, can increase code size while improving speed. This trade-off may be acceptable in environments with sufficient memory, but not in resource-constrained systems.
- **Complexity vs. Performance**: Complex global optimizations (such as interprocedural analysis) can offer large performance gains, but they may also increase compilation time and require more sophisticated analysis. This should be weighed against the performance benefits.

How to Measure Trade-offs:

- Compare the performance and resource usage metrics before and after optimizations. Assess whether the gains in execution time or memory usage justify the trade-offs in other areas.
- Run different scenarios with various inputs to understand how optimizations behave under different conditions (for example, small versus large inputs).

Continuous Monitoring and Iteration

Optimization is often an iterative process. After initial optimizations are applied, continuous monitoring and periodic revisits of the code are necessary to ensure that performance remains optimal as the code evolves.

How to Monitor and Iterate:

- Continuously profile and benchmark your application as it evolves and new features are added.
- Reassess optimizations after significant code changes to ensure that they are still providing the desired performance benefits.

Conclusion

In *Chapter 13, Machine-Independent Optimizations and Local and Global Techniques*, we explored various optimization strategies that improve the performance and efficiency of compiled code without relying on specific machine architectures. We covered **Local Optimization Techniques** which focus on optimizing individual basic blocks, and **Global Optimization Techniques**, which address optimization across multiple blocks and functions. The chapter also introduced **Data Flow Analysis**, a critical method for tracking variable values throughout the program. Practical examples using **LLVM Optimizations** provided a hands-on understanding of how these techniques are implemented in modern compilers.

Moving to *Chapter 14, Loop and Peephole Optimization*, we shift our focus to specific optimization techniques that improve the efficiency of loops and small sequences of instructions. **Loop Optimization Techniques** help enhance the performance of iterative processes, while **Peephole Optimization** targets minor, localized improvements in instruction sequences. This chapter will further explore these techniques with practical implementations using **LLVM Optimizations**, continuing the discussion of how to make compiled code more efficient and performant.

Points to Remember

- **Machine-Independent Optimizations** improve performance, without relying on specific hardware.
- **Local Optimizations** target small, specific code sections (for example, constant folding, dead code elimination).
- **Global Optimizations** improve the performance of the entire program (for example, function inlining, global common subexpression elimination).
- **Data Flow Analysis** helps identify opportunities for optimization by tracking how data moves through a program.
- **Trade-offs**: Optimizations often involve trade-offs between performance improvements and increased compilation time or complexity.
- **Local and Global Techniques Work Together**: Combining both types of optimizations enhances the overall efficiency of the program.
- **Efficiency Benefits**: Optimizations lead to faster execution, reduced memory usage, and smaller code size.
- **Portability**: Machine-independent optimizations ensure the program performs well across different platforms.

Multiple Choice Questions

1. **Which of the following is a machine-independent optimization technique?**
   a. Loop Unrolling
   b. Dead Code Elimination
   c. Instruction Scheduling
   d. Register Allocation
2. **What is the main purpose of data flow analysis in optimization?**
   a. To track the movement of control structures in the program
   b. To identify opportunities for reducing memory usage
   c. To identify and optimize redundant calculations
   d. To determine the execution time of each function
3. **Which optimization technique moves calculations that do not change the inside loops outside the loop?**
   a. Constant Folding
   b. Loop Invariant Code Motion (LICM)
   c. Function Inlining
   d. Global Common Subexpression Elimination
4. **What does constant folding do during compilation?**
   a. Moves constant values outside loops
   b. Evaluates constant expressions at the compile time

c. Eliminates unnecessary functions

d. Reduces the number of function calls

5. **Which of the following is NOT a common local optimization technique?**

a. Dead Code Elimination

b. Function Inlining

c. Loop Fusion

d. Global Common Subexpression Elimination

6. **Which technique involves replacing a function call with the function's body to reduce overhead?**

a. Loop Unrolling

b. Dead Code Elimination

c. Function Inlining

d. Peephole Optimization

7. **What is the main goal of global optimizations?**

a. To optimize small code segments

b. To improve the overall performance of the entire program

c. To reduce the compilation time

d. To identify unnecessary variables in loops

8. **What type of optimization aims to eliminate redundant computations across the program?**

a. Global Common Subexpression Elimination

b. Constant Folding

c. Loop Unrolling

d. Instruction Scheduling

9. **Which of the following is a trade-off when applying machine-independent optimizations?**

a. Decreased code size without any performance gain

b. Increased compilation time and complexity

c. Decreased performance with reduced code size

d. Increased memory usage and lower performance

10. **Which optimization technique aims to reduce the number of iterations in a loop by increasing the number of operations per iteration?**

a. Loop Fusion

b. Loop Unrolling

c. Loop Distribution

d. Function Inlining

Answers

1. b
2. c
3. b
4. b
5. d
6. c
7. b
8. a
9. b
10. b

Questions

1. Explain the concept of machine-independent optimizations. How do they contribute to improving the performance of a program?
2. What are the main differences between local and global optimizations? Provide examples of techniques used in each category.
3. Describe the technique of constant folding. How does it improve the efficiency of a program? Provide an example.
4. What is dead code elimination, and why is it considered an important optimization technique? Explain with an example of how dead code is identified and removed.
5. Discuss the concept of Loop Invariant Code Motion (LICM). How does it help optimize loops, and what are the potential benefits and challenges of this optimization?
6. Explain the process of function inlining and its benefits in terms of performance optimization. What are the trade-offs involved in using function inlining?
7. What is global common subexpression elimination, and how does it reduce redundant computations in a program? Provide an example to illustrate how this technique works.
8. How does data flow analysis assist in identifying optimization opportunities? Discuss its role in both local and global optimizations.
9. What are some of the trade-offs involved when applying machine-independent optimizations? How do developers balance performance improvements with increased compilation time and complexity?
10. How do local, and global optimizations complement each other? Discuss the relationship between the two and provide examples where both techniques are used together to improve program efficiency.
11. Explain the concept of interprocedural analysis in the context of global optimization. How does it help improve the performance of functions across different parts of a program?
12. What challenges might arise when implementing machine-independent optimizations? Discuss the common difficulties developers face and potential solutions.

13. In your opinion, which optimization technique covered in this chapter is the most effective for improving the performance of a program? Justify your answer with examples or scenarios where it would be particularly beneficial.

Key Terms

- **Machine-Independent Optimizations**: Techniques that improve program performance without relying on specific hardware features.
- **Local Optimization**: Optimizations applied to individual code segments, such as basic blocks or small functions.
- **Global Optimization**: Optimizations applied to the entire program or large sections of code to improve overall performance.
- **Constant Folding**: The optimization of expressions involving constant values at the compile time, rather than the runtime.
- **Dead Code Elimination**: The removal of code that does not affect the program's output, such as unused variables or operations.
- **Loop Invariant Code Motion (LICM)**: Moving calculations that do not change during loop iterations outside the loop to reduce redundant work.
- **Function Inlining**: Replacing a function call with the body of the function to reduce the overhead of function calls.
- **Global Common Subexpression Elimination**: Identifying and eliminating repeated expressions across the program to reduce unnecessary computations.
- **Data Flow Analysis**: A technique used to track how data moves through a program, helping identify optimization opportunities.
- **Trade-offs**: The balance between optimizing performance and the increased time or complexity of applying optimizations.
- **Loop Optimization**: Techniques that improve the efficiency of loops, such as unrolling, fusion, or parallelization.
- **Peephole Optimization**: A local optimization that looks for small patterns in the code and replaces them with more efficient alternatives.
- **Instruction Scheduling**: The arrangement of instructions in a way that maximizes processor efficiency and minimizes latency.
- **Redundant Code**: Code that does not contribute to the program's outcome and can be removed for optimization.
- **Compiler Optimization Passes**: The steps the compiler takes to apply various optimization techniques to the code.

CHAPTER 14
Loop and Peephole Optimization

Introduction

In *Chapter 13, Machine-Independent Optimizations and Local and Global Techniques*, we explored methods to enhance program performance, without relying on specific hardware. This included **local** and **global optimization techniques**, such as constant folding, dead code elimination, function inlining, and global common subexpression elimination. We also delved into the role of **data flow analysis** in identifying optimization opportunities and discussed the trade-offs involved in applying these techniques. It emphasized how combining local and global optimizations can lead to significant performance improvements across programs.

In *Chapter 14, Loop and Peephole Optimization*, we turn our focus to two critical optimization techniques: **loop optimization** and **peephole optimization**. Loops are a central part of many programs and are often performance bottlenecks, making their optimization essential. We will explore techniques, such as **loop unrolling**, **loop fusion**, and others that aim to improve loop efficiency. Additionally, **peephole optimization** examines small sections of code, replacing inefficient patterns with optimized versions to enhance performance. Finally, we will discuss the practical implementation of these techniques using **LLVM optimizations**, with examples to demonstrate their effectiveness.

This chapter builds on the concepts from the previous chapter, providing specialized strategies for optimizing specific parts of the code, with a focus on resource-intensive areas like loops and code sequences.

Structure

In this chapter, we will discuss the following topics:

- **Introduction to Loop and Peephole Optimization**
  - Importance of Code Optimization
  - Context and Applications of Loop and Peephole Optimization
  - Overview of Optimization Goals
- **Loop Optimization Techniques**
  - Understanding Loop Optimization
  - Common Loop Optimization Techniques
  - Trade-offs and Considerations in Loop Optimization
  - Impact of Loop Optimization on Performance
- **Peephole Optimization**
  - Definition and Purpose of Peephole Optimization

Introduction to Loop and Peephole Optimization

In the realm of program optimization, **loop** and **peephole optimizations** are two crucial techniques that specifically target code efficiency, focusing on reducing execution time and resource consumption. These optimizations play a key role in improving the performance of a program, especially in resource-constrained environments or performance-critical applications.

While **loop optimization** primarily targets repetitive structures in a program, aiming to minimize the overhead of repeated operations, **peephole optimization** deals with refining small, localized instruction sequences, making them more efficient. Both techniques work together to streamline the code, resulting in faster, smaller, and more efficient applications.

In this chapter, we will explore the fundamental principles behind **loop** and **peephole optimizations**, their importance in enhancing program performance, and the various strategies involved in applying these optimizations effectively.

Importance of Code Optimization

Code optimization is essential for improving the overall efficiency and performance of a program. By optimizing code, developers can ensure that applications run faster, consume less memory, and are more energy-efficient, all of which are crucial in a wide range of computing environments. The importance of code optimization can be highlighted in the following ways:

- **Improved Execution Speed**: Optimized code minimizes unnecessary operations, reducing the time it takes for a program to execute. This is especially important for performance-critical applications, such as games, real-time systems, and data processing tools, where speed is crucial for user experience and functionality.
- **Lower Resource Consumption**: Efficient code consumes fewer system resources, such as CPU, memory, and disk space. This is particularly important for mobile devices, embedded systems, and cloud environments where resources are limited. Optimizing code helps in reducing the load on hardware, leading to longer battery life in portable devices, and better overall system performance.
- **Scalability and Portability**: Optimized code is often more adaptable across different hardware and software platforms. It can scale better in environments with varying amounts of available resources. By reducing resource dependency, optimized code can perform well on both low-end and high-end systems.
- **Cost Efficiency**: By reducing resource usage, optimized code can also help in lowering operational costs, especially in cloud-based applications where resource usage directly

correlates with the cost. Code that runs more efficiently translates to fewer resources needed, which results in cost savings.

- **Energy Efficiency**: In power-constrained environments, such as mobile and IoT devices, code optimization is key to reducing power consumption. Efficient algorithms and minimized instruction sequences help lower energy usage, extending battery life, and contributing to environmental sustainability.
- **Improved Maintainability and Readability**: Code optimization not only focuses on performance but also on simplifying code structures. Cleaner, more efficient code is easier to maintain, debug, and extend. Optimizing code can involve removing redundant instructions and streamlining logic, making it easier for developers to understand and modify in the future.

Context and Applications of Loop and Peephole Optimization

In software development, optimizing code is crucial for improving performance and efficiency. **Loops** are often the most executed parts of a program, while **peephole optimization** focuses on fine-tuning small sections of code. Together, these techniques address both large-scale and localized inefficiencies, making programs faster, smaller, and more resource-efficient. Let us explore where and how these optimizations are applied in real-world scenarios.

Context of Optimization

Code optimization aims to maximize performance and efficiency by addressing areas where programs spend most of the time or resources. Two critical areas are **loops**—which are often the most frequently executed parts of a program—and **small instruction sequences**, where inefficiencies can significantly impact overall performance.

- **Loops**: Optimizing loops which execute repeatedly, reduces runtime and resource consumption, making a noticeable difference in performance.
- **Peephole Optimization**: By focusing on small patterns of instructions, this technique refines code efficiency at the micro-level, ensuring faster and more compact execution.

Applications of Loop Optimization

Some applications of loop optimization are listed as follows:

- **Scientific and High-Performance Computing**

  Loops in tasks, such as weather simulations, machine learning, or matrix operations are prime candidates for techniques, such as **loop unrolling** which the reduces iteration overhead.

- **Real-Time Systems**

  Optimizing loops ensures critical operations, such as sensor data processing, meet strict timing requirements. For instance, reducing loop overhead in an autonomous vehicle system enhances the decision-making speed.

- **Graphics and Animation**

  In gaming and visual rendering, loop optimization improves frame rates, ensuring smoother visuals, and better user experience.

- **Embedded Systems**

  In constrained devices, minimizing the loop execution time conserves power, and reduces, strain on hardware.

- **Compiler Efficiency**

  Compilers use techniques, such as **loop invariant code motion** to optimize repetitive calculations, saving time during execution.

Applications of Peephole Optimization

Some applications of peephole optimization are listed as follows:

- **Assembly Code Refinement**

  Peephole optimization improves assembly code by removing redundant instructions. For example, replacing add 0 or multiply by 1 with no-operations saves processing cycles.

- **Embedded Systems**

  Optimized small code sequences help save memory, critical in devices with limited storage.

- **Performance-Critical Code Paths**

  Frequently executed segments, such as library functions, benefit from peephole optimization to enhance the runtime efficiency.

- **Compiler-Generated Code**

  Compilers use peephole techniques to refine the machine code by replacing inefficient instruction sequences with better alternatives.

- **Improved Debugging**

  Simplified code resulting from peephole optimization is easier to debug and maintain.

Complementary Impact of Loop and Peephole Optimization

While **loop optimization** focuses on reducing the overhead in repetitive structures, **peephole optimization** ensures that even the smallest details in the code are efficient. Together, they provide a comprehensive strategy for improving both the macro and micro aspects of the program performance, resulting in robust and high-performing software across domains.

Overview of Optimization Goals

The primary purpose of code optimization is to enhance the efficiency, performance, and maintainability of the software. Optimization techniques, such as loop and peephole optimization, aim to achieve these goals by targeting the specific areas in the code where improvements can yield substantial benefits. The following are the key goals of code optimization:

- **Enhancing Execution Speed**

  The foremost goal of optimization is to reduce the time a program takes to execute. Techniques such as **loop unrolling** and **peephole optimization** help eliminate redundant operations and streamline execution paths, enabling faster program performance.

- **Reducing Resource Consumption**

  Optimized code minimizes the usage of system resources such as CPU cycles, memory, and disk I/O. This is especially critical in environments with limited resources, such as embedded systems and mobile applications.

- **Improving Energy Efficiency**

  Energy-efficient code is essential for devices with limited power capacity, such as smartphones and IoT devices. By optimizing computational overhead and reducing unnecessary operations, power consumption can be significantly lowered.

- **Minimizing Memory Footprint**

  Memory optimization ensures that programs use memory efficiently by reducing unnecessary variable usage, and avoiding memory leaks. This is particularly beneficial for applications running on systems with constrained memory.

- **Enhancing Scalability**

  Optimized programs can scale more effectively, handling larger workloads or increased user demands, without significant degradation in performance. Scalability is crucial for cloud-based and distributed applications.

- **Improving Code Maintainability**

  Optimization often results in cleaner and more structured code. For example, removing redundant instructions or simplifying code logic makes it easier to read, debug, and extend.

- **Reducing Cost**

  Efficiently optimized code reduces operational costs by requiring fewer computing resources which is particularly important in cloud-based systems where resource usage directly impacts expenses.

- **Supporting Portability and Compatibility**

  Optimized code is better equipped to perform consistently across various platforms and hardware configurations, enhancing software adaptability.

Loop Optimization Techniques

Optimizing loops is one of the most impactful ways to enhance a program's performance, as loops often account for a significant portion of execution time. By applying various optimization techniques, developers can reduce overhead, improve execution speed, and make code more efficient. This section explores key loop optimization techniques, their trade-offs, and their impact on performance.

Understanding Loop Optimization

Modern compilers play a crucial role in loop optimization, often automatically applying techniques, such as **loop unrolling**, **loop fusion**, and **strength reduction** during the compilation process. However, manual optimizations are sometimes necessary for highly specialized applications or to complement compiler efforts.

Loop optimization is a cornerstone of performance engineering, offering a path to significant improvements in speed, efficiency, and scalability. By understanding the principles and techniques behind it, developers can create robust, high-performing software systems.

Common Loop Optimization Techniques

Optimizing loops is critical for enhancing the performance of programs, as loops often dominate execution time. This section explores some of the most widely used loop optimization techniques, their applications, and benefits.

Loop Unrolling

Loop unrolling is a technique that involves replicating the loop body multiple times to decrease the number of iterations, and minimize the overhead of loop control operations, such as initialization, condition checking, and incrementing counters. This optimization enhances execution speed by reducing control instructions and enabling better utilization of the processor pipeline.

How It Works:

Instead of iterating over a loop one element at a time, loop unrolling performs multiple iterations in a single pass by duplicating the operations within the loop body.

Example:

Before Unrolling:

```
for (int i = 0; i < 4; i++) {
    a[i] = i * 2;
}
```

After Unrolling:

```
a[0] = 0;
a[1] = 2;
a[2] = 4;
a[3] = 6;
```

Partial Unrolling (for larger loops):

```
for (int i = 0; i < n; i += 4) {
    a[i] = i * 2;
    a[i + 1] = (i + 1) * 2;
    a[i + 2] = (i + 2) * 2;
    a[i + 3] = (i + 3) * 2;
}
```

Loop Fusion

Loop fusion is an optimization technique that combines two or more adjacent loops that iterate over the same data range into a single loop. The goal of loop fusion is to reduce overhead, improve data locality, and enhance cache performance by minimizing loop control operations and taking advantage of spatial locality in memory accesses.

How It Works:

Instead of executing multiple loops over the same range of data, loop fusion merges them into one. This reduces the need for redundant loop conditions and allows the program to process data more efficiently in one pass.

Example:

Before Fusion:

```
// Loop 1
for (int i = 0; i < n; i++) {
    a[i] = i * 2;
}

// Loop 2
for (int i = 0; i < n; i++) {
    b[i] = a[i] + 1;
}
```

After Fusion:

```
for (int i = 0; i < n; i++) {
    a[i] = i * 2;
    b[i] = a[i] + 1;
}
```

In this example, the two loops are combined into a single loop that performs both operations (setting values in a and then updating b).

Loop Inversion

Loop inversion is an optimization technique where a while loop is replaced with a do-while loop or vice versa. This change can help optimize the way a loop's condition is checked and executed, improving the efficiency of certain types of loops.

How It Works:

In a typical while loop, the condition is checked before the body of the loop is executed. In a do-while loop, the body of the loop is executed first, and then the condition is checked afterward. Loop inversion typically involves reversing the structure of a loop to take advantage of the behavior that best suits the specific use case, reducing the overhead of redundant checks.

Example:

Before Inversion:

```
int i = 0;
while (i < n) {
    process(i);
    i++;
}
```

After Inversion:

```
int i = 0;
if (i < n) {
    do {
        process(i);
        i++;
    } while (i < n);
}
```

In this example, the original while loop is converted into a do-while loop which can sometimes be more efficient in terms of control flow, depending on the compiler and hardware architecture.

Strength Reduction

Strength reduction is an optimization technique that replaces an expensive operation in a loop with a simpler, less computationally expensive one. This typically involves replacing costly arithmetic operations, such as multiplication or division, with cheaper operations such as addition or bit shifting.

How It Works:

The main idea behind strength reduction is to identify opportunities within loops where expensive operations can be replaced with equivalent but simpler operations, reducing the overall computational cost and improving performance.

For example, multiplying by a constant can often be replaced by an addition or a bit shift operation which are less expensive on most hardware architectures.

Example:

Consider the following loop where the program multiplies **i** by **10**:

Before Strength Reduction:

```
for (int i = 0; i < n; i++) {
    result = i * 10;
}
```

In this case, multiplying i by 10 is relatively expensive, especially if this loop is executed many times.

After Strength Reduction:

```
for (int i = 0; i < n; i++) {
    result = i + (i << 3);  // i * 10 is equivalent to i + (i << 3)
}
```

By replacing the multiplication with a shift operation (**`i << 3`**), the operation becomes more efficient. This works because multiplying by 10 is the same as adding **`i`** to **`i`** shifted left by **`3`** bits (that is, multiplying **`i`** by **`8`**) and then adding **`i`** to that.

Trade-offs and Considerations in Loop Optimization

Loop optimization techniques, such as loop unrolling, loop fusion, loop inversion, and strength reduction, can significantly improve the performance of software applications. However, these optimizations often come with trade-offs that need to be carefully considered to ensure that the benefits outweigh the potential downsides. Following are some key trade-offs and considerations to keep in mind when optimizing loops.

Code Size versus Performance

- **Trade-off**: While loop optimizations, such as unrolling can reduce loop control overhead, they can also increase the size of the code due to repeated instructions. This increase in code size may lead to higher memory usage, potentially affecting the cache and reducing overall performance.
- **Consideration**: The performance improvement achieved by reducing loop overhead should be weighed against the potential cost of larger code size, especially in memory-constrained systems or embedded applications. For example, loop unrolling is particularly useful for small loops but may not be effective for large loops with many iterations.

Increased Register Usage

- **Trade-off**: Techniques such as loop unrolling and loop fusion can lead to higher register usage. For example, unrolling a loop may require additional temporary variables to hold intermediate results, leading to increased register pressure.
- **Consideration**: Excessive register usage can cause spilling, where data is written to slower memory, reducing performance. Optimizing for performance might require balancing register usage to avoid bottlenecks. Profiling the application to identify potential register pressure issues is important when applying these optimizations.

Complexity and Maintainability

- **Trade-off**: Optimized loops, especially those using advanced techniques such as strength reduction or complex unrolling, can make the code harder to read and maintain. The more complicated the optimization, the more difficult it may be for future developers to understand and modify the code.
- **Consideration**: It is important to strike a balance between optimization and code readability. While performance is crucial, code maintainability should not be sacrificed, especially for large codebases or in collaborative development environments. Commenting and documenting optimized code is vital to ensure that future modifications are made with full understanding of the changes.

Dependence on Hardware Architecture

- **Trade-off**: Some loop optimizations, such as strength reduction and loop unrolling, are highly dependent on the hardware architecture. For example, while multiplication is often slower than addition or shifting on most processors, certain processors may have optimized hardware support for multiplication that minimizes this difference.
- **Consideration**: Before applying optimizations, it is important to consider the target platform's characteristics, including processor type, cache architecture, and memory hierarchy. Profiling tools can help determine whether specific optimizations will provide tangible benefits for the target hardware.

Trade-offs Between Loop Fusion and Memory Access Patterns

- **Trade-off**: Loop fusion can improve performance by reducing the loop overhead, and improving data locality. However, combining loops with different memory access patterns or memory access patterns that are not cache-friendly, can negate the benefits of fusion and even degrade performance.
- **Consideration**: When applying loop fusion, ensure that the loops being fused have compatible access patterns. If the access patterns result in cache misses or memory contention, fusion may reduce performance rather than improve it. It is often helpful to analyze memory access behavior to determine if fusion will be beneficial.

Impact on Compiler Optimization

- **Trade-off**: Manual loop optimizations may interfere with the compiler's ability to apply its own optimizations, potentially leading to suboptimal results. Some compiler optimizations, such as automatic loop unrolling or strength reduction, may be more efficient than manual efforts.
- **Consideration**: While it is important to optimize code manually in some cases, developers should rely on compiler optimization flags and features as much as possible. Compilers are often well-tuned for the target platform and can perform optimizations based on detailed knowledge of the architecture.

Applicability in Different Contexts

- **Trade-off**: Certain loop optimizations may be highly effective for certain types of workloads, such as numerical simulations or image processing, but less so for others, such as string manipulations or I/O-bound operations.
- **Consideration**: Always evaluate the specific needs of the application when selecting loop optimization techniques. In computationally heavy applications, loop optimizations are usually beneficial, but for I/O-bound applications, optimizing the loops may have minimal effect on performance.

Energy Consumption

- **Trade-off**: Optimized loops may increase energy consumption in some cases, especially if they involve more frequent memory access or lead to more power-hungry processor operations. Optimizing for performance might lead to higher energy usage, which could be a concern in mobile or embedded systems with limited battery life.
- **Consideration**: Consider the energy implications of loop optimizations, particularly in power-constrained environments. In some cases, less aggressive optimization techniques may provide a better trade-off between performance and power consumption.

Impact of Loop Optimization on Performance

Loop optimization plays a crucial role in improving the performance of programs, especially in computationally intensive applications. Since loops are often the most time-consuming part of many programs, optimizing them can result in substantial performance gains. The impact of loop optimization on performance can be viewed through multiple lenses, such as execution speed, memory usage, and power consumption.

Reduced Execution Time

One of the primary goals of loop optimization is to reduce the time it takes to execute loops. Several loop optimization techniques directly contribute to achieving this goal:

- **Loop Unrolling**: By reducing the number of iterations, and eliminating redundant calculations, loop unrolling decreases loop control overhead. This leads to fewer branch instructions, and can significantly reduce the time spent on executing the loop.

  Example: In a loop performing simple calculations, unrolling can eliminate the repeated checks and increments of loop counters, allowing multiple computations per iteration.

- **Strength Reduction**: This technique replaces costly operations, such as multiplication or division with less expensive operations like addition or bit shifting. This reduces the computational load within the loop, improving like execution speed.

  Example: Replacing i * 10 with i + (i << 3) (that is, multiplication by 10 with addition and bit shifts) reduces the computational overhead, speeding up the loop.

- **Loop Fusion**: Combining two loops that iterate over the same data can reduce the overhead associated with managing multiple loops. By minimizing control flow instructions, loop fusion enhances the performance of the program.

  Example: Two separate loops that iterate over arrays can be fused into one loop, reducing the number of loop control checks, and improving data locality.

Improved Cache Utilization

Cache memory is much faster than main memory, so optimizing memory access patterns can have a significant impact on like performance. Proper loop optimization improves cache locality which is essential for achieving faster data access.

- **Loop Fusion**: By combining loops that access the same arrays or data structures, loop fusion improves spatial locality. This increases the likelihood that the data required by consecutive iterations will be stored in the cache, reducing the cache misses and, improving performance.
- **Loop Interchange**: Changing the order in which loops are nested can enhance cache utilization. When loops are reordered to access memory sequentially (that is, row-major or column-major order), cache efficiency improves, leading to faster memory access.

  Example: Accessing elements in a two-dimensional array, row by row rather than column by column improves cache performance because modern caches are optimized for sequential access patterns.

Increased Parallelism

Optimizing loops can expose opportunities for parallelism which can be crucial for utilizing multi-core processors effectively. By minimizing dependencies between loop iterations, some loop optimizations enable the execution of multiple iterations simultaneously.

- **Loop Carried Dependency Removal**: Eliminating dependencies between iterations, where one iteration's result depends on the previous one, allows parallel execution of loop iterations. This can lead to significant speedups on multi-core systems.

Example: In loops where each iteration is independent of the others, parallelizing the loop allows multiple cores to work on different iterations simultaneously, reducing the overall execution time.

- **Loop Unrolling**: Unrolling loops not only reduces control overhead but can also expose more opportunities for parallelization. By splitting a loop into smaller chunks, you can assign each chunk to a different processor in a multi-core system.

Reduced Memory Usage

Memory access patterns can significantly affect the memory usage of a program. Some loop optimization techniques help reduce memory usage, especially in systems with limited memory resources.

- **Loop Unrolling**: While unrolling increases code size, it can also reduce memory access overhead. By processing multiple loop iterations at once, unrolling can reduce the frequency of memory accesses, leading to more efficient memory usage.
- **Strength Reduction**: Reducing the complexity of operations within loops also reduces the number of variables that need to be stored in memory, contributing to more efficient memory usage.

Energy Efficiency

In addition to improving performance, optimizing loops can also reduce energy consumption which is important in mobile and embedded systems where power efficiency is a concern.

- **Strength Reduction**: Replacing expensive operations such as multiplication and division with simpler operations such as addition or shifting can also reduce the energy required to perform these operations.
- **Loop Unrolling**: Reducing the number of iterations in a loop can lower the number of control flow instructions executed, thereby reducing power consumption in the processor.
- **Memory Access Patterns**: Optimized memory access can reduce the power spent on fetching data from memory, particularly in systems with tight energy constraints.

Scalability

Loop optimization can improve the scalability of software, especially for applications that need to handle larger data sets. Optimized loops allow programs to perform well even as the size of the input grows.

- **Parallel Execution**: By enabling the parallel execution of independent loop iterations, optimized loops can scale with the number of available processing cores, making it easier to handle large datasets efficiently.
- **Reduced Overheads**: By optimizing loops for smaller iteration counts or reducing unnecessary computations, programs become more scalable, handling larger workloads with fewer resources.

Trade-offs and Considerations

While loop optimization has significant performance benefits, it is essential to consider the trade-offs involved:

- **Code Size**: Some optimizations, such as loop unrolling, can increase the code size. This may negatively impact memory usage and can lead to higher cache miss rates if the code no longer fits in the CPU cache.

- **Maintainability**: Highly optimized loops can become harder to understand and maintain. It is crucial to find a balance between optimization and code readability, especially in large codebases.
- **Overhead of Optimization**: Not all optimizations are beneficial for every program. In some cases, the overhead of applying an optimization may outweigh the performance improvements it brings. Profiling tools should be used to identify the most impactful optimizations.

Peephole Optimization

Peephole optimization is a local optimization technique that focuses on small, localized patterns of instructions. The primary goal is to improve the efficiency of the generated code by replacing a small "window" or "peephole" of instructions with more efficient or simpler instructions. This technique is typically applied at the level of the generated assembly or intermediate code.

Definition and Purpose of Peephole Optimization

Peephole optimization refers to a series of small-scale optimizations that examine a small section or "peephole" of the program's code, often a few consecutive instructions, and attempt to replace them with more efficient alternatives. These optimizations typically occur at the assembly or machine code level after the high-level code has been compiled into intermediate representations.

The main purpose of peephole optimization is to improve the performance of the compiled code by reducing unnecessary operations, lowering the instruction count, improving CPU cache utilization, and enhancing other low-level aspects of execution efficiency. It is typically used to target specific inefficiencies in the final output without changing the program's logic.

Common Peephole Optimization Techniques

Peephole optimization techniques typically look for common patterns in a small set of consecutive instructions that can be optimized. Some common techniques include:

Instruction Replacement

Instruction replacement is a peephole optimization technique that involves substituting a sequence of instructions with a more efficient, often simpler, equivalent instruction. The goal of this optimization is to reduce the number of machine instructions executed, thereby improving both the speed and efficiency of the generated code.

The purpose of instruction replacement is to eliminate redundant or inefficient instructions that do not contribute optimally to the program's execution. By using a more efficient instruction (or a combination of instructions), the program can run faster, consume less memory, and execute with fewer processor cycles.

How Instruction Replacement Works:

Instruction replacement typically focuses on replacing a sequence of instructions with a single, optimized instruction that performs the same function. The sequence of instructions might include unnecessary intermediate steps or could be simplified using more advanced hardware instructions.

Example: Consider the following sequence of instructions:

```
MOV R1, 5       ; Load the value 5 into register R1
ADD R1, R1      ; Add R1 to itself (equivalent to multiplication by 2)
```

This sequence can be replaced with:

```
SHL R1, 1       ; Shift R1 left by 1 bit (equivalent to multiplying by 2)
```

Here, instead of performing an addition, a bit-shift operation is used which is a more efficient operation.

Types of Instruction Replacement:

- **Substitution of Arithmetic Operations**:

  Replacing expensive operations (such as multiplication or division) with cheaper alternatives (such as addition, subtraction, or bit-shifting).

  Example:

  Replace A * 2 with A << 1 (bitwise shift left, equivalent to multiplication by 2).

  Replace A / 2 with A >> 1 (bitwise shift right, equivalent to division by 2).

- **Reducing Redundant Operations:**

  In cases where an instruction sequence is repeated unnecessarily, replacing redundant code with a simpler or more direct approach is beneficial.

  Example:

  If a calculation such as MOV R1, R2 followed by MOV R2, R1 is found, it can be eliminated as it does not change any values.

- **Leveraging Special CPU Instructions:**

  Modern processors often provide special instructions that can perform multiple operations simultaneously or more efficiently than general-purpose instructions. These specialized instructions can be used to replace simpler ones.

  Example:

  Use SIMD (Single Instruction, Multiple Data) instructions to process multiple data elements in parallel, instead of performing the same operation multiple times.

Redundant Code Elimination

Redundant code elimination is a peephole optimization technique that focuses on removing unnecessary or duplicate instructions from the code. The goal is to eliminate operations that do not affect the final outcome of the program, reducing the number of instructions and improving execution efficiency.

The primary purpose of redundant code elimination is to streamline the code, removing operations that are executed but do not contribute to the program's results. This leads to more compact, faster, and efficient code, as redundant instructions waste CPU cycles and memory resources.

How Redundant Code Elimination Works:

Redundant code elimination identifies operations that are executed but have no effect on the program's state, such as:

Assignments that overwrite themselves:

If a variable is assigned a value and that value is immediately overwritten by another assignment without any use in between, the first assignment is redundant.

Example:

```
MOV A, 5
MOV A, 10  ; The first MOV is redundant because A is immediately overwritten
```

The first `MOV A, 5` can be removed.

Duplicate operations:

Redundant operations may occur when the same calculation or operation is performed multiple times, without any change in the inputs.

Example:

```
MOV A, B
ADD A, C
MOV D, A
ADD A, C  ; This second addition is redundant because it repeats the previous
operation on A
```

Here, the second **`ADD A, C`** is redundant and can be removed, simplifying the code.

Dead code:

Sometimes, instructions may never be executed because of conditional logic that prevents them from being reached. These instructions are considered dead code and should be removed.

Example:

```
MOV A, 5
CMP A, 10
JZ label
MOV B, 20
```

If the condition for the jump (`JZ`) is never satisfied, the **`MOV B, 20`** becomes dead code and can be eliminated.

Constant Folding in Peephole Context

Constant folding is a peephole optimization technique where expressions involving constant values are evaluated at compile time rather than runtime. This optimization simplifies expressions that consist entirely of constants, replacing them with their evaluated result. The goal is to reduce computation during program execution by eliminating unnecessary calculations.

The purpose of constant folding is to enhance the efficiency of the generated code by evaluating constant expressions during compilation. By doing so, the code size is reduced, and execution speed is improved since computations involving constant values are resolved before the program is executed.

How Constant Folding Works in Peephole Optimization:

Constant folding typically focuses on simplifying expressions that involve constants. The optimization scans the instruction sequence for expressions such as A + B, A * B, or other arithmetic operations where the operands are constants. Once identified, the compiler will compute the result, and replace the expression with the evaluated result.

Example:

```
MOV R1, 5
MOV R2, 10
ADD R1, R2  ; Adds R1 and R2, results in 15
```

After applying constant folding, this code could be optimized to:

```
MOV R1, 15  ; Directly assign the result of 5 + 10 to R1
```

In this case, the addition of **`5 + 10`** is computed during compilation, and the redundant `ADD` instruction is eliminated.

Types of Constant Folding:

There are different types of constant folding techniques, each focusing on optimizing different kinds of expressions. So, let us explore the key types of constant folding commonly used in optimizations.

- **Arithmetic Constant Folding:**

  In this case, arithmetic expressions that consist only of constant values are evaluated at compile time.

  Example:

  ```
  MOV R1, 3
  MOV R2, 4
  ADD R1, R2    ; This can be replaced by MOV R1, 7
  ```

- **Boolean Constant Folding:**

  Boolean expressions involving constants can also be evaluated at compile time.

  Example:

  ```
  MOV R1, 1  ; True
  MOV R2, 0  ; False
  AND R1, R2 ; Result is 0, as 1 AND 0 is False
  ```

  This could be replaced with:

  ```
  MOV R1, 0  ; Directly assign the result of 1 AND 0
  ```

- **Logical Constant Folding:**

  Logical operations, such as AND, OR, and XOR, that involve constant operands can be simplified during compilation.

  Example:

  ```
  MOV R1, 0
  MOV R2, 1
  OR R1, R2    ; OR between 0 and 1 results in 1
  ```

  The result of 0 OR 1 is 1, so this can be replaced with:

  ```
  MOV R1, 1
  ```

Trade-offs and Considerations in Peephole Optimization

Peephole optimization is a critical technique for improving the efficiency of compiled code by examining small windows (or "peepholes") of instructions, and making local improvements. While peephole optimizations can greatly enhance the performance and reduce code size, they come with trade-offs and considerations that must be carefully weighed to ensure optimal results. Below are the key trade-offs and considerations involved in peephole optimization:

Optimization Overhead versus Execution Benefits

- **Consideration:**

  Peephole optimization requires analyzing the generated code, and looking for opportunities to simplify or replace instructions. This process introduces additional overhead during compilation, which may increase compile time. However, this overhead is generally outweighed by the benefits of faster and more efficient runtime execution.

- **Trade-off:**

  While peephole optimizations result in faster execution and smaller binary sizes, they may come at the cost of a longer compilation time. In time-sensitive projects, this overhead could be a concern, especially for large codebases or iterative compilation processes.

- **Mitigation:**

  For projects that prioritize runtime performance over compile-time efficiency, peephole optimizations are highly beneficial. In situations where compilation time is a bottleneck, it may be worth evaluating the trade-off between optimizing code, and reducing compilation time.

Limited Scope of Optimization

- **Consideration:**

  Peephole optimization works by analyzing a small portion of the code (usually a few adjacent instructions) and applying optimizations locally. This means that peephole optimizations are limited in scope and may not address larger inefficiencies that could be resolved by global optimizations or other more extensive techniques.

- **Trade-off:**

  Although peephole optimizations can improve specific instruction sequences, they may not significantly impact performance in the context of a larger, more complex program. In some cases, global optimization techniques, such as loop unrolling or inlining, might be needed for better performance gains.

- **Mitigation:**

  Peephole optimization should be used as a complementary technique alongside global optimization strategies. While it is effective for localized improvements, it cannot address global inefficiencies that may exist in larger parts of the code.

Potential for Introducing Bugs

- **Consideration:**

  When performing peephole optimizations, especially through instruction replacement or simplifications, there is a risk of inadvertently changing the program's behavior, particularly when optimizations affect the program's side effects (for example, modifying global variables or handling I/O operations).

- **Trade-off:**

  While peephole optimizations can reduce code size and improve performance, they may also alter the original logic if not applied carefully. This can lead to bugs or unintended behavior, especially in code that involves complex state changes or side effects.

- **Mitigation:**

  Careful analysis of the context in which the peephole optimization is applied is necessary to ensure that the transformation does not affect the program's correctness. Rigorous testing should follow optimization to confirm that the optimized code behaves as expected.

Diminishing Returns for Simple Code

- **Consideration:**

  In some cases, the code being optimized may already be highly efficient or simple, meaning that applying peephole optimizations may yield only marginal improvements or none at all. For such code, further optimization may not produce significant benefits.

- **Trade-off:**

  If the program already contains a few inefficiencies, applying peephole optimizations may not lead to any noticeable performance improvement. This could result in wasted optimization effort, especially if the execution time or code size is already optimized to an acceptable level.

- **Mitigation:**

  For simple or optimized code, it may be better to focus on higher-level optimizations, or address other aspects of the program that could lead to greater performance improvements, such as algorithmic changes or memory management optimizations.

Code Clarity versus Optimization

- **Consideration:**

  Peephole optimizations may involve simplifying or transforming instructions to improve performance or reduce size. However, in some cases, these transformations can make the code harder to read or understand, especially for future maintenance or debugging.

- **Trade-off:**

  While peephole optimization can make the code more efficient, it may come at the expense of code clarity. If the transformed code is too convoluted or obscure, it may be difficult for developers to understand, debug, or modify later.

- **Mitigation:**

  It's important to strike a balance between optimization and maintainability. Applying peephole optimizations where they will have the greatest impact on performance without sacrificing readability is key. Commenting or documenting optimizations can also help future developers understand the changes.

Limited to Certain Instruction Patterns

- **Consideration:**

  Peephole optimization is most effective when specific, identifiable instruction patterns are present in the code. For example, replacing a sequence of instructions with a more efficient equivalent is useful when there is a clear pattern of redundant or unnecessary instructions. However, not all code patterns lend themselves to peephole optimizations.

- **Trade-off:**

  The effectiveness of peephole optimization depends on the presence of suitable instruction sequences. If the code does not contain these patterns or is already efficient, the benefit of applying peephole optimizations may be minimal.

- **Mitigation:**

  The compiler or optimization tool can be enhanced to identify a wider range of peephole optimization opportunities. Additionally, combining peephole optimization with other techniques, such as loop or interprocedural optimization can help address inefficiencies that may not be captured by peephole analysis alone.

Risk of Over-Optimization

- **Consideration:**

  Applying too many peephole optimizations to a program can lead to over-optimization where the code becomes excessively complicated in the pursuit of even minor performance gains. This may lead to maintenance difficulties and subtle bugs that emerge due to overly aggressive transformations.

- **Trade-off:**

  While optimization is generally beneficial, excessive or overly aggressive peephole optimizations can result in negative side effects such as increased complexity or hidden issues, making the program more difficult to maintain in the long term.

- **Mitigation:**

  Optimization should be done judiciously, with careful profiling and testing to ensure that the benefits outweigh the costs. Developers should aim for a balance between performance gains and code maintainability, applying optimizations only when they result in tangible improvements.

Limitations of Peephole Optimization

Peephole optimization is a valuable technique for improving code by simplifying or replacing small sequences of instructions. However, it comes with certain limitations that should be taken into account when deciding how and when to apply it.

Limited Scope of Optimization

Peephole optimization works by analyzing a small window or "peephole" of code (usually just a few consecutive instructions) and making improvements within that local context. While this can result in the elimination of redundant operations and simplification of instruction sequences, it cannot address larger-scale inefficiencies or complex optimization problems that require a broader view of the code.

Limitation:

Peephole optimization cannot optimize the program globally. For example, it cannot optimize loops, function calls, or large code structures without further techniques such as global or interprocedural analysis. This limits its effectiveness in complex programs where inefficiencies spread across multiple areas of the code.

Lack of Context Beyond Immediate Instructions

Peephole optimization relies on localized instruction patterns, meaning that it only considers the instructions directly around the optimization target. It does not have access to broader program context, such as the larger control flow, data dependencies, or the program's overall structure.

Limitation:

This lack of broader context can result in optimizations that are incomplete or even incorrect in certain cases. For example, it might replace instructions with a more efficient alternative that works well locally but causes issues in the overall program flow or logic when considered in context.

Risk of Code Transformation Bugs

Peephole optimization can sometimes lead to unintended side effects or errors when transforming instructions, especially in complex programs where the behavior of code might change due to small modifications. In some cases, the optimized code could behave differently, especially in situations involving side effects, branching, or unusual data dependencies.

Limitation:

Improper application of peephole optimization may introduce subtle bugs, particularly when the transformation modifies critical instructions that have side effects, such as modifying global variables, performing I/O operations, or relying on specific instruction ordering. Without careful analysis, peephole optimization can inadvertently break the intended functionality of the program.

Over-Optimization

In some cases, applying too many peephole optimizations, or applying them too aggressively, can result in "over-optimization." This refers to optimizing the code to a point where the benefits are minimal, but the complexity increases, potentially introducing maintenance issues.

Limitation:

Overzealous use of peephole optimization can lead to excessively complex code that is harder to maintain, debug, and understand. This complexity might outweigh the small performance improvements achieved through the optimization, making it more difficult for developers to work with the code in the future.

Inability to Optimize Dynamic or Runtime Values

Peephole optimization relies on recognizing constant values and optimizing based on those. However, it cannot optimize expressions where the values are dynamic or determined at runtime, such as values based on user input, program state, or external data.

Limitation:

If the code involves operations that depend on runtime values (for example, variables whose values are set at runtime or depend on user input), peephole optimization will have limited impact. The compiler cannot evaluate or optimize such expressions ahead of time, and therefore, peephole optimizations cannot be applied to these cases.

Dependency on Instruction Patterns

Peephole optimization is effective only when certain instruction patterns or redundancies exist. If the code does not contain the specific patterns that peephole optimization is designed to improve (such as redundant or unnecessary operations), the optimization will not provide any benefit.

Limitation:

The effectiveness of peephole optimization depends on finding the right instruction sequences. If the code does not exhibit common inefficiencies that can be optimized, the result may be a lack of improvement or even a degradation in performance if the optimization is not carefully implemented.

Complicated Control Flow Issues

Peephole optimization operates on small instruction sequences without considering the overall control flow of the program. Some optimizations that make sense in a local context might interfere with complex control flow structures such as loops, conditionals, or jumps.

Limitation:

Optimizations that are applied without considering the broader control flow can break logical structures, causing unintended program behavior or making the code harder to debug. For example, an instruction replacement might introduce a jump instruction or reorder operations in a way that negatively impacts the flow of control.

Limited to Simple Instruction Replacements

Peephole optimization is primarily concerned with simple instruction-level replacements. This works well for eliminating redundant instructions, simplifying arithmetic operations, or merging common subexpressions. However, it does not typically perform more complex transformations like loop optimizations or function-level analysis.

Limitation:

Peephole optimization cannot address more complex performance issues, such as memory access patterns, branch prediction optimizations, or cache utilization which require higher-level analysis. To fully optimize a program, additional techniques, such as loop optimization, function inlining, or interprocedural analysis are required.

Comparison of Loop and Peephole Optimization Techniques

Loop optimization and peephole optimization are essential strategies to enhance code performance. While both aim to improve efficiency, they focus on different levels and scopes. Below is a detailed comparison of their characteristics, applications, and impact.

Key Differences and Similarities

To fully understand the role of loop and peephole optimizations, it's essential to compare their focus, scope, and impact. While both aim to enhance code performance, they differ in their approach and scale of application. Let us explore their differences and shared characteristics to grasp their unique contributions to optimization.

Aspect	Loop Optimization	Peephole Optimization
Focus	Targets loops to reduce redundancy and improve efficiency.	Targets small sequences of instructions for simplification.
Scope	Operates on entire loop structures and control flow.	Operates within a small window of instructions.
Impact	Significant for compute-intensive applications.	Incremental improvements at the instruction level.
Examples	Loop unrolling, loop fusion, strength reduction.	Instruction replacement, redundant code elimination.
Complexity	Higher, requires analysis of data dependencies and flow.	Lower, involves straightforward pattern matching.
Use Cases	Improves performance for repetitive computations.	Ensures efficient execution of individual instructions.

***Table 14.1**: Comparison of Loop and Peephole Optimization Techniques*

When to Apply Each Technique

Choosing between loop and peephole optimization depends on the nature of the code and the performance goals. Some scenarios benefit from a broad approach to optimizing loops, while others require localized improvements. Understanding when to apply each technique ensures efficient and effective code refinement.

Loop Optimization:

Best Suited For:

- **Performance-Critical Applications**: Programs where loops are the most time-consuming part, such as data analysis, simulations, or gaming engines.
- **Repetitive Operations**: Scenarios involving repeated computations or processing of large datasets.

Example Use Cases:

- Improving the execution speed of nested loops in numerical computations.
- Reducing memory access overhead in multimedia or scientific software.

Peephole Optimization:

Best Suited For:

- **Code Refinement**: Ensuring efficient use of instructions in low-level or assembly code.
- **Eliminating Redundancies**: Targeting small inefficiencies in the compiled code, such as removing unnecessary operations.

Example Use Cases:

- Streamlining instruction sequences in a compiler backend.
- Reducing binary size for embedded systems or resource-constrained environments.

Example Implementations Using LLVM Optimizations

Low-Level Virtual Machine (LLVM) provides a versatile optimization framework that supports a wide range of techniques, including loop and peephole optimizations. This section explores how LLVM implements these optimizations to enhance performance and code efficiency.

Overview of LLVM Optimization Framework

LLVM's optimization framework operates at multiple levels to transform Intermediate Representation (IR) into a highly efficient machine code. It includes:

- **Analysis Passes**: Collect information about the code structure and behavior, such as control flow and data dependencies.
- **Transformation Passes**: Apply specific optimizations, such as loop unrolling, strength reduction, and instruction simplification.
- **Target-Specific Passes**: Optimize for specific hardware architectures, ensuring compatibility and efficiency.

LLVM's modular design allows developers to apply or customize optimization passes, making it an industry standard for compiler development.

Case Studies of Loop and Peephole Optimizations in LLVM

LLVM's optimization framework demonstrates how various loop and peephole optimization techniques can be practically applied to improve the efficiency and performance of the generated code. The following case studies provide an overview of the specific techniques, their implementation in LLVM, and their impact on real-world applications.

Loop Optimization Case Study: Loop Unrolling

Scenario:

Consider a scenario where a program contains a loop that iterates many times, performing simple arithmetic or memory operations on large datasets. While loops can be efficient, the control overhead, such as checking loop conditions and incrementing counters, can introduce performance bottlenecks.

Optimization Technique:

LLVM applies **Loop Unrolling** to this scenario. This technique involves duplicating the body of the loop to reduce the number of iterations, and minimize the overhead associated with checking loop conditions.

Implementation in LLVM:

- LLVM analyzes loops to determine the optimal unrolling factor, based on iteration count and hardware architecture.
- The **Loop Unroll Pass** is applied, duplicating the loop body multiple times. This minimizes the frequency of the branching operations, and enables better instruction-level parallelism.

Impact:

- **Reduced Branching**: Fewer condition checks are needed, improving the overall efficiency.
- **Better Parallelism**: More instructions are executed in parallel, leading to a higher performance.

Results:

- Significant speedup in numerical computations and simulations, such as matrix multiplications, where loops have predictable iteration counts.
- Performance improvements of up to 20%, especially in tasks that benefit from reduced loop control overhead.

Loop Optimization Case Study: Loop-Invariant Code Motion (LICM)

Scenario:

In some cases, loops contain calculations that produce the same result for each iteration (that is, the value does not depend on the loop variables). Repeatedly performing the same calculation inside a loop leads to redundant computations.

Optimization Technique:

LLVM applies **Loop-Invariant Code Motion (LICM)** which identifies calculations that produce the same result in every iteration of the loop, and moves them outside the loop.

Implementation in LLVM:

- LLVM analyzes the loop body to find expressions that are invariant (that is, their value does not change across loop iterations).
- These expressions are moved outside the loop, ensuring that the computation is done once, rather than repeatedly inside the loop.

Impact:

- **Efficiency Gains**: Eliminates redundant calculations inside the loop which is especially beneficial when loops perform computationally expensive operations.
- **Improved Performance**: Decreases CPU cycle usage, leading to more efficient execution.

Results:

- For applications as image processing, scientific simulations, or any task with nested loops, LICM can lead to noticeable improvements in execution time, reducing processing time by up to 15-20%.

Peephole Optimization Case Study: Instruction Combining

Scenario:

At the machine code level, generated code may contain inefficient or redundant instruction sequences, such as adding zero to a register or multiplying by one.

Optimization Technique:

LLVM's **Instruction Combining** optimization pass identifies such inefficient patterns and replaces them with simpler and more efficient alternatives. For example, x + 0 becomes x, and x * 1 becomes x.

Implementation in LLVM:

- LLVM uses pattern matching to detect and simplify redundant or trivial operations.
- The **Instruction Combine Pass** ensures that these unnecessary instructions are replaced, streamlining the code.

Impact:

- **Reduced Instruction Count**: Fewer instructions result in faster execution, especially for programs with tight loops or small code sections.
- **Smaller Binary Size**: Code size is reduced, making it more suitable for resource-constrained environments such as embedded systems.

Results:

- Measurable reductions in code size and faster execution in applications such as low-level system software and embedded device code, where efficiency is critical.

Peephole Optimization Case Study: Redundant Code Elimination

Scenario:

In the process of code generation, unnecessary instructions that do not affect the final output can still appear, such as dead code or calculations whose results are never used.

Optimization Technique:

LLVM's **Redundant Code Elimination** removes such instructions to reduce unnecessary computational work.

Implementation in LLVM:

- LLVM performs an analysis to identify and remove the code that does not affect the program's final output.
- Unused variables, unreachable instructions, and unnecessary calculations are eliminated during the compilation process.

Impact:

- **Optimized Execution**: Removes the overhead of executing redundant instructions.
- **Simplified Code**: Reduces complexity in the generated machine code.

Results:

- Faster execution for programs with unused or redundant computations. For example, eliminating redundant memory access or unnecessary variable assignments in loops and conditionals improves speed in large codebases.

Analyzing Optimization Results

The success of code optimization techniques, such as loop and peephole optimizations, must be measured and evaluated to ensure that they achieve their intended goals. Analyzing optimization results involves assessing performance improvements, resource utilization, and potential trade-offs. Here is a breakdown of the key aspects of this analysis:

Measuring Performance Improvements

- **Execution Time:**

  Compare the runtime of the program before and after applying optimizations. Optimizations, such as loop unrolling and fusion, typically result in faster execution.

- **Throughput and Latency:**

  Assess metrics, such as Instructions Per Cycle (IPC) to gauge how effectively optimizations utilize processor resources.

- **Benchmarking:**

  Use standard benchmarks or real-world test cases to validate improvements under different scenarios.

Evaluating Resource Utilization

- **Memory Usage:**

  Optimizations should aim to the reduce memory footprint, without introducing additional overhead. For example, loop fusion can minimize memory accesses.

- **Energy Consumption:**

  Particularly important for mobile and embedded systems, and lower energy consumption indicates a successful optimization.

Identifying Trade-offs

- **Binary Size:**

  While peephole optimizations may reduce binary size, some loop optimizations, such as unrolling, could increase it.

- **Compilation Time**:

  Aggressive optimizations may result in longer compilation times which can be a concern for large projects.

- **Maintainability**:

  Optimizations must not overly complicate the code, especially in scenarios where further development or debugging is required.

Validation through Tools

- **Profilers and Debuggers:**

  Tools, such as gprof, valgrind, or LLVM's profiling tools can provide detailed insights into the program's behavior, and highlight areas of improvement.

- **Performance Counters:**

  Hardware counters can offer a precise data about CPU usage, cache hits/misses, and branch prediction accuracy.

- **LLVM Analysis Reports:**

  LLVM provides passes that generate detailed optimization reports, showcasing the transformations applied, and their effectiveness.

Ensuring Correctness

- **Regression Testing**:

  Verify that optimizations do not alter the correctness of the program. This involves rigorous testing with edge cases and expected outputs.

- **Static Analysis:**

  Use static analysis tools to detect potential issues introduced by optimization passes, such as incorrect instruction reordering.

Conclusion

In this chapter, we delved into the critical techniques for enhancing the performance of the generated code. **Loop optimizations**, such as **loop unrolling**, **loop fusion**, and **strength reduction**, focus on reducing the control overhead, improving parallelism, and eliminating redundant calculations. Meanwhile, **peephole optimizations**, such as **instruction replacement** and **redundant code elimination** target low-level inefficiencies in the machine code, streamlining execution, and reducing the instruction count. By applying these optimizations, LLVM significantly improves both high-level structures and low-level instructions, ultimately leading to a more efficient and faster code.

As we conclude this chapter, we look ahead to *Chapter 15, Instruction-Level Parallelism and Pipelining*, where we will explore more advanced concepts related to **Instruction-Level Parallelism (ILP)** and **pipelining**. This chapter will cover how modern processors exploit these techniques to overlap instruction execution, with an emphasis on **superscalar execution** and **out-of-order execution**. These strategies enable processors to process multiple instructions simultaneously, maximizing throughput and overall system performance.

Points to Remember

- Techniques, such as **loop unrolling**, **loop fusion**, and **loop inversion** help reduce overhead and improve performance by making loops run more efficiently.
- Focuses on improving the machine-level code by eliminating unnecessary instructions, and simplifying complex ones (for example, **instruction replacement** and **constant folding**).
- Expands loops to reduce the number of iterations and the overhead of checking loop conditions.
- Combines two loops that operate on the same data, reducing overhead, and improving performance.
- Changes the structure of loops to make them more efficient, especially for complex branching conditions.
- Replaces expensive operations, such as multiplication with cheaper ones, such as addition or shifting to speed up calculations.
- Replaces unnecessary operations (for example, **x + 0** becomes **x**) to reduce the execution time.
- Removes code that does not affect the output, such as unused variables or unnecessary calculations.
- Simplifies constant expressions during compilation, saving the computation time during execution.
- Optimization techniques may increase the code size or reduce flexibility which can impact readability or portability.
- LLVM automates many of these techniques, improving the performance of real-world applications by optimizing both the high-level and low-level codes.
- Loop optimizations mainly help with numerical tasks, while peephole optimizations make the final machine code smaller and faster.

Multiple Choice Questions

1. What is the main goal of loop unrolling?
   a. To combine multiple loops into one
   b. To reduce the number of loop iterations and the overhead
   c. To improve branching within loops
   d. To invert loop conditions for better performance
2. Which of the following is an example of loop fusion?
   a. Combining two loops that iterate over the same data
   b. Replacing a multiplication operation with an addition
   c. Expanding a loop to perform more operations at once
   d. Changing the order of a loop to reduce branching
3. What does strength reduction aim to do?
   a. Replace multiplication or division with addition or shifting
   b. Replace expensive instructions with the simpler ones

   c. Combine multiple loops into one
   d. Remove the redundant code that does not affect the output
4. Which of the following is an example of peephole optimization?
   a. Combining loops that process a similar data
   b. Replacing x + 0 with x in the machine code
   c. Reducing the number of loop iterations
   d. Simplifying constant expressions during compilation
5. What is the purpose of constant folding in optimization?
   a. To evaluate constant expressions at the runtime
   b. To reduce the number of loops in a code
   c. To simplify constant expressions during compilation
   d. To merge two similar loops
6. What does loop inversion typically improve?
   a. The performance of nested loops
   b. The branching behavior in loops
   c. The number of instructions in machine code
   d. The size of the program code
7. Which of the following techniques focuses on eliminating unused code?
   a. Strength Reduction
   b. Redundant Code Elimination
   c. Loop Unrolling
   d. Peephole Optimization
8. Which optimization technique replaces expensive operations with cheaper alternatives, such as addition or bit shifting?
   a. Loop Fusion
   b. Strength Reduction
   c. Constant Folding
   d. Instruction Replacement
9. What is the main benefit of using LLVM optimization passes?
   a. Reducing the number of loops in a program
   b. Improving the performance of both high-level and machine-level code
   c. Increasing the program size for better performance
   d. Replacing constants with runtime calculations

10. What is a trade-off involved in loop unrolling?
    a. It can increase the code size but reduce the loop control overhead
    b. It reduces the number of instructions but increases branching
    c. It decreases program size but reduces performance
    d. It improves the runtime but reduces readability

Answers

1. b
2. a
3. a
4. b
5. c
6. b
7. b
8. b
9. b
10. a

Questions

1. Explain the concept of loop unrolling. How does it improve performance, and what are the potential trade-offs?
2. What is loop fusion, and how does it help in optimizing the code? Provide an example scenario where loop fusion is beneficial.
3. Describe the process of strength reduction. How does it replace expensive operations with simpler ones, and why is this important for optimization?
4. What is peephole optimization, and how does it help improve the machine code efficiency? Discuss some common techniques used in peephole optimization.
5. Explain constant folding, and its role in code optimization. How does it impact the runtime performance and compile-time computation?
6. Discuss loop inversion and its effect on loop performance. Provide an example where loop inversion can enhance the execution speed.
7. What is redundant code elimination, and why is it important for optimizing the code? How does this technique contribute to a cleaner and more efficient code?
8. Explain the relationship between loop optimization techniques, and the overall performance of a program. How do techniques, such as loop unrolling, fusion, and inversion affect the performance metrics?
9. Discuss the advantages and disadvantages of using peephole optimization in modern compilers. When is it most effective to apply peephole optimization?

10. How do LLVM passes improve code optimization? Provide examples of specific optimizations that LLVM handles in relation to loop and peephole optimizations.

Key Terms

- **Loop Unrolling**: Expanding a loop to perform multiple operations in one go, reducing loop overhead.
- **Loop Fusion**: Combining two similar loops into one to reduce extra work.
- **Loop Inversion**: Changing the order or structure of a loop to improve efficiency.
- **Strength Reduction**: Replacing expensive operations (such as multiplication) with simpler ones (such as addition).
- **Peephole Optimization**: A technique to improve the machine code by replacing or removing inefficient instructions.
- **Instruction Replacement**: Swapping out unnecessary instructions for more efficient ones.
- **Constant Folding**: Simplifying constant calculations during compilation instead of at runtime.
- **Redundant Code Elimination**: Removing code that does not affect the program's outcome.
- **Code Size Trade-off**: Balancing between reducing code size, and improving performance.
- **LLVM Passes**: Optimization steps in the LLVM compiler to improve the program performance.

Chapter 15
Instruction-Level Parallelism and Pipelining

Introduction

In *Chapter 14, Loop and Peephole Optimization,* we explored software-level techniques aimed at enhancing the efficiency of the compiled code. These included loop optimization strategies, such as loop unrolling and fusion, alongside peephole optimization which focuses on refining the small code segments to reduce the execution time, and improve resource utilization. Practical implementations using LLVM optimizations demonstrated how these strategies translate into real-world performance improvements.

Building on these concepts, this chapter delves into hardware-level optimization techniques that drive the modern processor performance. It introduces key ideas, such as pipelining, superscalar execution, and out-of-order execution which enable processors to execute multiple instructions in parallel, greatly enhancing the throughput. By examining practical implementations using modern processor architectures, this chapter highlights the critical role of these techniques in achieving high-performance computing systems.

Structure

In this chapter, we will discuss the following topics:

- Introduction to Instruction-Level Parallelism
  - Understanding Instruction-Level Parallelism (ILP), and Its Importance
  - The Role of Pipelining in Modern Processor Design
- Pipelining Fundamentals
  - Basic Concepts of Pipelining
  - Pipeline Stages
  - Pipeline Hazards
  - Techniques for Hazard Mitigation
- Superscalar Architecture
  - Overview of Superscalar Execution
  - Instruction Issue Techniques
  - Performance Advantages of Superscalar Execution
- Out-of-Order Execution Techniques
  - Understanding Out-of-Order Execution
  - Instruction Reordering Mechanisms
  - Hardware Components for the Out-of-Order Execution

 - Evaluating Performance Implications
 - Case Studies on Out-of-Order Execution in Modern Architectures
- Practical Implementations in Modern Architectures
 - Overview of the Current Processor Architectures (ARM, Intel, and AMD)
 - Implementation Case Studies of Pipelining, Superscalar, and the Out-of-Order Execution
 - Performance Analysis and Metrics from Real-World Implementations

Introduction to Instruction-Level Parallelism

Instruction-Level Parallelism (ILP) refers to the ability of a processor to execute multiple instructions concurrently during a single clock cycle. This parallel execution significantly improves the performance and speed of processors by making better use of the available hardware. The key goal of ILP is to enhance the efficiency of CPU execution by enabling multiple instructions to be processed simultaneously, rather than sequentially.

In modern processors, achieving high levels of ILP is crucial for improving the overall system performance. By leveraging techniques, such as pipelining, superscalar architectures, and out-of-order execution, processors can handle multiple instructions at once, reducing latency and improving the throughput. Understanding ILP is essential for designing and optimizing high-performance computing systems, especially as applications become more demanding.

This chapter delves into the concept of ILP, exploring its significance, how it is achieved, and its role in modern processor design, focusing on techniques that allow for the parallel execution of instructions.

Understanding Instruction-Level Parallelism (ILP) and its Importance

Instruction-Level Parallelism (ILP) refers to the ability of a processor to execute multiple instructions simultaneously, increasing the speed and efficiency of program execution. In simpler terms, ILP measures how many instructions can be processed at the same time within a single CPU cycle. This ability to parallelize work within a processor is a fundamental factor in modern computing performance.

ILP is important because it directly influences how quickly a program can run. By processing multiple instructions in parallel, the processor can handle more tasks within a shorter time, significantly boosting the performance. This is especially beneficial for applications that require heavy computation, such as simulations, multimedia processing, and complex algorithms.

The key advantage of ILP is its potential to increase the system throughput–meaning the number of operations that can be completed in a given period. However, achieving high ILP can be challenging, as it depends on the type of instructions being executed, and the processor's available resources. To take full advantage of ILP, processors often employ techniques, such as pipelining, superscalar execution, and out-of-order execution.

The Role of Pipelining in Modern Processor Design

Pipelining is a key technique that significantly enhances the efficiency and speed of modern processors by overlapping the execution of multiple instructions. It divides the instruction cycle into several stages where each stage performs a part of the instruction's execution. As one instruction moves through the stages, another instruction can enter the pipeline, allowing the processor to work on multiple instructions simultaneously. This overlapping of work leads to a substantial increase in the throughput, improving the overall performance of the processor.

In modern processors, pipelining helps maximize the use of CPU resources, ensuring that every part of the processor is continuously engaged in executing instructions. This approach reduces the idle time, increasing processing capacity and speed. Typical pipeline stages include instruction fetch, instruction decode, execution, memory access, and write-back, each of which handles a different part of the instruction cycle.

Despite its advantages, pipelining comes with challenges, such as **pipeline hazards** which occur when one instruction depends on the result of a previous instruction. These hazards can cause delays in execution. To mitigate this, modern processors use techniques, such as **branch prediction** which predicts the direction of branches to keep the pipeline full, and **data forwarding** which allows the data to be passed between stages, without waiting for the instruction to be written back.

Pipelining is an essential design feature for achieving high-performance processing in modern computers, from everyday devices to complex computing systems. Its role in optimizing the instruction throughput is indispensable, making processors faster, and more capable of handling demanding workloads efficiently.

Pipelining Fundamentals

Pipelining is an essential concept in computer architecture that allows for the overlapping of multiple instruction stages to increase the processor throughput. In simple terms, it enables the CPU to work on several instructions simultaneously by breaking them into smaller stages, similar to how an assembly line operates. This parallelism increases the efficiency of the processor, allowing it to handle multiple tasks at once, ultimately improving the overall speed of execution.

Basic Concepts of Pipelining

Pipelining is a crucial concept in modern processors that enhances performance by allowing multiple instruction phases to overlap. Just like an assembly line in manufacturing, where each step of the production process happens simultaneously for different products, pipelining enables multiple instructions to be processed in parallel across different stages. This method significantly reduces the overall processing time, and improves throughput.

In this section, we will explore the core concepts of pipelining, how it works, and how it boosts the processor performance.

Pipeline Stages

Pipelining divides the process of executing instructions into distinct stages, allowing the processor to work on multiple instructions at once. Each stage handles a specific part of the instruction cycle, ensuring that different instructions can be processed in parallel. The following are the typical pipeline stages in modern processors:

Instruction Fetch (IF) Stage

The **Instruction Fetch (IF)** stage is the first step in the instruction pipeline, tasked with retrieving the instruction that the processor will execute next. This stage is crucial because it sets the entire pipeline in motion.

1. **Program Counter (PC)**:

   The **Program Counter (PC)** holds the memory address of the next instruction to be fetched. Initially, it points to the start of the program. After fetching an instruction, the PC is typically incremented to point to the next instruction, preparing for the next cycle of fetching.

2. **Fetching the Instruction**:

   The processor uses the address stored in the **Program Counter (PC)** to fetch the instruction from the memory. This instruction is then loaded into the **Instruction Register (IR)**, from where it will be passed to the next pipeline stage (Instruction Decode).

3. **Memory Access and Latency**:

   If the instruction is not found in the processor's cache, it must be fetched from the slower main memory which can introduce delays due to memory access times. Effective caching and memory hierarchy (such as L1 and L2 caches) are critical in minimizing these delays.

4. **Updating the Program Counter**:

   After fetching the instruction, the **Program Counter (PC)** is updated to point to the next instruction. Normally, it increments by the size of the current instruction. However, in the case of **branch instructions** (conditional or unconditional jumps), the PC may be altered to reflect the target address specified by the branch instruction.

The efficiency of the **Instruction Fetch** stage is vital for optimizing the overall performance of the processor. Minimizing latency in memory access, improving cache hit rates, and handling control flow (branches) effectively, all contribute to a smoother pipeline and faster execution.

Instruction Decode (ID) Stage

The **Instruction Decode (ID)** stage is responsible for interpreting the instruction fetched during the **Instruction Fetch (IF)** stage, and preparing the necessary operands and control signals required for execution. This stage is critical in understanding the operation to be performed, identifying the resources it needs, and setting up the pipeline for the execution phase.

Here is how the **Instruction Decode (ID)** stage works:

1. **Instruction Parsing**:

   In the ID stage, the instruction fetched into the **Instruction Register (IR)** is split into its individual components. These components generally include the **opcode**, **operand fields**, and any additional flags or immediate values. The **opcode** indicates the operation to be performed (for example, ADD, SUB, and MOV), while the **operand fields** specify the registers or memory locations involved.

2. **Register Fetch**:

   The instruction, typically operates on data located in registers. The **register file** stores the data used by the CPU, and the **ID stage** accesses these registers based on the operands specified in the decoded instruction. For example, if the instruction specifies two registers as operands, the values in these registers are retrieved during the decode stage.

3. **Control Signal Generation**:

   Based on the decoded **opcode**, the **control unit** generates the appropriate control signals that are sent to various parts of the processor. These signals dictate the operation (for example, ALU operation for arithmetic instructions), which resources are needed (for example, read from registers or memory), and how the instruction interacts with the rest of the pipeline.

4. **Immediate Operand Handling**:

   Some instructions require immediate values, such as constants or literals. These are extracted directly from the instruction itself. If the instruction uses an immediate operand (for example, **ADD R1, R2, #5**), this value is directly passed to the next stages for processing.

5. **Dependency Detection**:

   The ID stage checks for data dependencies between instructions. This helps to detect if the current instruction depends on the result of a previous instruction that has not been completed yet. This is crucial for handling **data hazards**, and ensuring that the correct data is available, when needed.

6. **Branch Prediction (if applicable)**:

   In the case of branch instructions (such as **JUMP** or **BEQ**), the **Instruction Decode** stage works with the **branch predictor** to determine the likely path of execution. If the prediction is correct, it can help minimize, pipeline stalls. If the prediction is incorrect, the pipeline might experience delays due to mis-predicted branches.

7. **Preparation for Execution**:

   After the decode stage, the instruction is ready to be executed. All the necessary resources, such as the correct operands and control signals, have been set up, and the pipeline can move the instruction to the next stage (Execution).

The **Instruction Decode (ID)** stage is vital for the efficient execution of instructions. It ensures that the CPU understands each instruction's requirements, and prepares the necessary resources, enabling the smooth progression of the instruction through the pipeline. Efficient instruction decoding is essential for the overall CPU performance, as delays here can propagate through subsequent stages, reducing the processing speed.

Execution (EX) Stage

The **Execution (EX)** stage is where the main computation or operation specified by the instruction is carried out. This is the stage where the processor performs the actual work, such as arithmetic, logic, memory address calculation, or branch determination.

Here's how the **Execution (EX)** stage works:

1. **Arithmetic and Logic Operations**:

   In the **EX stage**, the Arithmetic Logic Unit (**ALU**) performs any calculations or logical operations, dictated by the instruction. For example:

   - For an **ADD** instruction, the ALU will add the values of two operands.
   - For a **SUB** instruction, it will subtract one operand from another.
   - Logical operations, such as **AND**, **OR**, or **XOR**, will also be carried out by the ALU.

2. **Address Calculation**:

   For memory-related instructions (such as **LOAD** or **STORE**), the **EX stage** is used to calculate the effective memory address. If the instruction requires accessing memory, the ALU computes the address by adding an immediate value or offset to the value in the register. This computed address will be used in the next stage to access the memory.

3. **Branch Decision**:

   For conditional and unconditional **branch instructions** (such as **BEQ**, **BNE**, or **JUMP**), the **EX stage** determines whether the branch condition is met. For example,

   A **BEQ** (Branch if Equal) instruction will compare two registers, and decide whether to branch or not, based on whether the two registers contain the same value.

   If the branch condition is satisfied, the **branch target address** is calculated which will be used in the next stage to decide the next instruction to fetch.

4. **Operand Processing**:

   During the **EX stage**, the operands that were retrieved during the **Instruction Decode (ID)** stage are processed. This might include combining values, performing shifts, or modifying registers, according to the operation specified in the instruction.

5. **ALU Control Signals**:

   The **Control Unit** generates specific signals that tell the ALU what operation to perform. For example, it can instruct the ALU to add, subtract, perform a shift operation, or compare values based on the instruction type. These control signals ensure that the ALU performs the correct operation on the operands.

6. **Flags Update**:

   If the instruction modifies a register or memory, the **EX stage** may also involve updating the processor status flags, such as the Zero, Negative, Overflow, or Carry flags, depending on the result of the operation. These flags can affect subsequent instructions, especially when branches or conditional instructions are involved.

7. **Pipeline Considerations**:

   If the instruction depends on previous instructions (for example, a result from an earlier instruction), the processor may need to handle the data hazards, ensuring that the necessary data is available before the instruction can execute. Techniques, such as **forwarding** (passing data between stages) or **stalling** (delaying execution) may be used to manage these dependencies.

8. **Preparing for Memory Access or Write-Back**:

   Depending on the type of instruction, after the **EX stage**, the instruction may either proceed to the **MEM** stage (if it involves memory access) or the **WB** stage (if it requires writing back to a register). For instance:

   Memory-related instructions (such as **LOAD** or **STORE**) will use the result from the **EX** stage (address computation) in the **MEM** stage.

   Arithmetic or logic instructions that modify registers will pass their result to the **WB** stage to write the result into the register file.

The **Execution (EX)** stage is crucial for performing the core operations of the CPU. The success of this stage determines the correctness of the instruction, and ensures that the data processing occurs as intended. Any delay or error at this stage can significantly impact the overall pipeline performance, affecting the speed of instruction processing and execution.

Memory Access (MEM) Stage

The **Memory Access (MEM)** stage is the point in the pipeline where data is either read from or written to memory. This stage occurs after the **Execution (EX)** stage, and it is crucial for operations that involve memory manipulation, such as loading data into registers or storing data from registers to the memory. The **MEM stage** can involve various types of memory operations based on the instructions being executed. Here is a breakdown of how it works:

1. **Data Read (Load Operations)**:

   For **LOAD** instructions (for example, LOAD R1, 100(R2)), the **MEM stage** is responsible for fetching the data from the memory. The **address** where the data should be read from is calculated during the **EX stage**, and in the **MEM stage**, the data is retrieved from the specified memory location. The data fetched is then sent to the next stage (usually the **Write-Back (WB)** stage) to be written to the appropriate register.

2. **Data Write (Store Operations)**:

   For **STORE** instructions (for example, STORE R1, 100(R2)), the **MEM stage** is responsible for writing the contents of a register (in this case, R1) to a specific memory location. The memory address where the data will be stored is again calculated during the **EX stage**, and in the **MEM stage**, the register's data is written to that address in the memory.

3. **Memory Address Calculation**:

   The **MEM stage** does not perform address calculation directly. Instead, the address for memory operations is computed earlier in the **EX stage**. However, the **MEM stage** relies on the address provided by the **EX stage** to either fetch data (for a **LOAD**) or write data (for a **STORE**).

4. **Handling Memory Hierarchy**:

   Modern processors use memory hierarchies to speed up access times, including **caches**, **main memory**, and **virtual memory** systems. During the **MEM stage**, the CPU will first check if the data is available in the **L1 cache**. If it is not, the CPU may check the **L2** or **L3 caches** or access the **main memory**. Access to memory can take multiple clock cycles depending on where the data is located, and this can introduce latency.

5. **Memory Hazard Handling**:

   The **MEM stage** can also introduce certain **hazards**, particularly **data hazards**. For example, if one instruction is writing data to memory and a subsequent instruction depends on that data (for example, trying to load the value from memory), there can be a hazard that needs to be managed. The processor may need to stall or use techniques such as **forwarding** or **out-of-order execution** to mitigate the hazard.

6. **Access Control**:

   Some instructions may require specific **access control** (such as **privilege levels** in protected memory systems). The **MEM stage** handles the control flow and access rights, ensuring that only valid memory addresses are accessed, and checking for issues such as **segmentation faults** or **page faults** in systems with virtual memory.

7. **Cache Management**:

   In the case of **cache misses**, the **MEM stage** may involve fetching data from slower memory levels, such as main memory. This can introduce a **memory latency penalty**, which is why **caching** is essential for improving the speed of memory access.

8. **Pipeline Interaction**:

   The **MEM stage** can create a bottleneck if memory operations are slow. This is why processors often have multiple **execution pipelines** to perform non-memory operations concurrently with memory accesses, increasing overall throughput.

The **MEM stage** is vital for tasks that involve memory operations, and its performance directly impacts the efficiency of the entire pipeline, especially in systems that handle large amounts of data or have complex memory hierarchies. Efficient memory management during this stage ensures faster execution and better overall performance of the processor.

Write-Back (WB) Stage

The **Write-Back (WB)** stage is the final stage of the pipeline in modern processor architectures. In this stage, the results of the execution are written back to the processor's registers or memory, making the data available for future instructions to use. This stage occurs after the **Memory Access (MEM)** stage, and is critical for completing operations, involving arithmetic or logical instructions.

Here is a breakdown of the **WB stage**:

1. **Register Write**:

   In the **WB stage**, the processed results of instructions, such as arithmetic or logical operations, are written to the destination register. For example, in an instruction, such as ADD R1, R2, R3, the result of adding the values in registers R2 and R3 is written into register R1 during the **WB stage**.

   After the execution of the instruction in earlier pipeline stages (such as the **EX** or **MEM** stages), the final result is available and stored in the appropriate register.

2. **Memory Write**:

   In some cases, the **WB stage** may also involve memory writes if a **store** instruction was performed in the earlier **MEM stage**. For example, in the STORE R1, 100(R2) instruction, after the memory address is calculated, and data is written in the **MEM stage**, the WB stage ensures that the store operation is fully completed.

3. **Finalizing Instruction Execution**:

   The **WB stage** is where the execution of an instruction is considered complete. Once the results have been written back to the registers or memory, the instruction is officially retired from the pipeline. This allows the next instruction in line to begin its execution in the pipeline stages.

4. **Data Forwarding**:

   The **WB stage** is often involved in **data forwarding** (also known as **bypassing**) for subsequent instructions that may need the results of an instruction that is currently being processed. For instance, if a register value that is being computed in an earlier stage is required by another instruction, the result may be forwarded directly from the **WB** stage to the next instruction in the pipeline, before it's fully written to the register file.

5. **Handling Multiple Data Types**:

   Depending on the instruction, the **WB stage** may involve writing back different types of data. For instance, in the case of a floating-point operation, the result will be written to a floating-point register, whereas for integer operations, the result will be written to an integer register.

6. **Exception and Interrupt Handling**:

   If an exception or interrupt occurs during the instruction's execution, the **WB stage** plays a crucial role in handling the recovery, and storing any necessary state before handling the exception. For example, if an instruction causes a **divide by zero** exception, the **WB** stage might need to ensure that any affected register is rolled back to its previous value, before the exception is processed.

The **WB stage** ensures that all results produced by an instruction are written back to the appropriate storage locations. It plays an essential role in completing the instruction's execution, making the final outcome available for future instructions to use, or for final output. Proper functioning of this stage is crucial for maintaining the processor's data flow, and ensuring that the pipeline works efficiently.

Pipeline Hazards

In pipelined processors, **hazards** refer to situations where the pipeline's normal operation is disrupted, potentially causing delays or incorrect execution. These hazards occur due to various dependencies between instructions or resource limitations, affecting the smooth flow of instructions through the pipeline. There are three primary types of pipeline hazards: **Structural hazards**, **data hazards**, and **control hazards**.

Structural Hazards

Structural hazards occur when there is a conflict over the use of shared resources in a pipelined processor. This happens when multiple instructions require access to the same resource simultaneously, and there are not enough resources to handle them at once, causing delays or stalls in the pipeline.

Key Concepts of Structural Hazards:

This section discusses the fundamental ideas behind structural hazards, focusing on the key elements that cause resource conflicts in a pipelined processor.

Structural hazards occur when a processor does not have enough hardware resources to execute multiple instructions at the same time. In a pipelined processor, this happens when instructions require the same resource–such as execution units or memory ports–at the same stage, causing delays. Essentially, structural hazards are about resource contention where the resources are insufficient to handle the volume of simultaneous instructions.

Causes of Structural Hazards:

Here, we explore the main reasons that lead to structural hazards in processors, with examples highlighting how insufficient resources can create pipeline stalls.

- **Insufficient Functional Units**: A functional unit, such as an ALU or multiplier, may be under-provisioned, leading to conflicts when more than one instruction requires it at the same time.

  Example: A processor with only one multiplier may face a hazard if two instructions that require multiplication are issued simultaneously.

- **Limited Memory Access Units**: In processors with a single memory access unit, multiple instructions needing memory access, such as load and store operations, can cause conflicts and delays.

  Example: If two instructions need to access memory at the same time, such as one instruction needing to read and another needing to write, a hazard arises.

- **Shared Instruction Fetch Resources**: When multiple pipeline stages need to access instruction memory, and there is not enough bandwidth, structural hazards can occur.

  Example: If different stages of the pipeline are fetching instructions simultaneously, this can cause congestion in the instruction memory unit, leading to delays.

Solutions to Structural Hazards:

In this section, we present methods to overcome structural hazards, including practical solutions that enhance processor efficiency, and reduce the impact of resource contention.

- **Resource Duplication:** One common solution is to add more resources, such as additional execution units or more memory access ports, to ensure that there are enough resources for simultaneous operations.

- **Pipeline Stalling:** In some cases, stalling the pipeline for one or more cycles may be the simplest solution, allowing the necessary resources to become available. However, this reduces the overall performance.

- **Resource Sharing and Scheduling:** Implementing more sophisticated scheduling techniques, such as dynamic scheduling, can help avoid conflicts by carefully managing how and when resources are used in the pipeline.

- **Out-of-Order Execution:** Some advanced processors use out-of-order execution, allowing instructions that do not depend on the result of a conflicting instruction to proceed, while waiting for the necessary resource.
- **Instruction Reordering:** Reordering instructions in the pipeline to avoid conflicts over the same resource at the same time can help mitigate structural hazards, allowing the processor to maintain a steady throughput.

Data Hazards

Data hazards occur when instructions that are close together in the pipeline depend on each other's data. These hazards happen when one instruction requires the result of a previous instruction, but that result is not yet available because the earlier instruction has not completed all stages of the pipeline.

Key Concepts of Data Hazards:

Data hazards occur when instructions that are close together in the pipeline rely on the same data. These hazards happen when one instruction needs the result of a previous instruction, but the previous instruction has not finished executing yet. Since pipelines break instructions into separate stages, data hazards can delay the processing of later instructions. There are three main types of data hazards: Read-After-Write (RAW), Write-After-Read (WAR), and Write-After-Write (WAW).

Causes of Data Hazards:

Data hazards occur when one instruction needs to read or write data that another instruction is modifying in the pipeline. These hazards are caused by the sequence of instructions and their dependencies on each other's results.

- **Read-After-Write (RAW) Hazard (True Dependency):** This occurs when an instruction needs to read a register that is being written to by a previous instruction. If the first instruction has not written the result to the register yet, the second instruction will have to wait.

  Example: Instruction 1 writes to register R1, and Instruction 2 tries to read from R1 before Instruction 1 has completed.

- **Write-After-Read (WAR) Hazard (Anti-Dependency):** This occurs when a later instruction writes to a register that an earlier instruction needs to read. The earlier instruction may get incorrect data if the later instruction writes to the register too early.

  Example: Instruction 1 reads from register R1, and Instruction 2 writes to R1 before Instruction 1 has completed reading.

- **Write-After-Write (WAW) Hazard (Output Dependency):** This occurs when two instructions write to the same register. The result of the second instruction could overwrite the result of the first instruction, causing an error if the first instruction hasn't yet been committed.

  Example: Instruction 1 writes to register R1, and Instruction 2 also writes to R1. If Instruction 2 writes to R1 before Instruction 1, it can overwrite the correct result.

Solutions to Data Hazards:

To address data hazards, several techniques can be employed, such as pipeline stalling, data forwarding (bypassing), out-of-order execution, register renaming, and instruction reordering, all aimed at reducing the performance penalties associated with data dependencies.

- **Pipeline Stalling:** One of the simplest solutions to data hazards is to stall the pipeline, until the required data is available. This approach is easy to implement, but it can introduce delays, and reduce performance.

- **Data Forwarding (Bypassing):** Data forwarding is a technique that allows the processor to send the result of a previous instruction directly to the next instruction that needs it, rather than waiting for the instruction to finish, and write to the register file. This technique helps to avoid the need for pipeline stalls.

  Example: If Instruction 1 produces a value for a register that Instruction 2 needs, the value can be forwarded directly from the execution stage of Instruction 1 to the decode stage of Instruction 2.

- **Out-of-Order Execution:** In modern processors, the out-of-order execution can help avoid data hazards by executing instructions that do not have data dependencies, first. Instructions that require data from a previous instruction can be scheduled to execute later, once the data is available.

  Register Renaming: Register renaming helps avoid WAR and WAW hazards by dynamically assigning a new register to store intermediate results, instead of reusing the same register. This helps prevent unwanted data overwriting, and ensures that the data is not incorrectly read or written.

  Example: If two instructions are trying to write to the same register, renaming allows each to use a different register, preventing one from overwriting the other.

- **Instruction Reordering:** Compilers can reorder instructions to reduce dependencies. By scheduling independent instructions in between dependent instructions, the compiler can keep the pipeline busy, while avoiding unnecessary stalls.

Control Hazards

Control hazards, also known as **branch hazards**, occur due to the uncertainty of the flow of control in the program. These hazards are typically caused by **branch instructions** which change the instruction flow based on conditions (for example, if, for, or while statements). Since the processor cannot know the target of a branch, until the branch instruction is evaluated, it may end up executing incorrect instructions before determining the branch outcome.

Key Concepts of Control Hazards:

Control hazards typically arise when there is a **branch instruction**. These instructions alter the flow of the program, causing the processor to wait and decide which instruction should be fetched next. If the wrong instruction is fetched, it leads to wasted cycles in the pipeline.

Causes of Control Hazards:

Control hazards occur primarily due to **branch instructions**, including:

- **Unconditional branches** (for example, goto or jump instructions)
- **Conditional branches** (for example, if-else statements that change the flow based on conditions)

When the processor encounters such instructions, it cannot immediately determine which instruction to fetch next, resulting in delays.

Solutions to Control Hazards:

To handle control hazards efficiently, processors use several techniques:

- **Branch Prediction:**

  The processor predicts whether a branch will be taken or not, before it is fully evaluated. If the prediction is right, the pipeline runs smoothly. If wrong, the pipeline is corrected, but some cycles may be wasted.

- **Speculative Execution**:

  The processor executes instructions based on the predicted outcome of the branch, even before the branch decision is confirmed. If the prediction turns out to be wrong, the incorrectly executed instructions are discarded, but it minimizes the idle time.

- **Delayed Branching**:

  In delayed branching, the instruction right after the branch is always executed first, regardless of whether the branch is taken. This helps keep the pipeline filled, while the branch is being resolved.

- **Dynamic Branch Prediction**:

  More advanced processors use dynamic techniques to predict branches with greater accuracy. By learning from previous program executions and patterns, the processor can predict branches more effectively, reducing the risk of pipeline stalls.

Techniques for Hazard Mitigation

In pipelined processors, hazards–like data, structural, and control hazards–can cause delays in instruction execution. To prevent performance bottlenecks, effective hazard mitigation techniques are essential. The primary methods for handling these hazards are **stalling**, **forwarding**, and **branch prediction**. The following is a detailed explanation of each technique:

Stalling and Forwarding

In modern processors, hazards such as data and control hazards can delay the execution of instructions. To mitigate these hazards and maintain efficient processing, two crucial techniques are employed: **stalling** and **forwarding**. Both methods aim to resolve issues that arise, when there are dependencies between instructions in the pipeline.

Stalling

Stalling also referred to as a "pipeline stall" or "bubble," is a deliberate pause introduced into the pipeline to resolve data, control, or structural hazards. It temporarily halts instruction execution until the dependencies or conflicts are resolved.

Causes of Stalling:

- **Data Dependencies**: When an instruction depends on the result of a previous instruction that has not yet been completed.
- **Structural Hazards**: When multiple instructions require the same hardware resource simultaneously.
- **Control Hazards**: Occur during branching, when the target instruction cannot be fetched immediately due to uncertainty about the next instruction.

How It Works:

The pipeline inserts idle cycles to allow dependent instructions or required resources to become available.

No new instructions are fetched, until the stalled instruction progresses through the pipeline.

Limitations:

- Reduces pipeline throughput as no useful work is done during the stalled cycles.
- Increases execution time, particularly for long dependency chains.

Forwarding

Forwarding, also known as bypassing, is a technique used to resolve data hazards by rerouting data directly from one stage of the pipeline to another, without waiting for it to be written back to the register file.

How It Works:

The result of an instruction is sent directly to subsequent instructions that depend on it, bypassing the register write and read stages.

This eliminates the need for stalling in many cases, as dependent instructions can use the data immediately.

Key Benefits:

- **Improves Pipeline Efficiency**: Reduces the number of idle cycles caused by data hazards.
- **Minimizes Delays**: Ensures that instructions relying on the same data can execute without significant waiting.
- **Limitations**: Requires additional hardware (bypass paths and logic) to detect dependencies and reroute data.
- May not fully eliminate hazards, especially in complex dependency chains.

Branch Prediction Strategies

Branch prediction is a technique used in modern processors to improve the flow of instruction execution by guessing the outcome of conditional branch instructions before they are fully evaluated. This allows the processor to preemptively fetch, and execute instructions based on the predicted branch outcome, reducing the performance penalties caused by pipeline stalls due to control hazards.

Branch instructions disrupt the sequential flow of the pipeline by introducing uncertainty about the next instruction to be fetched. To maintain pipeline efficiency, branch prediction strategies predict the outcome of these instructions, allowing the pipeline to continue fetching and executing instructions without waiting for the branch resolution.

How Branch Prediction Works

Branch prediction helps speed up processing by guessing the outcome of a branch instruction, before it is fully executed. In this section, we'll explain how this prediction works, and why it is important for keeping the pipeline running smoothly.

Prediction Phase:

In the **Prediction Phase**, the processor attempts to predict the outcome of a branch instruction before it is fully executed. This allows the pipeline to continue running without delays.

Key aspects of the prediction phase include:

- **Branch Target Buffer (BTB):** A cache that stores previous branch results which helps predict the target of future branches.
- **History Tables:** These track past branch outcomes to predict future behavior, based on previous patterns.
- **Static Prediction:** A basic method where branches are predicted with simple, fixed rules (for example, assuming a branch will either always be taken or not).

The aim is to minimize pipeline stalls by making accurate predictions that allow instructions to continue flowing smoothly.

Execution and Validation Phase:

In the **Execution and Validation Phase**, the processor performs the actual execution of the branch instruction, and verifies whether the prediction made in the previous phase was correct.

Key aspects of the execution and validation phase include:

- **Branch Execution:** The processor executes the branch instruction, and computes the branch target (the address of the next instruction to be executed).
- **Validation:** Once the branch instruction has been executed, the processor checks if the predicted outcome (whether the branch is taken or not) matches the actual result.
- **Corrective Action:** If the prediction is correct, the processor continues with the instructions in the pipeline. If the prediction is incorrect, corrective actions are taken, such as flushing the incorrect instructions, and refilling the pipeline with the correct ones.

This phase ensures that the processor can maintain efficient execution, even when predictions are wrong, by quickly handling and recovering from mispredictions.

Types of Branch Prediction Strategies

Branch prediction helps processors guess the outcome of a branch before it's fully determined, keeping the pipeline running smoothly. There are different strategies for making these predictions, each with its own strengths. In this section, we will look at the various types of branch prediction techniques used in processors.

Static Branch Prediction

Static Branch Prediction is a technique where the outcome of branch instructions is predicted at compile-time using fixed, predefined strategies, rather than at runtime. The prediction is based on simple rules or assumptions that are determined before the program is executed. In this method, the prediction is generally done by the compiler which uses knowledge about the structure of the program, such as loops or conditionals.

For example, **backward branches** (which are typically associated with loops) are often predicted to be taken, as they are expected to repeat. **Forward branches**, on the other hand, are frequently predicted to be not taken, as they typically represent conditionals that often do not transfer control.

The primary advantage of static branch prediction is its simplicity and low overhead since it requires no runtime tracking of branch history. The compiler makes the decisions before execution begins which means it doesn't need additional hardware support to track past behavior.

However, the major limitation of static branch prediction is its inaccuracy in handling branches that depend on runtime conditions, such as data inputs or user interactions. If the prediction is wrong, it can result in pipeline stalls and performance degradation, as the processor has to flush the incorrect prediction, and restart the execution.

Dynamic Branch Prediction

Dynamic Branch Prediction is a sophisticated technique used to improve the efficiency of modern processors by predicting the direction of branches at runtime. Unlike static prediction methods which rely on predefined assumptions, dynamic prediction adapts based on the actual behavior of the program as it runs. This method uses historical data to make decisions about whether a branch will be taken or not, allowing the processor to keep the pipeline full and minimize delays.

How It Works:

Branch History Table (BHT): Dynamic branch prediction relies on a structure called a Branch History Table (BHT), which stores the outcomes of previous branch instructions (whether they were taken or not). By looking at this historical data, the processor can predict the outcome of future branches with a high degree of accuracy.

Two-Bit Prediction: A common approach within dynamic prediction is the **two-bit predictor**.

This method tracks branch behavior using two bits, representing states, such as:

- **Strongly Taken**: The branch is highly likely to be taken.
- **Weakly Taken**: The branch is sometimes taken, but not consistently.
- **Weakly Not Taken**: The branch is sometimes not taken.
- **Strongly Not Taken**: The branch is highly likely to not be taken.

This method helps avoid fluctuations in prediction, offering a more stable approach than single-bit methods.

Global versus Local Prediction:

Global Prediction: Uses the history of all branches to predict the behavior of a given branch. This approach considers how branches behave across the entire program.

Local Prediction: Focuses on the behavior of individual branches, using the history of a specific branch to predict its future behavior.

Key Benefits:

- **Enhanced Prediction Accuracy**: Dynamic branch prediction adapts to the program's actual behavior, making it more accurate than static methods, especially in programs with unpredictable or complex branching patterns.
- **Increased Instruction Throughput**: By predicting branches accurately, the processor can avoid delays, reducing pipeline stalls, and allowing instructions to flow smoothly through the pipeline.

Challenges:

- **Hardware Complexity**: Dynamic branch prediction requires additional hardware resources such as the Branch History Table and prediction counters which can add complexity and power consumption to the processor.
- **Mispredictions**: Although dynamic prediction is generally more accurate, mispredictions still occur. When a misprediction happens, the processor must discard the incorrect instructions, leading to performance penalties.

Superscalar Architecture

Superscalar architecture is a processor design that enables the execution of multiple instructions in parallel within a single clock cycle. Unlike scalar processors that execute one instruction at a time, superscalar processors leverage multiple execution units, and advanced scheduling techniques to process instructions concurrently, significantly boosting performance.

Overview of Superscalar Execution

Superscalar execution is a key technique in modern processor design that allows multiple instructions to be executed in parallel within a single clock cycle. This approach goes beyond traditional scalar processors, which can only process one instruction at a time, by leveraging multiple execution pipelines and advanced scheduling mechanisms.

The primary goal of superscalar execution is to **maximize instruction throughput** and improve overall performance by exploiting Instruction-Level Parallelism (ILP). Through parallel processing, a superscalar processor can complete more operations in less time which is especially beneficial for computationally intensive applications.

Key Features of Superscalar Execution:

- **Multiple Execution Units**: Superscalar processors contain several execution units (for example, ALUs, FPUs and Load/Store units) that can perform operations simultaneously.
- **Parallel Instruction Issue**: The processor fetches, and issues multiple instructions to the available execution units in one clock cycle.
- **Instruction Scheduling**: Techniques, such as **static scheduling** (compile-time) and **dynamic scheduling** (runtime) determine the optimal execution order.
- **Hazard Management**: Mechanisms, such as forwarding, stalling, and branch prediction ensure smooth execution despite data or control hazards.

How Superscalar Execution Works:

1. **Instruction Fetch**: Multiple instructions are fetched together in a single cycle.
2. **Decode and Analyze**: Dependencies, and readiness of instructions are checked.
3. **Instruction Dispatch**: Independent instructions are dispatched to different execution units in parallel.
4. **Execution**: Instructions are processed concurrently across multiple pipelines.
5. **Write Back**: Results are written back to registers or memory.

This parallelism is what enables superscalar execution to achieve significantly higher performance compared to traditional scalar processors.

Instruction Issue Techniques

In superscalar processors, instruction issue techniques are crucial for ensuring efficient parallel execution of multiple instructions. These techniques decide how instructions are dispatched to various execution units. The goal is to minimize idle times and maximize throughput by ensuring that instructions are executed in parallel whenever possible. There are two primary types of instruction issue techniques:

Static Scheduling

Static scheduling refers to the process where the compiler determines the order of instruction execution at compile time before the program is run. This method involves analyzing the instruction dependencies and available execution units to create a fixed sequence of instructions that maximizes parallelism and minimizes potential hazards.

How It Works:

In static scheduling, the compiler inspects the program's instruction flow and identifies dependencies between instructions (such as data dependencies). Based on this analysis, it organizes instructions to ensure that instructions that do not have data dependencies on one another can be executed concurrently.

It ensures that instructions are scheduled to run in a way that avoids issues, such as data hazards, where one instruction depends on the result of another, and control hazards, which occur when the flow of control changes unpredictably (such as due to branches in the code).

Key Advantages:

- **Predictability**: Since the instruction schedule is set at compile time, there are no decisions to be made at runtime which simplifies the processor's design and results in lower overhead.
- **Simplicity**: Static scheduling does not require complex hardware mechanisms, making it more straightforward and cost-effective for simpler processor designs.
- **Reduced runtime overhead**: The absence of runtime scheduling decisions means that there is no extra delay incurred during execution, improving performance in certain cases.

Key Limitations:

- **Lack of adaptability**: Static scheduling does not adjust for dynamic conditions, such as variations in processor load or available resources which may reduce its efficiency in real-time execution.
- **Compiler-dependent**: The effectiveness of static scheduling heavily relies on the compiler's ability to analyze the program correctly and schedule instructions optimally. If the compiler makes suboptimal choices, the overall performance of the program may suffer.
- **Limited flexibility**: Once the schedule is fixed, it cannot adapt to runtime changes such as data being unavailable or resource contention, making it less suited for complex or unpredictable workloads.

In essence, static scheduling is a straightforward, predictable technique that works well when the instruction flow and dependencies are known in advance, but it lacks the flexibility needed to handle more dynamic, complex execution scenarios.

Dynamic Scheduling

Dynamic scheduling is a technique used by modern processors to manage the execution order of instructions at runtime, based on the availability of execution units and the status of instructions. Unlike static scheduling, where the instruction order is determined at compile time, dynamic scheduling allows the processor to make decisions about instruction execution on the fly, depending on actual runtime conditions, such as resource availability, data dependencies, and hazards.

How It Works:

In dynamic scheduling, the processor analyzes the instruction stream during execution and decides when to execute each instruction, allowing out-of-order execution. This means that if an instruction is waiting for data, the processor can execute independent instructions in parallel, even if they were originally scheduled to run sequentially.

The processor uses hardware structures, such as **Reservation Stations** and **Reorder Buffers** to track the status of instructions, ensuring that they are executed when their operands are available. The **Tomasulo algorithm** is a well-known technique used for dynamic scheduling that helps resolve data hazards, and maximizes parallelism.

Key Advantages:

- **Increased Parallelism**: Dynamic scheduling allows independent instructions to be executed in parallel, improving overall throughput and performance, especially on complex, multi-cycle processors.
- **Handling Hazards**: It is particularly effective at handling data and control hazards, as the processor can execute instructions out of order, when resources become available, thereby avoiding delays from waiting on dependent instructions.

- **Improved Resource Utilization**: By dynamically adapting to available execution units and avoiding idle processor cycles, dynamic scheduling maximizes the use of the available hardware resources.

Key Limitations:

- **Complexity**: Dynamic scheduling requires more sophisticated hardware and control mechanisms to track dependencies, manage execution orders, and handle out-of-order execution. This increases the complexity of the processor design.
- **Overhead**: The need for hardware to monitor and track instruction status introduces some runtime overhead which can slightly reduce performance compared to a simpler, statically scheduled processor.
- **Potential for Increased Power Consumption**: The additional complexity and hardware required for dynamic scheduling may lead to higher power consumption, especially in processors with high degrees of parallelism.

Use Cases:

Dynamic scheduling is widely used in high-performance processors, particularly those with multiple execution units and the ability to execute instructions out of order. Examples include modern **superscalar processors**, **out-of-order processors**, and **high-end server processors** where maximizing instruction throughput and minimizing execution stalls is critical to performance.

Performance Advantages of Superscalar Execution

Superscalar execution refers to the ability of a processor to issue multiple instructions per clock cycle. This is achieved through the use of multiple execution units that can work in parallel. Superscalar architectures significantly improve performance by increasing instruction throughput, enhancing the ability of processors to handle several instructions at once. Here are the key performance advantages:

- **Increased Instruction Throughput:**

  Superscalar processors can issue more than one instruction per clock cycle, which directly increases the number of instructions processed in a given amount of time. This higher throughput leads to faster execution of programs compared to scalar processors which can only process one instruction per cycle.

- **Parallelism:**

  Superscalar execution allows multiple instructions to be processed concurrently. By having multiple execution units, the processor can handle independent instructions simultaneously, such as arithmetic operations, memory accesses, and branch evaluations. This parallelism boosts the overall performance of the processor, particularly in computationally intensive tasks.

- **Better Utilization of Resources:**

  With multiple functional units working in parallel, superscalar processors can better utilize their hardware resources. For instance, while one execution unit processes an arithmetic instruction, another might be handling a memory operation. This parallel resource utilization minimizes idle times, leading to higher efficiency.

- **Reduced Instruction Latency:**

  Since superscalar processors can execute multiple instructions at once, the overall latency (the time taken to complete a sequence of instructions) is reduced. This is particularly beneficial for applications where the execution of many instructions is dependent on each other, as multiple instructions can be processed simultaneously.

- **Out-of-Order Execution:**

  Superscalar architectures often implement out-of-order execution, allowing the processor to dynamically decide the order of instruction execution based on resource availability. This feature helps avoid pipeline stalls that would otherwise occur if instructions had to wait for previous ones to finish, improving the overall throughput and performance.

- **Improved Handling of Branches:**

  Superscalar processors can improve branch prediction and handling. With multiple pipelines, the processor can speculatively execute multiple branches in parallel, reducing the performance hit caused by branch mispredictions. This ability to handle branches more efficiently results in a smoother flow of instructions.

- **Higher Clock Speeds:**

  Many superscalar processors are designed to achieve higher clock speeds, further enhancing performance. This is because the ability to issue multiple instructions per cycle often means that each instruction is simpler, allowing the processor to run at a higher frequency without sacrificing performance.

- **Optimized for Complex Workloads:**

  Superscalar execution is particularly beneficial for workloads that require heavy computational power, such as scientific simulations, multimedia processing, and gaming. These applications often involve a large number of parallelizable instructions, making them ideal candidates for superscalar processing.

- **Efficiency in Multi-threading:**

  Superscalar processors can also perform well in multi-threaded environments by executing different threads concurrently. By processing multiple threads at the same time, these processors improve performance in systems running parallel applications or multi-core architectures.

Out-of-Order Execution Techniques

Out-of-order execution (OoOE) is an advanced feature in modern processors designed to increase the throughput and efficiency of instruction execution. By executing instructions as soon as the necessary data and resources are available–rather than strictly following their order in the program–out-of-order execution can significantly reduce delays, resulting in enhanced performance.

Understanding Out-of-Order Execution

Out-of-order execution allows a processor to dynamically rearrange the sequence of instructions it processes. Instead of waiting for previous instructions to complete (for example, due to data dependencies), the processor executes independent instructions as they are ready. This technique effectively hides latency from slow operations, such as memory access or data dependencies, which otherwise cause delays in instruction processing.

Key Components of Out-of-Order Execution:

- **Instruction Queue**

  The instruction queue holds the instructions fetched from memory before they enter the pipeline. It acts as a buffer where instructions are initially stored.

- **Reservation Stations**

  Reservation stations temporarily hold instructions waiting for their operands (data) to become available. They allow the processor to execute instructions out of order, as long as the operands are ready.

- **Reorder Buffers (ROB)**

  Reorder buffers ensure that results of out-of-order executed instructions are committed in the correct program order. They hold instruction results temporarily, and commit them in the order they appeared in the original program.

- **Register Alias Table (RAT)**

  The RAT maps logical registers to physical registers, helping to manage and rename registers dynamically. This allows out-of-order execution to avoid issues related to register dependencies.

- **Execution Units**

  These are the parts of the processor responsible for executing the individual operations (for example, arithmetic, memory access, or logic). The processor dispatches instructions to the appropriate execution unit based on their type.

How Out-of-Order Execution Works:

The execution process is typically divided into several stages:

- **Fetch**: Instructions are fetched from memory, and placed into the instruction queue.
- **Dispatch**: The instructions are dispatched to reservation stations for execution. The dispatch mechanism also checks the availability of required resources (for example, registers and memory).
- **Execute**: Instructions that have their operands ready are sent to the appropriate execution unit, where they are executed out of order.
- **Commit**: Once the results are generated, they are written back to the register file in the order the instructions appear in the original program. This is done via the reorder buffer.

Instruction Reordering Mechanisms

The instruction reordering mechanism plays a central role in out-of-order execution. It allows independent instructions to be executed before those that are dependent on data. The processor uses dynamic scheduling to reorder instructions at runtime, ensuring that operations can be executed as soon as their required data is available, without disrupting the intended outcome of the program.

Types of Out-of-Order Execution:

Dynamic Scheduling:

This approach allows instructions to be dispatched and executed out of order by the hardware. It does not require static instruction scheduling by the compiler. Dynamic scheduling uses hardware-based components such as reservation stations, and reorder buffers to manage instruction execution dynamically.

Static Scheduling:

In contrast, static scheduling involves the compiler arranging the instruction sequence in an optimal way before execution. While less flexible than dynamic scheduling, static scheduling can still improve performance by reducing pipeline hazards and data dependencies.

Performance Benefits of Out-of-Order Execution:

- **Higher Instruction Throughput**

  Out-of-order execution allows independent instructions to be processed in parallel, leading to higher instruction throughput compared to sequential execution.

- **Reduced Pipeline Stalls**

  The technique reduces the impact of data hazards and memory latency, ensuring that the pipeline is kept busy, and resources are efficiently utilized.

- **Improved Resource Utilization**

  Out-of-order execution helps maximize the utilization of the processor's functional units by dynamically scheduling, and dispatching instructions to available execution units, keeping them active.

Challenges and Considerations:

- **Complexity in Hardware Design**

  Out-of-order execution requires complex hardware to manage resources such as reservation stations, reorder buffers, and register alias tables. This complexity can increase the cost and design time of processors.

- **Increased Power Consumption**

  The additional hardware for managing out-of-order execution can lead to higher power consumption, as more resources are engaged to handle dynamic scheduling and instruction reordering.

- **Dependency Management**

  While out-of-order execution can efficiently manage independent instructions, handling dependencies, particularly data hazards, and control hazards, remains a challenge that must be carefully managed through techniques such as branch prediction and register renaming.

Real-World Applications of Out-of-Order Execution

Modern processors such as Intel's Core i7, AMD's Ryzen, and ARM's Cortex-A series use the out-of-order execution to maximize their performance. These processors use large instruction windows, multiple execution pipelines, and sophisticated instruction scheduling mechanisms to execute a large number of instructions concurrently, leading to improved performance in tasks ranging from gaming to scientific computing.

Hardware Components for Out-of-Order Execution

Out-of-order execution relies on specialized hardware components that manage the reordering of instructions and ensure that instructions are executed efficiently, and in the correct sequence, while maintaining the integrity of the program's results. Two key hardware components involved in this process are **Reservation Stations** and **Reorder Buffers**.

Reservation Stations

Reservation stations are hardware buffers that temporarily hold instructions before they are executed. These stations track the availability of operands which may not be available immediately due to data dependencies between instructions. They allow instructions to be issued out of order, enabling the processor to execute instructions as soon as their operands are ready, rather than waiting for previous instructions to complete.

How It Works:

Each reservation station is associated with a functional unit, such as an arithmetic or load/store unit, and can hold multiple instructions that are waiting to execute. When an instruction enters a reservation station, it checks if all the required operands are available:

If the operands are already in the registers or have been produced by previous instructions, the instruction is dispatched directly to the functional unit.

If the operands are not yet available, the reservation station waits until they are ready, allowing other instructions that do not have dependencies to be executed in the meantime.

By using reservation stations, the processor can keep its execution units busy, minimizing idle time and improving overall throughput.

Key Benefits:

- **Reduced Instruction Stalls:** By allowing instructions to execute out of order, the processor can avoid pipeline stalls that would occur if instructions had to wait for previous ones to complete.
- **Increased Parallelism:** Instructions that do not have dependencies can be executed in parallel, significantly boosting the performance of the processor.

Reorder Buffers

The reorder buffer (ROB) is a crucial component that ensures that the results of out-of-order instructions are committed in the correct program order. Even though instructions are executed out of order, the final results need to be written back to the registers or memory in the order they were originally issued. The reorder buffer manages this by holding the results temporarily, and ensuring that they are committed at the right point in the program's execution.

How It Works:

When an instruction completes execution in the pipeline, its result is stored in the reorder buffer. The instruction itself may have been executed out of order, but its result is not committed (that is, written back to the register file) until all previous instructions have been completed. This ensures the correct program behavior.

The ROB keeps track of the status of each instruction and its result. It also ensures that results are written back to registers in the same order as the instructions were issued in the program.

Once all instructions preceding a given instruction have been completed, the instruction in the reorder buffer is committed, meaning its result is written to the register file.

Key Benefits:

- **Program Order Commitment:** Ensures that the results of instructions are written back in the correct order, maintaining the correctness of the program.
- **Efficient Handling of Speculative Execution:** The reorder buffer plays a vital role in handling speculative execution and branch mispredictions. It can roll back the execution state to a safe point in case of a branch misprediction.

Evaluating Performance Implications

Out-of-order execution is a powerful technique used in modern processors to increase throughput and reduce idle time, but its impact on performance can vary depending on the specific implementation and the workload. Evaluating its performance implications involves assessing how effectively out-of-order execution improves overall system efficiency, reduces bottlenecks, and ensures better resource utilization. Next, we break down key factors influencing performance in out-of-order execution and how they contribute to the processor's overall behavior.

Key Performance Implications:

- Increased Instruction Throughput
    - **Impact:** Out-of-order execution allows the processor to execute instructions as soon as their operands are ready, independent of the order in which they appear in the program. This reduces pipeline stalls, and increases instruction throughput, meaning more instructions can be completed in a given period.
    - **Effect on Performance:** This leads to better utilization of the CPU's resources, such as execution units, and improves the overall speed of instruction processing, especially in cases where there are many independent instructions.
- **Reduced Latency for Independent Instructions**
    - **Impact:** Independent instructions which do not have data dependencies, can be executed in parallel. This helps minimize the latency associated with waiting for previous instructions to complete, reducing the overall execution time.
    - **Effect on Performance:** Latency reduction is especially important in modern processors where multi-threading and high-speed execution are essential. Faster execution times for independent instructions lead to better application performance.
- **Better Utilization of Pipeline Stages**
    - **Impact:** Out-of-order execution keeps different stages of the pipeline busy by allowing instructions to flow through available stages as soon as possible. This helps prevent pipeline stalls that typically occur when instructions depend on each other's results.
    - **Effect on Performance:** A better-managed pipeline with fewer stalls translates to more efficient processing, particularly in pipelines that involve complex instruction sets or memory access patterns.
- **Increased Complexity and Power Consumption**
    - **Impact:** While out-of-order execution provides performance benefits, it also introduces complexity in hardware design. Managing instruction reordering and dependencies and maintaining the integrity of the program state requires additional hardware components (such as reservation stations, reorder buffers, and the instruction window).
    - **Effect on Performance:** The added complexity can result in higher power consumption and increased design costs. However, if managed well, the performance gains from out-of-order execution can outweigh these drawbacks, especially in high-performance applications where power efficiency is secondary to raw processing speed.
- **Branch Misprediction Penalties**
    - **Impact:** Out-of-order execution relies heavily on branch prediction to execute instructions speculatively. When branch predictions are incorrect, the processor must flush and re-fetch instructions, leading to penalties.
    - **Effect on Performance:** Branch mispredictions can significantly reduce the benefits of out-of-order execution, as the processor has to discard speculative instructions and restart execution. However, with advanced branch prediction strategies, these penalties can be minimized.
- **Impact on Memory Access and Cache Utilization**
    - **Impact:** While out-of-order execution can improve the performance of independent instructions, memory access instructions may still cause bottlenecks, especially if there is a high dependency on memory or cache misses.

- **Effect on Performance:** Efficient memory access is essential to fully harness the benefits of out-of-order execution. Techniques, such as memory access reordering, prefetching, and cache optimization can mitigate these bottlenecks, allowing for smoother execution.

Case Studies on Out-of-Order Execution in Modern Architectures

Out-of-order execution (OoOE) is a critical feature in modern processors, allowing them to maximize throughput and improve performance by executing instructions as their operands become available rather than strictly adhering to program order. Many modern CPU architectures, including those used in desktop, server, and mobile devices, have adopted out-of-order execution to optimize performance. The following are case studies of how out-of-order execution is utilized in several widely used processor architectures.

Intel Core i7 (Nehalem Microarchitecture)

The Intel Core i7 processor, based on the Nehalem microarchitecture, introduced significant improvements in out-of-order execution as part of its design. The Nehalem architecture used dynamic out-of-order execution to improve both single-threaded and multi-threaded performance.

Key Features:

- **Out-of-Order Execution:** The Nehalem architecture features a wide out-of-order instruction window (more than 200 entries) that allows the processor to execute independent instructions concurrently, even if they appear out of sequence in the program.
- **Execution Units:** It includes multiple execution units for integer, floating-point, and SIMD operations. The processor can dispatch multiple instructions to these units in parallel, exploiting instruction-level parallelism (ILP).
- **Advanced Branch Prediction:** To support out-of-order execution, the Core i7 utilizes sophisticated branch prediction techniques which help reduce penalties from branch mispredictions.

Performance Benefits:

The out-of-order execution capabilities significantly enhanced the performance of the Core i7, making it ideal for tasks such as gaming, video editing, and multitasking. It allowed the processor to make better use of CPU resources and reduced idle time, improving instruction throughput.

Challenges:

Despite its powerful out-of-order execution, branch mispredictions, and memory access delays can still introduce performance bottlenecks in certain workloads.

AMD Ryzen (Zen Architecture)

AMD's Ryzen processors, based on the Zen architecture, also incorporate out-of-order execution to enhance performance. The Zen microarchitecture is designed to provide high instruction throughput and efficient multi-threading performance, particularly in gaming and productivity applications.

Key Features:

- **Instruction Window:** The Ryzen processors feature an instruction window capable of handling a large number of instructions simultaneously, enabling efficient out-of-order execution and better ILP.

- **Decoupled Front-End and Back-End:** The design of the Ryzen processor decouples the front-end (fetch and decode) and the back-end (execution and commit), allowing for higher instruction throughput and minimizing pipeline stalls.
- **Advanced Load/Store Queue:** The out-of-order execution is complemented by an advanced load/store queue, which allows the processor to handle memory operations more efficiently without waiting for older instructions to complete.

Performance Benefits:

The out-of-order execution in Ryzen chips allows for higher frequency scaling and better utilization of execution units. This improves gaming performance, content creation, and multi-tasking capabilities.

The architecture is designed to efficiently handle multi-threaded workloads, making it suitable for high-performance computing tasks like scientific simulations, rendering, and data analysis.

Challenges:

Ryzen's performance in applications with high data dependencies or frequent memory access can be impacted, as even with out-of-order execution, memory bottlenecks can limit potential gains.

ARM Cortex-A57 (Big.LITTLE Architecture)

The ARM Cortex-A57, part of ARM's big.LITTLE architecture, is designed for mobile devices and aims to balance power efficiency with high performance. The Cortex-A57 incorporates out-of-order execution, allowing it to execute instructions in a non-sequential order when possible.

Key Features:

- **Out-of-Order Execution:** The Cortex-A57 features a wide out-of-order pipeline, supporting simultaneous execution of multiple instructions, which increases the efficiency of the core in scenarios with high instruction-level parallelism.
- **Branch Prediction:** ARM implements advanced branch prediction algorithms in the Cortex-A57 to reduce the penalty of branch mispredictions, further improving the efficiency of out-of-order execution.
- **Instruction Scheduling:** The Cortex-A57 uses dynamic scheduling to dispatch instructions to available execution units, making it capable of handling high-performance tasks while conserving power.

Performance Benefits:

The out-of-order execution helps the Cortex-A57 achieve strong performance in mobile applications, balancing power efficiency and processing speed. It is especially useful in running applications that require heavy computation, such as video decoding, 3D gaming, and multitasking on mobile devices.

By enabling multiple instructions to be executed in parallel, the Cortex-A57 can achieve higher throughput than simpler in-order cores, making it suitable for modern smartphone and tablet applications.

Challenges:

ARM processors in the mobile space face challenges in balancing performance with power consumption. Even with out-of-order execution, excessive execution unit usage can lead to increased power draw, which must be carefully managed to maintain battery efficiency.

IBM Power9 Processor

The IBM Power9 is a high-performance processor based on the Power architecture, which is used in enterprise servers, workstations, and supercomputers. The Power9 incorporates advanced out-of-order execution techniques to maximize processing power.

Key Features:

- **Wide Instruction Window:** The Power9 processor features an extremely wide instruction window, capable of handling hundreds of instructions in flight. This allows it to exploit instruction-level parallelism efficiently, even in workloads with complex data dependencies.
- **Multiple Execution Units:** It includes multiple integer and floating-point execution units, enabling the simultaneous processing of different types of instructions.
- **Branch Prediction and Speculation:** The processor uses highly sophisticated branch prediction and speculative execution techniques which help it maintain high throughput even in the presence of complex branches or loops.

Performance Benefits:

Out-of-order execution in Power9 processors significantly enhances the performance of high-end server and HPC (high-performance computing) workloads. By executing independent instructions out of order, the processor minimizes idle times, and accelerates complex calculations.

Power9 is particularly well-suited for large-scale simulations, data analytics, and enterprise workloads where high parallelism is essential.

Challenges:

Similar to other advanced out-of-order architectures, Power9 processors must manage the complexity of maintaining architectural state and handling speculative execution efficiently. Branch mispredictions can result in penalties, and managing the large instruction window requires advanced hardware and software coordination.

Practical Implementations in Modern Architectures

The evolution of processor architectures has led to significant advances in the way modern processors handle tasks such as pipelining, superscalar execution, and out-of-order execution. In this section, we explore how these techniques are implemented in current processor architectures, such as ARM, Intel, and AMD, followed by a performance analysis based on real-world implementations.

Overview of Current Processor Architectures (ARM, Intel, and AMD)

Modern processors are the backbone of computing systems, powering everything from smartphones to high-performance servers. Among the most prominent architectures in use today are those developed by ARM, Intel, and AMD. These processors are designed with various optimizations and technologies to cater to different performance needs, power requirements, and usage scenarios. The following is an overview of the three primary processor architectures, and their characteristics:

ARM Architecture

Advanced RISC Machines (ARM) is a leading architecture in mobile and embedded systems, known for its low power consumption and efficiency.

The ARM architecture is based on the Reduced Instruction Set Computing (RISC) principle, where the processor uses a simpler instruction set to reduce complexity, and improve the execution speed.

Key Features:

- **Power Efficiency:** ARM is designed to be power-efficient, making it ideal for mobile devices such as smartphones, tablets, and IoT devices.
- **Simplicity:** ARM processors use a simplified instruction set which reduces energy consumption and helps with faster clock speeds.
- **Scalability:** ARM's architecture is highly scalable, used in everything from low-power processors to high-performance chips in servers and desktops.

Use Cases:

- **Mobile Devices:** ARM processors dominate the mobile market, being used in smartphones, tablets, and other portable devices.
- **Embedded Systems:** ARM is a common choice in embedded systems for industrial applications, medical devices, and automotive systems.
- **High-Performance Computing:** With the release of ARM-based server chips (for example, Apple's M1, AWS Graviton), ARM has also begun competing in high-performance computing markets.

Intel Architecture

Intel, a dominant force in personal computing and servers, uses the x86 architecture which is a Complex Instruction Set Computing (CISC) architecture.

Intel's processors are widely used in desktops, laptops, and servers, and are well-known for their powerful performance in computationally-heavy tasks.

Key Features:

- **High Performance:** Intel processors are designed for maximum performance, featuring high clock speeds and multiple cores for parallel processing.
- **Hyper-Threading:** Intel's Hyper-Threading technology allows each physical core to handle multiple threads, improving parallel task performance.
- **Integrated Graphics:** Many Intel processors come with integrated graphics, enabling lower-cost solutions for users who do not need dedicated GPUs.

Use Cases:

- **Personal Computers:** Intel processors are widely used in desktops and laptops, from consumer models to high-performance workstations.
- **Servers and Data Centers:** Intel processors, particularly in the Xeon series, are used in enterprise servers and cloud computing where high throughput and scalability are crucial.
- **Gaming and Content Creation:** Intel CPUs are a popular choice in gaming systems and workstations, offering high performance for demanding applications, such as video editing and 3D rendering.

AMD Architecture

Advanced Micro Devices (AMD) is a competitor to Intel, offering processors based on the x86 architecture, similar to Intel. AMD is known for its high-performance processors, and has gained significant traction in the recent years with its Ryzen and EPYC series.

AMD processors provide competitive performance, often at a more affordable price point compared to Intel counterparts.

Key Features:

- **Multi-Core Performance:** AMD processors often feature more cores and threads than Intel counterparts, which is beneficial for multi-threaded applications, such as video editing, 3D rendering, and gaming.
- **Simultaneous Multi-Threading (SMT):** Similar to Intel's Hyper-Threading, AMD's SMT technology allows each core to handle two threads simultaneously, boosting parallel processing capabilities.
- **Advanced Manufacturing Process:** AMD's recent processors, such as those based on the Zen 3 architecture, have been built using cutting-edge 7nm manufacturing processes, improving energy efficiency and performance.

Use Cases:

- **Desktop and Gaming PCs:** AMD's Ryzen processors are widely used in gaming and high-performance computing, offering superior multi-core performance at competitive prices.
- **Servers and Data Centers:** The EPYC series is aimed at the server market, competing with Intel's Xeon in providing scalable solutions for data centers.
- **High-Performance Workstations:** AMD is increasingly being used in professional workstations for tasks, such as scientific computing, rendering, and AI research.

Implementation Case Studies of Pipelining, Superscalar, and Out-of-Order Execution

The implementation of advanced techniques, such as pipelining, superscalar execution, and out-of-order execution has significantly enhanced the performance of modern processors. These techniques enable processors to handle multiple instructions simultaneously, improving throughput reducing latency. The following are real-world case studies showcasing the application of these execution techniques in contemporary processor architectures.

Pipelining: Intel Core i7 (Nehalem Architecture)

Intel's Core i7 processors, which are based on the Nehalem architecture, utilize advanced pipelining to enhance processing performance. The Nehalem architecture includes deep pipelining, where instructions pass through multiple stages, to improve throughput.

Key Features:

- **Multiple Pipeline Stages:** The processor integrates several pipeline stages, such as instruction fetch, decode, execute, memory access, and write-back.
- **Out-of-Order Execution:** To keep the pipeline active and avoid stalls, the processor fetches and decodes instructions out of order.
- **Branch Prediction:** It uses branch prediction to preemptively guess the outcome of control flow instructions, and minimize delays due to branching.

Performance Impact:

- **Improved Throughput:** The deep pipeline structure allows the processor to execute multiple instructions concurrently which boosts throughput.
- **Reduced Latency:** Overlapping stages in the pipeline reduce the latency that would occur in a sequential processor.

Superscalar Execution: AMD Ryzen 3000 Series (Zen 2 Architecture)

The AMD Ryzen 3000 series, based on the Zen 2 architecture, utilizes superscalar execution, allowing the processor to issue multiple instructions per clock cycle, thus, improving performance by exploiting instruction-level parallelism.

Key Features:

- **Multiple Execution Units:** Zen 2 features multiple execution units capable of executing several instructions at once.
- **Simultaneous Multithreading (SMT):** Each core supports two threads simultaneously, increasing parallelism, and overall throughput.

Performance Impact:

- **Higher Performance:** The combination of superscalar execution and SMT results in higher clock speeds and better multitasking performance, especially in compute-intensive applications.
- **Increased Resource Utilization:** The processor uses multiple execution units more efficiently, leading to reduced idle times for execution resources.

Out-of-Order Execution: Intel Xeon Scalable Processors (Skylake Architecture)

Intel Xeon Scalable processors, using the Skylake microarchitecture, leverage out-of-order execution to enhance performance. Out-of-order execution allows the processor to execute instructions as soon as their operands are available, even if they are not in the original program order.

Key Features:

- **Reservation Stations:** These hold instructions waiting for operands, ensuring that resources are not blocked.
- **Reorder Buffers (ROB):** The ROB maintains the original program order for instructions to commit results in the correct sequence.
- **Branch Prediction:** Skylake processors use sophisticated branch prediction algorithms to minimize delays due to control hazards.

Performance Impact:

- **Increased Throughput:** Out-of-order execution keeps the execution units active, and reduces pipeline stalls, improving the processor's throughput.
- **Efficient Resource Usage:** Instructions are executed as soon as resources become available, preventing idle time for execution units, and improving overall performance.

Combined Use of Techniques: Apple M1 Chip (ARM Architecture)

The Apple M1 chip, based on ARM architecture, integrates pipelining, superscalar execution, and out-of-order execution into a unified system-on-chip (SoC). The M1 chip is designed for high efficiency in mobile devices, offering both high performance and low power consumption.

Key Features:

- **Unified Architecture:** The M1 combines multiple processing units (CPU, GPU, and neural engine) in a single chip, allowing for streamlined processing.
- **Advanced Pipelining:** The chip uses a pipeline structure to handle multiple instruction stages concurrently.
- **Out-of-Order Execution:** It employs out-of-order execution to enhance throughput by ensuring that instructions are executed as soon as the necessary resources are available.

Performance Impact:

- **Energy Efficiency:** Despite its high performance, the M1 chip maintains excellent power efficiency, which is critical for mobile devices, such as iPads and MacBooks.
- **Exceptional Performance:** The chip delivers strong performance for both single-threaded and multi-threaded tasks, benefiting applications ranging from productivity software to gaming and content creation.

Out-of-Order Execution and Superscalar Execution: IBM POWER9 Architecture

IBM's POWER9 processors incorporate both out-of-order execution and superscalar execution, designed for high-performance computing (HPC) and enterprise applications.

Key Features:

- **Multiple Pipelines:** POWER9 processors include multiple instruction pipelines that enable simultaneous instruction execution.
- **Execution Units:** The architecture supports a variety of execution units (integer, floating point, vector, and load/store units) to process a wide range of instructions.
- **Simultaneous Multithreading:** Each core in the POWER9 processor supports multiple threads, further improving parallelism.

Performance Impact:

- **Scalability:** The POWER9 architecture's ability to execute instructions out of order and across multiple pipelines makes it suitable for large-scale computing environments.
- **Enhanced Throughput:** The combination of superscalar and out-of-order execution ensures high throughput, even under high-demand workloads, such as artificial intelligence, machine learning, and big data processing.

Performance Analysis and Metrics from Real-World Implementations

Performance analysis of processor architectures that utilize pipelining, superscalar execution, and out-of-order execution is essential to understanding the effectiveness of these techniques in real-world applications. Various performance metrics and benchmarks are employed to evaluate how well these architectures perform under different workloads and conditions. The following is an overview of key performance metrics, and how they are analyzed in real-world implementations.

Throughput

Throughput refers to the number of instructions a processor can execute per unit of time. It is a measure of the overall processing speed of a system.

- **Real-World Example:**

  Intel Core i7 (Nehalem Architecture): The throughput of this processor is significantly improved due to pipelining and out-of-order execution. Multiple instructions can be in different stages of execution at the same time, increasing the number of instructions completed in a given period.

- **Performance Metric:** Throughput can be measured using benchmarks, such as the SPEC CPU, where higher throughput directly correlates with better performance in compute-intensive tasks.
- **Analysis:** In real-world scenarios, throughput is often tested by running a set of benchmark applications that simulate typical workloads, such as media encoding, gaming, and scientific computing. Processors with deep pipelines and out-of-order execution tend to perform better in these scenarios due to their ability to process more instructions concurrently.

Latency

Latency refers to the time it takes for an instruction or a set of data to travel through the processor pipeline, and produce a result.

- **Real-World Example:**

  AMD Ryzen 3000 Series (Zen 2 Architecture): The implementation of superscalar execution and multiple execution units in the Ryzen 3000 series helps reduce latency by allowing instructions to execute in parallel. This is especially noticeable in tasks, such as gaming, where low latency is crucial for smooth performance.

- **Performance Metric:** Latency can be measured in terms of cycle count or clock cycles taken to execute a specific instruction.
- **Analysis:** Processors with more advanced branch prediction and out-of-order execution techniques typically exhibit lower latency, as they can avoid pipeline stalls. Real-world tests, such as those used in gaming and simulations, measure the time delay between an input command and the visual output, which provides insight into how latency impacts user experience.

Energy Efficiency

Energy efficiency measures the amount of computational work that can be done per unit of the power consumed. This is especially important in mobile and embedded systems, where the battery life is a critical concern.

- **Real-World Example:**

  Apple M1 Chip (ARM Architecture): The M1 chip is a prime example of achieving high performance, while maintaining excellent energy efficiency. Its integrated architecture which combines CPU, GPU, and other components, reduces power consumption, without sacrificing performance, particularly in tasks, such as video editing and multitasking.

- **Performance Metric:** Energy efficiency can be calculated using the metric "performance per watt," which measures the computational power (instructions per second) divided by the power consumed.
- **Analysis:** In mobile devices, energy-efficient architectures such as the Apple M1 are tested in real-world scenarios, such as browsing, media playback, and light computing. Benchmarks such as Geekbench are used to assess the performance-to-power consumption ratio. The M1 chip, for example, demonstrates superior energy efficiency compared to traditional x86-based chips, making it ideal for long battery life in laptops and tablets.

Scalability

Scalability refers to a system's ability to handle an increasing amount of work, or its potential to be enlarged to accommodate that growth. In terms of processor architectures, it refers to how well the system can scale with more cores, threads, and resources.

- **Real-World Example:**

  IBM POWER9 Architecture: Known for its scalability, the POWER9 architecture uses multiple execution units, extensive out-of-order execution, and simultaneous multithreading (SMT) to support a large number of parallel tasks. This makes it well-suited for high-performance computing (HPC) environments where workloads need to scale across many cores.
- **Performance Metric:** Scalability is evaluated through stress tests that simulate workloads with increasing demands. Benchmarks, such as SPECint and SPECfp are used to test how well the processor performs as the number of cores and threads increases.
- **Analysis:** Scalability is tested in environments, such as cloud computing and server farms, where workloads grow significantly over time. Processors, such as the IBM POWER9 excel in scaling for large databases, enterprise applications, and AI workloads which require handling massive parallel computations across multiple processors or cores.

Instructions Per Cycle (IPC)

IPC is a key performance metric that measures the average number of instructions a processor can execute per clock cycle. It is a direct indicator of the efficiency of the processor's architecture, especially for pipelined and superscalar designs.

- **Real-World Example:**

  Intel Xeon Scalable Processors (Skylake Architecture): These processors feature high IPC rates due to their ability to execute multiple instructions per clock cycle through superscalar execution and out-of-order execution. The higher the IPC, the better the processor's ability to handle complex workloads.
- **Performance Metric:** IPC is often calculated using benchmarking tools, such as SPEC CPU, where the number of instructions executed in a test run is divided by the number of clock cycles taken.
- **Analysis:** A higher IPC typically indicates that the processor can handle more work at the same time, leading to better overall performance. Processors that use superscalar execution and out-of-order execution techniques generally exhibit higher IPC values, making them suitable for high-performance tasks, such as scientific simulations, video rendering, and AI processing.

Benchmarking Results

Benchmarking involves using standardized tests to evaluate the performance of processors in various domains, including gaming, productivity, and scientific computing.

- **Real-World Example:**

  AMD Ryzen vs. Intel Core i7: Benchmark tests, such as Cinebench and Geekbench are commonly used to compare the performance of AMD Ryzen and Intel Core i7 processors. The benchmarks assess performance in multi-core and single-core workloads, providing a clear comparison of how well each architecture handles different types of tasks.
- **Performance Metric:** Performance scores from these tests, such as the number of frames per second (FPS) in gaming benchmarks or the time taken to render a video, are used to evaluate processor efficiency in real-world scenarios.

- **Analysis:** Benchmarks provide a reliable way to evaluate, and compare the performance of processors in different workloads. For example, gaming benchmarks focus on GPU performance, while workloads such as 3D rendering or video editing emphasize CPU performance. These results help consumers, businesses, and developers understand the performance trade-offs of different processor architectures.

Conclusion

In *Chapter 15, Instruction-Level Parallelism and Pipelining,* we delved into how modern processors achieve higher performance through techniques, such as **pipelining**, **superscalar execution**, and **out-of-order execution**. The chapter also addressed common challenges, such as **structural, data, and control hazards** and discussed methods, such as **stalling, forwarding**, and **branch prediction** to mitigate these issues. We further explored **static and dynamic scheduling**, with real-world case studies from **ARM, Intel**, and **AMD** processors to demonstrate the practical applications of these techniques.

Looking ahead to *Chapter 16, Optimizing for Parallelism and Locality,* we will explore optimization strategies aimed at improving program performance. This includes techniques for **parallelizing workloads**, enhancing **data locality**, optimizing **cache usage**, and applying **loop transformations**. The chapter will also provide practical examples of implementing these optimizations using parallel processing tools, offering a deeper understanding of how to improve program efficiency in modern computing environments.

Points To Remember

- **Instruction-Level Parallelism (ILP):** Enhances performance by executing multiple instructions simultaneously.
- **Pipelining Fundamentals:** Divides instruction execution into stages to increase throughput.
- **Pipeline Hazards:** Structural, data, and control hazards disrupt pipelined execution.
- **Hazard Mitigation Techniques:** Include stalling, forwarding, and branch prediction strategies.
- **Superscalar Architecture:** Executes multiple instructions per cycle to maximize parallelism.
- **Static Scheduling:** Scheduling decisions made at the compile time to improve performance.
- **Dynamic Scheduling:** Hardware schedules instructions at the runtime for better flexibility.
- **Out-of-Order Execution:** Instructions are executed based on resource availability, not on the sequential order.
- **Performance Metrics:** Metrics, such as IPC, latency, and throughput evaluate processor efficiency.

Multiple Choice Questions

1. What is the main objective of Instruction-Level Parallelism (ILP)?

   a. To improve hardware efficiency

   b. To execute multiple instructions simultaneously

   c. To reduce memory usage

   d. To simplify processor design

2. Which of the following is NOT a type of pipeline hazard?
   a. Structural Hazard
   b. Data Hazard
   c. Resource Hazard
   d. Control Hazard
3. In pipelining, what is the role of the "Instruction Fetch (IF)" stage?
   a. To execute the instruction
   b. To fetch the instruction from memory
   c. To decode the instruction
   d. To write the results back to registers
4. What is the primary difference between static and dynamic scheduling?
   a. Static scheduling occurs at the runtime; dynamic scheduling occurs at the compile time
   b. Static scheduling occurs at the compile time; dynamic scheduling occurs at the runtime
   c. Static scheduling resolves hazards dynamically
   d. Dynamic scheduling eliminates the need for forwarding
5. What technique is used to resolve data hazards in pipelining?
   a. Stalling
   b. Branch Prediction
   c. Forwarding
   d. Superscalar Execution
6. What is a key advantage of the Out-of-Order Execution?
   a. It ensures instructions are executed in the program order.
   b. It increases instruction latency.
   c. It allows instructions to execute based on resource availability.
   d. It reduces pipeline stages.
7. Which hardware component stores instructions waiting to execute in the Out-of-Order Execution?
   a. Branch Predictor
   b. Reorder Buffer
   c. Reservation Station
   d. Cache Memory
8. What does "Superscalar Execution" enable in modern processors?
   a. Execution of one instruction per clock cycle
   b. Execution of multiple instructions per clock cycle

   c. Reduction of the memory access time
   d. Simplification of the control flow
9. Which branch prediction strategy uses historical execution patterns to predict outcomes?
   a. Static Branch Prediction
   b. Speculative Execution
   c. Dynamic Branch Prediction
   d. Pipeline Stalling
10. What metric is used to evaluate the processor performance in terms of instruction execution?
   a. Instructions Per Cycle (IPC)
   b. Cache Hit Rate
   c. Latency
   d. Resource Utilization

Answers

1. b
2. c
3. b
4. b
5. c
6. c
7. c
8. b
9. c
10. a

Questions

1. Explain the concept of Instruction-Level Parallelism (ILP) and its importance in modern processor design.
2. Describe the role of pipelining in improving the processor performance. What are the key stages of a pipeline?
3. What are pipeline hazards? Explain the types of hazards with examples.
4. Discuss the techniques used to mitigate pipeline hazards, including stalling, forwarding, and branch prediction.
5. What is Superscalar Architecture? Explain how it enables the execution of multiple instructions per clock cycle.

6. Differentiate between Static Scheduling and Dynamic Scheduling. Provide examples of where each is used.
7. Explain Out-of-Order Execution. How do hardware components, such as Reservation Stations and Reorder Buffers enable this process?
8. Discuss the performance advantages of Superscalar Execution. How does it compare to the traditional scalar execution?
9. Describe the differences between Static and Dynamic Branch Prediction strategies. What are the benefits of each?
10. Provide an overview of modern processor architectures, such as ARM, Intel, and AMD. How do they implement techniques, such as pipelining, superscalar execution, and out-of-order execution to optimize performance?

Key Terms

- **Pipelining:** A technique that divides the instruction execution into multiple stages, enabling parallel processing.
- **Pipeline Hazards:** Issues that prevent the next instruction from executing in the pipeline, including the structural data, and control hazards.
- **Structural Hazards:** Resource conflicts that occur when the hardware cannot support all the necessary operations.
- **Data Hazards:** Delays caused by dependencies between instructions accessing the same data.
- **Control Hazards:** Interruptions due to changes in program flow, such as branches.
- **Stalling:** A hazard mitigation technique that delays the instruction execution, until dependencies are resolved.
- **Forwarding:** A method of resolving data hazards by passing the data directly between pipeline stages.
- **Branch Prediction:** A strategy to minimize control hazards by predicting the outcome of branches.
- **Superscalar Execution:** A design where multiple instructions are issued and executed in parallel, during each cycle.
- **Static Scheduling:** Compile-time scheduling of instructions to optimize execution performance.
- **Dynamic Scheduling:** Runtime scheduling of instructions to overcome stalls, and improve efficiency.
- **Reservation Stations:** Hardware buffers that store instructions and data for out-of-order execution.
- **Reorder Buffers:** A hardware mechanism that ensures program instructions are retired in the correct order.
- **Latency:** The delay or time required to complete the execution of a single instruction.
- **Throughput:** The number of instructions executed per unit of time.

CHAPTER 16
Optimizing for Parallelism and Locality

Introduction

In *Chapter 15, Instruction-Level Parallelism and Pipelining*, we explored key performance-enhancing techniques, such as instruction-level parallelism (ILP), pipelining, superscalar execution, and out-of-order execution. We also addressed hazards–structural, data, and control hazards–and solutions, such as stalling, forwarding, and branch prediction strategies. Practical examples of processor implementations from ARM, Intel, and AMD were also discussed.

In *Chapter 16, Optimizing for Parallelism and Locality*, we will focus on optimizing performance through parallelization and locality techniques. This includes methods for improving data locality, cache optimization, and loop transformations. We will also examine how to apply parallel processing tools to implement these strategies effectively. This chapter builds on the concepts from the previous chapter, offering further insights into optimizing modern computing systems for parallel execution.

Structure

In this chapter, we will discuss the following topics:

- Introduction to Parallelism and Locality Optimization
  - o Overview of Parallel Computing
  - o Importance of Data Locality in Performance
- Parallelization Techniques
  - o Types of Parallelism
  - o Identifying Opportunities for Parallelization
  - o Tools and Frameworks for Parallel Programming
- Data Locality Optimization
  - o Understanding Data Locality
  - o Spatial Locality
  - o Strategies for Improving Data Locality
  - o Impact of Data Locality on Performance
- Cache Optimization
  - o Cache Architecture Overview
  - o Cache Performance Metrics
  - o Techniques for Cache Optimization

- Loop Transformations
  - Importance of Loop Optimization in Parallelism
  - Common Loop Transformations
- Example Implementations using Parallel Processing Tools
  - Case Studies of Parallel Code Optimization
  - Performance Analysis of Implemented Examples

Introduction to Parallelism and Locality Optimization

In this section, we introduce the core concepts of **parallelism** and **locality optimization** which are essential for improving the performance of modern computing systems. **Parallelism** involves breaking down tasks into smaller subtasks that can be executed simultaneously, leading to better resource utilization, and faster execution times. On the other hand, **locality optimization** focuses on organizing data and instructions in a way that maximizes the efficiency of memory access, reducing latency and improving the overall performance.

Overview of Parallel Computing

Parallel computing refers to the simultaneous execution of multiple tasks or processes, enabling faster and more efficient computation. It is based on dividing large problems into smaller, and independent sub-tasks that can be processed concurrently. By utilizing multiple processors or cores, parallel computing can significantly reduce the time required for processing complex calculations or large datasets, making it essential in various fields, such as scientific research, machine learning, data analytics, and simulations.

The concept of parallelism can be understood through two main approaches: **Task parallelism**, where different tasks or operations are executed in parallel, and **data parallelism**, where the same operation is applied to different chunks of data simultaneously. These two approaches are commonly implemented using different computational models, such as shared memory and distributed memory.

Key Concepts in Parallel Computing:

- **Task Parallelism**: Involves dividing a program into multiple tasks where each task can run independently on separate processors.
- **Data Parallelism**: The same operation is performed concurrently on different pieces of data, often using large datasets.
- **Synchronization**: Ensures that parallel tasks work together efficiently, and communicate correctly without causing conflicts or errors.
- **Load Balancing**: Involves evenly distributing tasks across processors to ensure that no processor is overloaded, improving resource utilization and overall efficiency.

Parallel computing models can be classified into:

- **Shared Memory Model**: All processors have access to the same memory space, enabling them to share data directly. Communication happens by reading or writing to the shared variables.
- **Distributed Memory Model**: Each processor has its own local memory, and data exchange happens via message passing over a network. This model is common in large-scale systems and clusters.
- **Hybrid Parallelism**: Combines both shared and distributed memory models to leverage the strengths of each, improving performance and scalability.

Parallel computing has become a fundamental component of modern computing, particularly in High-Performance Computing (HPC), where it addresses challenges in processing large-scale computations, simulations, and data-intensive applications. It also plays a crucial role in optimizing for speed and resource efficiency in diverse computing environments.

Importance of Data Locality in Performance

Data locality refers to the concept of accessing data elements that are located close to each other in the memory, optimizing the time it takes to fetch that data. Efficient data locality is critical for improving the performance of a program, especially in parallel and high-performance computing systems. The main idea is that processors tend to work more efficiently when the data they need is nearby, reducing the overhead associated with accessing the distant memory locations.

There are two main types of data locality:

- **Temporal Locality**: This refers to the reuse of specific data or instructions in a short period. If a particular memory location is accessed, it is likely to be accessed again soon. Caching is a key technique that exploits temporal locality by storing recently accessed data in faster, smaller memory closer to the processor.
- **Spatial Locality**: This refers to the concept that data elements stored near each other in memory are often accessed together. For example, in array-based computations, consecutive elements are often processed in sequence. By grouping the related data in the memory, and ensuring that the processor accesses them sequentially, spatial locality improves the efficiency of memory use.

How Data Locality Impacts Performance:

- **Cache Efficiency**: Modern processors use multiple levels of cache (L1, L2, and L3) to store the frequently accessed data. When the data exhibits good locality, it increases the likelihood that the required data is already in the cache, reducing the need for slow memory accesses.
- **Reduced Latency**: Accessing data stored in the processor's cache or close to it results in significantly lower latency, compared to fetching data from the main memory or further from the processor.
- **Minimized Bandwidth Usage**: Optimizing data locality helps reduce the demand for memory bandwidth. By accessing data that is already in close proximity, processors avoid frequent memory bottlenecks, and make better use of the available bandwidth.
- **Efficient Parallel Execution**: In parallel computing, data locality plays a critical role in ensuring that each processor or core can quickly access the data it needs, without frequent data sharing or waiting for remote memory accesses. This minimizes synchronization costs, and enhances the overall throughput of the parallel systems.

Parallelization Techniques

Parallelization is a process in which tasks are divided into smaller sub-tasks, and executed simultaneously across multiple processors or cores. This technique significantly enhances computational performance, especially for complex and data-intensive applications. By utilizing parallelism, the overall execution time of the programs can be reduced, making it a key concept in high-performance computing, scientific simulations, and real-time data processing.

Types of Parallelism

Parallelism can be categorized into two main types: Data parallelism and task parallelism. Each type has its specific use cases and optimizations.

Data Parallelism

Data parallelism is a type of parallel computing technique where the same operation is applied simultaneously across multiple data elements. It involves dividing a large dataset into smaller chunks and processing these chunks in parallel. This approach takes advantage of modern processors' ability to execute multiple tasks simultaneously, significantly speeding up computations, especially in data-intensive applications.

Key Concepts of Data Parallelism:

- **Data Decomposition**: The large dataset is broken down into smaller, independent pieces that can be processed concurrently. Each piece is assigned to a different processor or core.
- **Uniform Operation**: The same operation is performed on each piece of data. For example, applying a mathematical formula or performing a transformation on each element of an array.
- **Independent Execution**: Since the operations on each data element do not depend on others, each can be computed in parallel, making data parallelism highly efficient for tasks that involve repetitive operations over large datasets.

Advantages of Data Parallelism:

- **Speedup**: By distributing the workload across multiple processors, tasks can be completed much faster compared to sequential execution.
- **Scalability**: As the size of the dataset grows, data parallelism scales efficiently with additional processors or cores, ensuring that the performance improves with the availability of more computational resources.
- **Simplicity**: Data parallelism is often easier to implement, compared to task parallelism, as the same operation is applied to each data element, requiring less synchronization.

Applications of Data Parallelism:

- **Scientific Computing**: Operations, such as matrix multiplication, vector processing, and numerical simulations are ideal candidates for data parallelism where each computation can be independently applied to a different element or subset of the data.
- **Image Processing**: When manipulating large images (such as resizing, applying filters, or color adjustments), each pixel or region of the image can be processed independently.
- **Machine Learning**: In training machine learning models, especially in deep learning, large datasets are processed using data parallelism, where different parts of the data (for example, mini-batches) are fed into separate computational units simultaneously.

Tools for Data Parallelism:

- **Single Instruction, Multiple Data (SIMD)**: This hardware feature allows a single instruction to operate on multiple data elements at the same time. It is commonly used in vector processors and Graphics Processing Units (GPUs).
- **OpenMP**: An API for parallel programming that supports data parallelism through simple compiler directives for multi-core processors.
- **CUDA**: A parallel computing platform and application programming interface model created by NVIDIA, specifically designed for leveraging GPU resources for data-parallel operations.

Challenges of Data Parallelism:

- **Memory Access Patterns**: Efficient data parallelism requires careful attention to memory access patterns. If data is not stored in a way that allows efficient parallel access, performance gains may be limited.
- **Load Balancing**: Ensuring that each processor receives an equal amount of work is crucial. If

some processors finish their tasks earlier than others, they remain idle, which reduces overall performance.

Task Parallelism

Task parallelism is a parallel computing technique where different tasks or processes are executed simultaneously across multiple processors or cores. Unlike data parallelism, which operates on a single large dataset, task parallelism focuses on dividing a program into independent tasks that can be executed concurrently. These tasks often perform different operations, but they may operate on the same or different datasets.

Key Concepts of Task Parallelism:

- **Task Decomposition**: The program or workload is divided into independent tasks, each of which can be executed in parallel. Each task might involve a different computation or function, making task parallelism suitable for programs with diverse operations.
- **Independent Execution**: Tasks are designed to execute independently, meaning the execution of one task does not directly depend on the completion of others. However, some synchronization might still be necessary if tasks share data or resources.
- **Concurrency**: Task parallelism enables the simultaneous execution of multiple tasks, potentially reducing the overall execution time. Concurrency can occur when tasks are logically independent and can be processed in parallel without waiting for others.

Advantages of Task Parallelism:

- **Flexibility**: Task parallelism is highly flexible, allowing for the parallelization of complex workflows where different tasks can be performed concurrently. This makes it suitable for a wide variety of applications.
- **Resource Utilization**: It allows for better utilization of system resources, as different tasks can be assigned to different processors or cores, optimizing the use of computational power.
- **Scalability**: Task parallelism scales well with an increasing number of processors, as the number of tasks in a program typically grows with the complexity of the problem. More processors can be added to execute more tasks concurrently, improving performance.

Applications of Task Parallelism:

- **Multithreading**: In multithreaded applications, each thread can be treated as a separate task. For example, a web server may have different threads to handle incoming requests, allowing multiple users to be served concurrently.
- **Distributed Computing**: Task parallelism is central to distributed computing systems, where tasks are divided across different machines or nodes. For example, in cloud computing, different tasks might be distributed across servers to optimize performance.
- **Scientific Simulations**: Complex simulations, such as those in physics or biology, often involve running different tasks concurrently, such as calculating different parts of a model or simulating different conditions.
- **Data Processing Pipelines**: In data processing, tasks might include reading data, filtering it, transforming it, and writing the results. Each of these stages can be parallelized, making the system more efficient.

Tools for Task Parallelism:

- **OpenMP**: OpenMP provides constructs for parallel programming in C, C++, and Fortran, which can be used to parallelize tasks by distributing them across available cores.
- **Message Passing Interface (MPI)**: MPI is a communication protocol used in distributed

systems to enable parallel execution across different nodes or machines. It is commonly used for task parallelism in supercomputing environments.

- **Threading Libraries**: Libraries such as POSIX threads (Pthreads) and C++11 threads allow developers to create and manage parallel tasks within applications. These libraries provide mechanisms for task creation, synchronization, and communication.

Challenges of Task Parallelism:

- **Task Dependency**: While tasks are intended to be independent, in many cases, they can have dependencies, which means one task may require the result of another. Proper synchronization mechanisms need to be in place to handle dependencies.
- **Load Balancing**: Just like data parallelism, task parallelism requires efficient load balancing. If some tasks are significantly more complex than others, the processors assigned to those tasks may become bottlenecks, reducing overall performance.
- **Overhead**: Managing parallel tasks, including communication and synchronization between tasks, can introduce overhead, which may negate the benefits of parallelism if not handled effectively.

Identifying Opportunities for Parallelization

Parallelization is the process of dividing a program into smaller, independent tasks that can be executed concurrently to improve performance. To maximize the benefits of parallel computing, it is essential to identify which parts of the program are suitable for parallel execution. Proper identification of parallelizable tasks can lead to significant improvements in computational efficiency, especially for compute-intensive applications. The following are key strategies and methods for identifying opportunities for parallelization:

Analyzing Independent Operations

Look for sections of code where operations are independent of each other and can run simultaneously without affecting the outcome. For example, in loops where each iteration operates on different elements, these iterations can often be executed concurrently.

Example: In matrix multiplication, each element of the resulting matrix can be computed independently by multiplying corresponding elements from the input matrices. Each computation does not depend on others, making it a prime candidate for parallelization.

Loop-Level Parallelism

Loop-level parallelism occurs when a loop contains operations that can be executed in parallel, especially when the loop iterations are independent. Identifying loops with independent iterations is one of the most common strategies for parallelization.

Example: A simple for-loop that sums an array of numbers can be parallelized by dividing the array into smaller segments and having different threads sum each segment concurrently.

Method: Loop-carried dependencies (where an iteration depends on the result of the previous iteration) must be identified and avoided or reduced for successful parallelization.

Task-Level Parallelism

In many programs, different tasks or functions can be performed concurrently. For example, if the program involves performing different computations (such as image processing, data analysis, or simulation), these tasks may be independent and can run in parallel.

Example: In web scraping, while one thread retrieves data from one source, another thread can retrieve data from a different source without waiting for the first task to complete.

Data Parallelism

Data parallelism involves performing the same operation on different pieces of data. When the program has large datasets and applies the same operation to each element (such as in matrix operations, sorting, or image processing), these operations can be parallelized.

Example: Applying a function to each element of an array or matrix, such as performing a mathematical operation on each pixel of an image, can be done in parallel.

Identifying Bottlenecks

A bottleneck occurs when a particular section of code or operation consumes a disproportionate amount of time or computational resources. By identifying bottlenecks, you can focus parallelization efforts on those specific areas to reduce the overall execution time.

Example: In a simulation that requires complex calculations, parallelizing the most time-consuming calculations can significantly speed up the entire process.

Analyzing Task Dependencies

Understanding the dependencies between tasks is crucial for effective parallelization. Tasks that have data dependencies or require results from other tasks cannot be executed concurrently unless those dependencies are handled appropriately.

Example: In a program that computes a series of calculations, if the result of one computation is required by the next, parallelization can only occur if dependencies are reduced or eliminated, such as by using techniques like data partitioning or reordering.

Using Profiling Tools

Profiling tools analyze the performance of a program and identify the sections of code that take the most time to execute. These tools can help pinpoint areas where parallelization can be applied for improved performance.

Tools: Examples include Intel VTune, gprof, and Visual Studio's Performance Profiler. These tools provide insights into where bottlenecks occur and can highlight parts of the program that may benefit from parallelization.

Considering Hardware Architecture

The hardware architecture plays a significant role in identifying parallelization opportunities. Different processors (CPUs, GPUs) have varied capabilities and the ability to handle different types of parallelism. Understanding the hardware's architecture and its capabilities (such as the number of cores or SIMD instructions) is essential in determining where parallelization is most effective.

Example: A GPU with hundreds of cores may be well-suited for data parallelism, while a CPU with fewer cores may be better suited for task parallelism.

Divide-and-Conquer Algorithms

Divide-and-conquer algorithms, where large problems are broken down into smaller subproblems, are naturally suited for parallelization. Each subproblem can be solved concurrently and then combined to form the final result.

Example: Sorting algorithms such as quicksort or mergesort can be parallelized by dividing the dataset into smaller subsets and sorting them in parallel.

Using High-Level Parallel Programming Libraries

Many programming languages and libraries provide high-level abstractions for parallelization. These libraries often include parallel constructs for loops, task scheduling, and synchronization, making it easier to identify areas for parallel execution without needing to manually manage threads or processes.

Examples: OpenMP, Intel Threading Building Blocks (TBB), and the C++ Standard Library (with the C++11 thread library) provide tools to identify and implement parallelism.

Tools and Frameworks for Parallel Programming

Parallel programming requires robust tools and frameworks to simplify the implementation of parallelism, ensuring better resource utilization and performance. These tools help manage threads, memory, and inter-process communication while abstracting complexities. The following are widely used tools and frameworks for parallel programming:

OpenMP

OpenMP is a widely used Application Programming Interface (API) for shared-memory parallel programming, primarily in **C**, **C++**, and **Fortran**. It enables developers to create multi-threaded applications by simplifying the process of parallelizing code. OpenMP achieves this through **compiler directives**, **runtime library routines**, and **environment variables**. By marking sections of code to run in parallel, developers can efficiently utilize multi-core processors without significant restructuring of their programs.

Key Features and Explanation with Examples:

Basic Parallel Region:

The **`#pragma omp parallel`** directive is used to mark a region of code that runs concurrently on multiple threads.

Example:

```
#include <stdio.h>
#include <omp.h>

int main() {
    #pragma omp parallel
    {
        int id = omp_get_thread_num();
        printf("Hello from thread %d\n", id);
    }
    return 0;
}
```

Output Example:

```
Hello from thread 0
Hello from thread 1
Hello from thread 2
Hello from thread 3
```

In this example, multiple threads execute the same block of code concurrently. Each thread has a unique ID, which is obtained using **`omp_get_thread_num()`**.

Parallelizing Loops:

The **#pragma omp for** directive allows the iterations of a loop to be divided among multiple threads. This is particularly useful for computations where iterations are independent.

Example:

```
#include <stdio.h>
#include <omp.h>

int main() {
    int n = 10;
    int a[n];

    #pragma omp parallel for
    for (int i = 0; i < n; i++) {
        a[i] = i * i; // Calculate square of i
        printf("Thread %d calculated a[%d] = %d\n", omp_get_thread_num(), i,
a[i]);
    }
    return 0;
}
```

Output Example:

```
Thread 0 calculated a[0] = 0
Thread 1 calculated a[1] = 1
Thread 2 calculated a[2] = 4
Thread 3 calculated a[3] = 9
...
```

Here, OpenMP divides the loop iterations across the threads. Each thread computes part of the **array a[]** concurrently, improving performance.

Work-Sharing Constructs:

The section directive splits different tasks across multiple threads.

Example:

```
#include <stdio.h>
#include <omp.h>

int main() {
    #pragma omp parallel sections
    {
        #pragma omp section
        printf("Thread %d: Task 1\n", omp_get_thread_num());

        #pragma omp section
        printf("Thread %d: Task 2\n", omp_get_thread_num());
    }
    return 0;
}
```

Output Example:

```
Thread 0: Task 1
Thread 1: Task 2
```

In this case, the two sections are executed in parallel by different threads.

Synchronization and Data Sharing:

OpenMP provides mechanisms to handle data conflicts and race conditions through critical, atomic, and **reduction** clauses.

Example with Reduction:

```
#include <stdio.h>
#include <omp.h>

int main() {
    int sum = 0;

    #pragma omp parallel for reduction(+:sum)
    for (int i = 1; i <= 10; i++) {
        sum += i;
    }
    printf("Sum = %d\n", sum); // Expected output: 55
    return 0;
}
```

Output:

```
Sum = 55
```

Here, the **`reduction(+:sum)`** clause ensures that all threads contribute to the final sum without conflicts.

Advantages of OpenMP:

- **Ease of Use:** OpenMP requires minimal code changes to parallelize programs.
- **Portability:** It works across various platforms and compilers.
- **Scalability:** Efficiently utilizes multi-core processors for improved performance.
- **Control Over Data Scope:** OpenMP provides fine control over shared and private variables.

Limitations of OpenMP:

- OpenMP is limited to **shared-memory systems** and is not suitable for distributed systems.
- Excessive thread creation can result in overhead, reducing performance gains.
- It requires the programmer to ensure that parallel code is **thread-safe.**

MPI

Message Passing Interface (MPI) is a standardized and portable message-passing system designed for parallel computing in distributed memory systems. Unlike OpenMP which works in shared-memory environments, MPI is used for **inter-process communication** in systems where memory is distributed among multiple nodes or processors.

Key Features of MPI:

- **Distributed Memory Systems**

  MPI is specifically designed for parallel computing in **distributed-memory** environments, where each processor has its own local memory, and processors communicate by passing messages.

- **Point-to-Point Communication**

  MPI supports **point-to-point communication** which allows direct communication between two processes. This is useful for tasks such as data exchange between nodes in a cluster.

Example:

```
MPI_Send(&data, 1, MPI_INT, dest_rank, 0, MPI_COMM_WORLD);
MPI_Recv(&data, 1, MPI_INT, source_rank, 0, MPI_COMM_WORLD, &status);
```

Collective Communication:

MPI supports **collective communication**, enabling communication between multiple processes. This is typically used in operations such as broadcasting data to all processes, gathering data from all processes, and performing reductions (for example, summing values across processes).

Example:

```
MPI_Bcast(&data, 1, MPI_INT, root_rank, MPI_COMM_WORLD);
```

Synchronization Mechanisms:

MPI provides **synchronization** techniques for managing how processes coordinate their execution. These include barriers (synchronizing all processes), as well as locking mechanisms for mutual exclusion.

Example:

```
MPI_Barrier(MPI_COMM_WORLD);
```

Process Groups:

MPI organizes processes into groups and provides functions to communicate within specific groups of processes. This enables more efficient communication in large systems.

MPI Data Types:

MPI includes support for **custom data types**, allowing communication of complex structures such as arrays, matrices, or user-defined types.

Example:

```
MPI_Type_create_struct(...);  // Define a custom MPI data type
MPI_Send(&custom_data, 1, custom_type, dest_rank, 0, MPI_COMM_WORLD);
```

How MPI Works:

1. **Initialization**

   The MPI environment is initialized with **`MPI_Init`**, and processes are identified by unique ranks within a **communicator**, such as **`MPI_COMM_WORLD`**.

   Example:

   ```
   int rank, size;
   MPI_Init(&argc, &argv);
   MPI_Comm_rank(MPI_COMM_WORLD, &rank);
   MPI_Comm_size(MPI_COMM_WORLD, &size);
   ```

2. **Communication**

   Processes communicate using **`MPI_Send`** and **`MPI_Recv`**, sending and receiving data between different processes, possibly across multiple machines.

3. **Finalization**

   Once communication is complete, the MPI environment is finalized with `MPI_Finalize`. No MPI function can be called after this.

Example:

```
MPI_Finalize();
```

Advantages of MPI:

- **Scalability:**

  MPI is highly scalable and suitable for large-scale parallel applications running on distributed memory systems, including clusters and supercomputers.

- **Portability:**

  MPI is supported on a wide range of platforms, from small-scale systems to large supercomputers, making it a versatile option for parallel programming.

- **Flexibility:**

  MPI allows fine-grained control over communication patterns, enabling the design of complex parallel algorithms that meet specific performance needs.

- **Efficiency:**

  Since each process has its own memory, there are fewer concerns with memory contention, leading to better performance in systems where data is distributed.

Applications of MPI:

- **High-Performance Computing (HPC):**

  MPI is widely used in large-scale simulations, scientific computing, weather forecasting, and other HPC applications requiring massive parallelism.

- **Distributed Systems:**

  It is commonly used in distributed systems for data processing, machine learning, and big data analytics.

- **Parallel Algorithms:**

  MPI is ideal for implementing custom parallel algorithms that require high scalability and performance.

Threading Libraries

Threading libraries provide a set of tools and functionalities to manage and execute multiple threads concurrently in a program. Using these libraries, developers can harness the full potential of multi-core processors to improve the performance of applications. Two of the most popular threading libraries are **POSIX Threads** (Pthreads) and **C++11 Threads**, both of which offer distinct advantages and can be used depending on the application's needs.

Pthreads

Pthreads is a low-level, system-dependent threading library that follows the POSIX standard for threads. It is widely used in Unix-like operating systems and provides a lot of control over thread management, synchronization, and communication.

Key Features:

- Threads are created using the **`pthread_create`** function.
- Synchronization is achieved with mutexes, condition variables, and semaphores.
- Offers fine-grained control over thread management, which makes it suitable for complex multithreading applications.

Example:

```
#include <pthread.h>
#include <stdio.h>

void* print_message(void* arg) {
    printf("Hello from thread!\n");
    return NULL;
}

int main() {
    pthread_t thread;
    pthread_create(&thread, NULL, print_message, NULL);
    pthread_join(thread, NULL);
    return 0;
}
```

In this example, a new thread is created that prints a message to the console. The **`pthread_create`** function is used to spawn the thread, and **`pthread_join`** ensures the main thread waits for the spawned thread to finish before continuing.

Benefits:

- Provides low-level control for performance tuning.
- Suitable for advanced use cases requiring custom thread management.
- Offers compatibility across platforms that support POSIX standards.

Limitations:

- Complex syntax for managing threads and synchronization.
- Requires manual memory and resource management.

C++11 Threads

C++11 introduced a standardized thread library in C++, providing a high-level, object-oriented abstraction for managing threads. The syntax is simpler compared to Pthreads and integrates seamlessly with other C++ features.

Key Features:

- Threads are created using the **`std::thread`** class.
- Supports modern C++ features such as lambda expressions and Resource Acquisition Is Initialization (RAII).
- Simplifies thread management with automatic handling of resources.

Example:

```
#include <iostream>
#include <thread>

void print_message() {
    std::cout << "Hello from thread!" << std::endl;
}

int main() {
    std::thread t(print_message);
    t.join();
    return 0;
}
```

In this example, a thread is created using **`std::thread`**, and it executes the **`print_message`** function. The **`join()`** function is used to ensure the main thread waits for the newly created thread to complete.

Benefits:

- Provides a higher-level, simpler API for managing threads.
- Integrates with modern C++ features, making it easier to write and maintain multithreaded applications.
- RAII ensures automatic cleanup of resources, preventing memory leaks.

Limitations:

- Less flexibility for low-level control compared to Pthreads.
- May not be as efficient in certain specialized use cases due to its abstraction.

Java Threading

Java also provides a robust threading library built into its standard API. The Thread class and the Runnable interface are central to Java's multithreading model. Java handles much of the complexity of thread management, including automatic garbage collection and synchronization.

Key Features:

- Threads are created by extending the Thread class or implementing the Runnable interface.
- The Java Virtual Machine (JVM) abstracts platform-specific details, ensuring portability.
- Built-in synchronization mechanisms such as the synchronized keyword.

Example:

```
class MyThread extends Thread {
    public void run() {
        System.out.println("Hello from thread!");
    }
}

public class Main {
    public static void main(String[] args) {
        MyThread t = new MyThread();
        t.start();
    }
}
```

In this example, a custom thread is created by subclassing **`Thread`** and overriding the **`run()`** method. The **`start()`** method initiates the thread, which prints a message to the console.

Benefits:

- Easy-to-use API for thread creation and synchronization.
- Automatically handles memory management and garbage collection.
- Provides high portability across different platforms due to JVM abstraction.

Limitations:

- Limited control over low-level thread management compared to Pthreads.
- Performance may be slower in certain scenarios due to the JVM overhead.

Comparing Pthreads, C++11 Threads, and Java Threads

Key Differences:

- **Pthreads** offer the most control over threading, suitable for advanced use cases but are more complex to use.
- **C++11 Threads** provide a simpler, high-level interface with integration to modern C++ features, making them ideal for general-purpose multithreading.
- **Java Threads** offer portability and ease of use, particularly suited for applications running on the JVM, though with less control over low-level operations.

When to Use:

- Use **Pthreads** for low-level control and performance tuning in Unix-like systems.
- Use **C++11 Threads** for simpler, cross-platform multithreading in C++ applications.
- Use **Java Threads** for multithreading in Java-based applications, especially when targeting the JVM.

Data Locality Optimization

Data locality refers to the use of data elements that are close to each other in memory during the execution of a program. Optimizing data locality can significantly improve the performance of programs by reducing memory access time, minimizing cache misses, and making better use of the processor's cache. Efficient data locality ensures that data accessed together is stored together, allowing faster processing by maximizing cache hits.

Understanding Data Locality

Data locality is the principle that data that is used together should be placed together in memory to improve the speed of data access. Optimizing for data locality can reduce the latency of memory accesses and increase overall program efficiency. There are two primary types of data locality: **temporal locality** and **spatial locality**.

Temporal Locality

Temporal locality refers to the tendency of a program to access the same memory locations repeatedly within a short period of time. If a program accesses a specific memory location, it is likely to access the same location again soon. Temporal locality can be leveraged by keeping frequently accessed data in the cache, as cache memory is much faster than main memory.

Example: If a loop repeatedly accesses the same array element in consecutive iterations, that element exhibits temporal locality.

Optimization Techniques:

- **Cache-friendly algorithms**: Ensuring that the most frequently accessed data is kept in cache by reordering memory accesses.
- **Loop reordering**: Altering the order of loops to maximize cache hits for frequently accessed elements.

Spatial Locality

Spatial locality refers to the tendency of a program to access memory locations that are close to each other. When a program accesses a particular memory address, it is likely to access nearby addresses in the near future. Spatial locality can be exploited by arranging data structures in memory in a way that makes it likely that contiguous data will be accessed together, increasing cache hits.

Example: In a 2D array, accessing elements that are next to each other, such as `array[i][j]` followed by `array[i][j+1]`, demonstrates spatial locality.

Optimization Techniques:

- **Contiguous memory allocation**: Store data in contiguous memory blocks to ensure that accessing one element brings neighboring elements into the cache.
- **Block-based algorithms**: For large datasets, divide data into blocks that fit in the cache, ensuring better spatial locality.

Strategies for Improving Data Locality

Improving data locality is a critical optimization technique for enhancing performance by reducing memory access times and increasing the efficiency of cache usage. Effective strategies for improving data locality can significantly impact the speed of programs, particularly in computation-heavy or memory-bound applications.

Here are the key strategies for improving data locality:

Data Structure Design

Data structure design plays a pivotal role in improving data locality by organizing data in ways that make it easier to access in a cache-efficient manner. The goal is to ensure that data that is frequently accessed together is stored together, minimizing cache misses.

- **Arrays over Linked Lists**: Arrays allow for contiguous memory allocation, which improves spatial locality compared to linked lists that store elements in non-contiguous memory locations.
- **Compact Data Structures**: Use smaller and compact data types to reduce memory overhead and increase the likelihood that the data can fit into the cache.
- **Array of Structures (AoS) vs. Structure of Arrays (SoA)**: In certain situations, reorganizing data into a structure of arrays layout can lead to better performance. SoA groups similar data types together, which is more cache-friendly than AoS, where each structure contains multiple data types together.

Memory Layout Optimization

Memory layout optimization focuses on how data is arranged in memory to ensure that related data items are stored close together, maximizing cache efficiency.

- **Contiguous Memory Allocation**: Store related data items in contiguous memory locations to improve spatial locality. This ensures that when one element is accessed, neighboring elements are likely to be loaded into the cache as well.
- **Blocking or Tiling**: For large arrays or matrices, breaking data into smaller blocks (or tiles) that fit into the cache can lead to improved performance. This technique is particularly effective for matrix multiplications and other computationally intensive tasks.
- **Padding and Alignment**: Proper padding ensures that data structures are aligned to memory boundaries that are optimal for the hardware's cache system, reducing the chance of cache conflicts.

Loop Transformations

Loop transformations reorganize the order in which loops access data, making memory access patterns more cache-friendly.

- **Loop Blocking/Loop Tiling**: Breaking large loops into smaller, cache-sized chunks ensures that working sets of data remain in the cache. This technique can be particularly effective for matrix operations or nested loops accessing multidimensional arrays.
- **Loop Interchanging**: Changing the order of nested loops to access data in a more cache-friendly pattern. For example, accessing a 2D array in row-major order instead of column-major order can improve spatial locality.
- **Loop Unrolling**: Unrolling a loop can help reduce the overhead of branching and increase the number of operations performed in a single loop iteration, reducing cache misses by keeping relevant data in the cache longer.

Prefetching

Prefetching is a technique where data is moved into the cache before it is needed, reducing the time spent waiting for memory accesses.

- **Software Prefetching**: Using compiler directives or explicit code instructions to move data into the cache before it's needed. This can be done based on the prediction of future data accesses.
- **Hardware Prefetching**: Relying on the hardware to predict and pre-fetch data into the cache automatically. Modern processors use sophisticated algorithms to prefetch data that is likely to be accessed soon.

Cache Blocking (Also Known as Cache Tiling)

Cache blocking or **cache tiling** is a technique where the data is divided into blocks that fit within the cache's size. This ensures that working data remains in the cache, minimizing the need for slower memory access.

Example: For matrix multiplication, break the matrices into smaller blocks that fit into the processor's cache. This technique ensures that when the computation for one block is done, the required data is already loaded in the cache.

Blocking Algorithms

Blocking algorithms work by dividing the computational problem into smaller subproblems that can be computed independently. This ensures that data is accessed in small, localized chunks that fit into the cache.

Example: In a large matrix multiplication, the matrix is divided into smaller sub-matrices (blocks), and computations are performed on these blocks. This reduces the number of cache misses as each block is processed in memory contiguously.

Data Prefetching and Stream Buffers

Prefetching and **stream buffers** are often used to load large sequences of data into memory ahead of time, reducing cache misses. These techniques help to ensure that frequently accessed data is already available in the cache.

Impact of Data Locality on Performance

Improving data locality can lead to significant performance gains by reducing the number of cache misses, which are expensive in terms of latency. When the data is not in the cache, the CPU has to access slower main memory, resulting in performance degradation. By optimizing data locality, the program can:

- **Reduce Cache Misses**: Access patterns that exhibit good temporal and spatial locality reduce cache misses, which improves execution speed.
- **Improve Memory Bandwidth Utilization**: Optimized data locality ensures that memory is accessed in bursts that match the cache's capacity, thus maximizing throughput.
- **Lower Latency**: Reducing the time spent accessing data from main memory by improving locality can greatly decrease overall execution time.

Cache Optimization

Cache optimization plays a crucial role in enhancing the performance of computer programs by reducing the time spent on memory accesses. By improving how data is stored and retrieved from the cache, systems can execute programs faster, especially for memory-bound tasks.

The following is an overview of the concepts involved in cache optimization.

Cache Architecture Overview

Cache is a small, high-speed memory component situated between the processor and main memory (RAM). Its purpose is to store frequently accessed data to minimize the time it takes to fetch data from slower memory.

Levels of Cache: Modern processors typically feature multiple levels of cache:

- **L1 Cache**: The smallest and fastest cache, directly connected to the processor core.
- **L2 Cache**: Larger than L1 but slower, shared between cores in some processors.
- **L3 Cache**: The largest cache, shared across multiple cores, slower than L2 but still faster than main memory.

Cache Hierarchy: Data is first searched in the L1 cache, then L2, and finally in L3 (if applicable). If data is not found in any cache, it is fetched from the main memory.

Cache Performance Metrics

To evaluate cache performance, several metrics are considered, which help identify how effectively the cache is being used:

- **Hit Rate**: The percentage of memory accesses that find the required data in the cache. A higher hit rate indicates better cache utilization.
- **Miss Rate**: The inverse of hit rate, representing the percentage of memory accesses that do not find data in the cache, requiring a fetch from slower memory.
- **Miss Penalty**: The time it takes to retrieve data from main memory after a cache miss occurs. Reducing this penalty is critical for improving system performance.
- **Cache Bandwidth**: The rate at which data can be transferred to and from the cache. High bandwidth leads to better cache utilization.

Techniques for Cache Optimization

Optimizing cache usage can significantly improve performance. The following are some common techniques for cache optimization:

Cache Blocking

Cache blocking (or **cache tiling**) is a technique used to optimize the use of cache by dividing large data sets into smaller blocks that fit into the cache. This helps to ensure that data used in computations remains in the cache, reducing cache misses.

Example: In matrix multiplication, breaking matrices into smaller blocks allows each block to be loaded into the cache, reducing the need to access slower memory.

Cache-Friendly Algorithms

Cache-friendly algorithms are designed to minimize cache misses by ensuring that memory access patterns take full advantage of the cache hierarchy.

Example: Algorithms that access memory in a linear or row-major order are more cache-friendly than those that jump randomly across memory locations. A good cache-friendly algorithm minimizes memory access and ensures that data accessed together is stored contiguously.

Data Locality: Organizing and accessing data in a way that exploits temporal and spatial locality helps improve cache efficiency. Temporal locality refers to reusing recently accessed data, while spatial locality ensures that data stored close together is accessed sequentially.

Prefetching Strategies

Prefetching involves loading data into the cache before it is actually needed, reducing the time spent waiting for data fetches. This can be achieved through both software and hardware prefetching mechanisms.

- **Software Prefetching**: This is done by the programmer or compiler using specific instructions to preload data into the cache based on predictable access patterns. A common example is using `prefetch` directives in code to load data ahead of time.
- **Hardware Prefetching**: Modern processors automatically detect access patterns and prefetch data into the cache to reduce delays caused by cache misses.
- **Streaming Prefetching**: This technique is used when accessing large datasets sequentially. The processor prefetches data from memory into the cache in anticipation of the next accesses, ensuring that the data is available when required.

Loop Transformations

Loop transformations are optimization techniques used to improve the efficiency of loops in programming. By altering the structure of loops, these transformations help enhance performance by increasing parallelism, improving cache usage, and minimizing execution overhead. They are especially valuable in high-performance and parallel computing environments.

Importance of Loop Optimization in Parallelism

Loop optimization is a critical aspect of enhancing performance in parallel computing. Loops often constitute the most computationally intensive parts of a program, and optimizing them ensures efficient resource utilization, faster execution, and scalability across modern architectures. In the context of parallelism, loop optimization addresses both computational and memory bottlenecks, paving the way for better performance.

- **Enhancing Parallel Execution**

  Loops inherently offer a natural opportunity for parallelism, as their iterations can often be executed concurrently. Optimizing loops maximizes this parallel potential by minimizing dependencies between iterations and balancing workloads. For instance:

  - **Without Optimization**: Dependencies or inefficiencies in loop structure may restrict parallel execution.
  - **With Optimization**: Techniques such as loop unrolling or loop tiling restructure loops to reduce dependencies and facilitate efficient parallel execution.

- **Improving Cache Utilization**

  Optimized loops improve data locality, leading to better utilization of cache memory. Techniques such as loop tiling reorganize loops to access data in a cache-friendly manner, reducing memory access latencies and improving overall throughput.

  Example: In matrix multiplication, tiling allows smaller portions of the matrix to fit into the cache, avoiding repeated data transfers between memory and cache.

- **Minimizing Overhead**

  Inefficient loop structures can introduce significant overhead due to frequent branching and loop control operations. Optimization techniques such as loop unrolling reduce the number of iterations and control instructions, enhancing performance.

- **Reducing Execution Time**

  Optimized loops execute faster by leveraging parallelism and reducing redundant computations. For applications with repetitive tasks, such as image processing or scientific simulations, loop optimization can significantly cut down runtime.

- **Enabling Scalability**

  Loop optimization prepares programs for execution on high-performance systems with multiple cores or processors. By restructuring loops for parallelism, programs can scale effectively, making optimal use of the available hardware.

Common Loop Transformations

Loop transformations are essential techniques used to enhance program performance by improving parallelism and data locality and reducing computational overhead. They play a critical role in optimizing code for modern processors, enabling efficient use of resources and faster execution.

Loop Unrolling

Loop unrolling is an optimization technique that improves program performance by reducing the overhead associated with loop control and enhancing instruction-level parallelism. By executing multiple iterations of a loop within a single iteration, loop unrolling minimizes the number of branch instructions and enables the processor to better utilize its resources.

The primary idea behind loop unrolling is to decrease the number of iterations by replicating the loop body multiple times. This reduces the loop control logic (for example, comparisons, increments, and branching) and increases the opportunities for parallel execution of instructions within the loop body.

Example:

Consider a loop that sums the elements of an array:

Original Loop:

```
for (int i = 0; i < 4; i++) {
    sum += a[i];
}
```

Unrolled Loop (Factor of 2):

```
for (int i = 0; i < 4; i += 2) {
    sum += a[i] + a[i + 1];
}
```

Fully Unrolled Loop (Factor of 4):

```
sum += a[0] + a[1] + a[2] + a[3];
```

Advantages:

- **Reduced Loop Overhead**: By decreasing the number of iterations, fewer branch and increment operations are required, leading to faster execution.
- **Improved Instruction-Level Parallelism (ILP)**: The unrolled loop provides more instructions for the processor to execute concurrently, utilizing multiple functional units effectively.
- **Better Pipeline Utilization**: Reduces the frequency of branch instructions, minimizing pipeline stalls.

Limitations:

- **Code Size Increase**: Unrolling replicates the loop body, which can lead to a larger code size (code bloat), potentially impacting instruction cache performance.
- **Limited by Dependencies**: Loops with inter-iteration dependencies may not benefit from unrolling.
- **Optimal Factor**: Choosing the unrolling factor is critical; an excessively high factor may negate performance gains.

Practical Use Case:

Vector Processing in Multimedia Applications:

Loop unrolling is frequently used in multimedia and scientific applications, such as image processing, where operations such as adding or multiplying pixel values over an array can benefit significantly from unrolling.

Example:

```
for (int i = 0; i < N; i += 4) {
    output[i] = input[i] * factor;
    output[i + 1] = input[i + 1] * factor;
    output[i + 2] = input[i + 2] * factor;
    output[i + 3] = input[i + 3] * factor;
}
```

Loop Fusion and Fission

Loop Fusion and Fission are two important loop transformation techniques that optimize program performance by reorganizing the structure of loops. These techniques focus on improving data locality, reducing overhead, and enabling parallelism in computational tasks.

Loop Fusion

Loop fusion (or loop jamming) combines two or more loops with the same iteration space into a single loop. This can enhance data locality and reduce loop overhead.

Example:

Original Code:

```
for (int i = 0; i < N; i++) {
    a[i] = b[i] + c[i];
}
for (int i = 0; i < N; i++) {
    d[i] = a[i] * e[i];
}
```

After Fusion:

```
for (int i = 0; i < N; i++) {
    a[i] = b[i] + c[i];
    d[i] = a[i] * e[i];
}
```

Advantages of Fusion:

- **Improved Data Locality:** Accessing `a[i]` in the same loop where it is computed reduces cache misses.
- **Reduced Loop Overhead:** Fewer loop control instructions (for example, initialization, comparison, and branching) improve execution speed.
- **Energy Efficiency:** Combining loops minimizes redundant instruction execution.

Challenges of Fusion:

- **Dependency Issues:** Fusion is not possible if there are dependencies between iterations that cannot be resolved.
- **Increased Register Pressure:** Combining loops may require more temporary variables, potentially straining available registers.

Loop Fission

Loop fission (or loop distribution) splits a single loop into multiple loops, each handling part of the computation. This can reduce contention for resources and improve parallelism.

Example:

Original Code:

```
for (int i = 0; i < N; i++) {
    a[i] = b[i] + c[i];
    d[i] = a[i] * e[i];
}
```

After Fission:

```
for (int i = 0; i < N; i++) {
    a[i] = b[i] + c[i];
}
for (int i = 0; i < N; i++) {
    d[i] = a[i] * e[i];
}
```

Advantages of Fission:

- **Increased Parallelism:** Independent loops can be executed concurrently on separate processors.
- **Reduced Register Pressure:** Each loop may use fewer registers, allowing for efficient hardware utilization.
- **Improved Cache Behavior:** Smaller loops may work more effectively with the available cache.

Challenges of Fission:

- **Increased Loop Overhead:** Each loop requires its own initialization and control instructions.
- **Decreased Data Locality:** Splitting loops can lead to multiple accesses to the same data in memory, increasing cache misses.

Comparison of Fusion and Fission:

Aspect	Loop Fusion	Loop Fission
Purpose	Combines loops to reduce overhead and improve data locality.	Splits loops to improve parallelism and manage resources.
Effect on Overhead	Reduces loop overhead.	Increases loop overhead.
Effect on Locality	Enhances data locality.	May reduce data locality.
Dependency Handling	Requires careful analysis of dependencies.	Useful for isolating dependent sections.

Table 16.1: *Comparative Analysis of Fusion and Fission*

Loop Tiling

Loop Tiling, also known as **Loop Blocking**, is a loop transformation technique that optimizes memory hierarchy usage by dividing larger iteration spaces into smaller, more manageable blocks or tiles. This technique enhances data locality and improves performance, especially on modern architectures with deep memory hierarchies.

In many applications, such as matrix computations, loops iterate over large datasets that may not fit entirely into the cache. Loop tiling breaks these large iterations into smaller chunks or "tiles," which can fit into the cache, allowing the processor to reuse data effectively before it is replaced.

Example:

Original Code (Without Tiling):

```
for (int i = 0; i < N; i++) {
    for (int j = 0; j < N; j++) {
        C[i][j] = A[i][j] + B[i][j];
    }
}
```

After Tiling:

```
int tileSize = 64; // Tile size
for (int i = 0; i < N; i += tileSize) {
    for (int j = 0; j < N; j += tileSize) {
        for (int ii = i; ii < min(i + tileSize, N); ii++) {
            for (int jj = j; jj < min(j + tileSize, N); jj++) {
                C[ii][jj] = A[ii][jj] + B[ii][jj];
            }
```

```
        }
    }
}
```

In this example, **tileSize** determines the size of the blocks. Each block (or tile) of the matrix is processed independently, improving cache utilization.

Benefits of Loop Tiling:

- **Improved Cache Utilization:**

  By working on smaller chunks of data that fit into the cache, loop tiling reduces cache misses and increases cache efficiency.

- **Enhanced Data Locality:**

  Processing tiles ensures that data is accessed repeatedly while still in the cache, minimizing memory access latency.

- **Better Parallelism:**

  Tiled loops can be distributed across multiple threads or cores, allowing for efficient parallel execution.

- **Optimized for Modern Architectures:**

  Tiling aligns computations with the size of cache blocks or pages, leveraging hardware features effectively.

Challenges of Loop Tiling:

- **Choosing Tile Size:**

  Selecting an optimal tile size is critical. Tiles that are too small may not fully utilize available resources, while tiles that are too large may lead to cache thrashing.

- **Implementation Complexity:**

  Introducing tiling increases code complexity, requiring careful handling of boundary conditions and performance tuning.

- **Hardware Dependency:**

  Performance improvements depend on the underlying hardware, such as cache size and memory bandwidth.

Real-World Applications:

- **Matrix Multiplication:**

  Loop tiling is widely used in matrix multiplication algorithms to improve performance by reducing memory access costs.

- **Image Processing:**

  In image processing tasks, tiling optimizes operations such as filtering or convolution by focusing on smaller sections of the image.

- **Scientific Computing:**

  Tiling is common in simulations and numerical computations, where large datasets are processed iteratively.

Example Implementations using Parallel Processing Tools

In this section, we explore real-world examples of how parallel processing tools can be effectively utilized to optimize computational tasks. By leveraging powerful parallel programming frameworks, we can significantly enhance performance in various applications. The tools and techniques we cover, including OpenMP, MPI, and threading libraries, help us to break down complex problems into smaller, concurrent tasks that can be executed simultaneously across multiple processors or threads. These examples will demonstrate how parallel processing can be applied to a variety of domains, from scientific computing to data processing, and provide practical insights into how parallel programming frameworks improve efficiency and speed.

Case Studies of Parallel Code Optimization

Parallel code optimization is a crucial practice for improving performance in multi-threaded and distributed systems. The following are several real-world case studies that showcase the use of various parallel processing tools and techniques to optimize computational workloads effectively.

Case Study 1: Matrix Multiplication Using OpenMP

- **Problem:** Speed up the computation of matrix multiplication for large datasets in scientific computing.
- **Implementation:**

  OpenMP directives are added to parallelize the outer loop.

  Each thread handles a subset of rows in the resulting matrix.

  For example,

```
#pragma omp parallel for
for (int i = 0; i < N; i++) {
for (int j = 0; j < N; j++) {
       for (int k = 0; k < N; k++) {
              C[i][j] += A[i][k] * B[k][j];
       }
}
}
```

- **Results:**

  Achieved a 4x speedup on an 8-core processor with efficient workload distribution.

  Performance improved further by ensuring cache-friendly data access patterns.

Case Study 2: Sorting Large Data with MPI

- **Problem:** Sort a massive dataset that exceeds the memory capacity of a single machine.
- **Implementation:**

  Data is partitioned and distributed across multiple nodes using MPI.

  Each node sorts its partition using a local sorting algorithm (for example, QuickSort).

  A parallel merge is performed using MPI's collective communication functions.

- **Results:**

  Sorting time reduced by 80% when compared to single-node execution.

  Near-linear scalability achieved with minimal communication overhead between nodes.

Case Study 3: Image Processing with GPU Acceleration

- **Problem:** Perform real-time image filtering using computationally expensive convolution operations.
- **Implementation:**

  The convolution kernel is parallelized using CUDA or OpenCL.

  Each pixel is processed as an independent thread to apply the filter efficiently.

- **Results:**

  Reduced execution time by over 10x compared to CPU-based implementation.

  Performance improved by optimizing memory coalescing and minimizing kernel launch overhead.

Case Study 4: Multithreaded Web Server Using Pthreads

- **Problem:** Improve a web server's ability to handle concurrent requests.
- **Implementation:**

  Used Pthreads to create a thread pool.

  Each thread processes client requests independently, handling parsing, file retrieval, and response generation.

- **Results:**

  Server capacity increased by 5x, handling over 10,000 simultaneous connections.

  Thread pooling reduced thread creation overhead significantly, improving response times.

Case Study 5: Weather Simulation Using Hybrid MPI-OpenMP

- **Problem:** Simulate weather patterns over a large geographical area with fine-grained detail.
- **Implementation:**

  MPI is used to distribute regions of the simulation grid among nodes.

  Within each node, OpenMP parallelizes computations across cores.

- **Results:**

  Simulation time reduced by 70%.

  Efficient use of shared memory within nodes and distributed memory across nodes ensured scalability.

Performance Analysis of Implemented Examples

Performance analysis is crucial to understanding the effectiveness of parallelization and optimization strategies. It helps identify bottlenecks, measure speedup, and assess the overall efficiency of the implementation. The following are key aspects of performance analysis for the parallelized examples presented earlier, with an emphasis on metrics like speedup, efficiency, and scalability.

Matrix Multiplication Using OpenMP

Objective: Optimize matrix multiplication for large datasets.

Performance Metrics:

- **Speedup:** The execution time decreased by approximately 4x when using 8 cores. This indicates an almost ideal speedup.
- **Efficiency:** The efficiency (Speedup/Number of Cores) was around 0.5, which is typical for matrix multiplication as not all steps are parallelizable.
- **Scalability:** The performance scales well with more cores but could be limited by Amdahl's Law, where the serial portion (for example, memory access) limits further improvements.

Results:

Performance improved due to better distribution of the workload across multiple threads.

Cache-friendly data access patterns played a crucial role in optimizing memory access and improving performance by reducing cache misses.

Sorting Large Data with MPI

Objective: Sort massive datasets across distributed nodes.

Performance Metrics:

- **Speedup:** Achieved up to 80% reduction in sorting time compared to single-node sorting.
- **Scalability:** The performance scaled nearly linearly with the number of nodes (N = 4, speedup of 3.5x).
- **Communication Overhead:** The time spent on MPI communication (for example, data exchange between nodes during merging) was minimal, thanks to optimized message-passing strategies.

Results:

The hybrid approach of parallel sorting and merging resulted in significant time savings.

Network latency was optimized by using non-blocking communication during parallel merges.

Image Processing with GPU Acceleration

Objective: Accelerate convolution operations for real-time image filtering.

Performance Metrics:

- **Speedup:** A 10x reduction in processing time was achieved by utilizing GPU parallelism for pixel-level operations.
- **GPU Utilization:** The GPU's full computational power was leveraged, achieving close to 90% utilization during heavy computational tasks.
- **Throughput:** The system was capable of processing hundreds of images per second in real-time.

Results:

The use of shared memory and memory coalescing optimizations greatly improved GPU performance.

Execution time was drastically reduced compared to CPU-based implementations, with GPU memory access patterns crucial for optimal performance.

Multithreaded Web Server Using Pthreads

Objective: Improve the web server's ability to handle concurrent requests.

Performance Metrics:

- **Throughput:** The server was able to handle over 10,000 simultaneous connections, a significant increase from its single-threaded version.
- **Latency:** The response time per request decreased due to parallel request handling and minimized thread creation overhead.
- **Thread Efficiency:** By implementing thread pooling, the overhead of creating and destroying threads was significantly reduced, improving overall server performance.

Results:

Using Pthreads allowed for high throughput with a scalable architecture.

Thread synchronization and task allocation were key factors in reducing server latency.

Weather Simulation Using Hybrid MPI-OpenMP

Objective: Simulate weather patterns over a large area using hybrid parallelism.

Performance Metrics:

- **Speedup:** Achieved a 70% reduction in simulation time compared to a serial implementation.
- **Scalability:** The performance scaled well across both the shared memory within nodes (OpenMP) and distributed memory across nodes (MPI).
- **Efficiency:** The combination of MPI for node-level distribution and OpenMP for intra-node parallelism resulted in efficient use of system resources.

Results:

The hybrid MPI-OpenMP approach allowed the simulation to handle large-scale datasets while maintaining good parallel efficiency.

Optimizing both inter-node communication and intra-node parallelism was essential for improving performance.

Conclusion

In this chapter, we focused on optimizing parallelism and data locality to improve performance. We started with an introduction to parallel computing and discussed the importance of data locality for better cache performance. We covered parallelization techniques, such as data and task parallelism, and how tools such as OpenMP, MPI, and threading libraries help in parallel programming.

We also explored strategies for improving data locality, such as memory layout optimization and cache-friendly algorithms, along with techniques such as cache blocking and prefetching. Loop transformations, including unrolling, fusion, and tiling, were explained for optimizing performance. Real-world case studies demonstrated how these optimizations work in practice.

In the next chapter, we will shift our focus to interprocedural analysis and optimization. We will look at interprocedural data flow analysis, call graph construction, and inline expansion, which all help in optimizing function interactions. The chapter will also include examples of interprocedural optimizations using LLVM, showcasing how modern compilers can improve performance across function calls.

Points to Remember

- **Parallelism Optimization**: Enhancing performance by dividing tasks into smaller parallel operations.
- **Data Locality**: Optimizing how data is stored and accessed to reduce latency.
- **Cache Optimization**: Techniques, such as cache blocking and prefetching improve memory access times.
- **Loop Optimization**: Transformations, such as unrolling, fusion, and tiling optimize loops for parallel execution.
- **Data Parallelism**: Performing the same operation on multiple data points simultaneously.
- **Task Parallelism**: Executing different tasks concurrently to improve performance.
- **Tools for Parallelism**: OpenMP, MPI, and threading libraries are key tools for parallel programming.
- **Memory Layout**: Organizing data to make better use of the CPU cache.

Multiple Choice Questions

1. What is the primary goal of parallel computing?
   a. To increase memory usage
   b. To improve execution speed by performing multiple operations simultaneously
   c. To reduce the number of threads used
   d. To avoid using caches
2. Which of the following best defines data parallelism?
   a. Parallelism achieved by breaking down tasks into smaller tasks
   b. Parallelism in which multiple data elements are processed simultaneously
   c. Parallelism that involves running independent tasks concurrently
   d. Parallelism achieved by combining several different tasks into one
3. Which of the following is NOT a strategy for improving data locality?
   a. Data structure design
   b. Memory layout optimization
   c. Loop unrolling
   d. Temporal locality
4. What is cache optimization primarily aimed at?
   a. Increasing the size of the cache
   b. Ensuring that cache misses are minimized, and cache utilization is maximized
   c. Reducing the cache's access time
   d. Decreasing the cache's refresh rate

5. Which of the following loop transformations increases the number of operations performed within a loop to reduce the overhead of loop control?
   a. Loop fusion
   b. Loop unrolling
   c. Loop tiling
   d. Loop splitting
6. What is the main advantage of loop fusion in parallel computing?
   a. It reduces the memory usage by combining two loops.
   b. It improves cache performance by minimizing loop overhead.
   c. It enhances the parallel execution of different tasks.
   d. It increases the number of iterations in each loop.
7. Which of the following best describes loop tiling?
   a. The process of combining multiple loops into one large loop.
   b. Breaking a loop into smaller sub-loops to improve cache efficiency.
   c. A technique for reducing loop unrolling overhead.
   d. A process of eliminating loops that are not necessary.
8. Which parallel programming tool is primarily used for shared-memory programming?
   a. MPI
   b. OpenMP
   c. CUDA
   d. Pthreads
9. What is the main feature of the MPI framework in parallel computing?
   a. It provides automatic parallelization.
   b. It supports parallel programming on distributed memory systems.
   c. It is used for managing caches.
   d. It simplifies task parallelism.
10. How does performance analysis help in parallel computing?
    a. It checks for the correctness of the code.
    b. It identifies potential performance bottlenecks, and optimizes the resource usage.
    c. It reduces the size of the code.
    d. It automatically parallelizes the code.

Answers

1. b
2. b
3. c
4. b
5. b
6. b
7. b
8. b
9. b
10. b

Questions

1. What is parallel computing, and why is it important for performance optimization?
2. Explain the difference between data parallelism and task parallelism.
3. What are the key benefits of optimizing data locality in parallel programs?
4. How does cache optimization improve the performance of parallel applications?
5. What is loop unrolling, and how does it enhance parallel execution?
6. Describe the concept of loop fusion and its advantages in parallel computing.
7. How does loop tiling contribute to better cache utilization in parallel programs?
8. What is the role of OpenMP in parallel programming, and how does it facilitate parallelization?
9. Explain how the MPI framework supports parallel programming across multiple nodes or machines.
10. What are some of the performance analysis techniques used to evaluate the efficiency of parallel programs?

Key Terms

- **Parallel Computing**: The use of multiple processors or cores to execute tasks simultaneously for faster processing.
- **Scalability**: The ability of a system or algorithm to maintain or improve performance as the workload increases or as more resources are added.
- **Granularity of Parallelism**: Refers to the size of the tasks that can be parallelized, from fine-grained (small tasks) to coarse-grained (larger tasks).
- **Synchronization**: The process of coordinating parallel tasks to ensure correct execution order and data consistency.
- **Race Condition**: A situation in parallel computing where the behavior of a program depends on the sequence or timing of uncontrollable events.

- **Load Balancing**: The process of distributing tasks evenly across processing units to optimize resource usage and minimize idle time.
- **Vectorization**: The process of converting scalar operations into vector operations that can be executed concurrently.
- **Task Scheduling**: The method of assigning tasks to processing units, ensuring that tasks are executed efficiently in parallel systems.
- **Latency-Hiding**: Techniques used to minimize the impact of latency (such as memory or communication delays) in parallel programs.
- **False Sharing**: A performance issue in parallel computing where threads on different processors or cores accidentally access the same cache line, leading to unnecessary synchronization and performance degradation.

CHAPTER 17

Inter Procedural Analysis and Optimization

Introduction

The previous chapter covered parallelization techniques for multi-core utilization, data locality optimization to reduce memory latency, and loop transformations for efficiency, with practical parallel processing implementations.

Building on these concepts, this chapter delves into **Interprocedural Analysis and Optimization**, which focuses on improving program behavior across function boundaries. It introduces **interprocedural data flow analysis**, a technique to understand data dependencies and interactions between functions, enabling more comprehensive optimizations. **Call graph construction** is discussed as a tool to map function calls, providing a clear view of control flow in the application. Additionally, the chapter covers **inline expansion**, a method to replace function calls with their actual definitions, reducing overhead and enhancing execution speed. Through practical examples using tools such as LLVM's interprocedural optimization framework, this chapter equips readers with the skills to design more efficient programs by analyzing and optimizing function interactions.

Structure

In this chapter, we will discuss the following topics:

- Introduction to Interprocedural Analysis
  - o Scope of Interprocedural Analysis
  - o Importance of Interprocedural Optimization
- Interprocedural Data Flow Analysis
  - o Principles of Data Flow Analysis
  - o Techniques for Analyzing Data Flow Across Functions
  - o Challenges in Interprocedural Data Flow Analysis
- Call Graph Construction
  - o Overview of Call Graphs and Their Importance
  - o Methods for Constructing Call Graphs
  - o Applications of Call Graphs in Optimization Techniques
  - o Limitations and Considerations in Call Graph Analysis
- Inline Expansion Techniques
  - o Inline Expansion
  - o Advantages of Inline Expansion for Code Optimization

    - Guidelines for Applying Inline Expansion
    - Potential Disadvantages of Inline Expansion
- Implementations in LLVM
    - Introduction to LLVM Optimization Framework
    - Case Studies Demonstrating Interprocedural Optimization
    - Performance Evaluation of LLVM Implementations

Introduction to Interprocedural Analysis

Imagine a symphony where each instrument plays its part independently, without considering the overall harmony. The result would be chaotic and uncoordinated. Similarly, in software development, analyzing functions in isolation often overlooks the bigger picture. **Interprocedural Analysis** addresses this by examining how functions interact and influence each other, creating a cohesive and optimized program.

This analysis goes beyond the boundaries of individual functions, studying data flow, control flow, and dependencies across the entire program. By providing a holistic view of the code, interprocedural analysis enables developers to uncover inefficiencies, streamline performance, and ensure the program operates as a unified whole.

Scope of Interprocedural Analysis

The scope of interprocedural analysis is broad, covering various aspects of program behavior that span across functions.

Key areas include:

- **Data Dependencies:** Tracking how variables are passed, modified, and used across functions to ensure proper execution and identify optimization opportunities.
- **Control Flow Analysis:** Mapping the sequence of function calls and how execution paths are connected within the program. This helps in understanding the program's structure and potential bottlenecks.
- **Call Graph Construction:** Creating a visual representation of function relationships to provide insights into the program's architecture and identify areas for improvement.
- **Optimization Opportunities:** Techniques such as constant propagation, dead code elimination, and inline expansion are applied across multiple functions to enhance overall efficiency.

By addressing these areas, interprocedural analysis enables developers to optimize entire programs rather than isolated segments, leading to significant performance gains.

Importance of Interprocedural Optimization

Interprocedural optimization is a powerful tool for creating high-performing software systems. By analyzing the program as a whole, it uncovers inefficiencies and optimization opportunities that are often missed when functions are considered in isolation.

For example, **inline expansion**, which replaces function calls with their actual code, reduces overhead and improves execution speed. Similarly, identifying and eliminating unused variables or redundant computations across functions saves both memory and processing power.

The benefits extend beyond performance. Interprocedural optimization creates cleaner, more maintainable code, reducing the likelihood of errors and ensuring a smoother user experience.

For instance, in applications such as gaming or real-time data processing, where every millisecond matters, these optimizations can make a significant difference.

In a world where software complexity is increasing, interprocedural optimization is essential for ensuring that applications are scalable, reliable, and efficient. It transforms fragmented codebases into cohesive systems, delivering superior performance and robustness.

Interprocedural Data Flow Analysis

Interprocedural Data Flow Analysis is crucial for optimizing complex software systems by understanding how data is shared and manipulated across multiple functions. Unlike traditional data flow analysis, which focuses on individual functions, interprocedural analysis expands the view to examine the movement of data across function boundaries. This approach ensures that data dependencies are recognized, enabling better optimization and more efficient programs.

Principles of Data Flow Analysis

At its core, **Data Flow Analysis** tracks how values assigned to variables propagate through a program. For interprocedural analysis, this means analyzing not just what happens within a single function but also how data flows between functions. The goal is to ensure that no redundant operations occur and that data is passed efficiently across the program. By capturing the "flow" of data from one function to another, interprocedural analysis provides a more complete picture of a program's execution and potential optimization opportunities.

Techniques for Analyzing Data Flow Across Functions

Analyzing data flow across functions is essential for optimizing software systems. It helps track how data is transferred, modified, and utilized within and between functions, ensuring that inefficiencies are minimized and performance is optimized. Here are several key techniques used in interprocedural data flow analysis:

Call Graph Construction

A **call graph** represents the relationships between functions in a program. It is like a map that shows how functions are interconnected through function calls. By constructing a call graph, we can:

- **Visualize dependencies** between functions and identify where data is passed or modified.
- **Analyze reachability**, helping determine which functions impact a particular piece of data.

Example: In a program with a main function calling other helper functions, the call graph would show the flow from the main to each helper function, allowing us to track how variables are passed between them.

Interprocedural Slicing

Interprocedural slicing isolates relevant portions of code that influence a particular variable, even if they span multiple functions. This helps in focusing only on the critical code that impacts the desired data, making the analysis more efficient.

- **Data Slicing**: Tracks how data is passed and modified.
- **Control Slicing**: Understands execution paths and their effects on data flow.

Example: If a function calculates a value that is later passed to another function, interprocedural slicing helps identify all relevant code, even in different functions, that modifies this value.

Fixed-Point Computation

Fixed-point computation is an iterative process used to determine data flow across function calls. It involves:

- Starting with an initial approximation of data flow.
- Repeatedly updating the flow until no further changes occur (that is, the flow stabilizes).

This technique ensures that all data interactions are fully considered, even across multiple levels of function calls. It is particularly useful in large programs with many interdependent functions.

Example: In a program where several functions depend on each other's output, fixed-point computation ensures that all possible data flows are explored until the most accurate result is achieved.

Flow Sensitivity

Flow sensitivity considers the order in which functions are called and how this order affects data flow. This technique is essential because the sequence of function calls often dictates how data is manipulated.

- **Understanding Order**: Some functions might depend on the results of others, meaning the order of execution directly influences the final outcome.

Example: A function that sorts an array might behave differently when called before or after a filtering function, as the order of operations affects the data passed between functions.

Data Flow Propagation

Data flow propagation tracks how data is passed and altered as it moves through a program. This technique ensures that the correct data is transferred between functions, and unnecessary modifications are avoided.

- **Tracking Variables**: Ensures that variables are passed correctly from one function to another.
- **Optimizing Function Calls**: Helps identify redundant or unnecessary calls by tracking how data is modified.

Example: If a function calculates a value and another function uses this value, data flow propagation ensures that the correct value is used, without recalculating or modifying it unnecessarily.

Context-Sensitive Analysis

The **context-sensitive analysis** is used to understand how a function's behavior changes depending on its calling context. This is important because the same function might produce different outcomes when called in different situations.

- **Consider Calling Context**: By tracking the specific context in which a function is invoked, we can optimize the flow of data.

Example: A sort function might behave differently when called with an empty array compared to an array with 1,000 elements. Context-sensitive analysis ensures that we account for these differences when tracking data flow.

These techniques are crucial for a comprehensive understanding of how data flows across function boundaries, providing opportunities for optimization and performance improvements. By employing these techniques, developers can ensure their programs run more efficiently and are free from redundant operations.

Definitions and Uses in Interprocedural Contexts

Understanding key definitions and their applications in interprocedural contexts is essential for tracking and optimizing data flow across functions. Here, we will define some crucial concepts that are central to interprocedural analysis and explain how they are used in practice.

In and Out Sets

In the context of interprocedural data flow analysis, **In and Out sets** refer to the sets of variables or data that enter and exit a function. These sets help track how data is passed between functions and how it is modified within them.

- **In Set**: Represents the data that enters a function, that is, the inputs to the function, which could include parameters or global variables.
- **Out Set**: Represents the data that exits a function, that is, the outputs or the results of a function's execution.

Use Case: By analyzing the **In and Out sets**, we can optimize the transfer of data between functions, avoid unnecessary computations, and eliminate redundant variable assignments.

Reachability

In interprocedural analysis, **reachability** refers to the ability to determine whether a function can affect a particular piece of data. This helps track how data is manipulated across various function calls and how one function's output might impact another function's input.

- **Reachable Functions**: A function is said to be reachable from another if there is a direct or indirect call between them. Tracking the reachable functions is essential to understanding data flow across the entire program.

Use Case: Analyzing reachability allows us to determine which functions are responsible for modifying or using a specific data item, helping identify optimization opportunities such as function inlining.

May and Must Analysis

May and Must analysis distinguishes between different levels of certainty in data flow analysis:

- **May Analysis**: Determines whether a variable may flow through a function. This approach considers all possible paths and is useful when dealing with uncertain or indirect data flows.
- **Must Analysis**: Determines whether a variable must flow through a function. It provides a more precise, conservative approach, ensuring that certain data flows are tracked with higher certainty.

Use Case: May analysis helps in considering all potential outcomes, while **Must analysis** focuses on the most deterministic paths. These analyses provide varying levels of accuracy and efficiency for different optimization tasks.

Variable Handling and Parameter Passing Mechanisms

Handling variables and passing parameters between functions is at the core of interprocedural data flow analysis. Different mechanisms for passing data can influence how variables are handled across function boundaries and impact optimization strategies.

Pass-by-Value

In **pass-by-value**, a copy of the data is passed to the function. Any modifications made to the parameters inside the function do not affect the original data in the calling function.

- **Impact on Data Flow**: Since the original data is not modified, the flow of data is one-way, from the caller to the callee. This makes data flow easier to track because the original data remains unchanged.

Use Case: Pass-by-value is common for simple data types (for example, integers or floats) where the function doesn't need to modify the caller's data.

Pass-by-Reference

In **pass-by-reference**, the function receives a reference to the original data, allowing it to modify the data directly. This creates a two-way data flow where the function can both consume and modify the caller's data.

- **Impact on Data Flow**: The caller's data can be modified directly by the callee, making it more challenging to track data flow. Careful analysis is required to ensure that modifications are tracked across function boundaries.

Use Case: Pass-by-reference is useful for large data structures such as arrays or objects, where passing a copy would be inefficient. However, it requires careful tracking to avoid unintended side effects.

Return Values

A function can return a value to the calling function, which adds another layer of complexity to data flow analysis. Return values allow data to flow back to the caller, but this flow can be influenced by the function's logic and state.

- **Impact on Data Flow**: Return values provide a way for functions to output data, but their usage depends on the context in which the function is called. These return values can be used as inputs for subsequent function calls.

Use Case: Return values are crucial when dealing with computations that need to be shared across functions. Analyzing return values helps identify opportunities for optimization, such as inlining return statements or eliminating unnecessary function calls.

Global Variables

Global variables are variables that are accessible throughout the entire program. In interprocedural analysis, global variables can be modified by multiple functions, making them a critical factor in understanding data flow.

- **Impact on Data Flow**: Global variables can complicate data flow analysis because any function can modify them, leading to potential side effects that may not be immediately obvious.

Use Case: While global variables can simplify data sharing between functions, they require careful tracking to avoid unintended interactions and side effects. Optimization strategies may involve minimizing their use or ensuring they are only modified in well-defined ways.

Static vs. Dynamic Parameter Passing

- **Static Parameter Passing**: Involves passing fixed, known values during compile time, making data flow more predictable and analyzable.
- **Dynamic Parameter Passing**: Occurs at runtime, with values passed depending on the

function's execution context. This introduces variability and complexity into the analysis, as data flow can change dynamically based on runtime conditions.

Use Case: Static passing is easier to track, while **dynamic passing** requires more sophisticated analysis to account for runtime variability. Both methods play a role in optimizing data flow across function calls.

Challenges in Interprocedural Data Flow Analysis

Interprocedural data flow analysis is a powerful technique used to understand how data moves across multiple functions in a program. However, tracking data flow between functions presents several challenges. The following are some of the key issues encountered in this process:

Function Call Dependencies

In a program, functions often call other functions, passing and receiving data between them. This dependency between functions can complicate the analysis of data flow:

- **Function Call Order**: The order in which functions are called affects the flow of data. Understanding this order is key to tracking data correctly.
- **Data Modifications**: Data can be modified in one function and used in another, and determining how this affects the flow requires careful tracking.

Example: Imagine **Function A** calls **Function B**, and **Function B** modifies a variable that **Function A** uses afterwards. Analyzing the effect of this dependency requires understanding both functions' behaviors.

Challenge: Ensuring all possible function interactions and data modifications are accurately tracked without unnecessary repetition.

Handling Recursive Functions

Recursive functions, which call themselves either directly or indirectly, add complexity to data flow analysis. This is because the data flow can change depending on the depth of recursion.

- **Dynamic Data Flow**: Each recursive call may affect the state of the data differently, making it hard to track the flow across recursive levels.
- **State Persistence**: Maintaining the correct state across multiple recursive calls is challenging, as data might be modified at each level.

Example: In a recursive function such as the one used to calculate factorials, the function calls itself repeatedly, each time modifying the data passed in. Tracking how the data changes at each level of recursion is key.

Challenge: Preventing the analysis from becoming overly complex and ensuring that data modifications are correctly tracked across recursive levels.

Unknown Function Behaviors

Sometimes, especially when using external libraries or third-party code, the behavior of a function may not be fully known. This poses a challenge in interprocedural analysis since the impact of such functions on data flow cannot be easily predicted.

- **Opaque Functions**: When functions are external or their code is not available for analysis, it is hard to determine how they affect the data.

- **Assumptions**: In these cases, we might have to make broad assumptions or use approximations, which could reduce the accuracy of the analysis.

Example: If a function from a library modifies a global variable in ways that are not easily traceable, the data flow becomes difficult to model accurately.

Challenge: Dealing with unknown behaviors and making the right assumptions without compromising the accuracy of the analysis.

Global and Shared Variables

Global variables are accessible by multiple functions, which makes them harder to track. Modifications to global variables in one function can have ripple effects throughout the program.

- **Side Effects**: Changes to global variables can have unintended consequences in other functions, leading to complex data flow dependencies.
- **Concurrency Issues**: In multi-threaded programs, global variables may be modified simultaneously by multiple functions, which adds additional complexity to the analysis.

Example: Imagine a global variable counter that both **Function A** and **Function B** modify. The state of the counter in **Function A** will affect the behavior of **Function B**, and tracking this requires careful attention.

Challenge: Effectively managing and tracking global and shared variables, especially in concurrent programs.

Scalability of Analysis

As programs grow, so do the number of functions and their interactions. Interprocedural data flow analysis can become resource-intensive, making it difficult to scale for large programs.

- **Exponential Growth**: As the number of functions increases, so do the possible interactions and paths that need to be analyzed.
- **Resource Constraints**: Analyzing large programs can be computationally expensive and may require significant memory and processing power.

Example: In a large web application, there could be hundreds or even thousands of function calls, all of which need to be analyzed. As the program grows, the number of interactions and paths to consider increases exponentially.

Challenge: Ensuring the analysis scales effectively to handle larger programs without overwhelming system resources.

Addressing Context Sensitivity

Context sensitivity refers to the idea that the data flow analysis should consider the specific context in which a function is called. Ignoring the context may lead to inaccurate analysis, so it is crucial to address it for precise tracking of data flow.

Tailoring Analysis to Specific Contexts

When functions are called, they may behave differently depending on the input parameters, the current state of the program, or the surrounding functions. To ensure accurate data flow analysis, we must track these specific contexts:

- **Function Arguments**: The input parameters to a function can significantly impact the flow of data. Different inputs may cause different behavior, and analyzing the flow requires considering this variability.

- **Caller's State**: The global variables or the environment in which a function is called can also affect how data flows through that function.

Example: If **Function A** calls **Function B** with different parameters, **Function B's** behavior and data flow will vary based on those parameters. The analysis must track these different scenarios to be accurate.

Challenge: Maintaining separate data flow records for each unique function call context can be computationally expensive.

Context-Sensitive versus Context-Insensitive Analysis

- **Context-sensitive analysis** takes into account the specific calling context of each function, which leads to more precise results but can be more computationally expensive.
- **Context-insensitive analysis** treats all function calls the same, regardless of their calling context, which is faster but less accurate.

Example: If **Function A** calls **Function B** with different parameters multiple times, context-sensitive analysis would track each call individually, whereas context-insensitive analysis would treat all calls as the same.

Challenge: Balancing the trade-off between precision and efficiency when choosing between context-sensitive and context-insensitive analysis.

Handling Context Explosion

In large programs with many functions, the number of contexts to analyze can grow exponentially, a phenomenon known as **context explosion**. This can make context-sensitive analysis very computationally expensive.

- **State Explosion**: Each unique context adds more states to track, leading to increased complexity.
- **Optimization Techniques**: To address context explosion, techniques such as **context merging** or **summary-based analysis** can be used to consolidate similar contexts and reduce the computational burden.

Example: In a complex system, multiple recursive calls and different function arguments can lead to a large number of unique contexts, making analysis unmanageable.

Challenge: Managing the exponential growth of contexts to avoid excessive resource usage while maintaining accuracy.

Managing Summary Information

To make interprocedural analysis more efficient, **summary information** can be used to represent the effects of functions in a more abstract form, rather than repeatedly analyzing each function in detail.

Function Summary:

A **function summary** is a compact representation that captures the essential information about a function's data flow without detailing every internal operation. This allows the analysis to avoid reprocessing the same function multiple times.

- **Summary Creation**: Function summaries are created by abstracting out unnecessary details, such as local variables, while retaining key data flow information.
- **Efficiency Gains**: Using summaries reduces computational overhead by eliminating the need to perform redundant analysis.

Example: Instead of reanalyzing a large sorting function every time it is called, a summary of its effects (for example, it modifies a certain array) can be reused to track data flow more efficiently.

Challenge: Creating accurate and concise summaries that capture the necessary details without losing important information.

Summary Propagation:

Once summaries are created, they need to be propagated across the program to track how data flows between functions. This ensures that the data flow analysis remains consistent and up-to-date.

- **Updating Summaries**: Summaries must be updated whenever a function's behavior changes or when a new calling context is encountered.
- **Consistency**: It is essential that summaries remain consistent across the program to avoid errors in data flow tracking.

Challenge: Ensuring that the propagation of summaries is done correctly and efficiently, without introducing inaccuracies.

Call Graph Construction

A **call graph** is a crucial tool in program analysis, offering a visual representation of how functions interact with each other. It enables the analysis of dependencies, performance bottlenecks, and optimization opportunities. Let us now dive into the construction of call graphs, their types, and applications.

Overview of Call Graphs and Their Importance

A call graph is a directed graph where the nodes represent functions and the edges represent function calls. Call graphs are fundamental for:

- **Understanding Dependencies**: They highlight which functions depend on others, helping to detect tight coupling or circular dependencies.
- **Optimization**: By analyzing the graph, we can identify functions that are called frequently and may benefit from optimizations such as inlining or reordering.
- **Performance Analysis**: Pinpointing bottlenecks or unused functions that can be removed to reduce overhead.

For large programs, call graphs provide a roadmap to potential optimizations, making them indispensable in software analysis.

Methods for Constructing Call Graphs

There are various techniques for constructing call graphs, each suited for different types of analysis. These methods help software engineers and analysts understand the relationship between different functions in a program.

Static Analysis:

Static analysis tools examine the program's source code or intermediate code. These tools build a call graph by identifying function definitions and calls without executing the program. Tools such as **LLVM** or **Clang** are commonly used for this purpose.

- **Pros:** Provides a complete overview of all function calls, including those that may not be executed in a particular run.

- **Cons**: May produce an overly conservative graph that includes unreachable functions or irrelevant paths. However, static analysis is faster and does not require running the program.
- **Example**: A tool such as **LLVM's Clang** can analyze the source code and generate a static call graph, mapping out all function calls that can be made, regardless of whether the functions are invoked during runtime.

Dynamic Analysis:

On the other hand, dynamic analysis tracks function calls during the program's execution. Tools such as **gprof**, **Valgrind**, and **DTrace** can generate call graphs based on actual program behavior at runtime.

- **Pros**: Provides an accurate view of the program's behavior for specific input conditions, capturing real-world execution.
- **Cons**: Limited to the execution trace and may miss potential calls that are never triggered during the run. Additionally, it may not handle all execution scenarios, such as exception handling or multi-threading.
- **Example**: Using **gprof**, the execution of a program can be monitored, and a dynamic call graph is produced based on actual function calls made during execution.

Hybrid Analysis:

Combining static and dynamic analysis can offer the best of both worlds. For instance, static analysis provides an overview, while dynamic analysis adds precision by confirming actual function calls. This method can improve the overall accuracy of call graph construction.

Example: A hybrid approach may start with a static call graph to get a broad overview of function calls and then use dynamic analysis to fill in the details of actual execution.

Distinction Between Static and Dynamic Call Graphs

Here is a simple comparison between static and dynamic call graphs:

Feature	**Static Call Graphs**	**Dynamic Call Graphs**
Construction	Analyzed from source or intermediate code	Analyzed from source or intermediate code
Scope	Shows all potential function calls	Shows only executed function calls
Accuracy	May include calls that never occur	Reflects actual runtime behavior
Handling Indirect Calls	May not accurately capture dynamic dispatch or indirect calls	Accurately tracks indirect calls
Use Case	Useful for understanding program structure and dependencies	Useful for performance analysis and debugging
Limitations	Can be large and complex, may not reflect actual execution	Limited to observed executions, may miss unexecuted code
Example	Shows that `foo()` calls `bar()`, even if `foo()` never runs	Shows only function calls that occurred during execution

***Table 17.1**: Comparison between Static and Dynamic Call Graphs*

Handling Indirect Calls in Call Graphs

Indirect calls, such as those involving function pointers or virtual function calls, present a challenge in constructing accurate call graphs. These calls do not have a fixed target at compile-time, making it difficult to map out all possible interactions.

Challenges: Indirect calls are harder to represent because the actual function target is determined at runtime. In some cases, indirect calls are used in object-oriented programming with virtual methods or callbacks.

- **Static Approximation**: Static tools use heuristics or pointer analysis to estimate the targets of indirect calls, but this may not always be accurate.

  Example: A function pointer in C/C++ could point to different functions based on user input. Static analysis might try to include all possible target functions in the call graph, leading to over-approximation.
- **Dynamic Analysis**: During execution, the actual target of an indirect call can be tracked, providing an exact call path. However, it may not cover all potential calls if not all paths are triggered during execution.

  Example: In a C++ program, if an object is derived from multiple classes, dynamic analysis would allow us to track exactly which method is invoked through the virtual function mechanism at runtime.

Hybrid Methods: Combining static and dynamic analysis can help capture both potential and actual targets of indirect calls. Static analysis can identify possible indirect calls, while dynamic analysis refines the graph based on actual runtime behavior.

Applications of Call Graphs in Optimization Techniques

Call graphs play a key role in several optimization techniques, as they help identify performance bottlenecks, redundant code, and opportunities for parallelization. Here are some common applications:

- **Inlining**: By analyzing the frequency and size of function calls, call graphs help identify functions that could benefit from inlining. This can reduce function call overhead by directly embedding the function's code at the call site.

  Example: Small getter/setter functions that are called frequently could be inlined to eliminate the cost of the function call itself.
- **Dead Code Elimination**: Call graphs can reveal functions that are never called, allowing for their removal to reduce program size and improve efficiency.

  Example: A function that is never invoked or is only reachable through obsolete code paths can be safely removed from the program.
- **Interprocedural Analysis**: Call graphs enable analysis across function boundaries, which is essential for optimizations that span multiple functions, such as constant propagation, loop unrolling, and function specialization.

  Example: Analyzing the call graph helps determine which functions can be specialized for particular inputs to improve execution time.
- **Parallelization**: By identifying independent functions or determining which functions have no interdependencies, a call graph can assist in optimizing a program for parallel execution by enabling concurrent execution of independent functions.

  Example: A program with independent functions can be parallelized by identifying functions that do not rely on each other's results.

Limitations and Considerations in Call Graph Analysis

While call graphs are powerful, there are limitations:

- **Scalability**: For large programs, call graphs can become large and difficult to manage. Visualizing and analyzing large-scale call graphs may require significant computational resources.

  Example: A program with thousands of functions might produce a call graph with millions of nodes and edges, making it challenging to analyze manually.

- **Accuracy**: Static analysis may produce incomplete or overly conservative call graphs, while dynamic analysis is limited to specific execution paths. This may lead to missing important function calls or not capturing all execution scenarios.

  Example: A static call graph might include function calls that are never invoked, while a dynamic call graph might miss certain branches if not all input conditions are covered.

- **Handling Indirect Calls**: Indirect function calls are difficult to represent accurately in a call graph. Both static and dynamic methods may struggle with these types of calls, especially in languages that support polymorphism or callbacks.

  Example: In object-oriented programming, indirect calls through virtual functions or callbacks can be difficult to track and represent accurately in a call graph.

Inline Expansion Techniques

In software optimization, the efficiency of function calls plays a crucial role in performance. Each time a function is called, the program must pass control to that function and then return to the calling code, which introduces overhead. This overhead becomes more noticeable when small functions are called frequently. **Inline expansion** is an optimization technique designed to reduce this overhead by replacing the function call with a direct insertion of the function's body into the caller's code, effectively eliminating the need for the call itself. Here is a closer look at inline expansion and its impact on code optimization.

Inline Expansion

Inline expansion involves replacing a function call with the function's code at the location where the function is called. Instead of transferring control to the function and returning it, the body of the function is directly inserted into the caller. This reduces the overhead associated with the function call process, such as parameter passing, saving return addresses, and stack manipulation. The technique works best with small, frequently invoked functions, where the benefits of reduced function call overhead are more significant than the cost of copying the function's body.

Inline expansion is typically applied to small functions that have minimal code and are called many times. Functions such as simple mathematical operations, getters, or setters are ideal candidates for inlining.

Advantages of Inline Expansion for Code Optimization

Inline expansion offers several performance benefits, particularly when applied to small, frequently called functions. Some key advantages include:

- **Reduced Function Call Overhead**: By inserting the function's code directly at the call site, inline expansion eliminates the need for runtime function calls. This means no stack manipulation, no control transfer, and no return address management.

  Example: For a simple function such as add(a, b) that just returns the sum of two numbers, inlining the function would replace the call with a + b, avoiding the overhead of making a function call.

- **Improved Cache Performance**: Since the function's code is inserted directly in the call site, inline functions are more likely to be loaded into the instruction cache. This improves the locality of reference, reducing cache misses and increasing overall performance.

  Example: In a large program, if a small function is frequently called, inlining can help avoid jumping around the program, improving cache hits and making the execution flow smoother.

- **Potential for Further Optimizations**: Once a function is inlined, the compiler has more opportunities to optimize the combined code, including constant folding, loop unrolling, or even removing dead code. The inlined function is now part of the caller's code, giving the compiler more context to make smarter optimization decisions.

  Example: If an inlined function takes a constant as an argument, the compiler may calculate the result during compilation rather than at runtime, further improving performance.

Guidelines for Applying Inline Expansion

While inline expansion can yield significant benefits, it should be applied selectively to avoid negative consequences such as code bloat. Here are some guidelines to maximize the advantages of inline expansion:

- **Small, Frequently Used Functions**: Inline expansion is most effective when applied to small functions that are called many times. These functions should have minimal code (typically less than a few lines) to ensure that inlining them does not unnecessarily increase the size of the program.

  Example: A small function such as multiply(x, y) that multiplies two numbers would benefit from inlining because the function's body is small and the overhead of making a call is likely more costly than just performing the multiplication directly.

- **Avoid Inlining Large Functions**: Functions with large bodies should generally not be inlined, as doing so can lead to excessive code duplication, resulting in larger binary sizes and possibly reducing cache efficiency.

  Example: A large function such as sort() should not be inlined because copying its entire body wherever it is called would unnecessarily increase the program size and potentially decrease performance due to instruction cache misses.

- **Consider Compiler Settings**: Many modern compilers offer automatic inlining based on heuristics, such as function size and frequency of calls. While you can suggest inlining with the inline keyword in languages such as C++, it is important to trust the compiler's ability to choose the best functions for inlining.

  Example: In C++, you may use inline to hint the compiler to inline a function, but the compiler may still decide not to inline it if it is too large or infrequently used.

- **Measure the Impact**: Always measure the performance of your program before and after applying inline expansion. The benefits of inlining depend heavily on the function's size, frequency of calls, and the overall architecture of the program. Profiling tools such as **gprof** or **Valgrind** can help determine if inlining results in a performance improvement.

  Example: After inlining a function, profile the program to ensure that the inlining results in faster execution. If the program size increases significantly or the cache performance worsens, it may indicate that inlining was not beneficial.

Potential Disadvantages of Inline Expansion

While inline expansion can lead to performance improvements, it is not without its drawbacks. Here are some potential disadvantages of using this technique:

- **Code Bloat**: One of the main risks of inline expansion is **code bloat**. When a function is inlined at multiple call sites, it increases the size of the program because the function's code is duplicated everywhere it is called. This can lead to an increase in the size of the binary, which may cause inefficient use of memory or instruction cache.

  Example: If a small function is called 100 times in a program, inlining it would duplicate its code 100 times, leading to unnecessary code expansion that could negatively impact performance by reducing cache efficiency.

- **Increased Compilation Time**: Inline expansion can increase compilation time, especially for large codebases. The compiler needs to process each inlined function and insert its body at every call site, which can slow down the build process.

  Example: If you inline several small functions in a large program, the compiler may spend more time processing the code, potentially increasing build times.

- **Limited Benefits for Large Functions**: Inlining large functions can defeat the purpose of the optimization by significantly increasing the program's size, potentially reducing performance. Larger functions often have a larger impact on cache efficiency, and inlining them can make the program less efficient.

  Example: Inlining a large function such as matrixMultiply() would increase the size of the binary without providing significant performance benefits, as the inlined code would likely miss cache opportunities due to its size.

- **Interfering with Debugging**: Inline functions can make debugging harder, as stepping through inlined functions may not show the function's entry point in the call stack. This can make it difficult to trace the program flow during debugging sessions.

  Example: If a function is inlined and you try to set a breakpoint at the beginning of the function during a debugging session, the debugger might not recognize the function's original location, making it harder to track where the program's flow goes.

Implementations in LLVM

LLVM, a powerful compiler framework, offers a broad set of tools and libraries for optimizing software programs at various stages of the compilation process. Among these are key interprocedural optimizations, such as interprocedural data flow analysis, call graph construction, and inline expansion. This section explores the implementation of these optimization techniques in LLVM, providing practical insights and case studies for real-world applications.

Introduction to LLVM Optimization Framework

Low-Level Virtual Machine (LLVM) is an open-source, modular compiler infrastructure that provides a comprehensive framework for analyzing, transforming, and optimizing software. It is widely used due to its powerful, flexible optimizations and support for a variety of programming languages and platforms. LLVM allows developers to optimize code at different stages of the compilation process, providing detailed control over the performance characteristics of a program.

What Makes LLVM Unique?

LLVM is distinguished by its ability to optimize code across multiple programming languages and architectures. Here is a deeper look into why LLVM is a popular choice for developers looking to enhance performance:

- **Intermediate Representation (IR)**: At the heart of LLVM is its Intermediate Representation (IR), a platform-independent, low-level language that serves as a common ground for analyzing and optimizing code. IR abstracts away machine-specific details, making it easier to apply optimizations that work across various hardware and software environments.
- **Modular Optimization Passes**: LLVM's optimization framework is composed of various "passes," which are individual transformations applied to the code. Each pass targets a different aspect of the program, such as improving memory access patterns or reducing redundant computations. These passes can be combined in various ways to create custom optimization pipelines tailored to specific needs.
- **Extensibility**: One of the most powerful features of LLVM is its extensibility. Developers can create custom optimization passes to address specialized performance goals or system constraints. This flexibility makes LLVM suitable for both general-purpose and domain-specific optimizations.

Key Features of LLVM's Optimization Framework:

- **Rich Set of Optimization Passes**:

  LLVM offers an extensive range of built-in optimization passes. These passes can improve various aspects of a program's performance, such as optimizing loops, reducing memory usage, or eliminating dead code.

  For example, **loop unrolling** might be applied to reduce the overhead of loop control, or **constant propagation** could eliminate variables that do not change.

- **Target-Independent Optimizations:**

  LLVM applies optimizations to its IR, making these optimizations machine-architecture-independent. As a result, a single optimization pipeline can be used across different platforms, saving time and resources for cross-platform development.

- **Simplified Debugging and Analysis:**

  LLVM offers powerful debugging and analysis tools that help developers understand how optimizations impact their code. Tools such as **llvm-gdb** and **llvm-prof** allow developers to trace through code and analyze how optimizations influence runtime behavior, memory usage, and other critical metrics.

  Example: When inlining a function, developers can use LLVM's debugging tools to observe how it affects execution time and memory access patterns.

- **Advanced Interprocedural Optimizations:**

  Interprocedural optimizations work across function boundaries, analyzing the program as a whole. LLVM supports advanced techniques, such as **interprocedural data flow analysis** and **call graph construction**, which can significantly improve performance by optimizing how data flows between functions and reducing the overhead of function calls.

- **Scalable Performance:**

  LLVM's modular design ensures scalability, meaning it can be applied to small applications as well as large, complex systems. Whether optimizing a single function or a whole program, LLVM can handle transformations at different scales without sacrificing performance or efficiency.

Real-World Use Cases of LLVM Optimizations:

To better understand the practical application of LLVM, here are some common use cases where its optimization framework makes a significant difference:

- **High-Performance Computing (HPC):**
  In areas such as scientific computing or machine learning, where performance is paramount, LLVM's optimizations help reduce computational overhead. For example, **loop optimizations** can accelerate matrix multiplications in numerical simulations.
- **Embedded Systems:**
  In embedded systems, resources such as memory and processing power are often limited. LLVM can help reduce code size through optimizations, such as **dead code elimination** and **function inlining**, which are essential in making embedded systems more efficient.
- **Web Browsers and Graphics Processing:**
  Web browsers and graphics applications often rely on LLVM to optimize rendering performance. **Vectorization** and **loop unrolling** can be applied to improve graphics rendering speed, while **call graph analysis** helps identify and optimize critical functions.

LLVM's Optimization Process: A Closer Look

To see how LLVM optimizes code, let us walk through the general process:

1. **Translate Source Code to IR:**

   The first step in the optimization process is translating the high-level source code (for example, C and C++) into LLVM IR. This intermediate representation abstracts away machine-specific details while preserving the logic of the original program.

2. **Apply Optimization Passes:**

   After the code is represented in LLVM IR, various optimization passes are applied. Some of the most common passes include:

   a. **Loop Optimizations**: Reducing the overhead of loops through techniques such as unrolling or invariant code motion.

   b. **Dead Code Elimination**: Removing unused or redundant code that does not contribute to the program's output.

   c. **Inlining**: Replacing function calls with the function's body to reduce call overhead.

3. **Target-Specific Optimizations:**

   Once the general optimizations are applied, LLVM performs target-specific optimizations to tailor the code to a particular machine architecture. This can include low-level transformations such as register allocation and instruction scheduling.

4. **Code Generation:**

   Finally, LLVM generates machine code for the target platform. This machine-specific code is then ready for execution or further processing.

How LLVM Benefits Performance:

LLVM's optimizations can lead to tangible improvements in several areas:

- **Execution Time**: By applying optimizations such as **function inlining** or **loop unrolling**, LLVM can significantly reduce the time it takes for a program to execute, particularly in performance-critical applications.

- **Memory Usage**: Optimizations such as **dead code elimination** and **constant propagation** help minimize memory usage by removing unnecessary variables and operations, which is crucial in resource-constrained environments such as embedded systems.
- **Code Size**: LLVM can also reduce the size of the compiled binary, ensuring that only the necessary code is included. This can lead to faster loading times and more efficient use of storage.

Case Studies Demonstrating Interprocedural Optimization

Interprocedural optimization involves analyzing and optimizing a program across function boundaries, rather than just focusing on individual functions. These optimizations can provide significant performance improvements, particularly in large and complex software systems. The following are several case studies demonstrating the real-world impact of interprocedural optimizations using LLVM.

Case Study: Optimizing Scientific Computing Code

In scientific computing applications, performance is critical due to the complexity of algorithms and large datasets. Interprocedural optimization, specifically **interprocedural data flow analysis**, plays a key role in improving performance by analyzing how data is passed between functions. In this case study, LLVM was used to optimize a scientific computing compiler by applying techniques such as **constant propagation** and **dead code elimination**.

Optimization Outcome: The use of interprocedural analysis allowed LLVM to eliminate redundant calculations across functions, reducing both memory usage and execution time. As a result, large-scale simulations were able to run faster, and computational resources were used more efficiently.

Case Study: Embedded Systems with Memory Constraints

In embedded systems, memory and processing power are often limited, which requires careful optimization. Applying interprocedural optimizations, such as **call graph construction** and **function inlining**, helped reduce overhead in an embedded system used for real-time sensor data processing.

Optimization Outcome: LLVM's interprocedural optimizations allowed for better memory management, reduced code size, and improved execution speed. By analyzing data flow across functions, LLVM was able to eliminate unnecessary calls and consolidate smaller functions. This resulted in a more efficient embedded system with improved performance and reduced memory consumption.

Case Study: Web Browser Rendering Optimization

Web browsers rely on fast rendering of HTML, CSS, and JavaScript to deliver a smooth user experience. Interprocedural optimizations, such as **inline expansion** and **loop unrolling**, were applied to the browser's graphics rendering pipeline.

Optimization Outcome: LLVM's optimizations improved the performance of the rendering engine by reducing the time spent on function calls and eliminating redundant calculations. This led to faster web page loading and improved rendering performance, resulting in a better browsing experience for users.

Implementing Interprocedural Data Flow Analysis in LLVM

Interprocedural data flow analysis allows us to track how variables and values are passed across function boundaries in a program. This analysis is crucial for optimizing a program's overall performance, especially in large codebases where multiple functions interact with each other.

How Data Flow Analysis Works in LLVM

LLVM supports interprocedural data flow analysis through its powerful suite of analysis passes. The primary goal is to track how variables are passed across function calls and identify opportunities for optimization, such as **constant propagation** and **dead code elimination**.

1. **Pass Creation**: The first step is to create an LLVM pass that can traverse the call graph and propagate data flow information across function boundaries.
2. **Global Analysis**: Using global variables and function calls, LLVM tracks how values are passed between functions. If a variable is computed in one function but never used in another, LLVM can safely eliminate the computation.
3. **Optimization**: Once the data flow has been analyzed, LLVM applies various optimizations to reduce redundant computations, improve memory usage, and speed up execution.

This process allows LLVM to optimize a program not just within individual functions but across the entire codebase, improving performance at a global level.

Constructing Call Graphs within LLVM

A **call graph** represents the relationships between functions in a program. It shows which functions call which, providing an essential map for applying interprocedural optimizations. Call graphs are a key element in optimizing program performance, as they help identify functions that are frequently called or perform significant computation.

Importance of Call Graphs:

- **Identifying Hotspots**: By analyzing the call graph, you can identify functions that are called frequently and are candidates for optimization. These functions can benefit from techniques such as **inlining** or **tail call optimization**, which reduce the overhead of repeated function calls.
- **Reducing Redundancy**: The call graph also helps to identify functions that are never called, enabling LLVM to eliminate them, which reduces the code size and enhances performance.

Building a Call Graph in LLVM:

1. **Analysis Pass**: LLVM provides built-in passes to construct call graphs by analyzing the control flow of the program. This pass identifies function calls and builds a graph that shows the relationships between functions.
2. **Optimization**: Once the call graph is constructed, LLVM can apply optimizations. For example, functions that are called frequently can be inlined to reduce the cost of function calls. Recursively called functions can also be optimized using specialized techniques.
3. **Handling Recursion**: The call graph can also help identify recursive functions and apply optimizations to ensure that recursion does not negatively impact performance.

Applying Inline Expansion Techniques in LLVM

Inline expansion involves replacing a function call with the actual body of the function. This optimization eliminates the overhead of function calls, leading to faster execution and improved performance.

Advantages of Inline Expansion:

The following are the advantages of inline expansion:

- **Reduced Function Call Overhead**: By eliminating the need for function call setup (such as pushing arguments onto the stack), inline expansion can significantly improve performance, particularly in programs with frequent function calls.
- **Improved Cache Locality**: Replacing function calls with their bodies can lead to better cache utilization, as the code for frequently called functions is brought closer to the caller.
- **Performance Gains**: For small, frequently called functions, inlining can significantly reduce execution time by eliminating the overhead associated with function calls.

Challenges of Inline Expansion:

The following are the challenges of inline expansion:

- **Code Bloat**: Inlining many functions can result in a larger code size, which could negatively impact performance, especially if the code exceeds the cache size or leads to increased instruction cache misses.
- **Compilation Time**: Inline expansion can increase the compilation time, as more code needs to be generated and optimized.

Applying Inline Expansion in LLVM:

LLVM provides an **inline function pass** that identifies functions eligible for inlining. This pass replaces calls to these functions with their bodies, reducing the overhead of function calls. Generally, small functions with simple control flows are good candidates for inlining, while larger, more complex functions are left unchanged.

Performance Evaluation of LLVM Implementations

Performance evaluation is a crucial aspect of assessing the effectiveness of optimizations implemented using the LLVM framework. By measuring how well LLVM performs in real-world applications, developers can gauge the impact of various optimizations, understand their benefits, and identify any potential drawbacks. This evaluation process helps in fine-tuning the optimizations to achieve the best possible performance for a given system.

Defining Performance Metrics

Before diving into performance evaluation, it is important to define what "performance" means in the context of LLVM optimizations. Performance can be measured through several metrics, including:

- **Execution Time**: The time it takes for a program to run from start to finish. This is one of the most direct indicators of optimization success, especially for computationally intensive applications.
- **Memory Usage**: The amount of memory consumed by the program during execution. Optimizations such as **data flow analysis** can help reduce memory footprint by eliminating unnecessary variables and operations.
- **Code Size**: The size of the compiled code is another key metric. While some optimizations such as **inlining** can increase code size, they may also lead to faster execution due to better cache utilization. It is essential to strike a balance between reduced code size and enhanced performance.
- **Power Consumption**: For embedded or mobile applications, power consumption is an important factor. Optimizations that reduce the need for frequent memory accesses or excessive computational overhead can contribute to more energy-efficient execution.

- **Cache Utilization**: Efficient use of CPU caches can drastically improve execution speed. Optimizations such as **loop unrolling** or **inlining** help improve cache locality, thus reducing cache misses and improving performance.

Benchmarking LLVM Optimizations

To evaluate LLVM's performance, a series of benchmark tests are often conducted on real-world applications or synthetic programs designed to highlight specific optimization aspects.

The following are some common benchmarking techniques:

- **SPEC CPU Benchmark**: The Standard Performance Evaluation Corporation (SPEC) provides a suite of benchmarks that are commonly used for evaluating the performance of compilers and optimizations. These benchmarks include computationally intensive programs that can highlight the performance improvements brought by interprocedural optimizations.
- **Microbenchmarks**: These focus on the performance of specific components of the system, such as individual functions or algorithms. Microbenchmarks are useful for evaluating the impact of specific LLVM optimization passes such as **constant propagation** or **dead code elimination**.
- **Real-World Application Tests**: Running real-world applications through LLVM-optimized compilers provides a more comprehensive view of how optimizations impact overall system performance. For example, testing LLVM on web browsers or embedded systems can show how optimizations affect response times and memory usage.

Performance Gains from Interprocedural Optimizations

LLVM's interprocedural optimizations offer significant performance improvements by analyzing data flow across function boundaries and identifying opportunities for optimization. Some key gains include:

- **Reduced Function Call Overhead**: Techniques such as **inline expansion** eliminate the overhead of function calls by directly embedding function bodies in place of calls. This can drastically improve the performance of programs that rely on small, frequently called functions.
- **Better Cache Utilization**: By using **call graph construction** and **function reordering**, LLVM can optimize the layout of functions and data to improve cache locality, reducing the number of cache misses during program execution.
- **Dead Code Elimination**: Through **interprocedural data flow analysis**, LLVM can identify code that is not used anywhere and eliminate it, leading to smaller and more efficient binaries.
- **Constant Propagation**: LLVM can propagate constants across functions, reducing the need for redundant calculations and improving performance.

Analyzing the Trade-offs

While LLVM optimizations lead to significant performance improvements in many cases, there are trade-offs that need to be considered:

- **Code Bloat**: While **inline expansion** can improve performance, it may also increase the size of the compiled code. This is especially problematic in systems with limited memory or in applications where code size is critical, such as embedded systems.
- **Compilation Time**: Some optimizations, particularly **interprocedural analysis** and **call graph construction** can increase the compilation time. This is especially noticeable in large codebases. The benefits of optimization may be overshadowed by the longer build times in such cases.

- **Diminishing Returns**: As optimizations are applied, the performance gains may decrease. For example, after a certain point, adding more **inline expansions** may lead to higher code size without significant speed improvements.

Performance Testing Tools in LLVM

LLVM provides several tools and passes to facilitate performance testing and optimization analysis:

- **LLVM's opt Tool**: This tool allows you to apply different LLVM optimization passes to your code and compare the results. You can use it to experiment with various passes such as **function inlining**, **loop unrolling**, and **data flow analysis** to measure their impact on performance.
- **LLVM's perf Tool**: This is a Linux profiling tool that can be used in conjunction with LLVM to profile the performance of optimized applications. It provides detailed insights into execution time, CPU cycles, memory usage, and more.
- **LLVM's clang**: The Clang front-end compiler provides the option to apply optimization passes during the compilation process. The -O (optimization) flags in Clang allow you to specify different levels of optimization, from basic to aggressive, and evaluate how they impact performance.

Case Study: Performance Evaluation of LLVM in a Web Browser

Let us consider a case study where LLVM optimizations are applied to a web browser's JavaScript engine. Web browsers rely on the efficient execution of JavaScript for tasks such as rendering pages, executing scripts, and managing user interactions.

Before LLVM Optimization:

- **Execution Time**: JavaScript execution takes a noticeable amount of time, particularly when running complex scripts.
- **Memory Usage**: The browser consumes a considerable amount of memory due to inefficient memory management.
- **Code Size**: The size of the compiled JavaScript engine is relatively large, leading to slower load times.

After LLVM Optimization:

- **Execution Time**: By applying **interprocedural data flow analysis** and **inlining**, the execution time for JavaScript scripts is significantly reduced.
- **Memory Usage**: Dead code elimination and **constant propagation** reduce memory usage by eliminating unnecessary data and computations.
- **Code Size**: LLVM's optimizations result in a smaller compiled binary, which improves load times and reduces memory footprint.

Conclusion

In this chapter, we examined the critical role of interprocedural analysis and optimization in enhancing the performance of software systems. By exploring techniques such as **interprocedural data flow analysis**, **call graph construction**, and **inline expansion**, we understood how these methods enable compilers to optimize across function boundaries, leading to more efficient execution. We also addressed the challenges of **context sensitivity**, managing **summary information**, and dealing with **indirect calls** in call graphs, which add complexity to these optimizations. The practical applications of these techniques, particularly through the LLVM framework, demonstrated their potential to significantly improve performance, albeit with trade-offs such as increased compilation time or potential code bloat. The chapter highlighted the importance of carefully balancing these optimizations to achieve the best performance outcomes in real-world systems.

As we move into *Chapter 18, Case Studies and Real-World Examples*, we will take a closer look at how the concepts discussed in previous chapters are implemented in real-world scenarios. This chapter will delve into **case studies of compiler implementations**, examining the impact of interprocedural optimizations in various programming languages. We will also analyze real-world applications, such as web browsers and embedded systems, to see how these optimizations are applied and the challenges that arise during implementation. Finally, we will explore the solutions adopted to overcome these challenges, providing valuable insights into the practical application of optimization techniques in diverse domains.

Points to Remember

- **Interprocedural Optimization** improves performance across multiple functions, not just within individual functions.
- **Data Flow Analysis** tracks data across functions to eliminate unnecessary operations.
- **Call Graphs** map how functions call each other, helping optimize the program's structure and performance.
- **Inline Expansion** replaces function calls with the function code itself to reduce call overhead.
- **Challenges** include handling different contexts, indirect calls, and managing large amounts of summary data.
- **LLVM** is a powerful tool for applying interprocedural optimizations and analyzing program performance.
- **Performance Trade-offs**: Optimizations may increase compilation time or code size, so balance is key.
- **Real-World Impact**: Interprocedural optimizations are crucial for large systems such as browsers or embedded software.
- **Global Optimization**: Unlike local optimizations, interprocedural optimizations focus on improving the entire program's efficiency.
- **Context Matters**: Applying optimizations should be context-sensitive to avoid unnecessary overhead.

Multiple Choice Questions

1. What is the primary goal of interprocedural optimization?
   a. To optimize a single function independently
   b. To optimize across multiple functions for global efficiency
   c. To improve code readability
   d. To eliminate redundant variables in one function
2. Which technique helps track data flow across functions in a program?
   a. Inline Expansion
   b. Interprocedural Data Flow Analysis

   c. Dead Code Elimination

   d. Loop Unrolling

3. Which of the following challenges is associated with indirect calls in call graph construction?

   a. Reducing compilation time

   b. Handling dynamically determined function targets

   c. Improving code readability

   d. Simplifying code structure

4. In interprocedural optimization, which method eliminates unnecessary operations based on the flow of data?

   a. Constant Propagation

   b. Dead Code Elimination

   c. Inline Expansion

   d. Data Flow Analysis

5. What is a major trade-off when applying interprocedural optimization techniques?

   a. Increased program size vs. increased readability

   b. Reduced compilation time vs. better performance

   c. Increased code size and compilation time versus better performance

   d. Reduced code complexity vs. better performance

6. Which of the following frameworks is commonly used for implementing interprocedural analysis and optimization?

   a. Eclipse

   b. LLVM

   c. Visual Studio

   d. Jupyter Notebook

7. What does inline expansion involve in compiler optimization?

   a. Replacing function calls with the actual function code

   b. Removing unused code from the program

   c. Optimizing variable usage across functions

   d. Breaking down large functions into smaller ones

8. What does interprocedural data flow analysis primarily track?

   a. Function calls and returns

   b. The flow of data between variables and functions

   c. The program's execution speed

   d. Code readability and maintainability

9. Which of the following is a key benefit of using interprocedural data flow analysis?
   a. It reduces the need for function inlining
   b. It helps track the flow of variables and constants across function boundaries
   c. It eliminates all function calls
   d. It reduces program size by eliminating comments
10. What is the primary challenge in handling indirect calls during call graph construction?
   a. Indirect calls cannot be tracked at runtime
   b. The target function for indirect calls is not known at compile time
   c. Indirect calls slow down the execution of the program
   d. Indirect calls always lead to program errors
11. Which optimization technique removes code that does not affect the program's output?
   a. Loop unrolling
   b. Constant folding
   c. Dead code elimination
   d. Inline expansion
12. Which of the following is an example of a performance trade-off when applying interprocedural optimization?
   a. Increased code size versus reduced performance
   b. Reduced memory usage versus higher execution time
   c. Increased compilation time versus better runtime performance
   d. Simpler code structure versus better performance
13. Which technique allows a function to be replaced with its body to reduce the overhead of function calls?
   a. Dead code elimination
   b. Inline expansion
   c. Constant propagation
   d. Function inlining
14. Which of the following techniques does LLVM use for interprocedural optimization?
   a. File compression
   b. Function splitting
   c. Interprocedural data flow analysis
   d. Dynamic memory allocation
15. What does summary information in interprocedural analysis typically include?
   a. The physical memory locations used by the program
   b. High-level representations of function behavior

c. Exact execution timings of each function

d. The syntax of the entire program

16. What is one of the main reasons for using interprocedural optimization in large-scale software systems?

    a. To reduce the program's readability

    b. To minimize the need for debugging

    c. To optimize performance across the entire program

    d. To simplify the code structure

Answers

1. b
2. b
3. b
4. b
5. c
6. b
7. a
8. b
9. b
10. b
11. c
12. c
13. b
14. c
15. b
16. c

Questions

1. Explain the concept of interprocedural optimization, and how it differs from intra-procedural optimization.

2. Discuss the challenges involved in interprocedural data flow analysis, and how they are addressed.

3. What is the significance of call graph construction in interprocedural analysis? How do indirect calls affect call graph construction?

4. Describe inline expansion as a technique for code optimization. What are the advantages and potential disadvantages of using inline expansion?

5. How does the LLVM framework support interprocedural analysis and optimization? Provide examples of how it applies data flow analysis, call graph construction, and inline expansion.
6. What are the trade-offs to consider when applying interprocedural optimizations to a program? How does balancing compilation time and program performance impact optimization decisions?
7. Discuss the role of summary information in interprocedural analysis. How does it help in managing large-scale software projects?
8. Why is context sensitivity important in interprocedural optimization? Explain how optimizations may vary based on different program contexts.

Key Terms

- **Context Sensitivity**: The need to consider the specific context in which a function is used during optimization.
- **Indirect Calls**: Function calls whose target is not known at compile time, posing a challenge for optimization.
- **Summary Information**: High-level representations of a function's behavior used to optimize across multiple functions.
- **Dead Code Elimination**: The process of removing code that does not affect the program's output.
- **Constant Propagation**: Replacing variables with their known constant values to eliminate redundant computations.
- **Inlining**: Replacing function calls with the body of the function to reduce overhead.
- **Optimization Passes**: Steps in the compilation process that apply different optimization techniques.
- **Global Program Efficiency**: The overall effectiveness of a program after applying interprocedural optimizations.
- **Compilation Time**: The time required to compile the program, which may increase with more optimizations.
- **LLVM Passes**: Specific optimization and analysis steps provided by LLVM to transform and optimize code.

CHAPTER 18
Case Studies and Real-World Examples

Introduction

In *Chapter 17, Interprocedural Analysis and Optimization*, you explored how analyzing and optimizing across function boundaries can enhance program performance. You learned about **interprocedural data flow analysis**, which enables information sharing across functions, improving optimization potential. We also discussed **call graph construction**, a crucial tool for understanding function relationships, and **inline expansion**, which helps reduce function call overhead. To ground these concepts in practice, we examined **LLVM-based interprocedural optimizations**, giving you a real-world perspective on their implementation.

Building upon this foundation, *Chapter 18, Case Studies and Real-World Examples*, will take you beyond theory and into practical applications. You will explore **case studies of compiler implementations**, gaining insights into how optimizations are applied in different **programming languages** and real-world projects. Have you ever wondered about the real challenges faced by compiler designers? This chapter will not only introduce you to these challenges but also show you the innovative **solutions** used to overcome them. By the end, you will have a deeper appreciation of how compiler optimizations directly impact software efficiency and performance in real-world scenarios.

Structure

In this chapter, we will discuss the following topics:

- Foundations of Case Studies in Compiler Technology
  - The Role of Case Studies in Compiler Design
  - Importance of Practical Applications in Compiler Development
- In-Depth Analysis of Compiler Implementations
  - GNU Compiler Collection (GCC)
  - Low-Level Virtual Machine (LLVM)
  - Clang Compiler
- Compiler Applications Across Programming Languages
  - C/C++ Compiler Implementations
  - Java Compiler Implementations
  - Python Compilation and Interpretation
- Real-World Examples and Performance Analysis
  - Case Studies of Compiled Programs
  - Performance Metrics Across Languages

- Challenges in Compiler Development
    - o Common Development Obstacles
    - o Solutions Derived from Case Studies
- Emerging Trends in Compiler Technology
    - o New Technologies and Methodologies in Compiler Design
    - o Future Directions for Compiler Research and Development

Foundations of Case Studies in Compiler Technology

Compilers are at the heart of software development, transforming high-level code into executable machine instructions. While theoretical principles provide the foundation for compiler design, real-world case studies offer invaluable insights into how compilers are built, optimized, and adapted to different programming needs.

By examining case studies, we can explore the practical challenges and solutions that arise in compiler development. These real-world examples highlight how compilers optimize performance, manage errors, ensure security, and support multiple programming languages. They also shed light on the trade-offs developers face when balancing compilation speed, runtime efficiency, and resource usage.

This chapter delves into various case studies and real-world examples to illustrate how compiler technology evolves, adapts, and impacts modern software development. Through these insights, we gain a deeper understanding of compiler architecture, best practices, and emerging trends that continue to shape this essential field.

The Role of Case Studies in Compiler Design

Compilers are at the core of software development, ensuring that high-level programming languages are translated into machine-executable code. While theoretical principles provide the necessary foundation for compiler design, real-world case studies bring these concepts to life by showcasing their practical implementation. Through case studies, we gain a deeper understanding of how compilers handle performance optimization, error detection, trade-offs in design, and language-specific challenges.

Studying real-world compiler implementations allows us to see how different design choices impact efficiency, usability, and performance. Every compiler, whether it be GCC, LLVM, or Clang, has undergone various iterations and improvements over time. By analyzing these case studies, we can understand the decisions that shaped their development and how they continue to evolve to meet modern programming demands.

Case studies serve as valuable learning tools by offering insights into:

- **Performance Optimization**

  One of the primary goals of a compiler is to generate optimized machine code that improves execution speed and reduces resource consumption. Case studies help us see how compilers apply advanced techniques such as loop unrolling, register allocation, constant propagation, and inlining to enhance performance.

  For example, LLVM's optimization framework allows developers to fine-tune performance using a modular approach, making it one of the most widely used compilers in research and industry. By analyzing its implementation, we can understand how optimizations are structured, executed, and tested in real-world scenarios.

- **Error Detection and Handling**

  Compilers are not just responsible for code translation; they also play a crucial role in error detection and debugging. Case studies highlight different methods compilers use to identify syntax errors, report meaningful warnings, and recover from unexpected exceptions.

  For instance, Clang's diagnostic engine is known for its detailed and user-friendly error messages, helping developers quickly pinpoint and resolve issues in their code. By studying such implementations, we gain insights into how effective debugging mechanisms are integrated into compilers.

- **Trade-offs in Compiler Design**

  Every compiler must strike a balance between compilation speed, runtime performance, and memory efficiency. Some compilers prioritize faster compilation times, while others focus on code efficiency and optimization.

  A great example is Just-In-Time (JIT) compilation in Java and Python, where the compiler translates code at runtime rather than ahead of time. This approach improves execution speed but also introduces overhead. Through case studies, we can analyze the impact of such trade-offs and determine the best approaches for different applications.

- **Language-Specific Challenges**

  Each programming language has its own unique characteristics and compilation challenges. Case studies allow us to explore how compilers handle these differences effectively.

  - **C/C++ Compilers**: Focus on manual memory management and low-level optimizations.
  - **Java Compilers**: Generate bytecode for execution in the Java Virtual Machine (JVM), allowing portability across platforms.
  - **Python Compilers**: Deal with dynamic typing, interpretation, and runtime optimizations.

By examining compiler implementations for different languages, we can see how design choices shape their functionality and efficiency.

Learning from Case Studies to Improve Future Compilers

Case studies not only help us learn from past successes but also highlight common pitfalls and challenges in compiler development. They provide valuable lessons on:

Optimizing compilation workflows to enhance performance.

Improving debugging tools to help developers write error-free code.

Ensuring security measures to prevent vulnerabilities like buffer overflows.

Adapting compilers to modern architectures and emerging programming paradigms.

By leveraging these real-world examples, developers and researchers can refine existing compiler technologies and contribute to the development of faster, more reliable, and adaptable compilers for the future.

Importance of Practical Applications in Compiler Development

Compilers serve as the critical link between high-level programming languages and machine-executable code. They transform human-readable instructions into a form that the computer can understand and execute. While the theoretical concepts behind compiler design form the foundational knowledge, it is through practical applications that compilers are refined, optimized, and adapted to real-world needs. Without these applications, compilers would remain abstract tools without real-world relevance. Practical applications ensure that compilers not only function efficiently but also evolve in response to new programming paradigms, hardware architectures, and performance demands.

The role of practical applications in compiler development extends far beyond simple translation. It includes the ability to optimize performance, ensure security, improve error handling, and adapt to new technologies. Through real-world applications, compilers become more than just theoretical constructs; they are essential tools that developers rely on to create software that is efficient, secure, and robust.

Performance Optimization in Real-World Scenarios

In any software application, performance is a critical factor. A good compiler does not just translate code but also ensures that it runs as efficiently as possible. Practical applications of compilers help achieve performance optimization, which is especially important in domains where speed and resource usage are paramount, such as high-performance computing, gaming, and cloud applications.

Compilers employ various techniques to improve the performance of the generated machine code. Some common optimization techniques include:

- **Loop unrolling**, which reduces the overhead of looping by executing multiple iterations at once, thus speeding up the program.
- **Register allocation**, which efficiently uses CPU registers to reduce memory access and improve computation speed.
- **Inlining**, where function calls are replaced with the function's actual code to minimize the overhead that comes with calling a function.

For instance, the LLVM optimization framework is a widely used tool that allows developers to fine-tune performance for a wide range of applications, from scientific computing to AI-based models. By implementing such optimizations, developers can ensure that their programs run efficiently in resource-intensive environments.

Error Handling and Debugging Support

While performance is crucial, a compiler's ability to help developers identify and correct errors is just as important. In real-world software development, debugging is often a time-consuming and complex task. A practical application of compilers involves integrating error detection and debugging tools that help developers identify syntax errors, logic mistakes, and runtime issues as quickly as possible.

Compilers such as Clang are well-known for their clear and informative error messages. Unlike traditional compilers that often provide cryptic or vague errors, Clang offers detailed diagnostics with precise error locations and suggestions for resolving common issues. These messages help developers identify the source of the problem and correct it faster, reducing the overall time spent debugging.

Such error-handling mechanisms are invaluable in large-scale projects where finding the root cause of bugs can be a laborious task. By providing helpful warnings and immediate feedback, compilers not only improve software quality but also enhance developer productivity.

Security and Code Safety Enhancements

As security becomes an ever-growing concern in modern software development, compilers are increasingly designed to incorporate features that detect vulnerabilities and enforce safe coding practices. A well-designed compiler can help prevent common security issues such as buffer overflows, memory leaks, and undefined behaviors—problems that can lead to severe security vulnerabilities.

For example, modern compilers integrate security features such as stack canaries to protect against stack-based buffer overflow attacks and control flow integrity (CFI) to prevent attackers from manipulating the program's execution flow. Additionally, memory safety checks in languages such as C and C++ help avoid dangerous memory access violations. These security enhancements are crucial in industries where software integrity and data protection are paramount, such as in healthcare, finance, and cybersecurity.

The integration of such features demonstrates how practical applications in compiler development not only improve the safety and robustness of the software but also help developers write secure, error-free code from the start.

Adaptability Across Languages and Architectures

As technology advances, compilers must remain adaptable to new programming languages, hardware architectures, and operating systems. Practical applications of compilers enable them to support multiple languages and adapt to emerging hardware and development paradigms. A modern compiler needs to be more than just a one-size-fits-all solution—it must be flexible enough to cater to different languages and evolving technologies.

For instance, LLVM and Clang have been designed for modularity, making them suitable for a wide range of software development needs, from mobile applications to cloud-based systems. Furthermore, compilers such as the GNU Compiler Collection (GCC) support a broad set of languages, including C, C++, and Fortran, ensuring portability across various platforms.

Similarly, Just-In-Time (JIT) compilation used in Java, Python, and JavaScript enables runtime optimizations that improve execution speed for interactive applications. These features make it easier for developers to write code once and run it anywhere, whether on a mobile device, cloud platform, or server.

Enhancing Software Development Workflows

Compilers play an integral role in modern software development workflows. They impact build systems, integrated development environments (IDEs), and continuous integration/continuous deployment (CI/CD) pipelines. Practical applications of compilers within these tools help improve development efficiency by automating tasks such as code compilation, performance profiling, and bug detection.

In popular IDEs such as Visual Studio Code and JetBrains CLion, compilers are integrated to provide real-time code analysis, auto-completion, and error checking. These features make coding smoother and faster, allowing developers to write high-quality code without frequent context switching between the code editor and debugging tools.

Moreover, continuous integration systems rely on compilers to automatically build and test software, ensuring that new changes don't break the code and that performance remains consistent across iterations.

In-Depth Analysis of Compiler Implementations

Compilers are essential tools in software development, transforming code that developers write into machine-executable instructions. But they do much more than just translate code—they help improve performance, manage errors, and ensure compatibility across different platforms. To understand how compilers really work, it is useful to take a closer look at some of the most widely used ones, such as GCC , LLVM, and Clang.

In this section, we will dive into each of these compilers, looking at their key features, design decisions, and the challenges they have faced in development. We will also explore how they optimize code, improve performance, and impact real-world applications. By the end, you will have a clear picture of what makes these compilers stand out and why they are so important in modern software development.

GNU Compiler Collection (GCC)

The GNU Compiler Collection (GCC) is one of the most well-known and widely used compilers. It was originally developed as part of the GNU Project and has since evolved into a powerful and versatile tool that supports many programming languages, including C, C++, Fortran, Ada, Objective-C, and more. GCC has become an essential tool in the open-source software ecosystem, powering everything from small applications to large-scale systems.

Some of the key features that make GCC widely used include:

- **Multi-Language Support**: GCC can compile code written in a variety of languages, making it a versatile choice for developers working in different domains.
- **Optimization Levels**: GCC provides several levels of optimization, ranging from basic optimizations to aggressive performance improvements, allowing developers to tailor their code's performance.
- **Cross-Compilation**: GCC supports cross-compiling, which allows developers to generate executable code for different hardware architectures and operating systems from a single codebase.
- **Comprehensive Error Checking**: GCC has robust error checking, providing clear error messages and warnings that help developers identify and fix problems in their code.
- **Wide Platform Support**: GCC can be used on a wide variety of operating systems and platforms, including Linux, Windows, macOS, and many others.

Due to its flexibility, power, and wide platform support, GCC is a fundamental tool in the development process for a wide range of applications.

Design Choices and Implementation Challenges

While GCC's capabilities make it an excellent choice for many developers, its design also introduces certain challenges.

- **Monolithic Architecture**: GCC's architecture is relatively monolithic, which means that all components of the compiler are tightly integrated. While this helps maintain consistency, it can also make the system difficult to maintain and extend as new features and languages are added.
- **Complex Codebase**: As GCC supports multiple languages and platforms, its codebase has grown to be very large and complex. This can make it difficult to navigate, especially when trying to introduce new features or optimizations.
- **Balancing Portability and Optimization**: One of the major challenges faced by GCC is balancing the need for portability (ensuring it works on many different systems) with the desire to generate highly optimized machine code for a specific target system. Optimization techniques that work well for one platform may not be as effective on another, and developers must make careful decisions about which optimizations to implement.
- **Performance Concerns**: GCC's performance, especially when compiling large projects, has been a concern for some developers. Although there have been efforts to improve compile times, GCC's processing time can still be a limiting factor in very large codebases.

Despite these challenges, GCC has remained a robust, widely adopted compiler. Its flexibility, continual development, and strong community support have kept it at the forefront of compiler technology.

Low-Level Virtual Machine (LLVM)

LLVM, which stands for Low-Level Virtual Machine, is a modern, open-source compiler infrastructure that provides a collection of modular and reusable compiler components. Unlike traditional compilers, LLVM is designed as a framework that supports not only the compilation process but also advanced optimizations and code generation for a variety of programming languages.

LLVM is known for its flexibility, performance, and cross-platform capabilities, making it a popular choice in both research and industry for building compilers, interpreters, and other programming tools.

Architectural Innovations and Flexibility

LLVM's architecture is one of its biggest strengths, thanks to its modular design and Intermediate Representation (IR). This innovative approach separates different stages of the compilation process, allowing for great flexibility and extensibility.

- **Modular Design**: LLVM's modular structure means that the different parts of the compiler (front-end, optimizer, and back-end) are designed as independent, reusable components. This separation allows for easy updates, customizations, and the addition of new features without disrupting the whole system.
- **Intermediate Representation (IR)**: A central innovation of LLVM is its use of IR—a low-level, platform-independent representation of the source code. This allows LLVM to optimize the code before generating machine-specific instructions, making it easier to perform optimizations that can be applied across various platforms.
- **Cross-Platform Support**: LLVM can target a wide variety of hardware architectures, from x86 and ARM to emerging platforms such as RISC-V. Its modularity makes it easy to extend and support new target architectures.
- **Extensibility**: One of LLVM's most attractive features is its ability to be extended. Developers can create new frontends for different languages, add custom optimizations, or support new target architectures, all within the same LLVM framework.

Key benefits of LLVM's architecture:

- **Flexibility**: The separation of concerns between the front-end, optimizer, and back-end makes LLVM a highly flexible system that can support a wide range of programming languages and hardware targets.
- **Cross-Platform**: LLVM is capable of generating code for a variety of platforms, making it ideal for cross-compilation and multi-platform development.
- **Customization**: Its modularity allows developers to easily add custom optimizations and extend LLVM to suit specific needs, whether for new languages or architectures.

Advanced Optimization Techniques

LLVM is renowned for its extensive set of optimization techniques, which significantly enhance the performance, efficiency, and scalability of the generated machine code. These optimizations work on the Intermediate Representation (IR), which provides a platform-independent code representation, enabling LLVM to apply sophisticated transformations before generating the final machine-specific code.

Let us dive deeper into some of the key advanced optimization techniques LLVM employs:

Loop Optimizations

Loops are often a critical performance bottleneck in programs, and LLVM applies several optimization techniques to enhance loop performance:

- **Loop Unrolling**: This technique involves expanding the loop body multiple times to reduce the overhead of loop control. Instead of executing the same loop iteration several times, it performs multiple operations in a single iteration. This improves the program's parallelism and reduces the number of jumps or branches within the loop.
- **Loop Fusion**: When multiple loops operate on the same data, LLVM can combine them into one. This reduces overhead and improves cache locality, as multiple operations can be performed sequentially without redundant memory accesses.
- **Loop Invariant Code Motion**: In many cases, certain computations inside a loop do not change during each iteration (for example, calculations based on constants). LLVM moves such computations outside the loop to reduce redundant calculations and improve performance.

Dead Code Elimination

Dead Code Elimination (DCE) identifies and removes code that will never be executed or whose result does not affect the program's output. This includes: Unused variables, Unreachable code blocks, and Redundant computations.

By eliminating this code, LLVM reduces the size of the generated binary, leading to faster load times and improved performance in both time and space.

Constant Propagation

Constant propagation is an optimization where known constant values are substituted for variables that always hold a constant value. This allows the compiler to eliminate unnecessary operations and computations at runtime, which can result in faster code execution.

For instance, if the code contains a statement like:

```
int x = 5;
int y = x * 2;
```

LLVM can replace `x` with `5` in the second statement, turning it into:

```
int y = 10;
```

This avoids the need for a multiplication operation at runtime.

Function Inlining

Function inlining replaces a function call with the body of the function itself. This is particularly beneficial for small, frequently used functions because it removes the overhead of calling a function, including the jump instructions and stack frame management.

For example, instead of:

```
int add(int a, int b) {
    return a + b;
}
int main() {
    int sum = add(5, 3);
}
```

The function **add** can be inlined directly into the main function:

```
int main() {
    int sum = 5 + 3;
}
```

This reduces the overhead and can lead to significant performance improvements, especially in tight loops or small helper functions.

Profile-Guided Optimization (PGO)

Profile-Guided Optimization (PGO) uses real runtime data to inform optimization decisions. The idea is to gather profiling data about how often different parts of the code are executed during a representative run of the program. This information can then be used to optimize frequently executed code paths.

For example, if a certain loop is executed many times in practice, LLVM may apply more aggressive optimizations to that loop to maximize performance, such as loop unrolling or vectorization. Conversely, less frequently executed code may not receive such intense optimization, allowing the overall optimization process to focus on the program's critical performance paths.

Vectorization

Vectorization transforms scalar operations into vector operations, allowing a processor to perform the same operation on multiple data elements simultaneously (SIMD: Single Instruction, Multiple Data). This can significantly speed up applications that involve large datasets or heavy computational tasks, such as matrix multiplication or data processing.

For instance, instead of executing a loop that adds two arrays element-by-element:

```
for (int i = 0; i < n; i++) {
    C[i] = A[i] + B[i];
}
```

LLVM may apply vectorization to allow the CPU to process multiple elements in parallel, such as:

```
for (int i = 0; i < n; i += 4) {
    C[i] = A[i] + B[i];
    C[i+1] = A[i+1] + B[i+1];
    C[i+2] = A[i+2] + B[i+2];
    C[i+3] = A[i+3] + B[i+3];
}
```

This takes advantage of hardware capabilities such as AVX or SSE to accelerate the computation.

Interprocedural Optimization (IPO)

Interprocedural Optimization refers to optimizations that span across function boundaries. These optimizations analyze multiple functions in the program to improve performance as a whole. Key techniques include:

- **Inlining across functions**: Functions that are frequently called and small can be inlined even across function boundaries.
- **Constant propagation across functions**: Known constants in one function can be propagated to other functions, reducing redundant calculations.
- **Function specialization**: LLVM can generate specialized versions of functions based on the actual parameters passed at runtime, leading to more efficient code.

Interprocedural optimizations help LLVM understand the relationship between different functions, enabling it to make performance-enhancing decisions that may not be apparent within a single function's scope.

Target-Specific Optimizations

LLVM includes optimizations tailored to specific target architectures. By understanding the specific features of the hardware, LLVM can generate machine code that maximizes the processor's capabilities. For example:

- **Instruction scheduling**: LLVM can reorder instructions to take advantage of the CPU's pipeline and reduce instruction dependencies.
- **Vectorization for specific hardware**: LLVM generates code that utilizes Single Instruction, Multiple Data (SIMP) instructions such as AVX, AVX2, or NEON, depending on the target CPU.
- **Cache optimizations**: By analyzing memory access patterns, LLVM can adjust the code to improve cache locality, reducing memory latency.

These optimizations allow LLVM to generate highly efficient code specific to a given architecture, resulting in better performance.

Clang Compiler

Clang is a compiler front-end for the LLVM project, designed to provide fast and efficient compilation, a modern architecture, and a rich set of features for both developers and end-users. It is widely recognized for its user-friendly error and warning messages, making it a popular choice for software development. Clang is highly compatible with GNU Compiler Collection (GCC) but offers enhanced performance, better diagnostics, and more flexibility in terms of customization and integration with other tools.

Clang is particularly known for its modularity and its ability to integrate seamlessly with other tools in the LLVM ecosystem, including static analysis tools, debuggers, and profilers.

Features Unique to Clang

Clang stands out from other compilers due to several unique features that make it particularly attractive for developers:

- **Excellent Diagnostic Messages**: One of the standout features of Clang is its diagnostic messages, including warnings and errors. Clang is known for providing highly readable, detailed, and helpful error and warning messages, which often include suggestions for how to resolve issues. These diagnostics make it easier for developers to debug and improve their code.
- **Modular Architecture**: Clang's design is highly modular which means developers can easily reuse, extend, and integrate Clang's components into their own tools. This modularity makes Clang highly customizable, whether you are building custom static analysis tools, developing plugins, or working on custom optimizations.
- **Support for Modern C++ Features**: Clang has excellent support for the latest C++ standards, including C++11, C++14, C++17, and even experimental support for C++20 features. This makes Clang an ideal choice for developers working with cutting-edge C++ features, as it is generally faster to adopt new language standards than many other compilers.
- **Cross-Platform Support**: Clang can be used on a variety of platforms, including Unix-like systems (Linux and macOS), Windows, and embedded systems. Its cross-platform compatibility ensures it can be used for a broad range of development projects.

- **Integration with IDEs**: Clang integrates seamlessly with Integrated Development Environments (IDEs) such as Visual Studio, Xcode, and others, providing features such as autocomplete, code navigation, and on-the-fly error checking, greatly improving developer productivity.
- **Static Analysis:** Clang provides a powerful static analysis tool that can detect a wide variety of issues in the codebase, from memory leaks and null pointer dereferencing to potential security vulnerabilities. The integration of static analysis in the Clang ecosystem helps developers improve the quality and safety of their code.
- **Open Source and Extensible**: Like LLVM, Clang is open-source, which means that developers can contribute to its development, customize it for their needs, or build on top of it. This openness fosters a large and active community that continuously enhances Clang's capabilities.

Performance Metrics and User Impact

Clang is known for its performance, both in terms of compilation speed and the quality of the generated machine code. These performance metrics have a significant impact on the user experience, especially in large-scale projects or real-time systems where compilation time and runtime performance are critical.

- **Compilation Speed**: Clang's compilation speed is generally faster than many other compilers, including GCC, especially for large projects. This is due to its optimized parsing and code generation algorithms. Faster compilation times can significantly improve the development workflow, reducing the time developers spend waiting for their code to compile and allowing for faster iterations.
- **Memory Usage**: Clang is designed to be lightweight and memory-efficient. It tends to use less memory than other compilers, especially when handling large codebases. This is particularly useful in resource-constrained environments, such as embedded systems, where minimizing memory usage is a critical concern.
- **Code Optimization and Performance**: The generated machine code produced by Clang is highly optimized, providing excellent runtime performance. It often produces code that is as fast as or faster than the code generated by other compilers, thanks to LLVM's robust optimization techniques. Clang benefits from the extensive optimizations provided by LLVM, such as dead code elimination, constant propagation, and function inlining, which result in smaller, more efficient binaries.
- **User Experience**: The user impact of Clang's features is considerable, particularly for developers focused on improving code quality and development efficiency. The clear and helpful diagnostic messages make it easier for developers to fix bugs and improve their code. Moreover, the integration with IDEs and static analysis tools streamlines the development process by providing real-time feedback and identifying issues before they become serious problems.

For users working on performance-critical applications, the combination of fast compilation times, optimized machine code, and low memory usage can significantly improve the overall efficiency of the development lifecycle and runtime performance of the application.

Compiler Applications Across Programming Languages

Compilers are the backbone of most programming languages, translating high-level code written by developers into machine code that can be executed by a computer. Different programming languages have different needs and challenges when it comes to compilation. The techniques and strategies employed by compilers vary based on the language's features, design, and runtime characteristics.

In this section, we will explore compiler implementations across a range of popular programming languages: **C/C++**, **Java**, and **Python**. We will examine best practices, optimization techniques, performance implications, and how each language handles compilation and interpretation.

C/C++ Compiler Implementations

C and C++ are two of the most widely used programming languages for system-level and performance-critical applications. They allow developers to write software that interacts closely with hardware, making them indispensable for tasks that require high performance, such as operating systems, embedded systems, and game engines. However, compiling C/C++ code involves more than simply converting human-readable code into machine code. It is about optimizing that code to run as efficiently as possible on the target machine.

The C/C++ compilers are built with a set of tools and techniques aimed at transforming code into an optimized version that can execute quickly while consuming minimal system resources. In this section, we'll dive into some of the key practices, techniques, and performance considerations that influence how C/C++ compilers work.

When developing C/C++ code, it is essential to make the most of the compiler's optimization features. Here are some best practices and techniques that can significantly boost your program's efficiency:

- **Choosing the Right Compiler Flags and Optimization Levels**: Compiler flags are like instructions that tell the compiler how aggressively to optimize the code. For example, -O2 applies a standard level of optimization, while -O3 focuses on more aggressive performance improvements. It is often a matter of balancing speed and compile-time.

  The -g flag is helpful for including debugging information, while -pg enables profiling, which helps you identify performance bottlenecks during the development phase.

- **Incorporating Function Inlining**: Inlining is a common optimization strategy that reduces the overhead of function calls. By embedding function code directly at the call site, you can avoid the expense of pushing data to the call stack. This technique works best for small, frequently-used functions, but you need to be careful not to bloat the binary size.

- **Optimizing Memory Management**: Memory usage plays a critical role in the efficiency of C/C++ programs. Techniques such as loop unrolling and data alignment help improve memory access patterns, ensuring that the CPU caches are used effectively and reducing the chances of memory fragmentation.

  Allocating memory on the stack (where possible) is more efficient than using the heap, as stack memory is faster to allocate and deallocate.

- **Leveraging Link-Time Optimization (LTO)**: Link-Time Optimization is a process where the compiler performs optimizations across multiple files during the linking phase, rather than just compiling individual files. This allows the compiler to perform more comprehensive optimizations, such as eliminating dead code or performing interprocedural function inlining.

- **Profile-Guided Optimization (PGO)**: PGO involves running the program to gather real execution data, which is then fed back to the compiler to guide optimization decisions. This ensures that the most frequently executed code paths receive the most aggressive optimizations, helping to speed up execution.

- **Advanced Features for Maximum Efficiency**: Vectorization is one of the most advanced optimizations supported by modern C/C++ compilers. It enables the execution of the same operation on multiple data points in parallel, reducing computation time.

  Dead Code Elimination ensures that parts of the code that will never be executed are removed, reducing both binary size and execution time.

Loop Optimization involves techniques such as loop unrolling, reducing the number of iterations, and minimizing redundant calculations.

While all these optimization techniques offer significant performance gains, there are a few trade-offs that developers need to be aware of. It is not always a straightforward path, and the choice of optimization can impact various aspects of the program:

- **Balancing Compilation Time with Execution Speed**: Some optimizations, especially aggressive ones such as -O3 or -flto, may significantly increase the time it takes to compile your code. While this might be acceptable for production builds where speed is crucial, it could slow down the development cycle during testing or debugging. For such cases, you might choose less aggressive optimization levels, such as -O1 or -O2, to speed up compilation.
- **Managing Memory Usage**: Techniques such as inlining and vectorization can result in a larger binary size or higher memory usage. This can become a concern for systems with limited resources (for example, embedded systems or mobile devices). Developers need to weigh the benefits of performance against the cost in terms of memory consumption.
- **Execution Time**: Many optimizations improve execution speed, which is critical for time-sensitive applications. For example, loop unrolling can reduce loop overhead, and vectorization allows simultaneous processing of multiple data points. However, you must monitor how these changes affect the overall memory footprint, as the optimizations could lead to increased cache misses or longer load times in some scenarios.
- **Optimizing for Scalability**: If your application is designed to run on multi-core or multi-threaded environments, optimizations that focus on parallelism and Single Instruction, Multiple Data (SIMD) can dramatically improve scalability. These techniques allow tasks to be divided into smaller chunks and processed simultaneously across multiple processor cores, enhancing performance in multi-threaded applications.

Java Compiler Implementations

Java is a high-level, platform-independent programming language that relies on a two-step compilation process to achieve both flexibility and efficiency. Unlike traditional compiled languages such as C and C++, which generate machine-specific executable files, Java programs are first compiled into an intermediate format called bytecode. This bytecode is then executed by the Java Virtual Machine (JVM), allowing Java applications to run seamlessly across different operating systems and hardware architectures.

Java's compilation process plays a crucial role in optimizing performance while maintaining its "*Write Once, Run Anywhere*" philosophy. Java compilers, such as javac (the standard Java compiler) and Just-In-Time (JIT) compilers, work together to transform human-readable Java code into highly efficient machine instructions. This section explores Java's compilation model, the process of bytecode generation, and the role of JIT compilation in enhancing execution speed.

Bytecode Generation and JIT Compilation Insights

Java's compilation process is unique because it balances portability and performance, making it one of the most widely used languages in modern computing. Unlike languages such as C and C++, which directly compile source code into machine code for a specific platform, Java takes a two-step approach:

- **Bytecode Generation**: Java source code is first compiled into an intermediate representation called bytecode, making it platform-independent.
- **Just-In-Time (JIT) Compilation**: During execution, the Java Virtual Machine (JVM) dynamically translates frequently executed bytecode into native machine code, significantly improving runtime performance.

This approach allows Java applications to run on any device with a JVM, ensuring cross-platform compatibility while still benefiting from real-time performance optimizations. Let us explore these steps in greater detail.

Bytecode is an intermediate, low-level representation of Java source code. It consists of compact, platform-neutral instructions that can be executed by the JVM. When a Java program is compiled using the javac compiler, it produces .class files containing bytecode instead of machine-specific binary code.

The process of generating bytecode is the first step in Java's compilation pipeline. This step allows developers to write code once and execute it anywhere. The Java compiler (javac) transforms the human-readable source code into bytecode that the JVM can understand and interpret. But how exactly does this transformation take place, and what happens behind the scenes? Let us explore the steps involved in generating bytecode from Java source code.

1. **Writing Java Source Code**: Developers write Java programs in `.java` files.
2. **Compilation with javac**: The Java Compiler (javac) translates the source code into `.class` files, which contain bytecode.
3. **Execution in the JVM**: The JVM interprets bytecode or compiles it into machine code using JIT compilation.

Now that we have established how bytecode is generated, let us explore the significant advantages of bytecode in Java. Bytecode provides an intermediate layer between the source code and machine code, offering a powerful combination of portability, security, and flexibility. But what makes bytecode so powerful? Why is it such a critical component of Java's success as a cross-platform language? Let us dive into the benefits bytecode brings to the table.

- **Platform Independence**: The same bytecode can be executed on any system with a JVM.
- **Security and Stability**: Java programs run in a controlled execution environment, reducing the risk of security vulnerabilities.
- **Dynamic Optimization**: Since bytecode is structured, the JVM can apply runtime optimizations to enhance performance.

However, interpreting bytecode line by line can be slow. To address this, Java uses JIT Compilation, which dynamically translates frequently used bytecode into machine code for faster execution.

Just-In-Time (JIT) Compilation

JIT compilation is a technique where the JVM identifies frequently executed bytecode (hotspots) and compiles it into native machine code during runtime. This eliminates the need for repeated interpretation, significantly boosting performance.

To understand this process better, think of it as learning a new skill. When a person first learns a new task (such as typing), they do it slowly and carefully. Over time, they memorize common keystrokes and start typing much faster. Similarly, JIT compilation learns which parts of the code are frequently used and compiles them for quick execution.

Step-by-Step Process:

1. **Initial Interpretation**: The JVM begins by interpreting bytecode line by line.
2. **Hotspot Detection**: The JVM monitors execution and detects frequently used code segments, known as hotspots.
3. **Native Code Compilation**: The JIT compiler compiles these hotspots into optimized machine code.

4. **Performance Boost**: The compiled native code is stored and reused, avoiding the need for repeated interpretation.

Since JIT compilation only optimizes frequently used code, it ensures that less frequently executed parts remain interpreted, balancing performance and resource usage.

Types of JIT Compilation in Java

Java's JIT compiler operates at multiple levels to optimize performance based on different application needs.

- **Client Compiler (C1)**: Focuses on quick startup time, making it ideal for small applications.
- **Server Compiler (C2)**: Performs deeper optimizations, such as method inlining and loop unrolling, best suited for large, long-running applications.
- **Graal JIT Compiler**: Introduced in Java 9, Graal offers advanced optimizations using speculative execution and vectorization, providing high-performance computing capabilities.

Each of these compilers plays a critical role in ensuring optimal execution speed, while maintaining Java's flexibility.

JIT compilation offers several key advantages over traditional interpretation:

- Faster Execution Over Time: Since frequently used bytecode is converted into native machine code, execution becomes significantly faster on subsequent runs.
- Dynamic Optimizations at Runtime: Unlike static compilers (which optimize code before execution), JIT compilation allows the JVM to analyze actual runtime behavior and optimize the code accordingly.
- Balanced Resource Usage: Instead of compiling the entire program at once (which can be slow), JIT compiles only the most frequently used code, reducing unnecessary processing overhead.

To further improve Java's performance, the JIT compiler applies various advanced optimizations, such as:

- **Method Inlining**: Replaces function calls with actual function code, eliminating call overhead.
- **Loop Unrolling**: Expands loops to reduce branching, making execution more efficient.
- **Dead Code Elimination**: Removes unnecessary or unreachable code, improving execution speed.
- **Speculative Optimization**: Uses runtime profiling to predict execution patterns and optimize code accordingly.

These optimizations allow Java programs to execute much faster while still maintaining flexibility.

While JIT compilation improves Java's performance, it also presents some challenges:

- Increased Memory Usage: Since compiled native code is stored in memory, JIT compilation can increase RAM consumption, especially for large applications.
- Startup Delay: The JIT compiler requires time to analyze and compile frequently executed code, leading to slower startup times compared to statically compiled languages.
- Garbage Collection Impact: JIT compilation generates additional temporary objects and optimized code, which can put pressure on Java's Garbage Collector (GC) and impact overall performance.

Despite these challenges, JIT compilation remains a key factor in Java's ability to deliver high-performance applications.

Python Compilation and Interpretation

Python is known for its simplicity and flexibility, but what makes it truly unique is how it handles code execution. Unlike statically compiled languages such as C or Java, Python follows a dynamic, interpreted execution model that allows for greater flexibility at runtime. However, this also comes with trade-offs, particularly in terms of performance and efficiency. Understanding how Python compiles and interprets code is crucial for optimizing its execution and making the most of its capabilities.

Python uses a two-step execution process that includes both compilation and interpretation:

1. **Source Code to Bytecode**: When a Python script runs, the source code (.py file) is first compiled into bytecode (`.pyc` files stored in the `__pycache__` folder).

   This bytecode is an intermediate representation of the code, optimized for execution by the Python Virtual Machine (PVM).

2. **Execution by the Python Virtual Machine (PVM)**: The PVM reads and executes the bytecode line by line, dynamically interpreting instructions during runtime.

Unlike Java, which uses a Just-In-Time (JIT) compiler to convert bytecode into machine code, Python executes its bytecode directly within the virtual machine.

Since Python does not rely on static compilation into machine code, it offers greater portability across different systems, making it a preferred choice for scripting, web development, and data science applications.

Dynamic Typing Considerations and Performance

One of Python's defining features is its dynamically typed nature, meaning variable types are determined at runtime rather than during compilation. While this flexibility allows for rapid development and ease of use, it also introduces performance overhead.

Impact of Dynamic Typing on Performance:

- **Increased Execution Overhead**: Every time a variable is used, Python must check its type, which adds extra processing time compared to statically typed languages.
- **Memory Management Challenges**: Python relies on automatic memory management and garbage collection, which can introduce latency, especially in memory-intensive applications.

Optimization Techniques to Improve Performance:

- **Using Built-in Functions**: Python's built-in functions are implemented in C, making them significantly faster than manually written loops.
- **Leveraging Just-In-Time Compilation (JIT) with PyPy**: PyPy is an alternative Python implementation that uses JIT compilation to convert Python bytecode into machine code at runtime, leading to significant speed improvements.
- **Using Type Hints (PEP 484)**: While Python remains dynamically typed, adding type hints can help tools such as MyPy catch errors early and improve code optimization.

Despite its performance trade-offs, Python's ease of use, extensive libraries, and flexibility make it one of the most widely used programming languages today. Understanding its compilation model and the impact of dynamic typing can help developers write more efficient, optimized Python programs.

Real-World Examples and Performance Analysis

Compilers play a fundamental role in optimizing code execution, ensuring programs run efficiently across different hardware architectures. In this section, we explore real-world examples where compiler optimizations significantly impact performance. We will also conduct a comparative analysis of compiler outputs and evaluate performance metrics across multiple programming languages.

Case Studies of Compiled Programs

Analyzing real-world compiled programs provides valuable insights into how compiler optimizations impact execution speed, memory usage, and overall performance. By examining case studies across different languages and architectures, we can better understand how compilers transform high-level code into efficient machine code. Below are some notable case studies that highlight the role of compilation in real-world applications.

Performance Improvements in C/C++ Compilers: The Case of SPEC CPU Benchmarks

Overview: The **SPEC CPU benchmark suite** is widely used to measure the performance of compiler optimizations across various hardware platforms.

Key Observations:

- GCC and Clang apply **loop unrolling, vectorization, and register allocation** to improve execution speed.
- Optimizations such as **dead code elimination and function inlining** reduce redundant operations, enhancing CPU efficiency.

Impact: Programs compiled with aggressive optimization flags (for example, -O2, -O3, -march=native) show **significant runtime reductions**, sometimes by more than **20-30%**, depending on the workload.

Java's JIT Compilation in Enterprise Applications

Overview: In Java-based applications, the **Just-In-Time (JIT) compiler** dynamically compiles bytecode into optimized native code at runtime.

Key Observations:

- Java's **HotSpot JIT compiler** identifies frequently executed methods and recompiles them with **adaptive optimizations.**
- Techniques such as **escape analysis and speculative devirtualization** minimize runtime overhead.

Impact: Java applications, such as web servers and enterprise systems, experience **lower startup times and better throughput** due to runtime optimizations.

Example: The performance of **Apache Tomcat**, a Java-based web server, improves by over **40%** when running with **GraalVM's JIT compiler**, compared to standard HotSpot JIT.

Python Compilation and Performance Gains with PyPy

Overview: Python is typically interpreted, but **JIT compilers, such as PyPy** can significantly enhance execution speed by compiling frequently used code paths.

Key Observations:

- **PyPy's tracing JIT** optimizes repeated function calls by eliminating redundant computations.
- Programs involving **heavy looping operations and mathematical computations** benefit the most from JIT compilation.

Impact: Python applications running on PyPy can achieve **2x-10x speed improvements** compared to the standard CPython interpreter.

Example: In **scientific computing applications**, such as numerical simulations using NumPy, PyPy reduces execution time by over **50%**, making it a preferred choice for performance-intensive Python workloads.

GPU-Optimized Compilation: NVIDIA CUDA and LLVM-Based Compilation

Overview: Modern compilers optimize code for **parallel execution on GPUs**, improving performance in AI, gaming, and scientific computing.

Key Observations:

- **CUDA compilers optimize memory access patterns** to reduce latency.
- **LLVM-based GPU compilers**, such as ROCm for AMD GPUs, apply **warp scheduling and loop unrolling** to maximize efficiency.

Impact: Programs utilizing **CUDA or OpenCL optimizations** see performance improvements of **5x to 100x** compared to CPU-based execution.

Example: Deep learning frameworks, such as **TensorFlow and PyTorch** use compiler-optimized CUDA kernels, accelerating **neural network training by 10-50 times** on GPUs.

Effects of Compiler Optimizations on Performance

Compiler optimizations are crucial for improving execution speed, reducing memory usage, and enhancing overall efficiency. Let us explore **three real-world cases** where compiler optimizations have made a significant difference.

Web Browsers (Google Chrome's V8 Engine: JavaScript)

Optimization Applied: Just-In-Time (JIT) Compilation and Hidden Class Optimization

Impact:

- Earlier JavaScript engines interpreted code line by line, resulting in slow execution.
- JIT compilation dynamically translates frequently executed code segments into **machine code**, significantly improving execution speed.

Result: A **5× performance improvement** in web-based applications such as Google Docs and interactive web games.

Machine Learning Libraries (TensorFlow: C++)

Optimization Applied: Loop Unrolling and Vectorization

Impact:

- TensorFlow's deep learning models rely on highly optimized C++ routines for numerical computations.
- **Loop unrolling** reduces branching overhead, while **Single Instruction, Multiple Data (SIMD)** vectorization enables parallel processing of large datasets.

Result: Training deep learning models became up to **10× faster**, reducing computation time significantly.

Game Development (Unreal Engine - C++)

Optimization Applied: Function Inlining and Code Caching

Impact:

- Unreal Engine optimizes rendering loops and physics calculations using **function inlining** to eliminate function call overhead.
- **Code caching** precompiles frequently used shaders, reducing loading times.
- **Result**: A **significant improvement in frame rates**, from **30 FPS to 60 FPS**, providing a smoother gaming experience.

Comparative Analysis of Compiler Outputs

Compilers optimize code differently depending on their internal strategies. Let us compare how **GCC, Clang, and MSVC** handle a simple **matrix multiplication** task.

Test Case: Optimized versus Non-Optimized Code

Consider the following **C++ loop-based matrix multiplication**:

```
for (int i = 0; i < N; i++) {
    for (int j = 0; j < N; j++) {
        for (int k = 0; k < N; k++) {
            C[i][j] += A[i][k] * B[k][j];
        }
    }
}
```

With compiler optimizations enabled (`-O2` or `-O3`), execution times vary:

Compiler	Execution Time (Optimized)	Execution Time (Non-Optimized)
GCC 13	1.2s	3.5s
Clang 16	1.1s	3.2s
MSVC 2022	1.3s	3.8s

***Table 18.1**: Comparative analysis of compiler outputs*

Observations:

- Clang produced the fastest execution time due to aggressive loop vectorization.
- GCC performed well but had slightly higher execution time due to differences in memory access optimization.
- MSVC had the slowest optimized execution, possibly due to different register allocation strategies.

Performance Metrics Across Languages

The performance of compiled code varies across different programming languages. To highlight this, let us compare **sorting a list of 1 million integers** using **C++, Java, and Python.**

Test Case: QuickSort Implementation Across Languages

Language	Compiler/Interpreter	Execution Time	Optimization Level
C++	GCC 13	0.15s	-O3 (Full Optimization)
Java	OpenJDK 17 (JIT)	0.25s	JIT-enabled
Python	CPython 3.11	2.1s	No JIT Optimization

***Table 18.2**: Performance metrics across languages*

- C++ (GCC) was the fastest, benefiting from aggressive optimizations such as inline expansion and memory prefetching.
- Java (JIT-compiled) performed well, dynamically optimizing runtime performance.
- Python (interpreted) was the slowest, as it lacks low-level compiler optimizations.
- PyPy (JIT-enabled Python) can reduce execution time to ~0.6s, making Python more competitive.

Challenges in Compiler Development

Compiler development is a complex and evolving field that presents numerous challenges. From designing efficient optimization techniques to handling code errors and ensuring cross-platform compatibility, compiler engineers must overcome various obstacles. This section explores some of the most **common challenges**, the role of **error management in compiler design**, and **solutions derived from real-world case studies.**

Common Development Obstacles

Compiler development presents several challenges, including balancing performance and code size, ensuring cross-platform compatibility, and handling undefined behavior in programming languages. Addressing these obstacles is crucial for building efficient and reliable compilers that meet the demands of modern software development.

- Balancing Performance and Code Size: One of the biggest trade-offs in compiler design is between speed and memory efficiency. High optimization levels (for example, -O3 in GCC) may improve execution speed but can lead to increased binary size. Embedded systems (for example, IoT devices) require highly compact binaries, limiting optimization techniques.

  Example: The **LLVM compiler** offers different optimization levels (-Os for size, -O3 for speed), allowing developers to choose the best trade-off.

- Cross-Platform Compatibility: Modern applications must run on multiple architectures (x86, ARM, and RISC-V). Ensuring consistent behavior across platforms is difficult due to differences in instruction sets. Compilers must generate efficient machine code without breaking compatibility.

  Example: Clang's **cross-compilation support** enables developers to compile C/C++ programs for different platforms with a single compiler.

- Handling Undefined Behavior: Many programming languages (C, C++) have undefined behaviors, such as Integer overflows, Memory access violations, and Uninitialized variables

  Example: The **GCC sanitizers (-fsanitize=address)** help detect memory corruption issues at runtime, preventing crashes in production environments.

Code Optimization and Error Management

Code optimization and error management are crucial aspects of software development, focusing on improving performance and robustness.

Challenges in Code Optimization

Optimizing code without breaking functionality is one of the hardest parts of compiler development.

Difficulties include:

- **Loop optimization** (unrolling, vectorization).
- **Register allocation** (assigning variables to CPU registers).
- **Inlining functions without excessive memory use.**

Example: **JIT compilers (for example, HotSpot in Java)** dynamically optimize **hot paths** (frequently executed code) to improve runtime efficiency.

Error Detection and Debugging Challenges

Compilers must detect **syntactic, semantic, and runtime errors** while providing clear diagnostics.

Common issues:

- **Misleading error messages** (for example, a missing semicolon causing unrelated errors).
- **Incorrect warning suppression**, leading to undetected bugs.

Example: **Clang's detailed error messages** are preferred over GCC's, making debugging easier.

Solutions Derived from Case Studies

Real-world case studies provide valuable insights into overcoming compiler development challenges. By analyzing successful implementations, we can identify effective strategies for improving compilation speed, enhancing security, and refining debugging tools. This section highlights key lessons learned from major compiler projects.

Improving Compilation Speed (LLVM Case Study)

- **Problem**: Large projects (for example, Chrome) take **hours to compile**.
- **Solution**: LLVM introduced **incremental compilation** and **parallel processing**, reducing build times by **50%**.

Ensuring Security in Compiler Optimizations (GCC Case Study)

- **Problem**: Aggressive optimizations sometimes remove **security checks**.
- **Solution**: GCC's **-fstack-protector** flag adds **buffer overflow protection**, preventing vulnerabilities.

Enhancing Debugging Support (Clang Case Study)

- **Problem**: Developers struggle with **unclear error messages**.
- **Solution**: Clang improved error diagnostics with **color-coded output** and **precise suggestions**.

Best Practices and Lessons Learned

Developers can follow certain best practices to ensure efficient and maintainable compiler implementations. From modular design principles to optimizing for different hardware architectures, this section outlines essential guidelines and industry-proven techniques for building robust compilers.

- **Use modular compiler design**: Helps in debugging and future enhancements.
- **Provide clear and detailed error messages**: Makes debugging easier for developers.
- **Optimize for different hardware architectures**: Ensures compatibility across platforms.
- **Balance performance and memory efficiency**: Choose the right optimization strategy.
- **Leverage real-world benchmarks**: Continuously test compiler outputs on real applications.

Emerging Trends in Compiler Technology

As computing needs evolve, compiler technology continues to advance, incorporating new techniques to improve performance, efficiency, and adaptability. Modern compilers are no longer just tools for translating high-level code into machine code–they now integrate AI-driven optimizations, just-in-time (JIT) compilation, and hardware-specific tuning. These advancements allow compilers to generate faster and more efficient programs while adapting to the growing complexity of software development. This section explores the latest trends shaping compiler technology and how they impact programming and execution efficiency.

New Technologies and Methodologies in Compiler Design

The field of compiler design is constantly innovating to meet the demands of modern computing environments. Some of the **key advancements** include:

- **AI-Assisted Compiler Optimization:** Machine learning is being integrated into compilers to optimize code automatically.

  AI models analyze program behavior and predict the most efficient compilation strategy.

  Example: **LLVM's Machine Learning Guided Optimization (MLGO)** improves compiler heuristics for better performance.

- **Just-In-Time (JIT) Compilation Enhancements:** JIT compilers dynamically optimize code at runtime, adapting to real-world execution patterns.

  Modern JIT techniques reduce startup time while maintaining execution speed.

  Example: **GraalVM** enhances Java's JIT compilation for faster execution and lower memory overhead.

- **Hardware-Aware Compilation:** New compilers are designed to **leverage specific hardware architectures** (for example, ARM, RISC-V, GPUs).

  Optimized code generation ensures efficient utilization of **multi-core processors and specialized accelerators.**

  Example: **TensorFlow XLA (Accelerated Linear Algebra)** compiles machine learning models for GPUs and TPUs.

- **Secure and Privacy-Preserving Compilation:** With growing cybersecurity concerns, compilers now integrate **security-focused optimizations.**

Features such as **control-flow integrity (CFI) and memory safety enhancements** reduce vulnerabilities.

Example: **LLVM's SafeStack and Control Flow Guard (CFGuard) in Clang** protect against buffer overflows and code injection attacks.

Future Directions for Compiler Research and Development

The future of compiler technology is shaped by increasing demands for **high-performance computing, security, and adaptability**. Some key research directions include:

- **Quantum Computing and Post-Classical Compilation:** As quantum computing advances, new compiler frameworks are needed to handle **quantum circuits and qubit operations**.

  Example: **IBM's Qiskit compiler** translates quantum programs for quantum hardware execution.

- **Self-Optimizing Compilers:** Future compilers may include **autonomous learning mechanisms** that continuously optimize code based on real-time execution data.

  Example: Auto-tuning compilers that adapt to specific hardware configurations for improved performance.

- **Universal and Cross-Language Compilation:** The need for **multi-language interoperability** is growing, leading to the development of **universal compilers**.

  Example: **Multi-Level Intermediate Representation (MLIR)** supports multiple languages and execution environments, improving cross-platform compatibility.

- **Energy-Efficient Compilation:** With sustainability in focus, future compilers will optimize code for **low-power consumption** in edge computing and IoT devices.

  Example: **Compilers that generate energy-efficient binaries for mobile and embedded systems**.

Conclusion

Chapter 18, Case Studies and Real-World Examples, provided a practical perspective on compiler design by examining real-world implementations, optimization strategies, and performance analysis. Through case studies of widely used compilers such as GCC, LLVM, and Clang, we explored their architectural innovations, optimization techniques, and implementation challenges. These case studies highlighted how design decisions impact compilation efficiency, execution speed, and memory management.

Additionally, the chapter discussed compiler applications across various programming languages, focusing on how compilation differs in C/C++, Java, and Python. We examined the role of optimizations–such as inlining, loop unrolling, and dead code elimination–in improving program performance while addressing common challenges such as code efficiency, error handling, and balancing speed with accuracy.

Beyond specific compiler implementations, this chapter emphasized the importance of analyzing compiler outputs, comparing performance metrics, and understanding real-world optimization challenges. Emerging trends, such as AI-driven compiler optimizations, energy-efficient compilation techniques, and advancements in just-in-time (JIT) compilation, were also explored, giving insights into the future of compiler development.

Building on this knowledge, *Chapter 19, Hands-on Exercises and Projects*, will transition from theory to practice. This chapter will offer interactive exercises, sample compiler projects, and real-time code compilation activities, allowing learners to apply their knowledge in a hands-on environment. By working with various compiler tools and platforms, learners will deepen their understanding of compiler development and optimization techniques in real-world scenarios.

Points To Remember

- **Compiler case studies** provide insights into real-world performance improvements and optimizations.
- **GCC, LLVM, and Clang** each have unique features suited for different compilation needs.
- **Compiler optimizations** such as loop unrolling, inlining, and dead code elimination improve execution speed and efficiency.
- **Java uses bytecode and JIT compilation**, while Python relies on JIT-based interpretation for better performance.
- **Compilers are essential** for AI, embedded systems, and high-performance computing applications.
- **Challenges in compiler development** include balancing compilation speed, runtime performance, and security.
- **AI and machine learning** are transforming compiler technology with adaptive optimizations.
- **Quantum computing** requires specialized compilers to optimize quantum circuits and execution.
- **Energy-efficient and domain-specific compilers** are crucial for mobile, AI, and cloud computing advancements.

Multiple Choice Questions

1. What is one major advantage of using compiler case studies?
   a. They increase the compilation time.
   b. They provide insights into real-world performance improvements.
   c. They make debugging unnecessary.
   d. They reduce the need for code optimization.
2. Which of the following is a key feature of LLVM?
   a. Strictly interpreted execution
   b. Modular and flexible architecture
   c. Only supports C programming language
   d. Does not support JIT compilation
3. What makes Clang stand out from other compilers?
   a. It only supports Java compilation.
   b. It provides better error diagnostics, and faster compilation.
   c. It cannot be used for performance analysis.
   d. It is the slowest among the modern compilers.

4. Which optimization technique improves execution speed by reducing redundant calculations?
    a. Dead code elimination
    b. Loop unrolling
    c. Code obfuscation
    d. Manual memory management
5. What is the main purpose of JIT compilation in Java?
    a. To convert source code directly to machine code
    b. To execute bytecode at runtime for improved performance
    c. To eliminate the need for garbage collection
    d. To replace static compilation with manual memory management
6. How does Python improve execution speed in modern implementations?
    a. By using JIT compilation in PyPy
    b. By converting Python code directly to machine code
    c. By removing the Global Interpreter Lock (GIL)
    d. By preventing dynamic typing
7. Which of the following best describes profile-guided optimization (PGO)?
    a. Uses runtime data to improve compilation performance
    b. Reduces file size by removing all comments
    c. Slows down execution to improve debugging
    d. Converts machine code back into source code
8. Why is compiler optimization important for AI and machine learning applications?
    a. It increases the time required for model training.
    b. It enhances the computational efficiency and the speed.
    c. It limits memory access for deep learning models.
    d. It prevents models from using GPU acceleration.
9. What is a common challenge in compiler development?
    a. Ensuring compatibility with outdated programming languages
    b. Balancing compilation speed and runtime performance
    c. Avoiding the use of optimization techniques
    d. Reducing the number of supported languages
10. Why do quantum computers require specialized compilers?
    a. Quantum circuits operate differently from classical computing models
    b. Quantum computers use traditional binary execution
    c. Classical compilers are faster than quantum compilers
    d. Quantum compilers eliminate the need for memory management

11. Which of the following languages primarily relies on bytecode execution?
    a. C
    b. Java
    c. Assembly
    d. HTML
12. What is the primary benefit of using GCC for compilation?
    a. It is platform-dependent, and optimized for a single architecture.
    b. It supports multiple architectures, and provides extensive optimization options.
    c. It only compiles Java and Python code.
    d. It does not support inline assembly.
13. Which feature makes LLVM suitable for modern software development?
    a. Lack of modularity
    b. Support for Just-In-Time (JIT) compilation and optimizations
    c. Restriction to only C++ language
    d. No support for optimization techniques
14. Why is energy-efficient compiler technology important?
    a. It increases power consumption for better performance.
    b. It optimizes code execution to reduce energy usage in embedded and mobile devices.
    c. It only benefits quantum computing applications.
    d. It prevents software from running on low-power devices.
15. What is a key trend in compiler technology?
    a. Removing support for older programming languages
    b. Integration of AI-driven optimizations for smarter code compilation
    c. Eliminating optimization techniques in favor of faster compilation
    d. Using only static compilation methods

Answers

1. b
2. b
3. b
4. a
5. b
6. a
7. a

8. b
9. b
10. a
11. b
12. b
13. b
14. b
15. b

Questions

1. How do case studies in compiler design provide insights into real-world challenges and solutions?
2. Explain the key architectural innovations in LLVM and how they contribute to compiler flexibility.
3. Discuss the impact of Just-In-Time (JIT) compilation on Java's performance and execution efficiency.
4. Compare Python's interpretation and compilation process with traditional compiled languages such as C/C++.
5. How do compiler optimizations such as loop unrolling, dead code elimination, and inlining enhance program performance?
6. What are the major challenges in compiler development, and how can case studies help address them?
7. Explain the role of profile-guided optimization (PGO) in improving compiled program performance.
8. Why are energy-efficient compiler technologies important for mobile and embedded systems?
9. How do different compiler implementations affect performance across various programming languages?
10. Discuss emerging trends in compiler technology, including AI-driven optimizations and quantum computing compilers.

Key Terms

- **Cross-Compilation** – The process of compiling code on one platform to run on another.
- **Link-Time Optimization (LTO)** – A technique that optimizes the entire program at the linking stage.
- **Static Single Assignment (SSA) Form** – A representation used in modern compilers to simplify optimization.
- **Backend Compilation** – The phase responsible for generating machine code from intermediate representation (IR).
- **Intermediate Representation (IR)** – A low-level representation of code used for analysis and optimization.

- **Code Profiling** – The process of analyzing program execution to identify performance bottlenecks.
- **Memory Safety** – A compiler feature that prevents memory access errors like buffer overflows.
- **Garbage Collection Optimization** – Compiler techniques to improve memory management in languages like Java and Python.
- **Ahead-of-Time (AOT) Compilation** – Compiling code before execution to improve startup performance.
- **Vectorization** – A compiler optimization that transforms loops to use SIMD (Single Instruction, Multiple Data) for better performance.

Chapter 19
Hands-on Exercises and Projects

Introduction

Compiler development is a highly technical field that requires both theoretical knowledge and practical skills. While previous chapters focused on understanding **compiler architecture, optimization techniques, and real-world implementations**, this chapter emphasizes **hands-on learning** through structured exercises and projects. Practical experience is crucial in compiler design, as it helps reinforce key concepts and enhances problem-solving abilities.

This chapter provides a **step-by-step approach** to implementing various **compiler components**, allowing learners to gain hands-on experience in **lexical analysis, syntax analysis, semantic analysis, intermediate code generation, and code optimization**. Each section includes detailed explanations, code examples, and guided exercises to help learners develop a deeper understanding of how compilers process source code.

In addition to exercises, the chapter includes **sample projects** designed to help learners build functional compiler-related applications. These projects include **developing a Mini C Compiler, creating a Simple Python Interpreter, and designing a Domain-Specific Language (DSL)**. Each project covers essential concepts, such as **parsing, symbol table management, and optimization techniques**, giving learners a comprehensive understanding of compiler construction.

Furthermore, the chapter explores **real-time code compilation and analysis**, introducing tools, such as **LLVM, Flex, Bison, and ANTLR**. These tools are widely used in modern compiler development and play a crucial role in **lexing, parsing, and generating optimized machine code**. The section also discusses best practices for **debugging compilation errors, performance profiling, and optimizing generated code**.

By the end of this chapter, learners will have **practical experience in building and analyzing compiler components**, preparing them for more advanced topics in compiler research and development. This hands-on approach ensures that they can confidently apply their knowledge to real-world scenarios, making them proficient in **compiler construction, language processing**, and **optimization techniques**.

Structure

In this chapter, we will discuss the following topics:

- **Introduction to Hands-on Learning**
  - Importance of Practical Experience
  - Integration of Practical Experience in this Chapter

- **Practical Exercises on Compiler Components**
  - Lexical Analysis Exercises
  - Syntax Analysis Exercises
  - Semantic Analysis Exercises
  - Intermediate Code Generation Exercises
  - Code Optimization Exercises
- **Sample Compiler Projects**
  - Project: Mini C Compiler
  - Project: Simple Python Interpreter
  - Project: Domain-Specific Language (DSL)
- **Real-Time Code Compilation and Analysis**
  - Setting Up Development Environments
  - Analyzing Compilation Output
- **Application of Various Compiler Tools and Platforms**
  - Utilizing Flex and Bison for Lexer and Parser Creation
  - Exploring LLVM for Code Generation
  - Integrating Other Compiler Frameworks
- **Reflection and Discussion**
  - Lessons Learned from Exercises and Projects
  - Discussion on Challenges Faced and Solutions Found
- **Future Directions for Learning**
  - Further Resources for Compiler Development
  - Encouragement for Ongoing Learning and Exploration

Introduction to Hands-on Learning

Compiler design is a multifaceted field that requires a blend of **theoretical knowledge and practical implementation**. While concepts such as **parsing, code generation, and optimization** provide the foundation, **hands-on experience** is what truly strengthens understanding. By actively working with compiler components, learners can **experiment, debug,** and **analyze real-world scenarios**, gaining a deeper grasp of compiler behavior. This practical approach helps in translating abstract concepts into tangible solutions, making learning more effective and engaging.

Importance of Practical Experience

Practical experience is essential in compiler development because it bridges the gap between **theoretical concepts** and **real-world applications**. While understanding parsing techniques, optimization strategies, and code generation is crucial, hands-on learning allows developers to **apply these concepts effectively**. By directly engaging with compiler components, learners gain a **deeper understanding of how compilers function**, making them better equipped to tackle complex challenges in software development.

Learning about compilers is important, but actually working with them makes a big difference. Practical experience helps you **understand concepts better, solve problems efficiently, and gain**

confidence in building and debugging compilers. By applying what you learn through hands-on exercises, you can see how different parts of a compiler work together and improve your skills in real-world scenarios.

- **Enhances Concept Retention**: Implementing compiler components reinforces learning better than passive reading.
- **Develops Problem-Solving Skills**: Debugging errors in lexical analysis, syntax parsing, or code optimization builds logical thinking.
- **Fosters Hands-On Familiarity**: Working with **LLVM, Flex, Bison, and ANTLR** helps learners understand real-world compiler tools.
- **Improves Debugging Abilities**: Spotting and resolving **compilation errors, inefficiencies, and performance bottlenecks** is an essential skill.
- **Prepares for Industry Applications**: Many software development and systems programming roles require **compiler expertise**.
- **Encourages Experimentation and Innovation**: Hands-on learning allows developers to explore **new techniques in compiler optimization and design**.

Integration of Practical Experience in This Chapter

This chapter is designed to immerse you in **real-world scenarios** where you can directly apply the theoretical knowledge you have gained. The exercises and projects included provide hands-on experience that will help solidify your understanding of compiler design. You will be working with **compiler components** such as **lexical analysis, syntax parsing, semantic analysis**, and **code optimization** through practical coding tasks.

Each section in this chapter is structured to guide you through **practical exercises** and **projects** that reflect **real-world compiler development** challenges. You will start by creating basic components such as a **lexer** and **parser**, before moving on to more advanced tasks, such as implementing **type checking**, generating **intermediate code**, and exploring **code optimization techniques**.

Throughout the chapter, you will be using industry-standard tools and platforms, such as **Flex**, **Bison**, and **LLVM**, ensuring that the experience you gain is directly applicable to modern compiler development. This hands-on approach makes the learning process more engaging and ensures you gain a **well-rounded** understanding of compiler construction and optimization.

Practical Exercises on Compiler Components

In this section, we will explore various practical exercises that focus on the core components of a compiler. These exercises will allow you to understand the underlying mechanics and concepts behind the compilation process, helping you build a solid foundation in compiler construction. Each task is structured to give you hands-on experience with different stages of compilation, from lexical analysis to code optimization.

Lexical Analysis Exercises

Lexical analysis is the process of transforming raw source code into meaningful tokens. These tokens are the building blocks for further analysis and ultimately the generation of machine code. A lexer (or lexical analyzer) reads the source code and identifies the core components, such as keywords, operators, identifiers, literals, and symbols. This stage is crucial as it prepares the input for further compilation stages, such as syntax and semantic analysis.

Creating a Simple Lexer: Steps and Code Examples

Creating a lexer involves writing a program that breaks the input code into tokens, each representing a unique category of text, such as a keyword, identifier, or operator.

Steps for Creating a Simple Lexer:

1. **Defining Token Types**: The first step is to define what kinds of tokens the lexer should identify. These could include identifiers, keywords, operators, and literal values such as numbers or strings. We use regular expressions (regex) to define patterns for each token type.
2. **Scanning the Input**: Once the token types are defined, the lexer scans through the input code character by character, matching sequences of characters against the regular expressions defined for each token.
3. **Generating Tokens**: After each match, the lexer generates a token. A token consists of a type and a value. For instance, for the input `"x = 5 + 3"`, the lexer might generate the following tokens: ('**ID**', 'x'), ('**ASSIGN**', '='), ('**NUMBER**', '5'), ('**PLUS**', '+'), ('**NUMBER**', '3').

Here is a simple example of a lexer implemented in Python:

```
import re

# Define token types using regular expressions
token_specification = [
    ('NUMBER',   r'\d+'),             # Integer
    ('ASSIGN',   r'='),               # Assignment operator
    ('ID',       r'[A-Za-z]+'),       # Identifiers
    ('PLUS',     r'\+'),              # Addition operator
    ('MINUS',    r'-'),               # Subtraction operator
    ('SKIP',     r'[ \t\n]+'),        # Skip over spaces, tabs, and newlines
    ('MISMATCH', r'.'),               # Any other character (error)
]

# Combine all the regex patterns into one master pattern
master_pattern = '|'.join(f'(?P<{pair[0]}>{pair[1]})' for pair in token_speci-
fication)

# Lexer function to match tokens
def lexer(code):
    for match in re.finditer(master_pattern, code):
        type_ = match.lastgroup
        value = match.group(type_)
        if type_ == 'SKIP':
            continue  # Ignore spaces and newlines
        elif type_ == 'MISMATCH':
            raise ValueError(f'Illegal character: {value}')
        yield type_, value

# Test the lexer
code = "x = 5 + 3"
for token in lexer(code):
    print(token)
```

In this example:

Regular expressions are defined to identify numbers, identifiers, and operators, such as + and =.

The lexer function processes the code, matching text to the defined patterns and yielding tokens accordingly.

This is just one part of the lexer. Once implemented, this basic lexer can be expanded to handle more complex programming constructs.

Implementing Regular Expressions: Patterns and Testing

Regular expressions (regex) are a fundamental tool in lexical analysis. They allow us to define patterns for token types that the lexer can match against the source code. In this exercise, you will learn how to write regular expressions for common language constructs and test them.

Common Token Types:

- **Identifiers**: Typically, identifiers are variable names, function names, or any user-defined names. A common pattern to identify identifiers in many programming languages is:

  Pattern: [A-Za-z_][A-Za-z0-9_]*

This pattern matches any sequence starting with a letter or underscore, followed by any combination of letters, digits, or underscores.

- **Numbers**: Numbers are often integers or floating-point values. Here is a pattern to match integers:

  Pattern: \d+

For floating-point numbers, we can allow an optional decimal point:

  Pattern: \d+(\.\d+)?

- **Operators**: Operators such as +, -, =, and * are used in many programming languages. For simple operators, the pattern could be:

  Pattern: \+|-|=

Testing Regular Expressions:

After defining regular expressions, we need to test them to ensure they correctly match the expected tokens. The following is an example of how to test regular expressions in Python:

```
import re
#Define some common patterns
patterns = [ (r'[A-Za-z_][A-Za-z0-9_]*', 'identifier'),
             (r'\d+(.\d+)?', 'number'),
             (r'+|-|=', 'operator'),
]

#Sample code to test the regex patterns
test_cases = [
    "variable1", # should match identifier
    "123.45", # should match number
    "+", # should match operator
]

#Test function
def test_regex():
for pattern, label in patterns:
    print(f"Testing {label} pattern: {pattern}")
    for case in test_cases:
        if re.match(pattern, case):
           print(f"Match found for '{case}'")
        else:
           print(f"No match for '{case}'")

test_regex()
```

In this example:

We define several patterns for identifiers, numbers, and operators.

Then, we test each pattern against different test cases to ensure that the regex works as expected.

This is an important step in building a lexer, as it helps identify and refine the patterns needed to tokenize the input effectively.

Lexical analysis is the first step in building a compiler, where we break down the source code into meaningful tokens. Creating a lexer using regular expressions is an essential skill, and testing those regex patterns ensures that our lexer functions correctly. As you move forward with compiler design, understanding how to implement lexical analysis and how regular expressions help in this process will be key to building more advanced components, such as parsers and code generators.

Syntax Analysis Exercises

Syntax analysis is a vital phase in the compilation process, ensuring that the structure of a given input matches the syntax rules of the language. This stage is commonly handled by a parser. In this section, we will explore how to build a parser using **Yacc/Bison** and how to construct **Abstract Syntax Trees (ASTs)** to represent and optimize parsed expressions.

Building a Parser using Yacc/Bison

Yacc (Yet Another Compiler Compiler) and **Bison** are tools used to generate parsers for context-free grammars. The parser checks whether the input string (usually source code) conforms to the grammatical rules of the programming language.

Step-by-Step Guide to Building a Simple Arithmetic Parser:

Define the Grammar: The first step is to define the syntax rules (grammar) that describe valid expressions. For example, we can define a simple arithmetic grammar for expressions such as 3 + 5 * 2.

Example grammar for simple arithmetic:

```
%token NUM
%left '+' '-'
%left '*' '/'
%%
expression:
          expression '+' expression { $$ = $1 + $3; }
        | expression '-' expression { $$ = $1 - $3; }
        | expression '*' expression { $$ = $1 * $3; }
        | expression '/' expression { $$ = $1 / $3; }
        | NUM { $$ = $1; }
        ;
%%
```

- **`%token NUM`**: A token representing numbers.
- **`%left '+' '-'`**: Declares operator precedence for addition and subtraction.
- **`%left '*' '/'`**: Declares operator precedence for multiplication and division.

  The grammar defines the rules of expression parsing, where each rule matches an operation and calculates the result.

  The actions **`{ $$ = $1 + $3; }`** define the computation that takes place when a rule is matched, for example, adding two operands.

Lexer (Flex): Before the parser can work, we need a lexer (written in **Flex**) to tokenize the input. The lexer scans the input and returns tokens (such as numbers or operators) to the parser.

Example lexer code:

```
%%
[0-9]+  { return NUM; }
[+\-*/] { return yytext[0]; }
%%
```

The lexer matches sequences of digits and returns the NUM token for numbers.

It also returns operators, such as +, -, *, and /.

Compile and Run: Once you define the grammar and lexer, you can compile them using **Bison** (for parser generation) and **Flex** (for lexer generation). Then, compile the C code generated and run the parser.

Example command:

```
bison -d parser.y
flex lexer.l
gcc -o calculator parser.tab.c lex.yy.c -lfl
./calculator
```

When you run the program with input such as `3 + 5 * 2`, the output will be computed according to the grammar rules, following the correct precedence of operations.

Constructing Abstract Syntax Trees (AST)

An **Abstract Syntax Tree (AST)** is a tree representation that captures the hierarchical structure of an expression or program. Unlike a syntax tree, the AST simplifies the structure by removing unnecessary details such as parentheses, focusing on the core logical structure.

Let us explore how ASTs are constructed using the same example of arithmetic expressions.

Example 1: Arithmetic Expression 4 + 3 * (2 - 1)

Parsing the Expression:

The expression 4 + 3 * (2 - 1) is parsed in stages, following the operator precedence.

Step 1: The innermost operation is 2 - 1. The subtraction operator - becomes the root node of this subtree.

Step 2: The multiplication 3 * (2 - 1) is parsed, where * becomes the root, and 3 and (2 - 1) are its children.

Step 3: Finally, the addition 4 + (3 * (2 - 1)) becomes the top-level operation, where + is the root, 4 is its left child, and 3 * (2 - 1) is its right child.

AST Representation:

The AST for 4 + 3 * (2 - 1) is as follows:

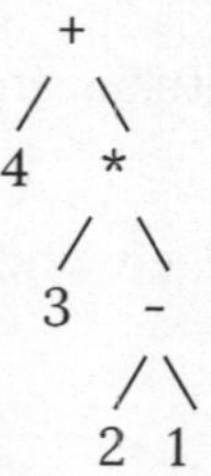

The root node + represents the addition operation.

The left child of + is 4; the right child is the multiplication *.

The multiplication * node has two children: 3 and the subtraction -.

The subtraction - node has two children: 2 and 1.

Example 2: Expression a + b * c

Parsing the Expression:

Step 1: Since multiplication has higher precedence than addition, the expression b * c is parsed first.

Step 2: The addition a + (b * c) is then parsed, with + as the root node and b * c as its right child.

AST Representation:

The AST for a + b * c is as follows:

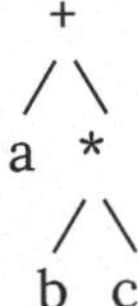

The root node + represents the addition operation.

The left child of + is a; the right child is the multiplication *.

The multiplication * node has two children: b and c.

Semantic Analysis Exercises

Semantic analysis plays a crucial role in ensuring that the program's meaning aligns with the language's rules. This phase involves checking for logical errors that may not be detected during syntax analysis. Semantic analysis focuses on verifying type correctness, symbol definitions, and scopes, ensuring that the program makes sense logically.

Type Checking Implementation

Type checking ensures that operations in a program are performed on compatible data types. For instance, adding two integers is valid, but adding a string to an integer is not. This process helps detect potential issues early, before code execution.

Key Concepts of Type Checking:

- **Type Systems**: These are rules that describe how types are used in a language. For example, strongly typed languages such as Java or C enforce strict rules about how different data types interact.
- **Static Type Checking** occurs at compile time. Languages such as Java or C++ perform this check.
- **Dynamic Type Checking** happens at runtime, and languages such as Python or JavaScript use this approach.

Example of Type Checking in Action:

Consider a simple language with two types: int and bool. A type checker must ensure that operations are performed between compatible types.

For example:

```
int x = 5;
bool flag = true;
x = flag; // Error: Type mismatch (can't assign a bool to an int)
```

In this case, the type checker would raise an error when attempting to assign a boolean to an integer variable, as this is not semantically correct in most programming languages.

Challenges in Type Checking:

- **Implicit Type Conversion**: Some languages allow implicit casting between types, such as converting an integer to a float. Handling such conversions while preserving accuracy and avoiding unexpected behavior can be challenging.
- **Type Polymorphism**: In languages supporting polymorphism (such as C++ or Java), where different types can be handled by the same code, type checking becomes complex because it must handle multiple types for a single operation.
- **Complex Expressions**: In more complex expressions, type checking needs to evaluate the types of intermediate results, adding an extra layer of complexity.

Symbol Table Management

A **symbol table** is a data structure that keeps track of identifiers (such as variable names, function names, classes, and so on.) and their associated information (such as type, scope, and memory location). The symbol table is essential for semantic analysis and type checking, allowing the compiler to track which variables are in use and where they are declared.

Structure of a Symbol Table:

A symbol table is typically implemented as a hash table or a tree structure to allow quick access to symbol information.

Each entry in a symbol table includes:

- **Symbol Name**: The identifier's name (for example, variable name, function name).
- **Data Type**: The type associated with the symbol (for example, int, bool).
- **Scope Information**: The scope in which the symbol is valid (local, global, function-level, and so on.).
- **Memory Location**: The address where the symbol is stored during execution.

Example of Symbol Table:

For the code:

```
int x;
float y;
```

The symbol table might look as follows:

Symbol Name	Type	Scope	Memory Address
x	int	Global	0x00001
y	float	Global	0x00002

***Table 19.1**: Symbol Table.*

Managing Scope in Symbol Tables:

- **Global Scope**: Symbols declared outside functions are globally accessible. They should be placed in the global section of the symbol table.

- **Local Scope**: Symbols declared within functions are only valid inside those functions. Each function should have its own local section in the symbol table, allowing the compiler to track scope changes accurately.

Handling Variable Redeclaration:

One of the challenges when managing symbol tables is ensuring that variables are not redeclared in the same scope. For example:

```
int x;
int x;  // Error: x is already declared in the same scope.
```

The symbol table helps detect such redeclarations by checking if a symbol already exists in the current scope before allowing the declaration.

Example of Symbol Table with Nested Scopes:

In languages that support nested scopes, such as functions within functions, the symbol table needs to track symbols at multiple levels. Here is an example for a code:

```
int x;              // Global scope
void foo() {
    int x;          // Local scope inside foo
}
```

The symbol table might look as follows:

Symbol Name	Type	Scope	Memory Address
x	int	Global	0x00001
y	int	Local	0x00002

***Table 19.2**: Symbol Table with Nested Scopes.*

Challenges in Symbol Table Management:

- **Dynamic Scoping**: Languages such as Python and JavaScript use dynamic scoping, where the scope can change based on runtime conditions. This requires a more complex symbol table structure to track symbols dynamically.
- **Nested Scopes**: Managing symbols in nested functions or blocks introduces complexity, as the symbol table must be capable of handling nested scopes and ensuring proper resolution of variable references.

Intermediate Code Generation Exercises

Intermediate code generation is a crucial step in the compilation process, where the high-level program is transformed into a lower-level intermediate form. This intermediate representation is independent of the target machine architecture, allowing the compiler to optimize the code before generating machine code.

One popular form of intermediate code is **Three-Address Code (TAC)**. This code represents operations in a form that uses three operands for each instruction, making it easier for the compiler to perform optimizations and eventually generate target-specific assembly code.

Generating Three-Address Code

Three-Address Code (TAC) is an intermediate representation of a program where each instruction consists of at most three operands. These operands typically include two source operands and one result operand. For example, an addition operation may look like:

```
t1 = a + b
```

Here, t1 is the result, and a and b are the operands.

Steps to Generate TAC:

1. **Identify Variables and Operations**: The first step in generating TAC is to examine the high-level code and identify variables and operations (arithmetic, logical, assignments, and so on).
2. **Temporary Variables**: Since TAC is used for optimization, the compiler often introduces temporary variables to hold intermediate results. These temporary variables are denoted with names, such as t1, t2, and so on.
3. **Translate High-Level Code to TAC**: Convert each operation into its equivalent TAC instruction, breaking down complex expressions into simpler ones.

Example Code Walkthrough:

Consider the following simple high-level code written in C:

```
x = a + b * c;
```

Let us break it down to generate the corresponding TAC:

Identify Expressions: The expression a + b * c involves multiplication and addition.

First, handle the multiplication: b * c.

Then, add a to the result of b * c.

Generate Temporary Variables:

We need temporary variables to hold intermediate results.

TAC Generation:

First, generate the multiplication:

```
t1 = b * c
```

Then, generate the addition:

```
t2 = a + t1
```

Finally, store the result in x:

```
x = t2
```

Thus, the corresponding Three-Address Code for the expression `x = a + b * c` is:

```
t1 = b * c
t2 = a + t1
x = t2
```

Step 1: `t1 = b * c` computes the product of b and c and stores it in a temporary variable t1.

Step 2: `t2 = a + t1` adds a to the result stored in t1 and stores the sum in t2.

Step 3: `x = t2` assigns the final result stored in t2 to the variable x.

This approach makes it easier for the compiler to optimize the expression, rearrange operations, and eventually generate the final machine code or assembly code.

Benefits of TAC:

- **Simplicity**: Three-Address Code simplifies the structure of high-level operations by breaking them down into smaller, manageable instructions.
- **Optimization**: Intermediate code, such as TAC, allows the compiler to optimize code before generating the final target code.

- **Portability**: Since TAC is independent of machine architecture, it facilitates optimizations and supports code generation for multiple platforms.

Consider the following C code for a more complex expression:

```
z = x * y + a - b / c;
```

To generate Three-Address Code, the compiler would perform the following steps:

1. **Multiply**: **t1 = x * y**
2. **Divide**: **t2 = b / c**
3. **Add**: **t3 = t1 + a**
4. **Subtract**: **t4 = t3 - t2**
5. **Assign**: **z = t4**

Thus, the final TAC would be:

```
t1 = x * y
t2 = b / c
t3 = t1 + a
t4 = t3 - t2
z = t4
```

This intermediate code can then be further optimized and transformed into efficient machine-level instructions for execution.

Code Optimization Exercises

Code optimization is one of the crucial stages in the compilation process, where the goal is to improve the efficiency of the generated code without changing its functionality. Optimizations can be applied at various levels of the compilation process, from high-level source code to low-level assembly or machine code. The primary aim is to make the code run faster, use fewer resources, or consume less memory.

Implementing Basic Optimization Techniques

In this section, we will focus on basic optimization techniques, with examples to illustrate their application. These techniques are simple but fundamental to the process of improving code performance.

Constant Folding

Constant folding is an optimization where constant expressions are evaluated at compile time rather than at runtime. This reduces the number of operations that need to be performed during execution.

Example: Consider the expression in C:

```
x = 5 + 10;
```

Instead of generating code to perform the addition at runtime, constant folding will calculate the result during compilation:

```
x = 15;
```

This optimization eliminates the need to perform the addition in the final executable, reducing both time and space complexity.

Implementation Steps:

1. Identify constant expressions (for example, `5 + 10`).
2. Evaluate them at compile time.
3. Replace the expression with the constant value.

Constant Propagation

Constant propagation is an optimization where the values of known constants are propagated through the program. This technique helps eliminate unnecessary computations when the values of certain variables are known and do not change.

Example: Consider the following code:

```
int a = 5;
int b = a + 10;
int c = b + 15;
```

After constant propagation, we can replace `a` and `b` with their values:

Eventually, we can replace `b` with `15`, resulting in:

```
int c = 15 + 15;
```

This leads to further simplifications:

```
int c = 30;
```

Implementation Steps:

1. Identify constant variables (for example, a = 5).
2. Propagate constant values across expressions that depend on them.
3. Simplify expressions using these constant values.

Dead Code Elimination

Dead code elimination is the process of removing code that does not affect the program's output. This is particularly useful in situations where variables are assigned values but never used or computations are performed but not needed.

Example: Consider the following code:

```
int x = 5;
int y = x * 2;
int z = 10;
y = y + 5;
```

If the value of **z** is never used, the compiler can eliminate the entire assignment to **z**:

```
int x = 5;
int y = x * 2;
y = y + 5;
```

This eliminates unnecessary computations and improves the code's efficiency.

Implementation Steps:

1. Analyze variables and operations to identify unused or redundant code.
2. Remove operations or assignments that do not affect the program's output.
3. Ensure that removing dead code does not change the program's behavior.

Loop Unrolling

Loop unrolling is an optimization technique that involves expanding the loop body to reduce the overhead of the loop control structure. This can result in fewer branches and better performance for certain types of loops.

Example: Consider the following simple loop in C:

```
for (int i = 0; i < 4; i++) {
    a[i] = b[i] + c[i];
}
```

By unrolling the loop, we can perform multiple iterations in a single loop pass:

```
a[0] = b[0] + c[0];
a[1] = b[1] + c[1];
a[2] = b[2] + c[2];
a[3] = b[3] + c[3];
```

In this example, the loop is unrolled to avoid the overhead of repeated incrementing, comparison, and branching. This can result in better performance when the loop body is simple and the number of iterations is known ahead of time.

Implementation Steps:

1. Identify loops with a small number of iterations that can be unrolled.
2. Replace the loop with manually written code that performs multiple operations in a single pass.
3. Ensure that unrolling does not introduce errors or change the behavior.

Common Subexpression Elimination

Common subexpression elimination is the process of identifying expressions that are computed multiple times and replacing them with a temporary variable to avoid redundant calculations.

Example: Consider the following code:

```
int a = x * y;
int b = x * y + z;
```

The expression `x * y` is computed twice, which is redundant. Instead, we can store the result in a temporary variable:

```
int temp = x * y;
int a = temp;
int b = temp + z;
```

This reduces the number of multiplications, improving the efficiency of the code.

Implementation Steps:

1. Identify repeated expressions that are computed multiple times.
2. Store the result of these expressions in a temporary variable.
3. Replace subsequent occurrences of the expression with the temporary variable.

Sample Compiler Projects

In this section, we will explore three practical compiler projects that provide a hands-on approach to understanding and implementing key concepts in compiler design and language processing. These projects are designed to cover different aspects of compiler construction, ranging from a simple C compiler to a Python interpreter and a Domain-Specific Language (DSL). Each project will include an overview of the goals and requirements, along with step-by-step implementation guides to help you through the process.

Project: Mini C Compiler

The Mini C Compiler project is an exciting opportunity to understand and apply the core principles of compiler construction. The goal of this project is to create a simple yet functional compiler for a subset of the C programming language, supporting key features, such as basic arithmetic operations, variable assignment, and conditionals. This project will give you hands-on experience in lexical analysis, syntax parsing, semantic analysis, and code generation.

Project Overview

The primary goal of the Mini C Compiler project is to design and implement a compiler that translates a simple C-like language into intermediate code or machine code. The focus is on creating a functional and extensible compiler for basic operations, supporting features such as:

- **Lexical Analysis**: Identifying and categorizing tokens from a C-like input program (for example, keywords, operators, variables).
- **Syntax Analysis**: Parsing the tokenized input to ensure correct syntax and structure (using grammar rules).
- **Semantic Analysis**: Ensuring that the code adheres to the semantic rules (such as type checking and variable declaration).
- **Code Generation**: Converting the parsed input into executable code (either assembly, intermediate code, or simplified machine code).
- **Error Handling**: Gracefully handling syntax and semantic errors, providing meaningful error messages for debugging.

Key Requirements:

- **Lexical Analyzer (Lexer)**: Tokenizes the input source code, breaking it down into manageable components.
- **Parser**: Validates the syntactical structure of the source code using a grammar.
- **Symbol Table**: Keeps track of variables and their types.
- **Type Checking**: Ensures operations are type-safe (for example, adding two integers or assigning integer values).
- **Code Generation**: Generates intermediate or assembly code for execution.
- **Error Reporting**: Catches both syntax and semantic errors and provides detailed feedback.

Step-by-Step Implementation Guide:

1. **Lexical Analysis (Lexer)**:

   The first step is to break the source code into tokens (keywords, identifiers, numbers, operators). For example, consider the code:

   ```
   int x = 10 + 5;
   ```

   The lexer would break this down into tokens such as:

   - INT

- IDENTIFIER(x)
- ASSIGN
- NUMBER(10)
- PLUS
- NUMBER(5)
- SEMICOLON

Implementation Tip: Use regular expressions to define token patterns (for example, [a-zA-Z_][a-zA-Z0-9_]* for identifiers).

2. **Parsing (Syntax Analysis)**:

   Once the source code is tokenized, the parser ensures that the tokens follow the correct syntax according to the language's grammar. The grammar can be defined using a context-free grammar (CFG). For example, a simple rule for an assignment could be:

```
 stmt -> IDENTIFIER ASSIGN expr SEMICOLON
expr -> NUMBER | IDENTIFIER | expr PLUS expr
```

   The parser will check if the input follows these rules and produce a syntax tree (AST). The AST represents the hierarchical structure of the code.

3. **Semantic Analysis**:

   This phase checks for logical consistency, such as ensuring variables are declared before they are used and that operations make sense for their types. For example:

```
int x;
x = 10 + "hello"; // Error: adding an integer to a string
```

   The **symbol table** will store information about declared variables (for example, type and scope), helping to perform type checking and catch errors such as undeclared variables.

4. **Code Generation**:

   After the code has passed lexical, syntax, and semantic analysis, the next step is to generate code. In this project, you can choose to generate intermediate code or assembly-like code. A simple statement, such as int x = 10 + 5; could translate to:

```
MOV R1, 10
MOV R2, 5
ADD R1, R2
MOV x, R1
```

   You could also generate an intermediate representation such as three-address code (TAC). The resulting code is the one that can be further optimized or executed on a machine.

5. **Error Handling**:

   Throughout the process, ensure that errors are handled effectively. The compiler should be able to report both **syntax errors** (for example, missing semicolons, unmatched parentheses) and **semantic errors** (for example, type mismatches, undeclared variables).

   Example error:

```
int x;
x = y + 10;  // Error: y is undeclared
```

Provide useful error messages, such as "undeclared variable 'y'", and indicate the line number and type of error.

Project: Simple Python Interpreter

The Simple Python Interpreter project focuses on creating a minimal interpreter for a subset of Python-like syntax. The goal is to understand the core components of interpreting a programming language, including lexical analysis, syntax parsing, semantic analysis, and execution. This project will provide insights into how programming languages are processed and executed by an interpreter, offering hands-on experience in building a functional language interpreter.

Project Overview

When building a project like the Simple Python Interpreter, several important design decisions shape its functionality and performance. These decisions determine how the interpreter processes code and handles various features. Let us explore some of the key design choices that guide the development of this interpreter.

Language Subset: The interpreter will support a basic subset of Python syntax, such as arithmetic operations, variable assignments, control flow (if/else), and function calls.

Supported Features:

- Variable declarations: `x = 10`
- Arithmetic operations: `x + y`, `x * 5`
- Conditionals: `if x > 5: ...`
- Basic function definitions: `def add(a, b): return a + b`

Unsupported Features:

- Advanced Python constructs such as object-oriented programming (OOP), file handling, and complex libraries will not be included for simplicity.

Execution Model: The interpreter will use an **evaluation-based approach**, where each line of code is parsed, analyzed, and executed directly.

Instead of compiling the code into intermediate code or machine code, the interpreter will **execute** the code immediately after parsing.

Core Components:

- **Lexer**: Tokenizes input Python-like code.
- **Parser**: Analyzes the syntactic structure of the tokenized code.
- **Evaluator**: Executes the parsed code.
- **Error Handling**: Detects syntax and runtime errors, providing meaningful feedback.

Step-by-Step Implementation Guide

Step 1: Setting Up the Lexer

A lexer (or tokenizer) is the first component of any interpreter or compiler. Its job is to break down the input source code into a sequence of tokens (for example, keywords, operators, and identifiers).

Consider an example,

```
Import re

# Define regex patterns for the tokens
TOKEN_PATTERNS = [
    ('NUMBER', r'\d+'),
```

```
        ('PLUS', r'\+'),
        ('MINUS', r'-'),
        ('TIMES', r'\*'),
        ('DIVIDE', r'/'),
        ('LPAREN', r'\('),
        ('RPAREN', r'\)'),
        ('ID', r'[a-zA-Z_][a-zA-Z0-9_]*'),
        ('WHITESPACE', r'\s+'),
    ]

    def lexer(code):
        tokens = []
        position = 0
        while position < len(code):
            match = None
            for token_type, pattern in TOKEN_PATTERNS:
                regex = re.compile(pattern)
                match = regex.match(code, position)
                if match:
                    if token_type != 'WHITESPACE':  # Ignore whitespaces
                        tokens.append((token_type, match.group(0)))
                    position = match.end()
                    break
            if not match:
                raise SyntaxError(f"Unexpected character at position {position}")
        return tokens
```

The **lexer** takes the source code as input and uses regular expressions to match specific token patterns.

The **`TOKEN_PATTERNS`** list contains the types of tokens (for example, numbers, operators, and parentheses).

For each match found in the code, the lexer appends the token to the tokens list, skipping any whitespace.

Step 2: Building the Parser

The parser takes the sequence of tokens generated by the lexer and checks if they follow the rules of the language. It constructs a syntax tree, which represents the hierarchical structure of the source code.

```
class ASTNode:
    def __init__(self, value, children=None):
        self.value = value
        self.children = children if children else []

def parse_expression(tokens):
    token = tokens.pop(0)
    if token[0] == 'NUMBER':
        return ASTNode('NUMBER', [token[1]])
    elif token[0] == 'ID':
        return ASTNode('ID', [token[1]])
    else:
        raise SyntaxError(f"Unexpected token: {token}")
```

In this example, we define an **`ASTNode`** class to represent the nodes of our abstract syntax tree (AST).

The **`parse_expression`** function processes the tokens and creates an AST by recognizing numbers or identifiers.

If the parser encounters an unexpected token, it raises a **SyntaxError**.

Step 3: Evaluation of the AST

Once the AST is built, the next step is to evaluate it. The interpreter will process the AST to produce a result based on the logic of the language.

```
def evaluate_ast(node):
    if node.value == 'NUMBER':
        return int(node.children[0])  # Return the numeric value
    elif node.value == 'ID':
        return variables[node.children[0]]  # Retrieve value from variables
    else:
        raise RuntimeError(f"Unknown AST node type: {node.value}")
```

The **evaluate_ast** function takes an AST node and evaluates its value.

If the node represents a number, it converts the string value to an integer.

If the node is an identifier (ID), it looks up its value in the variables dictionary, which holds the variable assignments.

Step 4: Adding Variables and Assignment Support

To add the ability to handle variables (such as x = 5), we need to extend our parser and evaluator.

```
variables = {}

def parse_assignment(tokens):
    var_name = tokens.pop(0)[1]  # Get variable name
    tokens.pop(0)  # Skip '='
    expr_node = parse_expression(tokens)
    variables[var_name] = evaluate_ast(expr_node)
```

The **parse_assignment** function extracts the variable name and parses the right-hand side expression.

It then evaluates the expression and stores the result in the variables dictionary.

Step 5: Putting It All Together

Now, we combine all of the preceding steps to process a simple Python program.

```
def interpret(code):
    tokens = lexer(code)
    while tokens:
        if tokens[0][0] == 'ID':  # If we encounter an identifier, it's an as-
signment
            parse_assignment(tokens)
        else:
            expr_node = parse_expression(tokens)
            result = evaluate_ast(expr_node)
            print(result)
```

The interpret function tokenizes the code, then processes each token.

If an assignment is encountered, it calls **parse_assignment**.

Otherwise, it evaluates the expression and prints the result.

If you input the following Python code into the interpreter:

```
x = 5
y = x + 2
print(y)
```

The output would be:

7

This basic interpreter can handle simple assignments and expressions. Of course, for a real-world interpreter, you would need more advanced features, such as handling various types of expressions (for example, addition, subtraction), supporting functions, and error handling.

Project: Domain-Specific Language (DSL)

A **Domain-Specific Language (DSL)** is a specialized programming language designed to solve problems in a particular domain, making tasks more efficient and intuitive. Unlike general-purpose languages, DSLs focus on simplifying specific operations, such as database queries, configuration management, or mathematical computations. This section explores how to design and implement a DSL, providing practical insights and examples to help you build one from scratch.

Designing and Implementing a DSL

A **Domain-Specific Language (DSL)** is a programming or scripting language designed for a particular application domain. Unlike general-purpose languages (such as Python or Java), a DSL focuses on specific tasks, making it more efficient for certain types of problems. Examples of DSLs include SQL (for database queries), HTML (for web structuring), and Regex (for pattern matching).

Steps to Design and Implement a DSL:

1. **Define the Purpose and Scope**
    a. Identify the problem domain that the DSL will address.
    b. Determine whether it will be an **external DSL** (standalone language with its own syntax) or an **internal DSL** (built within an existing language).

Example: A DSL for generating reports from a dataset.

2. **Design the Syntax and Grammar**

    Decide how the DSL will look. Will it be textual, visual, or a configuration-based language?

    Define keywords, structures, and rules for the language.

    Example syntax for a simple reporting DSL:

```
REPORT "Monthly Sales"
FROM sales_data.csv
FILTER region = "North America"
GROUP BY product_category
SHOW total_sales, profit
```

3. **Implement the Lexer and Parser**

    The lexer breaks down the DSL code into **tokens** (keywords, variables, operators).

    The parser organizes these tokens into a **structured representation** (Abstract Syntax Tree - AST).

4. **Develop the Interpreter or Compiler**

    The interpreter processes the AST and executes commands in real-time.

    If needed, the compiler can transform the DSL into another programming language (for example, converting DSL commands into SQL queries).

5. **Add Execution and Output Generation**

   Implement code execution, error handling, and result generation.

6. **Test with Real Use Cases**

   Validate the DSL with different inputs to ensure its reliability.

   Optimize performance for efficiency.

Example DSL Implementation

For this example, we will create a simple DSL for mathematical expressions

Step 1: Defining the DSL Syntax

Our DSL will support:

- Assigning variables
- Basic arithmetic operations (+, -, *, /)
- Printing results

Example DSL Code:

```
SET x = 10
SET y = 5
PRINT x + y
```

Step 2: Implementing the Lexer

```
import re

TOKEN_PATTERNS = [
    ('SET', r'SET'),
    ('PRINT', r'PRINT'),
    ('NUMBER', r'\d+'),
    ('ID', r'[a-zA-Z_][a-zA-Z0-9_]*'),
    ('EQUALS', r'='),
    ('PLUS', r'\+'),
    ('MINUS', r'-'),
    ('TIMES', r'\*'),
    ('DIVIDE', r'/'),
    ('WHITESPACE', r'\s+'),
]

def lexer(code):
    tokens = []
    position = 0
    while position < len(code):
        match = None
        for token_type, pattern in TOKEN_PATTERNS:
            regex = re.compile(pattern)
            match = regex.match(code, position)
            if match:
                if token_type != 'WHITESPACE':
                    tokens.append((token_type, match.group(0)))
                position = match.end()
                break
        if not match:
```

```
                raise SyntaxError(f"Unexpected character at position {position}")
        return tokens
```

This lexer scans the DSL code, and extracts tokens, such as SET, PRINT, ID, and operators.

The lexer **ignores whitespace**, and generates structured tokens for parsing.

Step 3: Implementing the Parser

```
class ASTNode:
 def init(self, value, children=None):
 self.value = value
 self.children = children if children else []

def parse(tokens):
 token = tokens.pop(0)
 if token[0] == 'SET':
 var_name = tokens.pop(0)[1]
 tokens.pop(0) # Skip '='
 expr_node = parse_expression(tokens)
 return ('SET', var_name, expr_node)
 elif token[0] == 'PRINT':
 expr_node = parse_expression(tokens)
 return ('PRINT', expr_node)
 else:
 raise SyntaxError(f"Unexpected token: {token}")

def parse_expression(tokens):
 token = tokens.pop(0)
 if token[0] == 'NUMBER':
 return ASTNode('NUMBER', [token[1]])
 elif token[0] == 'ID':
 return ASTNode('ID', [token[1]])
 else:
 raise SyntaxError(f"Unexpected token in expression: {token}")
```

The `parse()` function builds an **AST (Abstract Syntax Tree)** for variable assignments, and print statements.

`parse_expression()` handles mathematical values and variable names.

Step 4: Implementing the Interpreter

```
variables = {}

def evaluate(node):
    if node[0] == 'SET':
        variables[node[1]] = evaluate(node[2])
    elif node[0] == 'PRINT':
        print(evaluate(node[1]))
    elif isinstance(node, ASTNode):
        if node.value == 'NUMBER':
            return int(node.children[0])
        elif node.value == 'ID':
            return variables.get(node.children[0], 0)
    else:
        raise RuntimeError(f"Unknown node type: {node}")
```

`evaluate()` executes the parsed commands by storing variable values and printing results.

If a variable is referenced before being assigned, it defaults to 0.

Step 5: Running the DSL

```
def run(code):
    tokens = lexer(code)
    while tokens:
        ast = parse(tokens)
        evaluate(ast)

dsl_code = """
SET x = 10
SET y = 5
PRINT x + y
"""

run(dsl_code)
```

Output:

```
15
```

This example illustrates a **simple yet functional DSL** for arithmetic operations. By following this approach, you can extend your DSL with more advanced features, such as **loops, conditionals, and functions**. The key takeaway is that designing a DSL involves **defining a clear syntax, implementing lexing and parsing, and building an interpreter** to execute the DSL commands efficiently.

Real-Time Code Compilation and Analysis

Real-time code compilation and analysis are essential for ensuring that code is efficient, error-free, and optimized for performance. This section covers setting up development environments, debugging compilation errors, and profiling code execution to enhance efficiency.

Setting Up Development Environments

A well-configured development environment ensures seamless coding, debugging, and optimization. It involves setting up compilers, interpreters, debugging tools, and performance analyzers to streamline the development process.

Several tools and platforms enhance real-time code compilation and analysis. Some widely used options include:

- **GCC and Clang**: Popular C/C++ compilers for high-performance compilation
- **JVM and GraalVM**: Java-based runtime environments for Just-In-Time (JIT) compilation
- **PyPy and CPython**: Python interpreters optimizing runtime execution
- **LLVM**: A modular and flexible compiler framework for code generation and analysis
- **IDEs such as VS Code, JetBrains IntelliJ, and Eclipse**: Providing built-in compiler integrations and debugging features

To ensure an optimal development experience, consider these best practices:

- **Choose the Right Compiler**: Select a compiler that best suits your project's needs (for example, Clang for performance, GCC for cross-platform compatibility).
- **Optimize Compiler Flags**: Use appropriate optimization flags (-O2, -O3, -march=native) to enhance performance.
- **Leverage Build Systems**: Automate compilation with tools such as CMake, Make, or Gradle to manage dependencies efficiently.

- **Use Debugging Tools**: Utilize GDB, LLDB, or Valgrind for troubleshooting and memory management.
- **Enable Continuous Integration (CI)**: Automate compilation and testing to detect errors early in development.
- **Monitor Performance**: Profile execution time and memory usage with performance analysis tools, such as Perf, Valgrind, or JProfiler.

Analyzing Compilation Output

Compilation output provides valuable insights into the success or failure of code compilation. Understanding error messages, warnings, and optimization logs helps developers debug and refine their code for better performance and efficiency.

Key Aspects of Compilation Output Analysis:

- **Error Messages**: Identify syntax errors, missing dependencies, and undefined references.
- **Warnings**: Address potential issues that might not prevent compilation but could lead to runtime errors.
- **Optimization Reports**: Review compiler optimizations, such as loop unrolling, function inlining, and constant propagation.
- **Generated Assembly Code**: Inspect the intermediate assembly code to understand the efficiency of compiled instructions.

Debugging Compilation Errors: Common Pitfalls

Compilation errors can arise from various sources, including syntax mistakes, missing dependencies, or incorrect configurations. Understanding common pitfalls can help developers resolve issues quickly and efficiently.

Common Compilation Errors and Their Solutions:

- **Syntax Errors**: Caused by incorrect syntax, such as missing semicolons, unmatched parentheses, or invalid keywords.
- **Solution**: Carefully read the error message and locate the offending line of code.
- **Linker Errors**: Occur when the compiler cannot find the required libraries or symbols during linking.

  Solution: Ensure that all necessary libraries are included and correctly linked using appropriate flags (-L and -l).
- **Undefined References**: Result from missing function or variable definitions.

  Solution: Check for missing header files or unimplemented functions.
- **Segmentation Faults**: Occur due to invalid memory access.

  Solution: Use debugging tools such as GDB or Valgrind to track memory violations.
- **Compiler Version Mismatch**: Some features may not be supported in older compiler versions.

  Solution: Upgrade to a compatible compiler version or modify the code to align with the available features.

Proper debugging techniques save time and ensure code stability, making error resolution a crucial skill for developers.

Performance Profiling and Analysis Tools

Optimizing code performance requires identifying bottlenecks and analyzing execution efficiency. Profiling tools help developers track CPU usage, memory allocation, and function execution times.

Popular Performance Profiling Tools:

- **Gprof**: Used for profiling C/C++ programs by analyzing function call times.
- **Valgrind (Cachegrind & Memcheck)**: Helps detect memory leaks and analyze cache performance.
- **Perf (Linux Performance Profiler)**: Monitors CPU cycles, instructions per second, and bottlenecks.
- **JProfiler & VisualVM**: Java-based tools for monitoring heap memory and garbage collection.

Effective Strategies for Performance Analysis:

- **Identify Hotspots**: Use profiling tools to determine functions consuming excessive execution time.
- **Optimize Memory Usage**: Reduce unnecessary memory allocations and prevent leaks.
- **Leverage Compiler Optimizations**: Utilize optimization flags (-O2, -O3) to improve execution speed.
- **Parallelize Code**: Implement multithreading and vectorization to enhance performance.
- **Monitor System Resource Usage**: Track CPU and memory utilization to ensure optimal resource management.

Application of Various Compiler Tools and Platforms

Compiler development relies on a variety of tools and frameworks that simplify and streamline the process of code compilation and optimization. These tools range from lexical analysis to code generation and performance profiling. Leveraging these tools helps developers create efficient and robust compilers for different programming languages. This section will explore some of the most commonly used tools and platforms in compiler development.

Utilizing Flex and Bison for Lexer and Parser Creation

Flex and Bison are two powerful tools that automate the creation of lexical analyzers (lexers) and parsers, respectively. Lexers are responsible for scanning and tokenizing source code, while parsers analyze the syntactical structure of the code.

- **Flex (Fast Lexical Analyzer Generator)**: Flex is used to generate lexers from regular expressions. It helps define how the lexer should scan and match tokens in the source code.
- **Bison**: Bison is a parser generator that takes a grammar specification (written in a specific syntax) and generates the parser that can recognize and process the source code based on the grammar.

Practical Example: Creating a Lexer and Parser

Let us consider a simple calculator that supports addition, subtraction, multiplication, and division. We can define the following steps:

1. **Define Tokens**: The lexer (using Flex) will define the basic elements, such as numbers, operators, and parentheses.

```
%%
[0-9]+         { return NUMBER; }
[\+\-\*/]      { return OPERATOR; }
\t|\n          { /* skip white spaces */ }
%%
```

2. **Define Grammar**: The parser (using Bison) will define how the tokens relate to one another.

```
%%
expr    : expr OPERATOR expr    { /* perform operation */ }
        | NUMBER               { $$ = $1; }
;
%%
```

3. **Link Lexer and Parser**: Once Flex and Bison generate the lexer and parser, you can compile and link them into a program that will read an expression and evaluate it.

Exploring LLVM for Code Generation

LLVM (Low-Level Virtual Machine) is a versatile and modular compiler infrastructure that provides tools for code generation, optimization, and analysis. LLVM can take intermediate representations (IR) and generate highly optimized machine code for a variety of architectures.

Building Projects with LLVM

Using LLVM allows for more flexibility in the compilation process, as it can target multiple architectures without needing to redesign the backend.

- **Targeting Multiple Platforms**: LLVM allows you to generate code for different hardware platforms (x86, ARM, and so on) with minimal changes to the codebase.
- **Optimization**: It includes a range of built-in optimization techniques, such as constant folding, inlining, loop unrolling, and more.

For instance, in a project where we need to compile a custom language into machine code, we would:

- **Use LLVM's Frontend**: Parse the source code into an intermediate representation.
- **Apply Optimizations**: Use LLVM's powerful optimization passes to improve the generated code.
- **Generate Machine Code**: Use LLVM's backend to generate machine-specific code that can be executed on the target architecture.

Integrating Other Compiler Frameworks

Beyond Flex, Bison, and LLVM, there are various other tools and frameworks that can be integrated into the compiler development workflow. These tools can help with various tasks, such as syntax analysis, type checking, and code optimization.

Overview of ANTLR

ANTLR (ANother Tool for Language Recognition) is a powerful parser generator used to create lexers and parsers from grammar specifications. It is often used in projects where custom language support is needed.

Use Case: Suppose you are designing a domain-specific language (DSL) for data transformation. You can use ANTLR to create the lexer and parser that will interpret and process the DSL code.

How it Works: ANTLR reads grammar definitions (written in its syntax) and generates code that can parse the language and produce Abstract Syntax Trees (AST).

Example: Simple Arithmetic Expression Parser with ANTLR

Here is how ANTLR can be used to create a simple arithmetic expression parser:

Define Grammar:

```
grammar Expr;

expr   : term ((PLUS | MINUS) term)* ;
term   : factor ((MUL | DIV) factor)* ;
factor : NUMBER | LPAREN expr RPAREN ;
NUMBER : [0-9]+ ;
PLUS   : '+' ;
MINUS  : '-' ;
MUL    : '*' ;
DIV    : '/' ;
LPAREN : '(' ;
RPAREN : ')' ;
```

Generate Parser: ANTLR will generate a lexer and parser that can process arithmetic expressions, evaluate them, and return the result.

Parse Input: The generated parser can be used in your program to process and compute results for expressions such as 3 + 4 * 5.

The use of powerful tools, such as Flex, Bison, LLVM, and ANTLR can significantly streamline the process of developing compilers. These tools provide essential functionalities, such as lexical analysis, syntax parsing, and code generation which are crucial for building efficient and flexible compilers. Integrating these tools into your projects not only enhances the efficiency of the development process but also allows you to build custom compilers tailored to specific needs.

Reflection and Discussion

As we wrap up the hands-on exercises and projects, it is essential to reflect on the lessons learned, the challenges faced, and how to continue progressing in the field of compiler development. This section will dive into the key insights gathered from the practical experiences and how those can guide future learning. Additionally, we will discuss some of the common hurdles in compiler projects and how solutions were found. Finally, we will explore resources and ways to keep learning and improving in this area.

Lessons Learned from Exercises and Projects: Key Insights

Through the completion of various exercises and projects, several valuable lessons emerge. Here are some key takeaways:

- **Importance of Building Strong Foundations**: Understanding fundamental compiler concepts, such as lexical analysis, parsing, and code generation, is crucial. These concepts form the backbone of any project, and mastering them ensures smoother project development.
- **The Role of Optimization**: Compiler optimization is not just about improving performance; it is also about understanding the trade-offs between time complexity and space complexity. Learning how different optimizations (such as loop unrolling or dead code elimination) impact the generated code is essential for building efficient compilers.
- **The Interdisciplinary Nature of Compiler Development**: Compiler development brings together knowledge of programming languages, algorithms, data structures, and hardware

architectures. The experience of integrating these concepts into one cohesive system is both challenging and rewarding.

- **The Importance of Testing and Debugging**: Testing and debugging are indispensable in compiler development. The complexity of handling syntax, semantic analysis, and code generation requires thorough testing to catch errors early. Using tools for error reporting and debugging throughout the process helps prevent issues from snowballing into larger problems.

Discussion on Challenges Faced and Solutions Found: Community Insights

Throughout the compiler development exercises, several challenges are likely to arise. These challenges can vary from technical obstacles to conceptual hurdles. Here is a look at some common issues and the solutions developed either individually or with the help of the community:

- **Handling Complex Syntax and Grammar:**
  - **Challenge**: When working on parser generation, complex grammars can lead to ambiguous parsing or errors in recognizing valid input.
  - **Solution**: Leveraging powerful parser generation tools, such as Bison or ANTLR helps in creating parsers for more complex languages. Additionally, breaking down the grammar into smaller, manageable components can reduce the complexity of the task.
- **Integrating Lexical Analysis with Syntax Parsing:**
  - **Challenge**: Aligning the lexer and parser to work seamlessly often presents integration issues, especially when tokenization errors occur.
  - **Solution**: Properly synchronizing the lexer and parser through well-defined tokens and grammar rules, along with iterative testing, proved to be the key to overcoming this challenge.
- **Error Handling in Intermediate Code Generation:**
  - **Challenge**: Generating intermediate code (such as three-address code) often involves handling errors gracefully, especially when translating complex expressions.
  - **Solution**: Implementing comprehensive error-handling mechanisms, including error recovery strategies in intermediate code generation, ensures that the compiler can provide helpful feedback during the translation process.
- **Optimizing Code Without Breaking Functionality:**
  - **Challenge**: While optimizing generated code, ensuring that the functionality remains correct can be difficult, especially with aggressive optimizations.
  - **Solution**: Conducting rigorous regression testing, where optimizations are tested alongside various edge cases, helps ensure that performance gains do not lead to unintended side effects.

Future Directions for Learning

As technology and programming languages evolve, compiler design continues to advance in complexity and efficiency. The future of compiler development lies in several exciting areas that offer opportunities for further exploration and learning:

- **Integration with AI and Machine Learning**: The use of machine learning in optimizing compilers, such as automatic tuning of performance optimizations, is a promising field.

Research in AI-based optimization algorithms can revolutionize the way compilers generate and improve code.

- **Cross-Platform Compilation**: With the rise of cloud computing and multi-platform development, future compilers will focus more on enabling seamless cross-platform compilation. This includes compiling code that runs efficiently on different hardware and operating systems.
- **Optimized Just-In-Time (JIT) Compilers**: JIT compilers are becoming more sophisticated, and further advancements in this area can drastically improve performance, especially for languages such as JavaScript and Python that rely on dynamic typing and real-time compilation.
- **Better Support for Parallelism and Concurrency**: As hardware continues to evolve with more cores and parallel processing capabilities, compilers will need to do more to optimize code for concurrency. This will include advanced optimization techniques to harness the full power of modern processors.
- **Domain-Specific Languages (DSLs)**: The development of new DSLs that are optimized for specific industries (such as finance, bioinformatics, and data science) will continue to grow. These languages could provide simpler, more efficient ways to express complex problems.
- **Compiler Security and Protection**: With growing concerns about security vulnerabilities, compiler designers are beginning to focus on how compilers can detect and prevent common security issues, such as buffer overflows and malicious code injections.

Encouragement for Ongoing Learning and Exploration: Engaging with the Community

The world of compilers is vast and continually evolving, and ongoing learning is key to staying current. Here are a few ways to keep exploring the field:

- **Hands-on Practice**: Continue building small compilers or interpreters. Start with simple projects and gradually increase the complexity as you become more comfortable with the theory and practice.
- **Engage with Communities**: Join online forums and communities dedicated to compiler development. Participating in discussions, reading about others' experiences, and collaborating on open-source projects will expose you to a range of techniques and ideas.
- **Research and Academic Papers**: The field of compiler design has a wealth of academic research. Reading research papers and following conferences such as PLDI (Programming Language Design and Implementation) or POPL (Principles of Programming Languages) can help you stay up to date with the latest breakthroughs.
- **Contribute to Open-Source Projects**: Many compiler projects, such as LLVM and GCC, are open-source. Contributing to these projects can give you real-world experience and deepen your understanding of advanced topics.
- **Experiment with Compiler Construction Tools**: Explore different compiler tools, such as LLVM, ANTLR, Flex, and Bison, to gain a deeper understanding of their strengths and limitations. Building projects with these tools will expose you to the practical aspects of compiler design.
- **Explore Alternative Programming Paradigms**: Expand your knowledge by learning about alternative programming paradigms (for example, functional programming, logic programming) and their impact on compiler design.

By adopting a mindset of continuous learning and experimentation, you can stay ahead in the evolving world of compiler technology and contribute to the exciting advancements in the field.

Conclusion

As we wrap up this final chapter, it is clear that hands-on experience is truly the key to mastering compiler development. In this chapter, we moved beyond theory and dove into the exciting world of real-world applications, guiding you through practical exercises and projects that solidified your understanding of the core concepts of compiler construction.

By building your own lexer, creating parsers, and working through abstract syntax trees (AST), you have gained a hands-on understanding of how compilers break down and process code. These exercises were not just about writing code–they were about solving problems and making critical design decisions. You learned how to approach tasks step-by-step, from analyzing lexical patterns to optimizing performance.

The sample projects, such as the Mini C Compiler and Simple Python Interpreter, allowed you to take your skills further. These projects were more than just challenges–they were opportunities to see how a compiler really works in practice. With each project, you tackled different aspects of compiler design, and through trial and error, learned to refine your approach and make smarter design choices.

We also introduced you to powerful tools, such as Flex, Bison, and LLVM. These tools are industry standards, and now, you are equipped to use them effectively. You have seen firsthand how compilers are built using these frameworks, and you have learned the valuable skills of analyzing compilation output, debugging issues, and optimizing the code.

What is even more important is that we have only scratched the surface. The world of compiler design is vast and constantly evolving. The exercises, projects, and resources in this chapter have set the stage for your next steps. With your newly developed skills, you are ready to dive deeper, explore new tools, and take on more complex compiler projects.

So, as you close this chapter, remember that the journey does not end here. The field of compiler development is filled with endless opportunities for innovation and learning. Stay curious, keep experimenting, and never stop exploring. The skills and lessons you have learned here will be your foundation as you continue to grow and tackle even more exciting challenges ahead.

Points To Remember

- **Practical Exercises**: Hands-on activities help apply theory to real-world problems in compiler design.
- **Lexer and Parser Creation**: Building these components is crucial for understanding how a compiler works.
- **Abstract Syntax Trees (ASTs)**: ASTs break down code into manageable pieces, and are essential for compiling.
- **Type Checking and Symbol Tables**: Important for ensuring correct code behavior and structure.
- **Three-Address Code**: Intermediate code generation is a key step in turning code into machine-readable instructions.
- **Code Optimization**: Techniques, such as loop unrolling and dead code elimination improve code efficiency.
- **Real-World Projects**: Projects, such as a Mini C Compiler or Python Interpreter provide valuable hands-on experience.
- **Tools (Flex, Bison, LLVM)**: Industry-standard tools help build compilers efficiently.
- **Setting Up Development Environments**: A good setup is essential for testing, debugging, and compiling projects.

- **Debugging and Performance Analysis**: Understanding how to identify and fix errors is crucial for improving your compiler.

Multiple Choice Questions

1. **What is the primary focus of Chapter 19 in the context of compiler development?**
   a. Theory behind compiler design
   b. Hands-on exercises and practical experience
   c. Data structures used in compilers
   d. History of compilers
2. **Which of the following tools is mentioned in Chapter 19 for building a lexer and parser?**
   a. LLVM
   b. ANTLR
   c. Flex and Bison
   d. JavaCC
3. **What is an Abstract Syntax Tree (AST) used for in compiler construction?**
   a. To store the source code
   b. To visualize the structure of the program
   c. For debugging the code
   d. For type checking
4. **In the context of semantic analysis, what is the role of a symbol table?**
   a. To store machine-level code
   b. To check for type errors
   c. To store identifiers and their attributes
   d. To represent the program's flow
5. **Which of the following is a key component of code optimization?**
   a. Token generation
   b. Type checking
   c. Dead code elimination
   d. Parsing syntax
6. **Which project is an example given in Chapter 19 for creating a simple compiler?**
   a. Java Compiler
   b. Mini C Compiler
   c. Assembly Compiler
   d. C++ Compiler
7. **What is the primary advantage of using Flex and Bison in compiler design?**
   a. They help in code debugging.
   b. They are used for building lexers and parsers.

   c. They generate the final executable code.
   d. They handle semantic analysis.

8. **What does LLVM primarily help with in compiler development?**
   a. Building lexers
   b. Parsing syntax
   c. Code generation and optimization
   d. Type checking

9. **Which of the following is a recommended practice when setting up a development environment for compiler projects?**
   a. Use the latest versions of compilers without testing
   b. Avoid using version control tools
   c. Ensure proper configuration for tools and platforms
   d. Skip debugging steps to save time

10. **What is the purpose of debugging compilation errors?**
    a. To optimize the final output
    b. To find and fix errors in the code
    c. To generate machine code
    d. To analyze runtime performance

Answers

1. b
2. c
3. b
4. c
5. c
6. b
7. b
8. c
9. c
10. b

Questions

- Describe the steps involved in creating a simple lexer. What are the key components of a lexer, and how does it contribute to the overall compilation process?
- Discuss the process of building a parser using Yacc/Bison. How do tools like these aid in syntax analysis, and what are some common challenges faced during parser construction?
- What are Abstract Syntax Trees (ASTs)? How are they constructed, and why are they important in the compiler's translation process? Provide an example of an AST for a basic arithmetic expression.

- Define semantic analysis in the context of compilers. How does type checking help in ensuring the correctness of the source program? Explain with an example.
- Discuss code optimization techniques in compilers. Provide examples of some basic optimizations, such as dead code elimination or loop unrolling, and explain how they enhance the performance of the final output.
- In the context of the 'Mini C Compiler' project discussed in the chapter, and what are the key goals and requirements? Outline the step-by-step process involved in implementing this project.
- Describe the process of designing and implementing a Domain-Specific Language (DSL). What are the main considerations for developing a DSL, and how does it differ from general-purpose programming languages?
- What are the best practices for setting up a development environment when working on compiler projects? Discuss the tools and platforms that are recommended, and explain how they contribute to an efficient workflow.
- Discuss how performance profiling and analysis tools can aid in improving a compiler's efficiency. Provide examples of tools that are used for performance profiling, and how they help developers identify bottlenecks in code.
- Explain the role of LLVM in modern compiler development. How does it aid in code generation and optimization? Provide an example of how LLVM can be used to generate optimized machine code for a specific program.

Key Terms

- **Yacc/Bison**: Parser generators used to create parsers for compilers.
- **Abstract Syntax Tree (AST)**: A tree representation of the syntactic structure of the source code.
- **Semantic Analysis**: The phase in compilation where the meaning of the program is checked for correctness.
- **Type Checking**: Ensuring that variables are used with compatible data types in a program.
- **Symbol Table**: A data structure that holds information about variables, functions, and other identifiers.
- **Intermediate Code Generation**: The process of translating source code into a more abstract representation for optimization.
- **Three-Address Code**: An intermediate code form that typically uses three operands to represent operations.
- **Code Optimization**: Improving the performance of a code by reducing its size or increasing its execution speed.
- **Domain-Specific Language (DSL)**: A programming language designed for a specific task or domain.
- **Compiler Tools and Platforms**: Software tools used for building and working with compilers (for example, Flex, Yacc, LLVM).
- **Flex**: A tool used to generate lexical analyzers for compilers.
- **ANTLR (Another Tool for Language Recognition)**: A parser generator used for building parsers and interpreters for domain-specific languages.

Index

A

B

C

D

E

F

G

I

M

T

U

W

Y